ROUTLEDGE HANDBOOK OF SOCIO-LEGAL THEORY AND METHODS

Drawing on a range of approaches from the social sciences and humanities, this handbook explores theoretical and empirical perspectives that address the articulation of law in society, and the social character of the rule of law.

The vast field of socio-legal studies provides multiple lenses through which law can be considered. Rather than seeking to define the field of socio-legal studies, this book takes up the experiences of researchers within the field. First-hand accounts of socio-legal research projects allow the reader to engage with diverse theoretical and methodological approaches within this fluid interdisciplinary area. The book provides a rich resource for those interested in deepening their understanding of the variety of theories and methods available when law is studied in its broadest social context, as well as setting those within the history of the socio-legal movement. The chapters consider multiple disciplinary lenses – including feminism, anthropology and sociology – as well as a variety of methodologies, including: narrative, visual and spatial, psychological, economic and epidemiological approaches. Moreover, these are applied in a range of substantive contexts such as online hate speech, environmental law, biotechnology, research in post-conflict situations, race and LGBT+ lawyers.

The handbook brings together younger contributors and some of the best-known names in the socio-legal field. It offers a fresh perspective on the past, present and future of socio-legal studies that will appeal to students and scholars with relevant interests in a range of subjects, including law, sociology and politics.

Naomi Creutzfeldt and **Marc Mason** are based in the law school at the University of Westminster; **Kirsten McConnachie** is based in the law school at the University of East Anglia.

ROUTLEDGE HANDBOOK OF SOCIO-LEGAL THEORY AND METHODS

Edited by Naomi Creutzfeldt, Marc Mason and Kirsten McConnachie

LONDON AND NEW YORK

First published 2020 by Routledge

2 Park Square, Milton Park, Abingdon, Oxon, OX14 4RN
605 Third Avenue, New York, NY 10017

Routledge is an imprint of the Taylor & Francis Group, an informa business

First issued in paperback 2020

British Library Cataloguing-in-Publication Data
A catalogue record for this book is available from the British Library

Library of Congress Cataloging-in-Publication Data
Names: Creutzfeldt, Naomi, 1974– editor. | Mason, Marc (Law teacher), editor. | McConnachie, Kirsten, editor.
Title: Routledge handbook of socio-legal theory and methods / edited by Naomi Creutzfeldt, Marc Mason and Kirsten McConnachie.
Description: Abingdon, Oxon ; New York, NY : Routledge, 2019.
Identifiers: LCCN 2019014614 (print) | LCCN 2019017548 (ebook) | ISBN 9781138592902 (ebk) | ISBN 9781138592902 (hbk)
Subjects: LCSH: Sociological jurisprudence.
Classification: LCC K376 (ebook) | LCC K376 .R68 2019 (print) | DDC 340/.115–dc23
LC record available at https://lccn.loc.gov/2019014614

ISBN: 978-1-138-59290-2 (hbk)
ISBN: 978-0-367-78379-2 (pbk)

Typeset in Bembo
by Swales & Willis, Exeter, Devon, UK

We thank Mike Leach and Samuel Banda for their creative interpretation of socio-legal studies on the cover image.

CONTENTS

Contents

CONTRIBUTORS

Ben Bradford is Professor of Global City Policing at the Jill Dando Institute for Security and Crime Science, University College London. His research concentrates on procedural justice theory, and questions of trust and legitimacy in criminal justice contexts.

Victoria Brooks is Lecturer in Law at the University of Westminster. She is a writer and researcher on sexual ethics, and her book *Fucking Law: The Search for Her Sexual Ethics* is published by Zero Books (2019). Victoria experiments with philosophy and writing to communicate the experience of women's sexuality, while also using academic research methods that examine personal experience and what it can tell us about ethics and laws relating to sex. Victoria has published academic papers, book chapters and media articles on the theme of the body, sex and law.

Emilie Cloatre is a Professor of Law at the University of Kent. Her research focuses on the relationship between law and 'science in society', and in particular between law and medical practices. She is currently Principal Investigator on a Wellcome Investigator Award entitled, 'Law, Knowledges and the Making of "Modern" Healthcare', and co-Investigator on an ESRC project entitled 'Biomedicine and Beyond: The Social and Regulatory Dimensions of Therapeutics in Japan and the UK'.

Dave Cowan works at the University of Bristol and researches housing and property issues from a socio-legal perspective.

Richard Craven is a lecturer at the University of Leicester where he teaches administrative law and competition law. Richard's research studies economic regulation, specifically in relation to the regulation of government procurement in the United Kingdom and European Union. His research is socio-legal, using qualitative empirical methods and engaging with socio-legal theory and economic sociology.

Naomi Creutzfeldt is a Reader in Law at the University of Westminster. She teaches public law, civil and commercial dispute resolution and socio-legal research methods. Her interests in ADR, as pathways of informal dispute resolution, have a broader scope, addressing questions of access to justice, vulnerability and consumer protection. Her latest book is *Ombudsmen and ADR* (Palgrave, 2018).

Margaret Davies is Matthew Flinders Distinguished Professor at Flinders University. She is a Fellow of the Academy of Social Sciences in Australia, Fellow of the Australian Academy of Law, and author of five books on legal theory and the philosophy of property. Her latest book is *Law Unlimited: Materialism, Pluralism, and Legal Theory* (2017).

Benjamin Farrand is Reader in Law and Emerging Technologies at Newcastle University. He works on the interplay between law and politics in the regulation of new technologies and writes about security, lobbying and policy development in areas of uncertainty, with recent works including articles on emerging approaches to counterfeit control on the Internet, comparative approaches on biotechnology regulation in the EU and China, and the private regulation of cybersecurity.

Iginio Gagliardone is Senior Lecturer in Media and Communication at the University of the Witwatersrand, South Africa, and is Associate Research Fellow in New Media and Human Rights in the Programme in Comparative Media Law and Policy, University of Oxford. He holds a PhD from the London School of Economics and Political Science and has been living between Italy, Ethiopia, the UK and South Africa, researching the relationship between new media, political change and human development, and exploring the emergence of distinctive models of the information society in the Global South. His most recent publications include *The Politics of Technology in Africa* (Cambridge University Press), and *World Trends in Freedom of Expression and Media Development* (UNESCO Publishing). His latest book is *China, Africa, and the Future of the Internet* (Zed Books, 2019).

Thomas Giddens is Lecturer in Law at the University of Dundee in Scotland. He is a critical, comics and cultural legal scholar, with particular interests in visuality, aesthetics and epistemology. He is author of *On Comics and Legal Aesthetics* (Routledge, 2018), founding chair of the Graphic Justice Research Alliance and a member of the Editorial Committee for *Law and Humanities*.

Rebecca Hollander-Blumoff is a Professor of Law at Washington University School of Law in St. Louis, Missouri. Professor Hollander-Blumoff's research focuses on law and psychology in the context of dispute resolution. Her interdisciplinary perspective on legal dispute resolution uses psychological research and insights to better understand the role of legal actors, systems and norms. She also explores the relationship between human behaviour and dispute resolution systems, particularly in the context of legal negotiation and civil procedure. Professor Hollander-Blumoff previously served as the Chair of the Executive Committee of the Association of American Law Schools' Section on Civil Procedure. In addition to her undergraduate and law degrees from Harvard University, Professor Hollander-Blumoff holds a PhD in social psychology from New York University, where she formerly served as an acting assistant professor in the Lawyering Program, as well as a research fellow at the Institute of Judicial Administration. Professor Hollander-Blumoff has been a Visiting Professor of Law at Notre Dame Law School and Harvard Law School.

Rosemary Hunter is Professor of Law and Socio-Legal Studies at the University of Kent. She is a general editor of the Edward Elgar Research Handbooks in Law and Society and the Onati International Series in Law and Society, a Board Member of the Onati International Institute for the Sociology of Law and former Chair of the Socio-Legal Studies Association. She was one of the organisers of the English, Australian and New Zealand Feminist Judgments Projects and has also supported other feminist judgment projects around the world.

Matthew A. Jay is a social epidemiologist with a special interest in how epidemiological methods can be used to better understand the operation of law and its outcomes. His research focuses particularly on the use of administrative data and family law, and he also researches acute and chronic pain in children. Matthew graduated from the University of Westminster in 2012 with an LLB and from UCL in 2017 with an MSc in Social Epidemiology and he is currently pursuing a PhD at the UCL Great Ormond Street Institute of Child Health on the Children Act and educational outcomes.

Briony Jones is an Associate Professor in International Development in the Politics and International Studies Department of the University of Warwick. Her research takes place at the intersection between international development, transitional justice and peacebuilding. In particular, her work focuses on citizenship, reconciliation, political agency, the politics of intervention and the politics of knowledge production. She co-edited *Resistance and Transitional Justice* (Routledge, 2017) and currently leads an international project on *Knowledge for Peace: Understanding Research, Policy, Practice Synergies*. She is also an associate researcher at swisspeace and the University of Oxford and a member of the Working Group on Transitional Justice and SDG 16.

Richard Kirkham is a public lawyer who has a long-standing research interest in the ombudsman sector and administrative justice more generally. His publications include M. Hertogh and R. Kirkham (eds), *Research Handbook on the Ombudsman* (Edward Elgar, 2018) and *The Ombudsman Enterprise and Administrative Justice* (with Trevor Buck and Brian Thompson; Ashgate, 2011).

Jennifer Lander is Lecturer in Law at De Montfort University. Prior to joining Leicester De Montfort Law School, she held an Early Career Fellowship at Warwick's Institute of Advanced Study (2017–2018). Jennifer's current research explores the role of transnational law in natural resource-based development as a constitutional "mover and shaker", focusing on Central Asian and East African frontier economies. Her monograph *Transnational Law and State Transformation: The Case of Extractive Development in Mongolia*, is published by Routledge (2019).

Antonia Layard is a Professor of Law at the University of Bristol. She teaches and researches property and planning law, urban development and legal geography. Antonia has a particular interest in how we might be able to develop legal concepts of place and is completing her book *Law, Place and Maps* (Routledge, forthcoming). Recent funded projects include researching public space developments at the University of Bristol with Streets Imagined and "The Bus Project" with Room 13 and Hareclive Primary, researching bus use by children in South Bristol.

Kathy Mack is Emerita Professor, Flinders University. She received her BA (Magna cum Laude) from Rice University (Houston, Texas) and JD from Stanford Law School (California) and later an LLM from the University of Adelaide. Before coming to Australia, Kathy practised law in California, mainly criminal law. She has taught evidence, criminal law and procedure, civil procedure and dispute resolution, including interviewing and negotiation, at the University of Adelaide Law School as well as at Flinders. Since 1994, in collaboration with Matthew Flinders Distinguished Professor Sharyn Roach Anleu, she has been engaged in socio-legal research into the Australian courts and judiciary, beginning with an investigation of the production of guilty pleas and continuing with research into the everyday work of the judiciary. Their latest book is *Performing Judicial Authority in the Lower Courts* (Palgrave, 2017).

Marc Mason is Senior Lecturer at the University of Westminster. His interests include: the regulation of the Bar; diversity and inclusion, with a particular focus on LGBTQI+; and queer approaches to family law.

Kirsten McConnachie is Senior Lecturer in Law at the University of East Anglia. Her research focuses on law and governance in refugee situations, and she has a particular regional interest in South East Asia. She has published on topics including governance by armed groups, the history and management of refugee camps, legal pluralism and non-state justice systems, victimology in transitional justice and constitutional reform. She is the author of *Governing Refugees: Justice, Order and Legal Pluralism* (Routledge, 2014).

Carrie Menkel-Meadow is Distinguished Professor of Law and Political Science, University of California, Irvine, and Chettle Professor of Law, Dispute Resolution and Civil Procedure, Emerita, Georgetown University. She has been engaged in socio-legal research since 1980 and has published 15 books and more than 200 articles on dispute resolution, mediation, negotiation, the legal profession, legal ethics, the delivery of legal services and cause lawyering, feminist legal theory and gender in law, legal education and studies of globalization in law and legal education. She has served on the Boards of Directors of the Law and Society Association and the American Bar Foundation and the editorial boards of *Law & Society Review* and *Law & Social Inquiry*.

Kath Murray is a Research Associate at the University of Edinburgh. Her PhD investigated the rise of intensive stop and search in Scotland and prompted major legislative and policy reform. Her research interests include police powers and accountability, railway policing, policy-making on sex and gender identity.

Alexa Neale is Research Fellow in Historical Criminology at the University of Sussex. Her research and publications are in the areas of domestic murder, and race and capital punishment. She is shortly to commence a Leverhulme Early Career Research Fellowship (ECF-2018-448) at Sussex entitled 'Black Books: The Institutional Memory of Hanging and Mercy at the Home Office'.

Angus Nurse is Associate Professor, Environmental Justice, and Deputy Head of the Department of Criminology and Sociology at Middlesex University School of Law where he teaches and researches criminology and law. Angus has research interests in criminality, critical criminal justice, animal and human rights law, antisocial behaviour and green criminology. He is particularly interested in animal law and its enforcement and the reasons why people commit environmental crimes and crimes against animals. Angus is a member of the Wild Animal Welfare Committee and has previously worked in the environmental NGO field and as an Investigator for the Local Government Ombudsman. His books include *Policing Wildlife* (Palgrave Macmillan, 2015), *Animal Harm: Perspectives on why People Harm and Kill Animals* (Ashgate, 2013) and *Miscarriages of Justice: Causes, Consequences and Remedies* (Policy Press, 2018) co-authored with Sam Poyser and Rebecca Milne.

Elizabeth A. O'Loughlin is a Lecturer in Law at the City Law School, University of London (2018–). Prior to joining City Law School, Elizabeth was a PhD candidate at the University of Manchester, where she has worked on a European Research Council-funded study entitled 'A Sociology of the Transnational Constitution'. From July to August 2018, she was a Kathleen Fitzpatrick Visiting Fellow in Comparative Constitutional Law at Melbourne Law School. She was previously a teaching assistant at the University of Leeds, a researcher at the University of Sheffield, and has also worked in the Kenya Section of the International Commission of Jurists. Elizabeth holds a doctorate from the University of Manchester, an LLM (by research) from the European University Institute and an LLB from the University of Leeds.

Andreas Philippopoulos-Mihalopoulos is Professor of Law & Theory at the University of Westminster and Director of the Westminster Law & Theory Lab, a practising artist working on performance, photography and text pieces, and a fiction writer. He is the author of *Absent Environments* (2007), *Niklas Luhmann: Law, Justice, Society* (2010) and *Spatial Justice: Body, Lawscape, Atmosphere* (2014), as well as editor of several books.

Maayan Ravid is a doctoral student at the University of Oxford's Centre for Criminology where she researches intersections of border control, state penal power, race, gender and ethnicity. She completed an MSt in Socio Legal Research in 2015, also in Oxford's Faculty of Law. Maayan's academic work has coincided with more than a decade of grassroots activism alongside refugee and migrant communities in Israel.

Sharyn Roach Anleu is a Matthew Flinders Distinguished Professor of Sociology in the College of Humanities, Arts and Social Sciences at Flinders University, Adelaide, and Fellow of the Australian Academy of the Social Sciences. She is a past president of the Australian Sociological Association and the author of *Law and Social Change* and four editions of *Deviance, Conformity and Control*. She has contributed to the Master's programme at the International Institute for the Sociology of Law, Oñati, Spain. With Emerita Professor Kathy Mack, at Flinders University, she leads the Judicial Research Project, which undertakes socio-legal research into the Australian judiciary and its courts. Their latest book is *Performing Judicial Authority in the Lower Courts* (Palgrave, 2017), and, in 2018, Sharyn and Jessica Milner Davis co-edited *Judges, Judging and Humour* (Palgrave).

Alice Schneider is a DPhil candidate at the Oxford Centre for Socio-Legal Studies. Her thesis focuses on the recognition of information privacy as a case study of legal change in modern societies. Alice is also a Stipendiary Lecturer in Law at St Hilda's College, Oxford.

Lizzie Seal is Reader in Criminology at the University of Sussex. Her previous publications are on capital punishment, historical criminology, cultural criminology, transgression and gender representations of women who kill. She is currently engaged in two research projects: race and the death penalty in twentieth-century England and Wales, and reforming British law and policy on the global death penalty.

Charlotte Helen Skeet is a Lecturer-in-Law and a Co-Director of the Sussex Centre for Human Rights Research in the School of Law, Politics and Sociology at the University of Sussex (www.sussex.ac.uk/schrr/research). She is the academic convenor and lecturer for the Women and Human Rights module in the LLM/MA in International Human Rights, and for Feminism, Law and Society in the MA in Gender Studies at the University of Sussex. Research interests include gender and constitutionalism, post-colonial feminist legal theory and intersectionality theory. She convened the Intersectionality Stream for the Socio-Legal Studies Conference from 2010 to 2016.

Nicole Stremlau is Research Professor in the Humanities at the University of Johannesburg and Head of the programme on Comparative Media Law and Policy at the Centre for

Socio-Legal Studies of the University of Oxford. She has conducted extensive research in East Africa. Nicole is the recipient of a European Research Council grant to examine the role of social media in conflict and migration, with a specific focus on the Somali territories. Her recent books include *Media, Conflict and the State in Africa* (Cambridge University Press, 2018) and *Speech and Society in Turbulent Times* (Cambridge University Press, 2018).

Lisa Webley is Chair in Legal Education and Research, Research Director of CEPLER and Head of Birmingham Law School. She holds a Senior Fellowship at IALS where she is director of the National MPhil/PhD Legal Research Methods Training programme, which includes a range of socio-legal methods. She has conducted a range of empirical socio-legal projects using mixed methods approaches.

Julia Yesberg completed her PhD in Forensic Psychology at Victoria University in Wellington, New Zealand. Her research interests include the rehabilitation and reintegration of high-risk offenders, desistance, violence, neighbourhood policing and police power. She currently works as a researcher within the Mayor's Office for Policing and Crime in London.

PART I

Approaching socio-legal studies

1

SOCIO-LEGAL THEORY AND METHODS

Introduction

Naomi Creutzfeldt, Marc Mason and Kirsten McConnachie

We are delighted to present the first *Routledge Handbook of Socio-Legal Theory and Methods*, a collection that showcases the breadth of work animating contemporary socio-legal studies. Socio-legal studies has had an enormous influence on legal scholarship, challenging assumptions about (*inter alia*): the nature of law, rules and legal thought; the relationship between law and ethics, morality and religion; law, government and governance; and law and community; and providing an understanding of the meaning of legal culture and legal consciousness. In addressing these issues, socio-legal scholars have established conversations and collaborations across multiple disciplines, including sociology, anthropology, psychology, history, geography, politics, international relations, cultural studies, economics, philosophy and more. This work has been paradigm-shifting for many of us as individuals but has also transformed the realms of legal education and practice. A positivistic 'black-letter' approach to law is no longer the only or even dominant paradigm of legal education. It is fundamentally challenged by the growing number of law schools that offer a socio-legal approach to the study of law, in recognition of the importance of understanding the context of law, and the need to provide future practitioners, policymakers and researchers with the theoretical and methodological skills necessary to understand the world in which they will operate.

Socio-legal studies (and law and society research) has a strong history of engaging with political activism. It has been animated by a commitment to social and political change and a confidence that this was not (as some early doubters viewed it to be) incompatible with serious intellectual enquiry. In the US, *law and society* research emerged at a moment when social activism and post-war prosperity coincided to foster hope for progressive social change. Seeking to engage in research that would improve social policy and enable advocacy, law and society scholars aimed at connecting themselves with practitioners and policymakers. This encouraged new understanding of the ways in which law interacts and engages with its social environment. The *socio-legal studies* movement, particularly those sections of it influenced by legal realism, started to uncover law's limitations and prompted the exploration of the social context, including an increasing emphasis on empirical legal research. Continued questioning of authority and of conventionally held positivist legal thought encouraged the emergence of the *critical legal studies* movement. The history of these intellectual movements is discussed further by several contributors to Part I of this volume, particularly Creutzfeldt (Chapter 2)

3

and Menkel-Meadow (Chapter 3). An important insight that emerges from their work is the extent to which these movements in legal scholarship have consistently sought to *change things*, not just about the world around us but also in the legal academy itself. This includes the law school curriculum and the way that the 'socio-legal' fits within other disciplines and theories. It acquires new impetus as we recognise the importance of engaging early career researchers in this work, particularly at a time of increased pressures on researchers (e.g. casualization of academic employment, pressures to acquire external funding, research assessment processes) that may otherwise encourage them to play it 'safe' and avoid riskier, time-intensive – but enriching – engagement with multi-disciplinary research. Maintaining the health of socio-legal studies, and its commitment to social justice, requires new academics to enter the field with their own commitment to reflexive and responsive development of research and teaching approaches. Here we all share the responsibility to grow the field and to foster collaboration and exchange. We hope that this volume will play a part in supporting this endeavour.

'Law', 'society' and the relationship between the two constitute an endlessly generative subject. As research questions, disciplinary relationships, methodological techniques and sites of study evolve, so do the boundaries of the field as a whole. The sheer scope of work makes it very difficult to pinpoint precisely what socio-legal studies *is*. A discipline in its own right? A research approach? An orientation or way of understanding the world? A political commitment? At various times, each of these answers has been proposed (see further Part I to this volume). Similarly, the diversity of approaches makes it impossible and perhaps undesirable to define a canon for the field. At its broadest, the field of socio-legal studies might be defined as a way of seeing, of recognising the mutually constitutive relationship between law and society. That relationship is open to endless interpretation because law and society are both constantly changing. Any attempt to fix a precise definition of socio-legal studies will almost inevitably be stultifying, failing to do justice to the body of work that exists or predict its future iterations. In recognition of the disadvantages of definitional fixity, we have therefore chosen largely to side-step defining socio-legal studies and to concentrate this handbook instead on *doing* socio-legal studies. Socio-legal research is carried out through individual projects that adopt a variety of theoretical stances and methodological approaches. We felt there was a gap in the literature for a book that explored some of the variety of approaches that are possible in 'doing' socio-legal studies and profiled the diverse research themes, theoretical approaches and methodologies represented in contemporary socio-legal research.

This volume also reflects the evolution of socio-legal studies, in recognition that we, as editors, are part of what might be considered the 'third generation' of socio-legal scholars. The range of work collected in this handbook shows the enduring significance of some research topics, such as policing, judicial decision-making, capital punishment, race and gender. It also demonstrates the emergence of new research directions addressing new social and legal challenges such as identity, intersectionality, biotechnology, environmental crime, international development and political violence. Above all, it shows that there are many different types of research enquiry.

This handbook celebrates socio-legal scholarship and highlights the energy and originality in the field as it stands today. We are very pleased to have contributions from scholars at all stages of their career: from PhD students, early and mid-career academics, to internationally renowned socio-legal scholars. We are also very pleased to have contributions from a number of disciplines, reflecting the influence on socio-legal studies of history, geography, sociology, anthropology, economics and international development (see further Part II,

'Disciplinary and theoretical relationships'). Despite the range of work that this handbook includes, we cannot claim that this is a comprehensive overview of socio-legal studies – nor indeed would we try to. In particular, our collection is dominated by UK and US scholarship. We recognise this as a gap within the current volume and as an area that future handbooks may be able to respond to more effectively.

Finally, we wanted to make the handbook practically useful. Our aim was to provide the socio-legal community (established researchers, early career researchers and prospective researchers) with an accessible guide to theories and methods in socio-legal studies. We sought to produce a repository of contemporary socio-legal scholarship, certainly, but to do this from a practical perspective: what do socio-legal projects look like from the inside? How do socio-legal researchers conduct their work? What are some of the challenges that they faced? How did they resolve those difficulties? There are many research methods textbooks and many published works of socio-legal research, but hardly any books discussing the bit in the middle: how a particular method has been applied in a particular project. We chose to focus this handbook on that aspect – that is, the *process* of research – and encouraged our contributors to reflect on their use of a particular theory or method and what worked or did not. This was an opportunity for our contributors to discuss the motivations, doubts and anxieties of doing research, rather than focusing solely on their research findings. It is now an opportunity for our readers to peer behind the curtain of finished, published works and recognise the many choices, decisions and compromises that are involved in any major research project. We hope that this will instigate new theoretical and methodological conversations and inspire new research projects.

In summary then, this handbook aims to offer the reader a sample of the rich variety of theoretical and methodological approaches within the broad field of socio-legal studies. It is a collaboration and, as such, reflects an approach that has been at the heart of the development of socio-legal studies and is integral to the future of the field.

The organisation of the handbook

The range of ideas and approaches represented within the discipline and in our authors' work has made it challenging to settle on a broad organising framework for this handbook. All of our authors are talking about their own experiences of socio-legal research, and almost all contributions include some discussion of disciplinary issues, theoretical framing and methodological choices. However, most chapters profile one of these elements more than another, so we have grouped the volume around three core themes: (1) approaching socio-legal studies, (2) disciplinary and theoretical relationships and (3) methodological choices. These categories are not clear-cut, however, and many chapters overlap between and across these themes.

Part I, 'Approaching socio-legal studies', provides an overview of the historical evolution of socio-legal studies and focuses on themes that everyone pursuing a socio-legal research project will encounter. This part aims to encourage readers to learn from others' experiences and to uncover some of the realities that are usually left to discussions around dinner tables or to a rant with colleagues in a corridor. In this regard it is valuable to trace the evolution of socio-legal studies. The dynamic between individual researchers, institutional traditions and the law curriculum presented barriers and challenges that had to be (and still need to be) overcome. Creutzfeldt (Chapter 2) provides an account of some prominent voices in the making of socio-legal studies, revealing personal stories of strong beliefs, hard work and serendipity. As the field of socio-legal studies evolves, we cannot leave behind the wisdom of those who have set out some of the paths for us. Menkel-Meadow (Chapter 3) draws on her own experience as a pioneer in socio-legal studies to explore 'the uses and abuses' of socio-legal research in theory and method. This chapter offers a journey through key socio-legal ideas including law in social context, legal realism, legal pluralism, legal movements and institutions, the law in the books versus the law in action, law and culture, legal theory, ideology, and the role of law in social change.

A shift from the gestation of socio-legal studies as a field into the practicalities of conducting socio-legal research is presented in Chapters 4–9. Webley (Chapter 4) offers a structured guide to designing a socio-legal research project, addressing central 'how-to' questions and practical decisions of the research process. Philippopoulos-Mihalopoulos (Chapter 5) takes a different approach, challenging legal writing (and particularly legal essay writing) to move beyond familiar confines and embrace the possibilities of fragmentation and even formlessness. Socio-legal research is moving beyond traditional distinctions towards an emplaced, embodied and material understanding of law, but legal writing does not (yet) reflect this shift. Davies (Chapter 6) examines the use of critical theory in socio-legal studies and argues for recognition of theorising as an intellectual activity that is creative, exploratory and experimental; not separate from practice or from empirically based knowledge but interwoven with experience. Cloatre and Cowan (Chapter 7) consider the question of interdisciplinarity, recognising socio-legal studies as an inherently interdisciplinary endeavour but also acknowledging the challenges of interdisciplinarity for researchers operating in a disciplinary environment. They discuss their own experience of academic peer-review (and the phenomenon of "Reviewer 2") as a case study of interdisciplinarity in action.

Brooks (Chapter 8) reflects critically on ethical awareness in socio-legal research and the conceptualisation of risk in ethical review processes. Mason (Chapter 9) draws attention to another aspect of the research process, the concept of objectivity, and the extent to which objectivity is attainable or desirable. He uses thinking from feminist and queer theory to challenge research more broadly to consider the ethics of equating objectivity with distance and detachment. Murray (Chapter 10) examines the 'impact' agenda, an increasingly prominent metric for academic funding, appointments and promotions in the UK. Drawing on her own experience of conducting a politically sensitive and 'high-impact' research project, Murray reflects on implications of this agenda for the production of academic knowledge.

Part II, 'Disciplinary and theoretical relationships', explores the ways in which socio-legal studies has been informed by disciplinary and theoretical approaches originating outside law. Socio-legal studies has been a 'magpie discipline' that has picked up ideas from many other disciplines in the service of its own goals. This part explores some of those relationships and their application. Influential interdisciplinary relationships in socio-legal studies include those labelled as 'law and ...', such as sociology, anthropology, development, economics, social psychology and international development. These disciplinary relationships recognise and engage with different facets of law, whether as an institution, as a normative order or as a process that shapes and is shaped by human behaviour. Different disciplinary traditions have also brought different methodological approaches to bear on the study of law. Roach Anleu and Mack (Chapter 11) examine the nexus between law and sociology and discuss their use of empirical methods such as observational fieldwork and court-room observations in a large-scale study of judges, magistrates and their courts in Australia. Hollander-Blumoff (Chapter 12) explains the contribution that social psychology can make to socio-legal research and outlines her use of survey, self-report, simulated negotiation processes and behavioural coding approaches to study the importance of procedural justice in legal negotiations. Craven (Chapter 13) draws on his work on government procurement law to explore the relationships between law, economics and socio-legal studies.

Socio-legal studies in the UK and US is increasingly looking outwards, to examine law in its global context. Three chapters examine aspects of this work. McConnachie (Chapter 14) discusses the influence of anthropology in legal research, including enhancing understanding of law in everyday life, law in non-Western societies, legal pluralism and the use of ethnographic methods. Lander's chapter (15) considers similar themes, addressing the relationship between law and development, and her own fieldwork on extractive development (mining) and civil society in Mongolia. Jones (Chapter 16) considers some of the challenges faced by researchers working in post-conflict contexts or conditions of mass violence and examines how qualitative, empirical and fieldwork based research methods 'can add value to socio-legal research in the field of transitional justice'.

The final set of chapters in Part II all make use of distinctive theoretical approaches to generate new insights about how law functions, and its processes and consequences. Layard (Chapter 17) considers legal geography and 'the co-production of space, law and society'. Legal geography is a burgeoning research area that has utilised a variety of methods including empirical, ethnographic and mixed methods approaches. Layard argues for the contribution of 'reading law spatially' through critical legal analysis of cases and demonstrates this approach in an insightful analysis of *DPP v Jones* (1999). Moving from spatiality to temporality, Ravid and Schneider (Chapter 18) employ discourse analysis to explore the changing meaning of legal concepts over time, considering the use of 'infiltrator' as the dominant term for (some) categories of refugees and migrants in Israel.

Feminist approaches have a long presence and influence in socio-legal studies, as Hunter (Chapter 19) explains. Her chapter explores an emerging feminist socio-legal approach, that of feminist judgment projects which, through rewriting case decisions, 'interrogate and contest the practice of judicial decision-making and bring knowledge of gendered social experience to the process of judging' Skeet (Chapter 20) also recognises the importance of feminist approaches to law but adopts an intersectionality approach. Intersectionality has been highly influential in sociology but is perhaps less evident in law and socio-legal studies. Skeet's work on human rights adjudication and 'visibly Muslim women' demonstrates the potential value of intersectionality as a theoretical approach and a methodology in socio-legal studies, and, crucially, as praxis and a political commitment to social justice.

Part III, 'Methodological choices', showcases some of the many innovative research methods used by socio-legal researchers today and illustrates how methodological choices are adapting to new forms of data and new possibilities for data analysis. Many of the methodologies profiled centre on innovative readings of texts, histories and images. There is sometimes an assumption that socio-legal research projects are always empirical and interview-based. As this collection shows, that is far from the case.

Many of our contributors are engaging in documentary research, and their research shows the scope and possibilities for this work. Seal and Neale (Chapter 21) read with and against the grain of archive documents (including courtroom evidence) in researching race, racialisation and the death penalty in England and Wales (1900–1965). Their approach to archival materials sheds light not only on the legal context, but also on the lived experience of the working classes in the early 20th century and the racialised assumptions present in the criminal justice system. Nurse (Chapter 22) provides a narrative approach to reading texts that examines environmental protection through the narratives of state, NGOs and courts. In an analysis of 'legal aesthetics as visual method', Giddens (Chapter 23) uses multimodal readings of comics to develop a deeper understanding of law, legality and its expression, and takes this further to query all forms of legal knowledge, including academic practice. Kirkham and O'Loughlin (Chapter 24) take a systematic approach using content analysis to examine judicial decision-making in judicial reviews of ombudsmen. Farrand (Chapter 25) uses process tracing to examine large volumes of texts from various sources to understand the development of regimes around patentability of inventions derived from human embryonic stem cell research.

The final chapters discuss quantitative and experimental approaches. Yesberg and Bradford (Chapter 26) explore the potential value of experimental approaches in socio-legal studies, including problems and issues of validity, and illustrate the experimental approach with accounts of research looking at the impact of high-risk special treatment units on recidivism, and the effectiveness of a procedural justice intervention in policing (see also Hollander-Blumoff's Chapter 12 in Part II for discussion of simulated negotiation exercises).

Jay (Chapter 27) works with large data sets, and his chapter draws on insights from public health to demonstrate the use of epidemiological approaches to child protection law, arguing for a move towards evidence-informed law. Finally, Stremlau and Gagliardone (Chapter 28) look at hate speech and dangerous speech online, setting it in its historical, legal, political and social context and making links between hate speech, inequality and politics.

2

TRADITIONS OF STUDYING THE SOCIAL AND THE LEGAL

A short introduction to the institutional and intellectual development of socio-legal studies

Naomi Creutzfeldt*

Introduction

I have been engaged in socio-legal research projects since I started my career at the Centre for Socio-Legal Studies in Oxford. I kept searching for a text that would assist me in making sense of what socio-legal studies is and guide me through its methods and theories. I chose not to get lost here in a discussion about formal terminology of *law and society* or *socio-legal*. I will use the terms interchangeably as they have merged into a fluid descriptor of a strand of scholarship, method, and theory. Attending numerous workshops and conferences I encountered so many inspiring people and projects, I realized that there was a mass of lived experience and wisdom. Our volume starts to capture just this, showcasing the amazing work that is being done by socio-legal scholars today. But it is also important to reflect upon how we got here. In this chapter I bring together some of the stories that I believe to be significant for understanding the evolution of the field. I am inspired by stories of making a difference, having a moral purpose, and tracing this through institutional and individual narratives. Of course, these narratives are not firmly aligned; people follow different paths and have differing opinions and perceptions about events. When starting to dive into the research for this chapter I soon realized that it could only be a first step to a larger, more comprehensive, project.[1]

* I am very grateful to Carrie Menkel-Meadow, Rosemary Hunter, Mavis Maclean, Tom Tyler, David Sugarman, Phil Thomas, Sally Engel Merry, and Deborah Hensler for making time to be interviewed and to provide comments on earlier drafts of this chapter. I feel very humbled that my project found such enthusiasm and support from scholars I admire. Thanks also to Linda Mulcahy, Ian Loader, Kirsten McConnachie, and Marc Mason for comments on an earlier draft of this chapter.
1 I plan to write a book and engage more fully with the development of socio-legal studies around the world.

I begin this chapter from the premise that socio-legal studies is a fluid and continually developing area of scholarship. It is made up of clusters and approaches within it. One could define the evolving field as the 'empirical studies of law, legal institutions, actors, and legal processes', or as 'the gap between law on the books and law in action' (Pound 1910). 'Law and society is the study of how law is made, interpreted, enforced and experienced by those on whom law *acts*' (Menkel-Meadow, interview, 2018). Socio-legal studies fill both an intellectual space and a research space. Those in the field are motivated to affect policy and social change (some researchers do both, and others do one or the other). It allows us to cross disciplinary boundaries, to expand and mix mindsets, and to combine methods and theories. These spaces are complex and do not have to be empirically driven, politically oriented, or geared towards social change.

In this chapter I offer a map of the vast field of law and society. It is impossible to accurately reflect the various developments and serendipitous moments and events that led to the law and society of today. This chapter is written for scholars who might be new to the field and is divided into two parts. I start my reflections in the *here and now* by looking at the tangible institutional presence of law and society. I will focus on the historical and geographical development of law and society. Intellectual and social-political movements produced, over time, an institutional presence. These include professional associations, research and teaching centres, and specialized journals. In the second part of this chapter I turn to a few selected intellectual journeys that frame the institutional development of socio-legal studies. Rich interviews[2] offer a unique window into experiences of the development and growth of law and society. I realize that I am artificially separating things that happened alongside each other and are clearly intertwined. I hope though that the chosen structure will provide a helpful overview and introduction to the field of socio-legal studies.

My methodological approach informs the chapter structure. Initially, I searched for information in the public domain to get an overview of what has been written on law and society. I accessed the collections of 'conversations in law and society' at Berkeley[3] and Cardiff,[4] which are valuable resources for anyone interested in the field. At conferences in 2018 (SLSA in Bristol and LSA in Toronto), I was able to conduct face-to-face interviews (and others through Skype) with prominent scholars in the field. The interviews lasted between two and three and a half hours. I realized, while I was collecting data for my chapter and interviewing pioneers in the field, that I am doing an empirical study of socio-legal studies: I am not looking at minutes of meetings or what got published in journals. I designed an interview guideline that produced the three themes focused on below (intellectual formation, research and writing, politics and policy). I chose to present the interviews without my analysis to offer an account of how the interviewees experienced and saw themselves during the socio-legal movement. The combination of existing material and fresh empirical data allows me to give voice to some of the *personal* developments that coincided with and contributed to the *institutional* development of law and society.

---

2 Why did I select the people I interviewed for this chapter and not others? To be honest, I had to start somewhere and was fortunate that those who shaped the field were more than happy to share their story. I am by no means claiming to provide a comprehensive picture – I am providing a small window into personal stories that I was very interested to hear and that I hope will be of interest to readers.

3 www.law.berkeley.edu/research/center-for-the-study-of-law-society/conversations-in-law-and-society/

4 www.cardiff.ac.uk/research/explore/research-units/centre-of-law-and-society

Institutions of law and society

I trace developments of intellectual movements through their institutional manifestations. Starting with geographical roots, I discuss the institutions from a historical perspective, on a country-by-country tour of associations, journals, research centres, and teaching at universities. All these individual parts, of course, are tied together and influence each other. Restrictions on chapter length directed my focus towards developments in the USA and the UK. I chose these countries to showcase distinctive paths in the intellectual, institutional, and political developments of law and society.[5] There are noteworthy overlaps and cross-fertilization between the movements. Scholars of these movements produced associations, research centres, and journals. Journals foster and support the agenda of empirical research and have focused on a variety of socio-legal topics. The content of the journals, for example, is a good opportunity to trace the development of enquiries of socio-legal scholarship reflecting the interests and research agenda of the time (Cownie & Bradney 2017). Many academic publishers now have dedicated socio-legal series, producing monographs and edited collections.[6]

Today there are many law and society/socio-legal organizations around the world. Some of these are on the SLSA website (Table 2.1); however, I want to stress here that this list is not exhaustive and does not reflect the true diversity of socio-legal scholarship. There are many more countries with academics doing socio-legal research than are listed in the table.

To law from the outside: the law and society movement in the USA

The study of law and society rests on the belief that legal rules and decisions must be understood in context. Law is not autonomous, standing outside of the social world, but is deeply embedded within society. While political scientists recognize the fundamentally political nature of law, the law and society perspective takes this assumption several steps further by pointing to ways in which law is socially and historically constructed, how law both reflects and impacts culture, and how inequalities are reinforced through differential access to, and competence with, legal procedures and institutions.

(Levine 1990)

With its origins in the late 1950s and early 1960s, the field of law and society has always been interdisciplinary. Its early development has been well documented (Garth & Sterling 1998; Macaulay et al. 2007; Menkel-Meadow 1990; Mertz et al. 2016; Schlegel 1995). Challenging law as being self-directed, social scientists and legal scholars engaged in empirical research aimed at solving social problems and responding to current debates. The law and society movement is built upon interdisciplinary and multidisciplinary scholarship. This is apparent through the way in which research into social problems and empirical analyses are performed: through numerous methods and theories. Engel (1999) described law and society as having a greater focus on theory and substantive results than on the sophistication of the methods or an insistence on the superiority of any particular methods.

---

5 Intellectual movements have affected law and society scholarship, and law and society scholarship has had an impact on those movements: see Cotterell/Nelken in E. Örücü and D. Nelken (eds), Comparative Law: A Handbook. (2007) Oxford: Hart.
6 For example, Richard Hart left OUP to set up Hart Publishing as a specialist socio-legal press in the late 1990s; it is active in Oxford and New York and is now part of Bloomsbury.

Table 2.1 National and transnational bodies and global law and society/socio-legal organizations[7]

ALERTANET Latin American Network on Law and Society	http://alertanet.org/english.html
Argentinian Society for the Sociology of Law	www.sasju.org.ar
Asian Law and Society Association	http://alsa.sakura.ne.jp
Brazilian Association of Researchers in Sociology of Law	
Canadian Law and Society Association	www.acds-clsa.org
East Asian Law and Society – Collaborative Research Network	www.crn33-eals.org/Main.htm
Sociological Association for France – the Sociology study of Law and Justice Division	www.test-afs-socio.fr/drupal/RT13
German Association for Law and Society	www.rechtssoziologie.info/german-association-for-law-and-society
Irish Association of Law Teachers	www.ialt.ie
Israeli Law and Society Association	http://ilsa.huji.ac.il
Indian Sociology Society	www.insoso.org
Italian Association for the Study of Law and Society	
Japanese Association of the Sociology of Law	http://jasl.info/english_page
Law and Society Association (USA)	www.lawandsociety.org
Law and Society Association of Australia and New Zealand (LSAANZ)	www.lsaanz.org
Socio Legal Studies Association (UK)	www.slsa.ac.uk
International Institute for the Sociology of Law (Oñati)	www.iisj.net
International Association for Philosophy of Law and Social Philosophy	https://ivronlineblog.wordpress.com
Juris Diversitas: an international, interdisciplinary community for the study of legal mixtures and movements	http://jurisdiversitas.blogspot.co.uk/p/about-us_05.html
World Consortium of Law and Society	www.ijp.upt.pt/page.php?p=602
Research Committee for the Sociology of Law (International Sociological Association)	rcsl.iscte.pt/www.isa-sociology.org/en

7 www.slsa.ac.uk/index.php/socio-legal-associations; this list is not comprehensive, there are other organizations that have not been listed on the SLSA website.

A story of law and society can be traced through publications. Nader (1969) advocated for law *in* society rather than law *and* society. Socio-legal scholars embrace law as social, cultural, economic, linguistic, and ideological. Sarat (1990) builds an argument around an interviewee stating that 'law is all over'. The significance of the law being ever-present in our lives (in this case, of the welfare poor) helped understanding of how people think about law and use it to respond to problems. Embracing this view creates a challenge to set the boundaries for enquiry while drawing on other disciplines for methods, concepts, insights, and theories. There have been attempts at defining the field though textbooks and edited collections (Bonsignore et al. 2005; Calavita 2016; Cane & Kritzer 2010; Kidder 1983; Lempert & Sanders 1986; Macaulay et al. 1995, 2007; Sarat 2004; Travers 2010).

Abel (2010) offers a comprehensive overview of four decades of law and society scholarship. He looks at the development of ideas and research focus through the statements of the Law and Society Association (LSA) presidents and the content of the *Law & Society Review* (*LSR*). He concludes that scholarship ought to aim to promote progressive social change, and that social science should help law promote a liberal political agenda (p. 3). Law and society scholars embrace a wide range of epistemological perspectives. The 'pull of the policy audience' (Sarat & Silbey 1988) is a tempting outlet for reinforcing the status quo.

Caroll Seron (then the president of LSA) and colleagues (Seron et al. 2016) published a paper on the future of publishing by the LSA. Accompanying the development of law and society there was a complex and fraught relationship with critical legal studies (Seron and Munger 2017; Trubek 1984).[8]

Several socio-legal research centres were established. The people that work in research centres determine their intellectual focus and development. Each research centre typically has its distinctive focus and expertise, yet they all share a dedicated focus on the study of law in society. What these centres offer is a stimulating academic environment that enables students, staff, and visitors to meet and discuss ideas. There are opportunities for exchange, presentations of research projects, lectures, and seminars.

Founded in 1961, the Center for the Study of Law and Society in Berkeley[9] encourages and supports empirical research and theoretical analysis of the social consequence of law, including legal institutions and processes, the impact of law on individuals and groups, and social, political, and intellectual influences on law itself and legal activity. Although located in the UC Berkeley School of Law, the centre provides an environment where faculty and graduate students from many campus departments of the social sciences and humanities, as well as visiting scholars from the US and overseas institutions, regularly meet, present research papers, exchange ideas, and explore new concepts, perspectives, and research agendas. The centre's associated faculty and visitors are drawn from many disciplines, such as political science, sociology, economics, psychology, law, philosophy, and history.

The Berkeley programme is both in and out of the law school. It is a freestanding institution that is not much appreciated by 'conventional' law faculty. It offers the premier doctoral programme in socio-legal studies, awarding a PhD in jurisprudence and social policy. Law and society work at its best has been undertaken on the basis of critical mass *and* formal programmes or centres.[10] Today, UC Irvine is probably the 'biggest' law and society faculty,

8 See below on the influence on David Sugarman at Harvard during critical legal studies times.
9 www.law.berkeley.edu/research/center-for-the-study-of-law-society/
10 For example, in Wisconsin in the 1970s–2000 as well as at UCLA; UMass Amherst and UC Santa Barbara, Buffalo, University of Denver had leading law and society programmes that had no affiliation to law schools.

with both law school and non-law school members, but its own separate Department of Criminology and Law and Society (called CLS).

Law and Society Association

The roots and influence of LSA are in the social sciences. LSA was born in American Sociological Association meetings in the late 1950s to early 1960s. Political scientists, psychologists, and anthropologists with an interest in solving social problems united. Laura Nader conducted an anthropological study of variations in dispute processing. She had the first group of graduate students studying all over the world and compiled the first book looking at legal processes (not doctrine) comparatively (Nader & Todd 1978).

In 1964, responding to the availability of research funds and their own political and intellectual agendas, a multidisciplinary group of scholars created the Law and Society Association (Mather 2011). 'The Law and Society Association is an interdisciplinary scholarly organization committed to social scientific, interpretive, and historical analyses of law across multiple social contexts.'[11] This group had disciplinary backgrounds in anthropology, sociology, political science, law, psychology, history, and economics. The Association was founded by Professors Harry Ball, Robert Yegge, and Red Schwartz. Professor Ball became the first president of LSA, and Professor Schwartz became the first editor of the Association's journal, the *LSR*. With help from a grant from the Russell Sage Foundation, the first issue of the *Review* appeared in November 1966. For its first decade, LSA meetings were held in conjunction with the meetings of other major disciplinary associations. LSA held its own first national meeting in Buffalo, New York, in 1975. Three years later in Minneapolis, Minnesota, LSA held its first annual meeting. The Executive Office of LSA began at the University of Denver in 1971, moved to the University of Massachusetts at Amherst in 1987, and moved to the University of Utah in Salt Lake City in 2012.[12] LSA's main office moves regularly, depending on who agrees to be executive director of the LSA (a non-elective position chosen by the board).

Many intellectual movements such as civil rights, critical race theory, and feminist theory affected law and society studies (Menkel-Meadow & Diamond 1991; Seron & Munger 2017) in scholarship and in meetings and transmission of knowledge and creation of new categories. Law and society was internationalized by work on law and development, writing on legal education, and context. An early and important area where law and society work was internationalized was in research on the legal profession (Abel et al. 1988; Abel & Lewis 1989; Dezalay & Sugarman 1995; Dezalay et al. 1996; Halliday et al. 1998, 2007). The Working Group on Comparative Study of Legal Professions, which began meeting in 1980 and has met annually ever since, was an important vehicle for bringing together, and the Research Committee on Sociology of Law has nurtured law and society scholars transnationally.[13]

Japan and the Netherlands, for example, had strong early research traditions in law and society.[14] The Dutch were the first international participants to join the LSA conversations and attend meetings. The first International LSA meeting was in Amsterdam. The Japanese were

---

11 www.lawandsociety.org/commitments.html
12 www.lawandsociety.org/history.html
13 https://iwglp.wordpress.com/
14 For example: access to justice, dispute resolution, role of litigation in society, sociology of legal aid, lawyers and judges.

the first international members to join the LSA. LSA meetings started to take place regularly in international locations – Amsterdam, Glasgow, Berlin, Mexico City, Toronto, and so on.[15]

Law & Society Review. The LSA, through Wiley, publishes the *LSR* in four issues per volume per year. Founded in 1966, the *LSR* is regarded by socio-legal scholars in the US and other countries as one of the leading journals in the field.

Other prominent journals in the field are *Journal of Legal Studies* (1972), *Law & Social Inquiry* (1976), *Journal of Empirical Legal Studies* (2004), and *Annual Review of Law and Social Science* (2005).

Emerging in law: the socio-legal studies movement in the UK

The development of socio-legal studies in the UK was haphazard. In the early years of the 20th century, law graduates came from the 'golden triangle' of Oxford, Cambridge, and London Universities where the use of classic textbooks ensured that the legal education offered was doctrinal in nature (Cownie & Bradney 2018). As these graduates turned into law teachers, the doctrinal focus was continued in the law school curriculum. It lacked realism and was protected behind the strong walls of traditional legal teaching. Campbell and Wiles (1975) wrote a paper on the study of law and society in Britain and described competing schools of thought and their conflicting loyalties. The conflict at that time was between socio-legal studies and the sociology of law. 'The new socio-legal approach is regarded as subversive by some law teachers, and others believe it represents the indulgence of those who do not understand what is truly entailed in the study of law' (p. 585). Socio-legal studies was also seen as less rigorous than traditional sociology of law: 'Socio-Legal studies may be entered with a few newly learned techniques, but sociology of law demands commitment and application' (p. 607).

In the 1960s, the universities expanded, and there was a shortage of staff. Consequently, there were many job opportunities, and universities wanted to encourage a new generation of scholars and teachers. Some scholars went to the US for a period of time where they took part in or audited classes in law schools that were nothing like they had experienced in the UK. Law teaching seemed more appealing in the US, and the uncertainty, flexibility, and dynamics of law were explored. Maintaining the spirit of the late 1960s, the *radical* in the law was discovered as a different way of thinking of what law should do. UK law teachers were not solely influenced by US experiences. Several of those who studied in the US were also seriously affected/changed by working in developing countries and observing the legal reach of law in a new state and a struggling economy (Sugarman 2011).

The relationship between critical legal studies and law and society was very important for UK and US scholars (the relationship between socio-legal studies and the critical legal studies movement has also been very different in the UK and US, with the UK much more focused on continental philosophy).[16] Harvard Law School, and the scholarship associated with it, was influential in the 1980s in the US and thereby also affected the development of critical legal studies in other countries. Post-modernism, Marxism, and critical theory more generally were the drivers for change. Centres such as Berkeley or other US universities provided fertile breeding grounds for

---

15 www.lawandsociety.org/aboutmeetings.html
16 Especially important at Wisconsin and UCLA – feminist legal theory, critical legal studies, and legal education or 'The Fem-Crits Go to Law School' (Menkel-Meadow 1988); See Munger and Seron (1984).

new thoughts and enthused scholars to return to the UK and integrate a new style of teaching into the law curriculum. A new space was created for ideas and thinking. Alternatives to the study of law emerged and challenged the supremacy of doctrinal law (feminism and critical legal studies – the law in context movement gained a wide following).

A group of 20–25 young academics[17] set up a group that met informally to present and discuss papers on criminology and social science without any real structure (Phil Thomas, interview, 2018). Marxism and the sociology of law were critical to the motto of the movement: law is the problem not the solution. The group turned into a socio-legal group of the Society of Legal Scholars (then called the Society of Public Teachers of Law) in the 1970s. The first conference was held in Manchester in 1972. The group grew fast, with 150 members in the first year; over the next 20 years the socio-legal group became independent of the Society of Legal Scholars, and in 1990 the Socio Legal Studies Association (SLSA) was established (Thomas 1997).

Harris (1983)[18] outlines the shift experienced by academic lawyers who felt that something needed to be added to traditional legal scholarship, accepting that 'law was only one social phenomenon among many others' (p. 315) and needed to be understood in its social context. A further strand of interest developed towards the sociology of law. He argues that sociology, social policy, and social administration have been the greatest influence on the study and teaching of law in the UK. Here, the stark contrast with the development of law and society in the USA can be noticed. Whereas socio-legal studies in the UK is firmly rooted within the law schools, law and society scholars in the US are grounded in a variety of disciplines (political science, psychology, history, anthropology, and economics). Here, a distinction is clear between the greater link of law and society in the UK with clear policy ambitions (Genn 2008; Maclean & Kurczewski 2011), whereas the US has much less policy impact; there, the impact is focused on scholarship and teaching (Sarat & Silbey 1987).

In 1974, the Centre for Socio-Legal Studies (CSLS)[19] was established at Wolfson College in Oxford. The CSLS was part of a government programme to establish pure research centres, free of teaching and administration. There were four in the UK at that time, until Thatcher abolished the programme, and the host universities were expected to pick up the pieces. 'Oxford did not, there were only 2 jobs out of 11 or so continued. The rest of us had to find soft money … tough times!' (Mavis Maclean, interview, 2018). Donald Harris was the first director. A small group of like-minded interdisciplinary scholars found themselves in a position where they had no teaching obligations and had the opportunity to do research. CSLS engaged in the multidisciplinary study of law early on. The first large empirical assignment was a no-fault compensation project that was approached across the disciplines of the scholars represented (economics, social policy, law, psychology, etc.; Hawkins 1997).

Twining (1995) sets socio-legal studies in the context of development in higher education and academic law in England:

> The first twenty-one years of the CSLS spans almost exactly the same period [of funding, salary and professional status of academics deteriorating], which has been one of the most difficult in the history of higher education – an era in which we

---

17 The group was predominately male, but Maureen Cain was an influential participant. There was no one of colour.
18 The first director of the centre for socio-legal studies in Oxford wrote an article about the development of socio-legal studies in the UK.
19 www.law.ox.ac.uk/centres-institutes/centre-socio-legal-studies; www.nuffieldfoundation.org/sites/default/files/Law%20in%20the%20Real%20World%20full%20report.pdf

moved disjointedly and painfully from a small aggregation of institutions towards something approaching a mass 'system'.

(p. 35)

Twining goes on to state that socio-legal is only one of several significant intellectual trends within the discipline of law. Socio-legal has made a large contribution to the rethinking and reconceptualization of specialized fields in law, both traditional and new (ESRC 1994).

As well as in Oxford, there were socio-legal hubs in Warwick and Kent, and an exchange programme of scholars who went to Dar Es Salaam exposed them to African law, which changed the way an important cluster of scholars thought (see Phil Thomas below).

Socio-legal studies in the UK grew out of a shared desire to explore larger questions, to expand doctrinal enquiry into an empirical, evidence-based understanding of phenomena. Scholars were driven by their commitment to change the world and to challenge existing boundaries, to ask questions and explore phenomena that had no space in the current set-up, and to affect policy.

To sum up, the overall growth of socio-legal studies in the UK was more to do with serendipity than a structured organic development.

> Many actors contributed in different ways at different times. Also, then law was viewed differently to now: methods or empirical research were not a 'thing', there was a deep sense of political struggle, and some felt that it was their job to change the world.[20]

With the steady growth of universities and polytechnics came law graduates who were increasingly interested in socio-legal research. These graduates turned into teachers and slowly but surely turned socio-legal into a fixed part of the academic enquiry in many law schools.

The Socio-Legal Studies Association

The SLSA was formed in 1990 in the UK.[21] It grew out of the Socio-Legal Group, which for some years had provided an annual forum for socio-legal scholars to meet and disseminate their work. However, it was felt that there was a need for a more permanent organizational structure that would help to keep scholars in touch with each other, providing regular channels of communication and promoting and supporting the work of socio-legal academics.[22] SLSA promoted lots of new research spaces, to encourage people with ideas to thrive and grow and create and sustain an intellectual community.

The SLSA's launch was supported with a £4,000 loan from the Nuffield Foundation, administrative and financial support from the CSLS in Oxford, and seedcorn funding from academic institutions across the UK. The *Journal of Law and Society* also provided support (and still does) by distributing the *Socio-Legal Newsletter* to its mailing list. The SLSA has always welcomed members from around the world, and the initial list of 100 included individuals from the UK, Europe, USA, Singapore, Japan, and Australia.

The *Socio-Legal Newsletter* was launched in the spring of 1989 and, for many years, was the SLSA's main vehicle for communicating with members and non-members.[23] It

---

20 Phil Thomas, SLSA Bristol interview, 2018.
21 SLSA archive: http://ials.sas.ac.uk/library/archives/records-legal-education-archives-ials/socio-legal-studies-association-archive; British Library socio-legal archive: www.bl.uk/collection-guides/socio-legal-studies
22 http://ials.sas.ac.uk/library/archives/records-legal-education-archives-ials/socio-legal-studies-association-archive
23 Edited from Oxford by Nancy Drucker, the CSLS administrator, then edited and produced for several years by Penny Smith, Cardiff; thereafter Marie Selwood, the current editor, took over.

continues to be a keystone of the SLSA, publishing news about all the SLSA's activities and also features and reports about events, publications, and research of interest to socio-legal scholars worldwide. The first SLSA *Research Directory* followed in the spring of 1991. Later, an e-bulletin was established to provide members with more regular socio-legal news, and finally the website and weekly e-bulletin and a blog were launched to give members immediate access to the latest news and developments. The SLSA offers much more than an annual conference and thus has a wider reach than the LSA through providing research grants, training events, and support for workshops and seminars.

Over the years, the SLSA has grown and developed. A different UK university hosts the annual conference each year, which attracts more than 500 participants. Volunteers who sit on its Executive Committee run the SLSA.

Founded in 2016, the Centre of Law and Society at the University of Cardiff [24] is closely linked to the *Journal of Law and Society* and its activities; it aims to enable and raise the profile of high-quality socio-legal scholarship and education at Cardiff University. Cardiff offers a series of 'conversations in law and society' on its website.

Journal of Law and Society (*JLS*): 'The story of the JLS is closely linked with that of socio-legal studies in the UK. They were both formed about the same time (in the mid-1970s) as a spontaneous alternative to the Law School establishment, its pedagogy and its ideology' (p. 1).[25] Phil Thomas set up the journal in 1974 to provide an outlet for scholars with an interest in a socio-legal approach to law. *JLS* was born out of the spirit of 1968. 'While a wide range of theoretical influences (Marxism, feminism, sociology of law, critical legal studies, anarchism) and social movements influenced the early period of socio-legal studies and of the *JLS*; the catalyst was the weight of personal experience that a young generation of scholars had gained in the 1960s and their limited capacity to express it in the Law School as it then stood' (p. 2). The rationale for establishing the journal was to provide a vehicle for UK-based socio-legal scholars to promote their research. At the time there were only limited opportunities to place papers taking a socio-legal approach.

Social & Legal Studies: This is a leading international journal, publishing progressive, interdisciplinary, and critical approaches to socio-legal study. The journal was born out of a commitment to feminist, anti-colonial, and socialist economic perspectives on the study of law in 1993. It offers an intellectual space where diverse traditions and critical approaches within legal study meet. The journal particularly welcomes work in new fields of socio-legal study, as well as non-Western scholarship. In addition to its review section, the journal has developed an occasional innovative 'Debate & Dialogue' section. This feature allows more direct and immediate engagement between authors.[26]

---

24 www.cardiff.ac.uk/research/explore/research-units/centre-of-law-and-society; it was proceeded by Lancaster's Centre for Law and Society, which was established in May 2006, and was the first of its kind in England and Wales.

25 'The *Journal of Law and Society* at 40: History, Work and Prospects', https://onlinelibrary.wiley.com/page/journal/14676478/homepage/the_journal_of_law_and_society_at_40.htm

26 https://uk.sagepub.com/en-gb/eur/journal/social-legal-studies#editorial-board

International Journal of Law in Context:[27] William Twining and Robert Stevens established the Law in Context series for CUP (in 1970) and also founded the *International Journal of Law in Context*, published by CUP (first editors Carrie Menkel-Meadow and Michael Freeman). It was set up to be the first truly international law and society journal and is now publishing work from all over the world. Michael Freeman at UCL set up 'Law and ...' conferences and edited the Oxford series arising from them for 20 years.

Legal education and socio-legal studies

A good way to recognize how the field of socio-legal studies has established itself (or not) is to take a look at its presence in teaching curricula. Legal education in the US and the UK are very different and thus produce a different type of academic.

In the US, law is not an undergraduate subject. This means that everyone comes to law after being trained in a different discipline. As a result, law students are more mature and have received theory and methods training in other fields. Many of these students develop into professors who typically have PhDs in areas other than law (social psychology or economics, for example). This naturally builds bridges to other departments and facilitates collaborations. It also means that US law schools have scholars who do statistics: a space for that type of work is created. Empirical traditions in the US, therefore, have a strong quantitative component.

Law degrees in the UK, in contrast, start at undergraduate level. There is a strong history of theory and doctrine in teaching. Qualitative scholarship and methods are usually taught at postgraduate/PhD level. Not all universities offer a specific socio-legal syllabus, and socio-legal scholars are spread throughout UK universities' law schools. Socio-legal courses are available at several universities, including: the University of Glasgow, the University of Kent, the University of Exeter, Cardiff University, the University of Bristol, and the University of Oxford (Adler 2007).

The growth and development of schools of thought, disciplines, and methods happened while the institutional presence of law and society/socio-legal was establishing itself. In Chapter 1 and throughout this volume, different schools of thought, different disciplines, and different methods are showcased. The development of the field has been influenced by the national political agenda of the time, the type of research that got funded, and scholars' interest in a particular area of study. Some of these aspects will be explored through the interviews in the following section of the chapter.

In this section, I have provided a rough sketch of the development of socio-legal studies, with a focus on the USA and the UK. Of course, these are only two of many countries that have seen an expansion of socio-legal studies. Socio-legal movements have left their marks in different ways in the systems they developed. It is evident that, from being non-existent in research agendas, methods, or teaching curricula for most of the 20th century, socio-legal scholarship is now an established focus of scholarly and institutional interest.

27 www.cambridge.org/core/journals/international-journal-of-law-in-context

Individual paths in law and society/socio-legal studies

This section provides a space for excerpts of some of the voices[28] of the law and society movements. My decision to lightly interpret and present the interviews rather than analysing them more fully 'and to my own agenda' is intended for the benefit of new scholars to the field. Here, scholars recount their trajectory through socio-legal studies, with a focus on three key themes: intellectual formation; research and writing; and politics, scholarship and policy.

Intellectual formation

What was driving young academics in the 1960s–70s to pursue their path? What contributed to their intellectual formation? It turns out that, for those scholars I interviewed, shared narratives form around an appetite for exploring a world beyond and around law, being an activist, critiquing the doctrinal, and a healthy portion of serendipity. Discovering disciplines outside law, at a time when empirical explorations and socio-legal methods were not available in a law school, satisfied intellectual curiosity.

Carrie Menkel-Meadow[29]

My intellectual formation and interest was a combination of being a political activist and a clinician to teach students how law practice actually operated and how it should operate, normatively. Driven by the interest in more than law, I had a good sociology degree (Columbia Univ.) and when I think about my education, there was the formal degree and education that I have, but, actually, the way I thought about legal problems came from hanging around the social science departments. In the 70s very few people in the law schools were asking empirical questions. On a panel at the annual meeting of US Law professors (AALS) I was told not to engage with empirical research as it took too long and would not be valued by law schools.

I wrote an article on negotiation and legal problem solving that was rejected in all the law journals I submitted it to because there was no doctrinal law in the text. In the early 1980s the Centre for Public Resources was founded in New York City – a think tank for dispute resolution by corporate lawyers – not exactly my reference group. But, unbeknownst to me, in 1983/4 I was awarded the first ever prize for scholarship on dispute resolution. I was invited to a big, fancy award ceremony in New York City at the University Club on Fifth Avenue, where, when I was a child, no Jews, Catholics or women were allowed. It was a very establishment, white Anglo Saxon, Protestant club for Ivy League university graduates where the men did business and certainly no women. This building was next to the public library in New York City that I used to go to and was a place that I could never go into as a young professional (and poverty lawyer!), and the first time I go into the building is to get this award; and the award is in the *New York Times*! And 'the rest was history' in a sense that then, all of a sudden, my law school was very proud of me and

---

28 It is made up of interviews I held with: Carrie Menkel-Meadow (Chancellor's Professor of Law (and Political Science), University of California, Irvine); Rosemary Hunter (Professor of Law and Socio-Legal Studies, University of Kent); Phil Thomas (Emeritus Professor of Law, University of Cardiff); Mavis Maclean (Senior Research Fellow in Law, University of Oxford); Sally Engle Merry (Silver Professor of Anthropology, NYU College of Arts and Sciences); David Sugarman (Emeritus Professor of Law, Lancaster University); Tom Tyler (Macklin Fleming Professor of Law and Professor of Psychology, Yale Law School); Deborah Hensler (Judge John Ford Professor of Dispute Resolution, Stanford Law School).

29 Interview, Oxford, July 2018.

I was part of a group of academics that founded a field of teaching and study of negotiation, mediation and other ways of resolving disputes (the 'ADR' movement).

Sally Engle Merry[30]

I did my undergraduate degree at Wellesley College and my postgraduate degree in anthropology at Yale. At Brandeis University I then studied the law and did my dissertation in law and anthropology (an emerging field) in 1978. Questions about urban chaos and housing design for low-income people were very appealing to me. The Chicago school of sociology was very prominent then. I worked at Wellesley College for many years and then moved to NYU. I was interested in urban crime, architecture and housing, and female criminal activity. My research is, generally speaking, on who goes to court and why (more in the next section).

I attended my first LSA meeting (with 120 people) in 1980 in Madison and have been going ever since. LSA was then resolutely US focused, that was how it worked. (Scholarship was focused on mapping disputing patterns to counter claims about the litigation explosion. Why are the Americans so litigious?) I think that law and society is not a discipline in and of itself, rather a joining, a canon of many disciplines with an underlying sociology focus. We used social science to understand law, other fields were marginal and came and went. Until the 1990s the LSA remained US focused then it got more international. Now there is a 25% non-US based membership. There is a spin off East Asian group for example. LS did not have the pull of the Marxist movement in the 1980s, there was a love for Weber and Foucault.

Tom Tyler[31]

I did my PhD in Psychology, focussing on lab experiments. I then decided not to be attached to classic research in psychology, rather to go out and do fieldwork in real settings. That was my platform to do work that was valuable. My work spoke to different communities, law and management, economics. Law and Society celebrates diversity, I changed my work focus to topics of law and society. Having done that was a tricky move for my career: I just about got tenure. I had a clear trajectory and believed in what I was doing. My focus was on exploring legitimacy asking questions about why people accept court decision and this led me to procedural justice. I put legitimacy onto the agenda with my book in 2006 when the general opinion was that people just care about the outcome. People have lots of social stereotypes (Kahneman 2012) and research to date had not asked the people what they want.

In my opinion Law and Society has failed. Typically, US universities and law schools do not have a law and society programme. The University of California at Irvine is an exception. NYU dropped the programme and at Yale there is only one law and society scholar (me). Law and economics, on the other hand, has a serious representation in law schools; at Yale we have 8 in the faculty.

In many ways LSA is a space for second *real* interests. It gives scholars the space to talk about the law and get respect and status – in many ways it's people's passion – their reality is happening in parallel in their day jobs alongside tenure worries. The goals of LSA are to investigate the flaws in the legal system: gap studies (looking at the gaps between ideals and reality). Evidence is collected to produce social change (Galanter 1974; Macaulay 1985). The 1960s were a time of reform and change, there was idealism about the time and people were pushing for change.

---

30 Interview, LSA, Toronto, 2018.
31 Interview, London, May 2018.

Deborah Hensler[32]

I should start by saying that I am a political scientist, not a lawyer which means that I have a sort of 'outside–in' view of legal scholarship generally and also law & society scholarship.

As a high school student in the late 1950s I was interested in (what we would call today) ethnographic sociological analysis of communities (Lynd & Lynd 1959). For some reason, I was particularly interested in power and the distribution thereof. I majored in political science at Hunter College NYC and thought I wanted to go into politics, and was advised that I should first get a law degree. By happenstance, I met up with a young professor who was studying power structures and was trained in empirical survey methods, and hired me as his research assistant. In his freshman course he made us do field research, which was eye opening. Expanding my skills, I took a wonderful summer course at the University of Michigan Institute for Social Research, the leading such program in the US and learned sampling statistics and survey research methods from top scholars.

Talking to a friend of my older sister who was at Columbia University Law School made me think law school would be boring, and realizing I was unlikely to be a successful politician, I applied for a PhD in political science and sociology – I am a political sociologist, not a law and society scholar. I rejected an offer from Yale and decided to go to MIT where there was a new political science program offering empirical research training and a multidisciplinary perspective. At MIT I learned to be a policy analyst applying social science techniques to real policy problems. After leaving MIT, I did some consultancies for government making use of my empirical survey training.

In the late 1960s we moved to California, it was difficult to find a teaching job, I did not have my PhD yet and I encountered gender bias. I found a research position at UCLA and ended up running the survey centre there. I was contacted by the RAND corporation to give advice on survey research and 2 years later they invited me to work for them. After 6 years at RAND I was their most senior person in the field, not a good thing when you are still as young and inexperienced as I was. Just as I was thinking I needed to move on, my mentor at RAND announced a new programme, the 'Institute for Civil Justice,' was being created. A group of 5 RAND researchers, with different disciplinary backgrounds (law and psychology, economists, management science and me) formed the programme's first research team and was charged with developing its research agenda. Here is when my law and society story commenced. As background for this new role, I began to survey the existing empirical literature and began to read all the previous issues of *LSR*. Most of what I read, to be honest, I was not impressed by. The methods were not rigorous, the articles had a strong ideological left perspective and even though I am left of center myself, I don't think the purpose of academic research should be to make a political statement.

My first LSA meeting was around 1982 in Wisconsin in a small motel. After that, I began to engage with many law and society scholars: Bill Felstiner, Allan Lind, and, Tom Tyler in particular. Felstiner, Austin Sarat, and Bert Kritzer were just completing a ground-breaking study of federal court litigation with a major grant from the US Department of Justice. My early L&S work focussed on courts and court- connected ADR programmes, influenced by the early work of Lind and Tyler on procedural justice. I was fortunate to recruit Allan to RAND, later Robert MacCoun, and Judith Resnik. Then a traditional doctrinal scholar teaching at University of Southern California Law School,

32 Interview (Skype) July 2018.

joined up with us. Later I worked with Allan and Rob on a major research project on compensation claiming, which we modelled after work performed by Hazel Genn and her colleagues who were then at the CSLS at Oxford.

Mavis Maclean[33]

My first degree was in history. But in the 1960s the Oxford modern history syllabus closed with the end of the Second World War just as I began to get really interested. So for graduate study I went to the London School of Economics in 1968 and read for their new master's degree in Social Policy. Social Administration (implying clear but often merely descriptive study of social service provision) was being overtaken by the new focus on social policy (which was more exciting, sitting closer in analytical techniques to the study of public policy and politics). Though for a while both labels seemed to include the same people doing very much the same things.

When I was invited to join the new SSRC CSLS in Oxford in 1972 by Don Harris I found myself in a small group with two lawyers, one psychologist, two economists and two social policy people, all excited about working together to develop this new interdisciplinary activity. I was distressed by the impact of Thatcherism on our ability to identify and meet social need. I am hugely grateful to Don for whispering to me about the potential of law in society as a policy tool. After the large-scale survey work of compensation for accident victims (n = 3,000), Don introduced me to John Eekelaar, and we have worked together for nearly 40 years on family law and family policy, moving gradually from quantitative to qualitative research into the justice system.

My major concern at that time was the economic position of women after divorce. Mrs Thatcher in 1990 suddenly demanded a new child support system. I was invited into the then Lord Chancellor's Department, now Ministry of Justice, as an adviser, and am still there. I hasten to add my advice is rarely taken ... but the research function I helped to set up is thriving ... Throughout this life time of empirical policy oriented research my intellectual nourishment has come from the ISA Research Committee on the Sociology of Law, with its wonderful base in Oñati in the Basque country, and its nurturing of international networks, including my Polish collaborator Jacek Kurczewski who introduced me to the need to question every assumption, and to go and see for myself who is doing what.

David Sugarman[34]

Although intellectually curious for as long as I can remember, I was a 'late developer', and it was only at Further Education (FE) College that, with support from some wonderful teachers, the world of learning really opened up for me. My legal interests were and remain primarily historical and sociological – I want to know where law comes from, how and why it changes, and its impact on society.

During the second year of my undergraduate law degree (Hull University, 1967–70) I began to realize I could transcend the overwhelmingly doctrinal curriculum. My inspirational torts tutor, Ray Smith, recommended John Fleming's essay on remoteness and duty of care as control devices in liability for negligence (1968). The scales fell from

---

33 Interview, SLSA, Bristol, and paper for *JLS*, 2017.
34 Interview, IALS, London, May 2018.

my eyes as Fleming demonstrated how remoteness and duty of care were policy devices, and that the courts were doing politics. Some faculty were engaged with American Legal Realism and this contributed to my becoming a 'law and' person, as did the mid-late 1960's and my discovery of Edward Thompson and 'the new social history'. By my final year I had decided that I wanted to become an academic, and went on to Cambridge, focusing on directors' fiduciary duties. Most significant, however, was my first taste of teaching law. Spurred on by Bob Hepple (who became an important mentor), and under the aegis of the Cambridge Workers Education Association, I found teaching Labour Law to factory workers in and around Northampton to be both exhilarating and chastening. I learned far more than they, and hugely enjoyed the experience. Subsequently, Harvard (1975–76) changed my life – notably, the Law School classes I took or audited by Gary Bellow, Morton Horwitz (Sugarman 1980), Duncan Kennedy and Roberto Unger, and the Sociology Department's 'Introduction to Sociology' taught by Daniel Bell. The ideas they introduced to me remain important, as do the networks and friendships that arose from this experience, and which include Rick Abel, Bob Gordon, Dirk Hartog, Dave Trubek and Austin Sarat. My passion for history deepened. On returning home, I re-tooled with the help of Bill Cornish, who generously allowed me to audit his pioneering course on 'Law and Social Change in England, 1750–1950' (LSE), receiving strong and invaluable encouragement from Simon Roberts and William Twining.

My intellectual formation has also been influenced by participation in diverse groups and associations (including the Law and State Group, the Critical Legal Studies movement, the American Society for Legal History, LSA, SLSA, History Workshop, the British Legal History Conference and the Centres of Law and Society at Lancaster and Cardiff) and by subsequent opportunities to research and teach overseas, and the personal contacts that this has sustained.

Phil Thomas[35]

I was looking for more than law to study and explore. I went to the US and audited classes in a law school. Law teaching was more appealing and explored the uncertainty, flexibility and dynamic of law. I was exposed to a radically different way of thinking of what the law should do. Exploring the boundaries of law interdisciplinarily and interjurisdictionally was an exciting endeavour. Guided by a series of coincidences after spending time in the US and Africa I felt the way in which law was taught in the UK needed to be challenged. I knew there was more than the law I had been taught and explored questions to be asked from different disciplinary lenses.

In the 1960s/70s British universities were expanding and short of staff. This created a new space for self-expression, ideas and thinking. Law was viewed differently then than now; methods were not a thing, there was a deep sense of politics and struggle, we thought our job was to change the world. I was a political activist, a socialist and have experienced that politics and job always went together. There was no epiphany moment of coming together of like-minded scholars; socio-legal in the UK emerged out of a small group and a series of coincidences.

35 Interview, SLSA, Bristol, 2018.

Rosemary Hunter[36]

I was interested to learn about law and justice. But in my law degree in Australia in the mid-1980s I was not really learning about justice. I did a joint law and history degree which provided an additional lens, and I also took a new module on Law and Society which was taught by Richard Ingleby, one of Mavis Maclean's former PhD students from the Oxford CSLS. When I went to Stanford to do a doctorate in 1994 I learnt more about law and society approaches. My supervisor was Deborah Rhode, a prominent 'fem-crit', and my committee included Lawrence Friedman and Deborah Hensler. I already had an interest in critical approaches to law and feminism, and I became increasingly focused on people rather than the law, and the way law impacts on people's lives – something that can only be discovered empirically. My early development as a socio-legal scholar was formed more through mentors than formal teaching. This grew into continuous asking of questions and developing ideas leading me into both qualitative and quantitative empirical research, and the thrill of creating new knowledge.

To sum up, the brief insight into the intellectual formation of the interviewees, at similar times, illustrates how they were all motivated to explore phenomena beyond the pure legal. This influenced their pursuit of research agendas and writing.

Research and writing

Many factors influence research and publication agendas. These can range from personal interest, employer expectations, and political climate to funding priorities. The interviews showcased a strong appetite for exploring methodologies, gaining empirical insights, and working and thinking along interdisciplinary lines.

Carrie Menkel-Meadow

The first LSA meeting I went to, Susan Silby and Sally Merry gave a paper on mediation. They had a classic sociological taxonomy in juxtaposing different styles of mediation … and for me, it was like falling in love. It was reading Kalven and Zeisel's *The American Jury* (an empirical study comparing judicial and jury decision making). I thought this is the kind of work I want to do, I want to study how people do this work and look at different models that they are using in their work. So, it was very powerful for me and I contributed to that literature, on the legal process in action.

After having practised as a mediator in many different settings, I now return to Law and Society and feel a sense of estrangement. In order to be a very good analyst, you also have to have an insider's perspective: participation and observation. I feel that I would trust my own descriptions of mediation more than some outside researchers, who may be very well trained in empirical methods but who will have never sat in the seat of being a mediator, so don't understand the choices that a mediator has to make.

On an LSA plenary panel some years ago that I was on in Chicago – Jim Gibson (a quantitative political scientist) was making the argument that Law and Society had lost its positivist, quantitative soul. It was no longer doing hard science. It had moved into the narrative turn, to hermeneutics, and to postmodernism, and dominated by theorists.

36 Interview (Skype), July 2018.

Both theorists from the law school … (that was another critique, that the lawyers were taking over Law and Society), and there were fewer real social scientists in it. What's the soul of Law and Society? Is the tent big enough for humanities, narrative, postmodern theory? Austin Sarat founded the law and humanities group, and Ted Eisenberg, my former colleague at UCLA, the 'empirical legal studies' group. There has always a feeling of under-representation of economists at LSA. So there are still disciplinary issues in LSA. Sadly, Law and Society has largely 'failed' in really influencing American legal academia. In many ways law and economics has had a much greater impact in legal scholarship, education and the development of case law (see Chapter 3 in this volume). Seldom do US judges reference empirical work (see comments of Mavis MacLean for UK on this).

I had a whole other empirical career of studying women in the legal profession. I did a lot of studies and wrote a lot of articles. But, then I went off to do my international dispute resolution work, and although I would always be asked to give talks on women in the legal profession, I didn't really keep up that much with the data on that. And all of a sudden, now it's a very hot topic again and I am back to studying women in the legal profession and dispute resolution, including women as negotiators (combining some of the strands of my earlier empirical work).

So, when I say I pulled out of the politics of LSA and its governance I was just too busy doing, actually writing and I think I have taken teaching more seriously my whole career than many people. I think that legal education in other parts of the world is actually getting more interested in some of the experiential and socio-legal studies methods. So, they're looking for people who teach courses in addition to giving papers. So now I have taught in many countries outside of the US. Law and society is still my home in my head intellectually.

Sally Engle Merry

My work focuses on social justice. My first book was on urban crime (Merry 1981). Generally speaking I want to understand the problems people encounter – my role is that of a social critic and not social engineer. I then wrote a book on mediation (Merry 1990) building on anthropological work. My research was studying the litigiousness of Americans. More precisely, it is about average people that go to court for everyday problems and then lose control of their problems when handing them over to the courts. The way in which Marxism understood power was very helpful to my research, the focus on legal consciousness came out of these concerns about hegemony and power, and what preserves relations of power. The notion of culture was pushed and with that legal pluralism and legal consciousness was brought into the debate. They are great ways to conceptualize what was going on and thus helpful analytical tools.

Maintaining a focus on the dynamics of power, I then studied dispute resolution and colonialism through the lens of legal pluralism and anthropology in the UK and Africa. I did an ethno-historical study of lower courts in Hawaii (impact of US law on Hawaii society). I looked at the statistics of colonization to study the legal transformation and shift in legal consciousness.

Another research focus of mine is human rights and gender violence against women (in the early 90s). I looked at how local organizations mobilize; I studied vernacularization and the global Human Rights movement. Law and power helps us understand and access the human rights discourse. Human rights tell us that we have a right to make a claim. If the court does not respond to that claim we lose that right. My work is looking at that space.

I have been fortunate throughout my career to have institutional support for doing my research, as well as NSF grants (to look into how women's NGOs translate global into local, with Peggy Levitt).

More recently I have become interested in global governance and the use of indicators. How does one measure, how does one decide, is there a shared standard – who has the power to make these decisions? Again I looked at these questions through the lens of power and who has the power to make those decisions? Experts in the global north usually do quantifying about the global south without consulting those measured. Quantification of violence against women, human rights indicators, trafficking and government response to it are the topics of my recent work.

Tom Tyler

Persistence and adaptability are my two guiding principles. This allows me to deal with criticism – I never doubted what I did was important, if you believe in what you are doing then persevere. To be successful you need to be distinctive rather than mainstream. That might come with rejection and people not being ready for your ideas. Be pragmatic and don't take it personal when a paper gets rejected.

Deborah Hensler

Going back to my high school days, I was always interested in real people and daily lives. Some suggest that is 'because I am nosy'. Once the centre at RAND was established my research agenda was shaped by decisions made collaboratively by the research staff. Unlike most academics based at universities, we were oriented towards empirical research that could contribute to policy debates. We focused on identifying empirically testable assertions that underlined protagonists' arguments. Our research agenda was guided by what stakeholders (judges, legal practitioners, corporations and consumer groups) cared about: One of the big policy issues we worked on was how the legal system should respond to asbestos injury litigation in the early 1980s. In the process of trying to understand how courts were handling asbestos cases, we realized we were observing the birth of mass tort litigation. Over time, my research interests shifted from ADR which I focused on when I first began to engage in socio-legal studies to mass claims: how they arise, progress and are resolved both privately and publicly in courts. My interest in class actions arose from this, and class actions and other collective litigation have been my focus for the past 20 years.

Mavis Maclean

The key requirement for our field of study, whatever semantic issues may arise, is the need for sustainability. Our focus, our methodologies, and our methods of communication need to keep on developing in response to our changing environment if we are to make an ongoing and lasting contribution to the understanding of law in our society.

Since the Legal Aid, Sentencing and Punishment of Offenders Act 2012 which severely limited the scope of public funding for legal services, particularly in private family law, family lawyers have become rather jaundiced, and tend to see 'MoJ' as the Ministry for Limiting Access to Lawyers and Courts which is thought by many of us to limit justice, though there are some who some think a website and a mediator will do the job. This may well be the case, but we need evidence for the validity of this assumption: hence empirical socio-legal studies.

We were asked (at this launch of the Cardiff Centre) for a synthetic review of ideas, themes, areas, methodologies, and general theories in sociology of law and socio-legal studies, empirical legal studies, and law and society. We need, therefore, further semantic consideration, this time not relating to the description of institutions but of disciplines. This can be helpful if undertaken positively for what they reveal, but without any compulsion to be too anxious about the distinctions. The debates over the use of the terms sociology of law, socio-legal studies, law in society, law and economics, and empirical legal studies are sometimes thought to indicate confusion, or a lack of analytical rigor in the field. I would like to suggest that this is not the case but, rather, that these differences may well be seen as a reflection of the energy and movement in this area.

David Sugarman

My research and publications have been largely serendipitous – a consequence of my values, intellectual curiosity, penchant for inter-disciplinarity, and fortuitous invitations. My writing and teaching engage with law, history, politics and society, traversing diverse subject areas including legal history, company law, international human rights, law and literature, women's rights, legal life-writing, the legal profession, legal education, and European anti-discrimination law. I am not interested in preaching to the converted, but driven to engage with, and persuade, the widest possible audiences with clarity and evidence (and more recently, humour), and without excessive jargon. The interplay between law and politics, and linking law with economic and social structure and policy, have been paramount. Frequently, I set out a clear question and then use empirical research to address the issue. I am a middle-range thinker suspicious of loose generalizations that claim to have the answer to everything. You might say that I have spread myself too thinly, and that I am not, therefore, a role model for those who want to make it in academia.

Rosemary Hunter

I am interested in people's experience of law rather than law's internal stories about itself. My doctorate was a socio-legal study of feminist law reforms. Feminists have argued that criminal law silences women. Are civil and family law – particularly in relation to domestic violence, which has been the subject of feminist reforms – the same? How do those reforms operate in practice? I set out to explore these questions without much methodological knowledge. I had some interviewing experience from my history degree; I looked at other studies and read a lot of empirical work. In Australia a lot of the empirical work was done by activists, not at universities, and they were valuable sources. That kind of research may be small scale and not rigorously representative but it speaks a truth. I subsequently worked on big projects with interdisciplinary teams and mixed methods, often commissioned or grant-funded, and learnt a huge amount about methodology. After I came to England I was involved in developing the feminist judgments project.

In Australia only a few university law schools had a socio-legal focus. In 2006 I went to Kent, a critical socio-legal law school, there were many other socio-legal hubs: Warwick, Keele, Westminster, Birmingham, Leeds, Bristol, and the Oxford CSLS.

To conclude, common themes that emerge are that research and writing are influenced by a variety of factors that happen along the way. Inspiration and curiosity to pursue a research path can be driven 'from the inside' by a researcher's interest or 'from the outside' by a commissioned piece of research. A combination of both is probably what happens in most cases, and we cannot underestimate the role of politics and policy in some of these decisions.

Politics, scholarship and policy

Politics and funding are closely related. Each government and funding body has a set of areas that will get funding priority. There are a variety of incentives to support academic endeavours, especially in the development of large empirical projects and centres. Obtaining funding, being part of the policy debate, and engaging with stakeholders have grown to be more and more important for an academic career. However, the connection between politics, academics, and funding has always been demonstrable.

Carrie Menkel-Meadow

I have two chapters in the *Oxford Handbook of Empirical Legal Studies* (Cane & Kritzer 2010). One is an attempt to study the empirical conclusions around the claims and effectiveness of different forms of dispute resolution. The other chapter is on civil procedure, and I wrote it with Bryant Garth[37] on the extent to which empirical studies of legal process were used politically by policy makers. The government gave money to some researchers in order to promote faster, cheaper ways of disputing in a very political way, because our conservative Supreme Court justice, Warren Burger, wanted to get cases out of the court. Many Americans are very sceptical of government, but as progressive researchers, we wanted the government's support, because, without the money of the National Science Foundation or the National Academy of Sciences, you can't get really big research funded.

Per capita, if you looked at it, the amount of government funding and research in the United States is tiny as a function of GNP compared to many other countries. And so, some people never wanted to take NSF money, because they wanted to say what they wanted to say. And it's not like there was formal censorship, but there has been informal limitation. Every Republican administration in the United States has called for defunding important parts of the National Science Foundation, especially the so-called 'softer' sciences. Either the whole thing completely, which is mostly hard science, but certainly, Reagan, Bush, always proposed defunding the Law and Social Science programme. It's always been a tiny little part of NSF. But the Republican administrations have also called for defunding of the National Institutes of Health, which is cancer research. So, we've always had a very ambivalent relationship to government funding for research.

Sally Merry

I don't see myself as an activist but in the theoretical discussion I hope I am contributing to the debate about structures of power, empower some people to speak and not leave them in a position of powerlessness. My work reflects a continuity of concern about justice, about whose voices are not heard by the powerful. I am interested in investigating numbers, systems of power, and their remote and diffuse patterns.

There is always a good portion of serendipity in one's intellectual life, at least that is what I experienced. My work has a clear theoretical framework and link but the choice of topic usually happened in an unexpected moment.

The field has developed since the first LSA I attended in 1980. It has maintained its progressive politics. I worry that we move too far away from questions of power and law. We

---

37 People, processes, and politics of civil procedure.

need to continue to question how power operates and we need to continue to work on the perspective of the people who are powerless, addressing questions of inequality

Tom Tyler

I influenced theories of legitimacy and procedural justice *then* and *now* my work is influencing the police. It is important to maintain a balance in accepting speaking engagements; after all I am not a consultant. What I did, for example, is to design training based on procedural justice for the Chicago police. This programme can now be shared and taken advantage of without my constant engagement. One thing comes to mind in this context. I met John Braithwaite and he told me regarding policy – 'don't expect your name to get mentioned, you can't claim the credit.' It's an old persons game. Another important thing is not to get hooked into the games of colleagues. We all publish, speak, and have impact in different ways.

Deborah Hensler

It is a sad truth that empirical research on legal problems and policies is not well-funded. We see this with regard to pressing problems like access to justice for low income people, the promise and pitfalls of ODR, and immigration law. People care deeply about these issues and lobby for solution but usually they have no data and no interest in spending money to fund research – all funds are directed towards lobbying. The ground-breaking survey led by Kritzer et al. in 1979 for the US Department of Justice has never been repeated. A group of socio-legal scholars came together to try to get the Clinton administration to re-establish the office that had funded that research but without luck. The National Science Foundation (NSF), a major source of funding for academic research is organized largely along disciplines, which makes it challenging to fund law and society research. Interdisciplinary research is under-appreciated; disciplines rule and support maintaining disciplinary boundaries. A law and society program was established at NSF in the late 1980s, and thrived under the leadership of sociologist Felice Levine. My impression is that, in recent years, that program has made less of a mark on the field.

Although my personal research has benefited from law and society research and I have learned a lot from the leaders of the field, I see myself as more of a legal empiricist than a traditional law and society scholar. In part because my work is policy-driven rather than theory-driven. I think it's unfortunate that economists have defined the contemporary empirical legal studies movement and have spent some time in recent years arguing, in presentations and writing (Hensler 2017) that empirical legal studies were rooted historically in anthropology and sociology and that empirical research on law should celebrate multidisciplinarity and use a variety of methods, both qualitative and quantitative.

Mavis Maclean

We (as academics) can help government avoid 'elephant traps', which often accompany the search for developments which can both do good and save money, and perhaps argue effectively for reconsideration of an ill-advised venture. When a policy question arises we can offer a detailed description of what is happening in practice, rather than a view based on what is thought to be happening or should be happening (Maclean 2017).

As access to justice becomes overlain with discussion of mechanisms for alternative dispute resolution (ADR) and now online dispute resolution (ODR), I am thinking very hard about access (what is it?) to justice (what is it?) and whether mediators, interactive websites, and phone advisers do a good enough job for vulnerable parties? Or do lawyers (and courts) make a difference (they are creeping back into play in Australia, New Zealand, even parts of the United States)? In my view I think they do make an important difference, but the question of affordability remains. Must we focus now only on affordable justice? This is the topic of our current research, and it is demanding further methodological development to investigate such a large and ill-defined field.

Whether this kind of research activity should be described as sociology of law, socio-legal studies, or empirical legal studies is not an overriding concern, as long as the work is capable of long-term development. Ideally our work should be untroubled by semantics but fully sustainable!

David Sugarman

What one does is political. As George Orwell famously observed, there is no book genuinely free from political bias and every writer is in some sense a propagandist. Insight into our political-moral choices, and a willingness to listen and learn, point towards productive dialogue. I hope to contribute to debates about justice, power and inequality, and in a manner consistent with the best ideals and practices of the human sciences. The commissioned work that I have completed on women's rights, the treatment of rape victims and anti-discrimination law is the most explicit manifestation of these concerns. My conception of legal education and socio-legal studies is not narrowly academic. I have engaged with audiences, institutions and individuals beyond academia, through newspaper and magazine articles, radio and TV, and talks to schools and through the University of the Third Age. Inclusivity and diversity are important. Thus, I have argued that socio-legal studies would benefit from greater dialogue with currently marginalized disciplines, subjects, and audiences (Sugarman 2009, 2015, 2017). I strive to promote conversations about broadening legal education and scholarship, and the role and responsibilities of lawyers. A historicist sensibility attunes me to the peculiarities of place and time, and to questioning the status quo, institutional conservatism and the pressures of false necessity. Regarding the future, it is vital, but challenging, to give due weight to both the discursive and the material, to culture and political economy, and to law as ideology and violence.

Rosemary Hunter

In Australia in the early 1990s the Labor government had an interest in reform and research and I made some contributions to that agenda. When Labor lost in 1996 the Howard government came in and was not interested in my research. But there was an Australian Research Council grant scheme which funded work with industry partners and I found some state and federal government departments and agencies with agendas of mutual interest.

In the UK initially, I found it difficult to develop the kind of contacts with practitioners and policy makers that I had in Australia. The feminist judgments project, which is a more academic collaboration, was a different way of trying to achieve change. And I have gradually built up contacts, particularly in the family law field, often facilitated by Mavis Maclean's efforts to bring researchers and policy makers together. I remain wary of the pull of the policy audience, however (Hunter 2008). I choose to work in areas where I think there are current pressing problems, and I always maintain my independence and integrity as a researcher, even if that means providing an analysis or recommendations that are not welcome or popular.

To sum up, for most of the interviewees, being active in using their academic voice and having a political agenda played an important part in their career. The ambition to change the way things are done (e.g. in teaching curricula, research agendas, policy work) was a strong driver for change.

Conclusion

In this chapter I chose influential sites of socio-legal studies in the USA and the UK to trace institutional development. While providing an institutional overview, I also opened up windows onto some individual journeys to show that history matters for our appreciation of the field. Law and society is a constantly evolving field of scholarship made up of a multitude of individual intellectual journeys. The intellectual curiosity of its scholars has no boundaries and continues to build and expand the field by embracing its multidisciplinarity and questioning the connection between *the law* and *the social*.

One thing is clear; being a socio-legal scholar today means something very different to being a socio-legal scholar 50 years ago. When I conducted the interviews, I was struck by the emotions and enthusiasm about wanting to make a difference and needing to change the status quo. Might we speak of a generational culture, fuelled by passion to make change happen? My impression is that this sentiment of creation is lost today. We are part of a socio-legal space that has been created for us. There is undoubtedly room in this space to develop new theories, new research sites, and new agendas. The world today poses different questions to researchers and provides new challenges that have to be met with innovative approaches.

Having said that, among my colleagues (not all!) I observe a notion of *angst* guiding their agenda, rather than wanting to change the world. Worries about promotion, a tenured position, research funding, and publishing according to metrics set by institutions are at the forefront. Therefore, it is a continued challenge to the field to be brave, to push boundaries, and to keep questioning the status quo.

References

Abel, R. 2010, 'Law and Society: Project and Practice', *Annual Review of Law and Social Science*, 6 (1), 1–23.

Abel, R. L. & Lewis, P. C. (eds) 1988, *Lawyers in Society. The Civil Law World*. 3 vols. Vol. 2. Berkeley: University of California Press.

———. (eds) 1989, *Lawyers in Society. The Common Law World*. 3 vols. Vol. 1. Berkeley: University of California Press.

Adler, M. 2007, *Recognising the Problem: Socio-Legal Research Training in the UK*. Edinburgh: School of Social and Political Sciences, Edinburgh University.

Bonsignore, J., Katch, E., d'Errico, P., Pipkin, R., & Arons, S. 2005, *Before the Law: An Introduction to the Legal Process*, 8th edn. Belmont, CA: Wadsworth.

Calavita, K. 2016, *Invitation to Law and Society: An Introduction to the Study of Real Law*, 2nd edn. Chicago Series in Law and Society. Chicago: University of Chicago Press.

Campbell, C. M. & Wiles, P. 1975, 'The Study of Law in Society in Britain', *LSR*, 10, 547–578.

Cane, P. & Kritzer, H. (eds) 2010, *The Oxford Handbook of Empirical Legal Research*. Oxford: Oxford University Press.

Cotterell, R. 2007, 'Is it so bad to be different? Comparative Law and the Appreciation of Diversity', in E. Örücü & D. Nelken (eds), *Comparative Law: A Handbook*. Oxford: Hart, pp. 133–154.

Cownie, F. & Bradney, A. 2017, 'An Examined Life: Research into University Legal Education in the United Kingdom and the Journal of Law and Society', *Journal of Law and Society*, 44 (S1), S129–S143.

Cownie, F. & Bradney, A. 2018, 'Socio Legal Studies', in D. Watkins & M. Burton (eds), *Research Methods in Law*, 2nd edn., Abingdon: Routledge, pp. 40–65.

Dezalay, Y. & Garth, B. 1996, *Dealing in Virtue: International Commercial Arbitration and the Construction of a Transnational Legal Order*. Chicago: University of Chicago Press.

Dezalay, Y. & Sugarman, D. (eds) 1995, *Professional Competition and Professional Power: Lawyers, Accountants and the Social Construction of Markets*. London: Routledge.

Economic and Social Research Council. 1994, *ESRC Review of Sociolegal Studies*. Swindon: ESRC.

Engel, D. 1999, 'Presidential Address – Making Connections: Law and Society Researchers and Their Subjects', *Law & Society Review*, 33, 3–16.

Fleming, J. 1968, *An Introduction to the Law of Torts*, 2nd edn. Oxford: Clarendon Press.

Galanter, M. 1974, 'Why the "Haves" Come Out Ahead: Speculations on the Limits of Legal Change', *Law & Society Review*, 9 (1), 95–160. doi:10.2307/3053023.

Garth, B. & Sterling, J. 1998, 'From Legal Realism to Law and Society: Reshaping Law for the Last Stages of the Social Activist State', *Law & Society Review*, 32, 409–471.

Genn, H. 2008, *Judging Civil Justice*. The Hamlyn Lectures, Cambridge: Cambridge University Press.

Halliday, T. & Karpik, L. 1998, *Lawyers and the Rise of Western Political Liberalism. Europe and North America from the Eighteenth to Twentieth Centuries*. Oxford: Oxford University Press.

Halliday, T., Karpik, L., & Feeley, M. (eds) 2007, *Fighting for Political Freedom: Comparative Studies of the Legal Complex and Political Liberalism*. Oxford: Hart.

Harris, D. 1983, 'The development of socio-legal studies in the United Kingdom', *Legal Studies*, 3 (3), 315–333.

Hawkins, K. (ed) 1997, *The Human Face of Law; Essays in Honour of Donald Harris*. Oxford: Oxford University Press.

Hensler, D. 2017, 'The Role of Empirical Legal Studies in Legal Scholarship, Legal Education and Policy Making', in R van Gestel, H. Micklitz, & E. Rubin (eds.), *Rethinking Legal Scholarhip*, New York: Cambridge University Press, pp. 450–475.

Hunter, R. 2008, '"Would you like theory with that?" Bridging the divide between policy oriented empirical legal research critical theory and politics', *Special Issue: Law and Society Reconsidered Studies in Law, Politics, and Society*, 41, 121–148.

Kahneman, D. 2012, *Thinking Fast and Slow*. London: Penguin.

Kidder, R. L. 1983, *Connecting Law and Society: An Introduction to Research and Theory*. Englewood Cliffs, NJ: Prentice Hall.

Lempert, R. & Sanders, J. 1986, *An Invitation to Law and Social Science*. New York: Longman.

Levine, F. J. 1990, 'Presidential Address: Goose Bumps and "The Search for Signs of Intelligent Life" in Sociolegal Studies: After Twenty-Five Years', *Law & Society Review*, 24, 7–33.

Lynd, R. & Lynd, H. 1959, *Middletown: A Study in Contemporary American Culture*. Oxford: Harcourt Brace Javanovich.

Macaulay, S. 1985, 'An Empirical View of Contract', *Wisconsin Law Review*, 465–482. https://heinonline.org/HOL/LandingPage?handle=hein.journals/wlr1985&div=24&id=&page=&t=1558613755

Macaulay, S., Friedman, L. M., & Mertz, E. 2007, *Law in Action: A Socio-Legal Reader*. New York: Foundation Press.

Macaulay, S., Friedman, L. M., & Stookey, J. (eds) 1995, *Law and Society: Readings on the Social Study of Law*. New York: W. W. Norton.

Maclean, M. & Kurczewski, J. 2011, *Making Family Law: A Socio Legal Account of Legislative Process in England and Wales*. Oxford: Hart.

Mather, L. 2011, *Law and Society in The Oxford Handbook of Political Science*. R. Goodin (ed.). www.oxfordhandbooks.com/view/10.1093/oxfordhb/9780199604456.001.0001/oxfordhb-9780199604456-e-015

Mclean, M. 2017, 'Semantics or Sustainability: Socio Legal Research in Family Law, or Sociology of Law and Family Justice', *JLS*, 44, 61–73.

Menkel-Meadow, C. 1988, 'The Fem-Crits Go to Law School', *Journal of Legal Education*, 38 (1/2), 61–85.

Menkel-Meadow, C. 1990, 'Durkheimian Epiphanies: The Importance of Engaged Social Science in Legal Studies', *Florida State University Law Review*, 18 (1), 91–119.

Menkel-Meadow, C. & Diamond, S. S. 1991, 'Introduction: The Content, Method, and Epistemology of Gender in Sociolegal Studies', *Law & Society Review*, 25 (2), Special Issue on Gender and Sociolegal Studies, 221–238.

Merry, S. E. 1981, *Urban Danger: Life in a Neighbourhood of Strangers*. Philadelphia, PA: Temple University Press.

Merry, S. E. 1990, *Getting Justice and Getting Even: Legal Consciousness among Working-Class Americans*. Chicago, IL: University of Chicago Press.

Mertz, E., Macaulay, S., & Mitchell, T. W. (eds) 2016, *Translating Law-and-Society for Today's Legal Practice*. Vol. 1. Cambridge: Cambridge University Press.

Munger, F. W. & Seron, C. 1984, 'Critical Legal Studies versus Critical Legal Theory: A Comment on Method', *Law & Policy*, 6 (3), 257–297.

Nader, L. 1969, *Law in Culture and Society*. Chicago, IL: Aldine Press.

Nader, L. & Todd, H. 1978, *The Disputing Process: Law in Ten Societies*. New York: Columbia University Press.

Pound, R. 1910, 'Law in Books and Law in Action', *American Law Review*, 44, 12.

Sarat, A. 1990, '"The Law Is All Over": Power, Resistance, and the Legal Consciousness of the Welfare Poor', *Yale Journal of Law and Humanities*, 2, 348–379.

Sarat, A. 2004, *The Blackwell Companion to Law and Society*. Malden, MA: Blackwell.

Sarat, A. & Silbey, S. 1987, 'Critical Traditions in Law and Society Research', *Law & Society Review*, 21 (1), 165–174.

Sarat, A. & Silbey, S. 1988, 'The Pull of the Policy Audience', *Law and Policy*, 10, 97–166.

Schlegel, J. H. 1995, *American Legal Realism and Empirical Social Science*. Durham: University of North Carolina Press.

Seron, C. & Munger, F. W. 2017, 'Race, Law & Inequality, Fifty Years after the Civil Rights Era', *Annual Review of Law and Social Science*, 13, 331–350.

Seron, C., Savelsberg, J. J., Halliday, T., Liu, S., Morrill, C., & Silbey, S. 2016, 'Discussion Law & Society Review at Fifty: A Debate on the Future of Publishing by the Law & Society Association'.

Sugarman, D. 1980, 'Review Essay: M.J. Horwitz, The Transformation of American Law', *British Journal of Law and Society*, 7 (2), 297–310.

Sugarman, D. 2009, 'Beyond Ignorance and Complacency: Robert Stevens' Journey through Lawyers and the Courts', *International Journal of the Legal Profession*, 16 (1), 7–31.

Sugarman, D. 2011, 'A Special Relationship? American Influences on English Legal Education, c.1870–1965', *International Journal of the Legal Profession*, 18 (1–2), 7–57.

Sugarman, D. 2015, 'From Legal Biography to Legal Life-Writing: Broadening Conceptions of Legal History and Socio-Legal Scholarship', *Journal of Law and Society*, 42 (1), 7–33.

Sugarman, D. 2017, 'Promoting Dialogue between History and Socio-Legal Studies: The Contribution of Christopher W. Brooks and the "Legal Turn" in Early Modern English History', *Special Supplement: Main Currents in Contemporary Sociology of Law*, 44 (S1), S37–S60.

Thomas, P. 1997, 'Socio-Legal Studies: The Case of Disappearing Fleas and Bustards', in P. A. Thomas (ed), *Socio-Legal Studies*, Aldershot: Dartmouth, pp. 9–10.

Travers, M. 2010, *Understanding Law and Society*. London: Routledge.

Trubek, D. 1984, 'Where the Action is: Critical Legal Studies and Empiricism', *Stanford Law Review*, 36 (1/2), Critical Legal Studies Symposium, 575–622.

Twining, W. 1995, 'Remembering 1972: The Oxford Centre in the Context of Developments in Higher Education and the Discipline of Law', *Journal of Law & Society*, 22 (1), 35–49.

3

USES AND ABUSES OF SOCIO-LEGAL STUDIES

Carrie Menkel-Meadow[*]

Introduction: origin stories—the field's and mine

Many scholars have told origin stories of the socio-legal studies field, situating its beginnings in American legal realism, British law-in-context studies (Twining, 1978, 2012; Nelken, 2009), the American Sociological Association's sociology of law subdivision (Levine, 1990; Garth and Sterling, 1998), American desires to add social science rigor to legal and political movements for social change in the 1960s (see earliest issues of the *Law & Society Review*, 1966–1974) and the observation by both legal and social science scholars that law's impacts and institutions needed to be studied *empirically* to assess, among other things, the "gap" between the "law on the books" and the "law in action" (Pound, 1910; Friedman and Macaulay, 1969; Abel, 1973a, 2010; Macaulay, 1984; Friedman, 1986; Menkel-Meadow, 1990; Trubek, 1990; Calavita, 2016). Others have attempted to document a canon of classic works which define our field (Seron, Coutin, and Meeusen, 2013; Morrill and Mayo, 2015) or key concepts that define what we are studying: for example, Weberian "rationality" of the law (in regulatory and bureaucratic institutions; Hawkins, 1984; Ayres and Braithwaite, 1995); Durkheimian social statistics, patterning and other positivist empirically based claims (crime and divorce rates, court statistical studies and political attitude studies; e.g., Gibson, 2009), Marx-informed studies of class and power in law (e.g., Galanter, 1974); and more subtle influences of culture and everyday practices and understandings of law (e.g., Ewick and Silbey, 1998) as constituting a multiplicity of simultaneously existing systems of rules and norms, known as legal pluralism (Merry, 1988). Though economics was somewhat present at the multidisciplinary "birth" (mostly in the form of economic history; Hurst, 1964; Horwitz, 1977, 1992), more recent co-optation of socio-legal concepts and research by behavioral economics and psychologists has added some forms of empiricism to the study of the "efficiency" of laws and legal institutions (Posner, 1973, 1995; Langevoort, 1998, 2001).

Each of us who choose to work within these fields, concepts and ideas can probably remember what first drew us to the *multidisciplinary study of law and legal institutions* (see

[*] Special thanks to fellow travelers in these socio-legal fields who read and commented on this paper, Robert Meadow, Carroll Seron, Kitty Calavita and Naomi Creutzfeldt, and to my research assistants, Caleb Nissley and Sarah Salvini.

Garth and Sterling, 1998), which is how I define socio-legal studies (Sterett, 2015), or as one commentator famously put it "real law" (Calavita, 2016). Below, as illustrations, I recount some of the ways I conducted my own socio-legal research (primary research, secondary research, meta-analyses, synthetic analyses and some "mid-level" theory development in dispute resolution and negotiation). In the sections that follow I discuss a few notable examples of "good" uses of socio-legal research, in empirics, theory, policy and doctrinal treatments, and a few "abuses" or failures to properly use empirical data or other forms of socio-legal analysis.

For me, that first moment of "*Durkheimian epiphany*" (Menkel-Meadow, 1990) came when, as a young poverty lawyer, trained as an undergraduate in sociology by some of the leading scholars in that field at Columbia University, I was preparing for my first trial. My social scientist husband was studying regression analysis, time series and other empirical methods in the University of Michigan-Interuniversity Consortium for Political and Social Research, and I attended some of his classes (circa 1972). While preparing for trial and considering how a judge or a jury might draw conclusions from the evidence I was presenting, I read Kalven and Zeisel's now classic empirical study of *The American Jury* (1966). I fell in intellectual love. How could lawyers prepare a case, any case, without understanding the patterns and dynamics of the different kinds of decision makers they might appear before. Yes, every case has its own evidence, but judges and juries bring with them the sum of their human experiences. They are located in communities, in professions, in *societies* and in relationships (familial, religious, workplace, friendships) that are likely to affect how they process the evidence they hear and the decisions they make in any case.[1] How could anyone only read statutes, cases and documents, or even only interview witnesses as their legal preparation for a case? All cases are situated in ongoing *systems, institutions, communities, states, localities, societies and particular legal systems*. My study of sociology told me these things would influence decision making in cases and would vary in different matters, cases and locales. I was hooked. From that moment on, I worked to add social science to the rest of my own legal education (continuing in graduate sociology courses), later my practice as a poverty and civil rights lawyer, and then to my own teaching of trial advocacy, negotiation, discrimination law, civil procedure, legal ethics and the legal profession, and now international law.

From the moment I began to teach and research (and still practice) law, I always asked socio-legal (multidisciplinary, informed by different disciplines) questions:

1. With what assumptions are we working? How do we "know" what we think we know? What theories, ideas or frameworks are guiding our thinking (Mannheim's sociology of knowledge, 1929)? Where do they come from?
2. What are the statistical/quantitative patterns in this legal issue, case, matter, process (Durkheim, 1893, 1897)?
3. Who stands to gain/lose by particular processes, substantive laws, institutions (Galanter, 1974)?
4. What human processes, besides the desires for principle (jurisprudence; Hart, 1997) and rationality (Weber, 1954), inform and affect what people actually do inside legal institutions (psychology, emotion, culture, ethics, religion) as they act individually or in social groups (structural-functionalism; Parsons, 1951; neo-institutionalism)?

---

1 The classic expression of this in American legal folklore is that legal realism is the study of "what the judge had for breakfast" (Frank, 1949).

5. What other fields of multidisciplinary knowledge help us understand the role of law and legal institutions embedded in social interactions? Beyond the classic constituent fields of socio-legal studies (law, sociology, political science, psychology, history, anthropology, economics), what do we now learn from game theory, decision theory, organizational development and newer methods of quantitative (e.g., artificial intelligence and mass data mining) and cultural-qualitative analysis?

So, when, as a young legal scholar, I planned my first major research project (with the same aforementioned social scientist husband) to study how overworked poverty/legal aid lawyers allocated their work priorities, without fees as a motivating factor (US legal aid lawyers are salaried employees), we designed a triangulated study of several methods (*primary data collection*) to understand the possibility of a variety of different factors in work allocation decisions (see Meadow and Menkel-Meadow, 1983, 1985; Menkel-Meadow, 1998). With a research grant awarded by the United States National Science Foundation, we studied two sets of legal aid lawyers (one urban, the other rural), by conducting unstructured interviews, doing observations (we and trained research assistants "trailed" each lawyer for three random days of work and recorded, not privileged content, but particular tasks undertaken) and analyzing data from time sheets filled out by the studied attorneys for one random complete week of work. Multiple data sources provided several windows on work allocation decisions, with both aggregate and statistical analysis of most common work tasks undertaken, narrative explanations (both by the subjects of the study and by "external" observers) and analysis of formal work rules, supervisory and other standards of work. Though I was advised not to conduct this kind of lengthy, labor-intensive, data-driven, co-authored and *non-doctrinal* research before obtaining tenure in an American law school, I did it anyway.

I then encountered a first "abuse" of socio-legal studies. The Reagan administration in the 1980s sought vigorously to defund American legal aid, and a former law school classmate of mine in the federal government sought to have me testify about my data to demonstrate that legal aid lawyers were deciding "on their own" to sue the very government that was funding them and were choosing "leftist" political issues (e.g., school desegregation, immigration, abortion, consumer law reform and other kinds of class actions) to engage in social and legal redistribution projects rather than sticking to individual case processing (evictions, divorces, hearings for government benefits, etc.). Legal aid was not completely defunded, but at the time government funding was seriously reduced and has not yet, as of this date, recovered federal funding at equivalent levels, despite several Democratic administrations since. I was able to deflect "invitations" to testify as I knew my data would be "re-interpreted" by hostile political forces, but I voluntarily suppressed publication of some of my work due to fear of its misuse.

As a young scholar, bridging law and several other disciplines, my major early work was a *normative theory* of legal negotiation, drawing from work in political science, diplomacy, philosophy, game theory, sociology, social and cognitive psychology, anthropology, economics, decision theory and planning theory, in fact derived from observations I had made in my early poverty law practice, later expanded to all lawyering (Menkel-Meadow, 1984). I argued from these many different disciplines that the lawyer's default conception of scarce resources and distributive bargaining produced adversarial behaviors that in turn produced brittle, and often binary, outcomes which were often not efficient, social welfare-enhancing or appropriate for client needs. Instead, I proposed and outlined another "framework" (middle level theory) of conceptualization of integrative bargaining and behavior (itself derived from the early interdisciplinary work of Mary Parker Follett, 1995). This work, which coincided with larger cultural developments—the publication of *Getting to Yes* (Fisher and Ury, 1982) and later the fall of the Berlin Wall (see: Menkel-Meadow, 2013b; Menkel-Meadow, Love, Schneider, and Moffitt, 2018)—set the ground for my life's work as a conflict resolution scholar and practitioner.

My next Durkheimian epiphany came from *secondary analysis*. In what was, and continues to be, one of the most successful multinational socio-legal projects, Rick Abel (of UCLA) and Philip Lewis (Oxford Centre of Socio-Legal Studies) convened, over many years, a group of scholars of the legal profession to undertake a study of the legal professions in common, civil and "mixed" legal systems (18 different countries on five continents). It was finally organized into a three-volume study of *Lawyers in Society* (Abel and Lewis, 1988, 1989, 1995), and my task was to collate and analyze the data of the work of women lawyers in all countries participating in the study. I remember the "Eureka!" moment when, in completing my analysis, I noticed that women were present in some form as lawyers, judges or other legal professionals in all of the represented countries, but, when one analyzed the rank and status of particular occupations, women were always found in the least-valued or least-prestigious segment of the profession, evidencing the kind of occupational segregation being observed in most occupational sociology studies of the time (Menkel-Meadow, 1989). Today, these Durkheimian patterns of gender differences in the profession are ardently debated as scholars of the legal profession continue to report at national and gender levels of data collection (see Schultz and Shaw, 2003; Abel, Sommerlad, Hammerslev, and Schultz, 2019–2020) and debate the social meanings of gender (and now other) diversity in the legal profession. As a scholar of negotiation behavior, I continue to be involved in this project, arguing that women legal actors still work from gendered assumptions as perceived by others and enacted by themselves (Menkel-Meadow, 2012).

In a later project of a meta-analysis of empirical work on courts and civil procedure reform (which I co-authored with Bryant Garth, 2010), we explored the "uses" and "abuses" of the "commissioning" of empirical studies by courts and other interested legal bodies (both plaintiff and defense attorneys), seeking to justify or support particular policy outcomes and civil procedure rule changes. I was a "victim" of such demands when I conducted a study of the effectiveness of a mandatory arbitration program for a federal court, which was then used to lobby in Congress for the continuation of the program by interested officials seeking to reduce dockets, even though I felt the results were not sufficiently rigorous to publish them in a peer-reviewed social science journal. As another example, when I conducted a rigorous study of multiple forms of dispute resolution in a local city, suggesting some issues with the use of mandatory mediation in landlord–tenant cases, my report was not publicly revealed by the commissioning organization which wanted to promote the continuing use of mediation (without, in my view, adequate legal protections for some litigants appearing without counsel).

I relate these stories of my own social science and law experiences, as both a scholar and a commissioned consultant, to demonstrate what the rest of this essay explores more fully—socio-legal studies are essential for true understanding of how law and legal institutions operate, as embedded in other social processes and institutions. But, even with rigorous methods and testable theories, courts, political stakeholders and advocates are able to "use" socio-legal studies for theory development, data analysis and policy initiatives, but also socio-legal research may be ill used for advocacy or, more disturbingly, not used at all, or ignored when empirical claims are at issue. In the sections which follow I provide some examples of both.

"Good" uses of socio-legal studies: verifiable patterns of socio-legal behavior—ideas, empirics and policy

The best of socio-legal interdisciplinary work provides theories, concepts, testable hypotheses and robust empirical findings to understand the interaction of laws, legal actors (judges, lawyers, policy, juries, litigants and lay people) and legal institutions with the people and other institutions that are affected by law. Socio-legal scholars can study *law as the dependent variable* (law as affected by other social forces, processes and institutions) or *as the independent variable* (how does law affect other social institutions and the "acted upon" by law; Epstein and King, 2002; Epstein and Martin, 2014). Data collected to study law and legal processes can be quantitative—large aggregate data (as in court statistics, survey data or newer forms of large scale text analysis, as in the Comparative Constitutional project and "word cloud" analysis; see e.g., Law, 2017) or smaller sets of properly (randomly) selected samples of data. Data collection can be qualitative too, as in narratives, interviews, analysis of texts, use of focus groups and other methods. Those who study law and culture are often concerned with the mutually constitutive and interactive relations of law and the social (Mezey, 2015). Those who engage in socio-legal studies may be law trained or trained in one of the relevant social sciences (political science, sociology, psychology, anthropology, economics, history) or these days in both (joint degrees are increasingly common; George, 2006). Many scholars now identify as "socio-legal scholars" as an independent, if not methodologically uniform, discipline.[2] "Good" socio-legal studies have contributed new ideas or tropes about law and its enactment in social life, reported on relatively robust empirical patterns of behavior and been useful in some policy initiatives. I review a (non-systematic) sample of those here.

Socio-legal "tropes" or "memes"[3]

In considering what makes a "field" of intellectual study, we ask what questions does a field answer, and what knowledge do we gain by using the field's methods (Menkel-Meadow, 2007)? Socio-legal studies has already contributed some important ideas and tropes to the study of law that go beyond the arid formalism of jurisprudence (*what* is law, not *what does law do*) or doctrinal studies of law (what *is* the law).[4] Originally organized around the meme (first articulated by Roscoe Pound, 1910) that there were significant "*gaps*" between the *law* "*on the books*" and the "*law in action*," many socio-legal studies have been designed to demonstrate the law's actual operation or lack of efficacy (ignoring or desuetude [nonuse], distortion; Feeley, 1993; Edelman, 2016) or how formal law morphs into less formal forms

---

2 The international meeting of the Law and Society Association in Toronto in 2018 had 2,400 registered attendees.

3 I use "meme" here to connote a culturally repeated "idea"—in the case of socio-legal studies, more often "verified" in some quasi-scientific way. For the origins of the word meme, see Richard Dawkins (1976).

4 In earlier articles, I have asked what are the tropes, ideas or memes of law? What ideas or contributions to human knowledge come from the study of law alone? Even classic ideas of "due process," "equal protection" and "fairness" are derived from political philosophy and politics. "Ideas" of tort, contract, property—classic elements of law in both common law and civil law systems—are patterns of rules developed over time that permit social ordering and, like some forms of science, are subject to change as conditions change and more study reveals the need for different patterns, but in modern times it is often the observations of socio-legal studies that provide the evidence that rules should change or evolve (see Menkel-Meadow, 2001, 2007).

or social norms in practice (consider all the recent studies of race-based policing and criminal law in the United States, e.g., Richardson, 2015, 2017) or, as some socio-legal scholars have called it, "the color of law"—the social and legal construction of race and ethnicity through discriminatory or changing classifications (Mezey, 2003; Calavita, 2016).

Conventional uses of socio-legal methods include statistical measurements of legal phenomena to document how the law and its institutions do, in fact, operate (consider, as discussed below, the studies of racial disparities in the death penalty: Baldus, Woodworth, and Pulaski, 1990; the location and status of legal professionals: Abel and Lewis, 1988–1989; the impacts of different kinds of dispute processing on case management: Ali, 2018; Creutzfeldt, 2018; how lawyers and their clients interact and make decisions: Sarat and Felstiner, 1997; Kritzer, 2015; and variations in judicial and administrative decision making; Ramji-Nogales, Schoenholtz, and Schrag, 2011). Some other kinds of studies use a variety of data sources (aggregate data, semi-structured interviews, participant observations [or ethnomethodology in sociological terms]) to weave more intricate and interpretative explanations for the operation of law and legal institutions (see, e.g., Dezalay and Garth, 1996, on international arbitration and the legal and social construction of a transnational order; Utz, 1969, on regional variations in criminal justice plea bargaining and sentencing; Edelman, 2016, on the internalization and co-optation of civil rights laws in workplaces).

In addition to descriptions of how the law actually operates or is used by legal actors or those acted upon, socio-legal studies has also developed particular tropes or propositions (see Black, 1976, for an early effort to actually catalogue the propositions of socio-legal studies). The findings of Allan Lind and Tom Tyler (1988) in multiple studies of how lay people evaluate their experience of different structures in legal dispute resolution have emerged as a robust theory of *procedural justice*. People who use different kinds of legal processes (adversarial hearings vs. inquisitorial ones, mediation, arbitration, adjudication) rate their satisfaction with such processes by how fairly they are treated and how much "voice" they have, irrespective of outcome. This idea of procedural justice is one of the strongest replicated findings in socio-legal studies, now applied to the myriad new ways of resolving disputes (e.g., with alternative dispute resolution formats, ombuds, online dispute resolution and hybrid forms of dispute resolution; Menkel-Meadow, 2019). Recent studies suggest that the role of substantive outcome satisfaction, rather than only process satisfaction, may be variable by context (e.g., prison grievances; Jennes and Calavita, 2018), demonstrating how rigorous replication in different settings can provide more rigorous analysis of classic tropes.

The study of *dispute resolution* itself (Abel, 1973b; Nader and Todd, 1978; Gulliver, 1979) is one of the major interdisciplinary field constructions of socio-legal studies. Moving away from doctrinal studies of legal cases, legal anthropologists, then sociologists, psychologists and political scientists, began to look deeper into how "cases" are developed, from the now classic notion of "naming" (recognition of a wrong), "blaming" (attribution to someone) and "claiming" (formal attempt to get redress) (Felstiner, Abel, and Sarat, 1980–1981), to which I and others have added "reframing" for how lawyers and mediators might transform understandings of what disputes are really about (Menkel-Meadow, 1985). Other scholars now study the social construction of disputes, both the formal and the informal ways they are resolved (or not), and argue about whether a certain amount of disputing is healthy for a society to produce social change and to avoid the pacification or depoliticization of societies that seek to eliminate or reduce too much their conflict to produce false "harmony" (Nader, 1990).

Other broad memes produced by socio-legal theorizing include the idea of *legal pluralism* —the notion that multiple sets of norms or rules may exist in the same place at any one time, whether colonial and post-colonial legal systems, international legal orders, indigenous normative systems, formal legal federalism (national, state, provincial, local) or informal (e.g., workplace, religious, familial, peer [think teenager policing here!]) norms operating simultaneously with more formal rule systems. Socio-legal scholars now argue about whether multiple normative systems provide too much law or social control, or too much fragmentation for a unified understanding or enforcement (such as in the international legal order), or whether instead it offers points of resistance and multiple authorities to appeal to, or provides denser sets of regulatory regimes (Halliday and Shaffer, 2015). The socio-legal approach to legal pluralism has now spawned the larger field of *globalization*, focusing on both legal forms of globalization and social and economic interactions across borders (Menkel-Meadow, 2011).

The study of law in a social context has also produced ideas about how non-legal actors perceive and relate to law, through ideas of *legal consciousness, legal ideology* and the subfield of *law and culture*. Ewick and Silbey's (1998) study of "the common place of law" uses different data sources to explore how ordinary citizens stand "before," "with" or "against" the law, using both formal and informal normative orders. Like their study, I remember beginning a study of such informal ordering when my local movie theatre in Washington, DC announced ticket sales in advance for such blockbusters as the Harry Potter movies. Large groups of people began queuing weeks in advance, sleeping on the pavement to be able to buy tickets for the first showing of such films. As I began observations on a daily basis, it was clear the group had developed its own informal norms, enforced by the group with no formal police or legal action, such as bathroom breaks allowed without losing one's place, no substitutions of individuals in the queue, shared food and garbage runs, and cleared space for nearby shops. Repeatedly, over several years of release of these films, orderly young people created rules and policed themselves to act appropriately so that no formal police would be called. Rules so "enacted" seemed to carry over from one episode to another.

The concepts elucidated by socio-legal scholars should also be seen in their intellectual competition with other multidisciplinary fields (see "misuses" section below). Just after the founding of the Law and Society Association in 1964, the field of law and economics erupted onto the intellectual scene with writings by Richard Posner (1973) and others, arguing that a single trope "efficiency" to "maximize wealth" could be used to analyze the efficacy of all law. Law and economics turned out to be far more successful in its intellectual and law-policy project and captured not only intellectual capital, but also lawmaking authority, through appointments of lawyer-scholars to the judicial bench (Judges Posner, Easterbrook [Chicago school] and others) who could interpret and "make" the law with their tropes, and ideas. Does the fact that law and economics so "efficiently" reduced its theoretical claims to a very few tropes (such as efficiency and wealth maximization) account for its greater acceptability, as a doctrinal matter, than the more diffuse (and sometimes contradictory) findings and teachings of socio-legal studies?

In addition, two "breakaways" from the (US) Law and Society Association in the 1990s fragmented the multidisciplinary unity of the field. From the positivist, data-driven side, the *Journal of Empirical Legal Studies* was founded to publish only data-driven and empirical articles, and a group that formed around it (including Ted Eisenberg, 2011, Lee Epstein and others) began annual meetings to share empirical work and to train law professors in empirical methods.[5] At

---

5 An earlier effort to train law professors in social science methods, at the University of Denver in the early years of LSA, did not have much impact in the field or in drawing more law professors into rigorous empirical work (Garth and Sterling, 1998). More recently, LSA has run graduate seminars and other one-day programs for socio-legal "instruction" before the annual meetings of the society.

about the same time, another group began holding its own meetings and formed the Law, Humanities and Culture Association[6] to foster more narrative and humanities-based studies of law, including law and literature, popular culture and post-modernist approaches to the study of legal phenomena, and focused more on "external" interpretations and studies of the law, rather than those from within traditional legal interpretative traditions.

More recently, the sciences of cognitive and social psychology have produced a body of empirical work on *cognitive errors in human reasoning*, a great challenge to conventional notions of legal rationality and formalism (see, e.g., Kahneman and Tversky, 1974; Kahneman, 2013). This work has led to powerful studies of how such cognitive errors interact with legal phenomena, exploring implicit biases in all legal reasoning, behavior and decision making, now with special attention to, among others, racial and gender biases among judges, lawyers, police and other decision makers (Lawrence, 1987; Greenwald and Krieger, 2006; Jolls and Sunstein, 2006).

Modern socio-legal scholars (who also contributed a number of the founders of critical legal studies (CLS) in the United States and elsewhere in the 1970s and 1980s; Kelman, 1987; Trubek and Esser, 1989) have been especially concerned about who makes, interprets and enforces the law, including political theories of participation, critical race and feminist theories of exclusion in lawmaking and legal institutions, and what the social structure of knowledge and epistemology means for how the field develops its knowledge base and conceptualizes its studies (see, e.g., Menkel-Meadow and Diamond, 1991). CLS scholars (along with some socio-legal scholars), developed the "critique of rights" which challenged the notion that legal rights were at all effective in producing justice and reducing inequality. As all legal argumentation and doctrine could use *legal ambiguity* to provide arguments and decisions "on either side," the law itself was hopelessly (and politically) *indeterminate* (Kennedy, 1998). How much critical theory actually looks at empirical data is one of the continuing issues of intellectual contention (Munger and Seron, 1984).

Empirical findings: patterns of socio-legal behavior

If Durkheimian epiphanies mean anything it is the social science of seeing *patterns of "social facts"* emerging from rigorous empirical analysis. Our field is full of such studies, and I will review just a few here, each from different "constituent" disciplines, using different methods, to contrast with the "misuses" or "lack of use" discussed below.

Beginning with the first issue of the *Law & Society Review* (and before that from the constituent fields), articles and books and monographs have described, analyzed and evaluated the interaction of law, legal actors and legal institutions *with* and *within* society. Classic findings have produced data on the *legal needs of ordinary citizens* (Genn, 1999; Sandefur, 2014); *the operation of criminal and civil justice systems* (Utz, 1969; CLRP, Trubek, Grossman, Felstiner, Kritzer, and Sarat, 1983; Feeley, 1993); how *people perceive their encounters with legal institutions*, and *when they actually use them* (Merry, 1990); whether there are *patterns in judicial decision making* (associated with political party [Epstein and Knight, 1998;

---

6 The first meeting of this group was held at my then law school, Georgetown University, organized by Austin Sarat, Robin West and others of us at Georgetown. This group also now publishes its own journal, the *Journal of Law, Culture and Humanities*, drawing some theoretical, narrative and more humanities-based work away from the several leading socio-legal journals (*Law and Society Review, Law & Social Inquiry, Law & Policy*), or, as others might characterize it, providing more outlets of publication for different kinds of socio-legal work.

Epstein, Landes, and Posner, 2013], gender or other factors); and how *everyone in the legal system processes information and makes decisions* (Korobkin and Ulen, 2000; Guthrie, Rachlinski, and Wistrich, 2007), among other things. Where legal scholars have focused on doctrinal developments and often argue for law reform, often without any reference to empirical data (the last part of most law review articles), socio-legal scholars have been especially good at focusing on *non-uniform impacts* of *law* (various forms of *patterning by race, class, gender and other characteristics*), the *contextual conditions* that may be necessary for legal policies to be effective (Handler, 1986) and observations of the *"unintended consequences"* of the operation of laws and legal institutions.

Lauren Edelman's recent work (law and sociology; 2016) on the *"endogeneity" of law* in the co-optation of civil rights laws within workplaces and organizations is one example. Following on from earlier work by Kristin Bumiller (1988; on what actually happens to those who claim discrimination) and her father's legacy from political science (Murray Edelman, 1971, on "symbolic politics"), Edelman uses multiple data sets to provide both description and analysis of how equal employment opportunity officers and internal human relations departments bring law "inside" their organizations and thereby blunt the effectiveness of external regulation and litigation (where her empirical study of court decisions demonstrates that courts "defer" to companies' arguments of compliance through internal policies, even as the individual and aggregate stories of continuing discrimination are ignored or discounted; e.g., see *Wal Mart Stores v. Dukes*, 2011).

Similarly, decades of work on the *empirics of prosecution, policing, conviction, sentencing and incarceration*, from sociology, legal analysis and political science, describe how formal rules are ignored or manipulated to produce great disparities in stops, arrests, charges, convictions and incarceration (see, e.g., Provine, 2007, on disparities in cocaine arrests and charges). Many empirical studies of plea bargaining and incarceration (Alexander, 2010; Forman, 2017) also document that behaviors of all those with responsibility for criminal law enforcement (police, lawyers and judges) fail to comport with legal rules or non-racially motivated law enforcement. Many socio-legal studies document similar discriminatory patterns in housing, voting, employment and education (see summaries in Seron, 2016; Munger and Seron, 2017).

The socio-legal study of *regulation and compliance* (e.g., Hawkins, 1984; sociology, economics) also documents how regulation actually happens where some of the regulated comply with formal laws, others resist (including with bribery), and yet others internalize good practices and become "self-regulators" (Ayres and Braithwaite, 1995). Related to law enforcement and compliance are empirical studies of variations in *legal mobilization*, whether through group and collective actions or through individual uses of legal claiming opportunities (see, e.g., McCann, 1992).

Over decades of work, Elizabeth Loftus (psychology; 1996) has used *experimental methods* (laboratory studies) to demonstrate the inaccuracy of memories and much formal legal testimony. Legal anthropologists have also used intensive texts from courtrooms (and mediation sessions; see Greatbach and Dingwall, 1989) as data for *linguistic analysis* that demonstrates the actual *power dynamics of courtroom communication* (Conley and O'Barr, 2005). These studies use different, rigorous forms of empirical methods to cast doubt on the claims by many that the Anglo-American adversarial trial system and its formal evidence rules (or its alternatives) are best at producing both truth and justice. Others have focused on *presentation of evidence and arguments as scripts, jury decision making, using laboratory and simulation studies of group decision making* (Bennett and Feldman, 2014) or *observations of actual juries* (Hans and Vidmar, 1991; Diamond, Vidman, Rose, Ellis, and Murphy, 2003) to report on patterns of jury behavior; some of these may actually have policy impacts, as has the Arizona jury study (Diamond, 2007).

Well-constructed empirical studies in both laboratory and other simulated settings are now challenging the seemingly robust findings of economists and psychologists on elements of *prospect theory*, particularly *"the endowment effect"* (Plott and Zeiler, 2007; Klass and Zeiler, 2013), noting that earlier empirics supporting a theory of "ownership" distortions in bargaining behavior may, in fact, be more susceptible to contextual variation. (This is a particularly interesting finding to me as I have used endowment effect simulations in my negotiation classes for decades and found them far more variable than earlier research would suggest. I should have kept better continuous data sets myself!)

This is very far from an exhaustive set of examples of empirical studies drawn from a variety of disciplines that have combined with law to study law and legal institutions, but it hopefully demonstrates the rich contributions to our field from a variety of theoretical and methodological perspectives. Whether we have a true "canon" or not (let others argue about that; for me, canons are always changing in any field that keeps up-to-date with new developments), we do have a field—a field which is focused on understanding not only what law is, but what it can and cannot do. And so, I turn to socio-legal studies and policy.

Uses of socio-legal studies in policy

For readers of this handbook, from a variety of different countries and legal cultures, the question of the role of socio-legal studies in affecting policy is quite variable. In my own experience, although I have participated in many studies solicited by government agencies and courts (some pure research, others evaluative or goal-oriented), the use of empirical studies to actually affect policy has been quite limited or misused (see final section below). Within the socio-legal tradition, the United Kingdom and many European countries, as well as Australia and New Zealand, have asked social scientists to study and advise about legal phenomena (see, e.g., Genn, 2009) or to actually use findings from studies to make changes in policy (see Ali, 2018).

Within the American socio-legal field there has long been a healthy debate about whether socio-legal scholars should "feel the pull of the policy audience" (Sarat and Silbey, 1988) or should actively engage in policy-guided research. Though Sarat and Silbey cautioned against distortions by interested government officials of our "purer" scientific questions, Carroll Seron (2016), in her presidential address to the Law and Society Association, eloquently argued for the importance of engaged socio-legal research in policy, citing such examples as discrimination in housing, voting and policing, the efficacy of representation for indigent clients, regulation and mobilization, and the study of access to justice, as well as access to legal jobs, for the promotion of such enshrined democratic legal values as equality, fairness and justice. The quality of our health, education, housing, employment and environment depends on accurate assessment of what can be regulated by law and what cannot. Despite the ongoing debates in American socio-legal scholarship, the fact is socio-legal and empirical studies have been used in legal cases and in rule-setting and other policy making.

For American legal scholars, the first big bang moment in the use of social science in law was the development of the "Brandeis brief," a brief using social science data (and actually written by a feminist advocate, Josephine Goldmark)[7] in the case of *Mueller v. Oregon* (1908), which presented

---

7 Josephine Goldmark was Attorney (later Supreme Court Justice) Louis Brandeis's sister in law. She wrote the brief with feminist reformer Florence Kelley (Chused and Williams, 2016, 960). Notably, this brief also presented "foreign" (non-American) data and legislation, illustrating continuing issues around the use of "foreign" materials in American legal decision making (see Jackson, 2010).

data on the health effects of long days of work for women, in an effort (quite controversial among feminists today) to have the Supreme Court sustain limited working hours (the 10-hour day) as part of labor reforms. The law was sustained and ushered in an era of contest about how much states and the federal government could regulate labor and other economic and social issues (in brutal legal contests about regulation in an era of the ascendancy of capitalism set against the Depression of the 1930s).

The era of the Depression and the New Deal is often credited as both the founding and peak of the use of social science in policy making and legal realist scholarship (Schlegel, 1995; Twining, 2012). Many of the early legal realist scholars (mostly from Yale and Columbia law schools) moved into the Roosevelt government and argued for regulation and legislation (in securities, banking, corporate regulation, labor and social welfare) based on social science studies. In this period, empirical data were also marshaled for law reform (criminal law) and court procedural reform (Menkel-Meadow and Garth, 2010).

More controversially, social science studies played a role (it is contested how much of a role) in the landmark case of *Brown v. Board of Education of Topeka* (1954) in which the Supreme Court ordered desegregation of American schools and formally ushered in the era of (successful) civil rights litigation in the Supreme Court (Heise, 2005; Barnes and Chemerinsky, 2018).[8] Footnote 11 of the decision in *Brown* discussed the studies of social psychologists Kenneth and Mamie Clark, the "doll test," which demonstrated that black children preferred white dolls and thought black dolls were inferior (used to argue that "separate but equal" legal doctrine and school segregation produced feelings of inferiority and, thus, violated the Equal Protection clause of the Constitution in the provision of public education). Though the methods of the study were often criticized in scholarship, the Supreme Court did not evaluate or comment on the formal "validity" of the studies.[9] And—see below—it is interesting to note how, several decades later, the Supreme Court chose to ignore or not fully credit far more rigorous data on racial disparities in the death penalty (*McCleskey v. Kemp*, 1987).

Empirical studies can be commissioned to study a particular policy question (Wheeler, 1988), such as when I have been asked to study the effectiveness of court mediation and arbitration processes by comparing them with litigation, or to study the satisfaction of users with particular dispute resolution processes within organizations (e.g., the World Bank, the UN and the International Red Cross, for whom I have done such studies [unpublished]; but, see Creutzfeldt, 2018, for a published comparative study of one form of dispute resolution [ombuds], and Hazel Genn, 2010, for mediation in the UK). Alternatively, researchers may choose to study a legal phenomenon, such as whether changed pleading rules (such as those now demanded in civil rights cases in the United States) have had an effect on case filings and outcomes (Hannon, 2008), and such studies may ultimately affect rule drafting or legal change.

In the United States, socio-legal scholars have been asked to study such questions as whether civilians should be involved in reviewing policing decisions; what processes should

---

8 There actually were many civil rights cases before *Brown*; a few were successful, but most were not, and the *Brown* decision continues to be evaluated as not terribly successful in actually desegregating schools (see Rosenberg, 1991).

9 Since that time, there has been much discussion about whether courts should apply the *Daubert* doctrine (prejudicial screening of all scientific expert-presented evidence) to social science evidence in courts (such as in employment discrimination contexts (Renaker, 1996).

be used in different regulatory matters; what effects media might have on legal decision making (consider "the CSI" effect—jurors demanding more technical and forensic evidence after many years of TV shows exaggerating the validity of such evidence; see Goehner, Lofaro, and Novak, 2004; Kopacki, 2013); what legal interventions are most effective for compliance with regulations (e.g., health and safety); and what policies are most effective in social welfare, family law and immigration policies (Sarat and Ewick, 2015). In other cases, lawyers seek out social scientists as expert witnesses (as in statistical evidence for employment discrimination and public health cases) or to marshal data arguments for modern "Brandeis briefs." Unlike in many legal systems where the judge appoints a single expert to advise the court, American adversarialism (Kagan, 2003) has produced the "battle of competing experts" in many court and administrative proceedings, including health and medical science, gun forensics, accident mapping and a variety (less common) of social science questions. So, in some cases, empiricism is alive and well in our trials (even if trials are exceedingly rare these days—less than 2% of all cases filed in our federal court system result in trial [Galanter, 2004], though experts are still deposed in pre-trial discovery and have their reports considered in legal rulings and motions).

From its roots in trying to understand the lasting inequalities and imperfections in legal systems, the socio-legal field has been studying, for decades now, whether law can affect social change (Rosenberg, 1991; Epp, 2009), and lawyers and social movements have been efficacious in policy change and injustice correction (Cummings, 2018; Menkel-Meadow, 1998). This work has often (erroneously) assumed that social change advocated for by social movements will almost always be in one "progressive" direction (Southworth, 2008) or that progressive social change can only occur within a "sympathetic" democratic constitutional regime (see, to the contrary, Chua, 2014). The story of law and lawyers and those who resist the law in furtherance of broader goals of justice continues to unfold and be studied, especially in recent years, as contests between "progressive, liberal internationalists" and modern, anti-immigration nationalists have intensified, as evidenced by the UK's Brexit and the United States' conservative elections and anti-migration values spreading throughout the Western world. Socio-legal scholars in criminal, immigration, race and policing studies are, as I write this, designing studies to measure the actions and effectiveness of lawyers and other activists seeking to resist these developments.

Whether socio-legal studies is primarily an academic field or an "applied" one—as are urban planning, decision science and traditional law study—remains an ongoing (if, to me, arid) debate (Dagan, Kreitner, and Kricheli-Katz, 2018). As socio-legal studies, at least in the United States, was born of concerns for how to use social science to advance social justice (see Garth and Sterling, 1998), it seems appropriate to continue to see it being used effectively and rigorously. Now we turn to when that does not happen.

"Misuses" (or lack of use) of socio-legal studies

From the time of my first Durkheimian epiphany as a law student, I began to be hypersensitive to how often judges made empirical claims and statements in their opinions without any reference to empirical data. Others took note of this in a variety of textbooks and articles (see, e.g., Loh, 1984; Heise, 2002; Epstein and Martin, 2014; Monahan and Walker, 2014) designed to teach law students, lawyers and judges how to do, and understand the significance of, empirical research. Others have criticized whatever use the Supreme Court has made of empirical data in constitutional decision making or challenged the very notion that empirical data are important for judicial decision making (see, e.g., Zick, 2003; Edwards and Livermore, 2009).

In what has been the biggest rejection of rigorous social science in the courts thus far, the United States Supreme Court in 1987 rejected data from years of detailed study of the disparities in the use of the death penalty. In *McCleskey v. Kemp*, the Supreme Court refused to credit the decades of work done by David Baldus and his colleagues to document racial differences in death penalty punishment rates. In the case, a Georgia African-American man challenging his death penalty conviction asserted it was a "cruel and unusual punishment" (under the 8th Amendment) and a denial of "equal protection" (under the 14th Amendment of the US Constitution), where data robustly demonstrated that black men convicted of killing white victims were more than four times more likely to receive the death penalty than those convicted of killing black victims. Other racial disparities in death penalty sentencing had been demonstrated with high degrees of significance, but the court concluded that none of this met the constitutional standards of requiring "proof" of actual intent (rather than disparate treatment inferred from data) of discrimination (Ellsworth, 2012; Barnes and Chemerinsky, 2018). For a different approach, in Canada, see Perryman (2018). And, more recently, much of the litigation in constitutional same-sex marriage cases in the United States presented social science evidence about family relationships and childrearing (see, e.g., Hull, 2017).

For several years I taught a law and society seminar in a law school and, after introducing some of the classic works of the field and having papers presented by some of the leading American socio-legal scholars, asked students to read critically some major American decisions which relied on empirical statements about the world, but which did not examine any empirical data at all. Judges instead relied on their own "experiential" data and unsystematic personal observations rather than on rigorously and scientifically collected empirical data. Students were then asked to design a research plan for how to actually study the phenomenon at issue, to conduct a literature review of what empirical work had already been done on that question, and then to either (1) attempt a small-scale study of the phenomenon under review or (2) rewrite the opinion with proper references to existing empirical studies.[10] This seminar's purpose was for students to understand the role of empiricism in law and critically examine legal judgments, opinions and decisions for the rest of their lives and to notice when data are absent, ignored or misapplied.

Some have criticized the methodological weaknesses of much of what passes for empirical legal research (Epstein and King, 2002) and have urged that all law students and judges need to be better versed and educated in rigorous assessments of data analysis. This is extremely important for many reasons, but particularly because, as I have alluded to above, many of us have been "pulled by the policy audience's" request to "create" studies to "prove" predetermined desired policy goals, as in requests to justify various forms of legal process (e.g., mediation or litigation) or procedural rule reform (both criminal and civil), and especially with regard to desires to increase efficiency and reduce costs of some legal process without sufficient attention to other values (see Menkel-Meadow, Love, Schneider, and Moffitt, 2018, Ch. 14). Others accuse (rightly in some instances) some social scientist legal

---

10 One of the current projects of the socio-legal studies field is to "rewrite" leading judicial opinions in a variety of fields, but including the perspectives of empirical data and also the inputs of previously "excluded" groups, e.g., women, minorities, etc. (see Moran, 2010; Menkel-Meadow and Diamond, 1991; Hunter, Chapter 19, this volume).

(forensic) experts of being "bought" (or, worse, "whores") for particular "sides" of litigation and policy debates (see, e.g., Kousser, 1984).

More significant are the difficult epistemological issues of different standards of "proof" in the physical and social sciences and legal standards. Many expert witnesses and scholars have commented on the mismatch of the "beyond a reasonable doubt" standard in criminal law (in prediction testimony for example), and even the "preponderance of the evidence" standard in many civil matters does not square with the probabilistic standards of claims (depending on relative confidence levels) that can be made from empirical studies (see, e.g., Robbennolt, 2002; Greiner, 2008; Haack, 2014). Causal analysis in the social sciences does not match up with the legal standards for causation in any of its domains (torts, discrimination, environmental and epidemiological harm), and so empiricists and experts are disappointed they are not fully credited in legal proceedings, and lawyers and judges are often frustrated at their inability to use empirical research in a dispositive way.[11]

At the same time, there is the concern that socio-legal (and all social science data studies, as well as the newer forms of "algorithmic" logic with deep data mining), coding and quantification may tend to assimilate in coding boxes and classifications that which is not really uniform. I recall my own experience in listening excitedly to an early classic study of socio-legal studies at an LSA meeting (Susan Silbey and Sally Merry's classificatory study of mediators, 1986) and being influenced by their conceptualization of "settlers" (task-oriented agreement-seeking mediators) versus those who were more "therapeutic" and interpersonal in their orientations. Many decades later, as an experienced mediator of hundreds of matters, I find this classification system an artifact of simplistic conceptualization and the need to "codify" and reduce a great variety of mediator orientations, moves, techniques, goals and behaviors into simple, binary categories. As a mediator, I use many tools, techniques, goals and behaviors, and these depend greatly on context, the kind of matter, what is at stake, the parties, whether they have lawyers, and their many kinds of needs —I, and most of my mediator colleagues, do not fit neatly into these "either/or" boxes. I had similar reactions (in print) to the coding of so-called "similar" case types and courts in the RAND studies (Kakalik, Dunworth, Hill, McCaffrey, Oshiro, Pace, and Vaiana, 1996) of the effectiveness of ADR in the federal courts (Menkel-Meadow, 1997). As a practicing lawyer, I had litigated in both the Eastern District of Pennsylvania and the Central District of California, and these courts had very dissimilar caseloads and local legal cultures. From my having been inside both of these court systems, the comparisons in the large aggregated study of case treatments seemed inapposite to me.

Too much reliance on aggregate data for "predictive" models is also a potential misuse of empirical data in the legal system. Virginia Eubanks studied the use of algorithms and mass data sets to diagnose and predict who is likely to be neglecting and abusing children, failing to cooperate with electronic welfare and health benefit information requests, and eligible for housing benefits and assistance for homeless populations (Eubanks, 2018). This important work flags the epistemological, as well as methodological, differences in the algorithmic "predictive" thinking of our new age of artificial intelligence decision making, as contrasted to the legal standards of due process and individual adjudication "after," not "before," the facts have been "proven." Recently, the United States Supreme Court refused to grant review (certiorari) of a claim that it was a denial of due process to use algorithmic predictive models for risk assessment in criminal law sentencing (see *Loomis v. Wisconsin*, cert denied

---

11 These are depressing times for some of us empiricists, as many in the United States continue to deny the empirics of climate science!

June 26, 2017). Thus, judicial decision making can be problematic from both "too little" and "too much" data—depending how data are used and what legal standards are applied.

As I have come to be skeptical of judicial decisions that make empirical claims without empirical data and support, I now find myself sometimes equally skeptical of the empirical claims made in socio-legal studies that codify and classify phenomena, behaviors and people which I know are far more complex and context variable than empirical "measurements" permit in many studies.[12] Thus, after many decades in the field, I often find that what is being described with data sets, both large and small (e.g., many claims about ADR or litigation generically), doesn't ring true to me in situations where I have been a participant or witness to the phenomena described.[13] This has heightened my own respect for more nuanced ethnomethodological and participant observer studies, with long narratives and descriptions and fewer grander, more general claims. In other areas in which I work, such as gender difference in negotiation behavior, both aggregate and smaller case studies remain inconclusive, largely because different research designs in so many different contexts have produced such variable findings (see Menkel-Meadow, 2012, and Hollander-Blumoff, Chapter 12, this volume)—context really matters, and some things we study are highly interactive. Yes, ultimately, I still believe that all methods and different studies tell us something, but our field has not engaged in enough rigorous replication studies and iterated testing of findings.[14]

One notable "misuse" of socio-legal studies has, for me, been the "co-optation" of early socio-legal research (e.g., group decision making as in jury studies, "non-rational" factors in decision making, empirical studies of legal behavior) by law and economics scholars who now claim a new field of "behavioral economics" (Jolls, Sunstein, and Thaler, 1998; Ulen, 2013). After decades of classical economics "assumptions" about human behavior (and of "maximizing utilities"), in the late 1990s, law and economics scholars and social and cognitive psychologists began to realize that not all "men" (I use that word deliberately) reasoned exactly the same way, under all conditions, and that—aha!—decision making about legal and other matters might vary with context (see also Klass and Zeiler, 2013). Much of the work of behavioral economics has been extremely useful for the study of law, legal actors and legal institutions in many settings (e.g., plea bargaining; negotiating; legal decision making; resource allocation; incentive structures for legal compliance, including its use in many policy settings; risk analysis; regulatory policy [Sunstein, 2011]; environmental law; labor relations; and contracting generally), but the failure to read, cite and properly give attribution to those socio-legal scholars (particularly sociologists, psychologists and anthropologists) who have harvested these concepts—often with extensive data!—is academically shameful. This appropriation of concepts and decades of empirical work sadly demonstrates the failure to integrate a truly multidisciplinary field—we all still seem to work within silos

12 The Eubanks study (Eubanks, 2018) of the use of big data points out both underinclusiveness (no data from middle-class families for child neglect predictive models) and overinclusiveness (maintenance in the relevant systems of old or inaccurate data on income, housing, health conditions, etc.). The treatment of the surveilled poor in these systems may be the "canary in the mine" of how we all will be "judged" by our electronic data trails, whether they are accurate or not. In such systems, law may turn out to be either irrelevant or inept at monitoring and correcting basic information.

13 This has made me more responsive to complaints by judges, lawyers and political office holders who feel inadequately analyzed by many studies (see, e.g., Edwards and Livermore, 2009; Posner, 2009).

14 Most recently, in my own field, a natural experiment at the Wharton School at the University of Pennsylvania produced clear evidence that men had become more aggressive in laboratory negotiation simulations in a business school setting after Donald Trump's election! (Trump is a graduate of the Wharton School of business; see Huang and Low, 2017). Whether this finding will prove to be robust will require some kind of replication studies.

as we study the law from outside of doctrine. Legal economists seem to think that they have invented empiricism in law![15]

Implications: the limits of disciplinary thinking and a call for rigorous multidisciplinariety

From where will the Durkheimian epiphanies of the future come? This volume contains a set of many examples of law and ... disciplines. Examples are drawn from research being conducted all over the world now, not just in Anglo-American spheres of influence (or intellectual colonialisms?). Theory, methods, data and sources of interpretation are diversifying as our socio-legal field moves from studies of legal pluralism to actual migration of thought and globalization. As this volume attests, there is so much interesting work being done, it is hard to keep up with it all.

The expansion of studies of law and ... to so many new sites, with so many new kinds of data (major data sources from modern technology capture; Eubanks, 2018) and new lenses of interpretation, presents some challenges (e.g., Barnes, 2016)—some old, some new:

1. Does our field have (need) a canon? What are the key propositions of knowledge that characterize what we know about how law functions in society and how social forces structure law and legal institutions? What new concepts or tropes are we studying/should we be studying—for example, mixed "identity" and classifications (Mezey, 2003), "adjectival" constitutionalism, subnational and supranational legal systems (e.g., Shari'a law)?
2. Do we have clearly accepted methods (social science reliability, validity and causality standards, other measures of reliability)?
3. How much replication/cumulation of knowledge do we have/desire? (Should we be emulating the physical sciences, or do we have our own ways of evaluating knowledge production?)
4. How much should we commit ourselves to policy research? (Are we an applied science? How does this vary from legal culture to legal culture?)
5. Is the field committed to particular social/political/legal values (social justice, equality, democracy), or can it be a "neutral" or objective field of study?[16]
6. With what sense of ethics and responsibilities should we approach those we study? Beyond the now required institutional review boards for study of human subjects in most major universities (Schrag, 2010), what else do we owe those we study—beyond consent, explanations of our work and assistance in solving the problems we see (lack of housing, racialized policing, "crimmigration" or injustice; Menkel-Meadow, 2009)?[17]
7. With so many new comparative, global and diverse studies of socio-legal phenomena, what are our comparators? How do studies in legal regimes (constitutional, authoritarian), processes (litigation, alternatives to litigation, criminal, civil, administrative) and

---

15 There have always been a few economists within the sociolegal community in the United States, beginning with Willard Hurst and Morton Horwitz's economic histories. James Heckman at the American Bar Foundation (and a Nobel Economics prize winner) has long used extensive empirical data in his studies of school desegregation and the impacts of many social and economic reforms (Heckman and Krueger, 2003).

16 Anyone who knows the feminist, critical race and post-modern critiques of knowledge in the "post-canon" era knows there is no such thing as "neutral" knowledge, though our ethics of research provide some standards of aspiring to "objective" measures (see Harding, 1991; Moran, 2010).

17 For an important effort to delineate an ethics code for data scientists, programmers and system engineers of new computer/electronic/data system designers, see Eubanks, 2018, 212–213.

actors (lawyers, judges, police, tribunal officials) explain when so much of this is now hybridized, and nothing is a pure "ideal type"?

I will not belabor here the arguments I have made in many places (see, e.g., Menkel-Meadow, 2007) that essential to any modern legal education should be rigorous training in the constituent social sciences that comprise, affect and influence law, and the evaluation of its impacts. As our knowledge about law and legal institutions and their efficacy increases by study of more sites of norms and rules (internally and from "below"), as well as from outside (top–down for policy initiatives) and through the lenses of many more multidisciplinary fields (including hybrid fields such as urban planning, decision theory, artificial intelligence, cultural studies), no modern lawyer, judge, government official or bureaucrat should only study or know the "doctrine" of law, without understanding something about how that doctrine will (or will not) be used. Nor should they assume their "experiential" knowledge is superior to independent empirical findings. For those "outside" of the law (or the acted upon), it is even more imperative to know how the law on the books is still so far from the law (or justice) in action. In so many areas of legal and social policy, we need all the data and help we can get to learn what is happening on the ground and what policy or advocacy interventions work or do not work—consider current issues of worldwide migration; labor displacement and loss; "crimmigration"; ongoing discrimination and inequality on grounds of race, ethnicity, gender and class; human rights violations and enforcement; whether "rights" and legal movements are effective in producing more social change; and how the use of technology will alter our legal and social relations, perhaps forever. I look forward to many more studies, using many different methods, to expose the newest forms of Durkheimian epiphanies that should illuminate what the law promises us and when it fails.

References

Abel, Richard and Philip S.C. Lewis (1988, 1989, 1995) *Lawyers in Society: Civil Law, Common Law and Comparative Theories* (Berkeley and Los Angeles: University of California Press).

Abel, Richard C., Hilary Sommerlad, Ole Hammerslev and Ulrike Schultz (2019–2020) *Lawyers in Society Revisited* (London: Hart-Bloomsbury).

Abel, Richard L. (1973a) "Law Books and Books about Law" *Stanford L. Rev* 26: 175–228.

———— (1973b) "A Comparative Theory of Dispute Institutions in Society" *Law Soc. Rev* 8: 217–347.

——— (2010) "Law and Society: Project and Practice" *Ann. Rev. Law Soc. Sci.* 6: 1 23.

Alexander, Michelle (2010) *The New Jim Crow: Mass Incarceration in the Age of Colorblindness* (New York: Free Press).

Ali, Shala (2018) *Court Mediation Reform: Efficiency, Confidence and Perceptions of Justice* (Cheltenham, UK: Edward Elgar).

Ayres, Ian and John Braithwaite (1995) *Responsive Regulation: Transcending the Deregulation Debate* (Oxford: Oxford University Press).

Baldus, David C., George Woodworth and Charles A. Pulaski, Jr. (1990) *Equal Justice and the Death Penalty: A Legal and Empirical Analysis* (Evanston, IL: Northwestern University Press.).

Barnes, Mario L. (2016) "Empirical Methods and Critical Race Theory: A Discourse on Possibilities for a Hybrid Method" *Wisc* 2016: 443.

——— and Erwin Chemerinsky (2018) "What Can Brown Do for You? Assessing *McCleskey v. Kemp* as a Flawed Standard for Measuring the Constitutionally Significant Risk of Racial Bias" *Northwestern L. Rev.* 112: 1293–1336.

Bennett, Lance and Martha Feldman (2014) *Reconstructing Reality in the Courtroom* (New Orleans, LA: Quid Pro).

Black, Donald (1976) *The Behavior of Law* (New York: Academic Press).

Bumiller, Kristin (1988) *The Civil Rights Society* (Baltimore: Johns Hopkins Press).

Calavita, Kitty (2016) *Invitation to Law and Society: An Introduction to the Study of Real Law* (Chicago: University of Chicago Press).

Cane, Peter and Herbert Kritzer, eds (2010) *The Oxford Handbook of Empirical Legal Research* (Oxford: Oxford University Press.).

Chua, Lynette (2014) *Mobilizing Gay Singapore: Rights and Resistance in an Authoritarian State* (Philadelphia: Temple University Press.).

Chused, Richard and Wendy Williams (2016) *Gendered Law in American History* (Durham, NC: Carolina Press).

Civil Litigation Research Project (CLRP), David Trubek, Joel Grossman, William Felstiner, Herbert M. Kritzer and Austin Sarat (1983) *Civil Litigation Research Project Final Report* (Madison, WI: University of Wisconsin).

Conley, John and William O'Barr (2005) *Just Words: Law Language and Power* (Chicago: University of Chicago Press).

Creutzfeldt, Naomi (2018) *Ombudsman and ADR: A Comparative Study of Informal Justice in Europe* (Cham, Switzerland: Palgrave Macmillan).

Cummings, Scott (2018) "Law and Social Movements: Reimagining the Progressive Canon" *Wisc. Law Rev.* 2018: 441.

Dagan, Hanoch, Roy Kreitner and Tamar Kricheli-Katz (2018) "Legal Theory for Legal Empiricists" *Law Soc. Inquir.* 43 (2): 292–318.

Dawkins, Richard (1976) *The Selfish Gene* (Oxford: Oxford University Press).

Dezalay, Yves and Bryant Garth (1996) *Dealing in Virtue: International Commercial Arbitration and the Construction of a Transnational Legal Order* (Chicago: University of Chicago Press).

Diamond, Shari Seidman (2007) "Juror Responses to Scientific and Other Expert Testimony and how Judges Can Help" *J. Law Policy* 16: 46–67.

———, Neil Vidman, Mary Rose, Leslie Ellis and Beth Murphy (2003) "Inside the Jury Room: Evaluating Juror Discussions During Trial" *Judicature* 87: 54–58.

Durkheim, Emile (1893) *The Division of Labor in Society* (1997 reprint; New York City: Free Press).

——— (1897) *Suicide* (1951 reprint; New York City: Free Press).

Edelman, Lauren (2016) *Working Law: Courts Corporations and Symbolic Civil Rights* (Chicago: University of Chicago Press).

Edelman, Murray (1971) *The Symbolic Uses of Politics* (Champaign-Urbana, IL: The University of Illinois Press).

Edwards, Harry T. and Michael A. Livermore (2009) "Pitfalls of Empirical Studies that Attempt to Understand the Factors Affecting Appellate Decisionmaking" *Duke L. J.* 58: 1895–1990.

Eisenberg, Theodore (2011) "The Origins, Nature and Promise of Empirical Legal Studies and a Response to Concerns" *U. Ill. L. Rev.* 5: 1713–1738.

Ellsworth, Phoebe C. (2012) "Legal Reasoning and Scientific Reasoning" *Alabama L. Rev.* 63: 895–904.

Epp, Charles (2009) *Making Rights Real: Activism, Bureaucrats and the Creation of the Legislative State* (Chicago: University of Chicago Press).

Epstein, Lee and Gary King (2002) "The Rules of Inference" *U. Chic. L. Rev.* 69: 1–134.

——— and Jack Knight (1998) *The Choices Justices Make* (Washington, DC: CQ Press).

———, William Landes and Richard Posner (2013) *The Behavior of Federal Judges* (Cambridge, MA: Harvard University Press).

——— and Andrew D. Martin (2014) *An Introduction to Empirical Legal Research* (Oxford: Oxford University Press).

Eubanks, Virginia (2018) *Automating Inequality: How High Tech Tools Profile, Police and Punish the Poor* (New York: St. Martins Press).

Ewick, Patricia and Susan Silbey (1998) *The Common Place of Law: Stories from Everyday Life* (Chicago: University of Chicago Press).

Feeley, Malcolm (1993) *The Process Is the Punishment: Handling Cases in a Lower Criminal Court* (New York: Russell Sage).

Felstiner, William I.F., Richard L. Abel and Austin Sarat (1980–1981) "The Emergence and Transformation of Disputes: Naming Blaming and Claiming ..." *Law Soc. Rev.* 15: 631–654.

Fisher, Roger and William Ury (1982) *Getting to Yes: Negotiating Agreement without Giving In* (New York: Penguin). (Now in 3rd ed. with Bruce Patton, 2011.)

Follett, Mary Parker (1995) *Mary Parker Follett: Prophet of Management: A Celebration of Writings from the 1920s* (Pauline Graham, ed), (Boston: Harvard Business School Press).

Forman, James (2017) *Locking Up Our Own: Crime and Punishment in Black America* (New York: Farrar, Straus & Giroux).

Frank, Jerome (1949) *Courts on Trial: Myths and Realities in American Justice* (Princeton: Princeton University Press).

Friedman, Lawrence (1986) "The Law and Society Movement" *Stanford L. Rev* 38: 763–780.

――― and Stewart Macaulay (1969) *Law and the Behavioral Sciences* (Indianapolis: Bobbs–Merrill).

Galanter, Marc (1974) "Why the 'Haves' Come Out Ahead: Speculations on the Limits of Legal Change" *Law Soc. Rev* 9: 95–160.

――― (2004) "The Vanishing Trial: An Examination of Trials and Related Matters in Federal and State Courts" *J. Empir. Legal Stud* 1: 459.

Garth, Bryant and Joyce Sterling (1998) "From Legal Realism to Law and Society: Reshaping Law for the Last Stages of the Social Activist State" *Law Soc. Rev* 32: 409–471.

Genn, Hazel (1999) *Paths to Justice: What People Do and Think About Going to Law* (Oxford. Hart).

――― (2009) *Judging Civil Justice* (Cambridge: Cambridge University Press).

――― (2010) "Mediation: A Measured Approach" *J. Soc. Welfare Fam. L.* 2: 195–205.

George, Tracey E. (2006) "An Empirical Study of Empirical Legal Scholarship" *Indiana L. J.* 81: 141–161.

Gibson, James L. (2009) "Taking Stock of Truth and Reconciliation in South Africa: Assessing Citizen Attitudes Through Surveys" in *Assessing the Impact of Transitional Justice: Challenges for Empirical Research* (Hugo van der Merwe, Victoria Baxter and Audrey R. Chapman, eds), (Washington, DC: United States Institute of Peace Press, 173–190).

Goehner, Amy, Lina Lofaro and Kate Novak (2004) "Ripple Effect: Where CSI Meets Real Law & Order" *Time* November 1: 69.

Greatbach, David and Robert Dingwall (1989) "Selective Facilitation: Some Preliminary Observations on a Strategy Used by Divorce Mediators" *Law Soc. Rev.* 23: 613

Greenwald, Anthony G. and Linda Hamilton Krieger (2006) "Implicit Bias: Scientific Foundations" *Cal. L. Rev.* 94: 945.

Greiner, James (2008) "Causal Inference in Civil Rights Litigation" *Harv. L. Rev.* 122: 533–598.

Gulliver, P.H. (1979) *Disputes and Negotiations: A Cross-Cultural Perspective* (New York: Academic Press).

Guthrie, Chris, Jeffrey J. Rachlinski and Andrew Wistrich (2007) "Blinking on the Bench; How Judges Decide Cases" *Cornell L. Rev.* 93: 1–43.

Haack, Susan (2014) *Evidence Matters: Science Truth and Proof in Law* (Cambridge: Cambridge University Press).

Halliday, Terence and Gregory Shaffer, eds (2015) *Transnational Legal Orders* (Cambridge: Cambridge University Press.).

Handler, Joel (1986) *The Conditions of Discretion: Autonomy and Bureaucracy* (New York: Russell Sage).

Hannon, Kendall (2008) "Much Ado about Twombly? A Study on the Impact of *Bell Atlantic v. Twombly* on 12(b) 6 Motions" *Notre Dame L. Rev* 83: 1811.

Hans, Valerie P. and Neil Vidmar (1991) "The American Jury at 25 Years" *Law Soc. Inquir.* 16: 323–352.

Harding, Sandra (1991) *Whose Science? Whose Knowledge?* (Ithaca: Cornell University Press).

Hart, H.L.A. (1997) *The Concept of Law* (Oxford: Clarendon Oxford University Press).

Hawkins, Keith (1984) *Environment and Enforcement: Regulation and the Social Definition of Pollution* (New York: Clarendon Press).

Heckman, John and Alan Krueger, eds (2003) *Inequality in America: What Role for Human Capital Policy?* (Cambridge, MA: MIT Press).

Heise, Michael (2002) "The Past, the Present and Future of Empirical Legal Scholarship: Judicial Decision Making and the New Empiricism" *U. Ill. L. Rev.* 2002: 819–850.

――― (2005) "*Brown v. Board of Education*, Footnote 11 and Multidisciplinarity" *Cornell L. Rev.* 90: 279–294.

Horwitz, Morton (1977) *The Transformation of American Law 1780–1860* (Cambridge, MA: Harvard Univ. Press).

――― (1992) *The Transformation of American Law 1870–1960* (New York: Oxford Press).

Huang, Jennie and Corinne Low (2017) 'Trumping Norms: Lab Evidence on Aggressive Communication before and after the 2016 US Presidential Election', *American Economic Review*, 107 (5): 120–124.

Hull, Kathleen E. (2017) "The Role of Social Science Expertise in Same Sex Marriage Litigation" *Annu. Rev. Law Soc Sci* 13: 471–491.

Hurst, Willard (1964) *Law and Economic Growth: The Legal History of the Lumber Industry in Wisconsin 1836–1915* (Cambridge: Harvard University Press).

Kalven, Harry and Hans Zeisel (1966) *The American Jury* (Boston: Little Brown).

Kousser, J. Morgan (1984) "Are Expert Witnesses Whores? Reflections on Objectivity in Scholarship and Expert Witnessing" *Pub. Historian* 6 (1): 5–19.

Jackson, Vicki C. (2010) *Constitutional Engagement in a Transnational Era* (Oxford: Oxford University Press).

Jennes, Valerie and Kitty Calavita (2018) "It Depends on the Outcome: Prisoner's Grievances and Perceptions of Justice" *Law Soc. Rev.* 52: 41–72.

Jolls, Christine and Cass Sunstein (2006) "The Law of Implicit Bias" *Calif. L. Rev.* 94: 969–976.

———, Cass R. Sunstein and Richard Thaler (1998) "A Behavioral Approach to Law and Economics" *Stanford L. Rev.* 50: 5.

Kagan, Robert (2003) *Adversarial Legalism: The American Way of Law* (Cambridge, MA: Harvard University Press).

Kahneman, Daniel (2013) *Thinking Fast and Slow* (New York: Farrar, Straus & Giroux).

——— and Amos Tversky (1974) "Judgment under Uncertainty: Heuristics and Biases" *Science* 185: 1124–1137.

Kakalik, James, Terence Dunworth, Laural Hill, Daniel McCaffrey, Marian Oshiro, Nicholas Pace and Mary Vaiana (1996) *An Evaluation of Mediation and Early Neutral Evaluation under the Civil Justice Reform Act* (Santa Monica: RAND Institute).

Kelman, Mark (1987) *A Guide to Critical Legal Studies* (Cambridge, MA: Harvard University Press).

Kennedy, Duncan (1998) *A Critique of Adjudication (fin de la siècle)* (Cambridge, MA: Harvard University Press).

Klass, Gregory and Kathryn Zeiler (2013) "Against Endowment Theory: Experimental Economics and Legal Scholarship" *UCLA L. Rev.* 61: 2–64.

Kopacki, Christopher (2013) *Examining the CSI Effect and the Influence of Forensic Crime Television on Future Jurors* (Doctoral Dissertation, Virginia Commonwealth University).

Korobkin, Russell B. and Thomas Ulen (2000) "Law and Behavioral Science: Removing Rationality Assumption from Law and Economics" *Calif. L. Rev.* 38: 1051.

Kritzer, Herbert (2015) *Lawyers at Work* (New Orleans, LA: Quid Pro).

Langevoort, Donald (1998) "Behavioral Theories of Judgment and Decision Making: A Literature Review" *Vanderbilt L. Rev.* 51: 1499.

——— (2001) "The Human Nature of Corporate Boards: Law, Norms, and the Unintended Consequences of Independence and Accountability" *Geo. L. J. 89*: 797–832.

Law, David S. (2017) "The Global Language of Human Rights: A Computational Linguistic Analysis" *Law Ethic. Hum. Rights* 12: 1–34.

Lawrence, Charles R. (1987) "The Id, the Ego and Equal Protection: Reckoning with Unconscious Racism" *Stanford L. Rev.* 39: 317–355.

Levine, Felice (1990) "The Search for Signs of Intelligent Life in Sociolegal Studies: After Twenty Five Years" *Law Soc. Rev.* 24: 7–33.

Lind, Allan E. and Tom Tyler (1988) *The Social Psychology of Procedural Justice* (New York: Plenum).

Loftus, Elizabeth (1996) *Eyewitness Testimony* (Cambridge, MA: Harvard University Press).

Loh, Wallace D. (1984) *Social Research in Judicial Decision Making* (New York: Russell Sage).

Macaulay, Stewart (1984) "Law and the Behavioral Sciences: Is There any There There?" *Law Policy Q.* 6: 149–187.

Mannheim, Karl (1929) *Ideology and Utopia: An Introduction to the Sociology of Knowledge* (Harvest Press, 2015 reprint Martino Fine Books).

McCann, Michael W. (1992) *Rights at Work: Pay Equity Reform and the Politics of Legal Mobilization* (Chicago: University of Chicago Press.).

Meadow, Robert and Carrie Menkel-Meadow (1983) "Resource Allocation in Legal Services: Individual Attorney Decisions in Work Priorities" *Law Policy Q.* 5: 237–256.

Menkel-Meadow, Carrie (1984) "Toward Another View of Legal Negotiation: The Structure of Problem-Solving" *UCLA Law Rev.* 31: 754–842.

——— (1985) "The Transformation of Disputes by Lawyers: What the Dispute Paradigm Does and Does Not Tell Us" *Missouri. J. Dispute Res.* 2: 25–44.

———— (1989) "Feminization of the Legal Profession: The Comparative Sociology of Women Lawyers" in *Lawyers in Society: Comparative Theories* (Richard Abel and Philip S.C. Lewis, eds), (Berkeley: University of California Press), pp. 196–255.

———— (1990) "Durkheimian Epiphanies: The Importance of Engaged Social Science in Legal Studies" *Fla. St. L. Rev.* 18: 91–119.

———— (1997) "When Dispute Resolution Begets Disputes of Its Own: Conflicts among Dispute Professionals" *UCLA L. Rev* 44: 1871–1933.

———— (1998) "The Causes of Cause Lawyering: Toward an Understanding of the Motivations and Commitments of Social Justice Lawyers" in *Cause Lawyering: Political Commitments and Professional Responsibilities* (Austin Sarat and Stuart Scheingold, eds), (Oxford: Oxford University Press), pp. 31–68.

———— (2001) "Aha? Is Creativity Possible in Legal Problem Solving and Teachable in Legal Education?" *Harv. Neg. L. Rev.* 6: 97–144.

———— (2007) "Taking Law and … Really Seriously: Before, During and after 'The Law'" *Vanderbilt L. Rev* 60: 555–595.

———— (2009) "Are There Systemic Ethics Issues in Dispute System Design? And What We Should (Not) Do about It: Lessons from International and Domestic Fronts" *Harvard Neg. L. Rev.* 14: 195–231.

———— (2010) "Empirical Studies of ADR: The Baseline Problem of what ADR Is and what It Is Compared to" in *Oxford Handbook of Empirical Legal Research* (Peter Cane and Herbert Kritzer, eds), (Oxford: Oxford University Press), pp. 596–624.

———— (2011) "Why and How to Study Transnational Law" *Univ. Calif. Irvine Law Rev.* 1: 97–129.

———— (2012) "Women in Dispute Resolution: Parties, Lawyers and Dispute Resolvers—What Difference Does 'Gender Difference' Make?" *Dispute Resolution Mag.* April, 2012.

———— (2013a) "Regulation of Dispute Resolution in the United States of America: From the Formal to the Informal to the Semi-Formal" in *Regulation of Dispute Resolution—ADR and Access to Justice at the Crossroads* (F. Steffek, H. Unberath, R. Greger, H. Genn, C. Menkel-Meadow, eds), (Oxford and Portland, Oregon: Hart), pp. 419–454.

———— (2013b) "The Historical Contingencies of Conflict Resolution" *Int. J. Conflict Engage. Resolut.* 1: 32–54.

———— (2018) "The Origins of Problem Solving Negotiation and Its Uses in the Present" in *Discussions about Dispute Resolution* (Sarah Cole, Art Hinshaw and Andrea Kupfer Schneider, eds), (Oxford: Oxford University Press)

———— (2019) "Hybrid and Mixed Dispute Resolution Processes: Integrities of Process Pluralism" in *Comparative Dispute Resolution Research Handbook* (Michael Palmer, Marian Roberts and Maria Moscati, eds), (Chichester: Edward Elgar).

———— and Shari Seidman Diamond (1991) "The Content, Method and Epistemology of Gender in Sociolegal Studies" *Law Soc. Rev* 25: 221

———— and Bryant Garth (2010) "Process, People, Power and Policy: Empirical Studies of Civil Procedure and Courts" in *Oxford Handbook of Empirical Legal Research* (Peter Cane and Herbert Kritzer, eds), (Oxford: Oxford University Press), pp. 679–704.

————, Lela Love, Andrea Schneider and Michael Moffitt (2018) *Dispute Resolution: Beyond the Adversarial Model* 3rd ed (New York: Wolters Kluwer).

———— and Robert Meadow (1985) "Personalized or Bureaucratized Justice in Legal Services: Resolving Sociological Ambivalence in the Delivery of Legal Aid for the Poor" *Law Hum. Behav.* 9: 397–413.

Merry, Sally (1988) "Legal Pluralism" *Law Soc. Rev* 22: 869–896.

Merry, Sally (1990) *Getting Justice and Getting Even* (Chicago: University of Chicago Press).

Mezey, Naomi (2003) "Erasure and Recognition: The Census, Race and the National Imagination" *Northwestern L. Rev.* 97 (4): 1701–1767.

———— (2015) "Mapping a Cultural Studies of Law" in *The Handbook of Law and Society* (Austin Sarat and Patricia Ewick, eds), (Chichester, UK: Wiley Blackwell), pp. 39–55.

Monahan, J. and Laurens Walker (2014) *Social Science in Law: Cases and Materials* 8th ed. (New York: Foundation Press).

Moran, Rachel F. (2010) "What Counts as Knowledge? A Reflection on Race, Social Science and the Law" *Law Soc. Rev* 44 (3–4): 516.

Morrill, Calvin and Kelsey Mayo (2015) "Charting the Classics in Law and Society" in *The Handbook of Law and Society* (Austin Sarat and Patricia Ewick, eds), (Chichester, UK: Wiley Blackwell), pp. 18–36.

Munger, Frank (2017) "Race Law and Inequality: 50 Years after the Civil Rights Act" *Annu. Rev. Law Soc Sci* 13: 331–350.

———— and Carroll Seron (1984) "Critical Legal Studies vs. Critical Legal Theory: A Comment on Method" *Law Policy* 6 (3): 257–297.

Nader, Laura (1990) *Harmony Ideology: Justice and Control in a Zapotec Mountain Village* (Stanford, CA: Stanford University Press.).

———— and Harry Todd, eds (1978) *The Disputing Process: Law in Ten Societies* (New York: Columbia Univ Press).

Nelken, David (2009) *Beyond Law in Context: Developing a Sociological Understanding of Law* (Farnham: Ashgate).

Parsons, Talcott (1951) *The Social System* (London: Routledge).

Perryman, Benjamin (2018) "Adducing Social Science Evidence in Constitutional Cases" *Queen's L. J.*

Plott, Charles R. and Kathryn Zeiler (2007) "Exchange Asymmetries Incorrectly Interpreted as Evidence of Endowment Effect Theory and Prospect Theory?" *Am. Econ. Rev* 97 (4): 1449–1466.

Posner, Richard (1973) *Economic Analysis of Law* (New York: Wolters Kluwer Law & Business).

———— (1995) "The Sociology of the Sociology of Law" *Eur. J. Law Econ.* 2: 265–285.

———— (2009) *How Judges Think* (Cambridge, MA: Harvard University Press.).

Pound, Roscoe (1910) "Law in Books and Law in Action" *Am. L. Rev.* 44: 12.

Provine, Doris Marie (2007) *Unequal Under Law: Race in the War on Drugs* (Chicago: University of Chicago Press).

Ramji-Nogales, Jaya, Andrew Schoenholtz and Philip Schrag (2011) *Refugee Roulette: Disparities in Asylum Adjudication and Proposals for Reform* (New York: NYU Press).

Renaker, Teresa S. (1996) "Evidentiary Legerdemain: Deciding when *Daubert* Should Apply to Social Science Evidence" *Calif. L. Rev.* 84: 1657.

Richardson, L. Song (2015) "Police Racial Violence: Lessons from Social Psychology" *Fordham L. Rev.* 83: 2961–2976.

———— (2017) "Systemic Triage: Implicit Racial Bias in the Criminal Courtroom" *Yale L. J.* 126: 863–893.

Robbennolt, Jennifer K. (2002) "Evaluating Empirical Research Methods: Using Empirical Research in Law & Policy" *Nebraska L. Rev.* 81 (2): 777–804.

Rosenberg, Gerald (1991) *The Hollow Hope: Can Courts Bring About Social Change?* 2nd ed. (Chicago: University of Chicago Press, 2008).

Sandefur, Rebecca L. (2014) *Accessing Justice in the Contemporary USA: Findings from the Community Needs and Services Study* (Chicago: American Bar Foundation). Available at SSRN https://ssrn.com/abstract=2478040 or http://dx.doi.org/10.2139/ssrn.2478040

Sarat, Austin and Patricia Ewick (2015) *The Handbook of Law and Society* (Malden, MA: Wiley Blackwell).

———— and William Felstiner (1997) *Divorce Lawyers and Their Clients: Power and Meaning in the Legal Process* (Oxford: Oxford University Press).

———— and Susan Silbey (1988) "The Pull of the Policy Audience" *Law Policy Q.* 10: 97.

Schlegel, John Henry (1995) *American Legal Realism and Empirical Social Science* (Chapel Hill, NC: University of North Carolina Press).

Schrag, Zachary (2010) *Ethical Imperialism: Institutional Review Boards and the Social Sciences 1965–2009* (Baltimore: Johns Hopkins Press).

Schultz, Ulrike and Gisela Shaw, eds (2003) *Women in the World's Legal Professions* (Oxford: Hart).

Seron, Carroll (2016) "The Two Faces of Law and Inequality: From Critique to the Promise of Situated, Pragmatic Policy" *Law Soc. Rev* 50: 9–33.

————, Susan Bibler Coutin and Pauline White Meeusen (2013) "Is There a Canon of Law and Society?" *Annu. Rev. Law Soc Sci.* 9: 287–306.

Silbey, Susan and Sally Merry (1986) "Mediator Settlement Strategies" *Law Policy* 8: 7.

Southworth, Ann (2008) *Lawyers of the Right: Professionalizing the Conservative Coalition* (Chicago: University of Chicago Press).

Sterett, Susan (2015) "What Is Law and Society? Definitional Disputes" in *The Handbook of Law and Society* (Austin Sarat and Patricia Ewick, eds), (Chichester, UK: Wiley Blackwell).

Sunstein, Cass (2011) "Empirically Informed Regulation" *Univ. Chic. L. Rev.* 78: 4.

Trubek, David (1990) "Back to the Future: The Short, Happy Life of the Law and Society Movement" *Fla. St. L. Rev.* 18(1): 4–55.

———— and John Esser (1989) "Critical Empiricism in American Legal Studies: Paradox, Program or Pandora's Box" *Law Soc. Inquiry* 14: 3–67.

Twining, William (1978) *The Great Juristic Bazaar* (Farnham:Ashgate).

———— (2012) [reprint] *Karl Llewellyn and the Realist Movement* (Cambridge: Cambridge University Press).

Ulen, Thomas S. (2013) "Behavioral Law and Economics: Law, Policy and Science" *Sup. Ct. Econ. Rev* 21: 1.

Utz, Pamela (1969) *Settling the Facts: Discretion and Negotiation in Criminal Court* (Lexington, MA: Lexington Books).

Weber, Max (1954) *Max Weber on Law and Economy in Society* (Max Rheinstein, ed; Edward Shils, translator), (Cambridge, MA: Harvard University Press).

Wheeler, Russell (1988) "Empirical Research and the Politics of Judicial Administration: The Founding of the Federal Judicial Center" *Law Contemp. Prob.* 51 (3): 31–53.

Zick, Timothy (2003) "Constitutional Empiricism. Quasi-Neutral Principles and Constitutional Truths" *North Carolina L. Rev.* 115. https://dx.doi.org/10.2139/ssrn.466000

Cases Cited

Brown v. Board of Education of Topeka, 347 U.S. 483 (1954).

Daubert v. Merrell Dow Pharmaceuticals, Inc., 509 U.S. 579 (1993).

Loomis v. State (Wisconsin), 881 N.W. 2d 749 (2016).

McCleskey v. Kemp, 481 U.S. 279 (1987).

Mueller v. *Oregon*, 208 U.S. 412 (1908).

Wal Mart Stores v. Dukes, 564 U.S. 338 (2011)

4

THE *WHY* AND *HOW TO* OF CONDUCTING A SOCIO-LEGAL EMPIRICAL RESEARCH PROJECT

Lisa Webley

Introduction

This chapter sets out to explain why one may wish to interrogate a research question via socio-legal means, and to provide a structured way to go about such a project. It aims to be a starting guide to those less clear about socio–legal empirical projects rather than to be a comprehensive account of how to complete socio–legal research. It is the template that I use for research design and is just one perspective that those new to socio–legal research may wish to consider; there are a whole array of creative and individual approaches that one could chose to follow, many of which are set out in subsequent chapters. I have approached writing this chapter in this way as I am regularly contacted by nascent doctoral researchers and those new to this type of research who are keen to pursue socio–legal empirical methods but are unsure how and where to begin. I am also, less frequently, asked for advice by doctoral supervisors who are finding it a challenge to explain to their supervisees how to conduct this type of research. Much of what I say is, thus, a broad-brush encounter with the stages of a socio–legal research project and not a prescription of how it *must* be done. Projects are as diverse in approach and method as they are in substance. This is just one way of conceiving of a project.

This chapter will begin by considering, very briefly, what socio–legal research is. It will then delineate how you may set, or help others to set, an effective research question to provide a solid foundation for the study. Next it will turn to the role that the academic literature may play in assisting you to define your question yet further. It will examine whether you may wish to make use of a hypothesis or hypotheses to guide your method selection and the ways in which you test your findings. It will consider, in a nutshell, what data are, what we mean by research design, data collection and data analysis, and how to consider the ethical implications of your project. It will subsequently turn to conclusions about the key markers of academic quality: originality, significance and rigour, and how these can be harnessed further to improve the quality of your research.

Why socio-legal?

This whole book has been dedicated to a range of understandings about socio–legal research and its methods and techniques. I shall leave others to discuss these in a nuanced and detailed way (see, further, Cowan and Wincott, 2015; Feenan, 2013). It is worth considering at this stage, however, whether socio-legal research is the right kind of approach for your research project before embarking on how to accomplish the project.

Socio-legal research is the examination of how law, legal phenomena and/or phenomena affected by law and the legal system occur in the world, interact with each other and impact upon those who are touched by them. The 'socio' is about the societal context or impact of law and legal phenomena, rather than law in books. The 'legal' is more broadly defined than the text of the law (for theory of law, see Hart, 1961: ch. V; for theory of social world, see Durkheim, 1958: 1–13). Some who undertake this type of research come at is as sociologists, criminologists, social policy scholars and other forms of social scientist. Others are lawyers or humanities scholars. All seek to understand things in a particular environment or environments, some in theoretical terms and others in the field making use of empirical research methods. You will find examples of these varying approaches in this edited collection.

I was drawn to socio-legal research at the point when I realised that knowing what the law is, although very useful when advising a client, did not assist me to know how the law operates outside the court system and how it affects people who experience it or to know the extent to which the law works as it was intended. I became aware that there was a fascinating world around the text of the law, which included how people use law and why, how they act as lawyers, how individuals experience law and justice. That got me hooked on socio-legal research. I still teach doctrinal law – the text of law and how it is interpreted by the courts (Twining and Miers, 2010) – and that gets me part way along the journey to knowing what law is. I combine doctrinal research with socio-legal research when I want to know whether the law is in need of reform (Chynoweth, 2008: ch. 3; Hutchinson, 2002: ch. 5). I start with socio-legal research when I want to examine whether lawyers or other legal actors need different types of legal education and training, or whether the legal system is operating for the benefit of all rather than for those who have the financial means to instruct solicitors and barristers to act on their behalf in negotiations, mediation and/or litigation and so on. In short, if your research question is one in which you need to draw conclusions beyond what the law is, then socio-legal research may be an effective means to allow you to do so.

An approach to the staging of socio-legal research projects: the how

The question

The starting point for many socio-legal projects is a research question. Not all projects begin with one, but if your project is likely to be empirically driven then it helps to start with a clear idea of what you are seeking to do in the project, and a question can help to frame this. Sometimes the process begins with the objectives of the study being set out; other people begin with the question and set the objectives from there. Research questions are funny things in that, in the humanities, some social sciences and in law, they often first appear as a statement and not a question. That is, perhaps, because statements are often set as undergraduate and postgraduate assessments by faculty keen to engage students in a means by which they may critically discuss a proposition. And statements have their place. Experience has taught me, however, that a well-defined research question, ending in a question mark, is an important tool to help me to gain clarity about the aim of the project and to allow a focused literature review phase. Most statements can easily be converted into a proper question by the addition of a phrase such as 'To what extent does/is/can …'. There are other ways to phrase questions, of course. I have found that the addition of a question mark appears to help my brain focus on how something I am reading may help me to answer the starting research question, whereas a statement without a question mark appears to encourage my brain to seek to find a creative link between the statement and the thing that I am reading. The former, thus, allows me to zero in on evidence that assists me to an answer; the latter provides a means by which to broaden out the scope of my enquiry. Empirical socio-legal research questions benefit from a narrow, crisp focus, and so I encourage my doctoral students to deploy a proper question phrased in a single sentence at this stage of their project. Other types of socio-legal research, such as theoretical research, may benefit from the use of a statement instead.

The literature

Academics often tell their postgraduate students that they should undertake a literature review and rarely explain what one is. Yet students from undergraduate level onwards regularly engage in reviews of the academic literature and so are better placed than they believe when undertaking this phase. First, what is the literature for the purposes of a socio-legal project? The literature is all the academic work that has been published on the topic(s) directly relevant to your research question (see Bell and Walters, 2018: ch. 6). Thus, the more focused the question, and the better defined the key terms in the question, the easier it is to complete this phase of the research project. Time spent on refining the starting question is time well spent, as a broad research question will require an extensive literature review; a more targeted question will usually allow for a more focused and effective one.

The nuts and bolts of undertaking the literature review are well known to many, even if they are rarely set out systematically (for guidance on scholarly reading, research and feedback, see the *Law & Society Review* blog, 2017). I find it helpful to use my research question as the means by which to develop a battery of keywords that I can put into Google Scholar as the starting point from my literature search. I consider synonyms based on what words I think that academics may have used in projects similar to mine. Much of my research is into lawyers and their practice, and so I would use keywords that would likely capture articles and books written by other academics who have undertaken relevant studies, using words such as: lawyer, attorney, solicitor, barrister, legal professional, and so on. I may add in jurisdictional keywords: England and Wales, UK, Australia, and so on, and I may use Boolean operators such as 'AND' and 'NOT', as well as strategic use of quotation marks to enclose phrases in order to ensure that certain words occur together in the search algorithm, rather than simply occur in the same document. I use Google Scholar so as to minimise the presence of less authoritative sources in my search results. And I ensure that I am logged in to my institutional university account in another window, as Google Scholar will then direct me through to my university's electronic law library for sources that are behind pay walls but are accessible in full text format as a result of my university's subscription to that journal or publisher. I have found this to be the quickest way for me to search for relevant academic literature. I then follow the Google Scholar search with additional searches via my university subscription databases and the library catalogue, but more and more I find that these do not throw up new sources as Google Scholar becomes increasingly comprehensive.

The next phase of my literature review is to sort through the search results and download those that appear relevant. I do what we all do at this stage: I skim the first few lines of the search return for each source and see which look on point. I organise the sources I have downloaded into three folders (or in my case piles, as I often find it easier to print out key sources rather than read them on screen; I hope one day to be better at on-screen reading). In the first pile or folder I place those sources that seem to me to be absolutely on point to answer the question, those that may assist in answering an element of the question go into the second pile or folder, and those that now seem to be irrelevant go in the third pile or folder. I focus my attention on pile 1 sources for the note-taking phase of the literature review.

I make my notes in one running document on the computer, in which I have typed the research question in the header (so I keep it within my eyeline so as to ensure I retain focus), and I make my notes source by source, in sequence. I put the footnotes/references in as I go along (albeit not beautifully done), so that at the next stage I do not lose the page references or the citations for the material that I am noting down. I make sparse notes, having skimmed through the article at speed (usually the first read through is simply the introduction, first few paragraphs and the conclusions; the second read is the whole article at speed). My intention is to extract the findings (conclusions) that the academic author has set out that are directly relevant to answering my question. I am not making notes to understand that academic's study or to learn more about the topic; my notes are simply a means by which to pull out evidence of what others have found that may assist me to answer my research question. I indicate not just what the academic has found, but also *how* what they have found helps me to answer my question, and so there is some early-stage analysis in my notes even at this point. My notes are often only half a page of material per source, but each sentence will end with a footnote including a page reference to the exact point in the article or book where that finding was located. I repeat this approach for every source in pile 1, save the document as version 1, open it and save it again as version 2, and then I review it.

I have one main aim when I review my pile 1 source notes, which is to work out the repeating issues/themes/topics that other academics have discussed and concluded upon in the literature and that I have identified as important to my question. So, for example, if my research question were to be 'To what extent are there identifiable factors that contribute to inequality within the legal profession, and how may these be overcome?', I would find the literature replete with inequality findings associated with gender, ethnicity and race, parenthood, socio-economic group or class, university attended, disability, sexual orientation and age. As I work my way through my notes twice (the first time I would not spot the repeating themes for the early sources), I would jot down the repeating themes in the margin next to each source. Once done, I would then put each of those themes into the second version of my document as subheadings. And I would rearrange all the material in the second version so that all the material on gender was cut and pasted under the gender subheading, on race under the ethnicity and race subheading, and so on. This is why it is so important to have the footnotes/references in place at this stage, as the document goes from being organised by source to being organised by theme. I now have the makings of a thematic literature review, with all the evidence on gender, or race, in one place. This gives me an evidence base from which I may properly develop my analysis.

I then weigh that evidence under each subheading, look back at the question and ask myself how it helps me to answer the question – how does gender impact on inequality in the legal profession, and how this may be overcome? – and I add that sentence of analysis at the top of my paragraph. Following this, I rewrite all the evidence that comes after it (the material from my notes under the subheading) as the justification and evidence for my analysis so as to demonstrate how I got to my analysis. I then look back at my question again and ask myself how my analysis assists me in answering the question (the answer to 'I have concluded this, so what, who cares?') and add that sentence of conclusion or critical analysis to the end of the paragraph. I repeat that for each of the subheadings. Once I have finished this, I think about the order of my paragraphs so that the flow works as well as it can, I redraft the review again, make links between paragraphs, and may amend subheadings, group paragraphs under new ones or remove the headings altogether. I now have a functional literature review.

Finally, I work through the material in pile or folder 2 swiftly and add in anything that is relevant to my literature review. I may need to nuance some of the conclusions that I have reached to date, or I may be able to add in additional evidence in support of those findings. I do a quick check, too, that nothing in pile 3 is now relevant. And I may go back to and do an additional Google Scholar search now that I am clearer on my themes too. Once I am of the view that this stage of my literature review is complete, I read through it and redraft it in the light of my developing understanding. Importantly, I then consider which parts of my original research question have been satisfactorily answered by other academics through the studies that I have reviewed, and which parts remain unanswered. I redraft my research question on the basis of those elements not satisfactorily answered so far, and the new question becomes the one that I use to plan the empirical stage of my project. This is the foundation for my study, and it also provides me with my claim of originality, one of the hallmarks of quality, discussed in the section on 'Issues of wider relevance', below.

A theoretical framework?

Some scholars choose to answer their research question using a particular theoretical framework. A theoretical framework is an ideological or practical lens that holds certain things to be foundational as an explanation for how the world works (Anfara and Mertz, 2014). There are different 'levels' of theoretical lens, such as meta-theories, including postmodernism, critical realism and positivism, influenced by different approaches to ontology and epistemology (Sousa, 2010). At the next level down are theoretical lenses that seek to categorise or explain how particular aspects of the world work – for example, Bourdieu's human capital theory considers that there are a series of different markers of merit against which individuals are measured, known as different forms of capital. Each form of capital is defined, and they are all placed in a hierarchy of importance. Were I to be answering a question through the lens of Bourdieu's theory, I might need to undertake a literature review on Bourdieu's work so that I could, with dexterity, set out the key components of the theory; I might devote a whole section or chapter to this when I wrote up my study. Once I was clear on the components of the theory, their definitions and the way in which I would use the theory so as to construct my study design and analyse my data, I would then move on to plan my study as set out below.

A theoretical framework is a means by which to view the whole project; it underpins all the decisions that are made and how the data are analysed. But it is possible, instead, to use a theory purely at the data analysis stage so as to seek to explain findings that arise from the analysis of the data, as a way to set out why the findings are the way they are, rather than to underpin the whole project. Suffice to say that, at this stage in a project, it is important to know whether you wish to answer your research question through the lens of Marx, Foucault, Bourdieu, structural theories, political economy or something else. If so, you may need to spend time getting to grips with the theory and the elements that will inform and structure your study and your approach to data analysis. If not, you may instead move on to the next stage and consider theory at the data analysis stage. It is important to recognise, though, that most of us are always viewing the world through a theoretical lens, even if we are unclear what our ideological stance is. Our views are coloured by our understandings of the world, and those views may be hidden from our sight. And so, some supervisors and scholars argue that we all need to recognise our ideological framework, even if it is our own approach to the world rather than a framework defined by others, and thus we should interrogate our meta-theory of the world, regardless of whether we engage with individual theories. If not, we may become prey to ideological confirmation bias that skews our project findings as we progress through our study.

A hypothesis?

During the literature review, I sometimes get a sense of what I think the answer to my question is likely to be; that may be one answer or it may be a range of possible answers. This is perfectly legitimate, and in the natural sciences it would be normal to design an experiment to interrogate a likely answer, known as a hypothesis. Hypotheses are used to a limited extent in the social sciences, and even less frequently in the humanities. In a socio-legal context, we may need to be cautious about rejecting the use of a hypothesis out of hand, particularly for those of us who are trained as lawyers (Denzin, 2017). Without care, it is possible for us to design our study and analyse our data so that it becomes an act of advocacy for a particular answer, rather than a study with findings that emerge from the data. This is known as confirmation bias, and, although entirely normal for the human brain, it is problematic when we are undertaking scholarly work. And so, where I have a likely answer in mind, I harness the use of a hypothesis to minimise the chances that I will unconsciously confirm my biases. I set out the likely answer as a hypothesis and then design my study to seek to falsify or undermine it, not to seek to prove it right. This should, hopefully, counteract my bias, which is operating in the opposite direction (a desire to confirm what I think to be true). In the end, it is not important to the success of my project whether I disprove my hypothesis or hypotheses in whole or in part or whether I am unable to disprove it (and thus the answer may be correct). The answer is whatever it is, and the project is successful by virtue of it being undertaken in a rigorous way, rather than on the basis of a particular outcome.

The data

My next stage is to work through the types of data, the 'stuff' that I shall collect and analyse so as to be able to answer my question. There are lots of different ways of seeking to work out the data sources that may be relevant to the question. My preferred method is to split my post-literature review research question into its logically connected sub-questions and set out all the different types of people or 'stuff' that may allow me to answer each one. For my kinds of research question, the people may be, for example, lawyers in practice, judges, clients, legal academics and students, and sometimes members of the public. The stuff may be cases and statutes or a range of other types of document (law firm annual reports, arbitral awards, curricula and training materials etc.). It may extend to in-person observation of sites of legal engagement, whether court, lawyers' offices or law school clinics or classrooms. The range of sources is as broad as I am able to conceive of. I list them all, then consider which parts of my question those sources would assist with, how accessible they are and the practicalities associated with that, given my project schedule. I also consider the extent to which

I really want to use those sources, delete those that are either too challenging or are impractical and review which ones are left. Next, I need to consider whether those that are left will allow me fully to answer my question, and what caveats would I need to place on my findings were I to use some or all of these sources. I note all of this thinking down for the methods section or chapter of my project. I also consider whether I need to amend my research question in the light of the decisions I have taken on data sources.

Data collection and analysis

My next step is to consider how I shall collect the data I have identified as important to my research questions. Will I collect it via archival or database research (Platt, 1981; Scott, 1990), through a search of lawyers' offices or NGO websites, through interviews (face to face, telephone, Skype), questionnaires (online, on paper, self-administered by respondents or administered by me or others; Oppenheim, 1992), or observations in sites where decisions are being taken and/or roles being performed (Becker and Geer, 1970)? How shall I systematically record those data? Will I use a field notebook, will I record interviews, will the questionnaires self-code online or do I need to take paper copies and enter the data into a database? How will I pilot my approaches to data collection? Do I need to use a case study method (Gerring, 2004; Webley, 2016; Yin, 1994, 2013), a comparative method (Cotterrell, 2012; Örücü, 2006; Peters and Schwenke, 2000; Siems, 2014) or something else? These considerations are dealt with elsewhere in this collection and so I shall not address them here. You may wish to refer to the other relevant chapters in this regard.

There are decisions to be made about data analysis too, and each type of data may need a different form of analysis (Denzin and Lincoln, 2000; Gibbs, 2007; Miles and Huberman, 1994). There are traditions about the different ways in which one may analyse qualitative (narrative) and quantitative (numbers, statistical) data, although there is a good deal of overlap between some of these too (Epstein and Martin, 2010; Webley, 2010). Data analysis may refer to particular methods of extracting meaning from the data: grounded theory (Glaser, 1992; Glaser and Strauss, 1967; Strauss and Corbin, 1998), discourse (Taylor, 2001), thematic or content analysis (Bauer, 2000), or descriptive and inferential statistics (Cohen and Holliday, 1996; Desrosières, 1996; Wilkinson, 2000). Further, you may be overlaying a theoretical framework when analysing the data, and, if so, this will need to be factored in too. There are other things to consider – do you wish to make use of computer-assisted data analysis? This is usually a must in the context of statistical analysis of large data sets (SPSS, XL etc.), but it may be less clear cut when it comes to some forms of qualitative analysis. Some of us will use NVivo; others will use different software systems. And some may prefer to rely on more traditional pen-and-paper-type methods. Your decision will, in part, be linked to the size of your data sets and access to the software and any training you may need to be confident in its use. When I undertake quantitative analysis, I normally turn to SPSS as my software of choice; when undertaking qualitative analysis, I sometimes use NVivo and sometimes instead work without reference to computer assistance.

Research ethics

So far, we have considered a series of decisions about the focus of the study, the underpinning research question and sub-questions, the appropriate sources of data to assist with answering them, and how to collect those data and analyse them. We have not, however, considered the ethical implications that may arise from the study, and these will need to be thought through before ethical approval can be granted. Sometimes researchers can feel straight-jacketed by the formalised nature of the research ethics process, as if it is a hurdle that must be overcome in order to allow the study to proceed (Boon, 2005). But, if the process of ethical reflection can effectively be harnessed, it can lead to a much higher-quality, critically reflective and sophisticated research study that is clear on its impact on the academic community and wider society. I have found it worth spending time on this stage of the process to improve my study design.

The research ethics process is established, in part, to ensure that no-one is inappropriately harmed as the result of a research study. Harm is broadly defined to include psychological well-being as well as physical and other material harm; unethical harm is harm that we should have taken steps to mitigate or prevent either by changing our research protocol or by making a judgement about whether it is appropriate to conduct the research at all, given the effects that our study may have on others. To assess the ethical impact of a project we are usually asked to set out the study aims, the research question and sub-questions, any hypotheses, data sources, collection and analysis methods, along with any decisions we have taken in selecting those things. We are also usually asked to think through what we consider to be foreseeable risks as regards process and outcome: who could be affected, and how. I usually refer back to the Socio-Legal Studies Association Statement of Ethical Practice, but there are others that may be relevant to your disciplinary tradition and learned societies (e.g., see Ferdinand et al., 2007). Often there are detailed questions about certain types of data and their storage linked to legal requirements about data protection and data privacy too. By working through the research ethics process, we are forced to consider not just those who may be involved in the project but also those who may be touched by our findings; we reflect on the significance of our study and on its impact, on the rigour of our research design. These form part of the quality criteria for judging our research, set out below in the section on 'Issues of wider relevance'. Consequently, a robust approach to the research ethics process is a means by which we can test our study quality at the outset, and also generate the material we need for our research methods chapter too.

Findings: facts and inferences

Once I have collected my data and analysed them, I have a set of tentative findings that are particular to the data that I have collected – the people that I talked to, the cases that I read, those situations that I observed, the questionnaires that I have analysed. Assuming I have undertaken the data analysis systematically and in conformity to the meta-theory and the data analysis method that I am following, then I should have a robust set of specific findings. However, most of us in the socio-legal tradition will want to extend our findings beyond the individual situations that we have studied, and this is where things can get a bit more challenging. We are, in effect, drawing inferences from particular situations and reading those in to situations that we have not ourselves studied (King, Keohane, and Verba, 1996). We are going from individual contexts to more general ones. And that needs to be done with a degree of caution and humility so that inferences are not illogical and/or extended beyond our data's ability to evidence them (for particular concerns in the context of lawyers doing this, see Epstein and King, 2002). It is easier to attain generalizable findings when one has undertaken robust quantitative (statistical) data collection and analysis, because one of the features of this type of research is generalisability. In order to make universal claims, I would need to be sufficiently certain that my data set was either a population data set (containing everyone from the population I had studied) or a representative sample of those within the population. It would be inappropriate to make such claims for most qualitative or small-scale quantitative research (Webley, 2010); I need to write up my findings with care and indicate when I am drawing an inference – making a claim rather than stating what I consider to be an evidenced fact. This does not undermine the quality of my findings – far from it. It allows those reading my work to know when I am stating facts, when I am drawing inferences and when I am using theory to speculate on the likely explanation for those facts or inferences being as they are. This assists with my claim to analytical rigour, the final criterion against which much academic work is judged.

Issues of wider relevance

As indicated earlier in the chapter, the quality of academic work is often judged according to three main criteria: its originality, its significance and its rigour. They are the criteria used to assess doctoral theses and to assess academic work in the UK Research Excellence Framework process and similar exercises in other countries. I shall briefly examine each of these in the context of socio-legal empirical projects and indicate how they can be used to critique one's own draft research paper or thesis to increase its perceived quality and persuasiveness.

Originality, at first glance, appears to require sophisticated new ways of looking at the world. In fact, it is simply a way of judging what new insight has been produced through a study that was not previously known to the academic community. I need to know what is known already and what I have added to the sum of academic knowledge, and the literature review process is the way that I can both know this and demonstrate it. By the time that I have completed my literature review, I should know what has already been concluded on my question by the academic community and have identified a lacuna that my study will fill by answering my post-literature review question. The originality may be substantive – the nature of the question I have asked – or context-specific – the jurisdictional, temporal or specific case study context in which the question has been asked and answered. Sometimes, my study may be methodologically original, answering a question similar to that answered by a previous academic but using a different type of data, a different data collection method or a different means by which to analyse those data. Literature review and methods chapters provide us with the fora to prove originality claims. I have found that my claim is most persuasive when made upfront in my introduction so as to highlight the importance of my study by setting out what I have found and how it fills a gap in knowledge, or to confirm or refute earlier findings via different means or in a different context. I provide my justification in the literature and methods chapters or sections.

The significance of a study is a product of the critical analysis within it. It is, in essence, the explanation of how what we have found matters to the academic community. In what ways do our findings advance academic understanding, and why is that important and/or helpful? In some instances, the significance of the findings may extend beyond the academic realm and, if so, that may lead on to a discussion of recommendations that flow from the findings. I tend to add these claims to my introduction, immediately after my claim of originality, during the redrafting process following completion of my conclusions. Some people prefer to leave their claims to the conclusions chapter.

I have discussed the term 'rigour' as encompassing two different markers of quality: process rigour and analytical rigour. Process rigour addresses the research design decisions that we have made in designing our study, as well as how well we have executed those decisions when conducting our study (Webley, 2010, 2016). The research ethics process helps with claims to process rigour, not least as independent academics will have considered the decisions I have made and will have raised any concerns about quality as well as ethics at an early stage. In addition, I have found it worthwhile to keep a running note of all the decisions that I have taken in the conduct of my study, what has worked, what has not, and what amendments I have needed to make and why, so that I have all those details to hand for my methods chapter. I also consider carefully the limitations of my study, both the caveats as regards how I carried out the research and those relating to the inferences I have drawn too. Analytical rigour comes to the fore when I am seeking to reach conclusions from my data. I have found it helpful to ask myself what is proven by the data (to a legal standard), what is suggested by the data such that I may draw a reliable inference, and what I am seeking to explain by developing a theory or hypothesis that is speculative and that I or others may later wish to test through a subsequent study. I have developed those questions for myself so as to guide my self-critique of my findings, having at times overreached in my conclusions in the past. Others have different ways of checking the reliability of their findings.

Conclusion

I have set out one structured way to approach a socio-legal research project, via a series of stages. Of course, this oversimplifies the idiosyncratic and serendipitous nature of research and suggests a linearity to project planning and execution that is rarely seen in reality. Research questions are in a constant state of flux for most of us, much of the time. Projects can be brilliantly planned, and then confounding factors force us to retrace our steps and make different decisions about data and methods. The analytical stages of studies are far more mercurial than suggested too: sometimes, one brief moment of insight fundamentally changes how we 'read' the data, and that sets us off on a new and more interesting train of thought. A chance conversation with a colleague has, on more than one occasion, led me to see that my study results are wider-ranging than I had anticipated. Sharing findings at a work-in-progress stage can be really beneficial: a knowledgeable outsider's views may unlock connections between data. Self-critique and peer review are excellent means by which to improve the quality of a study at the planning, execution and write-up stages, and I am grateful for the time that others take to help me to reflect on my work. I hope that you are similarly supported by others too.

Further reading

A. Bryman *Social Research Methods* 5th Edition (Oxford: Oxford University Press, 2015).
P. Cane and H. Kritzer *The Oxford Handbook of Empirical Legal Research* (Oxford: Oxford University Press, 2010).
D. De Vaus *Research Design in Social Research* (London, Thousand Oaks, New Delhi: Sage, 2001).
T. May *Social Research Issues, Methods and Process* 4th ed. (Buckingham: Open University, 2011).
K. F. Punch *Introduction to Social Research Quantitative and Qualitative Approaches* 3rd ed. (London: Sage, 2013).

References

V. A. Anfara, Jr. and N. T. Mertz (eds) *Theoretical Frameworks in Qualitative Research* 2nd ed. (London, Thousand Oaks, New Delhi: Sage, 2014).
M. W. Bauer 'Chapter 8 – Classical Content Analysis: A Review' in M. W. Bauer, G. Gaskell and N. C. Allum (eds) *Qualitative Researching with Text, Image and Sound A Practical Handbook* (London, Thousand Oaks, New Delhi: Sage, 2000).

H. Becker and B. Geer 'Participant Observation and Interviewing A Comparison' in W. J. Filstead (ed) *Qualitative Methodology Firsthand Involvement with the Social World* (Chicago: Markham Publishing, 1970) 133–142.

J. Bell and S. Walters 'Chapter 6 Literature Searching' in *Doing Your Research Project: A Guide for First-Time Researchers in Education and Social Science* 7th ed. (Buckingham: Open University Press, 2018).

A. Boon 'Chapter 15 The Formalisation of Research Ethics' in R. Banakar and M. Travers (eds) *Theory and Method in Socio-Legal Research* (Oxford: Hart, 2005) 301–326.

P. Chynoweth 'Chapter 3 Legal Research' in A. Knight and L. Ruddock (eds) *Advanced Research Methods in the Built Environment* (Chichester: Wiley-Blackwell, 2008) 28.

L. Cohen and M. Holliday *Practical Statistics for Students* (London: Paul Chapman, 1996).

R. Cotterrell 'Comparative Sociology of Law' in D. S. Clarke (ed) *Comparative Law and Society, Research Handbooks in Comparative Law* (Cheltenham: Edward Elgar, 2012) 39.

D. Cowan and D. Wincott (eds) *Exploring the Legal Exploring the Legal in Socio-Legal Studies* (London: Palgrave Macmillan, 2015).

N. K. Denzin (2017) *Sociological Methods: A Sourcebook* (Routledge ebook, 2017) www.taylorfrancis.com /books/e/9781351489072

N. K. Denzin and Y. S. Lincoln (eds) *Handbook of Qualitative Research* 2nd ed. (Thousand Oaks, CA: Sage, 2000).

A. Desrosières 'Statistical Traditions: An Obstacle to International Comparisons?' in L. Hantrais and S. Mangen (eds) *Cross-National Research Methods in the Social Sciences* (London: Pinter, 1996) 17–38.

E. Durkheim *The Rules of the Sociological Method* (New York: Free Press, 1958).

L. Epstein and G. King 'The Rules of Inference' (2002) *University of Chicago Law Review* Vol. 69 No. 1 1–133.

L. Epstein and A. D. Martin 'Chapter 37 Quantitative Approaches to Empirical Legal Research' in P. Cane and H. Kritzer (eds) *The Oxford Handbook of Empirical Legal Research* (Oxford: Oxford University Press, 2010) 902–925.

D. Feenan *Exploring the 'Socio' in Socio-Legal Studies* (London: Palgrave Macmillan, 2013).

J. Ferdinand et al. 'A Different Kind of Ethic' (2007) *Ethnography* Vol. 8 No. 4 519–543.

J. Gerring 'What Is a Case Study and What Is It Good For?' (2004) *The American Political Science Review* Vol. 98 No. 2 341–354.

G. R. Gibbs *Analyzing Qualitative Data* (London, Thousand Oaks, CA, Delhi, Singapore: Sage, 2007).

B. Glaser and A. Strauss *The Discovery of Grounded Theory: Strategies for Qualitative Research* (Chicago: Aldine, 1967).

B. G. Glaser *Basics of Grounded Theory Analysis: Emergence vs. Forcing* (Mill Valley, CA: Sociology Press, 1992).

H. L. A. Hart *The Concept of Law* (Oxford University Press,1961) Chapter V.

T. Hutchinson 'Chapter 5 Social Science Methodologies for Lawyers' in *Researching and Writing in Law* (Pyrmont, Australia: Lawbook Co., 2002). https://legal.thomsonreuters.com.au/researching-and-writing-in-law-4e-book/productdetail/124535#description

G. King, R. Keohane and S. Verba *Designing Social Enquiry* (Princeton, NJ: Princeton University Press, 1996).

Law & Society Review A Brief Guide to Reading, Writing, and Giving Feedback in Socio-Legal Studies 18th October 2017 http://lawandsocietyreview.blogspot.com/2017/10/a-brief-guide-to-reading-writing-and.html

M. Miles and A. Huberman *Qualitative Data Analysis* 2nd ed. (Thousand Oaks, CA: Sage, 1994).

N. Oppenheim 'Chapter 8 – Question Wording' in N. Oppenheim (ed.) *Questionnaire Design, Interviewing and Attitude Measurement* (London, New York: Continuum, 1992) 119–149.

E. Örücü 'Methodological Aspects of Comparative Law' (2006) *European Journal of Law Reform* Vol. 8 29–42.

A. Peters and H. Schwenke 'Comparative Law beyond Post-modernism' (2000) *International and Comparative Law Quarterly* 49 800–834.

J. Platt. 'Evidence and Proof in Documentary Research: Some Specific Problems of Documentary Research' (1981) *Sociological Review* Vol. 29 No. 1 31.

J. Scott *A Matter of Record: Documentary Sources in Social Research* (Cambridge: Polity Press, 1990).

M. Siems *Comparative Law* (Cambridge: Cambridge University Press, 2014).

Socio-Legal Studies Association Statement of Ethical Practice www.slsa.ac.uk/images/slsadownloads/ethicalstatement/slsa%20ethics%20statement%20_final_%5B1%5D.pdf

F. J. Sousa 'Chapter 9 Metatheories in Research: Positivism, Postmodernism and Critical Realism' in A. G. Woodside (ed) *Organizational Culture, Business-to-Business Relationships, and Interfirm Networks series: Advances in Business Marketing and Purchasing* Vol. 16 (Bingley, UK: Emerald Books, 2010) 455–503.

A. Strauss and J. Corbin *Basics of Qualitative Research Techniques and Procedures for Developing Grounded Theory* 2nd ed. (Thousand Oaks: Sage, 1998).

S. Taylor 'Locating and Conducting Discourse Analytic Research' in M. Wetherell, S. Taylor and S. J. Yates (eds) *Discourse as Data: A Guide for Analysis* (London: Sage, 2001) 5.

W. Twining and D. Miers *How to Do Things with Rules: A Primer of Interpretation* 5th ed. (Cambridge: Cambridge University Press, 2010).

L. Webley 'Chapter 38 Qualitative Approaches to Empirical Legal Research' in P. Cane and H. Kritzer (eds) *Oxford Handbook of Empirical Legal Studies* (Oxford: Oxford University Press, 2010) 926–950.

L. Webley 'Stumbling Blocks in Empirical Legal Research: Case Study Research' (2016) *Law and Method*. doi:10.5553/REM/.000020

D. Wilkinson 'Analysing Data' in D. Wilkinson (ed) *The Researcher's Toolkit, The Complete Guide to Practitioner Research* (London: Routledge Falmer, 2000) 77–97.

R. Yin *Case Study Research Design and Methods* 5th ed. (Thousand Oaks, CA: Sage, 2013).

R. K. Yin *Case Study Research Design and Methods* 2nd ed. (Thousand Oaks, London, New Delhi: Sage, 1994).

5

WRITING BEYOND DISTINCTIONS[*]

Andreas Philippopoulos-Mihalopoulos

How to write beyond distinctions

Writing is all about distinguishing, not least what to include and what to leave out. So this chapter is not about writing without distinctions, but about becoming aware of the distinctions we habitually employ when writing about the law, and then making an effort to move beyond them. In what follows, I will be urging readers to leave behind at least a couple of distinctions. The first one, of a more formal nature, is that between socio-legal and critical legal writing. The second, referring more to the substance, is the distinction between text and context, or, to put it somewhat differently, law and matter (and with it, other disciplines, space, human and nonhuman bodies, objects, even ideas).

Ignoring at my peril Margaret Atwood's sound advice ('Writing itself is bad enough but writing about writing is surely worse, in the futility department', 2002: xvi), this chapter is about writing. The idea is to explore ways in which we can open up our writing practices beyond formal distinctions of who is what, or substantive distinctions of law on the one hand, and all other things on the other. We have been conditioned for too long to think, write and act according to turf divisions. These are insidious practices, employed in our writing in an often unthinking way, and embodied in the choice of authors we read, the conferences we attend, the law schools we seek employment in. Even the most progressive of us regularly indoctrinate our students with such distinctions.

This, however, is not just about writing. Legal research can never be 'just' writing. There is always a horizon, legal, political, social at large, and we are all gearing towards it. I assume here that the readers of this volume all share a broader horizon: the desire for a more just law. By artificially placing boundaries between, say, critical and socio-legal, interdisciplinary and disciplinary-focused, or personal ethnographic and 'objective' analysis of law (even in context), we debilitate the possibility of the united front we need to present in view of all the rather extreme challenges we are currently facing as scholars. These challenges are well known and appear equally on a micro (managerialism in universities,

[*] This text partly draws from my 2018 text 'To Have to do with the Law: An Essay' – my first ethnographic attempt and conscious writing on writing.

marketisation of research, quantification of teaching) and a macro level (global disregard of law, new geopolitical balances, insular nature of global political scene in terms of aid, environment and refugees, ecological degradation, and so on).

In the following two sections, I look into the above distinctions and the reasons for which they should be considered obsolete. In the next section ('Why do we all fail?'), I then point to our frequent reluctance truly to leave these behind and move into what Adorno has called the law of the essay, namely a manner of writing that allows for previously invisibilised elements to come forth. To do that, I argue we need to resist the urge for resolution ('Why must legal essays be disappointing?') and treat the essay instead as a body with its own, indeed legal, agency ('The essay as body?'). One way of doing this is by insisting on using the 'I' both as a semantic of personal responsibility but also as an indication of a collectivity ('How many am I?'). Another way is by allowing the text to unfold – indeed, we need to 'listen' to the text rather than always trying to impose a form on it ('What comes first, the idea or the writing?'). In the penultimate section, I sum up our responsibilities as legal scholars and writers, and I conclude with a listing divagation and a reminder of what is, hopefully, the most important reason for which we write: to allow for the emergence of a more just law.

Have we ever not been critical?

Let me start with the first distinction, that between socio-legal and critical. My argument is that the maintenance of the distinction does a disservice to both critical and socio-legal writing (traditionally understood). It implies that socio-legal writing cannot be critical – namely, theoretically informed with strong critical inclinations and potentially even a horizon-embracing vision of the future – and, respectively, that critical cannot be socio-legal – namely, pragmatically contextualised, in touch with an ever-evolving society the study of which often necessitates a broadly understood empirical approach. There is no doubt, of course, that several theoretical publications pay scant attention to how theory is translated into practice, or how, more broadly, theory can make a difference; likewise, a considerable amount of applied research is not interested in the benefits that more extensive theorisation brings in terms of diagonal, creative and unhinged thinking. But things are rapidly changing: a burgeoning number of scholars in the last decade or so have resisted such hard lines and have produced work that theorises practice and applies theory, if not in equal measure, at least without falling into an old-fashioned binary (out of a large body, see indicatively Bottomley and Wong, 2009; Grabham, 2016; Perry-Kessaris, 2017).

The distinction (and others, along the lines of 'high theory' versus grounded thought, concreteness versus abstraction, utopia versus pragmatism, and so on) has outlived its usefulness, except as a tool for turf preservation. It is perhaps understood that there is good legal thinking that is aware of its potential effect on reality, and that works on this in order to give direction to its theoretical development; and then, that there is not so good legal thinking that remains unconnected to reality and deliberately ignores its own transformative potential. Unless broadly understood as contextualisation, affective engagement and personal involvement, neither empirical studies nor mere theoretical work have a monopoly on reality.

In response to this, I have tried to sketch the concept of 'critical sociolegal' research (2015) and, more recently, the practice of 'law and theory' (2018b) as ways of moving beyond distinctions. This text is a continuation of the same project. It is my hope, however, that, increasingly, any need to come up with a category for the kind of research we are engaging in, both in this volume and in the wider academia, will eventually become obsolete.

What is the context of the law?

Considering the readership of this volume, there is no need to emphasise how a doctrinal focus on the letter of the law fails to understand what the law is. Context to the law is not what broccoli is to the tofu steak – the optional green bits. Rather, law's context makes the text of law, imbues it with relevance, links it to reality, fleshes it with matter, gives it a body and positions it in space and time. Context is text, and the distinction between the two is increasingly becoming outdated, whether we are talking about socio-legal, critical and/or interdisciplinary research. The relevant question now is, how best to include context when writing about the law.

The question bears considerable gravity: it has increasingly become the main challenge for and responsibility of a legal researcher. Ethical approval of empirical work is precisely about the careful filtering of the context into the text. Likewise, the question of which theory to choose and how to apply it is increasingly important, not just on a PhD level in terms of theoretical framework, but even earlier on in terms of undergraduate work that claims to engage with contemporary life. Theory needs to be there not only because it strengthens the legal argument, but also because it enriches it by opening it up to potential conflicts that the law habitually excludes. Finally, other disciplines enter legal thinking in the form of economics, gender and politics, or perhaps less traditionally in terms of space, time, corporeality, and so on.

The plethora of these considerations and the particular urgency with which they emerge (especially political, geopolitical and environmental issues) leave us with two options: either we carry on lamenting the loss of (a fantasy of) disciplinary sovereignty of law and resist the tide by reinstating the boundaries of law along traditional lines, or we accept that law is changing in line with reality, theory and other disciplines and becomes all the richer for this. In reality, I only see one option here.

Yet, there is one proviso: law's function remains distinct from other disciplines. However much we enjoy law's engagement with, say, anthropology, we are also aware of the fact that legal research is not anthropology. Rather, it can aspire to become a kind of, say, legal anthropology. This means that the text (in this case, the law) re-emerges from within the context: text and context, although in many ways identical, do not become one. Law's social function of binding expectations in terms of what is allowed and what is not is an important one. Although no doubt in a continuum with cultural, anthropological and socio-logical normative considerations, the law (the way it is understood in law schools) is still recognisable and can still be differentiated from other kinds of norm. Let us not become arrogant though: this is a spectrum, and law is only a form of intensification of the norma-tive, often aided by spatial (say, in a court of law) and temporal (say, in times of terrorist amber alert) conditions. What is deemed 'merely' cultural often ends up becoming 'solid' law, and vice versa.

Why do we all fail?

In what follows, I would like to zoom in on writing, especially legal essay writing, and the ways in which it can move beyond the above distinctions. I refer here predominantly to the art of scholarly essay writing, the type of writing we all engage with when reading or contributing to volumes such as this. There are, of course, other types of legal writing: case commentary, reports, textbooks, 'scholarship' writing, even funding applications. The kind of essay I am thinking of, however, is not limited to a formal understanding of an essay, whatever that might be, but potentially includes even the above kinds of writing and extends to any form of writing that analyses the law and its context. In that respect, all writing is essay writing – an attempt or a trial for both form and content.

This, however, is uneasy territory, as it upsets most of the ideas we have of what a legal essay is or should be, and consequently leaves us a little adrift, somewhat fumbling for the form we knew and trusted. Formlessness, however, has traditionally been considered an integral characteristic of the essay form, ever since Michel de Montaigne invented the term and to some extent the form of the 'essay' (*essai*, often translated as 'trial'). A lawyer by formation, Montaigne fought against the law with characteristic vehemence. Although his thoughts on law were convincing in many respects, it is our challenge to fight against some of these distinctions as well. In particular, Montaigne maintained that law cannot generate justice ('even our system of law, they say, bases the truth of its justice upon legal fictions', Montaigne, 1991: 603), in so doing maintaining a distinction between law and justice. And although there are different kinds of justice, and not every kind comes from law, we should also accept that there are different kinds of law too, and that the connection between them needs to be reinstated.

In order to reinstate this connection though, as I hope to do at the end of this essay, we need to think more broadly. The German philosopher Theodor Adorno (1984: 171) concludes 'The Essay as Form' with these words:

> the law of the innermost form of the essay is heresy. By transgressing the orthodoxy of thought, something becomes visible in the object which it is orthodoxy's secret purpose to keep invisible.

In other words, orthodoxy of thought keeps things invisible (presumably out of a desire to maintain status quo and disciplinary lines), whereas heresy, the law of the essay, brings these to the fore. But is this really how we think of our writing? Does the law of the essay really apply to essays on law? Do we really write essays (etymologically, trials and experiments) or do we sometimes feel as if we are filling in preformulated word documents? (I do.)

Without wanting unduly to challenge our volume editors (although I would like to challenge them a little), all contributors received, in good time, a very detailed outline of how the individual chapters should be formatted. I am not talking about referencing style and so on, but about the questions that each contribution is to be pondering on, neatly separated into easy-to-follow sections. (An example: the second section of each contribution is to be 'Analysis of one or more aspects of your experience applying this socio-legal theory/method … We do encourage contributors to take a reflective and reflexive approach, considering e.g.: What was your project and how did you use this theoretical/methodological approach? How did you use this theory/method and what would you do differently in the future? How were your research choices and outcomes shaped by aspects such as your positionality as a researcher and ethical implications/choices? What are the implications of your work for the development of this theory/method?') This is no doubt an expert editing attempt at making our (contributors) and their (editors) writing lives easier, and at achieving a much-valued consistency of outcome. Cheekily, however, my text is an ungrateful attempt at making my writing and their editing lives harder. I do not follow the suggested format, I answer only indirectly some of these questions, and I end up ignoring others. I hope I am not misunderstood as an arrogant trouble-maker: the above questions are excellent. Indeed, the editors ask for personal and textual positioning, future projections, practice-oriented facts – they ask of us to be *present* in what we write. But, at the same time, despite the fact that they explicitly state that they 'do not wish to be prescriptive about the content', and I believe them, they fail.

But we all fail. Let us go back to something even more basic: the writing of our students. Although the emphasis of my text here is not student writing, I employ it as an unambiguous indication of what we more or less impose on ourselves (as well as our students) as the 'appropriate' way of writing. So, to recall Adorno and the law of the essay: do we encourage, or at least tolerate, heresy? I have worked my way through many first-year student essays, the explicit objective of which is not so much the chosen topic but essay writing as such, researching and expressing, in short a first soft plunge into the world of academic writing. Year in, year out, they are asked to choose out of a list of topics (role of the judge, law and morality, statutory interpretation, and so on), and every year the absolute majority chooses the topic of juries. The majority among that majority form their topic along the lines of a seminar question in their handbook: 'What are the advantages and disadvantages of the jury system? Identify 2 or 3 points on each side of the debate'. The admittedly well-produced (not by me) handbook provides clear guidance on essay writing. For the introduction, for example, the main requirement is to:

> set out your approach to answering the question by mentioning briefly the issues you will cover. If you cannot do this then you are not clear on how you are going to approach answering the question. Go back to the question.

Following on, 'at the beginning of each paragraph state what the issue is'. And, as for the conclusion, emphatically 'do not introduce new ideas!' One of the oral instructions to students, about which I have an extended exchange every year with the programme responsible, is not to use the first-person personal pronoun. Passive voice, impersonal constructions ('it is submitted') or, at the very worst, 'we' is preferable.

Students (we!) mostly follow the guidelines, good students at least (we on what we think is a good day), and produce balanced, reasonably argued although understandably often hesitant and slightly wooden essays on juries. What is worrying though is that they regularly stop short of taking any position with regards to their chosen two or three points, and nearly always end up with a conclusion (and a whole text, for that matter) that does not introduce any new ideas (exclamation mark). I imagine that the argument is similar to that other argument that says you have to be able to master figurative painting first in order to move on to abstraction. I am certain that this is no longer considered valid, at least in trendy fine art schools, but there is something not altogether unattractive about it. You must first learn the basics, and only then fly. And, naturally, I am all too aware of the problems of incipient writing, and I have often found myself imparting to students, but also early career colleagues, the usual essay writing steps as if they were the truth.

But then, what do we sacrifice when we desire an essay to be merely an attempt and not a veritable trial? A trial of error and of bravado perhaps, but also a trial of judgement, of personal exposure and risk-taking? What do we lose when we only encourage well-formed, section-arranged consistency?

Why must legal essays be disappointing?

The essays we write about the law have a choice: they can either submit to the compulsion of the law to deliver a binary resolution: yes/no, guilty/not guilty, legal/illegal; or they can flow along the other, perhaps more honest, aspect of the law that never quite decides. This is that part of the law (or the essay) that lies in waiting for its interpreter/reader: as we said, law is inert until thrown into a context that animates it and indeed *makes* it the law. Whereas the former way of thinking about the law is the big adversarial spectacle, in the mode of dramatic trials and Netflix shows, the latter is the way law attempts to capture the future without, however, being able to dictate it. It is the law in its full potential: an opportunity to reinterpret reality. The choice of the legal essay and its author, to put it differently, is either to erect a fortress of a text along the lines of the court trial (an enclosure, a theological metaphor, a final testament)[1] or to assemble a text that is akin to a veritable *trial*, an experimentation with formats, ideas, facts, theories and disciplines. In short, a text that takes risks.

How can an essay achieve this? By allowing the writing to breathe. This potentially means many things, but, for legal thinking specifically, it means not being geared towards resolution but towards the unfolding process of writing. In other words, it means to side with new forms of law that are not adversarial but open, mediated, discursive, linked to practices of restorative and distributive justice rather than the still potent retribution models, and in so doing to keep an implicit but sonorous distance from the usual patriarchal structures that demand authorial stance and other delusions of control. It is not enough to pronounce such goals in our texts. Our texts need to perform them too: we need to produce less 'hierarchical' texts, as Andrea Lunsford calls the texts that are 'rigidly structured, driven by highly specified goals, and carried out by people playing clearly defined and delimited roles' (1990: 133).

We can draw inspiration from Montaigne's essays, famous for hardly ever culminating in any closure, grand finale or moral – in short, any definitive conclusion. As Philip Lopate (2013: 105) puts it,

> Montaigne's attraction to open-endedness or 'endlessness,' if you will, has a great deal to do with his seeking a balance, through the sifting of long experience and the acceptance of imperfection. Montaigne was a master of equilibrium; and equilibrium such as he advocated does not drive toward apocalypse or closure of any kind … He chose the essay as a form to develop, in part, because it offered him a way to circumvent too-hasty resolutions.

It is not merely a question of conclusion but of overall structure. Lopate (2013: 211) again: 'if you know already what all your points are going to be when you sit down to write, the piece is likely to seem dry, dead on arrival.' Why is that? Because then, the whole focus would be on the resolution. And we often conflate academic rigour with this need for resolution. It is impossible to perambulate, and thus take risks productively and creatively, if everything is predetermined. Direction, political views and ethical positions, yes; but perfectly pre-planned analysis neatly and descriptively laid out should not become the fate of academic writing.

An essay should harbour for the reader surprise, delight and disappointment, all at the same time. Surprise at the choice of topics, the way they have been approached, the new

---

1 'Enclosure not only symbolized the independence of law from political, commercial, and social space; it served to restrict access, limit vandalism, minimize the disruption of trial, and, perhaps above all, encourage deference to the administration of justice in a democratic society perpetually anxious about the authority of law and lawyers' (Spaulding 2012: 316).

connections with which they have been endowed. Delight at the same, but also at the turns of phrase, the choice of guiding metaphor or metaphors that will allow the essay to speak in other disciplinary languages and with a bifurcated force, a common front formed by reasoned argumentation and metaphorical completeness.

Above all, every essay must disappoint: if it is to be a trial, the essay needs to be the exact opposite of a court trial. It needs to remain incomplete and to embrace this very incompleteness with pride. This is because 'the usual reproach against the essay, that it is fragmentary and random, itself assumes the givenness of totality and thereby the identity of subject and object, and it suggests that man is in control of totality' (Adorno, 1984: 159). It is important that we relinquish the idea that our essays are little stabs at totality.

So, for a writing beyond distinctions, one needs to follow the desire of the essay. Fragment, open up, refuse to pass judgement! But: take position, thump on the side of the object in order to upturn it, flood it with other voices, break it up – and, in the process, break yourself up too.

The essay as body?

A good essay is not, of course, all fragmentation and incompleteness. There is something emerging from it, a discrete body of thought. On the back cover of his book *Essayism* (2017), a book that inspired me to think about writing, Brian Dillon writes:

> Imagine a type of writing so hard to define its very name means a trial, effort or attempt. An ancient form with an eye on the future, a genre poised between tradition and experiment. The essay wants above all to wander, but also to arrive at symmetry and wholeness; it nurses competing urges to integrity and disarray, affection and fragmentation, confession and invention.

This distinctly unlegal-sounding schizophrenia of aims is the core of an essay: both ancient and future, wandering wholeness, an emerging body of integrity amidst its own fragmentation. This is, therefore, another step towards an essay that moves beyond distinctions: the essay must emerge as an agent. Out of its words and phrases, a material body needs to be assembled. In other words, we need to understand that our writing lives beyond our intentions. It is prone to different readings, appropriations and misappropriations. It is in a continuous process of *becoming* – and that's ok.

Adorno (1984: 161) again: 'In the essay discreetly separated elements enter into a readable context; it erects no scaffolding, no edifice. Through their own movement the elements crystallize into a configuration.' The configuration is nothing other than the much-praised *consistency*. In order to be thought of as a material body and an agent that interacts and affects the way other agents (the law being one of them, but also the lawyers, the scholars, other disciplines, the planet as a whole) do, the essay needs to have a shape, an outline, both figuratively and in essayistic terms. A tidiness of sorts that to some extent subscribes to the order of wholeness and perhaps symmetry. Every body has a contour – we forget though that this contour can be fluid and ever-changing.[2]

---

2 How legal all those bodies of law, the *corpora juris* that pulsate with 'text, territory and terror' (Goodrich, 2006: 33), always channelled through sections and paragraphs. Goodrich has repeatedly shown us how text is body, and how what seems like mere legal textuality is a corporeal explosion. Matter is, after all, inescapable.

An essay worth its tentative name is a distinct body which, however, also forms part of a larger body, a collective effort to think and make the law more just. For this, the essay must engage with the space and time of its object: 'the essay comes so close to the here and now of the object, up to the point where that object, instead of being simply an object, dissociates itself into those elements in which it has its life' (Adorno, 1984: 162). Bring the object to life by pulverising it into zillions of particles of life-affirming materiality. Will life into the body of the essay by bringing its matter forth, even if this entails its disassembly, and link it up to other streams of thought and ideas that might not be obviously contiguous. This means: go deep into the legal technicalities and study the way the minutiae of law deposit themselves on every aspect of life in particular spaces and particular times. At the same time, do not lose sight of the larger task an essay sets out to fulfil: expose the coercive power of the law and embrace its transformative potential, *make* law and *live* law as part of our lives on this one planet that we have.

How many am I?

Should I be me when writing? The question is no longer whether research writing can present objective facts/truths (no), or whether bringing the 'I' in (in terms of pronoun and subject matter) renders the whole thing subjective (and, therefore, irrelevant or at best partial; yes, no, so what?). Nor is the question whether the law can be approached from the point of view of the 'I' (yes), or whether the 'I' must sublimate itself to the 'common person' (what is that?).

The question rather is whether the 'I' can move away from the atmospherics of the old distinctions – namely, bubbles of isolation that decree one's affiliation, readership, reference base and publication avenues – and into the collective body (of which the essay is part) that has the same desires as the author.

Once again, and at risk of simplifying, I would say that the desire of the wider critical socio-legal body is to make law more just, regardless of affiliations and modes of writing. Old distinctions can be things of comfort, zones of familiarity and tested grounds. But this is not an essay. One has to come out and reach for the identity of desire across the spectrum. This is the collective body that matters.

The only way of doing this is by remaining personal when writing (to recall our, wise after all, editors' suggestions. 'How were your research choices and outcomes shaped by aspects such as your positionality as a researcher and ethical implications/choices?') But we can go further: the body of the author has to become the text. For what is the law if not an embodiment? How can the law be understood unless through the bodies that make and undo and interpret and resist and ignore the law? And how better to communicate what we want to say, if not through the community of our bodies? This is the way to reach the wider body of desire for a more just law.

The 'I' is never in isolation but always part of a wider collectivity. The 'I' is multiple. Internally, 'the "I" is both contained and provisional – just as important, it is *dispersed*' (Dillon, 2017: 18; original emphasis). We are never just one body, operating in a single law-scape, in some sort of illusion of permanence. We are always multiple and dispersed. But this dispersion, seemingly a weakness, can be strategically enlisted. Use your dispersion, spread horizontally, take up your minoritarian positions and break free from the thinking that allowed the law to distance itself from its context. And follow the same strategy textually too: think of Bruno Latour's thick description of the Conseil d'Etat (2009), and its gravitational attraction for seemingly un-legal, unimportant details. This deliberate dispersion, this absent-minded focus, those centre-stage curios: these are often an effective way to flesh out the body of the law (see, e.g., Carr, 2016).

What comes first, the idea or the writing?

Time for a bit of sculpture: a good carver does not try to give a piece of wood a predetermined shape. Rather, she follows the waves of the wood, allowing for the shape to emerge from within its matter. Deleuze and Guattari write:

> it is a question of surrendering to the wood, then following where it leads by connecting operations to a materiality, instead of imposing a form upon a matter: what one addresses is less a matter submitted to laws than a materiality possessing a *nomos*.
>
> *(1988: 451)*

The same can be said of writing. We regularly forget that the text is also material. We must respect the materiality of our texts. We cannot just impose our enlightened selves on them. Listening to the *nomos* (i.e., the internal, rules) of materiality rather than imposing the law on matter means: use matter (the wood, the text), not by submitting it to a law (of predetermined structure and conclusion) but by allowing *through it* an emergence.

Listening to the object and its conditions of emergence is our way, as writers, to flesh out the strains, marks and wounds of the object itself: its gender oppression, its colonial exploitation, its heteronormative persuasion, its paternalistic force, its racial exclusion, its class slippage, its shaded mirroring of our own little worlds.

Listening to the text seems to be the exact opposite of the way we are taught (and the way we teach) to write. Unless you know exactly what you want to say, do not even start. Go back to the question. But how to know where the text will take you before you enter it? How to leave behind the all-consuming atmosphere of preconceptions, if not by listening to something else, something other?

In many respects, this is similar to the previous suggestion of letting the writing breathe – but with one important addition: the 'I' needs to be put aside for a moment. Losing the 'I' means surrendering fully to the text and its law, accepting vulnerability, facing our fragility before the law, and becoming aware of it. Effectively, facing one's vulnerability means becoming stronger, knowing one's context and dealing with it.

Once this has happened, the 'I' needs to be reinstated. It is needed in order to channel the elements of the text, to bring in consistency and to link up to the multiplicity of the community of the 'I'. In reality, of course, the 'I' never leaves the text – it just allows momentarily for a different priority. This 'I', now collective, immersed in the text, returns and takes up its responsibility.

The responsibility of writing beyond distinctions

At this point, as a summary before moving to the final part of the text, I would like to offer a list of suggested steps towards writing beyond distinctions on the basis precisely of these distinctions. These are not just pronouncements of 'what one should do' but lessons emerging from the current literature that tries to do exactly this, namely write beyond the standard distinctions and move into slightly unchartered territories of thinking about law. This is generally a more material, embodied and spatialised literature, often of feminist, queer or ecological persuasion.

So, with apologies for the inevitable violence of generalisation:

a. Writing beyond distinctions is not about ignoring distinctions but about actively engaging with them and questioning their relevance at all times.

b. The first distinction that needs to be confronted is that between critique and sociolegal positioning. At its most impoverished, this distinction refers to theory versus empirical studies. At its most nuanced – and closest to reality – this distinction is about the way in which our writing enters the world: an embracing of law's transformative potential and a problematisation of law's inherent inequalities, and an assembling of a common front, both theoretically and empirically engaged, against the various challenges that we are facing.

c. The second distinction that needs to be confronted is that between text and context. It is important that we understand law as material, embodied and spatialised, rather than only as textual, abstract and historicised. It is further important to remember that text partakes of materiality, is in itself material. A method of writing that makes use of the semantic and experiential 'I' fleshes out the embodiment of the law. (Legal) agency is a composition of the material and discursive, and, in that sense, an essay that engages with both these can be thought of as (legal) agent in itself. As a legal agent, the essay should be allowed to unfold, guided by its own materiality (including its occasional desire to remain incomplete and therefore disappointing) and not only by the author's intent.

d. The third distinction is that between legal technicalities and life (see also the following section on this). Law's embodied nature means that there is no matter without law, and no law without matter. The usual jurisprudential distinctions between norms/rules/laws are of limited use when it comes to thinking of the law as a spectrum. The input of other disciplines, such as anthropology, sociology, geography, and so on, is invaluable in rethinking this distinction.

e. The fourth distinction is that between writing and the idea of writing. It is important, of course, to have strong positions and concrete ideas when starting to write. It is very important to express these succinctly and clearly. At the same time, however, we should not be dealing with the text in an adversarial way, the sort of thing that must be fought and conquered in order to express our ideas. A text needs to be allowed to unfold creatively, without the constant vigilance of our preconceived, well-researched ideas. A text needs to perambulate in order to discover itself and the ideas (the ones we thought we had and others we did not expect we had) *while* being written.

f. The fifth distinction: the individual and the collective 'I'. Every 'I' is multiple. It always forms part of a larger body, that of a collectivity that shares the same desire. The writing 'I' needs to be fully personal and, at the same time, aware of the connection with other 'I's that desire that the law become more just.

g. The sixth distinction is that between law and justice.

(Long parenthesis: I used to despise bullet points or lists of any sort when I came across them in an essay. They would interrupt the flow and would introduce a staccato movement that usually had nothing to do with the way I wanted the rest of the text to be read. Perhaps they were a little too black-letter law for me, a little too theological even.

Recently, however, I started listing things. I started appreciating the reading rhythm of the bated breath. I felt a playfulness in the promise of completeness, and indeed of education, instruction even, in terms of 1, 2, 3, sections and paragraphs, this archetypically legal form. Maybe, I thought, I am coming closer to what everyone seems to think that the law is. But the playfulness I found most attractive was not the (subversive even) promise for completeness but exactly the opposite. Dillon (2017: 27) puts it well: 'The list, if it's doing its job, always leaves something to be invented or recalled, something forgotten in the moment of its making … something to be desired'. This space of 'to be desired' is also the space of other desires that upset our best-laid plans, and a *memento vanitatis* of our supreme delusion, very legal too, that we can list and contain everything neatly.

I felt another playful attraction to lists that was marking another delusion. Dillon (2017: 24) again: 'the appearance of a list in an otherwise narrative or polemic piece of prose intro-duces – more or less violently – a sudden verticality in the horizontal flow of the text.' This verticality, a habitual sign of authorial hierarchy and authoritative announcement (Braver-man, 2016), was playing directly with my own sense of authority as an author, of which I've never had a particularly high opinion ('death of the author', etc.). So I started appreciat-ing the awkwardness with which that vertical pole of 1, 2, 3, protruded in some sort of hypermasculine self-assertion from the horizontal and occasionally even deliberately poetic, whatever that is, flow of some of my texts, reminiscent of a shipwreck's mast sticking out of a flat sea. Lists became my own footnote for the alien authority we are supposed to feel when we write essays on law that are meant to instruct, educate, transform, help.)

What was the final distinction again?

Writing, in the ways I have tried to discuss so far, is an experiment, potentially person-ally exposing, treading on uncertain ground between and above disciplines, plunging into legal technicalities yet being conversant in theory, experimenting with formats, structures and given instructions, and in general challenging the law not only in terms of content, but also in terms of the text's format. The law of the essay is still a law: how to write a legal essay is often a blueprint exercise once the research has been done. But this is only the law that we have been accustomed to follow – the law that journal reviewers demand (but who are the reviewers if not us?), that the Research Excellence Framework (REF) panels in the UK want to read (and again, who are they if not us?), that our universities' internal committees expect and explicitly ask for. But one thing we must realise: that the law does not exist outside ourselves, our eyes that read and our fingers that type our reviews. Next time we ask for more 'consistency', let's think a bit about why we are asking for it. Are we not embodying a law (the law of textual ortho-doxy) that serves a specific disciplinary technique and a disciplinary closure that goes against anything that is actually happening not only 'out there' in 'real' life, but even in law: anyone who has sat through a trial will know that the law is always an interdiscip-linary excursus, moving from history to geography, biology to psychology, economics to ethics, science to media studies, gender studies to race theory (to mention just a few examples), and all that often in the ambit of a single argument.

As writers, we need to do justice to the law of the essay. We need to allow it to reveal the things that orthodoxy, to recall Adorno, wants to keep invisible.

Montaigne, as we have seen, believed that law cannot generate justice. Yet we know otherwise. We have seen, time and again, law delivering something akin to justice that can be peace, psychological closure, belonging, access to what is important to us, and so on. We have, however, also seen that often law does not deliver justice – on the con-trary, it sides with the fundamentally unjust and serves as a tool of oppression. Or, per-haps, that what the law delivers is justice only in name, and in practice is a bitter victory for all involved. This, however, does not interrupt the continuum between law and justice. We look into law in order to deliver something that feels just; that tries to guarantee that the same crimes will not happen again; that people will know what they can claim and will be empowered to claim it. We write about these instances because it is important.

A way to reinstate our faith in the connection between law and justice is by having one foot on the realistic (critiquing law, being harsh with its faults, catching out its foundational inequalities) and the other foot on the, broadly understood, utopian (embrace law's transformative potential, see its rhetorical and actual power, think theoretically about where it stands in relation to the rest of the world, consider the planet in all we think and do). Law's delivering justice is not a guarantee; nor, however, is a utopia. Justice itself is not utopian. On the contrary, justice is right here – but we need to open up to the possibility of seeing its connection to the law, and encouraging it.

Justice has been considered a bit of a dirty word, especially in some socio-legal circles that had had enough of the impossibilities of deconstruction and the fuzzy talk of things to come. But we need to divest justice of its messianic layer and focus on its everyday emergence as a thing that actually does occur. Justice is little more than an ethical positioning with regards to the issues at hand – as Jane Bennett (2010) writes, it is our responsibility to move away from noxious assemblages that compromise our ethics. This is what ethics is: a withdrawal with the subsequent debilitation of noxious assemblages, and a move into assemblages that have the potential of delivering justice. Following this, our responsibility as writers beyond distinctions is not only to withdraw from and resist problematic assemblages, thereby causing their destabilisation, but also to embrace such ethical moments where justice emerges.

Still, there is no final repose for a writer. While some things are rendered visible, other things necessarily become invisible. The essay constructs its own atmospherics of control, assembled by the collective desire of the writing 'I's to carry on (critiquing, constructing, transforming, analysing). Heresy can also become orthodoxy. It is hard to withdraw from this. It is lamentably comfortable, it is what the REF wants, it is what one's readers expect, and so on. But, at those points when the 'I' begins getting too comfortable, the 'I' needs to return and start *essaying*.

This is when the law of the text generates justice: when the text never rests, and more invisibilities are always revealed, especially the ones that were generated by our previous, well-meaning heresies. This is why our texts do not belong to us but to the readers who see our texts' invisibilities. The essay must never rest, the 'I' must never get complacent. This is not a shock strategy, or a marketing scheme to keep your readers reading. This is, simply put, our responsibility.

Further reading

In terms of interdisciplinary writing beyond distinctions, see:

Rosi Braidotti, 'A Theoretical Framework for the Critical Posthumanities', *Theory, Culture & Society*, 1–31, 2018, DOI: 10.1177/0263276418771486
John Law, *After Method: Mess in Social Science Research*, London: Routledge, 2004.

Out of a plethora of excellent works, some examples of legal essay writing beyond distinctions are:

Olivia Barr, *A Jurisprudence of Movement: Common Law, Walking, Unsettling Place*, London: Routledge, 2016.
Anne Bottomley, 'From Walls to Membranes: Fortress Polis and the Governance of Urban Space in 21st Century Britain', *Law and Critique* 18 (2), 171–206, 2007.

Irus Braverman, 'The Life and Law of Corals: Breathing Meditations', in A. Philippopoulos-Mihalopoulos and V. Brooks (eds), *Research Methods in Environmental Law: A Handbook*, Cheltenham: Edgward Elgar, 2018. 458–481.

Victoria Brooks, *Fucking Law (The Search for Her Sexual Ethics)*, London: Zero Press, 2019.

Margaret Davies, *Law Unlimited, Materialism, Pluralism, and Legal Theory*, London: Routledge, 2018.

Lucy Finchett-Maddock, *Protest, Property and the Commons: Performances of Law and Resistance*, London: Routledge, 2016.

References

Adorno, Theodor, 'The Essay as Form', *New German Critique*, 32, Spring–Summer, 151–171, trans. by Bob Hullot-Kentor and Frederic Will, 1984.

Atwood, Margaret, *Negotiating with the Dead: A Writer on Writing*, Cambridge: Cambridge University Press, 2002.

Bennett, Jane, *Vibrant Matter: A Political Ecology of Things*, Durham: Duke University Press, 2010.

Bottomley, Anne and Wong, Simone (eds), *Changing Contours of Domestic Life, Family and Law: Caring and Sharing*, Oxford: Hart, 2009.

Braverman, Irus, 'The Legal Life of Threatened Species Lists', in Irus Braverman (ed.), *Lively Legalities: Animals, Biopolitics, Law*, London: Routledge, 2016. 18–37.

Bruncevic, Merima, *Law, Art and the Commons*, London: Routledge, 2017.

Carr, Helen, 'Legal Technology in an Age of Austerity: Documentation, "Functional" Incontinence and the Problem of Dignity', in Cowan, David and Wincott, Dan (eds), *Exploring the 'Legal' in Socio-Legal Studies*, London: Palgrave Macmillan, 2016. 204–224.

Davies, Margaret, *Law Unlimited: Materialism, Pluralism and Legal Theory*, London: Routledge, 2017.

Deleuze, Gilles and Guattari, Felix, *A Thousand Plateaus: Capitalism and Schizophrenia*, trans. Brian Massumi, London: Athlone Press, 1988.

Dillon, Brian, *Essayism*, London: Fitzcarraldo, 2017.

Goodrich, Peter, 'A Theory of the Nomogram', in Goodrich, Peter, Barshack, Lior and Schütz, Anton (eds), *Law, Text, Terror: Essays for Pierre Legendre*, London: Routledge Glasshouse, 2006. 22–38.

Grabham, Emily, *Brewing Legal Times: Things, Form and the Enactment of Law*, Toronto: University of Toronto Press, 2016.

Latour, Bruno, *The Making of Law: An Ethnography of the Conseil D'Etat*, Cambridge: Polity Press, 2009.

Lopate, Philip, *To Show and to Tell: The Craft of Literary Nonfiction*, New York: Free Press, 2013.

Lunsford, Andrea, 'Composing Ourselves: Politics, Commitment, and the Teaching of Writing', *College Composition and Communication* 41, 71–82, 1990.

Montaigne, Michel de, *The Complete Essays*, trans. M. A. Screech, London: Penguin, 1991.

Perry-Kessaris, Amanda, 'The Pop-Up Museum of Legal Objects Project: An Experiment in "Sociolegal Design"', *Northern Ireland Legal Quarterly*, Special Issue on the Pop Up Museum of Legal Objects, 225–244, 2017.

Philippopoulos-Mihalopoulos, Andreas, 'A Sociolegal Metatheory', in Cowan, Dave and Wincott, Dan (eds), *Exploring the Legal*, Palgrave, 2015. 245–256.

Philippopoulos-Mihalopoulos, Andreas, 'To Have to do with the Law: An Essay', in Philippopoulos-Mihalopoulos, Andreas (ed.), *The Routledge Research Handbook on Law and Theory*, London: Routledge, 2018a, 475–496.

Philippopoulos-Mihalopoulos, Andreas, 'The *and* of Law and Theory', in Philippopoulos-Mihalopoulos, Andreas (ed.), *The Routledge Research Handbook on Law and Theory*, London: Routledge, 2018b. 1–12.

Spaulding, Norman, 'The Enclosure of Justice: Courthouse Architecture, Due Process, and the Dead Metaphor of Trial', *Yale Journal of Law & Humanities* 24, 311, 2012.

6

DOING CRITICAL-SOCIO-LEGAL THEORY

Margaret Davies

Introduction

Theory takes a variety of forms and is put to varying uses in socio-legal research. This chapter addresses methods of theory construction, that is, *doing* theory rather than applying theory or using it to frame empirical enquiries. My central questions are 'what is theory?' and 'how do you do it?'

I begin the chapter by addressing in outline the following preliminary matters: the nature of theory, socio-legal theory, and critical theory; the distinction between doing theory and applying theory; and the relationship of theory to change. The second part of the chapter considers some methodological parameters of my own theoretical work, taking as an example my recent book *Law Unlimited* (2017). This book represents an endeavour to consider afresh some of the classical questions of legal theory while suspending many of its constitutive limitations and distinctions. In a sense, the book is a thought experiment about the possibilities for understanding law if its conventional limits are temporarily removed. These limits relate both to the substance of law (for instance, that it is associated with a state) and its meta theoretical structure (for instance, the purported distinction of matter and meaning). I will close with some comments about the current challenges for critical socio-legal theory as it adapts to the challenges of ecological crisis and continuing consciousness of global injustices in the form of rampant capitalism, ongoing colonialism, and persistent social inequalities.

Theory and critical-socio-legal theory

Science does not rest upon solid bedrock. The bold structure of its theories rises, as it were, above a swamp. It is like a building erected on piles. The piles are driven down from above into the swamp, but not down to any natural or 'given' base; and if we stop driving the piles deeper, it is not because we have reached firm ground. We simply stop when we are satisfied that the piles are firm enough to carry the structure, at least for the time being.

(Popper 2002, 94)

Each object is in reality a small virtual volcano. There is continuity in the living: whereas theory entails a discontinuity, a cut, which is altogether the opposite of life … [Theory] is indispensable, at times, to make progress, but alone it is false. I resign myself to it as a dangerous aid. It is a prosthesis. All that advances is aerial, detached, uncatchable.

(Cixous and Calle-Gruber 1994, 4)

In this introductory section I consider first the nature of theory as an activity that defines and founds fields of scholarship but that also exists between and beyond disciplines. I then outline a view of theory as a dynamic and constantly changing activity – an exercise in transformation rather than definition. I briefly comment upon the distinctions between 'legal', 'socio-legal', and 'critical legal' theory before finally concluding that they can be (and increasingly are) fruitfully merged as 'critical-socio-legal theory' – an expansive theoretical and sometimes experimental space for understanding law.

First then, what *is* theory? There is no uncontested definition of theory: the term is used differently in different disciplines, but there are also controversies within disciplines about what theory is, as well as many commonalities across disciplines about certain types of theory. The best that can be attempted is therefore a description of different understandings of theory. Definitions of 'theory' sometimes contrast it with 'practice': theory is abstract knowledge whereas practice is material and enacted. In a social scientific or scientific sense, theory is often regarded as a general or underlying explanation of a connected set of facts, by contrast to the facts themselves. It can also, in a more scientific vein, be seen as the process of generating falsifiable propositions to be tested by empirical or experimental research (Popper 2002) or as the framework or paradigm that is paramount at a particular historical moment in scholarship (Kuhn 1996). Thinking of theory as different to facts is misleading because of the 'theory-dependence' of observation. Facts do not exist in and of themselves, but are construed in a framework of pre-existing generalities: 'the whole fabric of our knowledge is one matted felt of pure hypothesis' (CS Peirce, quoted in Joas and Knöbl 2004, 4). Moreover, the structure of language shapes what can be experienced, understood and expressed theoretically. As Sandra Harding says, 'when epistemological push comes to shove, we can never tell for sure whether we are responding to the compulsions of our language rather than those of our experience' (Harding 1986, 37, referring to WVO Quine).

We might think very broadly of theory as the interwoven concepts that infuse experience and knowledge at every level, as well as the processes of making these concepts explicit and of working with and against them in different ways. Theory would therefore appear in several forms: in perception and the articulation of meanings; in the concentrations and boundaries that differentiate one category from another (for instance, in the differentiation of 'law' from 'politics' and 'society'); in the generalisable knowledge about these different parts (legal theory, social theory, political theory); in the understanding of specific, practically oriented sub-parts of these categories (for instance, a theory of responsibility in criminal law, or regulatory theory); and in our thinking about how concepts are made and interrelate (meta-theory, or 'thinking about thinking'; Culler 1997, 15). Often, an effort is made to separate and formalise one of these layers of theory but this is in fact a difficult if not impossible task, because other layers remain implicit and are necessarily drawn into the process. Theory is normally reflective in that it attempts to subject its own presuppositions to critical examination, but it cannot hold everything in suspension at once. Sometimes theoretical presumptions are unstated and sometimes they are explicit; sometimes theory is essentially explanatory and predictive and sometimes it is normative: an explicit guide for action rather than a prediction of what will happen. All theories, however, are normative in the sense that they are guides for thinking.

The likes of social theory, political theory, literary theory, and legal theory are different exercises in that they address different subject matters and have been developed by reference to different disciplinary histories. As I have said, different disciplines have different theoretical traditions and definitions of theory. They have each narrowed it down in specific ways and refer to different canons of prior scholarship. However, there are also alignments between theory in many disciplines and significant mobility of ideas between them. Theorists and disciplines may be different, but many of their ideas and background frameworks are shared. Some of this is due to culture and very broad historical changes, such as the composite of transitions represented by the Enlightenment and modernity. Much of what scholars refer to as 'theory' has a distinctly European and masculine heritage and character. Within and sometimes beyond this context, there also exist generalised and less definable types of theory that seem to transcend disciplines or move between them. Feminist theory can be attached to a particular discipline but it also tends to be highly mobile and transferable across different subject areas (Ahmed 2000). The plurality of approaches collected under the names 'poststructuralism' and 'postmodernism' are similarly adaptable: wherever a prior body of thought has been defined by the precepts of modernism – the autonomous self, the narrative of progress, the assumption that foundational explanations or grand theories can be identified – postmodernism will have something to contribute. Many theorists are therefore influential in a range of disciplines.[1] Jonathan Culler describes theory as a 'miscellaneous genre' of 'works that succeed in challenging and reorienting thinking in fields other than those to which they apparently belong' (Culler 1997, 3). There is theory within particular disciplines, but theory *at large* has a more general influence.

Theory is sometimes understood as consisting of a relatively stable framework of explanatory or descriptive concepts – in other words, as something that can be used or applied in the process of understanding a field, analysing a set of data, or answering a question. Feminist theory, for instance, deploys a range of theoretical concepts – 'benchmark man', 'patriarchy', 'privilege', 'intersectionality', 'formal equality', 'substantive equality', 'compulsory heterosexuality', and many others – that provide the tools of feminist analysis and critique. Such concepts, however, are not pre-existent or fixed. They are adapted from elsewhere or created within the field. Culler describes theory as deploying 'moves' that can be used in different contexts (Culler 1997, 7). One powerful move, for instance, is demystification or denaturalisation:[2] exposing something that is widely understood to be 'natural' or as common sense as being in fact produced by the power relations associated with a discourse or ideology. This 'move' is frequently and productively applied in critical thought to illustrate the constructedness of ideas that have been taken for granted and to show how they are complicit in reproducing social power. Or, describing theory as a set of moves is itself a demystification of theory. To provide one more of potentially many examples, at its simplest, 'deconstruction' can be seen as a kind of move in which an accepted conceptual distinction (culture–nature, male–female, mind–body) is reversed so that the dominant term is seen as reliant on or secondary to the other.[3]

---

1 To take just a few examples, the following 20th- and 21st-century theorists are widely deployed in multiple disciplines: Simone de Beauvoir, Hannah Arendt, Michel Foucault, Edward Said, Jacques Derrida, Gayatri Chakravorty Spivak, Donna Haraway, Bruno Latour, and Judith Butler.

2 See Jane Bennett's helpful comments on the limits of demystification: 2010, xiv–xv.

3 As explained by Derrida: 'in a classical philosophical opposition we are not dealing with the peaceful coexistence of a vis-à-vis, but rather with a violent hierarchy ... To deconstruct the opposition, first of all, is to overturn the hierarchy at a given moment' (Derrida 1981, 41).

It is not possible to distinguish clearly between simply applying pre-existing concepts or performing theoretical moves and creating them, as even what is called 'application' of theory involves the renewal and reiteration of ideas. However, theory can be more or less focused on pushing the boundaries of thought, creating new concepts, or (more likely) adapting existing concepts to different circumstances, enlarging and merging them, and so forth.

Using a musical metaphor drawn from Schoenberg and Weber,[4] Theodor Adorno said that philosophy is not about formal analysis or fixed categories but about composition:

> instead of reducing philosophy to categories, one would in a sense have to compose it first. Its course must be a ceaseless self-renewal, by its own strength as well as in friction with whatever standard it may have. The crux is what happens in it, not a thesis or position – the texture, not the deductive or inductive course of a one-track mind.
>
> *(Adorno 2007, 33)*

Gilles Deleuze and Félix Guattari similarly wrote that philosophy 'creates [concepts] … and never stops creating them' (Deleuze and Guattari 1994, 33). In commenting on this point, Rosi Braidotti calls theory 'a form of organized estrangement from dominant values.' (2013, 77). I do not wish to enter here into discussion about the nature of any distinction between 'theory' and 'philosophy' or the niceties of the translations of these words: in the Anglophone world philosophy is regarded as a distinct discipline, but it also overlaps considerably with what is understood as theory at large as well as with the specific theory of non-philosophy disciplines. Speaking generally, the points made by Adorno and Deleuze–Guattari can also be made about theory: that it uses existing concepts, orders them, and applies them, but also extends, renews, and creates concepts. (*How* concepts are created is an interesting question, which I will return to in the next section.) The point made by Adorno about music is important: philosophy – or theory – is not a form or a stopping point but a process that goes on. It is endless and endlessly *emergent*. But, like music, it is also *performative*, which is to say, it brings something into being in a way that references, makes sense of, but also renews existing meanings (Blomley 2013; see also Ramshaw 2013).

The idea that change is inherent in theory, that it is not static or formal and cannot be reduced to a set of propositions, but rather unfolds through time, may make the very concept of theory and even more the process of doing it difficult to grasp. That is because it is, by definition, ungraspable. But this is also good news for theory and for theorists in a way, because it means that we are not locked into inherited concepts and can engage in conceptual transformations. We can, as many have argued, engage in theory that is prefigurative and even hopeful in the sense that it promotes a changing view of law (Cooper 2001, 2017; Davies 2007). At first glance, this may seem a suspect move for scholarship that is aimed at understanding a piece of the world. However, it is entirely defensible theoretically for the reasons explained above. Concepts are not timeless but have their own history and cultural location. They evolve and can be modified in many ways. Moreover, the notion of conceptual change is hardly new for legal theory. The founders of legal positivism, Jeremy Bentham and John Austin, promoted conceptual change on a grand scale and had political and

---

4 The Schoenberg reference immediately precedes this quotation in the text of *Negative Dialectics* and describes Schoenberg's attitude to 'traditional musicology', which is about form rather than the music itself. The metaphor of composition drawn from Weber is discussed later in *Negative Dialectics*.

reformist motivations (Hart 1958, 596; Campbell 1996, 74). They promoted a relatively self-contained view of law in legal positivism, which in their view would enable appropriate consideration of what law *ought to be* based on clarity about what it *is*. This intellectual and reformist project was extremely successful and dominated the 20th-century view of law.

As outlined above, theory often seems to move between disciplines and, in this sense – as a group of shared concepts and thinkers – it could be said to be one of several things that blur disciplinary boundaries. Despite the blurring, Western knowledge *is* organised according to a set of disciplines, and, although these may change over time, theorists always, of necessity, have some disciplinary background that includes and excludes certain material. Theory always emerges from a particular conceptual space and is practised by people with their own intellectual biographies. It is always about a specific area or set of concerns. This does not mean that theory is determined in any way by these pre-existing factors, because the combinations of disciplines, personal biographies, and objects are very considerable, as are the interpretations and performances of them. Theory is therefore never detached, but is always located or *situated* knowledge (Haraway 1988).

The situatedness of theory and, in particular, of the theorist has in the past assisted in delineating different subtypes of theory such as, for instance, 'legal theory', 'critical legal theory', and 'socio-legal theory'. (I have left the disciplinary qualifier 'legal' in these names as my concern here is with varieties of theory about law, but of course none of these forms of theory is self-contained.) There are no sharp lines between these forms of theory about law, and the intellectual trajectories of each of these terms is very complex. As subtypes of theory about law, they can be loosely and somewhat unsatisfactorily described by reference to several variables: intellectual reference points, disciplinary heritage, jurisdictional location, and the standpoint of the theoretical observer (see generally Douzinas and Geary 2005, 229–247). The complexity of these lines of influence inside and beyond the discipline of law means that they have never been unified as subtypes. For instance, the tradition of critical legal studies (CLS) in the US – which itself has complex lines of connection and disconnection with feminist and critical race theory – is different from CLS in other parts of the Anglosphere. All CLS traditions have some connection to, but are not wholly derived from, the critical philosophy ordinarily associated with the Frankfurt school of critical theory.

The terms 'critical legal', 'socio-legal', and 'legal' theory have at times suggested variable standpoints of the scholar vis-à-vis their theoretical object. The term 'legal theory' is perhaps the most common and can simply refer to all types of theory (explanation, analysis, speculation, critique, or conceptual reflection) about law. Denoting this broad coverage, it is sometimes called 'general legal theory' or 'general jurisprudence' (see Tamanaha 2001, xvi). However, the term 'legal theory' also has a narrower permutation as 'legal philosophy' and (sometimes) 'jurisprudence'. Although these terms can have a broader connotation, they are often associated with philosophically or juristically based approaches to legal theory in which the theorist adopts or accepts a self-consciously internal standpoint to state-based law (cf. Cotterrell 2014). This form of legal theory has been termed 'restricted legal theory' (Douzinas and Geary 2005, 10–11) to highlight its focus on state law as seen from the position of the legal insider. Much legal theory has been developed by scholars with a legal training, and it is often understood to be about how lawyers, judges, and legal academics understand law – that is, it is about a conventional understanding of law from the 'inside'.[5]

General legal theory)

5 Although some writers have attempted to distinguish 'legal theory', 'legal philosophy', and 'jurisprudence', in fact the distinction between them is contestable and, in my view, can be used more or less interchangeably (see also Dickson 2015, 210).

Theory and approaches dealing specifically with the social domain also bear several different names, each with a different heritage and resonance. By contrast to the inside, lawyer's, view of law represented by mainstream legal theory, the 'sociology of law' was traditionally presented as an empirically based *external* view of law that was implicitly critical of internalist legal theory. This position arose from the fact that social scientific accounts of law did not accept the methodological premise of mainstream legal theory that law is as the lawyers found it and assumed it to be (see e.g. Schiff 1976, 39). Sociology of law, and other approaches such as the anthropology of law, studied law and legal practices objectively as a set of facts, as things that can be observed by social scientists who may be, but are not necessarily, legally trained. Sociological theory of law has addressed more abstract questions of the structure and purpose of law, its social nature, and its relation to larger historical, economic, and political change. The more modern term 'socio-legal', used as the organising principle for this book, can be described in various ways in relation to both sociology of law (outside it) and legal theory (inside it) but is perhaps most simply understood as concerned with the intersections of law and society and the ways in which law and society are co-constitutive and co-existent (and therefore not separable). Socio-legal studies and its theory crosses disciplinary boundaries and has practitioners in many fields.

'Critical' legal theory also emerged as a reaction to the insider's view of law. Wacquant calls critique a 'solvent of *doxa*' or of common sense (2004) and describes two forms: epistemological, or Kantian, and social, or Marxian. Epistemological critique involves examining the foundations of knowledge 'in order to determine their cognitive validity and value' (2004, 97). Social critique looks at 'socio–historical reality and sets itself the task of bringing together the hidden forms of domination and exploitation which shape it so as to reveal by contrast the alternatives they thwart and exclude' (ibid.). He continues, '[the] most fruitful critical thought' brings these two traditions together and questions 'in a continuous, active, and radical manner, both established forms of thought and established forms of collective life … along with the social and political relations that obtain at a particular moment in a particular society' (ibid.). Critique can be critique of the foundations of conventional knowledge or it can be critique of power's social effects, but it often combines both things. Critical legal theory takes both forms, sometimes separately but often together. For instance, the critique of continuing colonialism in Australia addresses both the Eurocentric ideologies that underpinned colonialism and continue to structure the socio-political context *and* its continuing material social effects (Watson 1998; Kwaymullina and Kwaymullina 2010). Feminist legal critique considers the founding mythologies of positivist law as well as their frequent appearance in legal doctrine and decision making (Hunter et al. 2010; Douglas et al. 2014).

Delineations such as 'legal', 'socio-legal', and 'critical legal' theory are useful for broadly locating a text, a scholar, or a body of theory but should not be regarded as themselves fixed. In reality, the terms have never been conceptually distinct and are becoming less significant with the fading of certain 20th-century attachments, such as the distinction between theory and practice (Philippopoulos-Mihalopoulos 2018, 2). Critical theory is critique of social as well as epistemological formations. Although socio-legal theory has some relationship to and background in empirical studies of law and society, it is by no means constrained by a need for empiricism and is methodologically and theoretically interwoven with the critical tradition. Within and outside the discipline of law, both social and critical theory have strong connections to the European theoretical heritage of the 20th century. Rather than distinguish between these forms, therefore, it is preferable to collapse them into 'critical-socio-legal theory' or even 'legal theory' in a general sense. This inevitably brings into view a vast quantity of literature that at first sight is overwhelming. To return to Culler, 'one of the dismaying features of theory today is that it is endless. It is not something you could ever master, not a particular group of texts you could learn so as to "know theory"' (Culler 1997, 15). Nonetheless, the vastness of the literature provides considerable latitude for theorists to discover and reinvent their subjects. Theory is a space of truly endless potential as ideas can never be finished or stabilised: they rather tend to multiply and expand.

Doing theory and unlimiting law

It ought to be evident from the outline of theory above that my own theoretical instincts are to challenge rather than create or accept categorical definitions or structures. As a theorist, I find it difficult to maintain distinctions, including disciplinary distinctions, and in fact much of my theoretical work has taken the form of questioning pre-given boundaries and assumptions, at least insofar as they have been evident to me (which is not always). This approach undoubtedly reflects my own background in critical theory and feminist legal theory and results in what could be seen as either a lively cross-fertilisation or an uncritical merging of distinct ideas and intellectual traditions. As luck would have it, the scope of legal theory today is extraordinary and extraordinarily imaginative, meaning that the inspiration for moving beyond conventional boundaries is considerable.

Law Unlimited engages with a conventional theoretical question – 'what is law?' – and therefore has some commonalities with the mainstream legal theory of the 20th century. Apart from the question, however, there is perhaps not a great deal of continuity between my own approach and that of others who have asked it. In trying to define law, the main stream tradition of jurisprudence in the 20th century often focused on the limits and essence of law: that is, how law is different from nonlaw, and what characteristics are common to all legal systems (Tamanaha 2001, xiii–xvi). One problem of this theory has been how to delineate law from other behavioural guides such as social normativity and ethical precepts. This theory has focused on the limits and boundaries of law and tends to presume that law is different from nonlaw. Theory of law therefore consists of explaining how law *is* different from nonlaw and, in so doing, it narrows down a definition of law and an analysis of its essential characteristics. Typically, though not always, such legal theory takes state law as the central case of law and downgrades other forms of law – so-called 'traditional' and 'customary' law, as well as religious law and even international law – to a marginal or lesser status.

I took a different, more exploratory approach, which might be described as deploying three connected modalities: unlimiting law as well as examining its material and plural nature. In so doing, it was important not to prejudge the question by confining law to a particular type or tradition – as Douzinas and Geary say:

> Once the question [about law] has been posed as a 'what is' one, the answer will necessarily give a series of predicates for the word 'law', a definition of its essence, which will then be sought out in all legal phenomena. As a result, a limited number of institutions, practices, and actors will be included and considered relevant to jurisprudential inquiry and a large number of questions will go unanswered.
>
> *(2005, 10)*

This concern accurately captures the majority of what Douzinas and Geary call 'restricted' jurisprudence that has directly addressed the question 'what is law?' Like some others who preceded me, however, I felt that it was possible to consider the question in an inclusive rather than an exclusive way, and that answers to the question could take a variety of forms: they can be 'conditional, they can be inessential or plural, they can be temporally, spatially, or culturally specific, and they can also take the form of a narrative' (Davies 2017, 22). The first objective was to take an established question and answer it in a different way – to *unlimit* law rather than to limit it or define it.

This theoretical unlimiting of law brought into play two dimensions beyond the abstract and more exclusionary approaches – that is, the dimensions of plurality and materiality. Removing the limits that associate law with a state as singular and abstractly defined leads to an understanding of law that is both material and plural. Of course, this movement could be described in reverse: that starting with a view of law that is material and plural leads to a view of it as unlimited. In reality, the three dimensions are aspects of one and the same thing – a holistic image of law, or an unlimited, material, and plural law.

The emphasis on plurality is a consequence of detaching law from its identity with the state while critical pluralism links law to social and subjective meaning-making (Anker 2014). Prior critical and socio-legal theory has made the exclusionary foundations of restricted legal philosophy abundantly evident. In engaging with the most traditional question of such theory, it was not appropriate to accept its founding assumption – that law is associated with a state. At the same time, it was important to acknowledge that, in the West, law does have a dominant meaning associated with state law. In line with legal pluralist and broad socio-legal thought, I dealt with this apparent tension by regarding state law as one dominant form of law among many. State law is part of the extended field of legality, but is not itself definitive of law. It is theoretically reasonable to focus entirely on this one form, as many have done, as long as it is not regarded as the archetype of law (this qualification is frequently missing in the jurisprudential tradition).

Plurality and materiality are connected ideas – the one implicates the other. The perception of plurality emerges from acknowledgement of the contingency of accepted patterns of life and law. Things spill out beyond their conventional boundaries. Therefore, an equally important focal point for me was that law is as much about connection and relationships as it is about abstract definitions and difference. My aim was to consider the connectedness of law with other forms of normativity and with the active relations and material contexts from which law emerges. Materiality is not only the materiality of human social relationships but also the materiality of human connections with the physical world as theorised by legal geographers (Delaney 2010; Blomley 2011) and, more recently, by 'new' materialists and eco-theorists with a focus on the co-emergence of matter and meaning (Barad 2007; Philippopoulos-Mihalopoulos 2015; Grabham 2016).

Materialist and pluralist approaches are not new to legal theory (though there are new expressions of them), and my objective was not to develop new theory. Rather, my aim was to consolidate existing theory as well as to add a layer of meta-theory connecting the many different contributions that have been made against narrow and limited descriptions of law over the past century. As against limited, abstract, and singular conceptualisations of law, therefore, my aim was to point to some of the ways in which it could be seen as unlimited, material, and plural. The methodological question is how to go about constructing this theoretical view. As I outlined in the previous section, doing theory can itself be regarded as essentially about distilling essences and defining a field, or it can be regarded as experimental and a methodologically plural intervention in accepted and emerging ideas. I took the experimental and pluralist approach which, by definition, is unbounded and even a little random instead of patterned, and therefore cannot be distilled into a properly defined method. Nonetheless, some methodological strategies can certainly be identified in the work, and for my purposes here I would mention four – unlimiting; synthesising; flattening hierarchies; and prefiguring theoretical possibilities. I will describe each of these briefly.

Unlimiting

The overarching aim of *Law Unlimited* was to explore rather than define the concept of law, and, in order to pursue this aim, it was first necessary to try to identify and reflect upon the disciplinary, philosophical, cultural, and onto epistemological limits that – explicitly or impli- citly – constrained restricted legal theory. There are a great many of these limits, and a great many writers who have explored them from one location or another. Broadly speaking, they fell into two categories: first, characteristics of modernist Western ideology that were seldom discussed in classical legal theory but have surfaced strongly in critical-socio-legal theory; and second, characteristics of Western thinking about law as reflected mainly in legal positiv- ism. Into the first category about ideology at large, I put some rather broad factors:

- aesthetic ideas that theory should be orderly and neat;
- the principle of the presocial autonomous subject as an organising feature of legal and political thought;
- the distinctions of matter–meaning and body–mind and the dominance of mind and meaning (and consequentially idealism) in philosophy;
- the preference for singular over plural explanations; and
- the idea that theory should be stable rather than dynamic.

The second category – the limits of positive law and its theory – included:

- the distinction between restricted and general jurisprudence;
- the idea that there can be a defining characteristic of law;
- the tendency of efforts to *define* law to be parochial and Eurocentric;
- the imaginary that connects the legal subject to the sovereign;
- the idea that law is outside the self;
- the dematerialisation and displacement of law;
- the separation of law from politics and from social normativity;
- the hierarchical view of law as a top–down system of norms;
- the view that legal norms are most typically legislative and judicial pronouncements.

All of these limits have placed constraints upon legal theory and they have all been iden- tified and contested in critical-socio-legal theory. There are undoubtedly many others that I did not specifically include. Nonetheless, my first step in trying to move beyond these constraints was to collect them as ideas into a single place so that the extent of law's concep- tual limits could be clearly displayed. Having identified the limits, my aim was to begin to dismantle them, but, in terms of *unlimiting*, the process is not entirely clear and is perhaps more of a theoretical 'move' than a destination: it is not possible simply to discard the limits as they all do have an influence on the way that law is perceived, practised, and theorised. It is, however, possible to demystify them and to suspend them temporarily in the process of imagining different forms or expressions of law. This endeavour was underpinned by the other strategies outlined below.

Synthesising

It is always difficult to say what is new about a particular theoretical work. It is not the case that everything has already been said, because each saying or theorising constitutes a new iteration of ideas, in a new time and place, and usually in a new context. However, a great deal *has* been said, and it is very difficult for a theorist to carve out a space that is really distinctive. Theorising is intrinsically a collective activity, because it draws on the present state of thinking. But it is also personal, channelled through a particular knowing entity at a specific location and time. In writing *Law Unlimited*, I was not interested in multiplying the niceties of contrasting theoretical views or adopting a position with subtle differences to existing scholarship. Nor was I interested in defining the work by reference to a single discipline, subdiscipline, or group of theorists. It would be contradictory to unlimit the subject matter without also taking a broad view of legal theory's theoretical methods. A methodologically pluralist approach must accept that there may be some truth in different perspectives, and that different facets of law 'can be illuminated by theoretical shafts of light striking different parts of it from different directions and in different combination' (Dickson 2015, 213).

Explanations of law that come from quite different perspectives and deploy a range of methodologies illuminate it in differently valuable ways. Rather than limit the subject matter, therefore, and rather than try to insist upon a specific novelty, I took the approach that, in the first instance, the objective of the work would be to bring together, without unifying, the present state of general legal theory: in a sense it was a big-picture mashup of everything I found to be of interest to the themes of pluralism, materialism, and unlimited law. It was necessarily a personal view, representing the state of my own knowledge of and engagement with the theory (as is always the case). Many of the specific reference points were in 20th-century and early 21st-century legal thought – from early sociology of law, to legal positivism, realism, critical legal theory, legal geography, feminist legal theory, and other forms of thought about law. But I also drew heavily on the theory that floats between disciplines, the 'theory at large' that may have its own disciplinary base but that also links different disciplines, as well as recently produced legal theory concerning space, plurality, and materiality. The task was complicated but ultimately liberating because it enabled me to move freely across several traditions of law and theory.

There are dangers, of course, in such an unconstrained engagement with literature, which is that disciplines and traditions do exist, and contributions are usually forged within them. Disengaging from specific traditions risks effacing their specificities and nuances. In some disciplines, a problem crossing several disciplines would demand the input of several – even numerous – authors. Such an approach is difficult with theory, and hence the risks of crossing disciplines seem inevitable.

Flattening

As a theorist, it is very easy to start with ideas – usually as found in theoretical literature – and then wonder how these ideas, or a combination of them, apply to different contexts. One could, for instance, apply Derridean deconstruction to mainstream legal theory or use queer theory to critique the heteronormative narratives of law. Alternatively, the theorist can start with the process of trying to simplify the 'world's noisy multiplicity' into a set of theoretical ideas (Hayles 1999, 12). These are normal top–down and bottom–up practices for theory.

Key points for both materialist and pluralist theory are that ideas and imagined forms must not become rigid, and 'noisy multiplicity' must not be erased in the name of aspirations to rigour, consistency, and formal coherence. N Katherine Hayles warns against the 'Platonic backhand', where the inference from noise becomes in turn the 'original form' and is taken as a template against which everything is measured. It becomes, in other words, a top–down strategy and obscures, rather than explains, complexity (ibid.). For instance, many efforts to define law have notoriously ended (or started) with essentially European images of law and excluded ideas of laws originating in other places and taking other forms (Nunn 1997). Such definitions obscure as much as they explain.

Some of the dangers of rigidity can be addressed by adopting the perspective of flatness, which may take a variety of forms but can be summarised as insisting on the material connectedness of everything with everything else (including the researcher-observer; see Latour 2004). So-called 'flat ontologies', such as Actor–Network Theory, endeavour to look at the social–material networks and assemblages that produce entities such as law, the self, and the state. Rather than see such entities as pre-existing forms that can be taken for granted, flat ontologies see them as emerging from the interactions made and continually remade between people as well as between people and the nonhuman world. The idea of a flat ontology has been powerfully deployed in empirical social science to sidestep the structure–agency divide and to place the researcher or observer where she belongs – in the thick of the world, rather than as a neutral observer of it. It does not presume conceptual limits but rather traces the ways in which forms emerge from material relationships.

In terms of doing theory, it is the idea rather than the empirical practice of flatness that motivates – rather than a study based on observation of how things connect, relate, and assemble, a theoretical approach of flatness is essentially a reminder that ideational entities such as law or the self are *effects* as well as causes. Such an approach is, in other words, not entirely flat, and cannot be: although ideas are formed in everyday action, they also shape it (see Cooper 2014). The attitude of flatness shifts the theoretical focus away from a top–down use of pre-existing concepts as definitive of law to action, place, multiple connections, and matter.[6] Thus 'law' can be seen as an effect of ongoing and repeated socio-material actions *as well as* the concepts and imaginaries that influence action and relationships. The role of the theorist is not to study these actions and relationships as facts but to conceptualise the patterns and dynamics involved, relying where possible on the work of others who have studied elements of law–society empirically.

Flatness and verticality are metaphorical ideas and ought not to be taken too seriously. But the attitude of flatness does identify a specific ethos in socio-legal and other forms of theory in which everyday networks and relationships are regarded as essentially the basis for emergent ideas such as state-based law.

Prefiguring: be the change

Finally, the work was an exercise in 'prefigurative theory', a term I use by analogy to a style of political activism (Davies 2007). Prefigurative politics is an approach to promoting change in which people essentially try to enact the future in the here and now. In a practical sense, prefiguring is about actually creating alternatives, rather than expecting them to emerge at some point down the track when sufficient groundwork has been laid. Prefigurative politics encourages activists to get started with being the change rather than imagining a grand plan or model of change. It rests on an understanding that solid change is cultural, and so we may as well get on with it (see, generally, Swain 2019). Similarly, prefigurative *theory* aims

---

6 There is a clear resonance here with the sociology of law and legal realism of the earlier 20th century, some of which emphasised that acts are constitutive of law, rather than looking at law as constituting and affecting action.

to write change into current theory, partly using critique and analysis, but partly also by amplifying alternative explanations. The meta-theoretical justification for prefigurative theory lies essentially in the fact that theorists never do simply describe the world. Rather, they are constantly making choices and interpretations. Prefigurative theory works from the same justification as feminist judgements – it does not reject the basis from which it proceeds but rather performs it in a different way (Hunter et al. 2010).

In the language of classical legal philosophy, this hopeful methodology merges is and ought, in part by drawing out the ought buried in the is. But it also puts the imagination into practice, embedding it socially, even if in a limited way, and establishing pathways (actual and metaphorical) for future imaginings and future change (Cooper 2001, 2014, 2017). The pathway, after all, is made from repetition and builds over time: one event turns into a pattern and then into a normality and a norm (Davies 2017). This is as true of the neural pathways that set the conditions for the imaginable as it is of social practices that set the conditions for society and tracks on the ground that provide guidance on where to go. For me, the prefigurative effort in theory involves trying to work at once with a conventional present and with whatever this present forecloses or obstructs – for instance, with a positivist concept of law and with the extended social relations that enable it; or with binary concepts of gender identity as well as the material connections that make such identities a fiction or effect. Thinking of present structures such as law and identity in the same field as their complex non-legal and non-unitary foundations presents possibilities for both loosening and reconstructing concepts and forms of daily life.

Conclusion

Theory of some kind informs all scholarship, though it is not always articulated or explicit. Scholarship of law has often presumed the theory of legal positivism, the view that law is conceptually and institutionally separable from broader social normativity. Present critical-socio-legal theory offers far more expansive and imaginative resources for understanding law.

The process of doing theory does not have a singular methodology. Each theorist has their own practices, idioms, and background, and specific areas of theory have guiding questions and themes. Theory can be situated in and defined in relation to particular traditions or it can have a looser set of reference points and more pluralistic methodologies. It can adopt an approach that is descriptive and analytical or it can self-consciously endeavour to be normative and reconstructive. At present, much theory adopts a performative position, which is to say that it performs the present with a view to changing it.

Further reading

Ahmed, Sara. 2000. 'Whose Counting?' *Feminist Theory* 1: 97–103
Braidotti, Rosi. 2013. *The Posthuman*. Cambridge: Polity Press.
Cooper, Davina. 2017. 'Prefiguring the State.' *Antipode* 49(2): 335–356.
Deleuze, Gilles and Félix Guattari. 1994. *What is Philosophy?* Graham Burchell and Hugh Tomlinson trans. London: Verso.
Joas, Hans and Wolfgang Knöbl. 2004. *Social Theory: Twenty Introductory Lectures*. Cambridge: Cambridge University Press.
Philippopoulos-Mihalopoulos, Andreas ed. 2018. *Routledge Handbook of Law and Theory*. London: Routledge

References

Adorno, Theodor. 2007. *Negative Dialectics*. New York: Continuum.

Ahmed, Sara. 2000. 'Whose Counting?' *Feminist Theory* 1: 97–103

Anker, Kirsten. 2014. *Declarations of Interdependence: A Legal Pluralist Approach to Indigenous Rights*. Farnham: Ashgate.

Barad, Karen. 2007. *Meeting the Universe Halfway: Quantum Physics and the Entanglement of Matter and Meaning*. Durham: Duke University Press.

Bennett, Jane. 2010. *Vibrant Matter: A Political Ecology of Things*. Durham: Duke University Press.

Blomley, Nicholas. 2011. *Rights of Passage: Sidewalks and the Regulation of Public Flow*. London: Routledge.

Blomley, Nicholas. 2013. 'Performing Property: Making the World.' *Canadian Journal of Law and Jurisprudence* 26: 23–48.

Campbell, Tom. 1996. *The Legal Theory of Ethical Positivism*. Aldershot: Dartmouth Press.

Cixous, Hélène and Mireille Calle-Gruber. 1994. *Hélène Cixous, Rootprints: Memory and Life Writing*. Eric Prenowitz trans. London: Routledge.

Cooper, Davina. 2001. 'Against the Current: Social Pathways and the Pursuit of Enduring Change.' *Feminist Legal Studies* 9: 119–148.

Cooper, Davina. 2014. *Everyday Utopias: The Conceptual Life of Promising Spaces*. Durham: Duke University Press.

Cooper, Davina. 2017. 'Prefiguring the State.' *Antipode* 49(2): 335–356.

Cotterrell, Roger. 2014. 'Why Jurisprudence Is not Legal Philosophy.' *Jurisprudence* 5(1): 41–55.

Culler, Jonathan. 1997. *Literary Theory: A Very Short Introduction*. Oxford: Oxford University Press.

Davies, Margaret. 2007. 'Beyond Unity: Feminism, Sexuality, and the Idea of Law.' In *Sexuality and the Law: Feminist Engagements*, eds. Vanessa Munro and Carl Stychin, 151–170. London: Cavendish Press.

Davies, Margaret. 2017. *Law Unlimited: Materialism, Pluralism, and Legal Theory*. London: Routledge.

Delaney, David. 2010. *The Spatial, the Legal, and the Pragmatics of World-Making: Nomospheric Investigations*. London: Routledge.

Deleuze, Gilles and Félix Guattari. 1994. *What is Philosophy?* Graham Burchell and Hugh Tomlinson trans. London: Verso.

Derrida, Jacques. 1981. *Positions*. Chicago: University of Chicago Press.

Dickson, Julie. 2015. 'Ours is a Broad Church: Indirectly Evaluative Legal Philosophy as a Facet of Jurisprudential Inquiry.' *Jurisprudence* 6(2): 207–230.

Douglas, Heather, Francesca Bartlett, Trish Luker, and Rosemary Hunter, eds. 2014. *Australian Feminist Judgments: Righting and Rewriting Law*. Oxford: Hart.

Douzinas, Costas and Adam Geary. 2005. *Critical Jurisprudence: The Political Philosophy of Justice*. Oxford: Hart.

Grabham, Emily. 2016. *Brewing Legal Times: Things, Form, and the Enactment of Law*. Toronto: University of Toronto Press.

Harding, Sandra. 1986. *The Science Question in Feminism*. Milton Keynes: Open University Press.

Haraway, Donna. 1988. 'Situated Knowledges: The Science Question in Feminism and the Privilege of Partial Perspective.' *Feminist Studies* 14: 575–599.

Hart, HLA. 1958. 'Positivism and the Separation of Law and Morality.' *Harvard Law Review* 71: 593–629.

Hayles, N. Katherine. 1999. *How We Became Posthuman: Virtual Bodies in Cybernetics, Literature, and Informatics*. Chicago: Chicago University Press.

Hunter, Rosemary, Clare McGlynn, and Erika Rackley, eds. 2010. *Feminist Judgments: From Theory to Practice*. Oxford: Hart.

Joas, Hans and Wolfgang Knöbl. 2004. *Social Theory: Twenty Introductory Lectures*. Cambridge: Cambridge University Press.

Kuhn, Thomas. 1996. *The Structure of Scientific Revolutions*. 3rd ed. Chicago: Chicago University Press.

Kwaymullina, Ambelin and Blaze Kwaymullina. 2010. 'Learning to Read the Signs: Law in an Indigenous Reality.' *Journal of Australian Studies* 34: 195–208.

Latour, Bruno. 2004. *Reassembling the Social: An Introduction to Actor-Network Theory*. Oxford: Oxford University Press.

Nunn, Kenneth. 1997. 'Law as a Eurocentric Enterprise.' *Law and Inequality* 15: 323–371.

Philippopoulos-Mihalopoulos, Andreas. 2015. *Spatial Justice: Body, Lawscape, Atmosphere*. London: Routledge.

Philippopoulos-Mihalopoulos, Andreas, ed. 2018. *Routledge Handbook of Law and Theory*. London: Routledge

Popper, Karl. 2002. *The Logic of Scientific Discovery*. London: Routledge.

Ramshaw, Sara. 2013. *Justice as Improvisation: The Law of the Extempore*. London: Routledge.

Schiff, David. 1976. 'Socio-Legal Theory: Social Structure and Law.' *Modern Law Review* 39: 287–310.

Swain, Dan. 2019. 'Not Not but Not Yet: Present and Future in Prefigurative Politics.' *Political Studies* 67: 47–62.

Tamanaha, Brian. 2001. *General Jurisprudence of Law and Society*. Oxford: Oxford University Press.

Wacquant, Loïc. 2004. 'Critical Thought as Solvent of Doxa.' *Constellations* 11: 97–101.

Watson, Irene. 1998. 'Naked Peoples: Rules and Regulations.' *Law/Text/Culture* 4: 1–17.

7

'INDEFENSIBLE AND IRRESPONSIBLE'

Interdisciplinarity, truth and #reviewer2

Emilie Cloatre and Dave Cowan

Socio-legal studies as problematic

On one level, socio-legal studies is a curious discipline. Academics who profess such a specialism often seek to "characterize, classify, specialize" as Foucault (1977: 223) describes disciplines, in contradistinction to sovereign law. One consequence of socio-legal studies' openness has been its over-inclusiveness, such that, as Cownie (2004: 56) observed of her legal academic interviewees,

> Some of those describing themselves as "black letter" appeared to be adopting a very similar, not to say identical, approach to others who described themselves as "socio-legal", so that the line between legal academics adopting a doctrinal perspective and those adopting a socio legal perspective is not always clear.

This interweaving of doctrinal law and the socio legal represents one problematic – socio-legal studies has yet to cut off its law head. However, the search for boundaries proceeds, in part, because of an apparent desire of socio-legal scholars to bracket themselves off from the doctrinal lawyers. In a more recent vein, socio-legal scholars have looked in on law, making a series of insightful observations (Riles, 2005-06; and the chapters in Cowan and Wincott, 2017). As Blomley (2014) suggests, law both brackets in and produces non-law in that which it brackets out, and it does so through the technology of framing. Socio-legal scholars have spent a considerable amount of energy explaining technical legal knowledges. It is this technical knowledge that is, as the textbooks tell us, often contradictory (Cownie et al., 2010; Mulcahy and Stychin, 2010) and that begins the process of the accretion of the "constellation of elements" that builds into technical legal knowledge (Riles, 2011: 64). Perhaps also, it is this objectivity that provides the legal technique with its power – its seeming neutrality, a commonplace observation, as well as its insistence on relevance and market-centredness (Bankowski and Mungham, 1976: 7), points that are replicated in our "great" textbooks. Indeed, Bankowski and Mungham's lament remains the case:

> law is presented as capable of reproducing itself in the style of an hermaphrodite. Where "outside influences" are conceded, they are usually acknowledged in the form of a variant of the "Great Man Theory of History" thesis. ... Since law

textbooks encourage the idea that "the law" is somehow above "politics" or separate from it, then it is not surprising that they turn away from the study of how different conflicts of interests have impinged upon and shaped the law.

(Ibid.: 33)

By almost complete contrast, socio-legal studies sets itself up as interdisciplinary. It is rather peripatetic in the kinds of discipline with which it engages. And, this peripatetic interdisciplinary project is sometimes regarded as unproblematic, even though there are epistemological dangers. In his elegant essay on interdisciplinarity, Fish argues that there are limits to what is, or can be, possible. So, for example, he points out that "importing into one's practice the machinery of other practices" is problematic "because the imported product will always have the form of its appropriation rather than the form it exhibits 'at home'; therefore, at the very moment of its introduction, it will already be marked by the discourse it supposedly 'opens'" (Fish, 1994: 239). This problem of interdisciplinarity was at the heart of the debate in the late 1990s between Roger Cotterell (1998) and David Nelken (1998) about the allegiance of a "sociology of law", a kind of insider–outsider debate. That is, from where should the sociologist of law view their subject/object, and indeed whether a transdisciplinary approach is possible. The debate coalesces over the following argument:

> As sociology tries to understand law, law disappears, like a mirage, the closer the approach to it. This is because as sociology interprets law, law is reduced to sociological terms. It becomes something different from what it (legally) is; or rather, from what, in legal thought, law sees itself as being.

(Cotterell, 1998: 175)

This problem of interdisciplinarity becomes particularly marked in those "law and …" type enquiries that underpin much of socio-legal studies' cross-disciplinary excursions. In these kinds of foray, there is sometimes a kind of disciplinary imperialism being worked on, one way or the other, which emphasises a disciplinary disunity most particularly in the conjunction. Beginning from a laudable aim – to expand epistemological narratives – they can end up merely re-affirming law first; that is, we see the "and …" from the perspective of law (for similar arguments, see Nelken, 1993). We do not wish to suggest here that these studies have not expanded our appreciation of law, most significantly in implementation studies (which have produced the "gap problem" – that is, the gap between formal law and its implementation).

Other scholarship, particularly that influenced by what has been described as the Amherst Seminar (compare Trubek and Esser, 1989; Sarat, 1990), has moved beyond these oppositions towards an approach in which, empirically, law is intertwined with society. Ewick and Silbey (1998), for example, critique the "law first" tradition of scholarship, arguing that it has drastically narrowed our vision, and that, despite the research which shows that law "has no center and little uniformity, it is often implicitly assumed that the law is still recognizably, and usefully distinguishable from that which is not law" (p. 19). If we unhinge law from its institutional setting and think about the cadences of legalities in everyday life, "we must tolerate a kind of conceptual murkiness" (p. 35). Their sleight of hand was to make a shift from "law and society" to "law *in* society" (ibid.). As they put it, "[r]ather than something outside everyday social relations, legality is a feature of social interaction that exists in those moments when people invoke legal concepts and terminology, associating with law with other social phenomena" (p. 32). This move has led to a raft of scholarship, which has been concerned with the weave between legality and the everyday lives of people. Rather than focus on the law among some form of explicit or implicit hierarchy of exogenous actors, the shift to the everyday has produced some important findings about law's hegemony.

Part of that move has also involved a hollowing out of the meanings of law. Ewick and Silbey, for example, use the word legality "to refer to the meanings, sources of authority, and cultural practices that are commonly recognized as legal, regardless of who employs them or for what ends" (p. 22). Uncoupling formal law from legality in this sense has risks (Engel, 1998). Its breadth means that everything is potentially legal so that legality itself becomes meaningless, a container term; as Mezey (2001: 153) suggests, "the law is every-where so much so that it is nowhere". And, if that is the case, how do we speak to data that suggest that:

> more salient factors eclipse the force of law on conscious decision-making [by women in the street-level drug economy] and on their understandings of their situation. Economic realities, gender hierarchies, peer pressure, fear, the need for personal safety – all of these considerations call for extralegal (or quasi-legal) measures to ensure survival on the street.
>
> *(Levine and Mellema, 2001: 180)*

This approach has been most fully developed in what has come to be known as legal geography (see Layard, Chapter 17 in this volume). Braverman (2008), for example, demonstrated how different types of tree (pine and olive) identified the cultivation and non-cultivation of land in Israel and the occupied West Bank, becoming a legible marker of property rights because they are fixed (until uprooted, of course) and capable of being photographed as such. Trees, Braverman suggests, take on the form of enemy soldiers. Summarising the interactions between space and law, Blomley (2003: 30) has a neat expression when he "literally run[s] the words together, and refer[s] to the conjunction [space and law] as a 'splice'".

This broadening out of legality has also led to a focus on what is sometimes reified as "the social" or "society", as if its meaning is self-evident and can be presumed to exist. Even this label, however, has a crumbling edifice. So, for example, Fitzpatrick (1995: 102) argued that the social lacks any objective existence and poses a challenge for socio-legal studies: "whilst society depends on law for its possibility, law has to remain apart from it, resisting reduction in terms of society. Law then also marks a point at which society fails in its universal sweep and becomes impossible". A social study of law "debunk[s] the false beliefs that ordinary people entertain" about it (Latour, 2000: 110). Such findings began in laboratory studies, in which it was recognised that the production of scientific knowledge could not be studied without reconstructing the contexts in which that knowledge was produced (Callon, 1986; Latour and Woolgar, 1986). In her study of different scientific cultures, Knorr-Cettina (1999: 8) notes that expert systems constitute society. The social, in other words, is made up by its epistemic settings, which are themselves intertwined. As Latour (1999: 273) puts it, "The question: 'what links us together?' is not answerable in principle but in practice every time someone raises it a new association is made that does indeed link us together". In this version, power is operated not *in potentia* but "as the consequence of an intense activity of enrolling, convincing and enlisting".

In a particular brand of scholarship, this idea that the social is made up has been the product of a recognition that, in social science, we have focused far too much on the human actors and failed to give due attention to the way in which material stuff makes up the social. This is a point that is made also about size – rather than assume that bigger objects are most powerful, an empirically problematic point, power is said to be independent of size. As Callon and Latour (1981) suggest, a microbe exercises more power than the sovereign. Or, in a classic study, scallops proved rather more difficult to harvest than scientists hypothesised (Callon, 1984).

Perhaps as a result of its own social label, socio-legal studies has been slower than most of the other social sciences to build this set of understandings into its projects. It has achieved most purchase in socio-legal studies of technology and medicines (see, for example, Rooke et al., 2012; Cloatre, 2013). The recognition of the mutually constituting relationship between law and society, as well as Latour's own investigations into the Conseil d'Etat (Latour, 2010), provides a fruitful mode for this kind of enquiry and has produced some significant studies (Riles, 2011; Cowan and Wincott, 2015). Riles (2011: 72), for example, has demonstrated that legal technique has its own agency; as she puts it, "our tools also shape how we think, what we aspire to achieve, where we choose to go", even if we do so by acts of resistance (because such acts are always counterposed to those tools). It might be regarded as quite surprising that socio-legal studies has not taken on these insights, because law's interdependent relationship with documents and artefacts more generally is so well established that it is axiomatic.

In summary, there are significant issues with the label socio-legal and its apparently unquestioning adherence to interdisciplinarity. The idea that the socio-legal is something that can be the subject of study or studies raises further questions because it suggests that the object of study is unique and homogeneous, whereas the disciplinary gazes are potentially multiple. Further, it suggests that the socio-legal *can* be the object of study, of empirical observations, whereas so much is left invisible and unknown as a result of our ways of knowing. Like Knorr-Cettina (1999: 3), we advocate that we should be less interested "in the construction of knowledge" and more so "in the construction of the machineries of knowledge construction". In so doing, we can recognise, like good ethnographers, the significance of the enfolding of the material with the human. And, we can move towards what we have previously described as "a subtler understanding of law as a relatively fluid, changing, and uncertain set of practices" (Cloatre and Cowan, 2018).

Interdisciplinary problems in action: a case study

In this section, we use an anonymous review of a piece of our joint work as a case study of the problems of interdisciplinarity in the specific context of the university law school. We discuss our own #reviewer2, who regarded our paper as "fundamentally and hopelessly misconceived". This part is *not* by way of an ad hominem attack – quite the reverse, as the reviewer was expressing opinions that are commonly shared and accepted across much of legal academia. As ethnographers of everyday life, our purpose here is to examine the everyday life of peer review of interdisciplinary work. If, as has been suggested by the literature above, we read things from our own disciplinary perspectives, we should be interested in how others read our work. Further, we should also consider just how far doctrinal law concerns are from socio-legal concerns; or, to put it another way, to what extent are we all socio-legal now? If we treat this as a research question, peer review becomes a field for experimentation. Behind the superficial shadow of anonymity, one's work is read and critiqued.

In the first part, we set out the general argument of the paper on which Reviewer 2 was commenting, and our own (and colleagues') critique of that paper. We discuss our observations on the peer review process, as interdisciplinary academics. We then discuss Reviewer 2's reaction to it. We have assumed that Reviewer 2 is male (we do not *actually* know his gender or identity, because the peer review process operates through anonymity) because of the way he expressed himself, and because our personal experience of the brutal reassertion of what legal scholarship should be about, of the kind we share below, has tended to reflect particular gendered patterns in academia.

We wish to make just one negative point about the review at the outset. We are wizened old professors who have been in the "academic game" for a while. A negative notice is nothing new to us; our skins are collectively thick. However, we expect reviewers to show courtesy to an argument – even if they disagree with it – and to express their reviews in modulated tones (and journal editors to intervene when they do not). We have learned from this review, and we hope that readers of this chapter have the same reaction and will carry that through into their own reviewing practices.

Our paper

In 2017–18, we wrote a paper that brought our separate work together around the study of what we called "the legal consciousness of stuff". We sought to present a general argument that stuff has legal consciousness (this may be counterintuitive, though we redefined the term "consciousness" in the paper to expand its range).[1] We argued that,

> at times [stuff] is imbued with a consciousness and that consciousness is often legal. It is brought into effect by its interactions, enrolments, and translations with, and by, other stuff, which produce versions of legality in action. This means at least two things: first, stuff carries a form of legal consciousness that is unanticipated yet significant In shaping legalities; secondly, where stuff is at the core of what the law tries to do, it is always more than the passive recipient of legal framings, but can be transformative of legal relationships. The materiality of stuff can challenge the law, and always does more than is anticipated. Our argument is that this excess of material significance should not be overlooked when seeking to determine the effects of legal consciousness. Materiality evades and challenges the law; it transports its own scripts of legal consciousness, which are themselves translated and transformed by those legalities. Both in the governance of housing and medicines, stuff is what the law sets out to organise and regulate, yet stuff continues to frame those legal relations and possibilities on its own terms.

The examples we drew upon were selected from our separate studies. One study was about "shared ownership", a type of low-cost housing option that is sold as "ownership" but also as "part buy, part rent". It is a recognised form of social housing. In essence, the buyer buys a share of the property and rents the remainder from the landlord. Really, the relationship is one of a long lease, and there have been concerns expressed that buyers are unclear about the obligations they are taking on. There have also been concerns because of a recognition that the buyer's security is limited following a court decision in which the long lease was held to be a normal tenancy. Broadly, the landlord could obtain possession if there were rent arrears of more than two months.

In our paper, we drew on two examples from this study: first, the marketing brochure for particular developments. We argued that socio-legal studies has neglected such materials, but that they tell us much in the way they translate complex ideas into simple pictures and grids, which are then translated back into a vision of the expected buyer. In addition, we

---

1 For the sake of transparency, the paper appears on Cowan's researchgate site.

drew on a small nugget from an interview with a buyer, conducted during the project. The buyer had referred to cleaning up a sweetie wrapper outside her home. There was nothing unusual about that. However, it was the way in which the buyer used the sweetie wrapper – she had used it as a device to divide herself off from social rented housing. It was the kids living in social rented housing who dropped the sweetie wrapper, who didn't care about the estate; on the other hand, the act of cleaning it up performed her identity as different from – and, probably, better than – the social renters. It was an example of what the literature refers to as an act of selective belonging.

Second, we drew from examples in which medicines performed types of socio-legal relationship, to blur further the boundary between material vibrancy and legal consciousness. We interrogated, first, how to characterise the fields of relationships that surround so-called "counterfeit" medicines (a category that is highly uncertain) and how the materiality of certain drugs appears to carry and mediate particular types of legal existence. We argued that the markets of "fake" drugs are in part mediated by the particular legal assumptions that are embedded in particular types of drug, and that such embedding is not so different from what has been labelled as legal consciousness. Next, we described the many ways in which medicinal plants can reinvent themselves to escape legal categories and argued that reducing this legal vibrancy to one of human consciousness does not enable us to capture the socio-material processes at play.

Throughout, we were explicit about our provocation in the use of the term "consciousness", but argued that what has been captured under that label does not inherently and exclusively have to be human, and that legal consciousness scholarship may be missing some important forms of relations by focusing too much on humans.

Self-critique

We recognise now that we oversold the argument. Our friends and colleagues told us so. As one generously said,

> I'm afraid I don't think the paper's actually about legal consciousness. I read the paper as being about (in the very last words of the text) "the everyday operation of legalities". And I'm convinced by your argument about the importance of materiality and attention to "stuff".

Others, more directly, told us that they found it hard to see how stuff could possibly have a consciousness. For what it is worth, we now agree with those critiques. However, before we got to that view, we had submitted it to a journal.

We selected the journals (there were two) to which we submitted the paper carefully. Both had a reputation for publishing excellent, cutting-edge socio-legal articles. Both were "general" journals, in the sense that they are not aligned with any particular method or methodology, but publish papers that are concerned with law and legality. The first journal rejected the paper broadly for the same reasons as our friends and colleagues – their two reviewers were unconvinced by the legal consciousness framing of the paper, and the data being both international and national made it harder to generalise about stuff. The second journal rejected the paper. The first reviewer broadly shared the same views as the other reviewers.

At this point, we should say something about the review process used by leading journals. As a general rule, papers submitted to an academic journal are peer reviewed – that is, subject to review by other academics. It can, occasionally, be a bruising process, although the best peer reviews explain how a paper can be improved and the reviewer's reasons for their recommendation to the editor. Peer review is both a validating and self-validating process, in which the peer reviewer enacts both expertise over the field and judgement as to whether the paper itself contributes to that field.

Peer review for interdisciplinary scholarship – or scholarship that seeks to be interdisciplinary – can be particularly fraught with problems, in part because of the problems inherent in interdisciplinary research. For journal editors, the selection of reviewers frames the process. For socio-legal scholarship, and when publishing in "mainstream" law journals in particular, a danger is always to let the subject matter rather than methodology dictate that selection. The not-so-hidden secret in academia is about the vicissitudes of the review process – how reviewers differ in tone and substance about the same paper, how they critique a paper because it is not the paper they would have written, or how they might be abusive towards the author's perspective(s). In short, the review process offers a veneer to the selection process, and reviews might say more about the reviewer than the paper. Nevertheless, academics engage in it (as reviewers as well as authors) not just because it is a rite of passage, but also because it validates the paper. This method of judgement is built into academic lives; it has a hegemonic status within the academy; and, oddly, it is rarely the subject of written critique. We turn now to Reviewer 2's critique of our paper.

Reviewer 2: on "reality" and the purpose of scholarship

Reviewer 2 experienced a strong reaction to the paper, concluding a 1,900-word review as follows:

> The bright side is that the authors need not bother with revising and resubmitting. The fact that the framework of this piece has proven to be worse than useless frees them to get on with work in their areas – "shared ownership" and housing, generic/counterfeit drugs and medicinal plants – which, if the authors focus on reality including the actual law, could be genuinely useful and important.

We should not move on without commenting on the reviewer's requirement for us to "focus on reality including the actual law". This framing of the critique – that we had failed to focus on the real and the law, and that studies should be "genuinely useful and important" – makes important dual points about ontology and the very purpose of socio-legal studies. Both of these points are at the heart of the socio-legal problematic discussed above. As socio-legal academics of a particular "postish" bent, we appreciate that there is no single reality, but multiple realities. This is what the interdisciplinary endeavour tells us – reality is a question of perspective.

Postdisciplinary scholars might ask what purpose the real and reality serve. One answer is to trace this response back in the ways in which law has been taught and researched in university law schools in the UK. This story has been told many times (see, for example, Twining, 1967; Siems and Mac Sithigh, 2012). As Willock (1974: 3) put it, in a still-relevant thick description of the problems lawyers and sociologists have in working together:

> For the sociologist [law] is one regulator of human behaviour among many, a very precise and overt one, possibly one indispensable to social life, but with no claim to uniqueness. The lawyer sees it as marked off from other social controls, by its coercive force and by its official character. For [the lawyer] law is not a mere pressure to be identified, but an instrument to be wielded. [The lawyer] is not unaware of the shadowy shape of custom, but tends to dismiss it as either insignificant or belonging to the past. [The lawyer] distinguishes social sanctions from legal ones as being spasmodic, undirected and thus unpredictable.

One can discuss this tension between, on the one hand, the insularity of doctrinal law as taught in universities and, on the other hand, the growth of social sciences, both as a historical as well as an intellectual development. So, for example, in the 19th century, law "was seen as 'a practical' subject ... only ... learnt by practice and not by systematic, scholarly instruction" (Siems and Mac Sithigh, 2012: 659–60). The 20th century was marked by the growth of both the social sciences and university legal education, with the latter eventually largely displacing the "apprenticeship" model of entry to the legal professions. Ironically, from the 1960s, significant expansion of university legal education concerned with preparing students for practice ran alongside the growth of interest in and affinity of some academic lawyers with the (also expanding) social sciences – although the latter is probably most accurately seen as lagging somewhat behind the former (for example, the UK Socio-Legal Studies Association was only founded in 1990).

Tensions between law as social science and law as single unit discipline in its own right do emerge, often in unlikely moments. Whereas legal technicality is the subject of doctrinal law, suitably presented as a series of principles in textbooks, socio-legal scholars have tended to ignore such problems, regarding them as tedious or distasteful (Riles, 2005–06: 976). The power of legal technicality lies in its seeming neutrality, its apparently atheoretical stance, as well as its insistence on relevance and market-centredness (Bankowski and Mungham, 1976: 7). It is this which produces Reviewer 2's "reality", by which is meant a kind of truth about law.

Reviewer 2's rallying cry for scholarship that is "genuinely useful and important" reflects particular discussions that animated the broad socio-legal community in the 1970s and 1980s about what Sarat and Silbey (1988) described as "the pull of the policy audience". The concern was that socio-legal studies had lost its sociological edge; that, in seeking policy relevance, it had been captured by the policy audience such that it was no longer its own master. This call for relevance remains a tension within the socio-legal community and underlines the significance of the judgement of whether research is important or not. It also raises questions about the purpose of research – is it for academic endeavour (at the risk of speaking to a limited, echo-chamber audience) or to have an impact on that part of reality which is practice (at the risk of the sneering of sociologists). Such a binary is unlikely to represent "reality" – as impact case studies for the Research Excellence Framework are likely to tell us – but this question of audience does represent a consistent tension in academic life.

Reviewer 2 and "legality"

Reviewer 2 aimed the first part of his critique at the theoretical framing of the paper. It would be fair to say that he had a strong reaction to the way in which we used and developed the idea of legality and actors. His starting point was the familiar one that objects do not have consciousness, but he was less complimentary about our attempt "to bolt together and latch onto what they believe are prestigious works by others" – Ewick and Silbey's *The Common Place of Law* and the work of Latour and ANT scholars. As regards the former, he took issue with Ewick and Silbey's label of "legal consciousness", arguing that they were not talking about legality because "the practice involving the chair did not actually create any legal rights and the participants in the practice recognised that it did not". Further:

> If a practice does not create any legal rights, and those who practise it are conscious
> of this – conscious that they are asserting extra-legal rights – labelling such beliefs

and practices as "legal consciousness" is a bizarre denial of reality. Ewick and Silbey are US sociologists; if the discipline of sociology in the US wishes to foster bizarre denials of reality, that is their business. It is certainly not ours.

He then took on our argument that stuff can have a legal consciousness by reference to Latour's concerns that, "The hard-core natural sciences have aimed and claimed to be about active human agents discovering, manipulating, and characterising passive objects" (Latour, 2000: 116). However, as he put it, "No one was daft enough to swallow Latour whole and believe that things like chairs were conscious actors rather than objects".

> Sometimes borrowing from theorists in other disciplines is helpful, but not always; amongst other things, context matters. My knowledge of Latour's work comes from my extra-legal interests; legal scholars have overwhelmingly ignored Latour, for good reason. The essence and purpose of law has never been or purported to be the investigation and characterisation of passive objects; the essence and purpose of law is and always has been about evaluating human actions (including an evaluation of whether, even if the defendant has done some wrong, it is the sort of wrong against which the law ought to intervene). In this fundamentally different context, Latour's presentation of things as actors is worse than useless – as the authors' attempts to apply it demonstrate.

We will not comment in detail about Reviewer 2's analysis of Latour's ideas, simply because it is less relevant to our purpose here. However, the way in which Reviewer 2 frames his reading of Latour's work as "extra-legal" and that "legal scholars have overwhelmingly ignored Latour, for good reason" provides an important reflection on that socio-legal scholarship which has engaged with this work. Reviewer 2 is reminding us about the essence of law, which is to be neither challenged nor revisited because of the truths that it sets down. It is "extra", othered by its outsider performance; it cannot offer anything useful to doctrine and the reading of law because that is about human actions. This doctrinal reflection on Latour's oeuvre (and that of others in that tradition) might be critiqued as being blinkered (particularly because Latour has expanded his investigations to law), but it points to the proper disciplinary limits of law and critique in the academy, as envisioned by Reviewer 2.

Here, the process of peer review as a form of peer and expert engagement with socio-legal work also raises fundamental questions about who the experts of socio-legal scholarship are or should be; in other words, peer review operates not just as a gatekeeper for socio-legal work, but also as a validating device. To "get through" peer review, your peers must accept the validity of the ideas. Given Reviewer 2's understanding of "truth", "reality", "the essence of law", and what is most important in our work as legal scholars, Reviewer 2 offered his appreciation of the invalidity of our work certainly in the more limited sense of its appearance in a legal journal. In so doing, of course, he pointed out that with which we were already familiar about the problems of doctrinal law, and missed the point of our paper because it was extra-legal. This brings into question how strongly socio-legal writing can be regarded as a distinct field of expertise, against the classic thematic categories of legal fields.

On the substance of the review, the essential division between Ewick and Silbey and Reviewer 2 lay in the significance of the extended definition of legality, something that has no formal existence in law. This is both an important division for socio-legal studies and its relation to the academy, and a methodological division. Reviewer 2 was particularly animated by formal law and matters that are defined out as extra-legal. This problem is both

105

difficult and one on which there is legitimate disagreement in the academic community. After all, as Reviewer 2 suggested, labelling extra-legal matters as legal is, in one view, "a bizarre denial of reality" (ignoring the point about reality made in the previous part). It is a contradiction in terms. It also extends the meaning of law to the extent that, as Mezey (2001) suggests, it lacks coherence and meaning because everything can become legal.

Yet, if one suspends reality for a moment and considers the empirical findings of scholarship, what gives the chair in the snow its particular power is that the neighbourhood observes it. This is the methodological point about a shift in focus in socio-legal studies away from formal law, and what that might mean. It is – to use a slightly different expression – a norm of everyday life. In collapsing back into the everyday, socio-legal studies has found the way in which legality has this extended meaning in the mundane. This is not law backed by state sanction, but norms that are understood as such and that attract community opprobrium and reputational damage in the breaking. As Engel (1998: 141) suggests, "more often law is mediated through social fields that filter its effects and merge official and unofficial systems of rules and meanings".

Reviewer 2 and the irresponsible authors

In the substance of the review, we learn what Reviewer 2's version of reality looks like. Expressing himself in trenchant terms, Reviewer 2 commented about what he described as our "purported illustrations". As his comments on our readings of our examples unfold, we learn about what he sees as legitimate or non-legitimate ways to think about the law, which tells us something about the fragile place of socio-legal scholarship in the legal academy. In particular, the challenge to opening law up to critical, interdisciplinary analysis reminds us of how, in spite of its increased visibility, socio-legal scholarship is still built *against* a particular (doctrinal) canon.

To illustrate this, we use only the parts of the review that engage the example of shared ownership – this is both the example that Reviewer 2 comments upon in greater detail and sufficient to make our point. The reviewer felt that we should emphasise how shared ownership "truly works in practice" as a matter of law. Back on the comfortable terrain of "truth", Reviewer 2 explains in some detail what we knew anyway: the mechanics of shared ownership. We will spare readers the details of the scheme. What is of interest is Reviewer 2's conclusion: like us, he emphasised that there is a significant difference between how shared ownership is sold (including in the material brochures our paper considered), what shared owners themselves think it offers, and the legal relations that it formally creates:

> So the guff described in the marketing materials, and the beliefs of the interviewee – all about "ownership" – have nothing whatsoever to do with the actual law. They bear no relationship to the legal nature of these schemes or the legal position of the interviewee, and therefore bear no relation to reality. That is a genuinely important point, which deserves jumping up and down and screaming about – these schemes are practically fraudulent; and most people, even most lawyers, are not aware of this.
>
> Instead, the authors obscure the stark difference between these false representations/beliefs on the one hand and the law on the other through guff about "legalities" and "legal consciousness" defined in such a way as to assert that there is no difference between the law and false representations/beliefs about the law. That is indefensible and irresponsible.

Reviewer 2's concerns that our approach was "indefensible and irresponsible" must be addressed because, at heart, it raises methodological concerns about the absence of law. What if, in the everyday lives of research participants, formal law is entirely absent or negotiated around. This is not "bargaining in the shadow of the law", but a routinised irrelevance of law. Our approach to the shared ownership relation, as well as our focus on the representation of status through things, was "indefensible and irresponsible" because it ignored the significance of the particular underpinning document – the lease – which places the buyer in an appalling position. As Reviewer 2 pointed out, we should be jumping up and down about that. Reviewer 2 perhaps overextends himself in describing this as fraud, but rather makes our point for us because this is a colloquial rendering of fraud: it is the weaving of an extra legal version of fraud with everyday life. These schemes are not "fraud" as the law understands that term, in either criminal or civil law.

Doctrinal legal scholars have described the shared ownership relation by analogy with the fable about the emperor's new clothes. However, methodologically, this places law first and, in its reification of law, places law above everything (there is a kind of irony in Reviewer 2 being, in Ewick and Silbey's terms, "before the law" in his assessment). We knew and appreciated this. Our enquiry was methodologically different: how is shared ownership experienced and made sense of in everyday life? And, as a result, we were able to note how shared owners produce and construct "ownership" practically, weaving in formal legal appreciation of ownership as control over property, but also, and importantly for us, dividing themselves off from the other that is, renters. We sought to demonstrate – albeit unsuccessfully for Reviewer 2 – how shared owners express their version of legal ownership, abstracting themselves from other tenures (even though, ironically, they form part of those other tenures, as Reviewer 2 points out). This, in our view, remains a neglected aspect not only of legal scholarship, but also of the essence of law as lived experience.

Conclusion

Socio-legal scholarship, like all fields of knowledge, is permanently "in the making". New ideas continue to be imported and borrowed from an ever-increasing set of disciplines and resources, with a view to developing new insights into what law is about, how it works, and what it does, as well as what it might do. This comes with a number of difficulties. In this chapter, we explored three main sets of such difficulties. First, questions of identity: as socio-legal studies has evolved to assert itself as a distinct field of study, the precise nature of that distinctiveness has not always been clear. Institutional pressures for more interdisciplinary scholarship, as well as the numerical growth of scholars identifying as socio-legal, have meant that the boundaries between the interdisciplinary and the mainstream have at times lost salience. Second, socio-legal scholarship has rendered the boundaries of the "legal" fragile, at times to the point of effacement. This results in the possibility that law can be decentred as an object of analysis, but it also requires a proficiency in the interdisciplinary tools needed to explore broader social patterns that goes beyond the simple borrowing of ideas or methods. Third, socio-legal scholarship, in spite of its growth and increasing visibility, remains marginal in parts of the legal academy. Many of us have enjoyed careers where we can play with disciplinary boundaries and have enough of a community of interdisciplinary legal scholars that we have the luxury to forget about the precarity of such scholarship. Every now and then, however, we are reminded of our position, and indeed of the persistence of ideas about truth and reality within the legal academy.

References

Bankowski, Z., and Mungham, G. (1976). *Images of Law*, London: Routledge & Kegan Paul.

Blomley, N. (2003). "From 'what?' to 'so what?' Law and geography in retrospect", in J. Holder and C. Harrison (eds), *Law and Geography*, Oxford: OUP, 17–33.

Blomley, N. (2014). "Disentangling law: The practice of bracketing", *Annual Review of Law and the Social Sciences*, 10: 133–148.

Braverman, I. (2008). "'The tree is the enemy soldier': A sociolegal making of war landscapes in the occupied West Bank", *Law and Society Review*, 42(3): 449–482.

Callon, M. (1984). "Some elements of a sociology of translation: Domestication of the scallops and fishermen of St Brieuc Bay", *The Sociological Review*, 32(1): 196–233.

Callon, M. (1986). "The sociology of an actor-network: The case of the electric vehicle", in M. Callon, J. Law and A. Rip (eds), *Mapping the Dynamics of Science and Technology: Sociology of Science in the Real World*, Basingstoke: Palgrave Macmillan, 19–36.

Callon, M., and Latour, B. (1981). "Unscrewing the big Leviathan; or how actors macrostructure reality, and how sociologists help them to do so?", in K. Knoor and A. Cicourel (eds), *Advances in Social Theory and Methodology*, London: Routledge & Kegan Paul, 277–303.

Cloatre, E. (2013). *Pills for the Poorest: An Exploration of TRIPS and Access to Medication in Sub-Saharan Africa*, London: Palgrave Macmillan.

Cloatre, E., and Cowan, D. (2018). "Legalities and materialities", in A. Phillippopoulos-Mihailopolos (ed), *Routledge Handbook of Law and Theory*, London: Routledge, 433–452.

Cotterell, R. (1998). "Why must legal ideas be interpreted sociologically", *Journal of Law and Society*, 25(2): 171.

Cowan, D., and Wincott, D. (2015). "Exploring the legal", in D. Cowan and D. Wincott (eds), *Exploring the Legal*, London: Palgrave, 1–31.

Cowan, D., and Wincott, D. (eds) (2017). *Exploring the Legal*, London: Palgrave.

Cownie, F. (2004). *Legal Academics: Culture and Identities*, Oxford: Hart.

Cownie, F., Bradney, A., and Burton, M. (2010). *English Legal System in Context*, Oxford: OUP.

Ellickson, R. (1991). *Order without Law: How Neighbors Settle Disputes*, Cambridge: Harvard UP.

Engel, D. (1998). "How does law matter in the constitution of legal consciousness?", in B. Garth and A. Sarat (eds), *How Does Law Matter?* Fundamental Issues in Law and Society Research, Vol. 5. Evanston: Northwestern UP, 109–144.

Ewick, P., and Silbey, S. (1998). *The Common Place of Law: Stories from Everyday Life*, Chicago: University of Chicago Press.

Fish, S. (1994). "Why is interdisciplinarity so hard to do?", in S. Fish (ed), *There's No such Thing as Free Speech … and It's a Good Thing Too*, Oxford: OUP, 231–242.

Fitzpatrick, P. (1995). "Being social in socio-legal studies", *Journal of Law and Society*, 22(1): 105–112.

Foucault, M. (1977). *Discipline and Punish: The Birth of the Prison*, London: Penguin.

Knorr-Cettina, K. (1999). *Epistemic Cultures: How the Sciences Make Knowledge*, Cambridge: Harvard UP.

Latour, B. (1999). "On recalling ANT", in J. Law and J. Hassard (eds), *Actor Network Theory and After*, Oxford: Blackwell, 15–25.

Latour, B. (2000). "When things strike back: A possible contribution of 'science studies' to the social sciences", *British Journal of Sociology*, 51(1): 107–130.

Latour, B. (2010). *The Making of Law: An Ethnography of the Conseil d'Etat*, Cambridge: Polity.

Latour, B., and Woolgar, S. (1986). *Laboratory Life: The Construction of Scientific Facts*, New Haven: Princton UP.

Levine, K., and Mellema, V. (2001). "Strategizing the street: How law matters in the lives of women in the street-level drug economy", *Law and Social Inquiry*, 26(1): 169–185.

Mezey, N. (2001). "Out of the ordinary: Law, power, culture and commonplace", *Law and Social Inquiry*, 26(1): 145.

Mulcahy, L., and Stychin, C. (2010). *Legal Methods and Systems: Text and Materials*, London: Sweet & Maxwell.

Nelken, D. (1993). "The truth about law's truth", in A. Febbrajo and D. Nelken (eds), *European Yearbook of Sociology of Law*, Milan: Giuffrè, 87–163.

Nelken, D. (1998). "Blinding insights? The limits of a reflexive sociology of law", *Journal of Law and Society*, 25(3): 407.

Riles, A. (2005–06). "A new agenda for the cultural study of law: Taking on the technicalities", *Buffalo Law Review*, 63(4): 973.

Riles, A. (2011). *Collateral Knowledge: Legal Reasoning in the Global Financial Markets*, Chicago: University of Chicago Press.

Rooke C., Cloatre, E., and Dingwall, R. (2012). "The regulation of nicotine in the United Kingdom: How nicotine gum came to be a medicine, but not a drug", *Journal of Law and Society*, 39(1): 39–57.

Sarat, A. (1990). "Off to meet the wizard: Beyond validity and reliability in the search for a post-empiricist sociology of law", *Law and Social Inquiry*, 15(1): 155–170.

Sarat, A., and Silbey, S. (1988). "The pull of the policy audience", *Law and Policy*, 10(2–3): 97–166.

Siems, M., and Mac Sithigh, D. (2012). "Mapping legal research", *Cambridge Law Journal*, 71(4): 651–676.

Trubek, D., and Esser, J. (1989). "'Critical empiricism' in American legal studies: Paradox, program, or Pandora's box?", *Law and Social Inquiry*, 14: 3.

Twining, W. (1967). "Pericles and the plumber", *Law Quarterly Review*, 83(3): 396.

Willock, I. (1974). "Getting on with sociologists", *British Journal of Law and Society*, 1(1): 3–12.

8

ETHICAL AWARENESS AND SOCIO-LEGAL RESEARCH IN THE UK

Victoria Brooks

Introduction

Most of us will encounter an ethics review at some point in our careers. Most of the time, this will be simply to tick a box to say that our project raises no significant ethical issues. Usually, such a review will be a minor inconvenience, and, often, we will wonder at the point of ethical review. On occasions, the process will draw us in, as we will need to disclose to our institutions and/or research councils (the two major councils in the UK being the ESRC and the AHRC)[1] that our project involves, for example, human subjects or sensitive issues such as sexuality, criminal offences, or mental health. At this point, many of us will experience frustration and sometimes fear that our project will not be allowed to go ahead at all. Research ethics in the humanities, and more so in the narrower field of socio-legal studies, has not received the same level of attention and scrutiny as in the sciences. This is at once a shame and concerning. As we will see, research ethics and the bodies that apply them to our work (research ethics committees; RECs) have the power to bring us to reflect productively on not only the ethical position of our projects, but also our ethical position as researchers. As we will see, research ethics and the findings of RECs not only tell us about our field, our methods, and ourselves, but also the priorities, framings of risk, and prejudices and conventionally conservative ethics that are the foundation of the broader academic context within which we operate.

In what follows, I will set out an overview of research ethics processes that are likely to apply to a socio-legal project, the current criticisms of the frameworks that underpin research ethics in humanities fields, and the apparent biases of RECs. I will then move on to consider my own 'risky' sexuality project, and how this is a useful example that demonstrates both the power of research ethics and RECs and an occasional, yet urgent, need to be critical of research ethics in our particular field. In looking at this, I will also set out some strategies for dealing with a refusal of ethical approval, how this can be taken forward to ensure a project's continuation, how such a response can be dealt with productively, and how ethical awareness can be transformed into a positive and useful part of researcher development (De Wet, 2010).

---

1 The arguments I advance in this Chapter are targeted at the frameworks governing research at UK institutions. However, the points made in this article are likely to have broader application than the UK jurisdiction since much of the critique against ethical frameworks runs along similar lines.

The codes

It goes without saying that the process of ethical awareness must begin at the earliest possible stage of a project. There are several things that can impact on the timing of recourse to the procedure, which could range from reticence to engage in the process, simply not knowing it is necessary, or not knowing how to do it, to last minute changes in methodology or theoretical framework. Most projects, whether or not funded by a body external to the researcher's home institution, will be subject to the institution's ethics framework. It has been found that rash consideration of ethics and an assumption of a lack of ethical dimensions can be both 'erroneous and dangerous' (De Wet, 2010). Not only this, but such a position might render the researcher in contravention of research council guidelines, which require ethical awareness and engagement with RECs.

For socio-legal researchers, the Socio-Legal Studies Association (SLSA) has produced a 'living document' in the form of a Statement of Principles of Ethical Research Practice (SLSA, 2009). This document is designed to be read in conjunction with ethics guidance appropriate to each research project, which might be your specific institution's guidance and/or code of practice,[2] and it will likely include, whether or not you are externally funded, the ESRC Framework for Research Ethics (ESRC FRE; ESRC 2012). It should be noted that, if a project is funded by a different external body, such as a charity, then it will have its own ethical principles for the conduct of research, which also must be considered. It could be said, then, that there is guidance aplenty, with many papers and codes of practice and statements of principles to resort to, should you find yourself 'ethically' compromised during your project. It is also the case that you *must* engage with this process. Ethical awareness is not a choice, such that, if you are found to be in breach of these rules, you might find yourself in trouble at your PhD viva, or perhaps having your research funding removed, or, in extreme circumstances, you might find yourself splashed across the front pages of the *Daily Mail* and, potentially, without a job.

The process, at first glance, appears complex, anxiety inducing, and, to the most hardened empirical researchers, harmful to the production of free and exciting research (Burgess, 2007, cited in De Wet, 2010). I find myself fluctuating between all three of these possibilities, but I conclude that ethical awareness (albeit the processes and codes are problematic, as we shall see) can be hugely beneficial to a project, even (and especially if) the project is one that *confronts* and disrupts ethical codes and processes (although there are some caveats to this). But, before moving on to the problems with the process, I shall first look at the basic requirements and considerations and how an application for ethical approval for a socio legal project might look. It is worth mentioning that, at this point, any recommendations for navigating the process are drawn both from others and from my own engagement with ethical awareness.

The process

The ESRC FRE, which will be incorporated into most, if not all, research ethics frameworks (REFs), tells us that primary data collection will always raise ethical issues that must be addressed, whereas secondary use of data 'may' be uncontroversial, requiring only a 'light touch ethics review' (ESRC, 2012: 3). It is also the case that, once you indicate to your

2 See for example the University of Westminster Research Ethics Framework https://www.westminster.ac.uk/research/research-framework/research-ethics. Your own institution will have its own framework, which will incorporate and refer to external ethical guidance – most likely including the ESRC FRE.

research support team (your supervisors and so on), that you are planning to go into the field and carry out, for instance, interviews or observations, the requirement for some ethical engagement will become clear. It is also the case that, regardless of your methods, if your research involves a 'sensitive' subject matter, the requirement for ethical awareness will arise (and your supervisors, depending on their experience and research inclinations, may be panicking).

Although each institution will incorporate external guidance such as the ESRC FRE into its own frameworks, if you are attached to an institution, then your starting point will be your institution's application process for ethical approval. Each process will differ in terms of practical steps (it could be a paper/email form or a process using a virtual research environment) but will include similar 'triggers' for engaging more than a 'light touch ethics review'. There is no indication in the SLSA Principles as to what the headline triggers for a more in-depth review might be, specific to socio-legal research. The ESRC FRE gives institutions responsibility for establishing principles and policies, which include criteria for identifying the level of risk that a project entails and therefore the procedure to apply (ESRC, 2012: 8). The framework then goes on to set out the following categories that are *likely* to require a full, in-depth review: research involving potentially vulnerable groups or those lacking capacity; research involving sensitive topics (including participants' experience of sexuality, gender, race, political or illegal behaviour, experience of violence, abuse, or exploitation); research involving human tissue; research using secure or sensitive data; research involving deception; research involving psychological stress; research involving intrusive methods of data collection; research where the safety of the researcher might be at risk; research involving members of the public; research outside the UK or on the Internet; research through visual or vocal methods (where participants may be identifiable; ESRC, 2012: 8–10).

If your research fits into one of these categories, which is likely given their extensive coverage and the kinds of project that are likely to be undertaken by socio-legal researchers, then the ESRC FRE indicates that your research should be subject to a full ethics review (ESRC, 2012: 8–10). These categories are likely to be reflected in the institutional process, and, when you come to the 'risk' section of your institution's form and tick the box indicating that your research involves one of these areas, this will trigger a full ethics review. A full ethics review will involve consideration of your application by your institution's REC, following your institution's particular process for doing so. In the unlikely event that your research does *not* fall within the categories listed in the ESRC FRE and mirrored by your institution's 'risky' categories, then a 'light touch' review will be sufficient. A 'light touch' review, however, does not let you off the hook as far as ethical awareness is concerned. Although you will not be subject to the scrutiny of your REC, you will remain bound by the SLSA Statement of Principles of Ethical Research Practice and your institution's and the research council's codes of conduct/practice.

So far, the process seems, on the face of it, relatively clear, both in terms of the steps and in terms of the documents themselves that guide our ethical behaviour as researchers. However, this is far from the case. What the researcher will find is a huge area of uncertainty in the space that exists between the lines of these documents, containing these supposedly clear principles that guide a 'full ethics review'. This space of uncertainty is both problematic and productive, but, most importantly, it is a space in which researchers should demand (and receive) support mechanisms. It is also a space that might bring researchers into confrontation with institutional power within our discipline. It is crucial that socio-legal researchers, as part of 'ethical awareness', are conscious of the problems with these principles, as well as their protective purpose. This is particularly important given the power that RECs have in relation to our projects, and the impact that their findings can have.

Problems with research ethics, SLSA principles, and RECs

An ill-fit for the discipline

The first criticism of relevance to socio-legal researchers is that ethical clearance procedures in social science and the humanities tend to 'sprout' from procedures applied to the sciences (De Wet, 2010: 302). As we have seen, it is also the case that ethical frameworks for institutions and externally funded projects will always incorporate the ESRC FRE – a framework that is specifically designed for research in scientific disciplines. This ought not to be a surprise, as the origin of ethics review is in the sciences, with the process originally designed to prevent physical abuse and medical malpractice (Connor, Copland, and Owen, 2018: 401). Accordingly, the process is often thought of as not only unnecessary, but painfully bureaucratic – a perceived reality that will make most socio-legal researchers disengage (De Wet, 2010: 301).

Although an ethical framework will also incorporate the institution's own code of practice, and indeed the SLSA Principles, it is submitted that this does not render the overall ethical guidance any more focused on the specific demands of a socio-legal project. As De Wet argues, the positivist epistemological tenets of the ethical 'tick-box' exercise designed for the sciences simply does not fit with the demands of ethical practice in the social sciences (De Wet, 2010: 302). De Wet argues that the distance between the reality of the particular demands in humanities research and the design of the procedure has resulted in at once a disengagement with ethics review as a 'dead procedure' and a suspicion that it 'overregulates' research (De Wet, 2010: 303). This is not only potentially dangerous, but also sad, because ethical review, as we shall see, can be highly productive for a research project and supportive of the researcher.

For the socio-legal researcher, the inadequacy of ethics review processes is of particular concern, a concern that the ESRC FRE and the SLSA Principles of Ethical Research Practice do not fully address. Nouwen captures perfectly the very particular challenges of socio-legal research, particularly that which might well be deemed subject to a 'full review' as being 'risky' (Nouwen, 2014: 230):

> Practically, empirical socio-legal field research requires huge amounts of resources and time. Epistemologically, it suffers from the perennial identity crisis of social science as a science, given the limitations on its ability to demonstrate causality with anything like the certainty of natural sciences. Ethically, the context of research in situations of (post-)conflict continuously confronts the researcher with most difficult questions. Existentially, empirical socio-legal research can shake up the most basic assumptions, hopes, and expectations of the fieldworker … The challenges are huge, precisely because empirical socio-legal research takes place in the midst of a social world that is continuously changing and filled with contradictions, uncertainties, and inconsistencies.

The question is how an ethics framework that is specifically designed for the sciences can have any hope of covering the magnitude and variety of these challenges, all of which, I argue, have implications for research ethics: they are not just theoretical or academic challenges, these are resolutely real, carrying not only the possibility for unpredictable ethical demand for the research study, but also risk to the researcher *personally*. I shall come back to this point later, but the fact that a researcher can, and often is, left alone (potentially early on in their career) to deal with these challenges that do not fall within the categories of conventional risk – as set out by the ESRC and the SLSA, for example – is hugely concerning.

Risk: physical and reputational

In a way, it should not be a surprise that the SLSA Principles form a very 'legal' document. Each principle explains what is required of a responsible socio-legal researcher, including responsibility to junior researchers (Principle 3); acknowledgment of sources (Principle 4); safety and wellbeing (Principle 5); in great detail, the responsibilities of the researcher in relation to obtaining consent (Principle 7); confidentiality and data sharing (Principle 8); and a short and sweet section on social responsibility (Principle 9). I am afraid it is clear this document is focused on ensuring the protection of institutions and a notion of 'ethical' research that is far removed from the demands of the field, and the modern context of academia (De Wet, 2010: 313). Consequently, there is little in the way of protection that relates to the real risks to the researcher or evidence of a will to protect the innovative, demanding, and crucial field that is socio-legal work. In fairness, it is an inadequate supplement to a desperately inadequate framework. The reason for this begins with the conception of 'risk' that underlies both the ESRC FRE and the SLSA Principles.

The way in which risk is conceptualised is important, as this will inform the kinds of question that will be asked of a researcher, the kind of support needed/provided, and the overall productivity of the ethics review. This will also indicate, I claim, the priorities of the institution and the underlying assumptions about both the researcher and the socio-legal field. The risk that seems the most obvious will be physical risk to the researcher, with the resulting duty of care held by the institution as employer (SLSA Principles, Principle 5). Given the diversity of methodological enquiry and subject matter within socio-legal study, these dangers are likely to take on a variety of forms. Although this seems obvious and uncontroversial, the 'obviousness' of these dangers can hide a multitude of assumptions about both the researcher and researched (Lee-Treweek and Linkogle, 2001). For example, a concern about the physical safety of a female researcher going to a public sex beach for a socio-legal project is highly gendered – would the same question be asked of a man? What kinds of assumption are being made, and what does this say about both the institution and the field (Brooks, 2018)? Likewise, a lack of concern about a male researcher being assaulted in the field carries with it another set of gendered assumptions (Lee-Treweek and Linkogle, 2001). It is also the case that these kinds of physical risk will be the subject of scrutiny to the exclusion of 'softer' risks, such as emotional risk. When researching within a particular community in a particular place, the risks associated with isolation are real and serious (Sampson, 2017). There are risks, too, that might not even register with RECs, and certainly not in terms of the SLSA Principles, such as the potential for the dynamic of the field to render gaining informed consent, or ethical approval (as the field has changed or altered), impossible (Sampson, 2017). This has the effect of locating risk, and therefore responsibility, solely with the researcher in carrying out 'unsanctioned' work, and work that falls outside the Principles.

As universities have come under increased public scrutiny, reputational risk has become a heightened concern. This is particularly so as academic spaces have come to operate increasingly as businesses (Hedgecoe, 2016: 488). The particular kind of work that might cause the university a loss of 'prestige' or research funding is the kind of work that RECs are likely to be sensitive to (Hedgecoe, 2016: 494). As Hedgecoe argues, in the course of considering both student sex-work studies and terrorism studies, it seems to be the case that the ambit of RECs extends beyond legalistic duties of care, toward reputational harm (Hedgecoe, 2016: 494). It is also important to consider the personal risk to the researcher. As Massanari argues, with increased technology, social media use, and the ability to work with diverse kinds of community (some with extreme views), researcher visibility carries new forms of risk, which go beyond institutional reputation (Massanari,

2018: 7). Concern for reputation on the part of the SLSA takes the form of 'integrity' (Principle 2) to the discipline of socio-legal studies (SLSA Principles, Principle 2). I suggest that this focus, although well intentioned, does not make the researcher aware of the complexities associated with reputational risk, which for institutions is the priority, and integrity means institutional integrity – not integrity to your discipline (Connor, Copland, and Owen, 2018: 407).

The question then becomes one of how to navigate and mitigate these perceived risks (whether physical or reputational), if they are raised as a concern (either expressly or implicitly) as part of a full ethics review. Peter and Friedland suggest recourse to the researcher themselves, in assessing their own vulnerability in their particular project, might trigger closer, yet more flexible, engagement with RECs (Peter and Friedland, 2017: 115). Although it is not surprising that RECs attempt a protectionist stance, via focus on regulation, it is possible to form strategies to mitigate the distanced view that RECs take. This would also have the effect of undoing assumptions and researcher stereotypes, currently in operation with the consideration of both physical and reputational risk – moving from hypothetical assumed risk to actual risk (Peter and Friedland, 2017: 115). This approach of 'ethical mindfulness' is more a process and discussion than a judgement, 'recognizing and giving credence to feelings of discomfort, and being ethically reflexive' (Peter and Friedland, 2017: 115). This approach is an unconventional approach taken to risk and is not reflected in REFs. Yet, given that unconventional methodological and theoretical approaches in socio-legal studies are becoming the norm, we need an approach that fits.

Fear of innovative methods and reflexivity

If you are using an unconventional methodology, as well as researching within a 'risky' field, you are even more likely to be considered ethically 'risky'. A significant factor in the apparent increase in risk for socio-legal research is methodological innovation. Our research has become more critical of methods, and those of us doing qualitative work are taking our methodology itself as an object of critical concern. In doing so, we are doing work that fails to be captured by conventional risk frameworks and tick-box exercises, work that examines and disrupts power dynamics within the research process and moves toward researcher–participant collaboration (Connor et al., 2018: 401).[3] With research that prioritises social empowerment, we need an ethics framework that facilitates and empowers, but this, as we have seen, is not the case (Connor, Copland, and Owen, 2018: 401).

Reflexivity and methods that allow for reflexivity are being used with increasing frequency in socio-legal studies (Nouwen, 2014: 233). Reflexivity might be through the method itself (for instance, autoethnography or ethnography), or through the researcher's theoretical position, which takes account of the fact that analysis cannot be separated from the researcher who analyses and is, too, part of the world that she studies (Nouwen, 2014: 234). Nouwen finds that socio-legal research has been slow on the uptake for such work (with reflexive accounts often rejected for not being scholarly enough), but that such approaches are invaluable in dismantling the illusion that law, the object of our study, is external to us (Nouwen, 2014: 233). Nouwen claims that reflexivity relates clearly to intellectual honesty in disclosing the limitations and possibilities of research. With this being the

---

3 See also Victoria Brooks 'Fucking Research Ethics through Radical Method: autoethnography and the field of environmental law, in Andreas Philippopoulos-Mihalopoulos and Victoria Brooks (eds) Research Methods in Environmental Law (Elgar, 2017) for how radical methods (and theories) can cause disruptions to the ethical regimes of institutions.

case, it appears that honesty in our reflexivity and the impact of our methods and ourselves on our findings are essential ethical concerns.

However, it would seem apparent that socio-legal research is somewhat reticent to be open to creative and personal methodological enquiry (Nouwen, 2014: 233).[4] To be sure, it is one of the more adventurous disciplines, albeit the personal and political seem not to be a priority, as Nouwen suggests:

> Authors are expected to write up research by mentioning 'the facts', the theories, and possibly the methods. The relationship between facts, theories, methods, and the researcher, however, is rendered invisible, and so is the personal, social, and political character of research.
>
> *(Nouwen, 2014: 233)*

Yet, our ethical frameworks, the SLSA Principles included, do not provide guidelines on the necessity or the non-legalistic risks of doing such research and adopting such a position. What is worse is that we are left with a huge gap in our ethical frameworks, which will leave researchers unsupported in what can be a risky approach.

Hidden bias and the secret deliberations of RECs

The whisperings and debates of the REC, once our ethics reviews land on its desk, are as shrouded in mystery as jury deliberations, with no requirement to record or minute its deliberations or give full reasons for its 'verdicts', much less to disclose its biases. REC discussions take place in private, away from the researcher, who is not included in these conversations (De Wet, 2010: 313). An illusion is given of an objective body that can decide on the integrity of research that it is not doing and may well be outside its disciplinary expertise. The research may be highly controversial, and yet we endow the REC with the capability not only of judging its value and integrity, but of separating this judgement from broader institutional (legalistic and commercial) concern. Yet the impossibility and, I argue, danger of this position is largely ignored by the socio-legal community. Perhaps this is because the process seems comfortingly judicial!

I shall examine ways of navigating the biases, assumptions, blind spots, and uses of RECs in the following section. First, however, it is important to understand what kinds of bias might be encountered, and why they are inevitable, in order that we might develop individual and institutional strategies for ensuring they do not impact on the production of socio-legal knowledge. The majority of research concerning the bias of RECs is, unsurprisingly, in the medical and sciences field.[5] Yet this is also surprising, as bias as a social phenomenon of a person's subjective position is often the very subject matter of humanities and social sciences work. This gap in our knowledge is likely due to the discomfort and challenge of talking about the risks associated with cutting-edge socio-legal research.

In Halse's work on her experience as an REC chair, we find deeper, honest reasons for a problematic ethics decision in a sociology project, which takes us beyond the true but concealing conventional narratives of paternalism (Connor, Copland, and Owen, 2018) and safeguarding of the institution through legalistic framings of risk. Her work is also a clear articulation of the relation between a critique of RECs and self-interested neo-liberal

---

4 See also Brooks (2018).
5 See for example de Jong, van Zwieten, and Willems (2012).

institutional concern (Halse, 2011). Halse examines the ethics review of a (fictional) 'risky' socio-legal project by a PhD student (Mary) on the question of why married men with children use prostitutes (Halse, 2011: 242). We find through her work that the underlying ethical principles for such projects are of a conventional, rational kind, in which the researcher is presumed, somewhat unrealistically, to be: 'a rational being who abides by the decreed universalized norms of principlism even when this involves acting in ways that are counter to his or her subjective desires or rational self-interest' (Halse, 2011: 242).[6]

Mary's project seems to fall foul of this principle, owing to self-interest, or otherwise her personal investment in her project (her own marriage broke down owing to her husband's use of prostitutes; Halse, 2011: 247). Halse argues that personal insight such as this is a valuable tool in qualitative research, which is a point established in literature concerning reflexive positions.[7] What becomes troubling is that the standard against which projects are assessed is taken for granted as being based on an infallible catch-all principle that will guarantee ethical research (Halse and Honey, 2005: 2158). Halse and Honey have reasserted the argument that this is not the case, and that there ought to be an 'ethic of care and responsibility' in research (Halse and Honey, 2005: 2158).

What we do not learn from Halse's account, however, are the reasons for, and the impact of, the assumptions and self-interest of the REC members themselves. Bias in research on the part of the researcher is a well-rehearsed notion, with the notion of being objective being thoroughly rejected.[8] We have even been taught to move with bias, to look at it closely and embrace it for the lessons it will teach us about ourselves and our studies.[9] Responsibility for ethical research and upholding the 'integrity' of the ethical code is placed solely with the researcher and their supervisors. What about where the REC members themselves have an undisclosed, or unacknowledged, assumption or bias? Halse's confession does not go far enough. The stakes are too high for there to be a silence on this matter – if the production of knowledge and truly ethical research is at stake, then we need to know more. After all, the REC is formed of individuals with their own assumptions that they bring to the table in ethics reviews. I claim that this is a further reason why RECs must be opened up, so staff can observe them not only to stop them serving the interests of management and the neo-liberal institution (Hedgecoe, 2016: 497), but also to learn more about the assumptions applied to our work and to ourselves as socio-legal researchers. The following example of a real 'risky' socio-legal project examines why this is urgent and develops strategies for navigating the subjectivities of RECs.

Risky socio-legal work and ethical 'refusal'

There are many types of cutting-edge and challenging work in socio-legal research, including conflict and international criminal law (Nouwen, 2014), terrorism (Bakircioglu, 2010; Varona, 2013), drugs and childhood (Flacks, 2018), and mental health (Thom and Finlayson, 2011). Here, however, I will focus on sexuality work. This is because it is a field in which

6 The author demonstrates that this foundation is translated into, and applied in her decision-making processes, as a four-point framework of principles of research merit and integrity; justice; beneficence and respect.

7 See, for example, Mauthner, N and Doucet (2003).

8 See Donna Haraway's pioneering piece on partial perspectives and arguments against scientific objectivity, Donna Haraway (1988). For a socio-legal approach examining this position and method, see Mason, M in this volume (Chapter 9).

9 See, for example, Brooks (2018) and Brooks (2018) on autoethnography and the need for bias.

I can demonstrate problems with the ethical review process from personal experience, and because sexuality is notoriously loaded with uncomfortable truths, assumptions, and biases, many of which are silenced in an institutional space where we must be objective and distanced (Hedgecoe, 2016; Brooks, 2018).

I have rehearsed the details of my project on the ethics of sexuality elsewhere (Brooks, 2018). In short, the project was theoretical, but also included covert observations of a nudist and public-sex beach in southern France. I also considered the REC's correspondence in response to my ethics review application, which set out their concerns relating to my project in the same article (Brooks, 2018), but, for ease of use, I reproduce the main ones here:

- The Committee have serious concerns about your safety given you will be working off-campus with negligible support in a potentially dangerous environment where individuals nearby could be actively seeking a sexual encounter.
- The Committee were unclear how you would record the observations, for example would you propose relocating to improve the quality of your observations, and if so how would you be able to guard against suspicions being raised about your activity. Is it possible to undertake covert observations in this way and at the same time remain inconspicuous?
- Concepts of privacy could be contentious. While the research will be undertaken on a public beach, the individuals being observed may view their area as being a private or semi-private space. As there are quite strict laws in France relating to privacy has there been any assessment of the legality of the proposed research in the local context? Can you confirm that any proposed covert observations will only take place on people who are in a space that could be reasonably be observed by others, the individuals would have no expectation of privacy and that you will not follow individuals to better observe them should they go behind bushes/into caves, etc.?

To be clear, this correspondence was the response to my application for a full ethics review under the institution's procedure and framework. My application was refused at first instance, but, as we can see, the REC was keen for me to respond. In the end, this piece of correspondence has become career-shaping for me – forming a central point of analysis for my PhD and for my work after. I do not wish to criticise the REC for engaging as it did (and, from what I learned, there were protracted discussions on my application – although of course I do not know the content of these discussions). Nor will I undertake a sustained theoretical analysis of the concerns here, as I have done so elsewhere (Brooks, 2018). The important point here is to be aware of the types of question one might be asked, and to know that a refusal is not necessarily the end of the road. It is important, however, that we understand why these questions are asked, and why this points to gaps and assumptions within REFs.

We can see from the first concern above that we have a clearly gendered worry for my safety as a woman researcher. This, although perhaps well intentioned personally, is resolutely a concern framed through a legalistic, and indeed reputational, framing of risk. The risk assessment I had following my (eventual) ethical approval is testament to that, where the extent of the risk appeared to be that I would get sunburn from being on the beach. Interestingly, all sexual risks (perhaps STDs, consent, and so on) were ignored, together with any discussion of emotional risk. The two further concerns the REC raises are explicitly legalistic and connected to reputational concerns. We also find evidence of the depressingly familiar narrative of unproductive, yet well-intentioned, paternalism as a strategy for infantilising not only the participants in my study, but my position as a researcher (Connor, Copland, and Owen, 2018: 407).

In terms of how to deal with this kind of REC 'tussle', I would suggest, as far as it is possible, to embrace it. It can be quite a telling exercise about the subject matter itself, or otherwise the field, and not just about the REC and you as a researcher. Second, I think this first step is much easier if you have a supportive research team. I did, and this made the world of difference, meaning the response to the REC's refusal was a collective effort. I accept, however, that this might not always be the case, and that is why it is so important that we are openly critical about RECs and ethics review processes, and that researchers are adequately supported. This must be an ongoing process, as and when we find these 'gaps' in ethical review (Connor, Copland, and Owen, 2018: 405). The most concerning and urgent aspect of this is where we do see projects stopped in their tracks and where we suffer a huge loss to our discipline, undermining the core of the SLSA's principles, integrity in our discipline (SLSA Principles, Principle 2).

My project here is far from being unique in bringing a challenge to ethics reviews. Such projects can question academic institutional power and challenge the silencing of discussion as to sex. Hedgecoe gives the example of projects examining students who undertake sex work (Hedgecoe, 2016).[10] This project, at Kingston University, was remarkably similar to my own in terms of the REC's responses – reducing concerns to personal safety and thereby covering the true reputational concerns (Hedgecoe, 2016: 490). This, Roberts argues, demonstrates an institutional reluctance, that such research is: 'not only unwelcome, but actively discouraged' (Roberts, 2010, cited in Hedgecoe, 2016). Support of the researcher and true engagement with methods and gaining the keenest intellectual insight from the project are rejected in favour of upholding an institutional distance and shelter under the pretence of 'duty of care' (Hedgecoe, 2016: 490).

This situation ought to warn researchers undertaking 'risky' work that, frankly, their project is not given a full ethics review. If ethics is about integrity of the discipline, empowerment for participants, and support for researchers, then the procedure is simply not doing its job. The SLSA Principles, as the 'gap' filler for such work that the ESRC FRE is not designed to cover, do not help us in this regard. In short, I can say that, in terms of doing ethical research, the ethics review served only to demonstrate the lack of true and useful ethical awareness within institutions, and the need for a complete overhaul of the process. So, what is a researcher to do? How do we navigate these processes in the knowledge that they are inadequate for the needs of 'risky' socio-legal work?

Conclusions: strategies and support for socio-legal researchers

We are in a situation where REFs mirror the parameters and interests of commercially centred, REF- and TEF[11]-focused institutions. Ethical awareness processes are therefore fundamentally failing (Connor, Copland, and Owen, 2018: 411). It is important that researchers are aware of this, and are prepared to face and deal with the ethical unawareness of RECs. Most RECs will be open and ready for active conversations around research ethics and willing to turn a refusal into an approval. It is also possible that some may not be.[12] While the

---

10 See also feminist research on the discomfort and academic cultural anxiety of doing any kind of sexuality work, especially as a woman researcher – a position that has been a reality since the early 1990s. For example, Newton (1993); Irvine (2014) and De Craene (2017).

11 REF: www.ref.ac.uk/; TEF: www.officeforstudents.org.uk/advice-and-guidance/teaching/what-is-the-tef/.

12 See de Jong, van Zwieten, and Willems (2012): RECs must give advice on how to improve so as to prevent rejection of valuable research. This is not only a problem in social sciences and the humanities, but also in health and sciences ethical reviews.

'deliberations' of RECs remain a secret, without transparency as to their motives, it is diffi-cult to be sure if their concerns relate to the project's ethical dimensions – whether this relates to method or theory (Brooks, 2018). My overarching concern is avoiding the pre-vention of valuable work that contributes significantly to the field of socio-legal studies.

At the core of this concern is whether ethical frameworks are a good fit for the discipline and its unique demands. We have seen that this is not the case, and I argue that an urgent overhaul of the SLSA Principles and the key governing ethical framework of the ESRC FRE is required to fit with this reality. As we have seen, researchers have persistently argued that current frameworks do not fit the demands of social sciences and humanities work more broadly – in this jurisdiction and beyond.[13] I argue that, as socio-legal researchers, this reality affects us in a particular way, as our work is likely, in itself, to be operating at the forefront of challenging ethical and legal regimes. The good news here is that we are in a unique position to bring the required challenge. In doing so, I argue that the most useful and important ethical 'gap' that needs to be filled – and what socio-legal researchers must demand – is in researcher support as part of ethical awareness, as a process.

The importance of my research team and colleagues in the ethical review process was crucial. Without it, I would otherwise have considered the ethical refusal as a total block to my project. Research teams and supervisory teams ought to empower and advise and give the benefit of their experience. Further, informed, frank, and honest training ought to be given on the process and its importance, as well as the 'correct tools' to navigate it during staff and doctoral training (Connor, Copland, and Owen, 2018: 411). In addition, as emo-tional support is a serious gap in ethical consideration (Connor, Copland, and Owen, 2018: 405), there ought to be consideration of the risks of isolation and the emotional impact of a project. Such personal risks to the researcher are largely ignored and not framed as an institutional responsibility. Acknowledgement of these risks ought not to be a block to a project, but used as an opportunity to be aware and equipped. I would encourage, where possible, researcher support groups as an informal mechanism where researchers are under-taking demanding fieldwork. Although there are, in some cases, codes of practice relating to fieldwork, these tend not to focus on the needs of the researcher, but rather, again, on the legal protection of the institution (LSE, n.d.). Having spoken on research ethics in various institutions, I can attest to the desire to have such informal networks, and there is certainly a will to build them. Researchers must take an active role in creating and maintaining them.

By the nature of socio-legal work, its ethical demands can change with the field. The ethical approval you have gained may not cover you for a sudden need to change your methodology. In my case, I had approval for a non-participant methodology, whereas, once in the field, it was clear that I would become a participant.[14] Before I left to do my field-work, I asked what to do if this should happen, to which I was advised that I would need to seek further emergency approval, which, of course, is unrealistic. In these circumstances, I would have to retrospectively justify this change at my viva. However, this is not

---

13 See Owen (2002) in relation to Canada, Wynn et al. (2014) and Connor, Copland, and Owen (2018) in rela-tion to Australia; De Wet (2010) regarding South Africa, and see de Jong, van Zwieten, and Willems (2012) regarding the Netherlands.

14 The 'line' between researcher and participant continues to be contested. The closer that the ethics review pro-cess finds you to being 'part of the field', the greater the ethical concern. This is not unproblematic, with the collapsing of this line simultaneously challenging assumptions about researcher objectivity, and engaging closer ethical scrutiny. For an approach in 'risky' sexuality work, see Brooks (2018). Getting close to the line will also see you more likely to engage a need for ethics review, under the ESRC FRE (see pp8–10).

a satisfactory position and again testifies to the inadequacy and inflexibility of the framework that we have and the gaps that remain.

Ethical awareness can be a challenging but rewarding process. Just because it is difficult and the process is inadequate does not mean that we should not engage with it. In fact, this means that engagement and confrontation are even more important. As De Wet argues, we need to turn this into a radically confrontational conversation around ethical awareness (De Wet, 2010: 313):

> We have to instill an 'open knowledge system' where unrestricted debate, contestation and room for difference are accommodated and not inhibited by fears of authoritarianism and a conservative hierarchy.

We need a sustained and critical attitude to these processes and, as such, we must engage with them. As I have argued and as De Wet argues, this full engagement cannot happen while RECs remain closed, and documents and policies that form the framework are drafted in a vacuum (De Wet, 2010: 313). This cultural shift and the desired overhaul of the entire institution that is ethics review are not going to happen without, I would argue, some confrontation with institutional power and its conservative and restrictive academic and pedagogical agendas. They will not be achieved otherwise than through a wholesale change of culture and a framing of risk and the building of support mechanisms for researchers – a process that is not a bureaucratic tick-box exercise of control (Sampson, 2017: 13). My advice to new socio-legal researchers is to be prepared for a fight, but that fight will be worth it.

Recommended reading

Victoria Brooks 'Fucking Law (A New Methodological Movement)' (2018) *Journal of Organizational Ethnography*, 7:1 31–43.

Christine Halse and Anne Honey 'Unravelling Ethics: Illuminating the moral dilemmas of research ethics' (2005) *Signs*, 30:4 2141–2162.

Janice Irvine 'Is Sexuality Research 'Dirty Work'? Institutionalized stigma in the production of sexual knowledge' (2014) *Sexualities*, 17:5–6 632–656.

Geraldine Lee-Treweek and Stephanie Linkogle (eds) *Danger in the Field: Risk and ethics in social research* (Routledge, 2001)

SLSA 'SLSA Statement of Principles of Ethical Research Practice' (2009) retrieved from www.slsa.ac.uk/images/slsadownloads/ethicalstatement/slsa%20ethics%20statement%20_final_%5B1%5D.pdf (accessed on 20 August 2018).

References

Onder Bakircioglu 'A Socio-Legal Concept of Jihad' (2010) *International and Comparative Law Quarterly*, 59:2 413–440.

Victoria Brooks 'Fucking Law (A New Methodological Movement)' (2018a) *Journal of Organizational Ethnography*, 7:1 31–43.

Michael M. Burgess 'Proposing Modesty for Informed Consent' (2007) *Social Science and Medicine*, 65 2284–2295

James Connor, Simon Copland, and Jill Owen 'The Infantilized Researcher and Research Subject: Ethics, consent and risk' (2018) *Qualitative Research*, 18:4 401–415.

Valerie De Craene, 'Fucking Geographers! Or the epistemological consequences of neglecting the lusty researcher's body' (2017) *Gender Place and Culture* 24:3 449–464.

Jean Phillipe de Jong, Myra van Zwieten, and Dick Willems 'Ethical Review from the Inside: Repertories of evaluation in Research Ethics Committee Meetings' (2012) *Sociology of Health and Illness*, 34:7 1039–1052.

Katinka De Wet 'The Importance of Ethical Appraisal in Social Science Research: Reviewing a Faculty of Humanities' Research Ethics Committee' (2010) *Journal of Academic Research Ethics*, 8 301–314.

ESRC 'ESRC Framework for Research Ethics' (2012) retrieved from https://esrc.ukri.org/files/funding/guidance-for-applicants/esrc-framework-for-research-ethics-2010/ (accessed on 20 August 2018).

Simon Flacks, 'Drugs Law Reform, Performativity and the Politics of Childhood' (2018) *International Journal on Drug Policy*, 51 56.

Christine Halse 'Confessions of an Ethics Committee Chair' (2011) *Ethics and Education*, 6:3 239–251.

Christine Halse and Anne Honey 'Unravelling Ethics: Illuminating the moral dilemmas of research ethics' (2005) *Signs*, 30:4 2141–2162.

Donna Haraway 'Situated Knowledges: The science question in feminism and the privilege of partial perspective' (1988) *Feminist Studies*, 14:3 575–599.

Adam Hedgecoe 'Reputational Risk, Academic Freedom and Research Ethics Review' (2016) *Sociology*, 50:3 486–501.

Janice Irvine 'Is Sexuality Research 'Dirty Work'? Institutionalized stigma in the production of sexual knowledge' (2014) *Sexualities*, 17:5-6 632–656.

Geraldine Lee-Treweek and Stephanie Linkogle (eds) *Danger in the Field: Risk and Ethics in Social Research* (London, New York: Routledge, 2001).

LSE 'A Code of Practice for the Safety of Social Researchers' (n.d.) retrieved from webcache. googleusercontent.com/search?q=cache:lPKOv1ULgQUJ:www.lse.ac.uk/intranet/LSEServices/healthAndSafety/documents/SRA_%2520safety_code_of_practice.doc+&cd=5&hl=en&ct=clnk&gl=uk (accessed on 31 August 2018).

Adrienne Massanari 'Rethinking Research Ethics, Power and the Risk of Visibility in the Era of the "Alt-Right" Gaze' (2018) *Social Media and Society*, 4:2 1–9.

Natasha S. Mauthner and Andrea Doucet 'Reflexive Accounts and Accounts of Reflexivity in Qualitative Data Analysis' (2003) *Sociology*, 37:3 413–431.

Esther Newton 'My Best Informant's Dress: The erotic equation in fieldwork' (1993) *Cultural Anthropology*, 8 3–23.

Sarah Nouwen '"As you set out for Ithaka": Practical, epistemological, ethical, and existential questions about socio-legal research in conflict' (2014) *Leiden Journal of International Law*, 27 227–260.

Michael Owen 'Engaging the Humanities? Research ethics in Canada' (2002) *Journal of Research Administration*, 33:3 5.

Elizabeth Peter and Judith Friedland 'Recognizing Risk and Vulnerability in Research Ethics: Imagining the "what ifs?"' (2017) *Journal of Empirical Research on Human Research Ethics*, 12:2 107–116.

Andreas Philippopoulos-Mihalopoulos and Victoria Brooks (eds) *Research Methods in Environmental Law: A Handbook* (Cheltenham, UK, and Northampton, MA: Elgar, 2017).

Helen Sampson '"Fluid Fields" and the Dynamics of Risk in Social Research' (2017) *Qualitative Research*, 19:2 1–17.

SLSA 'SLSA Statement of Principles of Ethical Research Practice' (2009) retrieved from www.slsa.ac.uk/images/slsadownloads/ethicalstatement/slsa%20ethics%20statement%20_final_%5B1%5D.pdf (accessed on 20 August 2018)

Katey Thom and Mary Finlayson 'They're Not Really Doing "Normal" Psychiatry: The socio-legal shaping of psychiatric expertise in insanity trials' (2011) *Psychiatry, Psychology and the Law*, 20:1 46–59.

University of Westminster 'Research Ethics Framework' www.westminster.ac.uk/research/research-framework/research-ethics (accessed on 31 August 2018).

Gema Varona 'Who Sets the Limits on Restorative Justice and Why? Comparative implications learnt from restorative encounters with terrorism victims in the Basque country' (2013) *Onati Socio-Legal Series* 4:3 550–572.

L.L. Wynn, Mark Israel, Colin Thomson, Karolyn White, and Louise Carey-White 'A National Survey of Experiences with Ethics Review (2014) *The Australian Journal of Anthropology* 25:3 375–377.

9

ON OBJECTIVITY AND STAYING 'NATIVE'

Researching LGBTQI+ lawyers as a queer lawyer

Marc Mason[*]

Introduction

As researchers we are often concerned that our research both is, and appears to be, objective. For lawyers, too, objectivity is lauded as both attainable and desirable. This chapter is concerned with a moment in the planning of a research project where I had a (brief) crisis of conscience about my own ability to be objective. Writing this chapter (and a conference paper[1] that preceded it) has allowed me to take that moment and use it to build my understanding of what I believe to be a crucially important issue that we as researchers sometimes take as given.

This chapter arises out of a project on LGBTQI+ barristers.[2] In undertaking this research we set out to look at the experiences of barristers who identified as LGBTQI+ in order to determine whether their sexuality played any role in their working lives, whether it lead to any disadvantages, and how they dealt with this aspect of their identity. We carried out a survey of 126 barristers, QCs, professional training students, and pupils. This survey was delivered online and publicized as widely as possible.[3] We followed this up with face-to-face or telephone interviews with 38 of the respondents,[4] using a semi-structured interview guide. These interviews lasted for approximately an hour each and allowed us to explore in more depth some of the issues that were arising out of the survey.

[*] I am grateful to Naomi Creutzfeldt, Kirsten McConnachie, and Victoria Brooks for their encouragement and comments on earlier drafts of this paper. I am also grateful to Alison Eardley for providing the conditions to work on a first draft of the paper during a writing retreat.

1 SLSA Annual Conference, Bristol University, 27–29 March 2018.
2 With Steven Vaughan (UCL).
3 We were concerned to publicise beyond the LGBT support and social networks at the Bar (Freebar and BLAGG) because we were anxious not to limit our sample to those barristers who in some way engage with those networks, and therefore might have a particular experience. We distributed the survey with the help of the Bar Standards Board, the Bar Council, and the Inns of Court.
4 The final question in our survey was an invitation to participate in face to face interviews.

The research is currently being written up, but preliminary findings have been published (Mason and Vaughan, 2017). Findings so far have crystallized around a few themes. Of most interest to the profession so far appears to have been the prevalence of homophobia at the Bar.[5] For example, we found that 26.5% of our respondents had experienced discrimination relating to their sexuality, sometimes, often, or frequently (a further 25.6% reporting it had occurred, but rarely). This can be compared with the general working population where Stonewall found that 19% of LGB employees had experienced verbal bullying because of their sexuality. The interviews allowed us to observe that barristers tended to minimize these incidents and were reluctant to confront prejudice.

More theoretically interesting, to me at least, was the way these barristers constructed their identities. We found that 58% of respondents had actively concealed their sexuality in a work context, and 40% had lied about it. When we explored this further in interviews, it was clear that barristers were recognizing the concealable nature of this characteristic, and also some questioned the propriety of being out in the workplace. Some gave explanations that revealed underlying constructions of the workplace as places free from sexuality, and of LGBTQI+ identities being solely about sex. The recent #metoo movement has given the lie to the first construction, as indeed did some of our other responses, and made it easier to see the way in which the hegemony of heterosexual masculinity renders it invisible, giving the impression of an absence of sexuality, and in doing so serves the needs of that hegemony.

The research also allowed us to explore some of the more subtle ways that LGBTQI+ sexualities bring disadvantages in this context, particularly if they remain concealed. These included descriptions of the added cognitive work that results from having to be guarded in conversations while networking as well as negative impacts on general well-being. Conversely there was clear indication that the ability to 'bring your whole self' to your work and your relationship with clients was an advantage of being out, and, from some, that there may be recognition of an ethical or political requirement to be out, either in solidarity with those who are unable to conceal their sexuality or as a general opportunity to push back against normativity in what is otherwise a strongly conservative profession.

The driver for this chapter is a consciousness that arose that I shared a particular social location with, or proximity to, the participants in the research. I had disclosed in the participant information sheet that I was a self-employed barrister who had practised at the Bar and I came to realize during the interviews that I had been assuming that others would make assumptions about my sexual orientation simply from my engagement in this research, and perhaps from other aspects of my behaviour and presentation that may be readable. In the planning of the research I had viewed my professional status and experience as a strength that allowed me to understand the working environment of the research participants, but I had not really viewed my sexual orientation in the same way. My initial gut reaction to this issue had been to question my suitability to do the research, driven by concerns that were, at root, about objectivity and, in particular (on closer examination), a concept of objectivity tied up with distance and detachment. It is these questions that were the initial spark for the reflection and reading described in this chapter.

---

5 Headlines included 'Inns of Court accused of not doing enough to combat homophobia as research uncovers discrimination' (Hilborne, 2017), and 'Senior barrister told BPTC student "I don't trust fags like you", shocking new LGBT+ research reveals' (King, 2017) (with similar in Wareham, 2017).

The starting point is a fairly traditional conceptualization of objectivity, an example of which is:

> Objectivity (Objectivist, objective) refers to the removal of the persona (emotions, knowledge, experience, values and so forth) of the researcher from the research process. It is seen as central to the quality of research based on epistemological assumptions that truth can be determined as something distinct from particular contexts or participants.
>
> *(Somekh and Lewin, 2005, p. 347)*

Objectivity has variously been attributed to knowledge claims which are better supported than competitors, procedures which are assumed to be fair, often due to their standardization, and types of knowledge seeking communities. It is commonly associated with the concept of neutrality (Harding, 2014).

This chapter is based then on the journey I followed from a fairly naïve perspective on this issue, a perspective that I believe more easily gives me useful access to a process of discovery of various viewpoints. These questions allowed me to explore the literature on objectivity in methodology, and I, of course, found a fairly rich literature, particularly from feminist scholarship (see below), but also from critical race theory and research concerned with colonialism and neo-colonialism (e.g. Wagle and Cantaffa (2008), Kanuha (2000), hooks (1989), Daza (2008), Whitinui (2014); see also Skeet, Chapter 20, this volume). Each of these, of course, has its own particular concern and focus, as does the queer approach, which is influential on my thinking here (and in general). Queer theory is notoriously resistant to definition, and indeed resistance to definition, boundaries, and normative structures is one of its paradigmatic features. As Berlant and Warner (1995) describe, 'queer theory is not the theory *of* anything in particular, and has no precise bibliographic shape' (p. 344). For me, queer theory's interest and character lies in its rejection of normativity, binarism, and fixity, which has roots in its interest in sexuality and gender, and related dynamics of power, control, violence, and resistance, but which has potential to deploy its tools beyond this. See, for example, Marinucci (2016) and Warner (1993) on meanings of queer, Butler (2002) on queering kinship and race, and Halberstam (2011) on queering the concept of failure and applying queer theory to neo-liberalism. Its suspicion of normativity and boundaries and sensitivity to power structures have clear utility when we are considering the concerns around the controlling nature of the rhetoric of objectivity which unfold over the course of this chapter.

This journey to a richer understanding of 'objectivity' broadly followed four stages, and the same route underpins the structure of this chapter. First, I had the fairly swift realization that sharing a social location[6] does not preclude a robust analysis of that social location. I arrived at this position initially through consideration of ideas of management or auditing of subjectivity and a recognition that access and trust can be obtained through a degree of matching. Here, too, there was also an inkling of recognition of the absurdity of the alternative: that only straight people can research queers, only men can research women, only white people can research people of colour, and, importantly, the observation that the converse of each of these does not appear to be the practice. Next came the realization that in fact striving for objectivism in the traditional sense has long been abandoned by many scholars. Third was the realization that there is a viewpoint that considers objectivism not

---

6 Alternatively sharing a characteristic of interest to the research.

only unnecessary, but also undesirable and damaging. Finally, there was the discovery of a range of positions that each conclude that researching with a recognition and, to some extent, a utilization of the self or subjectivity can be particularly enriching and empowering and can lead to ways of looking at research where other values come into play that may feel more like they relate to ethics than to epistemology *per se.*

Difficulties achieving objectivity and benefits of membership: auditing, access, authority, and the problem of categories

Auditing

Researchers such as Peshkin (1988) demonstrate an auditing approach to subjectivity, suggesting a 'formal, systematic monitoring of self' (p. 20). This is not limited to characteristics, but also includes transient preferences and tendencies, such as justice seeking or a tendency to want to rescue. Although Peshkin recognizes some benefits from his audited subjectivities, the general tenor here is that these are to be recognized so they can be guarded against or confessed. For example, he talks of taming his subjectivity and considers the importance of giving himself a warning against 'perceiving just that which my own untamed sentiments have sought out and served up as data' (p. 20). He also claims that it can avoid the sense of producing an 'in-house' work, which would convey both permission to write and an interest in the subject's well-being or case and would avoid the risk of 'going native' as he describes it.

Access/trust

Although auditing guards against the risks that a researcher's social proximity might pose, proximity also offers direct benefits to the research, which should be acknowledged. One of these is the trust that might be gained from participants. This was surely part of my motivation for including my professional status, but is also one that applies to other aspects of identity. The idea being that LGBTQI+ individuals are more likely to trust that aspect of their experience to someone who is also LGBTQI+. That, as a result, they are more likely to participate in the research, and when they do so their responses are more likely to be freer. Justifications for this have included perceptions that the researcher is less likely to be biased and more likely to be accurate, a reduction in power relations between researchers and participants, or the promise of more effective communication (Rhodes, 1994, and Gunaratnam, 2003, cited in McDonald, 2013).

This is an aspect of the research process where the concealable nature of sexual orientation brings with it particular issues. Sexual orientation can be performed in countless ways and, where performance is ambiguous, can be assumed. On a practical level, Wagle and Cantaffa (2008) describe how a researcher's gayness can become questioned when it is performed differently to the way that gayness is performed by participants. On an ethical level, questions also arise as to whether there is a duty to disclose relevant characteristics, particularly where these are mistakenly assumed, given that the argument relating to recruitment suggests that social proximity matters to respondents (McDonald, 2013).

Authority/voice

It has been argued that the only site from which knowledge claims can be made about a particular group is from within that group, primarily owing to proximity to the experiences observed and contextual understanding (Smith, 2008, cited in McDonald, 2013). Taking a more moderate approach, are we able to hold that certain identities have more authority in making certain truth claims? As bell hooks (1989) does, do we say that those outside the social location can write and research, but questions will remain as to whether they are the most authoritative? Standpoint epistemology, discussed further below, has been described as a performance of marginalized groups who are seen as having a more complete view precisely because of their marginality and the need that this brings for an awareness of the dominant perspective in order to survive (Nielsen, 1990, cited in King, 1999).

From this perspective, then, in addition to access to participants and their viewpoints, membership of the group also brings with it an insider knowledge that has the potential to lend authority to claims made. In this, we begin to see a switching of the status quo where the distance currently equated with objectivity begins to be an obstacle to knowledge. We also detect signs that closeness might offer something more important, which I will return to in the next section.

The problem of categories

Although the ideas around matching participants to researchers seem attractive, there is also some uneasiness here. When we take our participants to be solely the characteristic that we are examining, which we also share, we are neglecting to consider all their other facets, some of which might not be shared, and we are in danger of assuming a shared experience that may in fact be quite varied. Gestalt theory reminds us that individuals are part of a broader phenomenological field within which different aspects emerge from the ground to be figural, depending on the individual and their current circumstances (Joyce and Sills, 2018). Adopting a presumption of stability and homogeneity within any category (race, gender, sexual orientation, etc.) ignores the instability and heterogeneity that we know in fact exists. There is also, at first blush, something quite un-queer about all this talk of categories. Queer theory has a tendency towards breaking down stable categories (Berlant and Warner, 1995), yet here we are seen to be reifying them to justify our research methodologies. One response is to accept this, and to acknowledge it as a provisional and pragmatic essentialism, although perhaps here the terminology of distance becomes useful; rather than considering a binary of shared/not-shared, what we are in fact discussing are degrees of closeness. That my respondents and I identify as LGBTQI+ does not mean that we share an identity, but rather that our social position is closer, at least on one dimension, so that, in a multidimensional social space, we come into closer proximity than if we occupied a different position on that dimension. It becomes an acknowledgement of a propensity to shared narratives or histories, but not a guarantee. This does, however, require us to take a more nuanced approach to assessing the degree of authority a voice has. Letherby (2011) cautions us that, 'if we accept a position which implies that there is only one (real, accurate, best) experience this can only be built upon the suppression of less powerful voices' (p. 68).

The problem of objectivity

Although I have so far been discussing ways in which I found excuses for straying into territory that risks losing objectivity, there are stronger positions that can be taken that suggest that, far from excusing ourselves when we stray into this territory, we should be going further and be taking a sceptical, if not hostile, view of the notion of objectivity. Katz Rothman (2007) reminds us of the duty to offer more than a distant, uninvolved approach:

> Our work of sense-making is a basic human job, done traditionally through story-telling. Whether the stories we use are our own, or those of our informants, or those we cull from tables of statistically organized data, we remain story-tellers, narrators, making sense of the world as best we can. Our ethical obligations go beyond what we owe our subjects – as urgently important as it is to protect them, to preserve their privacy and their feelings. We owe something too, to our readers and to the larger community to which we offer our work. Among the many things we owe them, is an honesty about ourselves: who we are as characters in our own stories and as actors in our own research.
>
> *(p. 15)*

This line of thinking has been pursued further by the adoption of visual or spatial metaphors (see Layard, Chapter 17, this volume) for the traditional concept of objectivity. Haraway (1988) adopts a visual metaphor, one that is familiar in the sense that we are used to discussions of viewpoints and perspectives, and indeed it is these that we are often anxious to avoid when we strive for objectivity. She describes how the drawing of boundaries of inside/outside a certain position is a 'power move'. In this account, the claiming of objectivity is the leaping of an unmarked body into a conquering gaze that allows it (him) to see without being seen. In claiming objectivity, the researcher claims for himself an identity free from characteristics that would make the research suspect. This very logic can be seen to be based on the problematization of marginalized identities, which are seen as marked, and the valorization of majority identities, which are viewed as unmarked. The claim of objectivity becomes a 'god trick' of seeing from nowhere in particular, an unmarked position without limits or responsibility. For Haraway, a more properly objective approach entails accepting that any view is from a particular and specific embodiment. There is no 'view-from-nowhere' or 'view-from-everywhere'. To acknowledge that this view is from a particular embodiment would acknowledge that knowing is never complete, but rather is always partial and constructed or stitched together imperfectly.

Whereas Haraway (1988) utilizes a metaphor of vision to examine the power dynamics involved in objectivity, Heshusius (1994) utilizes distance. For Heshusius, traditional objectivity is associated with distance between participant and researcher and, additionally, with control of that distance over which the researcher is deemed to have both responsibility and power. The objective researcher is exhorted to maintain a distance from their subject. The dangerously close researcher is encouraged to take pains to confess that closeness, to manage it, and to maintain objective distance. Heshusius describes how, when we are confronted with subjectivity, we seek to exclude, manage, or restrain it, and therefore fulfil our desire for control. However, in doing so, we are missing out on an important way of knowing. Instead, Heshusius calls for a *participatory consciousness* where we embed ourselves in what we seek to understand through a recognition of kinship. She describes how this involves an attempt to *be with* the other: 'I had to completely and nonevaluatively observe my personal reactions and in that attentiveness, dissolve (rather than manage or restrain) them, which opened up a mode of access that was not there before' (p. 19). The description of participatory consciousness does not call for either a particular distance from *or* closeness to the subject; rather it calls for an attempt to see the lives of participants in a way that echoes Roger's (1959) concept of empathy: an attempt to enter the world of the respondent.

For both of these theorists, adopting a critical approach to the traditional concept of objectivity is not simply about knowing better (although this can be read into each). It is, in addition, about an ethical imperative to challenge objectivity and, therefore, to challenge the underlying power structures in which it is complicit. Heshusius (1994), for example, is critical of approaches that 'manage' subjectivity as legitimizing the purported link between knowing and control of distance and, in doing so, leaving hidden power inequalities unchallenged. Using Haraway (1988), we can quite clearly see the radical power of claiming a perspective. The practice of drawing attention to one's perspective, in saying 'This is the location from which I am making claims', draws attention to the situated nature of *all* claims, even those that claim to be from nowhere. We shine a light on the unmarked position and, in doing so, mark it. In claiming a location, therefore, we not only gain access to insights in our own particular research projects, but we challenge implicit claims that allow privileged access to assertions of purity of knowledge.

I argue that looking at these ideas of distance and vision through a queer (or even just LGBTQ+) lens allows us also to think about how the myth of objectivity operates within us as individual researchers. If I am exhorted to control my subjectivity, and if this control strategy is internalized (and, to operate effectively, it must be), then there must be one 'I' doing the constraining and another 'I' being constrained. Looking at this in relation to concealable identifications and shiftable locations such as queerness allows us to raise particularly interesting questions. When I was, at the spark of this chapter, questioning my standing to do research because of a threat to objectivity, was that the unmarked 'I' speaking? That 'I', after all, is simply a white, middle-class, Western, cis-male. Was that the unmarked 'I' silencing the queer 'I'? As a gay, white, middle-class, Western, cis-male I have immediate access to a privileged unmarked position simply by hiding away the first of those descriptors. But what is the cost of that? And what if the descriptor I needed to drop was one that was inscribed on my body (e.g. woman, black) and therefore could not be dropped so easily and with such confidence that it would not be reinserted by a reader. And, in answering those questions, do I again find kinship with, and answers from, my research participants? Do I step down from a position of power as the researcher and (metaphorically) ask my participants how to be? In doing so, to give me answers around the cost of adopting the unmarked position, I would listen to the participants who said:[7]

> that I think I've spent such a long time hating myself, a long time being shut away, a long time not being as productive as I can be because I wasn't being the person I'm supposed to be.
>
> *(P15)*

> I think it's really important because I remember how unhappy I really was in university when I wasn't out and the efforts I made to lie about it ... People are human beings, they're going to ask you about your life, you know, where you go, what you do and there's only so far you can continue to avoid it.
>
> *(B23)*

---

7 All quotes from participants drawn from the publication referenced at Mason and Vaughan (2017).

And so actually, a big part of working with someone to get them to the place where they will give of their best as a witness and in terms of giving instructions … Then, for me, that extra bit beyond the sort of pure intellectual evaluation and advice is about actually relating to them as a real person and trying to get the best out of them, or get them to the best place for something. And I don't know how I would do that if I didn't use 'me', and an honesty and an authenticity with them.

(QC39)

I would also hear the participants who said:

And then I'm thinking do I want to confuse the picture anymore being a black person, being somebody of 30, by adding to the fact that you're gay.

(P15)

I think sometimes it's impossible really to separate that from the fact that I'm an ethnic minority and a woman because sometimes there's so many things, so many factors that make me 'other' that that one is the only one that isn't immediately obvious. So sometimes I think selfishly I make my life a little bit easier by slightly avoiding any questions [on sexuality] or anything that could bring it up in context where I just don't want to deal with it, I just don't want to deal with the reaction or with the awkwardness that the other person then feels because they've made a heteronormative assumption and then feel flustered about it. Sometimes I just don't really want to deal with it. And I don't like that, it's not something I'm happy about in myself, but I must admit that does happen.

(S27)

In addition to the ethical issue of choosing to conceal when others cannot and thus being complicit in oppressional dynamics, and the practical issue of always being at risk of failing to conceal, there is also a personal cost. For example, the description of a socially desirable 'I' silencing a more truly felt 'I' echoes with theories from person-centred psychotherapy of discrepancies between an ideal self which becomes manifest and an organismic self which remains hidden, leading to psychological distress (Rogers, 1959). The pressure or decision to conceal therefore becomes deeply anti-therapeutic.

Presence in research

If, after considering all of the above, I am to reach the conclusion that 'objectivity' as traditionally defined is, at least not always, necessary, or, as I think I do, that it is a concept that I have an ethical duty to hold as suspect, then where do I go from here? What other approaches do I have when considering the validity of my own, and indeed others', research? Participatory consciousness, standpoint epistemology, strong objectivity, and theorized subjectivity all offer approaches that are, in places, subtly different but provide a menu from which to draw tools to deal with the issues raised above. In this section, I offer up a summary of each before considering how they build upon each other, in the hope that it will afford the reader the opportunity to explore these ideas further:

Participatory consciousness

Heshusius (1994) asks, 'Don't we reach out to what we want to know with all of ourselves, because we can't do anything else?' She calls for us to engage in participatory consciousness, a mode of being that seeks knowledge through recognition of kinship and a 'being with' the subject rather than attempting separation through managed subjectivity. As she describes,

> It refers to a mode of consciousness, a way of being in the world, that is characterized by what Schachtel (1959) calls "allocentric" knowing (as contrasted to autocentric knowing), a way of knowing that is concerned with both "*the totality of the act of interest*" and with the "participation of the total person" (of the knower).
>
> *(Heshusius, 1994, p. 16; original emphasis)*

Here then we have an approach with degrees of identification and merging, of rejection of the necessity of individuation, objectification, and indeed subjectification as starting points for knowing and acceptance of the self as being epistemically related to the other.

Standpoint epistemology

Here we see a range of approaches that are founded on an understanding that some social locations can facilitate access to knowledge whereas others are epistemic blockages (Hammersley, 2011). They take as their starting point a conflict model of society, recognizing social inequality, in contrast to the consensus model that forms the foundation of objectivism (Harding, 2014). In an approach that evokes Oscar Wilde's statement (voiced by Lord Darlington) 'We are all in the gutter, but some of us are looking at the stars' (Wilde, 1893, p. 93), part of the reasoning of this approach is that those in marginalized positions have easier access to unexamined assumptions of the dominant group, either through their lived experience, which in part runs contrary to these assumptions, or through experiencing the impact of these assumptions (King, 1999). The approach also draws on the idea that those in dominant groups tend to have much less motivation to examine these assumptions, as any effect they have on them is likely to be positive, whereas for marginalized groups accessing these insights can lead to liberation (Hammersley, 2011).

As discussed above, this approach, in common with others, raises some concerns; however, these are not insurmountable. For example, there is a need to find a way to avoid both homogenization of categories and a setting up of a hierarchy of oppressions. This approach also seemingly implies a real, accurate, best experience, and, as Letherby (2011) points out, this seems inevitably to be built upon the suppression of less powerful voices. However, if we consider Haraway's (1988) reminder that all knowledge is partial and needs to be stitched together, we do, to some degree, ameliorate this position. King (1999) uses three criteria to assess standpoint work: representation, identification, and affiliation. Representation refers to the degree to which the writing evokes or connects to the phenomena that motivated the writing. Identification refers to the pragmatic essentialism of deploying a category in order that that category can be represented. King (1999) points out that, if this is not done, then standpoint epistemology cannot be leveraged against the dominant ideology. Finally, affiliation is the positioning of the writer in relation to the identified category. King (1999) suggests, 'As a writer, I must find the part of my self(ves) that registers a trustworthy parallel to the experiences of the subject I am describing/interpreting', while acknowledging that 'trust is a discourse that is conditioned by effective use of language' (p. 487).

Strong objectivity

Building on standpoint epistemology, Harding (2014) suggests research should be evaluated based on who is putting forward a knowledge claim and what its implications are, including, but not limited to, knowledge production, so that we also look at emancipatory aims and expose background structures and assumptions to scrutiny. Strong objectivity does not seek to abandon the valorization of objectivity, but rather deploys the decoupling of the concepts of objectivity and neutrality, particularly as it observes the way that neutrality can mask the value-laden and knowledge-distorting interests that constitute a project (Hammersley, 2011). Harding (2014) emphasizes the importance of extending what we consider to be 'methodology', and what we therefore consider to need an objective approach, to beyond the start of the research project. This, therefore, would include, for example, the decision to pursue a particular problem and ignore another. Brooks, in this volume (Chapter 8), demonstrates the importance of also including consideration of ethics approval as part of the process of 'methodology'.

Theorized subjectivity

Some of the approaches above seem inclined to deny any special status of the researcher. Theorized subjectivity allows this back in, to a degree. In common with other approaches, it acknowledges the personhood of the researcher and, in fact, claims that doing so 'could feasibly lead to the conclusion that our work is more objective, in that our work, if not value-free is value-explicit' (Letherby, 2011, p. 70) in that it allows us to acknowledge both the inevitability of bias (even from the unmarked position) and the usefulness of reflection. This approach retains at least some of the kinship found in participatory consciousness, in that it acknowledges that we all, researcher and researched, theorize our own subjectivities, but it also recognizes that the researcher, when doing so, benefits from training in second-order theorizing and also will often have access to multiple accounts (for example, through interview-based research). This allows the researcher to make use of what has gone before, while also remaining open to use of their own subjectivity.

Here, then, we have a range of approaches that, in combination (or perhaps individually), offer us a way out of the objectivity trap while allowing us to maintain a robustness and a trust in our research processes. From standpoint epistemology, we have an empowering realization that actually a marginalized position can not only be valid, but can also be one that motivates and strengthens our abilities to see and be critical of normative assumptions and to make knowledge claims that are in fact more robust. Strong objectivity adds to that an additional criterion upon which we evaluate research: the degree to which it meets emancipatory aims. Participatory consciousness encourages us to do this in a way that allows us to be more fully with research participants, whereas theorized subjectivity provides an understanding of how we can do this, how we can acknowledge and use our subjectivity, be with the research participant, yet still bring in our training and our specific position as researchers (which, after all, is clearly a part of our own subjectivity).

Intersections

Although some of the benefits discussed have been related to the researcher's social proximity to, or shared characteristics with, the specific issue examined, others may be more transferable. In the former category, issues of access or trust, and to some degree authority and voice, are clearly built upon proximity between researcher and researched and the (perceived or actual) knowledge gained from the researcher's lived experience which may be specific to the issue of concern. However, some of the ideas discussed above hint at an opportunity to work across intersections. The god trick highlighted by Haraway as the mechanism by which power is taken by those who are 'unmarked' (1988) begins to be dismantled by the unmarked position being put into sharp relief against our open acceptance of our markings. This emancipatory action is of service regardless of the type of marking, and indeed is surely stronger when the revealed markings collectively appear across a number of dimensions. Similarly, Heshusius's (1994) rejection of managed subjectivity is explicitly aimed at dissolving the purported link between knowledge and control of distance, which is complicit in allowing this unmarked body to see and not be seen (Haraway, 1988). Again, it seems to matter not in which dimension this control of distance is operating (as it appears to operate in all), and any dissolution of it is therefore of benefit. However, in addition to this one-for-all approach focused on the dismantling or erosion of power structures that detriment each, there is also support for the idea that experience of one area of subjugation allows, to a degree, a stronger claim to research in an alternative area. Haraway (1988) explains that the subjugated position is a vantage point with an advantage: vision is better from below in the sense that the subjugated standpoint is not an innocent one but is much more likely to be on to the god trick generally. '"Subjugated" standpoints are preferred because they seem to promise more adequate, sustained, objective, transforming accounts of the world' (Haraway, 1988, p. 584). This would seem to be true regardless of which characteristic has led to the subjugation. I also take a lead from some of the research participants who expressed the way that subjugation can lead to empathy across characteristics – for example:

> I'm known as being someone with good client care skills, I'm a good listener, I'm told that I'm sympathetic and empathic ... is it the sexuality side of my personality coming through? I think I do feel a more rounded barrister in that sense because of my sexuality. ... I think that when you are a member of a minority, you have a better understanding of how majorities and minorities interrelate.
>
> *(B19)*

Conclusion

The relatively small, and momentary, doubt that started this chapter has led to a complete rethinking of the way I see objectivity and research more generally. And I suggest it is a momentary doubt that would not have been available to me had I not been a queer (or alternatively female, or black, or HIV+, or migrant, or disabled, etc.) researcher. Having been persuaded of not just the unhelpfulness, but also the damaging nature of the traditional concept of objectivity, the conceptualization related to distance and disinterest, I am left open to a range of ways of thinking differently about the robustness and the value of research. These new ways of thinking will shape my research and my research agenda and also shape the way I evaluate the research of others. In doing so, there is no abandoning of the demand for quality, but rather a change in the way that I evaluate that quality, both in my own work and in that of others. In doing so, I am taking what I believe to be a more ethical, critical, and thoughtful approach through the use of the approaches listed on pages 131–132, not doctrinally but in a way that allows and requires a deeper, more reflective evaluation of quality. The insights from standpoint feminism relating to the need to shine a light on the unmarked perspective align with the idea that

> [q]ueer commentary has involved a certain amount of experimenting, of prancing and squatting on the academic stage. This is partly to remind people that there is

an academic stage and that its protocols and proprieties have maintained an invisible heteronormativity, one that infiltrates our profession, our knowledge.

(Berlant and Warner, 1995, p. 348)

Similarly, the tendancy of queer theory to reject boundaries and the potential it has to deploy its modes of understanding beyond its roots in thinking about sexuality and gender also have echoes in the insight from Haraway (1988) that, '[t]he knowing self is partial in all its guises, never finished, whole, simply there and original; it is always constructed and stitched together imperfectly, and *therefore* able to join with another, to see together without claiming to be another' (p. 586). The synthesis of these insights calls more widely for an approach to knowledge that is vigilant to stories that we are told, and that we tell, about who we need to be as researchers and how we relate to and differ from those we research. An approach that considers how we, queerly, reach across, dissolve, and question the imagined boundaries that we find between 'us' and our subjects and between and within disciplines to strive perhaps towards a productively undisciplined (Halberstam, 2011) approach to socio-legal research.

Further reading

Haraway, D. (1988) 'Situated Knowledges: The Science Question in Feminism and the Privilege of Partial Perspective', *Feminist Studies*, 14(3), p. 575.

Harding, S. (2014) '"Strong Objectivity": A Response to the New Objectivity Question', *Synthese*, 104 (3), pp. 331–349.

Heshusius, L. (1994) 'Freeing Ourselves from Objectivity: Managing Subjectivity or Turning toward a Participatory Mode of Consciousness?', *Educational Researcher*, 23(3), pp. 15–22.

McDonald, J. (2013) 'Coming out in the Field: A Queer Reflexive Account of Shifting Researcher Identity', *Management Learning*, 44(2), pp. 127–143.

Warner, M. (1993) 'Introduction', in Warner, M. (ed.) *Fear of a Queer Planet*. Minneapolis: University of Minnesota Press, pp. vii–xxxi.

References

Berlant, L. and Warner, M. (1995) 'What Does Queer Theory Teach Us about X?', *PMLA*, 110(3), pp. 343–349.

Butler, J. (2002) 'Is Kinship Always Already Heterosexual?', *Differences*, 13(1), pp. 14–44.

Daza, S. L. (2008) 'Decolonizing Researcher Authenticity', *Race Ethnicity and Education*, 11(1), pp. 71–85.

Halberstam, J. (2011) *The Queer Art of Failure*. Durham, NC: Duke University Press.

Hammersley, M. (2011) 'Objectivity: A Reconceptualisation', in Williams, M. and Vogt, W. P. (eds.) *The SAGE Handbook of Innovation in Social Research Methods*. London: Sage, pp. 25–43.

Haraway, D. (1988) 'Situated Knowledges: The Science Question in Feminism and the Privilege of Partial Perspective', *Feminist Studies*, 14(3), p. 575.

Harding, S. (2014) '"Strong Objectivity": A Response to the New Objectivity Question', *Synthese*, 104 (3), pp. 331–349.

Heshusius, L. (1994) 'Freeing Ourselves from Objectivity: Managing Subjectivity or Turning toward a Participatory Mode of Consciousness?', *Educational Researcher*, 23(3), pp. 15–22.

Hilborne, N. (2017) 'Inns of Court Accused of Not Doing Enough to Combat Homophobia as Research Uncovers Discrimination – Legal Futures', *Legal Futures*. Available at: www.legalfutures.co.uk/latest-news/inns-court-accused-not-enough-combat-homophobia-research-uncovers-discrimination (accessed: 24 February 2019).

hooks, bell (1989) *Talking Back: Thinking Feminist, Thinking Black*. London: Sheba Feminist.

Joyce, P. and Sills, C. (2018) *Skills in Gestalt Counselling & Psychotherapy*. 4th edn. London: Sage.

Kanuha, V. K. (2000) '"Being" Native versus "Going Native": Conducting Social Work Research as an Insider', *Social Work*, 45(5), pp. 439–447.

Katz Rothman, B. (2007) 'Writing Ourselves in Sociology', *Methodological Innovation Online*, pp. 11–16.

King, J. R. (1999) 'Am Not! Are Too! Using Queer Standpoint in Postmodern Critical Ethnography', *International Journal of Qualitative Studies in Education*, 12(5), pp. 473–490.

King, K. (2017) 'Senior Barrister Told BPTC Student "I Don"t Trust Fags like You', Shocking New LGBT+ Research Reveals – Legal Cheek', *Legal Cheek*. Available at: www.legalcheek.com/2017/09/senior-barrister-told-bptc-student-i-dont-trust-fags-like-you-shocking-new-lgbt-research-reveals/ (accessed: 24 February 2019).

Letherby, G. (2011) 'Feminist Methodology', in Williams, M. and Vogt, W. P. (eds.) *The SAGE Handbook of Innovation in Social Research Methods*. London: Sage, pp. 62–79.

Marinucci, M. (2016) *Feminism Is Queer: The Intimate Connection between Queer and Feminist Theory*. London: Zed Books.

Mason, M. and Vaughan, S. (2017) *Sexuality at the Bar: An Empirical Exploration into the Experiences of LGBT+ Barristers in England & Wales*. Available at: https://westminsterresearch.westminster.ac.uk/item/q2w44/sexuality-at-the-bar-an-empirical-exploration-into-the-experiences-of-lgbt-barristers-in-england-wales (accessed: 20 February 2019).

McDonald, J. (2013a) 'Coming Out in the Field: A Queer Reflexive Account of Shifting Researcher Identity', *Management Learning*, 44(2), pp. 127–143.

Peshkin, A. (1988) 'In Search of Subjectivity – One's Own', *Educational Researcher*, 17(7), pp. 17–21.

Rogers, C. R. (1959) 'A Theory of Therapy, Personality, and Interpersonal Relationships, as Developed in the Client-Centered Framework', in Koch, S. (ed.) *Psychology: A Study of a Science. Study 1, Volume 3: Formulations of the Person and the Social Context*. New York: McGraw Hill, pp. 184–256.

Schachtel, E. G. (1959) *Metamorphosis. On the Development of Affect, Perception, Attention and Memory*. New York: Basic Books.

Somekh, B. and Lewin, C. (2005) *Research Methods in the Social Sciences*. London: Sage.

Wagle, T. and Cantaffa, D. T. (2008) 'Working Our Hyphens Exploring Identity Relations in Qualitative Research', *Qualitative Inquiry*, 14(1), pp. 135–159.

Wareham, J. (2017) 'Senior Lawyers Tell Gay Students: "I don't Trust Fags like You"', *Gay Star News*. Available at: www.gaystarnews.com/article/gay-lawyers-facing-homophobia/#gs.o6CrzNn3 (accessed: 24 February 2019).

Warner, M. (1993) 'Introduction', in Warner, M. (ed.) *Fear of a Queer Planet*. Minneapolis: University of Minnesota Press, pp. vii–xxxi.

Whitinui, P. (2014) 'Indigenous Autoethnography: Exploring, Engaging, and Experiencing "Self" as a Native Method of Inquiry', *Journal of Contemporary Ethnography*, 43(4), pp. 456–487.

Wilde, O. (1893) *Lady Windermere's Fan*. 2009 reprint. Auckland, NZ: Floating Press.

10

THE POLITICS OF RESEARCH IMPACT

A Scottish case study

Kath Murray

Introduction: the impact agenda

The research impact agenda can be traced back to the 1993 UK White Paper *Realising Our Potential*, which put forward the argument that science, technology and engineering research should contribute more directly to the economy and society (Office of Science and Technology, 1993). The introduction of 'research impact' in the 2014 UK Research Excellence Framework (REF; the national appraisal mechanism for assessing university research) established the concept as a key institutional metric,[1] putting impact squarely on the social science agenda. By dint of this process, impact is now key to research funding. Boswell and Smith explain:

> accounts of the work that will be undertaken to achieve research impact ('pathways to impact') now form a significant section of grant application processes for the UK funding councils. The upshot is that obtaining core research funding and pro-ject-specific grants from publicly funded sources in the UK is now strongly dependent on researchers' abilities to respond adequately to questions about the non-academic value of their work.
>
> *(2017: 2)*

The key underpinning principle is accountability, coupled with utility. There are, as Ferguson points out, 'sound moral, ethical and financial arguments that publicly-funded academics should use their training and activities for the good of society' (2014: n.p.). The other side of the coin, as some academics have cautioned, is that the impact agenda, and attendant funding implications carries risks relating to academic freedom and agenda-setting, including the selection of research questions, and how 'institutions and academics prioritise their work' (ibid.). There is, for instance,

> a risk that current research funding policies, in the pursuit of short-term economic impact, may encourage a devaluation of basic research, and result in decisions to

---

1 Currently, the REF awards 20% of overall scores to institutions based on case studies of research impact (Boswell and Smith, 2017).

abandon, overlook or ignore research that may not yield immediate payoffs or solve concrete problems.

(Ibid.; see also Faust, 2010)

Partnership or legally binding contract working may also influence or restrict how evidence is disseminated (Walters and Presdee, 1998: 64; Hope and Walters, 2008: 15–19). In relation to policing research, Fyfe and Richardson observe that, although 'closer collaboration with police organisations brings many new research opportunities', it also creates challenges in terms of maintaining critical distance from sponsors (2018: 158; see also McAra, 2017). In a similar vein, academic discourse may be softened or 'tamed' by policy stakeholders (McAra, 2017: 785), findings used selectively, or publications released strategically (usually on a Friday) to minimise media or political scrutiny. As Hope and Walters state: 'When academics commissioned by government fail to produce the results which reinforce existing government policy and practice, the authorities will cherry-pick and highlight the most positive aspects of the research' (2008: 18). By the same agenda-setting logic, potentially sensitive research may simply fail to materialise, given that controversial or sensitive topics or projects are less likely to find willing partners, secure funding, gain access to data or take hold with policymakers. Although UK academic policy is to embed 'knowledge transfer as a permanent core activity in universities' (Pardoe, 2014: 1), as this chapter shows, it is clear that there is some evidence that stakeholders would prefer not to be transferred.

Set against the backdrop of major police reform in Scotland, namely the establishment of a single police service (Police Scotland) under the Scottish National Party (SNP) administration in April 2013, this chapter provides insights into the dynamics and politics of research impact in Scotland. The chapter is structured as follows. The first section looks at research impact within the context of Scottish criminal justice, and some of the broader policy and political challenges and obstacles. Building on these observations, the main body of empirical analysis, in the second section, examines the relationship between police reform in Scotland and the production and dissemination of critical policing research. To begin, the narrative describes the shift in the policing 'climate' (Loader and Sparks, 2010) as a result of police reform in 2013, from a 'cool', low-scrutiny environment to a heated climate, marked by intense political and media scrutiny (Murray and Harkin, 2017). Using a personal case-study approach, the narrative then shows how this shift impacted on my own doctoral research on stop and search in Scotland, undertaken between 2010 and 2014. The timing of the research is significant insofar that it coincided with the transition to a single force and the resulting politicisation of Scottish policing. The narrative describes the ease with which the fieldwork was carried out under the eight legacy forces and, conversely, how Scottish government and senior police officials sought to close down the findings under the newly established single police service (for a detailed account of these events, see Murray, 2017). Drawing the strands of analysis together, the chapter concludes with a commentary on the politics of research impact and some of the challenges of undertaking policing research under a single police force structure.

Research impact: challenges and obstacles

The practical challenges in relation to securing research impact are well established. By the same token, there are also a range of established strategies and guidelines available to social science researchers aimed at dealing with these challenges, including the well-established

Economic and Social Research Council (ESRC) Impact Toolkit (see also Reed, 2018). One of the main difficulties or challenges stems from the fact that policy-making is messy, often politicised and generally unpredictable. As Ferguson (2014: n.p.) observes, 'economic, political and social needs and priorities constantly change and cannot be accurately predicted in advance'. Nor are policymakers likely to engage with a single source of evidence (Cairney and Kwiatkowski, 2017). Drawing from psychology and policy theory, Cairney and Kwiatkowski (2017) set out various practical strategies to secure impact, from tailoring findings to different audiences to exercising discretion in order to exploit 'windows of opportunity' (Kingdon, 1984). Cognisant that the route to securing impact usually hinges on good relationships, trust and constructive engagement with policy partners, Cairney and Kwiatkowski also caution that speaking 'truth to power' may be counterproductive and – echoing Loader and Sparks's 'democratic underlabourer' or 'criminological diplomat' (2010: 146) – advise that 'effective engagement requires preparation, diplomacy, and good judgement as much as good evidence' (2017: 2; see also Turner, 2013). Yet, as the account in this chapter suggests, when research evidence is perceived as unpalatable or presents a threat to political, institutional and personal reputations, it may be that a more challenging or public approach is the only viable way for researchers to secure policy impact.

Post-devolution Scotland: criminology and the politics of research impact

Recent analysis by McAra (2017) provides useful insights into research impact in practice and captures the precarious relationship between academics and criminal justice policymakers in post-devolution Scotland. Tracing the shifting relationship between the Academy and the Scottish government, McAra (2017) details how key research findings from the Edinburgh Study of Youth Transitions and Crime (ESYTC)[2] on the criminogenic effects of the criminal justice system failed to gain traction under the early post-devolution Labour–Liberal administration. Situated within a youth justice policy landscape that broadly mirrored the Blairite 'respect' agenda,[3] as McAra explains, 'much academic research ran counter to the populist imperatives of a new government striving for legitimacy, and thus the influence of many scholars diminished', and the 'rising impact of the specialist advisor politicized the evidence base, with policy change being supported by partial readings of criminological knowledge or outright rejection' (2017: 784).

The election of a minority SNP administration in 2007 appeared to signal a shift in the relationship with the Academy, with the SNP government 'utilizing research evidence to build the intellectual case for "compassionate justice" as a distinctively Scottish approach to matters of crime and punishment' (ibid.: 772–3), thereby bringing the wider academic community into 'close dialogue with government and key institutions'. It is within this political setting that the ESYTC findings took hold and came to shape flagship Scottish government youth justice policies, notably the Whole Systems Approach (WSA) to youth offending, aimed at diversion and keeping young people out of the criminal justice system, and Early and Effective Intervention policies. Reflecting on this timeline, McAra observes that the 'Scottish experience has shown that research findings are generally only "listened" to and

2 The ESYTC is a large-scale longitudinal study of young people's pathways in and out of offending.
3 As part of the Respect Agenda, the 1997 Labour government introduced a range of sanctions including Anti-Social Behaviour Orders (ASBOs), curfew and dispersal powers, and parenting contracts and orders.

acted upon in very specific circumstances, namely where there is an intersection between the aims of government or specific institutional leaders and the criminological evidence' (ibid.: 784). Put another way, whether criminal justice researchers secure a foot in the policy door is likely to depend on, among other factors, political ideologies and priorities.

Although a more compassionate approach can be evidenced across a range of justice policies in Scotland, as McAra flags, there are nonetheless areas of contradiction, as well as 'evidence that Ministers will continue to play to populist pressures where this is perceived to have political traction' (ibid.: 773–4). The influence of the specialist advisor remains writ large in Scottish politics, with a small increase from twelve to fourteen advisors between the 2006 Labour–Liberal administration and the current SNP administration, and various policies remain out of kilter with the 'compassionate' narrative. Despite laying claim to a human rights-based agenda, until recently Scotland had one of the lowest minimum ages of criminal responsibility (MACR) in the world – just eight years. In 2019 the Scottish Parliament passed the Age of Criminal Responsibility (Scotland) Bill, which raised the MARC to twelve years – deemed the absolute minimum acceptable standard by the United Nations Convention on the Rights of the Child over a decade ago (UNCRC, 2007). It is, however, striking that it has taken nearly two decades to address a policy that runs counter to a wide body of research evidence (see Sutherland, 2016) and has real consequences in terms of future life chances, for what appear to be reputational reasons (Murray, forthcoming). In the penal field, rates of imprisonment in Scotland remain 'staggeringly high' (Howard League Scotland, 2018),[4] with nearly a fifth (18.7%) of the daily prison population in 2017 made up of people on remand (Scottish Parliament Justice Committee, 2018: 12). The Scottish government has also resisted ongoing calls to introduce prisoner voting, despite a series of European Court of Justice rulings that state that the UK ban on prisoners voting violates the European Convention on Human Rights (*Guardian*, 2018).

Arguably the most contradictory or unstable area of criminal justice policy in Scotland relates to the policing field, which has seen a temporal and geographical mix of both progressive and enforcement policies, from the widely acclaimed public health approach taken by Scotland's Violence Reduction Unit circa 2005 and onward and constructive use of 'campus cops' (Black et al., 2010) to hard-line approaches to stop and search and target-driven use of fixed penalties under the legacy Strathclyde police force (*Telegraph*, 2010). With its roots in the 'high levels of social and political conflict' in early twentieth-century Glasgow (Sparks et al., 2017), of particular significance here is the robust policing approach adopted in the Glasgow–Strathclyde area, which, as detailed next, transferred to Police Scotland under Scotland's first chief constable, Sir Stephen House, former chief constable of Strathclyde police force. Set against the backdrop of police reform in Scotland, the narrative shows how critical research on the intensive use of stop and search clashed with the dominant policing ideologies and strategies adopted by the new single service, and how, by dint of external political and media pressure, the research nonetheless gained a foothold, prompting legislative change.

Knowledge production and dissemination in hot and cold climates

The amalgamation of Scotland's eight forces into a single service in 2013 transformed the Scottish policing environment from a 'cool' climate, with low scrutiny and minimal political

---

4 Scotland has the ninth highest imprisonment rate in Europe according to Eurostat data (House of Commons Library, 2018).

engagement, to a heated and deeply politicised climate marked by contestation and intense media interest (Murray and Harkin, 2017). High-profile issues included the national roll-out of a Strathclyde-style enforcement-focused performance regime characterised by volume stop and search, the use of armed police on routine duties, as well as related concerns around accountability and a perceived democratic deficit (Loveday, 2018). As a rough marker of the instability brought about by reform, Scotland saw the departure of two chief constables (both in controversial circumstances), two Scottish Police Authority (SPA) chairs, two justice secretaries, several Police Scotland and SPA directors, and several SPA board members within the first five years of the new single service (Murray and Malik, forthcoming). With Scottish policing recast as a party-political SNP project and measure of government competency, reform broke the 'fundamental consensus around policing matters which had prevailed for much of the latter part of the twentieth century and early part of the twenty-first century' (Fyfe, 2015: 43) and brought reputational factors to the fore.

As detailed next, reform also changed the dynamics around academic research, introducing what might be described as a sense of nervousness and defensiveness around the production of critical academic knowledge. Drawing on personal experience, the narrative describes how my doctoral research on the uses of stop and search in Scotland proceeded smoothly under the eight-force legacy arrangement and, conversely, how Scottish government and senior police officials sought to 'neutralise' the findings in the heated post-reform climate (Mathiesen, 2004).

Knowledge production in a cool climate: researching stop and search

I began work on the doctorate[5] in 2010, under the long-standing eight-force structure (which dated back to 1975 and the regionalisation of local government). The main body of research and fieldwork was undertaken between 2011 and 2013, with final interviews in March 2013, just a few weeks ahead of the transition to a single service in April 2013. The key findings were published in January 2014, within the first year of the new single service (Murray, 2014), and the thesis was submitted in September 2014.

Aimed at explaining the rise of stop and search in Scotland, the project employed a range of qualitative and quantitative data sources and methods, including: statistical analysis of stop and search data detailing approximately 1.5 million encounters recorded between 2005 and 2010; analysis of thirty semi-structured interviews with serving and retired officers across a range of ranks; documentary analysis of secondary historical sources, including Hansard parliamentary transcripts, Cabinet papers and records lodged in the National Archives of Scotland; documentary analysis of press reports, police policy literature and police training guidelines; and observations of classroom training and a practical stop and search training session at the national Scottish Police College.

For the most part, the fieldwork proceeded smoothly. Senior officers spoke on the record and suggested further relevant contacts, and the legacy forces (Strathclyde, Lothian and Borders, Tayside) facilitated the research process, arranging interviews and, at times, assisting with travel. The Scottish Police College organised observation of stop and search training sessions, and each of the eight forces provided stop and search data in varying degrees of detail. Although the data requests were made under Freedom of Information

---

5 Case studentship, jointly funded by the ESRC and Scottish government.

legislation, many forces went over and above the basic requirements – for instance, the legacy Strathclyde force provided data formatted in SPSS.[6]

As the fieldwork progressed, it became apparent the project would be controversial and most likely high profile – albeit not in a way envisaged in the standard 'pathway to impact'. To briefly explain, at the time, the use of stop and search in Scotland was absent from the policing and political, described by one senior officer as a 'non-issue'.[7] Nonetheless, analysis of police force data showed a sharp rise in recorded searches between 2005 and 2010, with per capita search rates outstripping those in England and Wales nearly four times over by 2010. It was also evident that recorded searches fell disproportionately on teenagers. For instance, in 2010, search rates for sixteen-year-olds in the legacy Strathclyde police force outstripped the number of sixteen-year-olds. Related to these findings, the tactic was under-regulated, with most recorded searches undertaken on a non-statutory basis (without legal authority and nominally premised on consent).[8] Furthermore, in the absence of routinely published statistics or receipts for those searched, the tactic was unaccountable at an institutional and officer level. Aimed at providing key stakeholders[9] with adequate time to engage with the undoubtedly difficult emerging findings and to advise that the research would be published at some stage, the findings were shared in meetings and presentations between November 2012 and December 2013, thereby straddling the transition to a single force.

Knowledge dissemination in a heated climate

Just as the cooler climate of the eight-police-force structure facilitated the doctoral fieldwork, the heated climate of the single force at the point of dissemination had the opposite effect. In January 2014, the Scottish Centre for Crime and Justice Research published the key findings in an open-access report (Murray, 2014). Rejecting the key findings, senior officers developed a sixteen-point plan (Hutcheon, 2015b) aimed at setting the news agenda, pre-empting the report and managing critical opinion via a 'professional media messaging' campaign (Murray 2017: 511). Implemented in conjunction with government officials, the main plank of the strategy involved a national press conference staged two days ahead of the report's publication, at which the justice secretary announced new (and exceptionally high) stop and search figures to journalists and promoted the perceived benefits of the volume approach now adopted by Police Scotland. The attempt to close down the research was not, however, lost on the Scottish press (see also Hutcheon, 2015a, 2015b):

> Police Scotland knew a critical report on the tactic was imminent; they opted to pre-empt it. Justice Secretary Kenny MacAskill joined the single service at an event

---

6 This was owing to the volume of records, which exceeded the capacity of an Excel spreadsheet at the time.

7 This 'absence' became a key line of enquiry. The analysis showed how the standard coupling of stop and search and 'race' had blinded government and policing officials to the disproportionate impact of unregulated search practices on white working-class communities and argued that a failure to introduce basic accountability mechanisms or regulations allowed the tactic to flourish unimpeded.

8 In England and Wales, non-statutory stop and search was prohibited in 2003 owing to concerns about the 'consent' mechanism. See Police and Criminal Evidence Act 1984 (Codes of Practice) (Statutory Powers of Stop and Search) Order 2002, SI 2002/3075. See now Code A para.1.5.

9 These included the legacy Strathclyde police force, which accounted for about 80% of recorded searches and was alerted to the findings at an early stage, the Scottish government, Police Scotland, HM Inspectorate of Constabulary in Scotland and the Scottish Police Authority.

in Fife to welcome new national stop and search figures two days before the report, published by University of Edinburgh academic Kath Murray, entered the public domain. Given Murray's PhD project was funded by the Economic and Social Research Council (ESRC) together with the Scottish Government, the release date wasn't a secret. Indeed, asked by *Holyrood* if the two occurring in the space of 72 hours was purely a coincidence, assistant chief constable Wayne Mawson struggled to keep a straight face. It is not to say that Police Scotland's point of view on the tactic, which has been subject to sustained criticism since the single force came into being, is not valid. It is simply to say that the defensive display on show last month only helped to fuel claims that it is unwilling to listen to alternative ones.

(Robertson, 2014, n.p.)

Pathways to impact

Whereas evidence from the ESYTC had intersected with the ideological aims of the new SNP administration and gained support (McAra, 2017), in the case of intensive stop and search, the research evidence ran directly counter to the established Police Scotland and Scottish government position, promoting a hostile response. Both police and government officials remained wedded to the tactic – as a 2011 SNP manifesto commitment and signature policy of Chief Constable Sir Stephen House – and expressed no disquiet at the volume of recorded searches and lack of regulation or accountability (Salmond, 23 January 2014). Spinning the findings as evidence of the Scottish government's diversionary approach to youth justice, one official suggested: 'From a policy perspective (if this is the line taken) I think there is a need to link this to the wider [Scottish government] policy under [WSA] and keeping children out of the justice system' (email correspondence, cited in Murray, 2017: 513).

In practice, the Scottish government and Police Scotland's response meant the more conventional route to impact via diplomacy, negotiation and engagement with internal stakeholders remained closed. Nevertheless, via engagement with external stakeholders, the findings took hold in the media and Scottish Parliament and gained traction in the third sector, prompting criticism from the UN Human Rights Committee (*Guardian*, 2015). With mounting media and political pressure, the publication of a highly critical review by HM Inspectorate of Constabulary in Scotland in March 2015 acted as the final tipping point (HMICS, 2015). Broadly consistent with the original research findings and recognising the urgent need for reform, the review prompted the Scottish government to appoint an Independent Advisory Group (IAG) to review the regulation of stop and search and make recommendations to ministers. Passed in December 2015, the Criminal Justice (Scotland) Act 2016 enacted the IAG recommendations in full (Scott, 2015), thereby putting stop and search on a statutory basis, establishing a Statutory Code of Practice and bringing the era of under-regulation to a close.

Conclusion and further reading

Although the events detailed herein are undoubtedly an outlier, for the Academy, the account raises some difficult observations about the more uncomfortable pathways to impact that remain largely unacknowledged in the literature. First, from a personal perspective, producing research that publicly challenges existing institutional arrangements and powerful state actors is unnerving, stressful and at times, frightening. Although impactful in policy and legislative terms, the research also burned bridges and undoubtedly closed doors. In this respect, the account raises awkward questions about researcher status and the professional tensions that underpin the production and dissemination of critical research. Although 'outsider' status may afford researchers the freedom to articulate difficult issues in public, it can come at a professional and personal cost, arguably more so for postgraduate or early career researchers employed on insecure or precarious contracts. Outsider status is unlikely to be conducive to the type of networking that smooths and facilitates the research process, nor by the same token, is it conducive to longer-term career advancement. These reputational dynamics are more likely to be exacerbated in a small country such as Scotland, with its small, close-knit policy communities where most groups 'describe a fairly small world' and the 'usual story of everybody knowing everybody else' (Keating et al., 2009: 57, cited in Cairney, 2011: 79).

Second, there is a disjuncture between the type of output required by universities for career advancement (peer-reviewed journal publications, book chapters) and the output most likely to secure policy impact: open-access reports, briefings, blogs and social media. Both are time-consuming to produce, yet the latter carries little if any weight within the 'publish or perish' academic culture (Rawat and Meena, 2014). There is also a stark difference between defending an argument within the confines of the academic sector and/ or within closed policy circles and taking a public stance. Although social media strategies are part of the standard impact toolkit, maintaining or defending a position in this way can also open researchers to difficult exchanges and/or abusive comments.

Finally, the account provides insights into the dynamics of research impact under a single police service. It is clear that the single police service structure in Scotland has, at least potentially, significant implications for the production and dissemination of research and, relatedly, for academic impact. That governments and organisations sometimes seek to influence academic knowledge is not new (Loader and Sparks, 2010: 64). Yet, in Scotland, the single-force structure and concentration of power at the centre have greater salience in relation to the dynamics underpinning knowledge production and dissemination compared with less centralised arrangements. Crucially, a single force means a single point of access for researchers and reliance on gatekeeping practices that, in the heated post-reform climate, are more likely to be attuned to reputational implications compared with in the legacy era, as well as individual researcher reputations. Although it is not possible to nail down definitively, there is an anecdotal sense among policing researchers that research access in the post-reform era has become harder, with more hoops and hurdles. Nor is having a name for controversial research necessarily helpful in this respect.

The proximity of the police and the Scottish government, whereby the performance of the single police service is viewed as a measure of government competency, means research findings are more likely to be framed or spun in ways that lessen the possibility of research impact and/or diminish issues. For instance, Fyfe and Richardson describe how a Scottish government-funded evaluation of police reform was:

> carefully framed by the Government as an assessment of progress towards achieving its three strategic objectives for reform in terms of reduced duplication of back office services; improved access to national capacity and specialist expertise; and strengthened connections with communities [... whereas in fact the] reports make clear, however, that is not possible to reach any definitive conclusions in relation

to whether the aims of reform have been achieved but it has been able to highlight areas where there are continuing challenges and a lack of evidence.

(2018: 157)

These dynamics are likely to reinforce the overarching direction of policing research in the UK, whereby critical and theoretical work is 'eclipsed quantitatively by pragmatic policy orientated police research on crime control' (Reiner, 2010: 14). Arguably, one of the unintended consequences of the impact agenda is that critical research tends to be sidelined by research and funding arrangements premised on consensus partnerships between academics and stakeholders, or research *for* the police (Reiner, 2010; Squires, 2016). The upshot is that issues that might be viewed as the mainstay of critical criminology, at the time of writing, seem more likely to be taken up by investigative journalists than academic researchers.[10] For example, in Scotland there is relatively little critical academic research on policing structures and accountability mechanisms[11] or the discretionary exercise of police powers. This is not intended to critique more instrumentalist problem-solving approaches to policing research or the series of disciplines that constitute crime science. The overarching argument is about maintaining a range of perspectives and, importantly, providing robust research structures and mechanisms for academics to raise and address challenging questions.

Suggested further readings

Bastow, S., Dunleavy, P., and Tinkler, J. (2014) *The Impact of the Social Sciences: How Academics and Their Research Make a Difference*. London: Sage.

Hope, T. (2004) 'Pretend it works: Evidence and governance in the evaluation of the reducing burglary initiative', *Criminal Justice* 4 (3): 287–308.

McAra, L. (2017) 'Can criminologists change the world? Critical reflections on the politics, performance and effects of criminal justice', *British Journal of Criminology* 57: 767–788.

Murray, K. (2017) "Why have we funded this research?': On politics, research and newsmaking criminology', *Criminology and Criminal Justice* 17 (5): 507–525.

Turner, E. (2013) 'Beyond "facts" and "values": Rethinking some recent debates about the public role of criminology', *British Journal of Criminology* 53: 149–166.

References

Black, C., Homes, A., Diffley, M., Sewel, K., Chamberlain, V., and Ipsos MORI Scotland (2010) *Evaluation of Campus Police Officers in Scottish Schools*. Edinburgh: Scottish Government.

Boswell, C. and Smith, K. (2017) 'Rethinking policy 'impact': Four models of research–policy relations', *Palgrave Communications* 3. Available: www.nature.com/articles/s41599-017-0042-z

Cairney, P. (2011) *The Scottish Political System since Devolution from New Politics to the New Scottish Government*. Exeter: Imprint Academic.

Cairney, P. and Kwiatkowski (2017) 'How to communicate effectively with policymakers: Combine insights from psychology and policy studies' *Palgrave Communications* 37. Available: www.nature.com/articles/s41599-017-0046-8

Faust, D. (2010) *The role of the university in a changing world*, transcript of speech at the Royal Irish Academy, Trinity College, Dublin, 30 June [Online]. Available: www.harvard.edu/president/speech/2010/role-university-changing-world (accessed 17 July 2014).

10 Scottish policing issues taken up by investigative journalists include police access to mobile phone data, covert policing methods and the policing of animal rights activists.
11 See Malik (2017) for a notable example, and also Loveday (2018).

Ferguson, M. (2014) *The Research Impact Agenda: Defining, demonstrating and defending the value of the social sciences*. Australian Review of Public Affairs. Available: www.australianreview.net/digest/2014/08/ferguson.html

Fyfe, N. (2015) 'Policing Scotland post-reform; towards a shifting 'culture of control' and a new politics of policing', in Croall, H., Mooney, G., and Munro, M. (eds.) *Crime, Justice and Society in Scotland*. Abingdon: Routledge.

Fyfe, N. and Richardson, N. (2018) 'Police reform, research and the uses of "expert knowledge"', *European Journal of Policing Studies* 5 (3): 147–161.

Guardian (2015) 'UN human rights body criticises police stop-and-search powers in Scotland.' 24 July 2018.

Guardian (2018) 'Sturgeon pressed to allow prisoners to vote in Scottish elections.' 14 May 2018. Available: www.theguardian.com/uk-news/2018/may/14/sturgeon-pressed-allow-prisoners-vote-scottish-elections

HMICS (HM Inspector of Constabulary in Scotland). (2015) *Audit & Assurance Review of Stop and Search: Phase 1*. Edinburgh: HMICS.

Hope, T. and Walters, R. (2008) *Critical Thinking about the Uses of Research*. London: Centre for Crime and Justice Studies

House of Commons Library. (2018) *UK Prison Population Statistics*, Briefing paper CBP-04334. Available: http://researchbriefings.files.parliament.uk/documents/SN04334/SN04334.pdf

Howard League Scotland. (2018) *Critical Issues in Scottish Penal Policy: Inequality & Imprisonment*. 18 - September 2018. Available: http://howardleague.scot/news/2018/september/critical-issues-scottish-penal-policy-inequality imprisonment

Hutcheon, P. (2015a) 'Revealed: Police Scotland and Scottish Government tried to hamper research into stop-and-search.' *Sunday Herald*, 22 February 2015.

Hutcheon, P. (2015b) 'Revealed: How Police Scotland tried to undermine criticism of stop and search.' *Sunday Herald*, 16 May 2015.

Keating, M. (2009) *The Independence of Scotland: Self-government and the Shifting Politics of Union*. Oxford: Oxford University Press.

Kingdon, J. (1984) *Agendas, Alternatives and Public Policies*. New York, NY: Harper Collins.

Loader, I. and Sparks, R. (2010) *Public Criminology?* London: Routledge.

Loveday, B. (2018) 'Police Scotland: Challenging the current democratic deficit in police governance and public accountability', *Crime Prevention and Community Safety* 20 (3): 154–167.

Malik, A. (2017) *Steering from the Centre: The Scottish Police Authority and Police Governance in Scotland*. SIPR Research Summary No: 28. Scottish Institute for Policing Research.

Mathiesen, T. (2004) *Silently Silenced: Essays on the Creation of Acquiescence in Modern Society*. Winchester: Waterside Press

McAra, L. (2017) 'Can criminologists change the world? Critical reflections on the politics, performance and effects of criminal justice', *British Journal of Criminology* 57: 767–788.

Murray, K. (2014) *Stop and Search in Scotland: An Evaluation of Police Practice*. Glasgow: Scottish Centre for Crime and Justice Research.

Murray, K. (2017) ''Why have we funded this research?': On politics, research and newsmaking criminology', *Criminology and Criminal Justice* 17 (5): 507–525.

Murray, K. (forthcoming) *Soft Rain and Unfearties: Raising the Minimum Age of Criminal Responsibility in Scotland*. Glasgow: Scottish Centre for Crime and Justice Research.

Murray, K. and Harkin, D. (2017) 'Policing in cool and hot climates: Legitimacy, power and the rise and fall of mass stop and search in Scotland', *British Journal of Criminology* 57 (4): 885–905.

Murray, K. and Malik, A. (forthcoming) 'Contested spaces: The politics of strategic police leadership in Scotland', in Sivestri, M., Simpson, M., and Ramshaw, P. (eds.) *Police Leadership: Changing Landscapes*. Basingstoke: Palgrave Macmillan.

Office of Science and Technology. (1993) *Realising Our Potential: A Strategy for Science, Engineering and Technology*. White Paper (Cm 2250), Office of Science and Technology, London: HMSO.

Pardoe, S. (2014) 'Research impact unpacked? A social science agenda for critically analyzing the discourse of impact and informing practice', *Sage Open* 4 (2): 1–16.

Rawat, S. and Meena, S. (2014) 'Publish or perish: Where are we heading?', *Journal of Research in Medical Sciences* 19 (2): 87–89.

Reed, M. (2018) *The Research Impact Handbook*. Huntly: Fast Track Impact.

Reiner, R. (2010) *The Politics of the Police*. Oxford: Oxford University Press.

Robertson, A. (2014) 'Policing by consent', *Holyrood Magazine*, 3 February 2014.

Salmond, A. (2014) *Official Report: Meeting of the Parliament*. 23 January 2014. col. 26968.

Scott, J. (2015) *The Report of the Advisory Group on Stop and Search*. Edinburgh: Scottish Government.

Scottish Parliament Justice Committee. (2018) *An Inquiry into the Use of Remand in Scotland*. SP Paper 363. Edinburgh: Scottish Parliament.

Sparks, R., Jackson, L., Davidson, N., Fleming, L. and Smale, D. (2017) 'Police and community in twentieth-century Scotland: The uses of social history', *British Journal of Criminology*, 51 (1): 18–30.

Squires, P. (2016) 'Beyond contrasting traditions in policing research?' in Brunger, M., Tong, S., and Martin, D. (eds.) *An Introduction to Policing Research*. London: Routledge, 9–28.

Sutherland, E. (2016) 'Raising the minimum age of criminal responsibility in Scotland: Law reform at last?', *Northern Ireland Legal Quarterly* 67 (3): 387–406.

Telegraph (2010) 'Police targets "making officers behave like car salesmen".' 3 May 2010.

Turner, E. (2013a) 'Beyond "facts" and "values": Rethinking some recent debates about the public role of criminology', *British Journal of Criminology* 53: 149–166.

UN Committee on the Rights of the Child (UNCRC). (2007) General comment No. 10. Children's Rights in Juvenile Justice, 25 April 2007, CRC/C/GC/10.

Walters, R. and Presdee, M. (1998) 'The perils and politics of criminological research and the threat to academic freedom', *Current Issues in Criminal Justice*, 10 (2): 156–167.

PART II

Disciplinary and theoretical relationships

11

LAW AND SOCIOLOGY

Sharyn Roach Anleu and Kathy Mack

Introduction

Law is a complex social phenomenon of substantial and long-standing interest to sociologists. Legal phenomena can be subject to theoretical and empirical investigation using social science concepts and methods. At a macro level, sociology approaches law as an institution. It identifies linkages with other institutions such as political structures, economic relations, and cultural values and identifies relationships between legal institutions and other forms of social control or regulation. At a more micro level, social researchers investigate how various actors – lawyers, judges, social activists, and people in everyday life – experience, interpret, negotiate, and confront law, legal institutions, and legal discourse.

This chapter first considers the nexus between sociology and law. It then examines a research project investigating courts and the judiciary to illustrate some of the challenges of empirical research within legal institutions. One aspect of the project is observational field research, which has a long history in sociology and other allied social science disciplines, such as anthropology and socio-legal studies. The chapter describes the National Court Observation Study and reflects on its design strengths, limitations, and practical dimensions of undertaking the research. One facet is the many often-unanticipated micro-decisions researchers had to make during the planning and data collection phases, despite careful preliminary research and pilot testing.

Law and sociology nexus

For many sociologists, attention to law derives from broader concerns about social control, the division of labour, social change, knowledge, inequality, power, gender relations, violence, and so on. Sociological definitions of law stress its normative character. Sociological discussions of law are often concerned with the legal responses to behaviour that violates laws and so concentrate on criminal law and its operation.

Despite law and sociology being distinct disciplines and professions with separate concepts, language, and understandings of research, they share subject matters. Both are concerned with social relationships, values, social regulation, obligations, and expectations arising from particular social positions and roles. Relationships between law and society –

between legal institutions and social processes – are sometimes framed as a question of the relative autonomy of law (Tomlins 2007). In different ways, sociological theorists from Weber, Marx, Durkheim, Parsons, and Luhmann to Habermas consider 'law as a subject by locating it contextually as the dependant variable in a context of social and economic phenomena' (Tomlins 2000: 958; and see Roach Anleu 2010), though there is disagreement about how permeable law is to external forces.

Other approaches to the law and sociology nexus show that almost any aspect of social life can be subject to legal regulation; any social issue, setting, or process can involve issues that become legal issues and problems that are juridified (Ewick and Sibley 1998). This suggests that law is an independent variable influencing the meanings of such concepts as property, ownership, contract, trust, responsibility, guilt, and personality (Cotterell 1998). For Bourdieu (1987), law is a constitutive force. The juridical field, like any social field, is shaped by internal protocols, assumptions, values, and characteristic behaviours, all of which are amenable to sociological analysis.

It is useful to distinguish between sociological inquiry into institutionalised legal settings and law in ordinary or everyday settings. Legal institutions, organisations, and settings present distinct challenges to field research and data collection, as in the observational field research described in this chapter.

Observational research in court

Observational research is a well-established, though resource-intensive, strategy to study the performance of professional work and organisational settings, including courtrooms (Carlen 1976; Fielding 2011; Hunter 2005; Mack and Roach Anleu 2010; Rock 1993; Travers 2007; Ward 2017). The design of observational field research can vary widely in terms of the level of participation of the observer(s), the way the data are recorded, and the number and range of settings and/or participants observed, and whether and how it is combined with other kinds of data. Two pioneering studies of lower criminal courts rely on court observations within different research designs. Mileski's (1971) examination of courtroom encounters and the disposition of cases in a first-instance criminal court in one US city involved direct observation of 417 cases over a three-month period. She recorded and quantified the number and types of offences observed, the presence of legal representation, the plea, the disposition, and duration of the encounter between defendant and the court. She also classified the 'judge's manner toward the defendant ... into four categories: good-natured, bureaucratic, firm, and harsh' (1971: 523) and quantified these judicial demeanours. Mileski found the most frequent demeanour is routine and bureaucratic, displayed in three-quarters of the encounters. Judges were rarely harsh or good-natured, and were formal or firm only in some encounters (14%). Her typology of demeanour has been developed further in subsequent court observations of judicial behaviour (e.g. Hunter 2005; Mack and Roach Anleu 2010; Ptacek 1999).

Carlen adopted an ethnographic approach in her study of stipendiary and lay magistrates in London courts. She also applied concepts from dramaturgical sociology and the work of Goffman (1959) and Garfinkel (1956). Carlen undertook observations in the courtroom and in the gaoler's office, combining these with other kinds of data. She notes:

> At this court my frequent requests to speak to the stipendiary magistrates and their clerks were never refused ... I had long tape-recorded discussions with probation officers, or just hung around, sporadically talking to any policemen, defendants or solicitors who were waiting outside the courtroom.
>
> *(1976: xii)*

Her research details the many ways courtroom interactions and the relations between the magistrate and the prosecution serve to marginalise the (unrepresented) defendant. Despite a veneer of legitimate authority, 'mechanisms of repressive social control ... lurk behind, and render absurd, the judicial rhetoric of the possibility of an absolute social justice' (1976: 128).

Rock extended this research design in a study of the Crown Court (1993). More recently, Jacobson et al. undertook 'many [200] hours of observation of court hearings' combined with 'extensive interviews with victims, witnesses and defendants; interviews with professionals and practitioners who work in or around court' to investigate 'the essential features of the Crown Court process' (2015: 1).

> Observation was a core element of the research carried out for this study. It was undertaken on the basis that it would provide the most detailed insight into how the Crown Court operates on a day-to-day basis and, particularly, into the nature of the interactions between court users and professionals in court.
>
> *(Jacobson, Hunter and Kirby 2015: 17–18)*

Observation is necessarily partial, and 'what is observed must be recorded, written up, or transformed into field notes which become a representation, necessarily selective, of what occurred' (Roach Anleu et al. 2015: 377). There are several strategies that can enhance observational data and reduce inevitable, and perhaps inadvertent, partial coverage of highly complex social situations: (i) notetaking, (ii) relying on several researchers, and (iii) combining observations with other methods and sources of data.

(i) *Notetaking*: Typically, observers make field notes during observations (Emerson, Fretz, and Shaw 2011). For example, Booth (2012) recorded her observations of 18 sentencing hearings in field notes that she transcribed within a few hours following the hearing. A study of a problem-centred court indicates that '[f]ield notes were written in a small notebook during observations and typed within twenty-four hours' (Fay-Ramirez 2015: 215). Similarly, a study of a family court that entailed observations of child welfare proceedings over a one-year period specifies: '[d]uring the hearings, a detailed log was maintained' (Lens 2016: 707).

(ii) *Several researchers*: This can entail data collection by multiple researchers who separately observe different courtrooms, or the use of two or more observers at the same time in the same courtroom, recording observations independently. In one study involving 12 data collectors, the preliminary testing of the data recording sheet and the abilities of the researcher to complete the forms entailed two observers sitting in each of the courts and independently completing the forms. Later, the forms were compared, and questions with the largest discrepancies in answers were isolated. To overcome differences, a 'Manual for Answering the Questionnaire' was supplied to each observer, 'whose duty it was to familiarise himself or herself with its contents prior to the commencement of the main study' (Legal Studies Department, La Trobe University 1980: 32). After this testing, observers undertook observations separately.

(iii) *Multiple methods*: To remedy inevitable partiality, observational data can be mixed with data obtained or created from other methods, such as interviews (e.g. Fay-Ramirez 2015; Moore 2007; Schuster and Propen 2010), or documentary sources such as court files or transcripts of recordings of the court sessions observed (e.g. Booth 2012). Court observations can be one component of a qualitative or ethnographic research design. In her study of one of New York City's busiest lower criminal courts, Kohler-Hausmann's two years of fieldwork encompassed 'extensive ethnographic observation in courtrooms and interviews with judges, defense attorneys, prosecutors, defendants, and various court personnel ... between one and three full days per week sitting and observing various misdemeanour courtrooms' (2013: 359). Research design might also incorporate shadowing, where the researcher follows a specific participant in a setting over an extended period, observing and recording their activities, conversations, and interactions with others. Shadowing provides opportunities for asking questions immediately as they arise and seeking explanations for why this person did or did not do or say certain things. Shadowing allows access to both front-stage and back-stage locations of the setting (Goffman 1959; McDonald 2005). Swedish research investigating emotions in court included shadowing where two sociologists, each at different courts, followed a judge or prosecutor at work for several days, observing them during court hearings, and in their office, and conducting semi-structured interviews (Wettergren and Bergman Blix 2016).

The National Court Observation Study

Since 2000, the Judicial Research Project[1] of Flinders University has undertaken multimethod, sequential, empirical socio-legal research into the judiciary, studying the everyday work of judges and magistrates[2] and their courts in Australia. The Project deploys a distinctive combination of social science research methods and legal knowledge to gather empirical evidence aimed at understanding the judiciary as a professional occupation. It applies sociological concepts such as emotional labour, job satisfaction, performance of everyday work, professionalisation, and work–family conflict to a population – the judiciary – not previously studied from this perspective (Roach Anleu and Mack 2017). This sociological approach represents a significant departure from the more conventional legal conception of the judge as prestigious, eminent, and having a somewhat mystical status as the embodiment of law.

Observational fieldwork is a key component of the Judicial Research Project's investigation of the daily work of judicial officers in court (Emerson 1981). This aspect of the project studies the ways judicial officers deliver decisions, their demeanour, time management, and interaction with other participants – defendants, defence representatives, prosecution, and others. The fieldwork was conducted in Australia's lower courts, called magistrates courts in most jurisdictions, and the Local Court in New South Wales and the Northern Territory. One aim of the research design was to observe a range of courtrooms throughout Australia, rather than undertake deep ethnographic research in only one or two courts. The emphasis on national scope was generated in part by having all magistrates and local courts in Australia as formal collaborating organisations in the research project.

This study entailed a nearly constant process of decision-making, ranging from very broad to very concrete and specific, throughout all phases of the research, from design

---

1 For details see: www.flinders.edu.au/law/judicialresearch
2 Generally, in Australia, the term 'magistrate' refers to judicial officers in lower courts. 'Judge' refers to those who preside in the higher (intermediate or supreme) state, territory, or national courts, except in the Northern Territory where magistrates were given the title judge in 2016. Australian magistrates are paid judicial officers, with legal qualifications, and are appointed until a fixed retirement age. In this chapter, the term 'judicial officer' refers to any member of the judiciary, regardless of court level or type.

through implementation, data collection, data analysis, and publication. First, we needed to establish the purpose of the study, the questions it would address, and its scope, and then develop a concrete, feasible research design to accomplish these goals. This required decisions such as whom to observe, in which locations, and what information to record and how. Once data collection was underway, many further, often micro-, decisions needed to be made, some of them unanticipated. For example, during data entry, research assistants noticed that, occasionally, the space on the code sheet for the defendant's postcode was blank. This created ambiguity between matters where the defendant had no fixed address, and hence no postcode, and those where there were no address data available. It was decided to use the code 9999 for no fixed address and blanks to indicate missing data. When making such decisions, it is essential to be reflexive about these moments, and, if practicable, to record the decision and the reasons for making a particular choice.

Planning and design

The court observation study involved balancing several aims: to conduct observations in each state and territory; to undertake more observations in larger jurisdictions; to include metropolitan, suburban, and regional locations; to observe entire days; to include men and women of a range of ages and experience as magistrates; and to observe court days constituted by comparable kinds of matters. Preliminary observations of diverse criminal and civil matters in 23 magistrates courts throughout Australia, from March to December 2003, enabled the development of a detailed research strategy and data collection method.

We settled on the general criminal list as the most appropriate aspect of magistrates' everyday work to observe in detail. Over 95% of the criminal (and civil) work in Australian courts commences and is finalised in these lower courts (Australian Government Productivity Commission 2018). All jurisdictions have a criminal list, variously termed the arrest list, the mention court, or criminal court list. Non-trial proceedings – the preliminary stages of criminal cases such as deciding bail applications, determining requests for adjournment, standing down matters (for hearing later the same day), setting dates for other procedures, including trials, as well as taking guilty pleas, ordering pre-sentence reports, and passing sentence – constitute the criminal list. The kinds of offence that appear on the criminal list include drink driving, theft, assault, and some drug offences. These lists run regularly on specified days of the week or daily in the largest courts. The criminal list is part of the work of most magistrates at some point in their career, and sometimes throughout their entire careers, and is a setting that vividly depicts the nature, variety, seriousness, and volume of cases in these courts. We decided to exclude observations of trials as part of the research design. As most defendants plead guilty, trials are a small proportion of the very many cases that magistrates and their courts process, though the trials that do occur can take up a substantial portion of magistrates' time.

Implementation and data collection

Data collection took place over an 11-month period between August 2004 and July 2005. Thirty court sessions were observed in 20 locations, including all capital cities, five suburban, and four regional locations in Australia. Most observation sessions covered the same magistrate in one court from the beginning to the end of the day in court. On three occasions, a magistrate who had presided in a previously observed session was observed a second time conducting another session. Thus, the study comprises 30 sessions of 27 different magistrates. Although it was not ideal to observe a magistrate more than once, we decided it was preferable to losing the opportunity to undertake the observation of a scheduled session, as rescheduling was often not practicable, especially when the field research was interstate. The magistrates observed include men and women of varying ages and judicial experience and closely parallel the profile of the Australian magistracy as a whole in terms of gender, age, and years served as a magistrate.

The unit of analysis is the matter. That is, the matter is the entity on which we decided to collect the data and to aggregate this along several dimensions to enable identification of patterns and tendencies in magistrates' everyday work. A 'matter', for our purpose, was when each defendant's case was called, whether the defendant actually appeared in person or by video link or not at all. If two or more co-defendants appeared together, that was one 'matter'. If a case was called, then stood down and recalled later, that was two matters, as it represented two separate events. Defined in this way, the study comprises 1,287 matters.

To enhance reliability and limit subjectivity, every court session was observed by two researchers, simultaneously recording observations independently (Roach Anleu et al. 2015). For nearly all the sessions, the observers were Kathy Mack and Sharyn Roach Anleu together; one was always an observer. In a busy criminal court, many events occur at once, and the capacity of one person to observe and record is necessarily limited. Observation is a very personal and subjective experience; having two observers enables extensive and reflexive discussions of researchers' interpretations of events and behaviours observed (Holmes 2015).

To aid notetaking, we developed a template to record the same kind of information about each matter observed and a second template to record general information about the court session and court context, with space for additional notes. To reduce the amount of writing for each observer and provide options to tick or circle, these templates were preprinted. These templates – the matter code sheet and the session code sheet – facilitated quantification of data and analysis using statistical analyses.

The templates were pilot-tested in three different magistrates courts. It became obvious that the original matter code sheet design could not work: as the unit of analysis was each matter, and some matters happen very quickly,[3] it was not possible to observe and record all the information sought within the time frame of a single matter. We redesigned the template to record all the information needed on a single double-sided sheet of A4 paper, including space to write in any additional comments. This was accomplished by developing very brief, structured response categories labelled with abbreviations or numbers and by reducing the information to be collected. This also entailed decisions about what information not to record.

At the outset, we intended to record whether the magistrate referred to information or factors that might affect the process or outcome of the case. Based on the preliminary observations, we had developed a list of some 15 possible remarks (including an 'other'

---

3 Data from the court observation study show that the time taken for a single matter ranged from 15 seconds or less for 5% of the matters observed to 30–40 minutes for 11 matters (< 1%). One quarter (25%) of all matters were dealt with in less than one minute, half of all matters were completed in only two minutes and 20 seconds, and nearly all matters observed (95.0%) were dealt with in less than 15 minutes. The average time per matter was four minutes and 13 seconds. Note that these were not trial proceedings but were preliminary processes such as applications for bail, or guilty pleas and sentences.

category) reflecting factors such as time and time management, the victim, or a guilty plea. Given the range of issues this list encompassed, and the time it took to hear and observe the magistrate and then translate that information into one or more of the categories, it became clear that recording the information was not feasible and would generate too much missing data. At this point, we decided that such data were beyond the scope of this Study. Ultimately, the study was able to capture this kind of information for nearly all sessions observed, through transcripts of the proceedings, data that were not anticipated when the initial research design was developed.

During the course of the observations, we became aware that, in some courts, the sessions observed were being audio-recorded. It then became our routine practice to request audio tapes, electronic audio files, or typed transcripts (paper or electronic) that might be available. These were supplied, in one form or another, for all but one jurisdiction, where proceedings are not recorded. Where we obtained an official audio tape or digital recording, it was transcribed within the Judicial Research Project, rather than using a commercial transcription firm, to maximise accuracy and confidentiality.

While we were sitting in court, it was important not to react visibly to the proceedings, nor to display any emotion, to reduce obtrusiveness and limit any kind of disruption as much as possible (Bergman Blix 2009; Wettergren 2015). At times this was difficult – for example, to ensure that we did not drop bundles of papers or accidently set off the alarm on the small timers we each had.

During court proceedings, each researcher completed a separate code sheet for each matter. In order to clarify the meaning of the categories and abbreviations on the matter code sheet, we developed a detailed set of instructions. These aimed to maximise consistent interpretations of observations between the two observers and across the many different matters in different times and places. Throughout the observation process, aspects of the instructions were refined and elaborated to accommodate unanticipated events, situations, or interpretations. For example, the first version of the instructions provided for recording the magistrate's demeanour. After a few observations, it became clear that magistrates change their demeanour during a matter. We decided to revise the instructions to specify how to record primary and secondary demeanours.

After each session, in the late afternoon and into the evening, the two observers carefully compared their notes on the matter and session code sheets. This involved completing parts of the form that might have been left blank or correcting any slight mistakes that might have occurred owing to the rapidity of the matters, and ensuring that the template was being completed consistently in light of the instruction sheet. It also involved discussing areas of agreement and disagreement and reflecting on perceptions of the events and behaviours observed. This reflexive analysis included considering our feelings during, or in response to, court proceedings. For example, in some matters, we felt sympathetic to a defendant when the magistrate was being harsh and condescending or when the facts of the case demonstrated difficulties in their circumstances or family situation. In other situations, we empathised with the magistrate who expressed frustration in response to missing paperwork, absent defendants, or insufficiently prepared legal representatives.

From our initial court visits, we found that, from observation alone, it simply was not possible to consistently hear or identify the information needed from what occurred in court. Some details, such as the defendant's demographic data or the offence(s), are only available from court files. Because the criminal list is so busy, and files are needed for multiple functions within a brief time period (e.g. to arrange release on bail), organising this access depended on coordination with court registry staff. In most locations, a third researcher was located in the registry extracting details from the files – either paper or electronic – after the magistrate's decision and after court staff had completed working on them. This included checking information such as the defendant's age, postcode, prior offences, or the nature of the charges. Given the often numerous and mixed offences in one matter, plus jurisdictional differences in defining offences, six broad offence categories were used for the Study: property crimes, crimes against persons, driving, consequential (breach of an earlier court order – for example, non-compliance with a bail condition or breach of a sentencing order), and other (e.g. weapons offences or disorderly conduct). Each category had subcategories – for example, property crimes were separated into: shoplifting, vandalism, burglary or related, and other.

The use of standardised recording sheets with detailed instructions, the capacity to cross-check some data with the court files, and having two researchers observe the same events in court and discuss their observations immediately all increase the validity of the research strategy and confidence that the events observed have been reliably captured. The unanticipated availability of transcripts for nearly all matters enabled a richer qualitative, textual analysis of the matters observed. Other themes and patterns discernible in the transcripts include magistrates' use of humour, discussions about guilty pleas, and evidence of emotion and emotion work.

Data collection: coordination with the courts

Undertaking the court observation research entailed ongoing coordination with, and support from, each magistrate observed and the many court staff working in the courtroom and in the registry. Despite considerable pre-planning and generous assistance from magistrates and court staff, there were unanticipated difficulties. In addition, courts, especially lower courts, are busy places, often under-resourced and under-staffed, and so it can be difficult to identify time for participating in research. Advance scheduling is challenging, as court schedules can change at the last minute, and court business takes precedence over research.

For example, many courts outside major cities or metropolitan locations do not run general criminal lists every day, and so court observations could only occur on specific days. In some regional locations, other matters are scheduled in the same session as the criminal list, such as applications for family violence orders or even trials. Late listing or personnel changes might require unanticipated rescheduling of travel plans. On one occasion, we learned that half the magistrates in an interstate court would be away during our scheduled research visit. In another instance, legal aid lawyers were attending a conference on the day of our planned visit, and so we had to cancel the field research.

Before we visited a court, each magistrate who might be observed was sent information detailing the research strategy. Because of the varied and changing scheduling practices, it was rarely possible to identify in advance the specific magistrate who would be conducting the criminal list, either because the roster was not prepared as far in advance as we needed for our planning, or because of last-minute changes. The cover letter introduced us as researchers, stated explicitly the purposes of the court observations, what would happen to the resulting data, and gave assurances of anonymity and confidentiality. It also stressed that the research was not in any way a performance evaluation of either an individual magistrate or a particular court. The letter also indicated that the magistrate could decline by returning a card to the researchers in an enclosed stamped envelope, with guarantees that this decision would remain confidential to the researchers. A separate information sheet provided details of the research project and the rationale for the court observation research strategy. This process was needed to comply with the research ethics requirement for informed consent from human subjects of social research, even though the court proceedings observed were open to the public. (This process contrasts with an earlier Australian court observation study in which it was decided not to inform the court of the researchers' presence but to sit anonymously in the general body of the court and record what was seen and heard [Legal Studies Department, La Trobe University 1980]).

Later, as part of scheduling specific dates and locations, we again attempted to directly contact any magistrate who might be observed, to provide another confidential opt-out opportunity. Such contact was not always possible, as rosters are sometimes not set until a week or even a day before. For each court visit, wherever possible, we offered to meet with any magistrate either before or after the court observations to answer any questions or to hear any views. These conversations were not recorded formally, though sometimes field notes were made.

For each location we proposed to visit, we contacted the court staff well in advance to explain the nature and purpose of the research and to seek their assistance in facilitating our observations and access to the court records. On the day before the first scheduled court observation, at least one of the researchers visited the court to meet with relevant staff, and sometimes the magistrate, to answer any questions about the research project, view the courtroom, and obtain a copy of the list of the next day's cases.

Arranging where observers are located in a research setting is often complex. An observer's physical location in the courtroom inevitably shapes the range of participants and activities that can be observed. Given the nature of a courtroom layout, observers had to be close enough to the bench and bar table to see and hear participants, with sufficient space for paperwork and rapid note-taking, as well as aiming to be as unobtrusive as possible. Locations ranged from seats in the public gallery or chairs against the wall at the side of the courtroom to chairs in areas set aside for the press. Wherever located, the observers sat side by side.

In each courtroom, informal norms operate about who sits where in the public gallery and where legal practitioners and other participants or observers, including journalists, are seated. These norms can be different in different courtrooms. On a few occasions when court was adjourned during a session, lawyers approached one or both observers and asked about our presence and activities, attesting to their implicit assessment that we were 'out of place'. In their research in the English Crown Court, Jacobson, Hunter, and Kirby (2015) indicate they sat mostly in the public gallery, though on occasion they were asked to sit in the seating reserved for probation officers and other officials. By comparison, in her research on judges and their work in and out of court, Darbyshire sat – 'in and out of court' – beside the 40 judges she observed, shadowed, and interviewed (2011: 2).

Reflections on research design

This observational field research involves snapshots of many cases at various points from initiation to resolution. Individual cases were not tracked from commencement to completion, though some matters were entirely resolved in only one appearance. As the primary research focus was on magistrates and their daily work, tracking cases to assess how long any particular matter was in the court system before being finalised was beyond the parameters of the study.

This court observation research examines judicial conduct and associated activities in the courtroom, including magistrates' face-to-face interaction with other courtroom participants. It shows the ways in which interrelations with various court participants shape the performance of judicial authority; the courtroom is more than a legal setting: it is a social 'interaction order' (Goffman 1982). Law as an institution must be realised in the everyday practices of magistrates.

The design reflects a trade-off between and a combination of quantitative and qualitative data (Bryman 2006). 'Observations … are inherently limited in what they can reveal about participants' internal states' (Craciun 2018: 973). The research did not directly investigate magistrates' motives, intentions, experiences, or feelings and so cannot make claims about their subjectivities or the emotions they experienced. Nor did it directly investigate the perceptions or experiences of prosecutors, defence lawyers, or defendants or other recipients of the judicial decisions communicated, or any others in the courtrooms observed, except to the extent that any participant announced their thoughts, perceptions, or feelings in court. As the data were collected in a public setting – open courtrooms – we were not able to observe the many other decisions regarding a criminal case that are made outside the courtroom. For example, in some jurisdictions, the first request for an adjournment is granted at the registry counter; in others, this is a decision made by a magistrate. Magistrates may make their decision about a sentence during an adjournment and announce it in court. Nonetheless, there were occasions when the courtroom was less 'public' and we could observe less-formal proceedings, including humorous banter among magistrates and other professional or regular participants (defence lawyer, prosecution, and clerk). In some courts, plea discussions between the defence representative and the prosecution could sometimes be seen and heard in the courtroom before the magistrate entered, during an adjournment, or even during court proceedings.

This observational fieldwork enabled the capture of many aspects of magistrates' everyday work, including interactional dynamics in the natural setting of the courtroom. This methodology can incorporate 'the complex, chaotic and often confusing nature of court proceedings and the frequency with which they were interrupted for a wide array of reasons; and the juxtaposition of elaborate formality with informality, and of high drama with tedium' (Jacobson, Hunter, and Kirby 2015: 18).

The distinct languages, concepts, rules, and frameworks of law and sociology can present challenges for social research in legal settings. For example, judicial officers can be unfamiliar with social science and sceptical of sociology's value or relevance to their daily work. Some socio-legal researchers experience the judiciary as 'a "hard-to-reach" group' (Cowan et al. 2006: 548). Gatekeepers erect and maintain barriers, and judicial officers enjoy 'high status and professional remoteness' (Dobbin et al. 2001) and have very strong concerns about the confidentiality of any information they provide (Hunter, Nixon, and Blandy 2008: 87). Developing and managing -positive relations with the judiciary and the courts are essential to undertaking sociological, empirical socio-legal research in this setting (Bergman Blix, and Wettergren 2015).

Court observations and socio-legal research

Observational field research can be available for other socio-legal researchers. Courts are open public locations, providing vibrant, rich research settings. As Mileski notes, observation 'allows the opportunity to investigate the situational factors that may be associated with various kinds of cases and their dispositions' (1971: 475), but which are not captured by court statistics or records or in transcripts. Such empirical research enables direct observation of ordinary as well as unusual events and participants in the natural setting of the court.

Court observation studies demonstrate the range and complexity of daily activities and decisions in courts, which are usually not visible to the wider public. Most people have not been in court and may rely on (often-sensational) reports and cultural representations via television, movies, or social media to form a view about courts and judicial practices. Such views can depart widely from the daily activities, practices, and decisions that occur in the actual courtroom settings. The National Court Observation Study was large scale and resource-intensive in terms of time and financial cost to plan, undertake, and analyse the resulting data. There are many good examples of smaller-scale court observation studies, which can investigate local practices, especially when mixed with other sources of data (e.g. Fay-Ramirez 2015; Lens 2016; Schuster and Propen 2010; Travers 2007).

As disputing becomes more private and moves out of public courtrooms, sometimes into private dispute resolution spaces, opportunities for relatively unobtrusive observational fieldwork might be reduced. For example, virtual courtrooms – where people are in several different locations participating in a hearing via their computer – may be impossible for a researcher to access.

Conclusion

For the sociologist, legal settings, situations, incidents, and actors are embedded in social life and processes. Observational fieldwork can provide valuable insight into complex socio-legal settings, such as courtrooms, and provides opportunities for investigating intersections between law and sociology. It can be combined with other research methods, in particular interviews conducted before or after the observations, and/or with transcripts of the proceedings observed and court files, as was the case in the study described here. Observational fieldwork can also vary in scale. As with all research projects, multiple decisions must be made, including assessments about the feasibility of the research and the budget. Most important is to identify the research question(s) that the data will and can address.

Acknowledgements

We appreciate funding, financial, and other support from the Australian Research Council (LP0210306, LP0669168, DP0665198, DP1096888, and DP150103663), Flinders University, as well as the Australasian Institute of Judicial Administration, the Association of Australian Magistrates, and many courts and their judicial officers. We are grateful to several research and administrative assistants over the course of the research, and most recently to Colleen deLaine, Rhiannon Davies, Jordan Tutton, and Rae Wood. All phases of this research involving human subjects have been approved by the Flinders University Social and Behavioural Research Ethics Committee.

Suggested further readings

Becker, Howard S. 1998, *Tricks of the Trade: How to Think About Your Research While You're Doing It.* Chicago, IL: Chicago University Press.
Bourdieu, Pierre 1987, 'The Force of Law: Toward a Sociology of the Juridical Field', *Hastings Law Journal* 38: 814–853.
Lofland, John, David Snow, Leon Anderson, and Lyn H. Lofland 2006, *Analyzing Social Settings: A Guide to Qualitative Observation and Analysis*, 4th ed. Belmont, CA: Thomson Wadsworth.
Halliday, Simon and Patrick Schmidt 2009, *Conducting Law and Society Research: Reflections on Methods and Practices.* Cambridge: Cambridge University Press.
Small, Mario Luis 2011, 'How to Conduct a Mixed Methods Study: Recent Trends in a Rapidly Growing Literature', *Annual Review of Sociology* 37: 57–86.

References

Australian Government Productivity Commission 2018, *Report on Government Services: Courts* (Chapter 7). Canberra: Steering Committee for the Review of Government Service Provision.

Bergman Blix, Stina 2009, 'Emotional Participation: The Use of the Observer's Emotions as a Methodological Tool When Studying Professional Stage Actors Rehearsing a Role for the Stage', *Nordic Theatre Studies* 21: 28–38.

Bergman Blix, Stina and Åsa Wettergren 2015, 'The Emotional Labour of Gaining and Maintaining Access to the Field', *Qualitative Research* 15: 688–704.

Booth, Tracey 2012, '"Cooling out" Victims of Crime: Managing Victim Participation in the Sentencing Process in a Superior Sentencing Court', *Australian & New Zealand Journal of Criminology* 45: 214–230.

Bourdieu, Pierre 1987, 'The Force of Law: Toward a Sociology of the Juridical Field', *Hastings Law Journal* 38: 814–853.

Bryman, Alan 2006, 'Integrating quantitative and qualitative research: How is it done?', *Qualitative Research* 6(1): 97–113.

Carlen, Pat 1976, *Magistrates' Justice*. London: Martin Robertson.

Cotterell, Roger 1998, 'Why Must Legal Ideas Be Interpreted Sociologically?', *Journal of Law and Society* 25: 171–192.

Cowan, Dave, Sarah Blandy, Emma Hitchings, Caroline Hunter, and Judy Nixon 2006, 'District Judges and Possession Proceedings', *Journal of Law and Society* 33: 547–571.

Craciun, Mariana 2018, 'Emotions and Knowledge in Expert Work: A Comparison of Two Psychotherapies', *American Journal of Sociology* 123: 959–1003.

Darbyshire, Penny 2011, *Sitting in Judgment: The Working Lives of Judges*. Oxford and Portland OR: Hart.

Dobbin, Shirley A., Sophia I. Gatowski, Gerald P. Ginsburg, Mara l. Merlino, Veronica Dahir, and James T. Richardson 2001, 'Surveying Difficult Populations: Lessons Learned from a National Survey of State Trial Court Judges', *Justice System Journal* 22: 287–307.

Emerson, Robert M. 1981, 'Observational Field Work', *Annual Review of Sociology* 7: 351–378.

Emerson, Robert M., Rachel I. Fretz, and Linda L. Shaw 2011, *Writing Ethnographic Field Notes*, 2nd ed. Chicago, IL, and London: University of Chicago Press.

Ewick, Patricia and Susan S. Sibley 1998, *Common Place of Law: Stories from Everyday Life*. Chicago, IL: University of Chicago Press.

Fay-Ramirez, S. 2015, 'Therapeutic Jurisprudence in Practice: Changes in Family Treatment Court Norms over Time', *Law & Social Inquiry* 40: 205–236.

Fielding, Nigel G. 2011, 'Judges and Their Work', *Social & Legal Studies* 20: 97–115.

Garfinkel, Harold 1956, 'Conditions of Successful Degradation Ceremonies', *American Journal of Sociology* 61: 420–424.

Goffman, Erving 1959, *The Presentation of Self in Everyday Life*. New York: Doubleday Anchor.

Goffman, Erving 1982, *Interaction Ritual: Essays on Face-to-Face Behavior*. New York: Pantheon Books.

Holmes, Mary 2015, 'Researching Emotional Reflexivity', *Emotion Review* 9: 61–66.

Hunter, Caroline, Judy Nixon, and Sarah Blandy 2008, 'Researching the Judiciary: Exploring the Invisible in Judicial Decision Making', *Journal of Law and Society* 35: 76–90.

Hunter, Rosemary 2005, 'Styles of Judging: How Magistrates Deal with Applications for Intervention Orders', *Alternative Law Journal* 30(231–36): 46.

Jacobson, Jessica, Gillian Hunter, and Amy Kirby 2015, *Inside Crown Court: Personal Experiences and Questions of Legitimacy*. Bristol: Policy Press.

Kohler-Hausmann, Issa 2013, 'Misdemeanor Justice: Control without Conviction', *American Journal of Sociology* 119: 351–393.

La Trobe University Legal Studies Department 1980, *Guilty, Your Worship: A Study of Victoria's Magistrates' Courts*. Bundoora: La Trobe University.

Lens, Vicki 2016, 'Against the Grain: Therapeutic Judging in a Traditional Family Court', *Law & Social Inquiry* 41: 701–718.

Mack, Kathy and Sharyn Roach Anleu 2010, 'Performing Impartiality: Judicial Demeanor and Legitimacy', *Law & Social Inquiry* 35: 137–173.

McDonald, Seonaidh 2005, 'Studying Actions in Context: A Qualitative Shadowing Method for Organizational Research', *Qualitative Research* 5: 455–473.

Mileski, Maureen 1971, 'Courtroom Encounters: An Observational Study of a Lower Criminal Court', *Law & Society Review* 5: 473–538.

Moore, Dawn 2007, 'Translating Justice and Therapy: The Drug Treatment Court Networks', *British Journal of Criminology* 47: 42–60.

Ptacek, James 1999, *Battered Women in the Courtroom: The Power of Judicial Responses*. Boston, MA: Northeastern University Press.

Roach Anleu, Sharyn 2010, *Law and Social Change*, 2nd ed. London: Sage.

Roach Anleu, Sharyn and Kathy Mack 2017, *Performing Judicial Authority in the Lower Courts*. London: Palgrave.

Roach Anleu, Sharyn, Stina Bergman Blix, Kathy Mack, and Åsa Wettergren 2015, 'Observing Judicial Work and Emotions: Using Two Researchers', *Qualitative Research* 16: 375–391.

Rock, Paul 1993, *The Social World of an English Crown Court: Witnesses and Professionals in the Crown Court Centre at Wood Green*. Gloucestershire: Clarendon Press.

Schuster, Mary Lay and Amy Propen 2010, 'Degrees of Emotion: Judicial Responses to Victim Impact Statements', *Law, Culture and Humanities* 6: 75–104.

Tomlins, Christopher 2000, 'Framing the Field of Law's Disciplinary Encounters: A Historical Narrative', *Law & Society Review* 34: 911–972.

Tomlins, Christopher 2007, 'How Autonomous Is Law?', *Annual Review of Law and Social Science* 3: 45–68.

Travers, Max 2007, 'Sentencing in the Children's Court: An Ethnographic Perspective', *Youth Justice* 7: 21–35.

Ward, Jennifer 2017, *Transforming Summary Justice: Modernisation in the Lower Criminal Courts*. Abingdon and New York: Routledge.

Wettergren, Åsa 2015, 'How Do We Know what They Feel?' In *Methods of Exploring Emotions*, eds. Helena Flam and Jochem Kleres. London: Routledge, pp. 115–124.

Wettergren, Åsa and Stina Bergman Blix 2016, 'Empathy and Objectivity in the Legal Procedure: The Case of Swedish Prosecutors', *Journal of Scandinavian Studies in Criminology and Crime Prevention* 17: 19–35.

12

LAW AND SOCIAL PSYCHOLOGY METHODS

Rebecca Hollander-Blumoff

Introduction

Legal systems are, at their core, about social psychology. Social psychology is the study of how the individual and her environment interact to shape behavior, and such connections are inextricable from the law's focus on how to shape human behavior. Areas of study at the intersection of law and social psychology include more traditional areas of focus that have long been studied by researchers, such as jury decision-making and eyewitness testimony, as well as more recent and innovative intersections, such as the role that cognitive biases play in driving human behavior.

In the past several decades, there has been a burgeoning group of scholars focusing on the intersection of law and psychology in areas including juries, dispute resolution, criminal law, decision-making in litigation, and procedural justice. This group includes scholars such as Phoebe Ellsworth, Shari Diamond, Valerie Hans, Janice Nadler, Jeff Rachlinski, Donna Shestowsky, and Tom Tyler, just to name a few. Scholars in law and psychology employ a variety of methodological approaches in their research, including (but again, not limited to) lab studies (Ellsworth, 1989), scenario research (Rachlinski, 1996), field studies (Shestowsky, 2014), and self-report surveys (Tyler, 1988). Of course, all of these methodological approaches have benefits and disadvantages. Lab studies allow controlled settings where manipulation of subjects can clearly allow causal inferences to be drawn, but may lack external validity or reliability. Scenario research similarly allows for a high degree of control over the stimuli presented to participants, but may fail to capture nuances of real life, as well as failing to place the subject in a real position of caring about an outcome. Field studies have an unparalleled level of external validity and verisimilitude, but they are messy and expensive, and causal inferences may be impossible to draw. And self-report is relatively straightforward and inexpensive, asking participants to give information about themselves (a topic they should know well), but may be susceptible to bias or inaccuracies in reporting. For that reason, a particular research area can benefit from attacking a problem through a variety of methods, understanding that an amalgamation of results across a variety of methods helps to support the strength of findings in any one study.

My own research on the role of procedural justice in negotiation draws on at least two strands of past research – the body of research on procedural justice in psychology and the body of research on negotiation. In addition, because the research project I will be discussing in this chapter involves the perceptions of both parties to a negotiation, it incorporates some of the work from the field of interpersonal perception in psychology. Each of these research areas has traditionally relied on different methodology. In the field of procedural justice in psychology, researchers have attempted to understand how, when, and why fair treatment during a decision-making process matters to individuals receiving a decision at the hands of a particular decision-maker. The vast bulk of that research has relied on simply asking individuals to assess their treatment by a decision-maker through self-report. Most of this research has relied on asking individuals to call to mind a specific situation, such as a recent encounter with a legal actor, or a particular experience in court or inside a legal process. After asking individuals to think about a particular incident, individuals are asked first about the features of the encounter and then about their assessments of the encounter and their subsequent behavior afterwards. In negotiation research, scholars have relied on a combination of self-report (Becker and Curhan, 2018; Schneider, 2002), measured outcomes (Rogers et al., 2017), and observational and behavioral coding (Filipowicz et al., 2011; Wilson, 2016), although behavioral coding in legal negotiation had not, to my knowledge, previously been employed. In interpersonal perception, researchers have used both self-report and behavioral coding to measure self-perceptions, perceptions of others, and accuracy. In the project I discuss below, I used a combination of self-report and behavioral coding, including a focus on the connection between those variables.

Research on legal negotiation and procedural justice

As the field of procedural justice in psychology has developed over the last four decades, research inquiries have become increasingly sophisticated. The field has coalesced around the conclusions of the most fundamental and basic research showing that fair treatment played a separate and independent role, apart from a fair or a favorable outcome, in guiding individuals' assessments about the final decision. In context after context, this finding was reaffirmed. But more complicated questions remained – why did individuals care so much about fair process? What was the ultimate and long-term effect of believing that a process was fair? And what were the factors that shaped assessments of fair process? That is, what were the features of a process that an individual might reliably judge as "procedurally just"?

As answers started to emerge for the first several questions, the last question became particularly important. A growing body of research studies indicated that procedural justice perceptions were meaningful to people not merely as a proxy for having a fair or favorable outcome, but rather, because of what procedural justice indicated about their standing in their society and their group (Tyler, 1989). In addition, procedural justice perceptions were shown to be critical to individuals' belief that decision-making systems were legitimate and, in turn, to their willingness to abide by the decisions or follow rules that the relevant system produced (Tyler, 1990). Thus, the stakes for procedural justice grew ever higher. If being able to provide fair treatment to individuals was meaningful not because of what it might mean for their outcomes but rather because of a more fundamental connection with their identity and their self-image – and if providing fair treatment in a legal system increased perceptions of legitimacy and, in turn, willingness to comply with the law – then ensuring that individuals experienced fair process was critical. For scholars who want to use the findings of the work in social psychology to improve our legal system, exploring the answer to what constitutes a fair process is thus invaluable.

Research into the underlying behaviors that helped individuals decide that they were treated fairly proceeded apace, but the methodology that researchers used was unchanged –

the paradigmatic approach relied on self-report, analyzing what people said about their experiences along a variety of dimensions, such as voice and trust, and analyzing the relationship between those reports and individuals' ultimate assessments about fairness. Because procedural justice research was deeply concerned with the subjective experience of the individual, there was little focus on procedural justice research that sent independent coders to assess the fairness of a process from a third-party perspective.

With respect to the body of research in negotiation, I note here that the study of legal negotiation differs in some important ways from the study of ordinary negotiation in psychology and in organizational behavior and has unique challenges (Hollander-Blumoff, 2005). In these last disciplines, researchers have conducted a vast number of lab studies that pair individuals in a negotiation exercise and measure the effects of variables of interest, including, just to name a few, relationships, strategies, cognitive biases in decision-making, and social value orientation (De Dreu et al., 2007). But this inquiry is more difficult in the particular context of legal negotiation; simply pairing subjects (often college students) to negotiate a dispute or a transaction does not capture significant dimensions of the legal setting. The parties involved in a legal negotiation must have some legal training and need an awareness of the legal framework that governs the dispute or transaction at hand. This renders legal negotiation, a subset of regular negotiation, potentially different in a meaningful way from other types of negotiation, leading to questions of external validity if the conditions of a legal negotiation are not present in the research setting.

In addition, legal negotiation is particularly hard to study in the field because of ethical concerns and access issues. Many lawyers would doubtless not be eager to see their negotiation behavior subject to study by a third party, not to mention that confidentiality and ethics concerns might present a bar to observation. Also, of course, no potential manipulation is possible in a real legal setting; clients are not likely to consent to be assigned to an experimental condition varying the behavior of their lawyers when there could be real and meaningful consequences. Scenario research might be possible, but a low response rate might be problematic, because the sample of practicing lawyers is extremely busy, and selection bias for those who might choose to respond might skew the results significantly. Self-report studies of practicing attorneys in the legal community have been plagued by some of these problems; for example, Schneider's 2002 study had a 29 percent response rate, and Hinshaw and Alberts (2011) had a 28 and 16 percent response rate among the two groups they sampled.

Antecedents of procedural justice in legal negotiation: the instant project

In my own research on legal negotiation, I began with a focus on establishing that procedural justice was even relevant to the context of two individuals engaged in a bilateral legal negotiation process without any decision-making authority present. In light of the significant differences between negotiation and other, more authority-driven, processes, establishing the basic premise that individuals' fair treatment mattered was a key first step. In the legal world, this hypothesis was often met with some skepticism and disbelief.

My research used two data sets, each consisting of approximately 400 individual surveys for 200 dyads of negotiation partners. The participants in the study were first-year students at a large law school in the United States, who engaged in a simulated legal negotiation (as part of their course work) in which they attempted to resolve a legal dispute involving a contractor and a homeowner. The participants played the role of lawyers for each party and were videotaped during their negotiation. Parties were allotted up to forty-five minutes to negotiate; immediately after each negotiation, the parties completed a comprehensive questionnaire asking about their experience during the negotiation, including specific assessments about aspects of their own and the other party's behavior, as well as more general assessments about the negotiation process and the negotiation outcome. Thus, after each negotiation, we had each individual negotiator's recorded perceptions of her own behavior and the other's behavior, each negotiator's general assessments about the negotiation process and outcome, and a tape of the negotiation in its entirety.

For the initial part of this research, trying to determine whether or not procedural justice made a difference in how individuals perceived their negotiations, we used a traditional, self-report survey methodology in our analysis. (For a comprehensive analysis of survey design and survey analysis, see Krosnick et al., 2014.) The results showed that individuals who rated their process of negotiation as fairer were more likely to say that they would recommend the agreement reached to a hypothetical client and that it formed the basis of a good long-term solution to the negotiated dispute (Hollander-Blumoff and Tyler, 2008).

As I note above, self-report is not without its methodological concerns, although some of these concerns may have been less salient in my survey. For example, because we had a class population engaging in the negotiation simulation and survey process, we had an almost 100 percent response rate. In addition, the students knew that the survey would be used as part of the debriefing by the course professor around the negotiation exercise. This may have increased the truthfulness of the self-report, but, at the same time, there was no way to be sure how seriously the participants took the survey process, and the students may have wanted to appear as positively as possible in the eyes of their professor and fellow students. The participants did not receive any compensation for completing the survey, as it was taken as part of their coursework. This may have led to more honest answers, because the survey would potentially be discussed with a professor at a later time, or it may have led to less care being taken with the survey responses. As with any type of study, noting and assessing the potential limitations or issues around validity are critical.

Another question around the design of the survey was how to create a useful scale for assessing behavior. We ultimately used a 6-point Likert scale in which participants were forced to either choose from an "agree" or a "disagree" category, rather than allowing them to select "neither agree nor disagree"; this was a design choice that may have skewed responses from individuals who were agnostic or uncertain about a particular behavior or judgment. In addition, there were a multitude of questions on the survey; in retrospect, there were too many, and this may have led to nondifferentiation, the problem of responding by taking the shortcut of rating multiple objects identically (Krosnick et al., 2014).

But, once evidence amassed (Hollander-Blumoff and Tyler, 2008; Kass, 2008) to support the relatively straightforward premise that procedural justice in negotiation did matter and played a meaningful role in shaping judgments about the negotiation, my research focus shifted to an inquiry into how fair process might be defined in the context of a negotiation process. As noted above, research on the antecedents of procedural justice judgments traditionally relied on survey research, just as the primary underlying research on the role of procedural justice had done (Lind et al., 1997). Using regression analysis, researchers could look for the connection and relationship between an ultimate assessment of fairness and potential underlying features of fair treatment, such as having a voice in the process, being treated with courtesy and respect, considering the decision maker to be neutral and unbiased, and trusting the decision maker. That is, a survey instrument could ask questions about, for example, the level of trust in the decision maker or the degree of courtesy such a decision maker displayed and then examine statistically the degree of influence that these factors played in the final rating of fair process.

In my research into the antecedents of procedural justice judgments in negotiation (Hollander-Blumoff, 2017), I first used my own survey instruments to engage in this same process. To assess the procedural justice antecedents during the negotiation, I ran regressions to determine the degree of influence that a variety of potential antecedent factors might play in shaping fairness assessments. This yielded results that suggested that one party's judgments about the level of voice, courtesy/respect, and trust that he or she experienced from the other side during the negotiation all related significantly to that party's judgments about procedural justice (with courtesy/respect being the strongest factor), but that neutrality did not play a significant independent role. But negotiation is, in fact, different than the paradigmatic experience of a third-party decision-making process. One key difference, of course, is that there is no third-party authority "providing" a process. The process of legal negotiation is wholly dynamic, completely shaped by the behavior of both parties, in a way that, for example, a litigant could never shape the process of a trial in front of a judge, an arbitration (in which a neutral arbitrator rules on a dispute), or even a mediation (where a third-party neutral mediator facilitates negotiation between parties). Thus, the antecedents that were established in those other contexts were different in a fundamental, qualitative way.

And, as a related matter, those third-party authorities in those other contexts typically had some set of rules and structures that bound their behavior, or at the least provided a helpful benchmark which a participant in the process might use to guide their assessments both of fair process and of the antecedent factors. For example, rules about judges recusing themselves can shape perceptions both of neutrality and of fairness. Standards and norms governing behavior in the courtroom could help guide decisions about whether a party was treated with respect or courtesy. Knowing that an arbitrator adhered to the prescribed rules of arbitration and was a member of a professional society of arbitrators could help determine whether she was perceived as trustworthy.

In negotiation, in some ways, all bets are off. Very few legal rules help to shape norms about behavior in negotiation. Relying on participants' assessments exposed the biggest weakness of self-report and survey research – the subjective nature of perception. Who among us does not know someone who often feels ill-used or mistreated, or someone who is quick to smile and shrug off misbehavior? The range of ways in which individuals differentially perceive the same actions – often exacerbated by differences of race, sex, gender identity, power differentials, and a multitude of other factors – makes relying on self-report in a context that is largely rule-free a complicated proposition. Even after survey results suggested which factors played the biggest role in shaping fairness assessment, it remained to be seen what kinds of behavior in a negotiation would reliably yield general perceptions of fair treatment – or, as an intermediate matter, which behaviors would reliably yield perceptions of the specific antecedent factors, such as providing voice or acting with courtesy.

This question ultimately led me to a decision to engage in behavioral coding (Heyman et al., 2014) of my set of negotiations. This was particularly exciting because we could look at the behavior not solely in the isolation of pure coding by third-party neutral coders, but could also assess the viewed behavior in the context of the perceptions of the parties themselves by analyzing the relationship between the survey data and the coding data. This opportunity was both exciting and overwhelming. As shown in Figure 12.1, there were at least nine distinct types of variables collected. Each variable might relate to one party to the

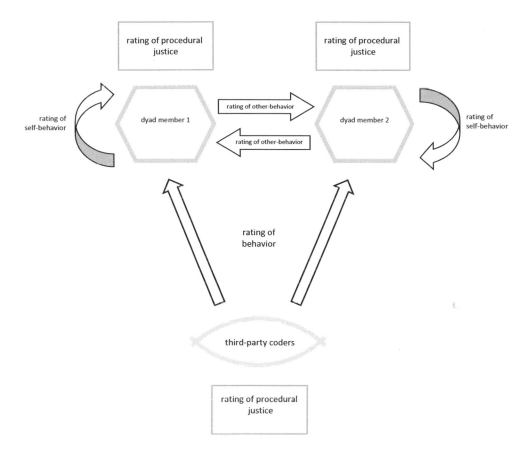

Figure 12.1 Variables collected

negotiation or two parties to the negotiation, and might be a self-report variable of one's own behavior, a self-report variable of the other party's behavior, a perception of the negotiation as a whole, or, lastly, a reported variable of either one or both of the negotiators, or the negotiation as a whole, from a neutral third-party observer.

Although the use of a pre-existing and pretested coding scheme would be convenient, the disadvantage of such an approach is clear: "existing coding systems might not be a good match for one's hypotheses" (Heyman et al., 2014). In this case, there was no set of procedural justice codes for negotiation available, nor was I aware of an available set of codes related to procedural justice behavior in another context. In pilot testing, with the help of my original two coders, I developed a set of 38 variables for behavior that seemed potentially to relate to one of the four typical clusters of procedural justice antecedents: voice, courtesy/respect, trust, and neutrality. These behaviors were conceptualized as either very specific (for example, one party revealed a specific piece of information to the other party – potential for trustworthiness) or broader (one party interrupted the other party – denial of voice). After multiple iterations of reviewing videotaped negotiations to assess the likely presence and clarity of these variables, this list was winnowed down to 27 variables (see Appendix A for a list of these variables in the coding manual). Even then, this was too many, and in future research I would (and would advise other researchers to) focus on far fewer variables.

Behavioral coding systems may be topographical (measuring the occurrence of behaviors) or dimensional (measuring the intensity of behaviors; Heyman et al., 2014). We focused on a topographical system using a classic technique in behavioral coding – unit coding. The idea in unit coding is that each utterance receives a code for what it does/says. One challenge with unit coding is to recognize when one utterance stops and another begins: short interjections may not break one utterance into two or more, but a longer interjection may do so. An exclusive code-per-unit system proved to be challenging in the negotiation context because each party would often make a multifaceted statement during the negotiation. We quickly determined that it was important to relax the coding so that each unit could be coded for as many categories as it fit. This had the potential to make the coding more nuanced and sophisticated, but also more challenging. Would we check each unit for complete consistency between coders? Or check each unit–code pair? Or simply each negotiation as a whole? We ultimately did not assess each unit independently for reliability, but assessed reliability at the level of the entire negotiation, as our end goal was to explore the holistic negotiation interaction, rather than any one particular time period or unit of the interaction. A more in-depth discussion about reliability analysis appears below.

Our coding system was both global (making assessments about coders' broad perceptions of behavior) and microbehavioral (counting incidences of smaller, fine-grained behavior), which in retrospect was too much for any one coder to manage. Microbehavioral codes also can cause problems even for experienced coders; Heyman et al.'s (2014) observation that "coders can almost never get or maintain adequate interrater agreement on such a large number [of] codes" proved to be true in this case. Because the videos were long (up to 45 minutes), we broke down our coding sheet into five-minute intervals to help keep track of where each coder was during the video while watching. Each coder also was keeping track of both parties to the negotiation simultaneously, although we later determined that it might make more sense to code for each party's behavior during one discrete viewing per party. This would result in three total viewings per coder, if not more.

In addition, because the coding was side-specific, each coder had to keep track of which negotiator was speaking and what code (and its relevant code number) might be available. Most codes were the same (for example, acting in a contentious manner), but some codes could only apply to one side or the other. So each coder had to remain aware of which party to the negotiation was on which side of the negotiation at all times. Originally, the Excel spreadsheet that the coders used had blank columns, which enabled the coders to label who was sitting on the left and who was sitting on the right by side, because coding left-to-right for negotiators sitting right-to-left proved confusing and counterintuitive to coders. Because the videos were webstreamed for viewing, coders had a difficult time using an electronic Excel sheet to code while simultaneously watching the videos. We thus made the decision to hand-mark Excel sheets while viewing the videos and then enter the data electronically thereafter. This was both time-consuming and allowed for another layer of potential error.

Ultimately, technologists at the Center for Empirical Research on the Law at Washington University were able to develop an embedded data collection system, which created a web interface that listed the variables below a live video, in two columns directly below each speaker. This interface provided coders the opportunity to simply "tick the box" any time they heard the relevant negotiator meet the qualifications of the particular code. All of these data were captured in CSV form behind the scenes and, from there, they were easily subject to migration into a software package such as SPSS. This technological innovation was game-changing for this research project, in that it made the actual coding process more intuitive and straightforward, streamlined the data collection process, and eliminated a host of potential errors.

Despite the technology intervention, interrater reliability remained the most significant challenge in this project. There were multiple options for making an assessment of reliability, and additional complexity was added because some videos were coded by two coders and others were coded by three or more coders. I measured reliability for video-coded variables in two distinct ways. First, I used the average measures reliability statistic produced by a one-way random effects intraclass correlation for two ratings of each video. For those ratings, I used data for every video that was coded by only two coders and, for all the other videos, I selected the two sets of coding from the most experienced coders. In relevant cases, data were ipsatized within coder (that is, transformed into ratings relative to the individual coder's average rating). Second, I analyzed reliability by calculating Krippendorff's alpha (K alpha), a specialized and conservative measurement tool for reliability of content coding when multiple coders are present and some data have been coded by a subset of coders.

I ultimately ran all analyses using mean video ratings for all coders. Adding coders typically increases reliability, and so my reliability figures as presented theoretically may represent a slight underestimation of actual reliability. Although interrater agreement was not as high as desirable, I noted in my results that findings based on behavioral coding may be published even when interrater reliability is below textbook standards (Vazire, 2010). Also, as Krippendorff (1980, p. 147) noted, stringent standards for reliability "may be relaxed considerably" in exploratory studies. Dichotomous variables had different optimal interrater reliability metrics than continuous variables. Some of our variables were, by their nature, dichotomous – for example, either a potentially damaging piece of information was revealed or it was not revealed. But other variables were potentially continuous – such as how many times a particular negotiator uttered a unit that was contentious in nature. Reliability for most of my variables was continuously too low for traditional research. However, interrater reliability standards can be relaxed in the setting of behavioral coding and also in exploratory research, both of which were present here. An effort to train coders, eliminate codes that appeared to be of marginal value, engage with coders regarding their differences at weekly meetings, and work harder to clarify the nature of each code in the coding manual yielded results, but interrater reliability remained stubbornly lower than optimal.

Taking a step back from the project, it became clear to me that, just as individuals engaged in the negotiation might perceive behavior differently based on their own personality, identity, pre-existing or current dynamic with the other party, or other factors, so, too, the coders brought their own issues to the table. Our coders were not artificial intelligence but rather human beings with their sets of judgments, concerns, experience, and preconceptions. As an example, one might consider the case of interrupting. What we were seeking was a variable that would be reverse-coded to reflect voice during the negotiation. The operationalization of voice was a reverse-coding of how often a party would be cut off while speaking, with the idea that someone who felt that they had not been permitted to speak fully would perceive a lower degree of voice than a party who had not been interrupted. And yet individuals often spoke over one another in a way that was not consistently perceived by coders as interrupting in a negative sense. That is, there was little consensus on what constituted a voice-depriving interruption. Social norms, differences in communication, gender roles, and other factors made the "neutral" assessment of interruption, among other variables, quite difficult. And other potential voice-related variables that we pilot-tested, such as active listening, proved to be simply useless after coding efforts were completely unsuccessful.

As another example, one underlying behavioral variable relating to trustworthy behavior was whether a participant had made an untruthful statement. I did not anticipate the difficulty with rating statements that were false; that is, it seemed initially that, because coders could read all of the background material that participants reviewed, it would be relatively simple to code for when a participant made a statement that was untrue as compared with the background material. And yet coders did not always agree regarding untruthfulness, because sometimes they perceived that a statement was close to the truth and was one potential interpretation, rather than untruthful, or sometimes they perceived that the participant did not intend to be untruthful but had merely made a mistake. We thus honed this variable so that it was only coded when a participant made a "self-serving false statement," meaning that the lie made was in favor of the participant's own interest and against the other party's interest. However, we included in the coding manual a specific instruction that the coder did not have to believe that there was an "intent" to lie. Ultimately, although we developed a better code for the kind of behavior that we thought might reasonably relate to untrustworthy behavior, differences in perception among coders made this effort more difficult than anticipated.

Finally, another methodological dimension to this project involved the use of dyadic data, which presented a tremendous opportunity but simultaneously required a special statistical analysis. Dyadic data are data in which individual measurement is taken, but for assessments of behaviors that occur at the level of a dyadic (two-person) interaction. That is, the data are essentially linked, and thus nonindependent, at the two-person negotiating dyad level; the exact same interaction is occurring for two study participants, but it is measured separately through the eyes of each party. Having perspectives from both parties to the negotiation regarding their opinions about their own and the other party's behavior, coupled with observational data from a third-party coder, allowed us to investigate questions including, but not limited to, how accurate each party was regarding her own and the other party's fairness-related behaviors; whether assumed similarity (the notion that one perceives the other as doing what oneself is doing) played a role in guiding behavior; whether parties were in agreement with respect to their behavior; and whether certain aspects of fair treatment were more likely to yield agreement among the parties with respect to its presence or absence. I used the social relations model (Kenny and Albright, 1987) to guide me in thinking about how to assess the accuracy and the general nature of interpersonal perception. Because the data were dyadic, I also conducted an analysis using multilevel modeling, treating the dyad as the unit of analysis in order to control for nonindependence of the dyadic partners. This required a bit more research and investigation into the proper statistical technique (Kenny et al., 2006).

Future directions

Conducting this particular research project suggested to me the potential interest and relevance of several future inquiries. One idea might be to turn the tables on the problem and, instead of understanding the coders to provide "objective" data, one might, rather, treat the coders themselves as the participants in the study. To try to develop a taxonomy of negotiation behavior that reliably translates into "fair process", one potential direction might be to record a handful of videos of negotiation behavior and ask coders to code for specific behaviors and for global assessments of fairness of process. This would allow researchers to manipulate behavior during the negotiation in order to see whether certain types of behavior could reliably be perceived as either fair or unfair, or, on a more granular level, whether certain behaviors are reliably perceived as providing voice, or as demonstrating courtesy and respect, or as fostering trust and promoting neutrality. This focus would be likely to give cleaner data on how individuals perceive negotiation behavior through a fairness lens.

But this approach, too, has its flaws. It might be less helpful in understanding the experience of an actual party to the negotiation. Theoretically, there may be a divide between how an observer and a participant perceive the same events. This "staged video" approach would not be able to reach that issue. In addition, on more practical notes, one would want to construct a "staged" video that looked largely unscripted and fluid, as a real negotiation would, but that contained particular behaviors that a researcher was most interested in examining. As my own experience, described above, suggests, it may take significant iterations of pilot efforts to isolate behaviors, especially in a setting as dynamic as the negotiation context.

Another potential direction might be to ask participants to engage in a live negotiation with a confederate who has been instructed to negotiate in a particular manner, using behavior that is predicted to be more or less promoting of each of the four clusters of procedural justice behavior. For example, a confederate might engage in "voice-providing" or "voice-depriving" behaviors, and a range of participants who engage in the same negotiation context with that confederate could be asked for their assessments around those four factors, as well as around their ultimate perceptions of fair process. This would have the advantage of attempting to assess the same behavior, but it would have significant hurdles in implementation. For example, even if the confederate has specific instructions, she may find it more or less difficult to maintain that behavior in light of whatever behavior the participant chooses to engage in. That is, negotiation is dynamic, and so any "script" or instructions given to one party might have the potential to be difficult to adhere to in a given situation or, if adhered to, to not apply well in a particular context and appear stilted and unnatural, introducing a confounding variable.

A different approach might be to code purely during a short slice of time. Watching videos that could last 45 minutes or longer increased the likelihood that coders got tired or confused. It might be worth analyzing some portion of time, such as the first and/or last five minutes of the interaction for procedural justice behaviors. This could add a layer of primacy/recency effects that might be interesting to explore, but it also would, by definition, leave out significant chunks of negotiation interaction that could be exceptionally meaningful. A time-sequential approach is another possible approach to this type of data, exploring whether fairness-related behavior at Time 1 has a significant effect on fairness-related behavior at Time 2.

Finally, one choice we made early on was to ignore differences of gender, race, or other person-specific variables in our analysis. This is a choice that I might revisit if I were running this project again. The questions of differences in negotiator behavior, and of perception across those differences, were ones that had the potential to swamp the project entirely. And our pairings were random, meaning that we did not have even samplings of male–male, male–female, and female–female pairings. And we did not collect any information on self-identification with race, gender or ethnicity. Nonetheless, I still have concerns that looking at these differences might have yielded important insights.

Ultimately, using behavioral coding in conjunction with survey data is a challenging and exhausting effort. It provides unparalleled richness, but is fraught with potential pitfalls. I recommend Heyman et al. (2014) and Krosnick et al. (2014) for excellent overviews of both behavioral coding and survey approaches. In addition, Kenny and Kashy (2014) provide a thoughtful discussion of the special challenges of, and statistical methods appropriate for, using dyadic data. The two research methods I have focused on here offer a complementary perspective; the bias that might be present in self-report can be mitigated by the efforts of third-party coders. Yet the very richness that makes the project so intriguing and promising is also a source of concern. In light of the multitude of ways in which the data can be connected and analyzed, I recommend that a researcher undertaking such a project hew carefully – at least initially – to a somewhat narrow focus as she embarks on this endeavor. A broad exploratory effort like the one I have described above yields fascinating tentative results, but it is important to think about ways in which such a project could be streamlined and honed so that the results are meaningful and reliable.

Appendix A

Guidelines for negotiation coding

Unit coding: The negotiations are coded according to units. A unit is what gets a code. Each unit can receive no code, one code, or more than one different code but <u>a single unit cannot get the same code twice</u>. A code is given only when the unit itself provides an unambiguous example of the code. If a unit can be interpreted in an alternative way that warrants a meaning different from the code, the code should not be given.

A "unit" is everything said by one negotiator in between what the other negotiator said.

For example:

Negotiator 1: I don't know that this will allow my client to recover any of his losses.
Negotiator 2: We can't help it if your client underestimated the costs. The subcontractor problem had nothing to do with my client. That had nothing to do with a two-week delay.
Negotiator 2: An arbitrator would not find that the two-week delay has any legal relevance.
Negotiator 1: The loss I'm not blaming on your client, but the two-week rush was your client's fault. A court would consider those things.
Negotiator 1: But I think we can call it a deal.

This contains 3 units. The different statements by the same negotiator that are made consecutively are still part of the same unit.

★★EXCEPTIONS★★

non-substantive response: When one negotiator's continuous statement is interjected by the other's non-substantive verbal acknowledgement (e.g. um-hum without showing approval or rejection, mere repetition of the first negotiator's statement), the first negotiator's continuous statement is counted as one unit, and the other's non-substantive response is not counted.

Example 1:

Negotiator 1: I think we could install the steps and the portable sweepers ...
Negotiator 2: Right.
Negotiator 1: ... and put in the small fence.

This is counted as one unit because Negotiator 2's interjection is a non-substantive response that is not a meaningful response to Negotiator 1's statement.
Example 2:

Negotiator 1: We need the steps and the portable sweepers ...
Negotiator 2: Oh no!
Negotiator 1: ... and the landscaping.

This is counted as two units – one unit for Negotiator 1's continuous statement and one unit for Negotiator 2's interjection. Negotiator 2's interjection expresses rejection of Negotiator 1's statement and therefore it is a meaningful response and should be counted as a unit.

mere repetition/clarification: When one negotiator repeats himself or herself in exact wording on a clarification request by the other negotiator, the whole exchange by the two negotiators should only be counted as one unit.
Example 3:

Negotiator 1: What is your top priority?
Negotiator 2: We have to have the steps.
Negotiator 1: Sorry?
Negotiator 2: We have to have the steps.

Only the first statements of both negotiators should be counted as units (i.e. two units in total), because the second statements are for clarification purpose, and Negotiator 2's second statement is an exact repetition of the first.

DICHOTOMOUS VARIABLES – only code, if disclosed, once per designated speaker

ROCHS: R's car accident

1. Only code the first time a lawyer discloses/asserts this fact to the other lawyer.
2. Code if the other lawyer restates/asserts this disclosure.
3. Can be somewhat indirect (e.g. "my client suffered a serious back injury in February"), but should get at the main point of this disclosure.

ROCHS: R in debt/no profit

1. Only code the first time a lawyer discloses/asserts this fact to the other lawyer.
2. Code if the other lawyer restates/asserts this disclosure.

ROCHS: R's cost of labor

1. Like the competitor's bid, it should have some reference to money, not value.

2. Should be reiterated by Rochs to be coded for Rochs (e.g. Kanat: "His cost for the steps is $2,000." Rochs: "Okay, the steps are $2,000 at cost.").
3. Questions are excluded.

KANAT: tiles are K's fault

1. Only code the first time a lawyer discloses/asserts this fact to the other lawyer.
2. Code if the other lawyer restates/asserts this disclosure.
3. Can be somewhat indirect (e.g. "my client/your client mistakenly ordered the wrong tiles"), but should get at the main point of this disclosure.

KANAT: R not allowed on prop

1. Only code the first time a lawyer discloses/asserts this fact to the other lawyer.
2. Merely mentioning that Rochs only had 2 weeks at the end of March to complete the project is not enough. It must be disclosed that Kanat forbade Rochs on the property in early March.

KANAT: competitor's bid

1. Code when mentioned with reference to some kind of monetary value.
2. Questions are excluded.
3. Do not code references to "value" or "worth."
4. Only references to actual bids are coded, or self-serving false statements about bids (e.g. "Stevens said he could do the sweepers for $4,000.").

CONTINUOUS VARIABLES – code all instances in separate units

discuss negot. process

1. Explicitly talking about the process. This category is a little vague, but all talk that refers to the process, and not the content, should be coded.
2. For example, "How do you want to start?" or "Let's talk about the sweepers before we talk about the steps."

intent to reach agreement

1. Code statements like "I hope we come to agreement today." Mere affirmation of those statements doesn't count, but something like "We hope so as well" does.

absolve other from blame

1. Explicitly absolving other from blame, e.g. "This is not your fault."
2. Can include expressions like "That wasn't your responsibility" or "That wasn't within your control."

absolve self from blame

1. Explicitly absolving self from blame, e.g. "This is not my fault."

2. Can include expressions like "This was not my responsibility" or "I had no control over that situation."

apologetic

1. Code statements like "my client is really sorry" or "we apologize for x."
2. Do not code statements like "we feel really bad" or "this situation sucks."
3. Code apologies between negotiators, external to the negotiation itself (e.g. "I'm sorry it's taking me so long to find these numbers.").
4. Do not include fake apologies or non-apologetic uses of "sorry."

contentiousness

1. Code all and only explicit name-calling and/or insults.
2. Will rarely occur.

interrupting

1. Not just talking over, but in a rude way.
2. Also trying to change the content of the conversation. Redirecting the conversation. Making a contrary point in the midst of someone else's statement.

self-serving false statements

1. Only code false statements that would serve the interests of the person making them. For example, Kanat's attorney claiming that the competitor's bids are lower than they really are, or Rochs's attorney claiming that Rochs's prices are higher than they really are.
2. Code self-serving false statements that seem unintentional.
3. Code any statement that is both SSFS and fits some other category, e.g. the cost of Roch's labor and SSFS, or the purpose of the pool and SSFS.

self-serving omissions

1. Code failure to disclose information that one party has. E.g. Rochs: "What did the competitor bid for the installation of the automatic sweepers?" Kanat: "I really don't know."
2. Code a self-serving omission even when it seems unintentional.

contract language

1. Not just talk of the contract, but a reference to something specific within the contract.
2. If the other party agrees, only code if she reiterates with contract language.
3. Also code instances of getting out the contract or diagram and pointing.

industry stand.

1. Code for use of the words "industry" and/or "standard."
2. If it is unclear whether the lawyer is referring to an industry or legal standard, code as industry standard.

legal stand. for product

1. Code for statements like "building code", "safety regulation" or "illegal pool."
2. Must use some kind of legal term.

legal cases

1. Code when a specific reference to a legal case is made.

subst. performance

1. Should include mentionings of "frustrates the purpose," "economic waste," and "idiosyncratic taste," and "substantial performance."
2. Code statements that are not exact but close enough given the context (e.g. "Digging up the entire pool is very wasteful.").

purpose of the pool

1. Code all mentionings of the pool's "purpose."

mention of poss. arbitration

1. Code statements where it is expressed that arbitration exists as an alternative to negotiations, but in a non-threatening manner.
2. If a party mentions an outcome while discussing arbitration, should be coded only as "likely arbitration outcomes" and not double-coded as both "mention of possible arbitration" and "likely arbitration outcomes."

likely arbitration outcomes

1. Code when there's a reference to some result of arbitration, whether specifically monetary or just a vague outcome.

threat of arbitration

1. Expressions of willingness and/or intention to proceed to arbitration.

positive expressions of fairness

1. Code positive expressions of fairness, e.g. "that's fair" or "well, that's not unfair." Can include use of "justice" as a synonym.
2. Do not code expressions of the principle of fairness, e.g. "my client is interested in fairness."

negative expressions of fairness

1. Code negative expressions of fairness, e.g. "that's not fair" or "I don't think that's fair at all!" Can include use of "justice" as a synonym.

fairness as concept (no valence)

1. Code all other expressions of fairness that are non-evaluative, i.e. have neither a positive nor negative valence
2. Examples include: "My client really cares about fairness", "Well, there's also the issues of fairness …"
3. Also include expressions using "unfair", e.g. "We are not interested in an unfair outcome."

Further readings

Grisso, T. and Brodsky, S., eds. 2018. *The Roots of Modern Psychology and Law: A Narrative History.* Oxford: Oxford University Press.

Kovera, M.B. and Borgida, E., 2010. Social psychology and law. In Fiske, S., Gilbert, D., and Lindzey, G., eds., *Handbook of Social Psychology*, 5th ed., Hoboken, NJ: John Wiley, pp. 1343–1385.

Monahan, J. and Walker, L., 2011. Twenty-five years of social science in law, *Law & Human Behavior*, 35(1), pp. 72–82.

Nadler, J. and Mueller, P., 2017. Social psychology and the law. In Parisi, F., ed., *Oxford Handbook of Law & Economics.* Oxford: Oxford University Press, pp. 124–160.

References

Becker, W. and Curhan, J., 2018. The dark side of subjective value in sequential negotiations: The mediating role of pride and anger. *Journal of Applied Psychology*, 103(1), pp. 74–87.

De Dreu, C., Beersma, B., Steinel, W., and Van Kleef, G. A., 2007. The psychology of negotiation: Principles and basic processes. In Kruglanski, A. and Higgins, E., eds., *Social Psychology: Handbook of Basic Principles*, New York: Guilford Press, pp. 608–629.

Ellsworth, P., 1989. Are twelve heads better than one? *Law and Contemporary Problems*, 52(4), pp. 207–224.

Filipowicz, A., Barsade, S., and Melwani, S., 2011. Understanding emotional transitions: The interpersonal consequences of changing emotions in negotiations. *Journal of Personality and Social Psychology*, 101(3), pp. 541–556.

Heyman R., Lorber, M., Eddy, J., and West, T., 2014. Behavioral observation and coding. In Reis, H. and Judd, C., eds., *Handbook of Research Methods in Social and Personality Psychology*, 2nd ed., New York: Cambridge University Press, pp. 345–372.

Hinshaw, A., and Alberts, J., 2011. Doing the right thing: An empirical study of attorney negotiation ethics. *Harvard Negotiation Law Review*, 16, pp. 95–163.

Hollander-Blumoff, R., 2017. Formation of procedural justice judgments in legal negotiation… *Group Decision and Negotiation*, 26(1), pp. 19–43.

Hollander-Blumoff, R. and Tyler, T., 2008. Procedural justice in negotiation: procedural fairness, outcome acceptance, and integrative potential. *Law & Social Inquiry*, 33, pp. 473–500.

Hollander-Blumoff, R., 2005. Legal research on negotiation. *International Negotiation*, 10(1), pp. 149–164.

Kass, E., 2008. Interactional justice, negotiator outcome satisfaction, and desire for future negotiations: R-E-S-P-E-C-T at the negotiating table. *International Journal of Conflict Management*, 19, pp. 319–338.

Kenny, D. and Albright, L., 1987. Accuracy in interpersonal perception – a social-relations analysis. *Psychological Bulletin*, 102(3), pp. 390–402.

Kenny, D., Kashy, D., and Cook, W., 2006. *Dyadic Data Analysis.* New York: Guilford Press.

Kenny, D. and Kashy, D., 2014. The design and analysis of data from dyads and groups. In Reis, H. and Judd, C., eds., *Handbook of Research Methods in Social and Personality Psychology*, 2nd ed., New York: Cambridge University Press, pp. 589–607.

Krippendorff, K., 1980 *Content Analysis: An Introduction to Its Methodology.* Beverly Hills, CA: Sage.

Krosnick, J., Lavrakas, P., and Kim, N., 2014. Survey research. In Reis, H. and Judd, C., eds., *Handbook of Research Methods in Social and Personality Psychology*, 2nd ed., New York: Cambridge University Press, pp. 404–442.

Lind, E., Tyler, T., and Huo, Y., 1997. Procedural context and culture: Variations in the antecedents of procedural justice judgments. *Journal of Personality and Social Psychology*, 73(4), pp. 767–780.

Rachlinski, J., 1996. Gains, losses, and the psychology of litigation. *Southern California Law Review*, 113, pp. 114–185.

Rogers, T., Zeckhauser, R., Gino, F., Norton, M., and Schweitzer, M., 2017. Artful paltering: The risks and rewards of using truthful statements to mislead others. *Journal of Personality and Social Psychology*, 112(3), pp. 456–473.

Schneider, A., 2002. Shattering negotiation myths: Empirical evidence on the effectiveness of negotiation style, *Harvard Negotiation Law Review*, 7, pp. 143–233.

Shestowsky, D., 2014. The psychology of procedural preference: How litigants evaluate legal procedures ex ante.. *Iowa Law Review* 99(2), pp. 637–710.

Tyler, T., 1990. *Why People Obey the Law: Procedural Justice, Legitimacy, and Compliance.* New Haven, CT: Yale University Press.

Tyler, T., 1989. The psychology of procedural justice: A test of the group-value model. *Journal of Personality and Social Psychology*, 57(5), pp. 830–838.

Tyler, T., 1988. What is procedural justice? Criteria used by citizens to assess the fairness of legal procedures. *Law and Society Review*, 22(1), pp. 103–135.

Vazire, S., 2010. Who knows what about a person? The self-other knowledge asymmetry (SOKA) model. *Journal of Personality and Social Psychology*, 98(2), pp. 281–300.

Wilson, K., 2016. Personality similarity in negotiations: Testing the dyadic effects of similarity in interpersonal traits and the use of emotional displays on negotiation outcomes. *Journal of Applied Psychology*, 101(10), pp. 1405–1421.

13

SOCIO-LEGAL STUDIES AND ECONOMICS

Richard Craven

Introduction

This chapter is about socio-legal studies and the study of markets and economic behaviour. This territory is typically the preserve of economics; the chapter reflects on the relationship between law, economics and socio-legal studies.

Mainstream economics – or "neoclassical economics"[1] – is "the science which studies human behaviour as a relationship between ends and scarce means" (Robbins, 1935, p. 115). For its critics, since the marginal revolution in the 1870s, inspired by Benthamite utilitarianism and the success of the natural sciences, notably physics (Mirowski, 1989), mainstream economics has sought to position itself apart from the other social sciences: it is an objective, mathematical science of human behaviour. In this view, the other social sciences are inferior: it is only economics, the most scientific of the social sciences, that can provide value-free analysis – prized by policymakers and politicians (Earle et al., 2016; Fourcade et al., 2015). The discipline can struggle to engage with the other social sciences, including law (Swann, 2016), and is often lampooned with the label the "dismal science" – today, mainly owing to the way economics approaches behaviour as removed from its social and historical context (Hodgson, 2001; Milonakis and Fine, 2009a).

In light of the above, it is perhaps understandable that socio-legal studies (as with sociology) enjoys uneasy relations with economics. Though socio-legal studies/law and society can be a broad – law in context – church, and despite efforts to carve out a place for economics in socio-legal studies (see, for example, Ogus, 2006), it has mainly been left for 'law and economics' to make use of insights from economics, using these to critique law and legal institutions. The law and economics movement in the United States has enjoyed

---

1 Neoclassical economics is a form of mathematical economics that came to dominate the mainstream after World War II. Paul Samuelson's "Economics" textbook, first published in 1948, is often recognised as the beginning of this period (Samuelson and Nordhaus, 2005). Today, "neoclassical economics" is often used in a derisory way to refer to the lack of diversity within mainstream economics. This, however, is arguably misleading, as there does exist diversity of opinion and approach within the mainstream. In particular, the mainstream has evolved over the years, e.g. accepting new institutional economics and, more recently, behavioural economics, and economists working in these areas are very unlikely to identify as neoclassical (see Arnsperger and Varoufakis, 2006).

marked success. This is owing, in the main, to the pioneering work of groups of academics at the University of Chicago – including Nobel Laureates[2] Ronald Coase, George Stigler, Milton Friedman and Gary Becker, as well as the jurist and academic Richard Posner (see Sanchez-Graells, 2018, for a useful overview of the literature) – and academics in Virginia – notably, James Buchanan (also a Nobel Laureate) and Gordon Tullock. Law and economics is prominent in law schools across the US, and, though it has failed to penetrate UK law schools in the same way, law and economics arguments have a major pull on policymakers around the globe.

A strained relationship between law and economics and socio-legal studies will be the subject of the first part of the next section. I will, as much as possible, relate the discussion to my own thinking around my own area of research – to do with economic regulation and, specifically, the regulation of government contracts (e.g. private finance initiative/ public–private partnership contracts) and procurement. Much UK public procurement regulation derives from the European Union, which regulates procurement for economic (the internal market) reasons; government procurement represents significant economic activity – 15–20% of EU GDP. Detailed, technical procedural rules are in place, based around principles of transparency, non-discrimination and equal treatment. It is in commercial areas, such as this, that law and economics analysis is most prevalent (e.g. Sanchez-Graells, 2015). Indeed, related subjects, such as competition/antitrust law and tax law, have been transformed by law and economics.

My current research looks at the government's use of procurement to pursue objectives collateral to the main buying purpose and value for money, such as achieving industrial, social and environmental policies. At present, I am interested in the interpretation and operation of law promoting "social value" across UK government procurement.[3] This social value regulation, particularly when looking at procurement in local government, appears at odds with how, since the 1980s, the UK has sought to regulate government procurement. Over the past 40 years, ideas from mainstream economics have been central to the regulatory strategy. For example, with acrimonious relations between central and local government, law and economics – specifically public choice theory (discussed in the next section) – provided a justification for transforming service delivery at local level through policies such as compulsory competitive tendering, in which services, traditionally delivered inhouse by local government, would be contracted out to private businesses.

My research entails qualitative research methods – observation of and interviews with people involved in local government contracting. This approach, in revealing the complexity of individuals' perceptions and experiences, is at odds with the simplifications and generalisations that are needed for the mathematical models of human behaviour found in mainstream economics. The second part of the next section therefore discusses how I am currently utilising heterodox ideas on economics, namely economic sociology, in order to complement law and economics approaches. The chapter concludes by looking at opportunities for socio-legal studies to build bridges with mainstream economics, and law and

---

2 Economics is the only social science with its own Nobel Prize. However, unlike the Nobel Prizes for outstanding contributions for humanity in chemistry, literature, peace, physics, and physiology or medicine, which were first awarded in 1901, the economics prize was established in 1968 by the Swedish central bank. These prizes are not technically a Nobel Prize, and are officially titled the Sveriges Riksbank Prize in Economic Sciences in Memory of Alfred Nobel.

3 Public Services (Social Value) Act 2012.

economics, as well opportunities for a more plural law and economics movement – a post-crash law and economics.

Socio-legal studies and law and economics

Researching with the "dismal science"

The first part of this section will reflect upon the relationship between legal studies, socio-legal studies in particular, and mainstream economics, which inevitably colours my own research agenda. The interaction between legal studies and mainstream economics has mainly come about because economists have turned their attention to law, bringing with them core tools and concepts from mainstream economics. It is through this law and economics work that many socio-legal scholars, myself included, will engage with mainstream economics. This section of the chapter will therefore begin with a description of two pioneering figures in law and economics: Coase and Becker. In the descriptions, we see law, in essence, subject to audit by economics – economic efficiency[4] representing the sole evaluative measure (Davies, 2010). Little value is given to familiar legal notions, such as justice and fairness.

Coase's "The Problem of Social Cost" (Coase, 1960), one of the most cited journal articles in both law and economics in the US, represents the watershed moment for law and economics. In the article, Coase takes aim at welfare economics in particular Arthur Pigou's arguments on market failure – that is, sometimes economic activity will have social costs and benefits that are not reflected in market prices, known as "externalities". In Pigovian welfare economics, a negative externality (e.g. health risks due to passive smoking) is a market failure that justifies regulatory intervention (e.g. banning smoking in enclosed workplaces). Coase disagrees, radically: it is a one sided assessment, ignoring the costs surrounding regulatory intervention – for example, the way in which bans or fines might hamper business. In the article, rather than refuting Pigou's thesis with mathematical models – as would be the norm in economics – Coase works through a number of practical illustrations, for example drawn from English tort law, some of which, such as *Sturges v Bridgman*,[5] will be very familiar to undergraduate law students in the UK. Coase uses these examples to argue that, absent transaction costs and provided legal rights are well defined and enforceable, market intervention is undesirable. If left alone, the producer and consumer of a negative externality will ultimately negotiate an efficient outcome, regardless of who holds the legal rights. This aspect of the article – which Stigler would label the "Coase Theorem" – would become an established part of economic theory.[6]

Becker's work, branded "economics imperialism" (Milonakis and Fine, 2009b), ventures into the territory of other social sciences. Becker takes insights from economics, developed in order to understand how markets operate, and uses them to understand behaviour in non-market situations. Posner would go on to take this approach even further, and Becker's

COASE

BECKER

---

4 There are different definitions of efficiency. However, though this is important, there is insufficient space to expand on this is the chapter.
5 [1879] 11 Ch D 852.
6 Despite the success of the Coase Theorem, this is not the central message in the article. Coase accepts that in the real world the presence of transaction costs could potentially undermine a negotiated, market solution. He is thus equivocal about the desirability of market intervention, and his main point is to caution against intervention relying only on "blackboard economics".

influence is still prominent today, for example in the *Freakonomics* series (Dubner and Levitt, 2005). Lawyers will likely be familiar with how Becker approaches criminal behaviour (Becker, 1968). He posits that decisions about whether or not to commit crimes can be looked at in the same way as market decisions – as the result of rational cost–benefit calculations by individuals: the individual will weigh up, among other things, the likelihood and severity of punishment against anticipated benefits resulting from an unlawful act. In order to deter more crime, therefore, which is not – from Becker's perspective – necessarily desirable, policymakers must simply increase its cost – that is, up the risk of detection, apprehension, conviction and punishment, and/or the severity of the punishment.

The powerful arguments, above, stimulate important socio-legal contributions, notably work studying the role of social norms (see, for example, Ellickson, 1991), which has prompted adaptations in law and economics. This sort of socio-legal work, emphasising the social aspects of market behaviour, is an important supplement to law and economics. For example, if law and economics provides a starting-point analysis, social research methods can then elaborate on its accuracy and the appropriateness of approaching behaviour from solely the economics perspective. However, despite some successes, socio-legal studies in the above vein can misunderstand what law and economics is trying to do (McCrudden, 2006). It can be all too easy to set economics up as an "intellectual straw man" – painting an exaggerated picture of economists' claims that one can then quite easily show to be simplistic and prone to errors (Fourcade, 2018). Because of this, socio-legal studies/law and society and law and economics often talk "past one another rather than engaging in dialogue" (Edelman, 2004, p. 182).

This is, arguably, unfortunate, as both of these branches of legal research would stand to benefit from greater interaction. Nevertheless, problematically, there is a general perception of tension between socio-legal studies/law and society and law and economics, especially pronounced in the US, with the two pitted in ideological opposition (Edelman, 2004). Law and economics is associated with an agenda around right-wing economics, whereas socio-legal studies is framed as left-leaning. The aims and values of traditional law and economics can appear at odds with the social ethos behind much socio-legal scholarship, and important law and economics work, such as that of Coase and Becker (above), struggles to accept logic, distinct from the economic, that we might recognise as grounded in "the social" (see Cotterrell, 2006). In the words of von Hayek, a pivotal figure in the development of Chicago law and economics,

> the term 'sozial' is the weasel-word par excellence. Nobody knows what it actually means. But it is definitely true that a social market economy is no market economy … social justice is not justice – and I am afraid a social democracy is no democracy either.
>
> *(Ptak, 2009, p. 128)*

In my own area of study, because government buying is a significant area of economic activity, this ideological tension has been especially noticeable. In particular, a fascinating exchange took place between leading scholars around the legality, under EU procurement law, of governments deviating from a commercial focus when buying, and looking to achieve sustainability objectives. The EU restricts governments from using procurement in this way – that is, as a policy tool – and the precise scope for including sustainability considerations is uncertain and controversial. A debate was triggered when Sanchez-Graells put forward an "economics informed" argument (Sanchez-Graells, 2010). Sanchez-Graells proposes a competition-orientated approach to the interpretation of EU procurement law,[7] which portrays the inclusion in government procurement of sustainability policies, which risk distorting the competitive process, as problematic. This was countered by a variety of arguments, one being that it provides a basis for "neoliberal" policy prescriptions advanced by the European Commission (Kunzlik, 2013).[8]

The above debate, in part, prompted my own research agenda on the subject, as I am now keen to provide an alternative economics-informed perspective. There appears little to justify an ideological opposition between law and economics and socio-legal research. Law and economics does not have to be tied to right-wing economics, just as socio-legal studies will not always occupy a position on the left (Donahue, 1988). Ideas from economics, which often carry great sway among policymakers and in society more generally, are available for socio-legal researcherers to make use of. As Chang notes, "[t]o exaggerate only slightly, if you are clever enough, you can justify any government policy, any corporate strategy, or any individual action with the help of ... economics" (Chang, 2014, p. 126). However, there is little sign of socio-legal research (e.g. in recognised socio-legal journals) recognising mainstream economics as an available tool.[9]

In this way, my socio-legal work is benefiting from my explorations into economic theory and traditional law and economics. However, an important limiting factor is mainstream economics' reliance on mathematics. Mathematics has been a prerequisite of disciplinary expertise in economics since the 1970s: it relies "on a set of reasoning tools that economists call 'models': small mathematical, statistical, graphical, diagrammatic, and even physical objects that can be manipulated in various different ways" (Morgan, 2012). Arguably, it is this dependence on mathematics that prevents total colonisation of law by economics (Cotterrell, 1998, p. 178), but it also works the other way: limiting legal scholars from appropriating any other than the most basic tools of economics. For those lacking access to the requisite mathematical expertise, there are other avenues, such as economic sociology, which provides an alternative and, for me, more attractive approach to understanding how markets operate. The second part of this section, below, discusses how my current research looks to economic sociology to add to our understanding of government contracts markets.

Value/s in government contracts and procurement law

This section will detail my current research, which studies the interpretation and application of government's social value duty and, in doing so, social constructions of law and value in government contracts markets. In studying value, the research strikes at the core of economics, as well as at a long-standing divide between economics and sociology. The section will begin, therefore, with discussion on the importance of value to mainstream economics, before relating this discussion to the regulation of local government. The section then moves on to consider the way economic sociology is informing my work.

---

7 Following reforms in 2014, a principle of competition can now be found in the EU public procurement rules. It did not exist (explicitly) at the time Sanchez-Graells was writing.
8 Sanchez-Graells clarified his argument in a later edition of his book (Sanchez-Graells, 2015).
9 Campbell and Lee's criticism of the response of the Department of the Environment, Food and Rural Affairs to the 2001 foot and mouth epidemic based on Coase's caution against reliance on "blackboard economics" is one exception to this (Campbell and Lee, 2003).

The roots of mathematical marginalism found in mainstream economics today lie in debate around value. In the 1870s, the marginal revolution – in which Jevons, Walrus and Menger put forward similar ideas on "marginal utility" – transformed economics, introducing a subjective notion of value. This strongly countered the objective, labour theories of value found in classical political economy (e.g. those of Smith and Ricardo) and Marxian political economy and shifted the focus of economic analysis away from production, towards consumption. Henceforth, money was simply a measure of the "utility" (well-being) consumers derive from commodities, and, in essence, the "value" of a commodity is an individual's willingness to pay for it. Consequently, value – in economics – is little more than a synonym for price. This notion of value would give rise to *homo economicus*: individuals are rational agents who are constantly calculating, rank-ordering opportunities according to their preferences and choosing the option that maximises individual utility. This fiction enables economists to model consumer behaviour mathematically.

In studying the regulation of government and, more broadly, the evolution of "the New Public Management" across public-sector administration over the past 50 years, the economic conception of the individual is prominent. This is mainly because of the influence of public choice economics, most influential in the 1980s under "New Right" governments. Public choice, associated with the Virginia School and figures such as Buchanan and Tullock, takes law and economics into the territory of political science. Economics is used to critique the state – for example, democratic politics, government and bureaucracy. We are to regard politicians and bureaucrats with distrust: they are individualistic utility maximisers. Bureaucrats – owing to inappropriate individual and organisational incentives, such as minimal competitive pressure and the lack of the private-sector profit motive and threat of bankruptcy – should be expected to pursue their own selfish interests over the public interest. The policy answer to this is the discipline of competition, such as through requiring public services to be put out to competitive tender. In addition, legal rules would be used to constrain the discretion enjoyed by bureacrats – for example, under s.17 of the Local Government Act 1988 – to align local authority purchasing decision-making with that of economically rational, profit-seeking corporations; there was no longer space for political and social values: local government was forbidden to take into account non-commercial considerations, such as labour standards, when awarding contracts.

Decades of the New Public Management have ingrained corporate and managerialist culture and values across government, including procurement departments. This, coupled with continued pressure for cost savings, means that, today, a common criticism levelled at government contracting is the over-emphasis on price, and this subject has gained attention in the media owing to links made between lowest-price tendering and the collapse of the major government contractor Carillion plc in 2018, and even procurement decision-making in relation to the Grenfell Tower fire in 2017. For some, the answer is to bring contracts back in-house and rely more on the state. The present government, however, sees "social value" procurement as an important part of the answer.

The social value duty, found in s.1 of the Public Services (Social Value) Act 2012, requires public bodies to "consider" how procurement may be used to improve an area's "economic, social and environmental well-being". The provision appears at odds with the New Public Management and mainstream economics. To contextualise this legal duty, and understand this apparently quite different means of regulating government procurement, I have therefore had to engage with literature speculating on the post-New Public Management, economic sociology and more mainstream aspects of economics, such as behavioural economics.

To put my current approach, above, into context and to make a case for its socio-legal significance, it is necessary to consider more the relationship between economics and sociology. This is because, while economics was constructing theories on consumer behaviour and markets for much of the twentieth century, these subjects were neglected by sociologists. Many put this down to "Parsons' Pact", which refers to the way in which Talcott Parsons – who had moved from Harvard's Economics Department to its newly established Sociology Department (Camic, 1987) – envisaged a particular, complementary role for sociology, alongside economics, in the social sciences (Parsons, 1937). Economics was to be a general science of rational human behaviour (value), whereas irrational behaviour was to be the focus of sociology (values; Velthuis, 1999).

This territory demarcation broke down in the 1970s: law and economics ventured into the terrain of sociology, and, soon afterwards, sociologists, notably Harrison White (White, 1981) and Mark Granovetter (Granovetter, 1985) responded, turning their attention to market behaviour and institutions. This work saw sociologists "free[ing] themselves from their inferiority complex and becom[ing] more confident in their own contribution to the analysis of economic processes (some of which, like network analysis, has influenced recent economic research)" (Fourcade, 2018, p. 1).

Today, the (new) economic sociology is arguably the most vibrant and prosperous area of sociology. However, work here tends to neglect law and legal institutions. In recent years, there have been numerous calls trying to spur on research that targets the meeting-point of economics, sociology and law, including proposals for research agendas on "an economic sociology of law" (Swedberg, 2003), a "sociology of law and the economy" (Edelman and Stryker, 2005), and, the purposely clunky, "econo-socio-legal approach" (Perry-Kessaris, 2013), which serves to emphasise the "interconnectedness that characterises the intersections between economic and legal aspects of social life, and ought to characterise the way we think about these intersections", coined by Perry-Kessaris (Perry-Kessaris, 2015, p. 58).

The "economic life of law" – in the words of Perry-Kessaris – represents an important, maturing area of socio-legal studies that scholars are approaching in different ways. A concept of "embeddedness" – a vague term, briefly found in Polanyi's *The Great Transformation* (Polanyi, 1944) and used by Granovetter in his "founding manifesto" for the (new) economic sociology (Granovetter, 1985) – provides the foundations for much of this work. Granovetter is critical of two extreme positions, the "undersocialised" view of human action found in economics – one of rational, self-interested behaviour, minimally affected by social relations – and the "oversocialised" view found across sociology – in which actors slavishly adhere to a social script designed by the social environment. Granovetter's alternative is to see behaviour as embedded in networks of social relations (i.e. interpersonal connections; see Ashiagbor, 2018, for a recent application of the idea in the context of development law). In studying law in the economy, socio-legal scholars are using different models under this overarching embeddedness framework. For example, Cloatre uses Actor-Network Theory (ANT) in analysing the meaning given to the WTO's Trade Related Intellectual Property Agreements and pharmaceutical patents in Djibouti (Cloatre, 2013), and others have utilised the idea of "networks of communities" (Cotterrell, 2010; Perry-Kessaris, 2011). Alternatively, Swedberg suggests that socio-legal researchers might look to the classical sociologists – in particular, Max Weber – whose wide-ranging studies on economy and society engaged with core institutions such as law (Swedberg, 2003).

The literature around economic sociology is rich, and, as economic sociology continues to venture into the traditional territory of economics, new possibilities are revealing themselves. In studying what compliance with the social value duty – a vague, general duty – means to actors in field, and, in essence, perceptions of value in government procurement, aspects of my current work engage with the French heterodox tradition of *économie des conventions* (the economics of conventions). Part of the attraction of this method was its burgeoning popularity in the social sciences, other than law, but also it provides a means for me to understand fundamental shifts over time in the thinking around how we regulate procurement.

Économie des conventions might be seen as part of institutional economics: conventions are, in essence, the most informal institutions. It is based around mainstream economics, but departs from it in order to explain how autonomous agents coordinate in the face of uncertainty. This scholarship rejects *homo economicus*, found in economics, in which rationality comes before coordination. Instead, according to convention theory, rationality emerges in coordinated action, as actors interpret different social situations. In this way, convention theory, which is growing in popularity across Europe and in the US, as more texts are translated, is an opportunity to investigate new terrain in economic sociology, "to abandon the dualisms of value versus values and economy versus embedded social relations" (Stark, 2000, p. 16), and might be important, going forward, for socio-legal researchers wanting to understand law's place in the formation of rational behaviour (Lang, 2013).

More specifically, I am seeking to utilise Boltanski and Thévenot's "pragmatic sociology of critique" to study the interplay between value and values underpinning government contracts and procurement law, policy and practice (Boltanski and Thévenot, 2006). In their "pragmatic sociology", the focus is on the critical operations of actors actually involved in economic and social disputes (which, for these theorists, is overlooked in Bourdieu's critical sociology), the specific justifications and criticisms actors put forward, and the outcome (including its stability) of the dispute. Boltanski and Thévenot explain that, for justifications/ criticisms to be considered legitimate, actors must ground these in a recognised mode of evaluation, which they call "orders of worth". They identify six orders of worth – inspiration, domestic, renown, civic, market and industrial – which correspond to higher common principles that coexist in the social world (derived from political philosophy).

My research, in seeking to understand local government procurement markets, therefore employs this theoretical framework in analysing data from observations of practice, interviews with actors involved in practice (e.g. procurement officers and government lawyers) and policy documents. The analysis brings out the contests between value – emphased by public choice theory in the era of the New Public Management – and political and social values – a popular topic in the post-New Public Management literature – in the development and reform of legal rules (e.g. debates over the reform of EU public procurement law in 2014), as well as actors' evaluations in practice – for example, interpretations of legally grey text or how actors approach a general legal duty, such as "best value" found in the Local Government Act 1999 or social value in government contracting in England and Wales, and how these evaluations change over time, especially in response to "critical moments", such as the Carillion collapse and the Grenfell Tower fire.

Post-crash law and economics

The thrust of my present research can be seen as taking socio-legal studies into what has been the recognised terrain of economics, to explore the role of law in economic sociology. This work is heterodox in relation to the mainstream economics that informs much law and economics. However, arguably, there are hints that this bifurcation is breaking down. The 2007–08 financial crisis and, across Europe, the societal consequences of austerity economics have highlighted blind spots within mainstream thinking and weaknesses within the economics profession. Indeed, at times, the challenge to the mainstream has been direct: "even Keynes was exhumed, if not entirely rehabilitated, as a justification for once again saving capitalism from the capitalists" in the government rescue of the banking sector (Peck, 2013, p. 135). This is bringing to the fore, not only a fresh wave of exciting socio-legal research (see, for example, Baars and Spicer, 2017), but also enthusiastic campaigning – originating from economics students, in the main – for reform and greater pluralism in economics. These campaigns potentially offer a pathway to opening up what would be beneficial dialogue between law and economics and socio-legal studies, paving the way for a broader law and economics, a post-crash law and economics. There are similar movements in the US, in particular where an emerging "law and political economy" agenda is gaining momentum. This entails teaching and research on law and economics from a more critical standpoint.[10] This section will briefly discuss the campaign for pluralism in economics, before moving on to consider two areas that, in addition to the economic sociology discussed in the second section, offer possible bridges between law and economics and socio-legal studies.

There are now numerous campaigning organisations around the globe, such as Rethinking Economics (www.rethinkeconomics.org/), that seek pluralism in economics, especially around curriculum reform in higher education (Earle et al., 2016). Rethinking Economics originated from a group of students, the Post-Crash Economics Society, at the University of Manchester and is now "an international network of students, academics and professionals". The campaign seeks to promote different "schools" in economics – for example, post-Keynesian economics, Austrian economics, evolutionary and institutional economics, feminist economics, ecological economics, complexity economics and Marxian political economy (to name but a few) – that continue to be widely maligned as heterodox. These different approaches emphasise different aspects and offer different perspectives and, thus, alongside the mainstream, may contribute to "a fuller, more balanced understanding of the complex entity called the economy" (Chang, 2014, p. 161). In addition, Rethinking Economics takes issue with the poor gender balance in the economics profession.[11]

The campaign for pluralism takes encouragement from the apparent acceptance of behavioural economics into the mainstream: the behavioural economist Richard Thaler won the Nobel Prize in 2017. Many mainstream economists can therefore point to the current popularity of behavioural economics when defending the profession from the attack that it represents an echo chamber in which heterodox views are problematically snubbed. The basic concept in behavioural economics – that the ability of agents to make rational, utility-maximising decisions is limited – is nothing new. Clearly, business (such as the advertising

---

10 The Law & Society Association (LSA; www.lawandsociety.org/) approved a Law and Political Economy Collaborative Research Network (CRN 55) in 2018, and there were two well-attended panels at the LSA annual conference in Toronto in June 2018. This activity is linked to a variety of projects: Class Crits (www.classcrits.org); The Association for the Promotion of Political Economy and Law (APPEAL; www.politicaleconomylaw.org); and the Law and Political Economy Blog (www.lpeblog.org). A new peer-reviewed journal for interdisciplinary research on law and political economy is also in the process of being established. This is provisionally titled the *Journal of Law and Political Economy* (accessed 6 September 2018).

11 The Royal Economics Society Women's Committee Survey, 2016, reports that women make up 28% of the total academic economics workforce in UK higher education institutions, increased from 17.5% in 1996; 15.5% are employed at professor level (see www.res.org.uk/view/art3July17Features.html). It is also reported that the number of women studying economics at higher education institutions in the UK has dropped, from 30% in 2000 to 26% in 2017 (www.bbc.co.uk/news/business-41571333). It is also noteworthy that, since 1969, only one woman has been awarded the Nobel Prize in Economics, Elinor Ostrom (2009).

industry) has long taken advantage of these human weaknesses, and socio-legal scholars, particular those working in consumer law, will likely be familiar with Herbert Simon's concept of "bounded rationality" (Simon, 1957) – the idea that agents, rather than seeking to maximise utility, must necessarily "satisfice" owing to cognitive limitations; that is, they do not have access to all the information required and, even if they did, their minds would struggle to process it adequately in the time available.

The rediscovery of behavioural economics by the mainstream, since the financial crisis, derives from the experimental work of psychologists Daniel Kahneman, awarded the Nobel Prize in 2002, and Amos Tversky (Kahneman, 2012). Their empirical experiments go further in demonstrating how individuals are prone to biases and habits and are social – all of which prevents them from making rational, consistent, utility-maximising decisions.

The social value law, which I am currently studying, places a weak duty on public bodies to "consider" how their procurement will contribute social value. Rather than mandating a course of action, I argue that the law here is, in effect, seeking to "nudge" public bodies towards a concept of value broader than lowest price. Arguably this suggests that new economic ideas underly regulation in the post-New Public Management. The idea of nudging derives mainly from the work of Richard Thaler, a behavioural economist, and the lawyer Cass Sunstein, who worked together at the University of Chicago. In their work, Thaler and Sunstein promote what they title "liberal paternalism": a middle course between laissez-faire and command and control. They argue that regulatory objectives can best be achieved through the design of strategies that take into account those cognitive susceptibilities that the behavioural sciences and behavioural economics show to occur. Thaler and Sunstein's bestselling book, *Nudge – Improving Decisions about Health, Wealth and Happiness* (Thaler and Sunstein, 2008), made waves among policymakers. In the US, Sunstein was appointed head of the Office of Information and Regulatory Affairs under Barack Obama; in the UK, in 2010, David Cameron established the Behavioural Insights Team ("The Nudge Unit"), once part of the Cabinet Office, now private (Campbell, 2017).

In the acceptance of behavioural economics into the mainstream, we see mainstream economics responding to criticism that it is too heavily devoted to the notion of rational individualistic agents (i.e. *homo economicus*) and recognising that the human mind is fallible. This behavioural turn in Chicago law and economics potentially represents an area of reconciliation between law and economics and socio-legal studies. The interdisciplinary field of behavioural economics attracts significant attention from within legal studies in the US and Europe. But, arguably owing to legitimate scepticism around nudge, socio-legal work engaging with nudge and behavioural economics is slow to emerge.

In addition to behavioural economics, dialogue around institutions offers scope for interaction between law and economics and socio-legal studies. Neoclassical economics was not always so dominant within the mainstream. In the early part of the twentieth century, although mathematical marginalism held a strong position in England, economics was relatively pluralistic: various distinct schools of thought were prominent in the discipline, including, in particular, historical economics in Germany, the Austrian school and, in the US, evolutionary and institutional economics – a non-mathematical approach to economics, closely related to economic sociology (discussed above), in which the focus is upon habits, social norms and other formal and informal rules in the economy (Hodgson, 2004). In the US, what, for some, is to be regarded as "the first great law and economics movement"[12] is

---

12 Though, for Duxbury, the suggestion that this was a "movement" is an exaggeration (Duxbury, 1995).

actually attributed to interaction between institutional economists and the legal realists – the forerunners to today's law and society community (Hovenkamp, 1990; Creutzfeldt, Chapter 2 in this volume). In these studies, law's role is not simply regulating markets (the focus of law and economics today – see above): law plays a constitutive part in markets (Edelman and Stryker, 2005; Lang, 2013).

Lang takes this further to argue that law defines relations between market participants, but also functions in "the ongoing production of market participants with the recognizable dispositions, motivations, and cognitive characteristics of the calculative homo economicus" (Lang, 2013, p. 158). There have been fruitful collaborations between law and (old) evolutionary and institutional economics (Deakin et al., 2017), as well as between socio-legal studies and the new institutional economics (Stephen, 2018). New Institutional Economics grew out of Coase's work on transaction costs (see above) and is mostly associated with Oliver Williamson and Douglas North; it adopts core tenets of neoclassical economics, including methodological individualism and rational choice theory, while looking at the ways institutions shape market behaviour. Regrettably, however, there is little sign of a refreshed, ambitious law and institutional economics, which Lang's writing appears to hope for.

At one time, prior to the financial crisis, law academics wanting to impact on policy and practice may well have been cautious about investing in heterodox economics. This can no longer be the case. Heterodox economists – some of whom claim to have predicted the financial crisis years in advance, such as Steve Keen and Ann Pettifor – who were once shunned by the media, have seen their careers reenergised. Also, though the mainstream continues to disregard them, in view of the "maladies of the UK economy", heterodox viewpoints are impacting on policy (Blackburn, 2018). It is reported that the leadership of the UK's Labour Party draws on, alongside mainstream contributions, radical work from think tanks such as the New Economics Foundation (https://neweconomics.org) and the Centre for Labour and Social Studies (CLASS; classonline.org.uk; Blackburn, 2018, p. 19), and the party's industrial strategy is influenced by heterodox economists, notably Mariana Mazzucato[13] and Ha Joon Chang. This highlights opportunities for socio-legal academics to engage more with heterodox economics, and, increasingly, this is happening, even in areas beyond those such as development law (Ashiagbor, 2018) and environmental regulation (Parker and Haines, 2018) that lend themselves more to this.

Conclusion

The chapter has reflected upon the relationship between socio-legal studies and economics. It makes two main points. The first relates to a perceived antagonism based on the ideological divide between law and economics and socio-legal studies. It argues that this divide is frequently unhelpful, and that these two branches of legal studies would benefit from more dialogue and interaction. The popularity of behavioural economics potentially opens a pathway with which to do this. In doing so, there is scope for a wider community of law and economics: one that incorporates the mainstream, but also complements this by recognising heterodox viewpoints, such as economic sociology.

13 Additionally, Mazzucato has influenced the Conservative government's industrial strategy and has also had the ear of Alexandria Ocasio-Cortez, the socialist politician who made waves when she unexpectedly won the 2018 Democratic primary in New York's 14th congressional district (the general election took place in November 2018).

Recommended reading

Black, J. (2013). "Reconceiving Financial Markets – From the Economic to the Social". *Journal of Corporate Law Studies* Vol. 13(2). 401

Davies, W. (2014). *The Limits of Neoliberalism: Authority, Sovereignty and the Logic of Competition*. London: Sage.

Edelman, L.B.; Stryker, R. (2005). "A Sociological Approach to Law and the Economy". Chapter 23. In Smelser, N.J.; Swedberg, R. (eds.). *The Handbook of Economic Sociology*. Princeton and Oxford: Princeton University Press. 2nd Edn.

Lang, A. (2013). "The Legal Construction of Economic Rationalities?". *Journal of Law and Society* Vol. 40 (1). 155; Chapter 8. In Ashiagbor, D.; Kotiswaran, P.; Perry-Kessaris A. (eds.). *Towards an Economic Sociology of Law*. New York: Wiley.

Fourcade, M. (2010) "Price and Prejudice: On Economics, and the Enchantment/ Disenchantment of Nature". Chapter 2. In Beckert, J. Aspers, P. (eds.). *The Worth of Goods*. Oxford: Oxford University Press.

Perry-Kessaris, A. (2014) "The Case for a Visualized Economic Sociology of Legal Development". *Current Legal Problems* Vol. 67(1). 169.

References

Arnsperger, C.; Varoufakis Y. (2006). "What is Neoclassical Economics? The Three Axioms Responsible for Its Theoretical Oeuvre, Practical Irrelevance and, thus, Discursive Power". *Panoeconomicus* Vol. 53 (1). 5.

Ashiagbor, D. (2018). "Theorizing the Relationship between Social Law and Markets in Regional Integration Projects". *Social and Legal Studies* Vol. 27(4). 435.

Baars, G.; Spicer, A. (2017). *The Corporation: A Critical, Multi-Disciplinary Handbook*. Cambridge: Cambridge University Press.

Becker, G. (1968). "Crime and Punishment: An Economic Approach". *Journal of Political Economy* Vol. 76(2). 169.

Blackburn, R. (2018). "The Corbyn Project". *New Left Review* Vol. 111. 5.

Boltanski, L.; Thévenot, L. (2006). *On Justification: Economies of Worth*. Princeton, NJ: Princeton University Press.

Camic, C. (1987). "The Making of a Method: A Historical Reinterpretation of the Early Parsons". *American Sociological Review* Vol. 52(4). 421.

Campbell, D. (2017). "Cleverer than Command?" *Social & Legal Studies* Vol. 26(1). 111.

Campbell, D.; Lee, R. (2003). "'Carnage by Computer': The Blackboard Economics of the 2001 Foot and Mouth Epidemic". *Social & Legal Studies* Vol. 12(4). 425.

Chang, H-J. (2014). *Economics: The User's Guide*. London: Pelican Books.

Cloatre, E. (2013). *Pills for the Poorest: An Exploration of TRIPS and Access to Medication in Sub-Saharan Africa*. Basingstoke: Palgrave Macmillan Socio-Legal Studies.

Coase, R. (1960). "The Problem of Social Cost". *Journal of Law and Economics* Vol. 3. 1.

Cotterrell, R. (1998). "Why Must Legal Ideas be Interpreted Sociologically". *Journal of Law and Society* Vol. 25(2). 171.

——— (2006). "From Living Law to the 'Death of the Social': Sociology in Legal Theory". In Freeman, M.D.A. (ed.). *Law and Sociology: Current Legal Issues*. Oxford: Oxford University Press. 16.

——— (2010). "Transnational Networks of Community and International Economic Law". In Perry-Kessaris, A. (ed.). *Socio-Legal Approaches to International Economic Law: Text, Context, Subtext*. New York: Routledge. 151.

Davies, W. (2010). "Economics and the 'Nonsense' of Law: The case of the Chicago Antitrust Revolution". *Economy and Society* Vol. 39(1). 64.

Deakin, S.; Gindis, D.; Hodgson, G.M.; Huang K.; Pistor K. (2017). "Legal Institutionalism: Capitalism and the Constitutive Role of Law". *Journal of Comparative Economics* Vol. 45(1). 188.

Donahue, J.J. (1988). "The Law and Economics: The Road Not Taken". *Law & Society Review* Vol. 22. 903.

Dubner, S.J.; Levitt, S. (2005). *Freakonomics: A Rogue Economist Explores the Hidden Side of Everything*. New York: Penguin.

Duxbury, N. (1995). *Patterns of American Jurisprudence*. Oxford: Clarendon Press.

Earle, J.; Moran C.; Ward-Perkins, Z. (2016). *The Econocracy: The Perils of Leaving Economics to the Experts*. Manchester: Manchester University Press.

Edelman, L.B. (2004). "Rivers of Law Contested Terrain: A Law and Society Approach to Economic Rationality". *Law & Society Review* Vol. 38. 181.

Edelman, L.B.; Stryker, R. (2005). "A Sociological Approach to Law and the Economy". Chapter 23. in Smelser, N.J.; Swedberg, R. (eds.). *The Handbook of Economic Sociology*. Princeton, NJ and Oxford: Princeton University Press. 2nd edn., 527.

Ellickson, R. (1991). *Order without Law*. Cambridge: Harvard University Press.

Fourcade, M. (2018). "Economics: The View from Below". *Swiss Journal of Economics and Statistics* Vol. 154(5). 1.

Fourcade, M.; Ollion, E.; Algan, Y. (2015). "The Superiority of Economists". *Journal of Economic Perspectives* Vol. 29(1). 89.

Granovetter, M. (1985). "Economic Action and Social Structure: The Problem of Embeddedness". *American Journal of Sociology* Vol. 91(3). 481.

Hodgson, G. (2001). *How Economics Forgot History: The Problem of Historical Specificity in Social Science*. London and New York: Routledge.

———— (2004). *The Evolution of Institutional Economics*. London: Routledge.

Hovenkamp, H. (1990). "The First Great Law & Economics Movement". *Stanford Law Review* Vol. 42 (4). 993.

Kahneman, D. (2012). *Thinking, Fast and Slow*. London: Allen Lane.

Kunzlik, P. (2013). "Neoliberalism and the European Public Procurement Regime". *Cambridge Yearbook of European Union Law* Vol. 15. 283.

Lang, A. (2013). "The Legal Construction of Economic Rationalities?" *Journal of Law and Society* Vol. 40 (1). 155.

McCrudden, C. (2006). "Legal Research and the Social Sciences". *Law Quarterly Review* Vol. 122 (Oct). 632.

Milonakis, D.; Fine, B. (2009a). *From Political Economy to Economics: Method, the Social and the Historical in the Evolution of Economic Theory*. London and New York: Routledge.

———— (2009b). *From Economics Imperialism to Freakonomics: The Shifting Boundaries between Economics and Other Social Sciences*. London and New York: Routledge.

Mirowski, P. (1989). *More Heat than Light: Economics as Social Physics: Physics as Nature's Economics*. Cambridge: Cambridge University Press.

Morgan, M. (2012). *The World in the Model: How Economists Work and Think*. New York: Cambridge University Press.

Ogus, A. (2006). *Costs and Cautionary Tales: Economic Insights for the Law*. London: Bloomsbury.

Parker, C.; Haines, F. (2018). "An Ecological Approach to Regulatory Studies?" *Journal of Law and Society* Vol. 45(1). 136.

Parsons, T. (1937). *The Structure of Social Action. Volume 2*. New York: McGraw-Hill.

Peck, J. (2013). "Explaining (with) Neoliberalism". *Territory, Politics, Governance* Vol. 1(2). 132.

Perry-Kessaris, A. (2011). "Reading the Story of Law and Embeddedness through a Community Lens. A Polanyi-Meets-Cotterrell Economic Sociology of Law". *Northern Ireland Legal Quarterly* Vol. 62. 41.

———— (2013). "Anemos-ity, Apatheia, Enthousiasmos: An Economic Sociology of Law and Wind Farm Development in Cyprus". *Journal of Law and Society* Vol. 40(1). 68.

———— (2015). "Approaching the Econo-Socio-Legal". *Annual Review of Law and Social Science* Vol. 11. 57.

Polanyi, K. (1944). *The Great Transformation: The Political and Economic Origins of Our Time*. New York: Rinehart.

Ptak, R. (2009). "Neoliberalism in Germany: Revisiting the Ordoliberal Foundations of the Social Market Economy". In Mirowski, P.; Plehwe, D. (eds.). *The Road from Mont Pelerin: The Making of the Neoliberal Thought Collective*. Cambridge, MA: Harvard University Press. 98.

Robbins, L. (1935). *An Essay on the Nature and Significance of Economic Science*. London: Macmillan. 2nd edn.

Samuelson, P.; Nordhaus, W. (2005). *Economics*. London: McGraw Hill. 18th edn.

Sanchez-Graells, A. (2010). *Public Procurement and the EU Competition Rules*. Oxford: Hart. edn.

Sanchez-Graells, A. (2015). *Public Procurement and the EU Competition Rules*. Oxford: Hart. 2nd edn.

———— (2018). "Economic Analysis of Law, or Economically Informed Legal Research". Chapter 8. In Watkins, D.; Burton,, M. (eds.). *Research Methods in Law*. London: Routledge, Taylor & Francis. 2nd edn. 170.

Simon, H. (1957). *Models of Man, Social and Rational: Mathematical Essays on Rational Human Behaviour in a Social Setting*. New York: Wiley.

Stark, D. (2000, January). "For a Sociology of Worth". Available at www.researchgate.net/publication/251651120_For_a_Sociology_of_Worth

Stephen, F.H. (2018). *Law and Development: An Institutional Critique*. Cheltenham: Edward Elgar.

Swann, P.G.M. (2016). "The Econocracy: The Perils of Leaving Economics to the Experts". *Prometheus* Vol. 34(3-4). 231.

Swedberg, R. (2003). "The Case for an Economic Sociology of Law". *Theory and Society* Vol. 32(1). 1.

Thaler, R.; Sunstein, C.R. (2008). *Nudge: Improving Decisions about Health, Wealth, and Happiness*. New Haven, CT; London: Yale University Press.

Velthuis, O. (1999). "The Changing Relationship between Economic Sociology and Institutional Economics: From Talcott Parsons to Mark Granovetter". *American Journal of Economics and Sociology* Vol. 58(4). 629.

White, H. (1981). "Where Do Markets Come From?" *American Journal of Sociology* Vol. 87(3). 517.

14

LAW AND ANTHROPOLOGY

Kirsten McConnachie

Introduction

Law and anthropology are both very broad fields of study. This chapter focuses on the areas where they intersect, notably in questions of legal form and function. A relationship between law and anthropology has operated in both directions: anthropologists have adopted law and legal systems as a site of study, and lawyers have used anthropological methods and insights to inform their work. The different starting points are sometimes reflected in different terminology (with anthropologists describing their work as "anthropology of law", and lawyers engaging in "legal anthropology"). Donovan and Anderson (2003: x) also suggest that different theoretical orientations can be distinguished, in that "legal anthropologists tend to limit their inquiries into problems of how law is used, while 'anthropology and law' anthropologists consider also what law is".

Even when converging on a shared interest in law and legal process, anthropology and law represent very different (and arguably not very compatible) intellectual traditions. The disciplinary orientation of law is formalist and centralist; it is located in "codes, courts and constables" and premised on the state's exclusive authority to write and enforce laws. Anthropology challenges these conventions of law as doctrinal and statist. Through its use of ethnography, attention to law in non-Western cultures and law in everyday life, anthropology expands understanding of what law is and where it is to be found, shaking legal assumptions of rigid formalism and encouraging awareness of law's presence in society and its relationship to culture. The fundamental incompatibility of these approaches would seem to make for an awkward relationship. Clifford Geertz (1983) famously described the anthropology of law as an unnatural hybrid, a "centaur discipline", and Nader (2005: 72–73) argues for "separate but equal arenas: we do different things" and claims to be

> sceptical if not contemptuous of lawyers who claim the title of anthropologist merely because they are studying the law of everyday life or native peoples; they may find the experience stimulating, but they have little grasp of what ethnographic work entails.

Regardless of such disapproval, many lawyers have drawn on anthropological theory and methods to inform their work and research, and the relationship between anthropology and law has been one of the most significant and enduring interdisciplinary relationships in socio-legal studies. Donovan and Anderson (2003: 3) characterise anthropology and law as occupying equal standing "in a position of balanced reciprocity [...] neither discipline is independent of, parasitic upon, or subordinate to the other." The disciplines may indeed have equivalent intellectual heft, but, in their interdisciplinary relationship, anthropology has perhaps been the more influential contributor. Nader (1996: vi) views this as another cause for concern:

> intellectually the anthropology of law gave to the movements [of law and society and critical legal studies] perhaps more than we received. "Our" terrain – the non-western other – our approaches and methods such as participant observation, and what we had learned about social and cultural processes through ethnography, fil-tered into other disciplines. Notions of critique and comparison, culture and local knowledge, and the various ideas about pluralism and perception had now moved horizontally into sister disciplines, albeit in altered forms.

Marcus and Pisarro (2008: 3) similarly suggests that anthropology suffered from its relationship with law (and other disciplines) as "the agendas of anthropological research became almost wholly shaped and defined by the interdisciplinary movements with which it associated". Whether or not anthropology has been diminished by its disciplinary openness, it has inarguably made its mark on the production of knowledge in socio-legal studies. Attempting to define anthropology's contribution to the study of law, Franz von Benda-Beckmann (2008: 11) suggested it can best be understood as an "accumulation of features" including attention to legal pluralism and "the totality of legal ideas"; legal schemes of meaning and the social significance of law; a cosmopolitan and comparative perspective; historical orientation; sensitivity to contextual differences; use of extended field research for data collection; and a relationship to a wider legal anthropological tradition.

A simpler way of describing the relationship might be to say that anthropology asks a question that is often never considered by lawyers: what is law? And to what extent can the label of law be applied to non-formal normative orders? This question has been much debated, with different positions from the view that "law" implies a level of institutionalisation and formalisation (and that this is necessary to distinguish law from mere etiquette or social practices) to support for a more expansive use of the term to encompass cultural and customary practices of dispute resolution, which may be uncodified but carry norm-setting and norm-sanctioning powers nevertheless (Pirie 2013; Roberts 1998; Gluckman 1969; Good 2015). As von Benda-Beckmann (2008: 6) recognised,

> It makes a great difference whether or not one limits the category of law to what lawyers call law, and whether or not one is interested in all kinds of social processes in which law gets involved, or specifically only in "legal" processes.

Which standpoint is taken is particularly important when it comes to the acceptance or otherwise of legal pluralism. Legal pluralism challenges legal centralism (i.e. the belief that law is in the exclusive control of the nation-state) by recognising that dispute resolution and order maintenance occur outside the formal legal system. Often called "customary" and "traditional" systems, another contribution of anthropology to law has been to reveal that many such systems are both more recent and more adaptive than they are taken to be (Chanock 1985; and, on the role of history in legal anthropology, see also Gordon 1984; Starr and Collier 1989; Benton 2002).

Earlier work on legal pluralism included classics of the ethnographic tradition that established "customary" justice practices and non-Western normative orders as a site of serious scholarship (Malinowski 1926; Evans-Pritchard 1990). Later work was more attentive to dynamics of colonisation, decolonisation and postcolonialism, still questioning the state's supposed monopoly on law but now also recognising law as a site of struggle and going beyond mere acknowledgement of the co-existence of different orders to track the relationships between them. This work is often situated with reference to Sally Falk Moore's (1973: 720) concept of the "semi-autonomous social field", which

> has rule-making capacities, and the means to induce or coerce compliance; but it is simultaneously set in a larger social matrix which can, and does, affect and invade it, sometimes at the invitation of persons inside it, sometimes at its own instance.

A concern with relationships between normative orders has been extremely influential in research on the creation and dissemination of human rights norms and their impact on local and global structures (Goodale and Merry 2007; Cowan et al. 2001). This work, and a wider literature on legal anthropology of human rights, can be understood in relation to a resurgence of interest in legal pluralism in international development (particularly in relation to access to justice agendas) as well as in relation to the operation of law in a transnational world (Benda-Beckmann et al. 2009; Anders 2015). Influential work in this area has included Merry's (2006) work on global norms on violence against women, as well as studies of the International Criminal Court (Clarke 2009) and other mechanisms of transitional justice (Wilson 2001).

The expansion in focus from legal orders operating "below" the level of the state to legal orders and institutions "above" the state has been adopted by other disciplines concerned with understanding globalisation and its institutions. A "global legal pluralism" approach within international relations, political science and international law uses the language of legal pluralism without the concomitant anthropological contextualisation of law and process. This work is concerned less with the observed relationships and lived realities of legal pluralism and more with the recognition of multilevel governance in international relations (Burke-White 2005; Berman 2007). Other disciplinary relationships have been more novel, notably geography, which has encouraged attention to law's relationship with space and spatiality (Blomley et al. 2001; Braverman et al. 2014) and recognition of multiscalar governance (Valverde 2015).

Anthropology and ethnography

Anthropology's greatest contribution to knowledge may well be one of method. The ethnographic method was for many years "an essential identity marker of anthropology", bound up with the quest to comprehend "the other" (von Benda-Beckmann 2008: 7). The centrality of ethnography to anthropology's production of knowledge came under serious scrutiny with the landmark collection *Writing Culture* (Clifford and Marcus 1986), which drew on poststructuralist theory of Barthes, Foucault and others to interrogate ethnographic texts and the methodological process that produced them. The questions asked in this collection still resonate a generation later: who is producing ethnographic research? For whom? What are the power relations embedded in this process? What is the value of the texts that are being produced? Should they be read as fact, rhetoric or fiction? The conversations resulting from *Writing Culture* encouraged a new generation of researchers to reorient the ethnographic encounter from one underpinned by quasi-colonial assumptions (an objective researcher encountering an exotic other) to one underpinned with awareness of power, knowledge, reflexivity and subjectivity. This included feminist researchers who sought to define new ways of being as a researcher, activist and citizen (Enslin 1994: 543–544), as well as indigenous researchers and insider-ethnographers seeking to shift the terms of research from its colonial and neocolonial paradigm (Smith 1999).

These days, extended fieldwork is no longer considered a rite of passage for anthropologists, and the anthropologist as ethnographer is no longer a foregone conclusion. This is a change that has been driven perhaps in part by the critical investigation of ethnographic process and writing described above. It has also been the result of a less formulaic approach to methods, which has seen a rise in quantitative studies and purely theoretical work in anthropology (Gupta and Ferguson 1997). However, there are also less-encouraging drivers of the move away from ethnography, including the changing conditions of academic labour. Ethnography is time-consuming and unpredictable and produces knowledge that is not amenable to direct replication. This is out of step with trends in information production, which increasingly privileges the creation and manipulation of "data" (statistically valid numbers, large-scale surveys, replicable findings) over the more subjective "knowledge" that is gained by immersion, questioning and reflecting. Mark Duffield (2018: 51–52) characterises this as a shift "from knowledge to data" and explains:

> Ethnographic fieldwork allows for interruption and expects delay. It gives people time to speak, to account for and justify their claims. It creates time and opportunities for causal examination, verification and refutation. Data on the other hand is only useful it if emerges quickly and is immediately operational. [...] Participant observation cannot be rushed. Ideas and conjectures grow at walking pace, and insights and discoveries worthy of the name reveal themselves slowly.

A privileging of remote data over the laborious acquisition of ethnographic knowledge has had consequences for anthropology. The devaluing of anthropology is apparent in departmental closures and even, in Poland, a political decision to erase anthropology as an independent discipline and subsume it within a new field of "Culture and Religion" (Goździak and Main 2018). There are fewer anthropology departments for students to attend, fewer resources to support their research and more onerous requirements of ethical approval, risk assessment and institutional approval. In the UK, these pressures are compounded by strict PhD completion timelines, whereby a single student's failure to submit their PhD thesis within the prescribed four-year period may result in a reduction or withdrawal of Research Council funding to that student's department. This system cannot tolerate the "delay" of ethnographic research, establishing another disincentive for students to embark on it.

A case study: law and anthropology in a refugee camp

To recap then, anthropology's influence on socio-legal studies can be seen in sites of study (local and everyday settings rather than courts and prisons), theoretical approaches (legal pluralism) and ways of thinking (critically, comparatively). There is also a clear and lasting influence on methodologies, particularly in the use of extended fieldwork, ethnography and participant observation to conduct socio-legal research. These were all features that I drew upon when I came to design my doctoral research, conducted between 2007 and 2011 among Karen refugees from Myanmar living in camps in Thailand. In this research project I set out to study the administration of justice among refugees and to analyse the refugee camp as a legally pluralistic space, shaped by refugee-led dispute resolution systems, the Thai national justice system, human rights norms propounded by international humanitarian agencies, and the rules and codes of non-state armed groups. I published the findings of this research in a number of articles, reports and a monograph (e.g. McConnachie 2012, 2014). My PhD was completed in law but included a substantial anthropology component, including dual supervision by the law and anthropology departments. To strengthen my understanding of anthropology, I read very widely, audited an undergraduate module in anthropology and secured funding from leading anthropology institutes, including the Wenner-Gren Foundation and the Royal Anthropological Institute (having applied with the view that, if I could persuade these institutes of the validity of my research, I was evidently on the right track). I explain all of this to show that my involvement with anthropology was not dilettantism but a genuine effort to develop a theoretical and methodological approach that was suited to my research topic. The discussion below explains in more detail how I approached this research and some challenges I encountered.

Research methods: fieldwork, ethnography and action research

Ethnographic and fieldwork-based research methods are well suited to research with refugees for a number of reasons (and, indeed, the research that has gone furthest in recognizing refugees as active participants in their own lives and societies is found in anthropology; Peteet 2005; Malkki 1995). Cultural immersion can offer a (very partial) corrective to the voicelessness of refugees by facilitating analysis and research outputs that are firmly rooted in their lived realities. Yet ethnographic research in refugee camps remains relatively rare, perhaps for the same reasons that Piacentini (2007: 152) cites for the rarity of ethnographic research in modern prisons: access is difficult, in terms of both navigating bureaucratic channels and a perceived (or actual) threat of violence or danger.

My primary research site was a refugee camp on the Thai–Myanmar border, which was primarily populated by Karen refugees and was located several hours' drive from the nearest town, with very limited transport out of the camp and no access to phone or internet. This meant that I had to conduct my camp-based data collection without the possibility of asking for advice from supervisors or colleagues. However, the physical isolation of the camp did not negate other features of globalisation and modern global governance. The refugee camp where I was based was remote, but its conditions were shaped by transnational networks (of advocacy, diaspora and politics), humanitarianism and development practices, and human rights discourses. Nader (1969) famously called for anthropological research to "study up" and make connections between different sources of authority at all levels. I followed this advice by designing a research approach that was not restricted to the experiences of refugees in camps but also actively researched the activities and perspectives of Thai authorities, international humanitarian agencies and non-state armed groups. These relationships were not a "vertical slice" (Nader 1980) but a networked field of intersecting actors and sources of power. The refugee camp environment was affected by flows of money, goods, ideas and people, and the stakeholder groups that I was studying (i.e. refugees, Thai authorities and international agencies) had multiple points of interconnection. Observing these connections and relationships was one of the ways in which my research attempted to collapse global/local distinctions.

My research approach also diverged from the classical anthropological stance of an "objective observer" in favour of an action research approach. Action research approaches essentially combine applied social science research with action intended to progress social welfare (Reason and Bradbury 2001; Whyte 1991). Action research also confronts the myth of a sole researcher/anthropologist by situating the researcher in clear relationships with members of the community and key informants (Jacobsen and Landau 2003; McTaggart 1991). I incorporated an action research element into my research by teaching English to refugee students throughout much of my fieldwork (of course, I ensured that the school, students and camp leaders were all aware from the outset that I was a researcher). My work as a teacher offered important advantages, including a role in the community that was both highly respected and more comprehensible than that of "PhD student" or "researcher". An affiliation with a school, rather than a civil society organisation or international agency, also helped to avoid co-option into a particular agenda or interest group. My fellow teachers and students played a very important role in my research. They answered my questions, assisted with translation and helped me make contact with camp leaders, judges, victims and perpet-rators of crimes, but they also introduced me to their families, invited me to weddings, bap-tisms and other events and generally enfolded me into their lives. However, teaching also involved a large time commitment and an added sense of responsibility to perform the role effectively. It reduced my ability to focus only on my research themes, while, conversely, enabling me to see and experience camp life in a more immersive fashion, as a member of a community (school, students, educators) rather than solely as an observer.

In total, I conducted fifteen months of fieldwork during my doctoral research. The pri-mary benefit of this extended period of research time was the additional rigour provided by the opportunity of testing data collected over an extended period and against multiple sources. Particularly in camp-based interviews, I primarily used formal interviews as an access point rather than an end-point to a relationship. After the interview, I would almost always be asked to visit again; when I did so, I would not conduct a formal recorded inter-view but would simply chat. In this less-formal and -contrived setting, over repeated con-versations, I was able to discuss the same topics repeatedly. This was powerful as it enabled me to triangulate my information and check my understanding of the person's views. It also distinguished my approach from the vast majority of research encounters that refugees experienced, which tended to be conducted in one-off interviews or focus groups.

Being present in the camp for a sustained period of time allowed me to ask more ques-tions, but it also gave me the time to answer questions that camp residents had for me; it allowed me to build friendships and to engage in a more equal and authentic interaction than is possible in a formal interview setting. The notion that ethnography transcends alterity risks being simplistic or even condescending (i.e. fieldwork as a "journey" for the researcher to discover empathy through encountering the Other). I was acutely aware of the limitations of research fieldwork and of my ability to fully understand the experience of Karen refugees. As Susan Sontag (2003: 113) famously wrote in *Regarding the Pain of Others*, "We can't imagine how dreadful, how terrifying war is; and how normal it becomes. Can't understand, can't imagine". Yet I also came to appreciate the value of *attempting* to understand and the importance of "being there" to that task. Spending time among people, eating, sleeping, talking and walking: in these ordinary everyday tasks I found a measure of connection and understanding that was immensely valuable personally and for my research.

Research challenges: access

If the time to build relationships was probably the clearest benefit of extended fieldwork, the biggest challenge was its unpredictability. Field research is not a controlled environment and requires constant adjustment and reassessment to check whether research goals are actu-ally being met. Two major research challenges that I had to navigate were securing field-work access and language. Access to the refugee camps in Thailand is closely controlled by

Thai authorities, and I needed to negotiate access at multiple levels, including at the level of the refugee community. Initially, I sought a partnership with a refugee-led women's organisation which has mass membership across all camps and operates an extensive range of programmes that reach out to all members of the refugee community. This organisation is a crucial "knowledge broker" between international organisations and the refugee community and thus was a valuable entry point into the community. This relationship initially seemed very constructive, and we reached an agreement that, if I taught for three months at a "leadership" school for Karen women outside the refugee camp, the organisation would then facilitate my research access to the camp. After I had taught English at the leadership school for three months, I was informed that the organisation had adopted a new policy not to assist researchers and therefore would not help arrange my access to the refugee camp or assist with my data collection in any way. This was a very difficult moment. My entire PhD research topic depended on securing extended research access to the camps, and my plan for achieving that – built carefully over months – had collapsed. I had "lost" three valuable months of research time and found myself back at the beginning, with no idea how I would secure access to the camps and whether I would be able to carry out my research at all. Fortunately, and serendipitously, I was able to connect with a camp-based school that was willing to secure my research access in exchange for me providing teaching. However, there was a fraught week or so where it seemed as though my research project might have ended almost before it began.

Another challenge in my research was language. I was researching the experiences of Karen refugees, almost all of whom speak at least one Karen language (typically S'gaw) and/or Burmese. A minority of refugees also speak English. Before my fieldwork began, I obtained a set of S'gaw Karen language materials and sought private tuition to learn the S'gaw alphabet and some basic phrases. My Karen language never developed to fluency, but I was able to hold short conversations and to understand the general flow of discussion. I conducted all interviews either in English or with a translator. Of course, this was far from ideal. In the novel *Irrawaddy Tango*, Law-Yone presents a thinly veiled portrayal of Burmese politics and the Karen insurgency. In one scene (Law-Yone 2003: 167–168), she describes an encounter between a foreign aid worker and members of the insurgency:

> "Tell us your hopes and fears", I remember one relief worker, an orange-haired American woman, saying to a major at the Jesu camp. Sandhurst was there to translate. "She's asking about your hopes and fears," he said to the young major. "We have lots of fears, tell her," said the Jesu, a sardonic type. "And no hopes anymore. Not a single one." The men had a good laugh, then Sandhurst turned to the American woman. "He fears the tyranny of the central government and hopes for democracy." The relief worker took this down in a notebook, wasting a whole page, I noticed, on a few lines of her long, extravagant, slanting script.

This short paragraph deftly highlights three main problems with translation: the power of the translator to corrupt a message, the desire of translators (and often interviewees too) to produce the answer they sense the fieldworker desires, and the potential for faux-pas in the simplest of tasks, such as writing on a piece of paper. When the research subject is an area of professional vocabulary – such as law – translation is even more problematic, either because the language requires a specialist vocabulary that a translator does not have, or because the issues under discussion are sensitive and discussed in ambiguous or euphemistic terms. This was evident in my research in relation to crimes of sexual violence. For example, a case where two refugee women had been raped by a Thai soldier was described by one interviewee as "he had two girlfriends" and by another that "he was in love with two girls". I became more familiar with potential euphemisms with time and learned to ask follow-up questions to try to ascertain the "true" nature of an encounter and whether it was consensual or not. I also made consistent efforts to triangulate my data and verify reports from multiple sources. Ultimately, I was confident that the conclusions I reached were valid, but my failure to acquire fluency in S'gaw Karen was certainly the biggest weakness of my methodology and my biggest regret in this research project. With several years' hindsight, I can recognise the factors that contributed to this outcome, including a strict PhD completion timetable and a fieldwork approach that committed me to spending much of my day teaching English (rather than learning Karen) and travelling between multiple sites (rather than remaining in the same area consistently for the duration of my research). Perhaps I would have been more alert to these risks if I had embarked on this research as a "trained" anthropology student rather than as a lawyer.

Research challenges: ethics

There is a growing literature on "dangerous" or "difficult" fieldwork that discusses the potential risks to health and personal security of conducting research in conflict zones (Sriram et al. 2009; Nordstrom and Robben 1995). My work with refugees involved very little personal risk or danger, but it has over the years presented a challenging emotional dimension. Core questions that I grappled with included: how to conduct the research without bringing any harm to anyone; how to make the research meaningful; and how to stay cognisant of power relations and processes of knowledge construction. I kept these questions constantly under consideration, as is perhaps inevitable in ethnographic research, which, as Fassin (2006: 523) argues, "is characterized by its informality. It blurs the boundaries between research and life. Fieldwork is everywhere".

Research ethics and procedures for ethical approval in fieldwork are another area where academic norms have changed enormously over recent decades. Of course, I had completed the necessary procedures for institutional ethics approval, but this was at best a starting point for the consideration of ethical questions arising from my research. When I started data collection, it became quite clear that ethical research choices would require ongoing assessment of my research goals and purposes as well as any possible unintended consequences of my research activities. Questioning the inability of scholarly research to contribute to a practical alleviation of suffering, Bourgois (2007: 288) suggests that researchers working in conflict zones should approach fieldwork ethics as entailing something much more human and much more moral than the typical ethics barometers of "informed consent" and notification. As a researcher, I pursued accuracy and methodological integrity at all times, but I also recognised that I was not a wholly disinterested observer. Where possible, I sought to help people and community organisations in practical ways, always through teaching and volunteering, sometimes with writing and research, sometimes with direct financial support. I found choices surrounding money and practical support to be among the most difficult of my research, requiring a balancing between the desire to help, awareness of my limited resources, and the possible implications for research integrity. I tended to balance these choices in favour of research integrity, trying to ensure that the rate of pay I provided to research assistants and translators was not excessive, and that I never gave money to research participants in exchange for information. These rules seemed to provide a minimum threshold to protect the integrity of the data that I collected. In retrospect, however, if I regret anything in my choices about money, it is that I was not generous enough.

I gave a great deal of thought to methodological choices and to maximising rigour and accuracy in data collection. This reduced but could not entirely eradicate anxieties about my qualification to speak for others and doubts about my understanding and interpretation. The refugee camps are complex societies, with many connections and relationships to be traced and untangled. The relationship to Myanmar alone creates webs of communication (between armed groups, between geographical areas, between Thailand and Myanmar) that could take decades of study to fully understand. Even the process of intellectualization at times felt like a betrayal, in a context of deep need that demanded practical action. I was conscious of both the non-essential nature of academic research and the very daunting task of attempting to represent the complex social order that I had experienced within the refugee camps.

Identity and positionality

Challenging ethical questions were also triggered by consideration of power relations and positionality. A number of aspects of my identity during this research project – Western, teacher, politically and geographically mobile – may be considered to accord an element of power that could make genuinely equal engagement difficult, if not impossible. This was exacerbated by the circumstances of a refugee situation, where it is impossible to be a true "participant-observer" while retaining mobility, freedom and personal security. An ongoing challenge during my research was related to my status as a white foreigner. Calls for ethnography to be "decolonised" are often premised on an assumed or implied local resentment to foreign researchers and to the arrogance of the ethnographic model: "it galls us that Western researchers and intellectuals can assume to know all that it is possible to know of us, on the basis of their brief encounters with some of us." (Smith 2005: 1). At the outset of my research I expected to encounter such resentment but found that I was instead treated with extreme deference as a white foreigner (*gawlawah*). My status as gawlawah was a challenge throughout my fieldwork, serving both as an asset (nothing could be denied me) and as a barrier to deep interactions (nothing could overcome my essential otherness). I was frequently told by interviewees how much they admired and welcomed white people and how happy they were that I was spending time with their community. Of course, this could be seen as simple flattery, and in some cases it probably was. However, I also came to perceive such statements as operating within a more nuanced process of claims-making. The historical role of white foreigners among the Karen is far from distinguished, but many Karen refugees embraced their relationship with the colonial past, minimising acts of betrayal while reifying acts of generosity. I was repeatedly told the story of a British soldier, Major Seagrim (known as "Grandfather Longlegs" among the Karen), who commanded Karen forces against the Japanese in World War II, voluntarily surrendered himself to prevent reprisals against local villagers and was executed. This conformed to a story-telling pattern that positioned white foreigners as rescuers or allies and Burmans as the exploiters.

Ferguson (2006: 154–175) notes that, for researchers steeped in postcolonial critiques of power, race and class, it is challenging – even embarrassing – to encounter people who do not reject a colonial heritage but actively admire and emulate it. Bhabha (1994) has explained such mimicry in terms of resistance, as a subversive reclaiming and reworking of colonial practices. Ferguson is not persuaded by this explanation, which does not account for apparently earnest acts of mimicry such as those I encountered among Karen refugees.

Instead, Ferguson suggests that mimicry might be read as a claim for a *relationship*, a claim to encourage a sense of responsibility through a reminder of past connections. Emphasising positive experiences of British colonisation and British people was one way in which refugees sought to encourage in me a sense of connection and responsibility for their suffering. This was also made explicitly, in requests to "tell your people about us" and "don't forget about us". I took these requests seriously and tried to respond to them by publishing academic writing, by writing reports for refugee-led organisations and by delivering many talks and op-eds about the refugee camps. Nevertheless, this was a very limited contribution and no doubt far less effective than my interlocutors had hoped or expected.

Law, anthropology and the future of interdisciplinarity in the UK

This chapter has outlined the importance of the relationship between law and anthropology to the development of socio-legal studies and within my own research. Anthropology's contribution to socio-legal studies has been profound, opening new avenues for understanding fundamental questions about the nature of law and its operation in society. Of course, this is just one of many disciplinary relationships now visible in legal research. Sullivan (2002: 1217) writes: "In the beginning there was law. Then came law-and. Law and society, law and economics, law and history, law and literature, law and philosophy, law and finance [...]." These disciplinary relationships offer new ways of thinking about law, indicate different questions to ask and suggest different methodologies for asking them. Yet the core work of a law academic remains "teaching lawyers the tools of practice" (Sullivan 2002: 1217). This establishes a potential tension between the research value of interdisciplinarity and the career consequences of conducting it, which is reflected in contradictory incentive/disincentive structures for interdisciplinary research.

On the one hand, leading social sciences funding bodies in the UK such as the ESRC, British Academy and Leverhulme Trust strongly encourage interdisciplinary research, increasingly making it a priority or prerequisite in funding calls. On the other hand, the everyday life of academic communities and university administration continues to be structured around defined disciplines. This certainly applies to teaching and course design, but also to conferences and other research events, academic journals and monographs, and academic promotions criteria. Most processes for review and scrutiny of academic work are also arranged around single disciplines, including such career-consequential processes as the UK's Research Excellence Framework. Interdisciplinarity offers the possibility of expanding research parameters, but it comes at the risk of being perceived as a "dabbler", operating on the peripheries of two disciplines rather than at the heart of one. As such, interdisciplinary researchers are likely to face additional anxieties regarding, for example, where they should submit their work, who will be reviewing it, and whether their work will be fairly judged by reviewers who have no familiarity with their research approach.

One recent study found that these "institutionalised disincentives to interdisciplinarity" are particularly acute for doctoral and early career researchers, who have not yet found permanent academic positions: "Too much interdisciplinarity early on could be career suicide", one respondent suggested (British Academy 2016: 18). Successful interdisciplinary research requires *time*, which is increasingly absent for academics at all stages. PhD students in the UK are already subject to increasingly strict pressure to submit their thesis within four years and to increasingly high expectations for teaching experience and academic publications in order to secure a permanent post or postdoctoral fellowship. Those embarking on interdisciplinary work not only need to acquire expertise in two disciplines rather than one, but may also find it harder to establish themselves as part of an academic community and to gain teaching experience in "core" undergraduate subjects. This was my experience, to some extent. I was a PhD student in law, and so my peers were largely not conducting fieldwork, and I did not have a cohort of friends and colleagues to share my research experiences with. This created a fairly extreme contrast between challenging yet hugely busy and sociable fieldwork followed by a lonely period of processing data and writing up. Choosing examiners for my thesis was another challenge – should it be someone from law or anthropology? What were the potential risks and benefits of each? (We opted for examiners from law, who were generous and enthusiastic about my work; my anxieties had been unnecessary.) In the years subsequently, I have been fortunate to find academic jobs, but it has always been a challenge to develop a teaching allocation in line with my research interests. Such challenges are common, but, in effect, interdisciplinary researchers may face additional hurdles in networking, publishing, building an academic identity and finding a permanent academic job. These hurdles are particularly difficult for early career researchers in a job market that is increasingly precarious and reliant on short-term contracts rather than permanent posts (Jones and Oakley 2018).

For such reasons, the British Academy study mentioned above concludes that interdisciplinary research is best conducted in a less "risky" career period, by more established researchers. Of course, more established researchers face a different set of disincentives for interdisciplinarity, in terms of losing an already-acquired academic identity and in terms of finding time to develop mastery in a second discipline in the face of existing research, teaching, administration, supervision and management responsibilities. These realities of modern academic life, combined with the shift "from knowledge to data" (Duffield 2018) discussed in the introduction, suggest a number of disincentives to interdisciplinary ethnographic research and particularly to extended periods of fieldwork. If this trend continues, it will likely become harder for young researchers to embark on extended fieldwork and interdisciplinary research projects, which would undoubtedly be a loss for socio-legal studies.

Further reading

J.K. Cowan, M. Dembour and R. Wilson (eds). (2001) *Culture and Rights: Anthropological Perspectives*, Cambridge: Cambridge University Press.

A. Gupta and J. Ferguson (eds). (1997) *Anthropological Locations: Boundaries and Grounds of a Field Science*. Berkeley: University of California Press.

S.F. Moore, ed. (2005) *Law and Anthropology: A Reader*, Malden: Blackwell.

A.C.G.M. Robben and J.A. Sluka. (eds). (2012) *Ethnographic Fieldwork: An Anthropological Reader*. Malden, MA: Blackwell.

J. Starr and J.F. Collier (eds). (1989) *History and Power in the Study of Law: New Directions in Legal Anthropology*, Ithaca, NY: Cornell University Press.

References

Anders, G. (2015) Law at its limits: interdisciplinarity between law and anthropology, *The Journal of Legal Pluralism and Unofficial Law*, 47(3): 411–422.

Benton, L. (2002) *Law and Colonial Cultures: Legal Regimes in World History, 1400-1900*. Cambridge: Cambridge University Press.

Berman, P.S. (2007) Global legal pluralism, *Southern California Law Review*, 80. 1155.

Bhabha, H.K. (1994) *The Location of Culture*. New York: Routledge.

Blomley, N., Delaney, D. and Ford, R. (eds). (2001) *The Legal Geographies Reader*. Oxford: Blackwell.

Bourgois, P. (2007). Confronting the Ethics of Ethnography: Lessons from Fieldwork in Central America. In A.C.G.M. Robben and J.A. Sluka, eds. *Ethnographic Fieldwork: An Anthropological Reader*, pp. 318–330. Malden, MA: Blackwell.

Braverman, I., Blomley, N., Delaney, N. and Kedar, A. (2014) *The Expanding Spaces of Law: A Timely Legal Geography*. Stanford, CA: Stanford University Press.

British Academy. (2016) *Crossing Paths: Interdisciplinary institutions, careers, education and applications*. www.thebritishacademy.ac.uk/interdisciplinarity

Burke-White, W. (2005) International legal pluralism, *Michigan Journal of International Law*, 25: 963–979.

Chanock, M. (1985) *Law, Custom, and Social Order: The Colonial Experience in Malawi and Zambia*. Cambridge: Cambridge University Press.

Clarke, K. (2009) *Fictions of Justice: The International Criminal Court and the Challenge of Legal Pluralism in Sub-Saharan Africa*. New York: Cambridge University Press.

Clifford, J. and Marcus, G. (eds). (1986) *Writing Culture: The Poetics and Politics of Ethnography*. Berkeley: University of California Press.

Cowan, J., Dembour, M., Wilson, R. (2001) *Culture and Rights: Anthropological Perspectives*. Cambridge: Cambridge University Press.

Donovan, J.M. and Anderson, H.E. (2003) *Anthropology & Law*. Oxford and New York: Berghahn.

Duffield, M. (2018) *Post-Humanitarianism: Governing Precarity in the Digital World*. Bristol: Polity Press.

Enslin, E. (1994) Beyond writing: Feminist practice and the limitations of ethnography, *Cultural Anthropology*, 9(4): 537–568.

Evans-Pritchard, E. (1990) *Kinship and Marriage among the Nuer*. Oxford: Clarendon.

Fassin, D. (2006) The end of ethnography as collateral damage of ethical regulation? *American Ethnologist*, 33(4): 522–524.

Ferguson, J. (2006) *Global Shadows: Africa in the Neoliberal World Order*. Durham, NC and London: Duke University Press.

Geertz, C. (1983) *Local Knowledge: Further Essays in Interpretive Anthropology*. New York: Basic Books.

Gluckman, M. (1969). Concepts in the Comparative Study of Tribal Law. In L. Nader, ed. *Law in Culture and Society*, pp. 349–373. Chicago: Aldine.

Good, A. (2015) Folk models and the law, *Journal of Legal Pluralism and Unofficial Law*, 47(3): 423–437.

Goodale, M. and Merry, S. (2007) *The Practice of Human Rights: Tracking Law between the Global and the Local*. Cambridge: Cambridge University Press.

Gordon, R.W. (1984) Critical legal histories, *Stanford Law Review*, 36: 57–125.

Goździak, E. and Main. I. (2018) Erasing Polish anthropology? *Anthropology News* website. December 7, 2018. www.anthropology-news.org/index.php/2018/12/07/erasing-polish-anthropology/

Gupta, A. and Ferguson, J. (eds). (1997) *Anthropological Locations: Boundaries and Grounds of a Field Science*. Berkeley: University of California Press.

Jacobsen, K. and Landau, L. (2003) *Researching Refugees: Some methodological and ethical considerations in social science and forced migration*. UNHCR Working Paper No. 90.

Jones, S.A. and Oakley, C. (2018) *The Precarious Postdoc: Interdisciplinary Research and Casualised Labour in the Humanities and Social Sciences*. Durham: Working Knowledge www.workingknowledgeps.com/wp-content/uploads/2018/04/WKPS_PrecariousPostdoc_PDF_Interactive.pdf

Law-Yone, W. (2003) *Irrawaddy Tango*. Evanston, IL: Northwestern University Press.

Malinowski, B. (1926) *Crime and Custom in Savage Society*. New York and London: Harcourt Brace Kegan Paul.

Malkki, L. (1995) *Purity and Exile: Violence, Memory and National Cosmology Among Hutu Refugees in Tanzania*. Chicago: University of Chicago Press.

Marcus, G. and Pisarro, M. (2008) The end(s) of ethnography: Social/cultural anthropology's signature form of producing knowledge in transition, *Cultural Anthropology*, 23(1): 1–14.

McConnachie, K. (2012) Rethinking the "refugee warrior": the Karen National Union and refugee protection on the Thai–Burma border, *Journal of Human Rights Practice*, 4(1): 30–56.

McConnachie, K. (2014) *Governing Refugees: Justice, Order and Legal Pluralism*. Abingdon: Routledge.

McTaggart, R. (1991) Principles for participatory action research, *Adult Education Quarterly*, 41(3): 168.

Merry, S.E. (2006) *Human Rights and Gender Violence: Translating International Law into Local Justice*. Chicago: University of Chicago Press.

Moore, S.F. (1973) Law and social change: the semi-autonomous social field as an appropriate subject of study, *Law and Society Review*, 7(4): 719–746.

Nader, L. (1969). Up the Anthropologist: Perspectives Gained from Studying Up. In D. Hynes, ed. *Reinventing Anthropology*, pp. 284–311. New York: Pantheon Press.

Nader, L. (1980). "The Vertical Slice": Hierarchies and Children. In G. Britain and R. Cohen, eds. *Hierarchy and Society: Anthropological Perspectives on Bureaucracy*, pp. 31–43. Philadelphia: ISHI Press.

Nader, L. (1996) *Law in Culture and Society*. Chicago: Aldine.

Nader, L. (2005) *The Life of the Law: Anthropological Projects*. Berkeley: University of California Press.

Nordstrom, C. and Robben, A. (eds). (1995) *Fieldwork under Fire: Contemporary Studies of Violence and Survival*. Berkeley: University of California Press.

Peteet, J. (2005) *Landscape of Hope and Despair: Palestinian Refugee Camps*. Philadelphia: University of Pennsylvania Press.

Piacentini, L. (2007). Researching Russian Prisons: A Consideration of New and Established Methodologies in Prison Research. In Y. Jewkes, ed. *Handbook on Prisons*, pp. 152–173. Collumpton: Willan.

Pirie, F. (2013) *The Anthropology of Law*. Oxford: Clarendon.

Reason, P. and Bradbury, H. (eds). (2001) *Handbook of Action Research: Participative Inquiry and Practice*. London: Sage.

Roberts, S. (1998) Against legal pluralism, *Journal of Legal Pluralism*, 42: 95–106.

Smith, L. T. (1999) *Decolonising Methodologies*. London: Zed Books.

Smith, L.T. (2005) *Decolonising Methodologies: Research and Indigenous Peoples*. London and New York: Zed Books.

Sontag, S. (2003) *Regarding the Pain of Others*. London: Penguin

Sriram, C., King, J., Mertus, J., Martin-Ortega, O., and Herman J. (eds). (2009) *Surviving Field Research: Working in Violent and Difficult Situations*. Abingdon: Routledge.

Starr, J. and Collier, J. (1989) *History and Power in the Study of Law*. Ithaca: Cornell University Press.

Sullivan, K.M. (2002) Foreword: interdisciplinarity, *Michigan Law Review*, 100(6): 1217–1226.

Valverde, M. (2015) *Chronotopes of Law: Jurisdiction, Scale and Governance*. Abingdon: Routledge.

von Benda-Beckmann, F. (2008) Riding or killing the centaur? Reflections on the identities of legal anthropology, *International Journal of Law in Context*, 4(2): 85–110.

von Benda-Beckmann, F., Benda-Beckmann, K., and Griffiths, G. (2009) *The Power of Law in a Transnational World*. Oxford: Berghahn Books.

Whyte, W.F. (1991) *Participatory Action Research*. London: Sage.

Wilson, R.A. (2001) *The Politics of Truth and Reconciliation in South Africa: Legitimizing the Post-Apartheid State*. Cambridge: Cambridge University Press.

15

DOING 'LAW IN/AND DEVELOPMENT'

Theoretical, methodological and ethical reflections

Jennifer Lander

Introduction

> Whatever the response, the claim to expertise in optimising the lives of others is a claim to power, one that merits careful scrutiny.
>
> *Tania Li, The Will to Improve (2007: 5)*

One would be hard-pressed in today's world to find someone who had not encountered the idea of 'development'. In fact, the commonly held belief that a spectrum of development defines the global political economy is evidenced in the ubiquity of the terms 'developed/developing world', 'First World/Third World' and even 'Global North/Global South'.[1] The use of these common frames to describe the unequal distribution of resources and power in the world demonstrates just how pervasive the idea of development has become not only within spheres of intellect and influence (e.g. policy-making, civil society and academic research), but also as a popular ideology. As James Ferguson (1990: xiii) put it in the preface to his book about development strategies in Lesotho almost three decades ago:

> It seems to us today almost non-sensical to deny that there is such a thing as 'development' or to dismiss it as a meaningless concept, just as it must have been virtually impossible to reject the concept 'civilisation' in the nineteenth century, or the concept 'God' in the twelfth. Such central organising concepts are not readily discarded or rejected, for they form the very framework within which argumentation takes place.

---

1 In this chapter, I predominantly use the terms Global South and Global North to avoid the hierarchical association with the term '*Third* World' countries, as well as to suggest that development inequalities run across (and within) national borders as well as between them. However, some scholars I cite continue to use the term Third World to denote a radical third approach to international law and politics, such as the Third World Approaches to International Law (TWAIL) movement. I also occasionally put 'developing' and 'development' in quotation marks when I want to emphasise that these terms are contested.

The concept of *development*, initially used in relation to the modernisation of states and economies, today frames issues as wide-ranging as trade and investment policy, infrastructure, standards of living, wealth distribution, human rights, gender justice, environmental sustainability and institutional change. It has become the dominant rationale and measure for the progress of societies. Despite this dominance, its meaning continues to be contested, with new indicators emerging periodically, from the basic needs approach in the 1970s, to the human development indices of the 1990s, to the Sustainable Development Goals today. While debates continue within academic, policy and civil society domains about how to understand and 'do' development, the concept continues – tenaciously – to hold its position as the 'dominant problematic' (ibid.: xiv) of organised efforts to improve society. Perhaps *because* of contestations and failures, the substance of the concept of development has consistently been revived (ibid.), although rarely losing the fundamental commitment to economic productivity and growth (Trubek & Santos, 2006: 6).

For lawyers and legal scholars, the field of 'development' has opened new opportunities for research and practice since its emergence after the Second World War. Joining economists, political scientists, geographers, anthropologists and sociologists, legal scholars have sought to contribute to debates about development as an idea, as well as to intervene in development practice. Because development itself has become a multifaceted concept, law and development has taken on an inherently interdisciplinary character as a 'node' (ibid.) between the study of economics, law and institutions. Unfortunately, this interdisciplinary location easily lends itself towards the technocratic and depoliticised patterns of thinking and acting common to mainstream economics and black-letter law. In particular, the methodology of mainstream economics, based on mathematical modelling and quantitative studies, continues to dominate mainstream thinking about development. The theory of change that underlies this methodology perpetuates the decontextualised calculation of legal institutions as facilitators of stability, efficiency and competition for market transactions. Consequently, this theory privileges an approach to legal interventions in development characteristic of institutional economics, which generally positions law as a managerial force to mitigate the crisis-prone nature of global markets.

While acknowledging that there are some practical merits associated with the celebrated 'problem-solving' (Trubek, 2012: 235; de Moerloose, 2017) character of law and development approaches, the tendency to work *within* the system often precludes the possibility of shifting the parameters of the 'given framework for action' (Cox, 1981: 128 129). The reality that must be kept at the forefront of this problem-solving field is that the 'social, political and economic arrangements affecting the global systems of production, exchange and distribution' (Strange, 1994: 18) – that is, the global political economy – are by no means neutral or just. These arrangements inevitably reflect the values of the 'arrangers', those who are invited to the table, those who benefit from the current composition (ibid.). Tinkering with the current system without seeking to transform it buttresses the status quo, which should be a primary concern to all law and development scholars, particularly given the history of the field, as will be explained shortly.

I believe that the task for the *socio-legal* scholar engaged in the field of law and development is precisely this: to step back from the juggernaut of development discourse and reflect on the sociopolitical processes and effects that law is being harnessed to produce, intentionally or unintentionally, in the global political economy (see Schneiderman, 2013b). This is not to say that there are no practical solutions to be offered as well. However, there is sociological and political significance in the assumptions about 'development' that inform the decisions made by elites or experts on behalf of others, whose lives may be heavily impacted by the changes pursued by practitioners and justified by scholars. As David Kennedy (2006a: 95) aptly put it, 'political choices are often presented in vocabularies of economic and legal expertise that obscure the political stakes of development policy making'. It is the task of the socio-legal researcher to make explicit the social processes and political stakes regarding the distribution of power and resources (ibid.) that are involved in any law and development project or policy. There is an urgent need for socio-legal research to engage with fundamental, baseline questions about the purpose, process and effects of law and development activities to 'expand the possibilities for thinking critically about what is and what might be' (Li, 2007: 2).

Sixty years of law and development scholarship: an overview of the field

1950s–1960s: law as instrument for national development

The first academic field of law and development in the 1950s and 1960s was founded on a similar set of assumptions as its contemporaries in political science and development economics, which were seeking to explain and promote the modernisation of the state and the economy. These lines of enquiry were animated by a common concern to theorise and explicate an economic, political and legal blueprint for capitalist development led by the state (Trubek & Santos, 2006: 1). The modernisation blueprint focused on developing 'four societal features' associated with the advanced liberal capitalist democracies of the West: 'bureaucratic governmental apparatus, capitalist market systems, "generalised universalistic legal systems" and democratic political systems' (Tamanaha, 2011: 209). In part, modernising scholarly endeavours were popular in the mainstream schools of politics, economics and law because this research agenda dovetailed with the foreign policy interests of the United States. In the race against Soviet communism, academic theories that championed liberal capitalist development models provided a legitimising rationale for U.S. involvement in making sure that newly independent states in the so-called Third World aligned with the West.[2]

The United States became a major source of economic assistance to European states after the Second World War ended in 1945. Concerned that European states might be vulnerable to Russia's communist influence, the United States intervened to unilaterally provide economic aid packages, with the condition that the recipients were willing to adopt certain liberal democratic and capitalist features. Whereas most Eastern European states rejected the offer of assistance, the majority of Western Europe accepted, as well as a few outliers such as Greece and Turkey. In June 1948, the economic assistance package known as the Marshall Plan was passed in the United States Congress through the Foreign Assistance Bill. The Marshall Plan's success in reversing the fortunes of Western Europe within four years inspired further export of the model to Asia, Africa and Latin America (Packenham, 1973: 34–35). As Trubek and Galanter (1974: 1085) point out, it is impossible to disentangle the

---

2 One could argue that a parallel movement of law and development scholarship was occurring in the Soviet Union; Soviet-inspired constitutional reforms legitimised central economic planning, and socialist legal theory made overt connections between legal forms and economic development (Trubek, 2012: 236). However, this 'law and development movement' did not style itself as such, nor was it the root of the contemporary academic field, consequently falling outside the scope of this chapter.

roots of law and development as a field of academic enquiry from its association with 'legal development assistance' programmes in the United States.

The first wave of Western law and development scholarship and practice bought into the fundamental assumption of the Marshall Plan, that economic productivity and growth were key to the realisation of democratic peace and the formation of 'modern', independent states. The economic – or material – aid delivered through development assistance was to be accompanied by technical assistance programmes, intended to act as a bridge to achieving the goals of political modernisation: political pluralism, electoral democracy, mass education, freedom of speech, national identity – that is, the tenets of liberal constitutional democratic systems found in the United States and the United Kingdom (Packenham, 1973: 198). Notably, the assumptions of American developmentalism in the 1950s and 1960s rested on the consensus at the time that *legal* institutions were fundamental to realising these twin goals of state modernisation (Tamanaha, 2011: 209).

The idea that legal systems have historically played an important role in developing capitalist economic systems was not new, but the idea of 'systematic legal reform projects' (Trubek, 2016: 303) to actively create and institutionalise capitalist models of development was particular to the post-war era. Law's unique capacity to effect change quickly, seemingly without the heavy baggage that often hamstrings politics, made it seem like an ideal institutional driver to catalyse structural reform in 'developing' societies. This faith in law's efficacy as an instrument of social change underpinned the first wave of law and development scholarship (Merryman, 1977: 462–463; Trubek & Santos, 2006).

To conclude this section, it is worth reiterating the key theoretical and methodological questions that animated law and development studies in the 1950s–1960s. To do so, I will draw on some insights from David Trubek (2016: 304–305), who reflected on four decades of law and development scholarship in a recent article. As a period of optimism about development, law and development studies were characterised by faith that (a) law could be an *instrument* for developmental change (e.g. as a key field for reform to catalyse economic growth and institutionalise liberal political systems), (b) 'modern law' could be transplanted from 'developed' Western states, (c) legal reform implied the adoption of liberal legality, and (d) changing legal culture through legal education would automatically produce legal modernisation (which would in turn promote and dovetail with economic and political modernisation). The methodology used in law and development scholarship was consequently one heavily characterised by legal positivism and formalism: scholars promoted legal education and legislative reforms animated by the assumption that pushing through new laws, legal institutions and education systems would automatically promote development. Underlying all of this was a 'progressive credo' (Merryman, 1977: 458) that change was not only possible but achievable through formal legal interventions.

1970s–1980s: critical deconstruction and socio-legal assessment of law and development

In the 1970s, cracks began to emerge in the field of law and development, as some scholars began to experience 'moral doubt' (Trubek & Galanter, 1974: 1080; Gardner, 1980; Snyder, 1982) about the legitimacy of exporting legal ideas and models to the so-called Third World, as well as questioning their impact. Writing in the early 1970s, David Trubek and Marc Galanter, perhaps unwittingly, pioneered a new generation of law and development studies with their critical piece entitled 'Scholars in Self-Estrangement: Some Reflections on the Crisis of Law and Development Studies in the United States' (1974). Trubek and

Galanter critiqued the law and development movement's motive as lacking normative legitimacy: why should 'developing' countries adopt liberal legal models at the behest of the U.S. government? They also offered a fairly damning assessment of the assumption that 'any improvement of legal institutions in the Third World will be potent or good' (ibid.: 1080), pointing to the fact that 'legal change may have little or no effect on social economic conditions in Third World societies and, conversely, that many legal "reforms" can deepen inequality, curb participation, restrict individual freedom and hamper efforts to increase material well-being' (ibid.). This assessment coincided with wider socio-legal critiques of the distance between the law in books and the law in practice in Western jurisdictions as well in the Global South, which fundamentally challenged the instrumental assumptions of the initial law and development movement.

The timing of the publication of 'Scholars in Self-Estrangement' was a remarkable coincidence with – or even possibly contributed to – the decline in law and development studies as a field of research and of practice (Merryman, 1977; Trubek, 2016). After the optimism of the first official United Nations 'Development Decade' (1960s), the once emerging field of law and development 'began to lose momentum' in the mid to late 1970s (Trubek, 2016: 302). One of the key reasons for this loss of momentum was the decline of U.S. development agency and foundation funding for law and development scholarship (Trubek, 2016: 309), partly as a consequence of mixed results from law and development initiatives (ibid.) and also owing to waning commitments to internationalism in U.S. foreign policy following intensified Cold War tensions. Another dimension was that law and development scholars recognised the moral and practical problems of their generally well-intentioned efforts to use law in the service of development, even though critical voices such as Trubek and Galanter intended their critique to 'improve and enlarge the field, not to end it' (ibid.: 305). The recognition that law could not be wielded as a straightforward instrument for development was undoubtedly influenced by voices from the Third World contesting the influence of the United States – and the Soviet Union for that matter – in trying to determine their developmental trajectories through the terms of aid, trade and foreign policy.

The 1950s and 1960s had seen the birth of an alternative movement of legal scholarship in the Global South that criticised the ways in which international law secured the interests of Western powers (Anghie & Chimni, 2003: 79–80; Chimni, 2007). These 'third world approaches to international law' (TWAIL) focused on the historical oppression of Southern peoples through colonisation and the perpetuation of colonial relations through the Western states' abuse of their power through the international legal system (Khosla, 2007: 297), which dovetailed with new theories about the active 'underdevelopment' (e.g. Frank, 1966) of the Third World through its inferior insertion into the global economic order (e.g. Wallerstein, 1974, 2004). Early TWAIL scholarship expressed great faith that the international legal system, if transformed, could be a source of justice and equality because it recognised the sovereignty of all states (ibid.; Anghie & Chimni, 2003). The TWAIL movement animated and was animated by political coalition movements between states in the Global South, such as the Bandung Conference in Indonesia in 1955. During the 1970s, coalition-building between 'developing' countries led to the delivery of a set of proposals to the United Nations demanding the establishment of a New International Economic Order that favoured sovereignty, economic justice and greater control over the terms of international trade and investment.

In the context of an increasingly plural international legal discourse, it is not surprising that the formalist, universalist approach to law and development faced a legitimacy crisis.

This crisis was deepened by the rise of new intellectual currents within legal theory, notably legal pluralism and critical law and society movements. Both of these movements, inspired by legal scholars' engagements with anthropology and sociology, as well as critical development theory, took a more contextual and critical approach to the role of 'modern law' in development. Legal pluralists perceived the law and development movement as the imposition of an external social order on pre-existing forms, tending to emphasise the relativity – rather than superiority – of Western legal systems often highlighting their export as a form of imperialism. For legal pluralists, the presence of multiple formal and informal systems of ordering is normal in all societies and, consequently, they rejected the construction of legal pluralism as a 'problem' to be solved (Tamanaha, Sage, & Woolcock, 2012: 2). In fact, legal pluralist approaches to law and development emphasised the way 'traditional' or customary forms of law enabled strategic avoidance of unwanted forms of state control over community resources (e.g. through land registration; Benda-Beckmann, 1989: 138).

In a similar vein, the critical law and society approach emphasised the way that any law reform effort is invariably conditioned by the social, historical, political and economic context in which it occurs. Not only does law reflect its sociopolitical context, it actively constitutes and enables particular patterns of power relations. Critical law and society approaches began to critique the dominant framing of law as a constraint on the exercise of power, seeing the way law might constrain certain forms of power (e.g. state/public) and enable others (e.g. commercial/private). Many socio-legal scholars developed a critical standpoint towards claims of law's neutrality, as well as an ambivalence about its progressive potential. Notably, in the 1970s and 1980s, new hubs of scholarship shaped by TWAIL, law in context and legal pluralism were established in universities in both the Global South and North, inspired largely by South–North collaborations.[3]

1990s onwards: law as an instrument for the global market

An instrumental interest in the role of law for development was resurrected in the 1980s with the rise of new economic theory that explicitly linked 'the role of institutions with the performance of economies' (North, 1991: 97). The fall of the Soviet Union was timely for this renewed attention to the instrumental relationship between law and development, particularly animated by the question of how former socialist states could 'transition' into liberal capitalist democracies (Kennedy, 2006b: 96). The second boom of law and development initiatives and scholarship in the 1990s had many striking parallels with its predecessor in the 1950s and 1960s. Both periods were characterised by faith in legal reform as a means – first for state change and then for market creation – as well as a more general optimism that there was a blueprint for economic development, largely based on Western models of capitalism. It was imagined, in the first instance, that development could occur through state 'modernisation' and industrialisation, and, in the second instance, that by adopting the institutions to engage in 'free' market exchange, economic development would almost certainly occur. Based on these assumptions, law and development became a multi-billion-dollar industry in the 1990s, far larger than the first wave (ibid.: 312; Trubek, 2006: 81).

In the early 1990s, law reform was a fundamental part of 'structural adjustment' packages offered by international financial institutions (IFIs) to post-Soviet countries in the wake of

---

3 For example, a 'Law in Development' programme led by Upendra Baxi, Abdul Paliwala and William Twining was established at the University of Warwick in the 1980s.

economic collapse; these were consequently extended to other crisis-afflicted states in the Global South through the 1990s. 'Structural adjustment' typically involved a complete overhaul of a country's legal infrastructure as a condition of debt relief and fiscal stimulus. Despite the enthusiasm for reform on the part of international and national reformers, the implementation of structural adjustment through 'shock therapy' (Sachs, 1994)[4] had a devastating impact on the targets of this institutional experimentalism (Trubek & Santos, 2006: 6). Most post-Soviet states faced lower socio-economic outcomes than they had during the Soviet period and lost most of their industrial base during this time as well (Klein, 2007). This was, of course, not surprising to the critical tradition of law in development and TWAIL scholars, who continued to critique 'one-size-fits all' models as at best misguided and at worst a new form of legal and political imperialism. The devastating impact of structural adjustment on societies in the Global South as well as the increase in capitalist predations in deregulated manufacturing, mining and agriculture sectors in the 1990s also prompted a wider critique of the empty promises of market-led development, joining prominent TWAIL contestations about the legal rules and regulations governing trade and investment (Chimni, 2007).

Later in the 1990s and early 2000s, practitioner, academic and activist influence on IFIs and national governments challenged the one-size-fits-all discourse dominating development assistance initiatives and programmes (Ordor, 2015: 335–338). Sustainability, human development, participation, poverty reduction and the need for effective states reframed the former emphasis on market reforms and the narrow focus on growth (Trubek, 2012: 238), informed by new currents of development theory, such as Amartya Sen's concept of development as freedom. This new agenda re-centred the state to some degree as an actor in development, partly fuelled by the explicit linkages drawn between development, radicalisation and national/global security in the post-9/11 context (Duffield, 2007). Although some call the deconstruction of the one-size-fits-all approach a complete 'reconceptualisation of development' (Ordor, 2015: 336), the underlying economic model has remained essentially the same in terms of its fundamentals (Tan, 2011; Adelman, 2018). However, the *framing* of development has at least changed, reflected in new policy paradigms such as the Human Development Index (Merry, 2014) and the Comprehensive Development Framework of the World Bank. Despite some reservations about actual progress made, the now-mainstream articulation of development as a process of holistic change includes social and environmental dimensions in addition to economic and institutional goals (Trubek, 2006; Ordor, 2015). Associated with these changes in thinking about development is a corresponding shift in ideas about the inherent value of law and legal institutions: 'legal reform is now justified whether or not it can be tied directly to growth' (Trubek & Santos, 2006: 9).

As an academic field, law and development studies has become increasingly fragmented (Trubek, 2016), focusing on different areas of 'development' as the concept widened to include human rights and democracy, environmental sustainability, security, social justice, as well as rule of law (May, 2014; de Moerloose, 2017). As many academics, influenced by the critical tradition, shied away from narrowly growth-oriented or productivist accounts of

---

4 According to Sachs in 'Understanding Shock Therapy' (1994) the crises afflicting post-Soviet economies were to be addressed through 'the rapid introduction of the six core institutions of capitalism' (1994: 29): (1) a monetary system based on a stable, convertible currency; (2) freedom of international trade and foreign investment; (3) private property rights; (4) private ownership of a high proportion of national assets; (5) corporate control of large enterprises; and (6) a social safety net.

development, the field shed some of its universalist baggage in favour of a more relativist approach whereby 'contextual factors are of overriding importance in defining both the appropriate ends of development and feasible strategies for attaining them' (Trebilcock, 2016: 333). This shift towards relativism even within the mainstream academy has created a new opportunity for socio-legal scholars to contribute contextual accounts of law's multifaceted relationship with development, as a practical project and a normative goal.

The fragmentation of law and development studies seems to be a natural consequence of a field defined by two concepts that appear increasingly to be 'moving targets'. Development, as was expressed above, has come to mean many different things to different actors and institutions. The context of globalisation has done no less for law (Kennedy, 2006a), in the sense that law's relationship with development is no longer simply about transplanting or reforming national legal institutions. The legal norms and forms that govern development projects and processes are increasingly transnational in character, both in terms of crossing jurisdictional boundaries (i.e., local, national, international, global) and in terms of heightened interlegality – 'the relations and interactions between co-existing legal orders' (De Sousa Santos, 2002; Twining, 2012: 121). This pluralisation is further hybridised by the blurring of clear boundaries such as those between public and private law-making, and hard and soft law. Legal transnationalisation, pluralisation and hybridisation have been largely occurring in response to complex governance challenges within the global economy (Halliday & Shaffer, 2015), where solely state (public) or market (private) responses can no longer be relied on to contain, mitigate or reverse the various crises that continue to accompany 'development.' Whereas some are optimistic about the proliferation of legal forms to address gaps in national and international governance (Zumbansen, 2012), others see the emergence of 'multiple, fragmented and often contradictory legal regimes' (Cutler, 2013: 722) as the new, almost irresistible '"common sense" of transnational capitalist legality' (ibid.).

Reflections on 'doing' law and development today: a socio-legal study of natural resource-based development in Mongolia, and how it came about

As is hopefully clear by now, the field of law and development has evolved and grown over the past sixty or so years. Its growth has been horizontal as well as vertical, as the distributed centre of the field of study is characterised more by poles than any sense of consolidation. If the field was once critically described as 'a vortex of conceptual and semantic confusion' in the late 1970s (Merryman, 1977: 457), there is a sense that the 'vortex' has become even more fluid and dynamic. The story of law and development's formation as a distinctive field is largely a history of experimentation, characterised by trial, error and ongoing cycles of critique. This is partly because of the quickly changing social, economic and political context following the end of the Second World War, and the swiftly evolving legal forms that have accompanied this most recent period of globalisation (Cutler, 2003; Frerichs, 2017).

The contemporary field is a broad church, comprising universalists ('there are clear pathways to development that can be replicated'), relativists ('development is contingent on context') and critics ('power relations underpin development processes'). Of course, these are fairly crude characterisations but, nonetheless, serve to illuminate the shape of the field. The universalist camp continues to promote a positive – and positivist – view of law's development-inducing properties. Whereas the universalists are bent on getting the formula just right, the relativists are equivocal about the idea that there is a formula in the first place, and the critics are sceptical about the power processes and implications of formula creation and implementation. The common questions raised by these latter two groupings of scholars tend to reflect concerns about context and power: What level or form of law is to be engaged in the pursuit of development? What contextual factors will impact the outcomes? Who benefits? What are the implications for the 'losers' in the inevitable power struggles over resources and decision-making?

Despite the variety of scholarship that exists under the law and development banner, empirical curiosity and the desire to change, improve or resist features of the world order drive scholars of all stripes. There has always been, and hopefully always will be, the impulse for the law and development scholar to address the real world in their research. The main difference between scholars is not their motivation but their methods and the theoretical toolkit they use to identify, diagnose and address problems. This is where the intellectual conflicts in law and development studies emerge; 'universalists' tend to be drawn to quantitative methods and abstract theory (e.g. positivism, legal formalism, game theory), whereas contextualists and critics identify more closely with mixed or qualitative methods and grounded theory (e.g. sociology of law, legal pluralism). The following sections will provide an overview of my own research and its relationship to law and development as a field.

Identifying the theoretical, methodological and ethical stakes of research: what, how and why

Since 2012, I have been researching the legal politics of mining in Mongolia, associated with that country's integration into the global economy as a competitive exporter of minerals.[5] Mongolia has arguably been a test case for the second boom of law and development theory, undergoing structural adjustment as a post-Soviet satellite state in the early 1990s and, since then, working to create the legal institutions necessary to become a competitive state in the global economy. Seeking a global market-led development strategy, successive Mongolian governments have focused on creating a legal framework as well as a conducive political environment to attract foreign investment to explore and exploit the country's extensive mineral resources. Mongolia's pursuit of an extractive development strategy since the late 1990s presented a unique opportunity to understand the significance of the process by which states adopt the political and legal infrastructure to support foreign investment. In my doctoral thesis, I argued that this process should be understood in terms of state transformation and de facto constitutional change (see Lander, 2017; forthcoming).

Although the 1992 democratic constitution commits the Mongolian state to the pursuit of plural pathways of development, based on 'national specifics' as well as global trends (Article 5.1), the story of mining in Mongolia is one where national preferences and interests have been systematically subordinated to transnational regulatory preferences and interests. Not only have the constitutional aspirations to developmental pluralism been undermined, but state power has been reorganised in practice along three fundamental axes to create a stable investment environment. This reorganisation has occurred across national state institutions, between national and subnational branches of government, and in relation to the governance of civil society. These sites of legal and political reordering have constitutional implications, impacting the practice of the separation of powers, the balance between central state management and self-government, and state–society relations. These reordering processes were largely achieved through legal mechanisms, constraining the kind

5 Mongolia has a wide mineral base, with substantial deposits of coal, copper, gold, fluorspar, iron, silver and uranium.

of 'risky' politics that had been perceived as disruptive to investor confidence. Purging nationalist politics from the national state through legal mechanisms has been a fundamental part of consolidating an extractive development strategy in Mongolia.

When I started the research process, I was not really concerned with the potential constitutional ramifications of natural resource-based development. I was initially interested in the way that mining in the South Gobi region of Mongolia had precipitated claims by Mongolian herders against mining companies, and the way these claims were framed by activists and NGOs. The theoretical framing of the research at that point was about citizenship, and how mining might be shifting national sensibilities of belonging, reflected in the claim-making strategies of herders. However, the fieldwork I undertook in Mongolia in 2014 and 2015 forced me to reconsider the assumptions I was making.

Ironically, the really illuminating 'finding' of my first fieldtrip in 2014 was the relative *absence* of civil society voices defending herders' rights in the terms that I expected (i.e., on the basis of national citizenship). Instead, the majority of activists and advocates seemed quite prepared to engage with the government and mining companies as collaborative partners in governance, with herders being positioned as 'traditional' stakeholders consulted on a case-by-case basis. The more radical social movements that had been calling on the government to reform the mining regime to protect national public interests and citizens' rights had faced criminal sanctions in 2013, leading many mainstream civic voices to distance themselves from conflictual strategies of engagement with the government and the private sector. The criminalisation of radical movements dovetailed with the offering of new financial and political incentives for civil society to engage more 'constructively' on mining issues – that is, participating in governance as a third party rather than contesting the mining sector from the outside.

The moves made by the apparatus of the state to depoliticise civil society indicated a much bigger story of change than the one I had initially set out to investigate. Following a major decline in foreign investment in 2012–2013, the government had started to systematically target sources of political instability that were impacting the legal environment. In particular, social movements, subnational governments and Parliament were seen as exposing the state to investors' ire by contributing to real and perceived political risk. Targeting these three sources of political risk involved a three-level programme of reform: within the central institutions of the state (intra institutional), between national and subnational levels of government (inter-institutional); and in relation to organised civil society and citizens (state–society relations). The distinctive influence of norms derived from *transnational* investment law about the rule of law and political risk mitigation underpinned these reforms in Mongolia's mining regime.

What had begun as a relatively straightforward curiosity into the claim-making strategies of Mongolian pastoralists shifted register into a much more holistic research agenda about state change, development, and law under conditions of economic globalisation. I began to analyse the development of mining legislation, the context and content of mining investment agreements, national development policy and state history, and the role of different actors (i.e., NGOs, IFIs, mining companies, government officials, investor lobby groups) in influencing the legal shape of Mongolia's natural resource-based development strategy. In 2015, during the second phase of fieldwork, I conducted more than forty interviews with different actors from these sectors to gain further understanding of the relationship between the state, investors and civil society, as well as to triangulate the evidence from the primary legal and policy sources.

Commitments to 'law in context' and inductive methodologies shaped the kinds of question I engaged in the context of researching Mongolia's mining regime from a socio-legal standpoint. The methodological back-and-forth movement between the legal text, context and subtext (Frerichs, 2013, cited in Amanda Perry-Kessaris, 2013: 6) deconstructed the formalist toolkit I did not even realise I had inherited about the relationship between development and law.[6] This deconstruction enabled me to construct a new theoretical framework based on an integrated analysis of social change induced by the global conditions of extractive development, considering the redistribution of decision-making power within national institutions, the scope of subnational government and the redrawing of legitimacy boundaries for civil society. Thus, rather than focusing on a single dimension of law's relationship with development (i.e., through the lens of citizenship), the interrelationships between apparently unrelated legal aspects of the mining regime, such as socio-environmental governance, investment law and administrative law, were illuminated.

Developing a comprehensive insight into the way that economic development strategies depend on particular legal and political transformations would be enough to categorise my research as a 'contextual' approach to the study of law and development. However, I could easily see how such a rich sociological account could be used to promulgate more of the same in other development contexts, just as descriptive anthropological insights were used by colonial administrations to deepen the scope of their rule. The ethical implications of how this research might be used by national government bureaucrats and international development technocrats have pushed me to become more explicitly evaluative about its normative stakes and to put my own cards on the table. This is a very important secondary step to make, because there are real dangers of instrumentalism in the current renewal of law and development studies, even in the 'contextual' tradition that now allegedly dominates the field (de Moerloose, 2017). For example, contextual analyses of how law can be seen to facilitate the efficiency and stability of global capital investment obscure the power relations that underpin these legal-economic configurations and the political options that have been foreclosed by them. Because of the real links between scholarship and practice in the field (Trubek, 2012), and the history of development projects going awry (Tamanaha, 2011), socio-legal researchers in law and development have an ethical duty to reflect – with urgency – on the relationship between the explication of context and the potential (mis)uses of that research. Or, indeed, to simply be honest about their own normative orientation to questions of law and development.

Conclusion: prepositions versus conjunctions and why they matter for socio-legal research in law and/in development

I was lucky enough to do my PhD research in a school of law that not only valued but pioneered critical, contextual approaches to the study of law and development. The Warwick School has always insisted that the choice of prepositions when it comes to law's relationship with development is crucial. This approach differentiates the contextual and critical scholarship from the universalist in the wider umbrella of law and development studies. For the contextual/critical scholar, law is always ever-present *within* 'development'

---

6 As Amanda Perry-Kessaris also writes in *Approaches to the Study of International Economic Law*, 'socio-legal approaches consider not only legal texts, but also the contexts in which they are created, destroyed, abused, avoided, and so on; and sometimes their sub-texts' (2013: 6).

initiatives. The rubric 'law *in* development' at least linguistically commits the socio-legal scholar to understanding law as a social process constitutive of the political and economic structures that enable or demand 'development'. Although 'law and development' is used fairly ubiquitously to refer to the field, the conjunctive – 'and' – implicitly externalises law's relationship to development. The effect of this is that law can be more easily framed as being an objective, unitary 'thing' that relates instrumentally to development.

Although instrumentalism has arguably always been a tendency and a temptation for law and development scholars, the fact of legal globalisation exacerbates it in some ways. Law has become the solution for almost every kind of social problem imaginable, reflected in the proliferation of soft law principles and standards that are quickly gaining ground to govern the cracks between jurisdictional boundaries and harder forms of law (e.g. national legislation and international treaties). For solutions-oriented law and development scholars, the contemporary period is one of renewed optimism (Lee, 2017).

However, some predict that there are dragons ahead, if they are not here already (Tan, 2018; Vandenhole, 2018). The proliferation of legal measures and forums makes it possible for conflicts over resources and power to be conveniently shifted away from public spaces of debate and reflection into technical legal spaces of rules application (Koskenniemi, 2007; Schneiderman, 2013a; Gill & Cutler, 2014). Furthermore, the development of a global legal market for principles, remedies and adjudicatory forums threatens to turn law and justice into commodities (Frerichs, 2017), as well as creating new sites and holders of authoritative legal power outside traditional systems of accountability (Garth & Dezalay, 1996; Cutler, 1999; Schneiderman, 2008). As law increasingly becomes commodified, and legal subjects are revalorised as 'stakeholders', we can clearly see the language and mechanisms of the market remaking imaginaries of law and social justice. Furthermore, the proliferation and diffusion of law defies any limit to what can be incorporated into its systems. What is urgently needed, more than ever, is sustained socio-legal analysis to keep 'power at the heart of the study of law and legal institutions' (Tan, 2013: 29) in order that myopic, market-friendly law-making might be prevented from becoming the unchallenged development common sense of the twenty-first century.

Suggestions for Further Reading:

Chimni, B. S. 2007. 'The Past, Present and Future of International Law: A Critical Third World Approach.' *Melbourne Journal of International Law* 8(2): 499–514.

Cox, R. 1981. 'Social Forces, States and World Orders: Beyond International Relations Theory.' *Millennium: Journal of International Relations Theory* 10(2): 126–155.

De Sousa Santos, B. 2002. *Towards a New Legal Common Sense.* Madison, WI: University of Wisconsin Press.

Ferguson, J. 1990. *The Anti-Politics Machine: Development, Depoliticisation and Bureaucratic Power in Lesotho.* Minneapolis, MN: University of Minnesota Press.

Li, T. 2007. *The Will to Improve: Governmentality, Development and the Practice of Politics.* Durham, NC: Duke University Press.

Trubek, D. & Santos, A. (eds.) 2006. *The New Law and Economic Development: A Critical Appraisal.* Cambridge: Cambridge University Press.

Reference list

Adelman, S. 2018. 'The Sustainable Development Goals, Anthropocentrism and Neoliberalism.' In D. French & L. Kotze (eds.) *Global Goals: Law, Theory and Implementation*, pp. 15–40. Cheltenham: Edward Elgar.

Anghie, A. & Chimni, B. S. 2003. 'Third World Approaches to International Law and Individual Responsibility in Internal Conflicts.' *Chinese Journal of International Law* 2: 77–103.

Benda-Beckmann, F. von. 1989. 'Scapegoat and Magic Charm: Law in Development Theory and Practice.' *Journal of Legal Pluralism* 28: 129–148.

Chimni, B. S. 2007. 'The Past, Present and Future of International Law: A Critical Third World Approach.' *Melbourne Journal of International Law* 8(2): 499–514.

Cutler, A. C. 2013. 'Legal Pluralism as the "Common Sense" of Transnational Capitalism.' *Onati Socio-Legal Series* [online] 3(4): 719–740. Available at: http://ssrn.com/abstract=2327501

Cutler, C. 1999. 'Locating "Authority" in the Global Political Economy.' *International Studies Quarterly* 43: 59–81.

——— 2003. *Private Power and Global Authority: Transnational Merchant Law in the Global Political Economy.* Cambridge: Cambridge University Press.

de Moerloose, S. 2017. 'Law and Development as a Field of Study: Connecting Law with Development.' *Law and Development Review* 10(2): 179–186.

De Sousa Santos, B. 2002. *Towards a New Legal Common Sense.* Madison, WI: University of Wisconsin Press.

Duffield, M. 2007. *Development, Security and Unending War: Governing the World of Peoples.* Cambridge: Polity Press.

Ferguson, J. 1990. *The Anti-Politics Machine: Development, Depoliticisation and Bureaucratic Power in Lesotho.* Minneapolis, MN: University of Minnesota Press.

Frank, A. G. 1966. *The Development of Underdevelopment.* Boston, MA: New England Free Press.

Frerichs, S. 2013. 'Law, Economy and Society in the Global Age: A Study Guide.' In A. Perry-Kessaris (ed.) *Socio-Legal Approaches to International Economic Law: Text, Context, Subtext.* Abingdon: Routledge, pp. 36–49.

——— 2017. 'The Rule of the Market: Economic Constitutionalism Understood Sociologically.' In P. Blokker & C. Thornhill (eds.) *Sociological Constitutionalism.* Cambridge: Cambridge University Press, pp. 241–264.

Gardner, J. A. 1980. *Legal Imperialism: American Lawyers and Foreign Aid in Latin America.* Madison, WI: University of Wisconsin Press.

Garth, B. & Dezalay, Y. 1996. *Dealing in Virtue: International Commercial Arbitration and the Construction of a Transnational Legal Order.* Chicago, IL: University of Chicago Press.

Gill, S. & Cutler, C. 2014. *New Constitutionalism and World Order.* Cambridge: Cambridge University Press.

Halliday, T. C. & Shaffer, G. 2015. *Transnational Legal Orders.* Cambridge: Cambridge University Press.

Kennedy, D. 2006a. 'The "Rule of Law", Political Choices and Development Common Sense.' In D. Trubek & A. Santos (eds.) *The New Law and Economic Development: A Critical Appraisal.* Cambridge: Cambridge University Press, pp. 95–173.

Kennedy, D. 2006b. 'Three Globalisations of Law and Legal Thought: 1850–2000.' In D. Trubek & A. Santos (eds.) *The New Law and Economic Development: A Critical Appraisal.* Cambridge: Cambridge University Press, pp. 19–73.

Khosla, M. 2007. 'The TWAIL Discourse: The Emergence of a New Phase.' *International Community Law Review* 9: 291–304.

Klein, N. 2007. *The Shock Doctrine: The Rise of Disaster Capitalism.* New York: Henry Holt.

Koskenniemi, M. 2007. 'The Fate of Public International Law: Between Technique and Politics.' *The Modern Law Review* 70(1): 1–30.

Lander, J. 2017. 'The Law and Politics of Foreign Direct Investment, Democracy and Extractive Development in Mongolia: A Case Study of New Constitutionalism on the "Final Frontier".' PhD thesis, University of Warwick.

Lander, J. Forthcoming. *Transnational Law and State Transformation: The Case of Extractive Development in Mongolia.* Abingdon: Routledge.

Lee, Y. S. 2017. 'General Theory of Law and Development.' *Cornell International Law Journal* 50: 415–471.

Li, T. 2007. *The Will to Improve: Governmentality, Development and the Practice of Politics.* Durham, NC: Duke University Press.

May, C. 2014. *The Rule of the Law: The Common Sense of Global Politics.* Cheltenham: Edward Elgar.

Merry, S. E. 2014. 'Global Legal Pluralism and the Temporality of Soft Law.' *The Journal of Legal Pluralism and Unofficial Law* 46(1): 108–122.

Merryman, J. H. 1977. 'Comparative Law and Social Change: On the Origins, Style, Decline and Revival of the Law and Development Movement.' *American Journal of Comparative Law* 25: 457–491.

North, D. C. 1991. 'Institutions.' *The Journal of Economic Perspectives* 5(1): 97–112.

Ordor, A. 2015. 'Tracking the Law and Development Continuum through Multiple Intersections.' *Law and Development Review* 8(2): 333–360.

Packenham, R. A. 1973. *Liberal America and the Third World: Political Development Ideas in Foreign Aid and Social Science*. Princeton, NJ: Princeton University Press.

Perry-Kessaris, A. (ed.) 2013. *Socio-Legal Approaches to International Economic Law: Text, Context, Subtext*. Abingdon: Routledge.

Sachs, J. 1994. *Understanding Shock Therapy*. London: Social Market Foundation.

Schneiderman, D. 2008. *Constitutionalising Economic Globalisation: Investment Rules and Democracy's Promise*. Cambridge: Cambridge University Press.

———— 2013b. 'Power and Production in Global Legal Pluralism.' In A. Perry-Kessaris (ed.) *Socio-Legal Approaches to International Economic Law: Text, Context, Subtext*. Abingdon: Routledge, pp. 98–117.

———— 2013a. *Resisting Economic Globalisation: Critical Theory and International Investment Law*. Basingstoke, UK/New York: Palgrave Macmillan.

Snyder, D. 1982. 'The Failure of Law and Development.' *Wisconsin Law Review* 3: 373–396.

Strange, S. 1994. *States and Markets*, 2nd edn. London: Pinter.

Tamanaha, B. Z. 2011. 'The Primacy of Society and the Failures of Law and Development.' *Cornell International Law Journal* 44: 209–247.

Tamanaha, B. Z., Sage, C. & Woolcock, M. (eds.) 2012. *Legal Pluralism and Development: Scholars and Practitioners in Dialogue*. Cambridge: Cambridge University Press.

Tan, C. 2011. 'The New Biopower: Poverty Reduction Strategy Papers and the Obfuscation of International Collective Responsibility.' *Third World Quarterly* 32(6): 1039–1056.

———— 2013. 'Navigating New Landscapes: Socio-Legal Mapping of Plurality and Power in International Economic Law.' In A. Perry-Kessaris (ed.) *Socio-Legal Approaches to International Economic Law: Text, Context, Subtext*. Abingdon: Routledge, pp. 19–35.

———— 2018. 'Beyond the "Moments" of Law and Development: Critical Reflections on Law and Development Scholarship in a Globalised Economy.' Conference paper presented to Law and Development: Theory and Practice, Humboldt University, Berlin, 6–7 July.

Trebilcock, M. 2016. 'Between Universalism and Relativism: Reflections on the Evolution of Law and Development Studies.' *University of Toronto Law Journal* 66(3): 330–352.

Trubek, D. 2006. 'The "Rule of Law" in Development Assistance: Past, Present and Future.' In D. Trubek & A. Santos (eds.) *The New Law and Economic Development: A Critical Appraisal*. Cambridge: Cambridge University Press, pp. 74–94.

———— 2012. 'The Owl and the Pussy-Cat: Is There a Future of "Law and Development?"' *Wisconsin International Law Review* 25(2): 235–242.

———— 2016. 'Law and Development: Forty Years after "Scholars in Self-Estrangement".' *University of Toronto Law Journal* 66(3): 301–329.

———— & Galanter, M. 1974. 'Scholars in Self-Estrangement: Some Reflections on the Crisis in Law and Development Studies in the United States.' *Wisconsin Law Review* 4: 1062–1102.

———— & Santos, A. 2006. 'Introduction: The Third Moment in Law and Development Theory and the Emergence of a New Critical Practice.' In D. Trubek & A. Santos (eds.) *The New Law and Economic Development: A Critical Appraisal*. Cambridge: Cambridge University Press, pp. 1–18.

Twining, W. 2012. 'Legal Pluralism 101.' In B. Z. Tamanaha, C. Sage & M. Woolcock (eds.) 2012. *Legal Pluralism and Development: Scholars and Practitioners in Dialogue*. Cambridge: Cambridge University Press, pp. 112–128.

Vandenhole, W. 2018. 'Towards a Fourth Moment in Law and Development?' Conference paper presented to Law and Development: Theory and Practice, Humboldt University, Berlin, 6–7 July 2018.

Wallerstein, I. 1974. *The Modern World System I: Capitalist Agriculture and the Origins of the European World-Economy in the Sixteenth Century*. New York: Academic Press.

———— 2004. *World-Systems Analysis: An Introduction*. Durham, NC: Duke University Press.

Zumbansen, P. 2012. 'Defining the Space of Transnational Law: Legal Theory, Global Governance, and Legal Pluralism.' *Transnational Law and Contemporary Problems* 21(2): 305–336.

16

QUALITATIVE DATA AND THE CHALLENGES OF INTERPRETATION IN TRANSITIONAL JUSTICE RESEARCH[*]

Briony Jones

two souls [...] dwell in many scholars: the one that wants to clarify and explain, and the one that is confused by the complexity of the issues confronted.

(Nouwen 2014, 234)

Introduction

This chapter focuses on the question of interpretation and how qualitative research methods can be used to add value to socio-legal research, specifically in the field of transitional justice. Transitional justice is defined by two key characteristics: the search to find justice and in so doing to articulate a response to violations that are often referred to as "unthinkable" or "unspeakable"; and a project of action that imbues policy, practice, and research with a normative agenda and moral impediment shaping the way we "see" the societies we work in. Because "the methods applied to human rights research reflect an understanding of the values and aims of the human rights discourse itself" (Andreassen, Sano, and McInerney-Lankford 2017, 1), these key characteristics of the field have led to the elevation of certain epistemologies of transitional justice that give primacy to the legal, to the quantifiable, and to the explicit. Among the "unprecedented project of knowledge production about armed conflict, conflict resolution and post-conflict reconstruction" that accompanied the Cold War ascendency of what is referred to as the liberal peace (Lewis 2017, 22), transitional

* I would like to thank the Swiss National Science Foundation and the Swiss Development Cooperation for their generous funds for the project *Knowledge for Peace: Understanding Research, Policy, Practice Synergies* (www.knowledge -for-peace.org). This book chapter was written in the framework and time of the research undertaken as part of this project. I would also like to thank Olivia Marshall for her invaluable work as a research assistant and compilation of a bibliography that was used for the writing of this chapter.

justice researchers, policymakers, and practitioners have developed a preference for technical knowledge that is professionalised, internationally mobile, and already legible to the field rather than a challenge to it (Nesiah, cited in McAuliffe 2017, 180). This is a function partly of the dominance of legal ways of knowing and also of the demands of a field that is perhaps dominated by what Corbridge has referred to in the international development context as the "dirty worlds of practical policy making" (2007, 202). As such, the explicit, the knowable, and the measureable gain prominence.

In her reflections on recent publications on research methods and human rights, Schmidt commented that "[o]ne of the biggest challenges facing researchers and practitioners working in transitional justice is the urgent need to create an evidentiary foundation that justifies and facilitates decision making in policy and practice" (2011, 159). In the last 15 years there has been an increasing focus on impact and whether or not causal relationships can be established between transitional justice interventions, such as tribunals and truth commissions, and their intended outcomes, such as respect for human rights, democracy, or reconciliation. A good example of this is the well-known *Transitional Justice Database Project* (www.tjdbproject.com/), which has given rise to a series of publications including one by Payne, Olsen, and Reiter in which they claim to "confirm for the first time that transitional justice has a positive effect on democracy and human rights" (2010, 982). If we understand transitional justice as a set of policies or inputs with outcomes that can be measured, it is not an unproblematic exercise in description, it is an exercise in representation of the "problem" and of the "solution". For it "is in giving words to the unspeakable that we can start to understand it, but that we also as interlocutors, shape the nature of that which we name" (Palmer, Jones, and Viebach 2015, 177). If violence is something knowable and addressable, then the solution must be something applicable, replicable, generalizable, and measurable. Transitional justice is not therefore something that is experienced, interpreted, or contested. Nouwen suggests that this may be partly to do with the object of much research on transitional justice: the law, an object that is (incorrectly) constructed as external to the lawyer. Even in the domain of socio-legal research, which is more open to reflexivity, Nouwen finds that the personal, social, and political character of research is most often rendered invisible (2014, 233).

Previously dominated by the law and legal practices (McEvoy 2007), transitional justice has expanded into an interdisciplinary field with contributions from sociology, anthropology, and political science, among others. This rapid growth in interdisciplinary academic research on human rights (Andreassen, Sano, and McInerney-Lankford 2017, 1) invites us to consider the promises and challenges of different research methods. In this chapter, I will explore what qualitative enquiry can offer to socio-legal studies scholars who are interested in researching and understanding transitional justice processes. Socio-legal studies' concern with the law as a social phenomenon, and with the epistemological implications of this (McKnight 2015), invites us to engage directly with research methods that do not seek to objectify or separate the law from the contexts in which it is applied. Indeed, socio-legal studies scholars are preoccupied with ongoing reinterpretation of the law, with its "text, context, and subtext" (McKnight 2015, 111), which demands more interpretivist approaches focused on subjectivities rather than objectivities. Thus, it is relevant to ask: What are the challenges of such approaches when concretely applied? Who interprets? What effect does such interpretation have? Importantly, not all interpretations of transitional justice are 'equal' in their ability to demand an audience and to shape either perspectives or acts.

Qualitative enquiry, broadly speaking, does not seek to direct learning but consciously leaves open the research encounter, allowing the messiness of complex lives to be seen and heard and included. Methods that are included under the category of qualitative enquiry can include narrative interviews, semi-structured interviews, observation, and life stories. In the chapter that follows, I will first provide an overview of key works that utilise qualitative enquiry in socio-legal studies, particularly with reference to transitional justice. I will then reflect on how my own challenges of operationalising qualitative methodologies in the field have sometimes led to crises of interpretation, but how such crises are not necessarily impasses as they can also prompt creative responses and more reflective research.

Naming the unknowable: qualitative methodologies in transitional justice research

In response to an increasing volume of work that seeks to measure the impact of, and evaluate and quantify, transitional justice processes, Dancy writes that:

> Practices deployed and administered in the name of justice do not readily lend themselves to simple empirical evaluation. Justice is not easily observed or measured, its attached meanings and symbols cannot escape cultural particularity and it will always be the controversial subject of ideological and political contestation, rather than causal certitudes.

(2010, 355)

However, the impulse to "know" more and in certain ways has led scholars and practitioners alike to seek an evidence-based transitional justice. An evidence-based transitional justice is one that is informed by empirical research which allows an assessment of communities' needs and attitudes, provides rigorous measurement of potential and actual impacts of transitional justice, and tests hypotheses leading to a better understanding of how to confront past violations of human rights (Pham and Vinck 2007, 233–234). Within this tradition, interpretivist accounts are believed not to offer the possibility of generalizability, or the possibility of establishing baselines on which to build and judge (Dancy 2010, 370; Pham and Vinck 2007, 234). These judgements are thought to be crucial if transitional justice research is to be able to tell us which policies work and what adjustments should be made in practice (Payne, Tricia, and Andrew 2010). It is not the purpose of this chapter to contest the legitimate concern with evidence-based transitional justice drawing on large N data sets. This work reminds us that, as researchers, we cannot escape the "dirty worlds of practical policy making" (Corbridge 2007, 202) in which our objects and subjects of research are embedded. What this chapter explores is the possibility of an evidence-based transitional justice that draws on qualitative methodologies.

There are scholars who have undertaken this important work highlighting the value of what we can learn from qualitative approaches to transitional justice research. To name but a few excellent studies, there are Millar's (2011) qualitative study of local experiences of truth-telling in Sierra Leone, Ingelaere's (2015) ethnographic and multi-method approach to researching Kinyarwanda identity formation in post-genocide Rwanda, Robins and Wilson's (2015) participatory action research with Nepalese victims, and Dancy and Wiebelhaus-Braham's (2015) qualitative comparative analysis of the timing and sequencing of transitional justice in Latin American countries. I would argue that all of these studies demonstrate the ethical value of foregrounding the voices of those who are the subjects of the research and give us substantive information on which policy and practice discussions can be based. This is because the way in which transitional justice has been, and continues to be, experienced is itself a significant form of "evidence" for transitional justice design and intervention. It is, therefore, of continuing frustration that evidence-based transitional justice implies a need for large N studies, for quantitative methods, and for more positivist approaches leading to "results" that are generalizable. Indeed, "empirical" is often misread as "quantitative" in an epoch in which counting and measuring are dominant and in which "[e]mpirical research that is limited to indexing, quantifying, and counting thus risks misrepresenting an inherently political concept such as 'justice' as a value-neutral unit that can be multiplied by the application of technical expertise" (Nouwen 2014, 230).

Nouwen outlines a series of challenges that confront socio-legal researchers conducting empirical research in conflict situations "in the midst of a social world that is continuously changing and filled with contradictions, uncertainties and inconsistencies" (2014, 230):

1. practical challenges of the time and resources required;
2. epistemological challenges of the difficulty in demonstrating causality to the same extent as is possible in the natural sciences; and
3. existentially as the basic hopes, assumptions and expectations of the field researcher can be challenged.

Indeed, there is a substantial amount of emotional labour involved in transitional justice research (Simić 2016), research that requires the researcher to directly engage with traumatic subjects, to navigate complex and sensitive contexts, and to come into contact with different actors in a nuanced moral landscape. In addition, transitional justice as a practical project means that many researchers have "invested too much of their lives in this project" (Nouwen 2014, 229) and are too professionally invested in the processes they are seeking to evaluate (Roht-Arriaza 2009), whether for human reasons of outrage and sympathy for others' experiences of violence or for reasons of professional entanglement. Miller has claimed that,

> [t]he role of international actors in the process of spreading the ideas and ideals of the "movement" of transitional justice has not yet been fully explored in the literature, perhaps because of (at least in part) the tendency of scholars or ex-commissioners to become consultants to, rather than fully external critics of, the enterprise.
>
> *(2008, 290)*

This lack of external criticism is the case not only because of the nature of the subject matter itself – large-scale violations of human rights – but also because of the broader context in which transitional justice research sits: a lack of consensus over what it is and who it is for. This lack of consensus (Dancy 2010, 361) does not sit well with positivist and quantitative methodologies. Unlike these, "interpretivism aims at understanding the ways in which deviation can be construed as purposeful or meaningful" (Dancy 2010, 363). Interpretivism is thus often linked with qualitative methods such as narrative interviews, life histories, or observation. These methods offer a "depth and richness of response that illuminates the dynamics of the process under study ... [and] can also identify more complex themes such as social identity and the power of religious beliefs" (Pham and Vinck 2007, 234). The depth and richness, however, also lead to two key challenges: the difficulty of fully grasping an object defined as "transitional justice" and the burden of interpretation. The burden of interpretation, which is the concern of this chapter, may explain why transitional justice researchers

> do not readily turn their analytical lenses inwards and talk about their ethical and methodological journeys and interactions in a personal way. Those who do disclose in a reflective way are rare since they are willing to expose themselves to the possibility of being "accused" of limiting their findings.
>
> *(Simić 2016, 102)*

Such exposure, however, is incredibly valuable for the way in which it humanises the field and breaks down the false dichotomy between "subjective" and "objective" researchers (Simić 2016, 109). The challenges of conducting socio-legal research in these contexts can themselves be research findings (Nouwen 2014, 250). It is with this idea in mind that we now turn to a series of short accounts of my use of qualitative research methods in transitional justice research and the need to navigate the burden of interpretation.

Challenges as findings: reflecting on qualitative methods in transitional justice research field experiences

This section seeks to offer a reflexive account of the use of qualitative methods and the challenges of interpretation when conducting fieldwork on transitional justice. Transitional justice is an expansive and expanding set of ideas, policies, and practices, and, for the purposes of this chapter, it is important to highlight that my own research endeavours have focused specifically on how the supposed beneficiaries experience transitional justice, the politics of transitional justice as a set of interventions, and the politics of knowledge production for and by transitional justice actors. This has led to work on a diverse set of themes including citizenship, education, reconciliation, truth commissions, democracy, and civil society. Motivated primarily by the underpinning conceptual questions that are raised when one focuses on the subjectivities of experiences of justice, I have also conducted fieldwork in a diverse set of countries including Sri Lanka, Uganda, Bosnia-Herzegovina, and Côte d'Ivoire. In the midst of this diversity of subjects and contexts, there has nonetheless been a consistency in the approach taken. I have exclusively used qualitative methods underpinned by an interpretivist approach, which allows an exploration of subjectivities, complexities, and complications that cannot be captured by more quantitative studies interested in correlation and causality.

My reflections included here draw on experiences and publications spanning the last decade. In particular, the aspect of mobility and movement between field sites, university employers, and subjects of study is relevant for a more reflexive account of research methods in practice. Such mobility has meant that, although my research experiences are broad, allowing for connections to be made between varied concepts and empirical settings, they do not in all cases reach the kind of depth that an area studies scholar or anthropologist might seek. As a political scientist working on socio-legal subject matter, I have often had to become familiar with new country contexts and new languages and have thus often relied on "third parties" who are in fact central to the fieldwork: gatekeepers, peers, and interpreters. This added layer, as we shall reflect on further below, adds an additional dimension to the burden of interpretation that faces the researcher who operationalises qualitative methods.

One of the methods that I have used most frequently has been the interview, and specifically the narrative interview. Narrative interviews focus on stories that individual people tell about their lives, but, through these stories, the narrative method connects the individual experience to the broader contexts in which that individual is embedded; "it is through narrativity that we come to know, understand and make sense of the social world, and it is through narratives and narrativity that we constitute our social identities" (Somers 1994, 606). In this sense, narrative interviews are not confined to only being a research method but are also part of how we as humans make sense of ourselves in the context of our lives. The narrative interview must, in this sense, always be seen as shedding a light on what stories can be told and the conditions of their being witnessed (Leydesdorff, Dawson, Burchart, and Ashplant 1999, 13). This means that the researcher as a witness must tread a careful line between the technicalities of the narrative method and the ethical aspect of bearing witness to the story of another.

As far as the practicalities are concerned, the broad structure of a narrative interview requires a series of prompting questions but perhaps also additional prompts such as photographs or quotes from others. The method encourages an open dialogue in which the interviewee tells a story that places life events in a sequence and gives to each part its significance in relation to the whole (Misztal 2003, 5–6). The interviewee does the majority of the speaking, but it is the researcher who, in the end, transcribes, analyses, and represents the story through her/his academic work.

Because the narrative interview is a form of "strategic communication" (Jovchelovitch and Bauer 2000, 65), the method presents the researcher with a series of choices of interpretation that include, among others:

- Do I interrupt the story for clarification or correction?
- Do I take at face value what is said or question it when "inconsistencies" appear?
- Do I triangulate what is being said to me with other sources of information?
- How do I represent the story in later written work or conference presentations?

When using this method, I also faced additional challenges that arise when working in a non-mother tongue language and when working in contexts of contested truths. To address, first, the implications of working in a non-mother tongue language, this is not uncommon practice for researchers engaged in fieldwork, but it is often written out of the story of research for fear of introducing messiness and reducing the credibility of the claims being made by the researcher. Indeed, a full acknowledgement of the presence of an interpreter and the way in which this shapes the process of knowledge production does present certain challenges. Temple stresses that interpreters are active in the process of constructing research, and that,

> an analytic engagement with how they come to know what to do, is an important component in understanding the nature and status of the findings. When the translator and the researcher are different people the process of knowledge construction involves another layer.

> *(1997, 614)*

This is a layer that is not just about the technical exercise of interpreting words from one language to another, but also includes the positionality of the interpreter vis-à-vis the researcher and the research participant. An interpreter is never neutral, and one cannot assume a direct relationship between languages, values, meanings, and identities (Temple 2008, 357–358). Given the multiple and continually mediated constructions of field identities (Srivastava 2006), it cannot be assumed that a narrative interview encounter is predictable, easily read, or simply interpreted.

During fieldwork in Bosnia-Herzegovina, I employed a young, male, Muslim interpreter who lived and worked in the town where the fieldwork was being conducted.[1] He was not a professional interpreter, but had an excellent command of English and understanding of the nuances of the field context. In this sense, he was at once an interpreter and, at the

---

1 I have written more extensively about this elsewhere (Ficklin and Jones 2009).

same time, a local adviser and "fixer", offering wisdom on who to interview and how to interpret their words. Following the 1992–1995 war, the former language of Serbo-Croat is now known as three different official languages: Bosnian, Serbian, and Croatian. Although they are mutually intelligible, the choice of words and emphasis is highly political, and I was reliant on the interpreter to navigate this, to put the interviewee at ease, and to set the political tone. Each interview therefore required additional time for us to prepare together and to debrief, carefully going through the interview and the interpretation and discussing his choices. This was in many ways a painstaking process in a context of time pressure. But it also illuminated aspects that I would not have identified or been able to analyse by merely listening to his English language words and taking them at face value.

The interpreter I worked with saw his role as more interventionist than I did. He often made judgements about interviewees that were based on his assumption of greater insight and local knowledge, dismissing their words, suggesting they speak to a different point as they have "misunderstood", or summarising that which he deemed to be less relevant. He was an active presence in the interviews not just because of these decisions he would make about how he would technically interpret the words, but also in the way he would engage with the interviewees, some of whom he would know, and some of whom would know him. Personal exchanges would precede or perhaps interrupt the interview. The narrative would therefore occasionally become a three-way conversation, and again the interpreter would manage the dynamic, disturbing the open-ended nature of the method with his own questions or summaries of what was "important". He occasionally stopped the interpretation if he felt the tone was incorrect, in one case because the interviewee was, in his view, flirting with me. These challenges required innovative responses from me in situ but also greater planning around the interview encounter. Given the open-ended nature of the method, the sensitivities of the context, and the presence of the interpreter, it was necessary to plan extra time to communicate openly with the interpreter, to prepare for interviews, and to debrief. The emotional labour of the work (Simić 2016) was not to be underestimated, especially as the interviewee in many ways directed the subject matter and raised subjects she/he deemed most relevant. This emotional labour was undertaken by all of those who were part of the encounter. The research method, with its focus on the story, demanded an analysis not only of the words spoken, but also of the contexts in which they were spoken.

The narrative interview holds value in the emphasis it places on the interviewee themself telling their story and managing the relationship between the chronological and non-chronological aspects – that is, the events and the meanings attached to them. In a field that has been criticised for marginalising the voices of those who have been affected by violence and who are the supposed beneficiaries of transitional justice interventions (Madlingozi 2010), it makes ethical and also analytical sense to choose methods that, in theory, foreground the voices and subjective experiences of those actors. However, experiences of violence are not always easy to unpick, and there is rarely a clear line that can be drawn around one single type of "victim" or between a "victim" and a "perpetrator". This means that field researchers may find themselves seeking out, analysing, and representing the voices of those who are not positioned in a morally clear-cut way. While researching the case of Côte d'Ivoire, I conducted interviews with Ivorians who were challenging the transitional justice process, namely the International Criminal Court case against former President Laurent Gbagbo and the national Dialogue, Truth and Reconciliation Commission. I "listened to, analysed and repeated statements made by actors who have placed themselves, or been placed by others, in opposition to many of the normative and moral claims of transitional justice advocates" (Jones and Fatogoma Adou 2017, 3). Learning from an approach taken by

Rauschenbach et al. in their interviews with those accused by the International Criminal Court for the Former Yugoslavia (2015), I did not intend to judge the veracity of the content of the interviews, nor did I intend to take a moral position on the interviewees' explicit aim to disrupt the transitional justice process. However, such a pretence to neutrality, especially when using qualitative methods, is a false and unachievable one. The subject matter of human rights violations and the reality that many researchers in this field are both personally and politically committed to a more just world mean that the way in which the interviewees' words are heard and the way in which the researcher interprets them are part of this political, personal, and moral negotiation.

During the interviews, I[2] faced a dilemma of how to establish enough rapport to ensure that the interviewee felt comfortable to tell their story, while at the same time experiencing discomfort with regards to the provision of a platform that the interviewee could mobilise to promote (in their words) their "fight" against transitional justice in Côte d'Ivoire. Indeed, there were frequent exchanges prior to or following an interview that made it clear that the interviewee was hoping that the interview opened up a new, legitimate space for the expression of her/his views. On one occasion, an interviewee explicitly told me that he would advertise the fact of the interview within his network in order to gain credibility from the fact that a researcher from the United Kingdom was interested in his views and activities. This was an unintended consequence of the research encounter, but not one that I could assume no responsibility for. When analysing and reproducing the words spoken in the interviews, I had to make decisions on a case-by-case basis about whether to render the words as truthfully as possible, thereby taking them at face value, or whether and how to place them in an analytical context that reduced their credibility based on the moral judgements made by myself and the reader. I often felt a split, incompatible loyalty to myself as an academic, to my Ivorian colleague and co-author, and to my interviewees who often believed I was generating a new opportunity for them to disseminate their ideas and activities.

Despite my desire to share the burden of interpretation with others – my interviewees, interpreter, gatekeepers – concrete experiences of using qualitative methods, specifically narrative interviews, illustrate that this is not easily done. Contexts of contested truths, morally ambiguous positionality, and often working in a non-mother tongue language render the open and explorative nature of the qualitative method also a challenge. It is, however, a challenge worth embarking on, as the messiness itself constitutes a finding that can be useful for this kind of research. Unexpected alliances or animosities between interpreters and interviewees add contextual detail and unsettle pre-existing assumptions. For example, during fieldwork in Bosnia-Herzegovina, I once tried to prevent my interpreter from joining me for an interview with someone who had been accused of war crimes against Muslims. However, when we arrived for the interview, the interpreter and interviewee greeted each other as family friends. I learned the valuable lesson that the very simplicities that I had been seeking to challenge through my research were there in my own assumptions. Listening to the stories of those in morally ambiguous positions vis-à-vis the transitional justice process also helps us to look anew at why certain actors may seem to reject a specific intervention or process. During fieldwork in Côte d'Ivoire, placing myself in the morally challenging position of providing a platform for those fighting against the transitional justice

2 I would like to extend special thanks to my colleague Adou Djané Dit Fatogoma of the Centre Suisse de Recherches Scientifiques à Abidjan Côte d'Ivoire, and to acknowledge the joint fieldwork and publications. In this chapter, however, I intend to speak only for myself and to reflect on my own research practice.

process enabled me to learn more about the plurality of perspectives in society, rather than avoiding the "bad guys" as other researchers would so often do, sure of their motives. At its core, qualitative research is a process of contextualisation, and this is something that is so important and sorely needed in transitional justice research. In recent reflections on the state of the field, Pablo de Greiff, the former United Nations Special Rapporteur on Truth, Justice, Reparation and Guarantee of Non-Recurrence, made reference to the "cookie cutter approach despite ourselves" (de Greiff 2017, n.p.) and called for differentiation between cases, identification of nuances, and more explanatory work able to compete with the increasing focus on standardisation.

Some reflections on unsettling "the expert" in transitional justice research

In the context of transitional justice research, the power of interpretation is particularly relevant. Experiences of large-scale, systematic violations of human rights place the interviewee in an almost automatic position of vulnerability, though this should not be confused with powerlessness. There is a stark distinction between those whose stories are being told and those who are retelling the stories and the audiences for both. As Madlingozi has written of the research encounter with the "transitional justice entrepreneur": "despite writing critically and passionately about the situation of the victim, the victim is not only left in the same position but this encounter could be an act of further violence and dispossession" (2010, 210–211). The most well-meaning scholars and practitioners can be complicit in this act of dispossession, or even in the ongoing violence of the hegemony of the law (Campbell and Turner 2008, 378). As a political anthropologist, Kelsall has illustrated with impressive effect the way in which the Special Court for Sierra Leone was unable to allow a full space to the victims' and witnesses' cultural ways of knowing, and instead the lawyers "applied linguistic techniques to excavate a particular version of the truth from a contested history" (2006). Certain voices are marginalised by the application of the law itself through a transitional justice process, and those who are framed as the "experts" are most often not those who are part of the affected communities. They are internationally mobile professionals who can reproduce the relevant models and transfer them between contexts (McAuliffe 2017, 180).

An acknowledgement of the interconnection between research, methods, and expertise is an important underpinning and also emerging reflection for this chapter. The way in which we choose to research transitional justice and the human rights violations that it addresses shapes not only what we can claim to know and the legitimacy it garners, but also the very objects of our enquiry. Carpenter has written that, "the process of researching human rights is in fact intimately connected with the practice of constructing human rights" (2012, 364). It is all the more important, then, that we:

- reflect extensively and reflexively on the research methods we choose and the frameworks in which the chosen research methods are embedded; and
- are honest about the practicalities of their operationalisation.

In transitional justice research, the previous domination of legal ways of knowing has been gradually challenged by work from socio-legal studies scholars, political scientists, anthropologists, sociologists, psychologists, and development studies scholars. McKnight writes of the need to "play" with the law on the sociological stage in order to discover "the law's existence as a phenomenon of other disciplines without wholly becoming a product of those disciplines" (2015: 121). This shift and opening up to alternative, equally valid ways of knowing has occurred perhaps in tension with a second shift towards a concern with impact, causation, and quantification. Scholars now grapple with which methods "count" and in what ways they can ensure their research retains relevance. In work that addresses directly the question of choice of methods and approach of methodology in transitional justice research, Dancy comes to the following conclusion, which is worth quoting at length:

> Observers should continue to use positivist logic to make arguments about consequences, building on correlations that otherwise might not have been noticeable, but they should do so with clearly stated assumptions about the way in which they choose their cases and why they understand these cases to be of a certain type. Interpretivists and critical theorists should continue to vivisect the body of assumptions on which these statements of correlation are based, while also attempting to discover the relations between observables and unobservables that constitute the social world. Without contributions from each way of thinking, responsible judgments about programs in the pursuit of social goods like justice cannot be made.
>
> *(2010, 376)*

This debate about which methods "count" needs to be connected with the debate over whose knowledge "counts". For it is not only a choice about how to generate useable and useful data, but also a choice about how we conduct research in contested contexts where assumptions about the objectivity of truth and of the objectivity of the law are unsettled. The subjectivity of knowledge that is highlighted by qualitative methods has the potential to enrich research on transitional justice. If we accept a subjectivity of knowledge, and if we seek it out through our research, then we can highlight the multiple positionalities of those who speak, those who listen, and those who reply. However, this potential creative dialogue between positions and actors cannot be realised if the subjectivity of knowledge is obfuscated by narratives of the universality of human rights or the knowability of one kind of justice. We would miss an opportunity for learning through such dialogue and, furthermore, run the risk of doing harm through the marginalisation of certain positionalities and the rendering invisible of certain experiences.

Recommended further reading

Jovchelovitch, Sandra and Martin W. Bauer. 2000. "Narrative Interviewing." In *Qualitative Researching with Text, Image and Sound*, edited by. Bauer, Martin W. and George Gaskell, 57–74. Thousand Oaks, CA and New Delhi: Sage.

Leydesdorff, Selma; Dawson, Graham; Burchart, Natasha and T.G. Ashplant. 1999. "Introduction: Trauma and Life Stories." In *Trauma and Life Stories: International Perspectives*, edited by. Lacy Rogers, Kim; Leydesdorff, Selma and Graham Dawson, 1–27. London, New York: Routledge.

Misztal, Barbara A. 2003. *Theories of Social Remembering*. Maidenhead and Philadelphia: Open University Press.

Nouwen, Sarah M.H. 2014. "As You Set Out for Ithaka: Practical, Epistemological, Ethical and Existential Questions about Socio-Legal Empirical Research in Conflict." *Leiden Journal of International Law* 27(1): 227–260.

Palmer, Nicola; Jones, Briony and Julia Viebach. 2015. "Introduction: Ways of Knowing Atrocity: A Methodological Enquiry into the Formulation, Implementation, and Assessment of Transitional Justice." *Canadian Journal of Law and Society* 30(2): 173–182.

Reference List

Andreassen, Bard A., Sano, Hans-Otto and Siobhán McInerney-Lankford. 2017. "Human Rights Research Method." In *Research Methods in Human Rights: A Handbook*, edited by Andreassen, Bard A.,

Sano, Hans-Otto and Siobhán McInerney-Lankford, 1–13. Cheltenham and Northampton: Edward Elgar.

Campbell, Colm and Catherine Turner. 2008. "Utopia and the Doubters: Truth, Transition and the Law." *Legal Studies* 28(3): 374–395.

Carpenter, Charli. 2012. "'You Talk of Terrible Things so Matter-of-Factly in This Language of Science': Constructing Human Rights in the Academy." *Perspectives on Politics* 10(2): 363–383.

Corbridge, Stuart. 2007. "The (Im)possibility of Development Studies." *Economy and Society* 36(2): 179–211.

Dancy, Geoff. 2010. "Impact Assessment, not Evaluation: Defining a Limited Role for Positivism in the Study of Transitional Justice." *The International Journal of Transitional Justice* 4: 355–376.

Dancy, Geoff and Eric Wiebelhaus-Braham. 2015. "Timing, Sequencing, and Transitional Justice Impact: A Qualitative Comparative Analysis of Latin America." *Human Rights Review* 16(4): 321–342.

de Greiff, Pablo. 2017. "Bridging the Research-Practice Gap: Applied Transitional Justice Research". Presentation made in Oxford June 2017 available as a podcast at: https://podcasts.ox.ac.uk/bridging-research-practice-gap-applied-transitional-justice-research

Ficklin, Lisa and Briony Jones. 2009. "Deciphering 'Voice' from 'Words': Interpreting Translation Practices in the Field." *Graduate Journal of Social Science* 6(3): 108–130.

Ingelaere, Bert. 2015. "Learning 'To Be' Kinyarwanda in Postgenocide Rwanda: Immersion, Iteration, and Reflexivity in Times of Transition." *Canadian Journal of Law and Society* 30(2): 277–292.

Jones, Briony and Djané Dit Fatogoma Adou. 2017. "Reading the 'Uncivil' in Civil Society Resistance to Transitional Justice in Cote d'Ivoire." *Political Geography* https://doi.org/10.1016/j.polgeo.2017.10.004

Jovchelovitch, Sandra and Martin W. Bauer. 2000. "Narrative Interviewing." In *Qualitative Researching with Text, Image and Sound*, edited by Bauer, Martin W. and George Gaskell, 57–74. Thousand Oaks, CA and New Delhi: Sage.

Kelsall, Tim. 2006. *Culture under Cross Examination: International Justice and the Special Court for Sierra Leone*. Cambridge: Cambridge University Press.

Lewis, David. 2017. "The Myopic Foucauldian Gaze: Discourse, Knowledge and the Authoritarian Peace." *Journal of Intervention and Statebuilding* 11(1): 21–41.

Leydesdorff, Selma; Dawson, Graham; Burchart, Natasha and T.G. Ashplant. 1999. "Introduction: Trauma and Life Stories." In *Trauma and Life Stories: International Perspectives*, edited by Lacy Rogers, Kim; Leydesdorff, Selma and Graham Dawson, 1–27. London, New York: Routledge.

Madlingozi, Tshepo. 2010. "On Transitional Justice Entrepreneurs and the Production of Victims." *Journal of Human Rights Practice* 2(2): 208–228.

McAuliffe, Padraig. 2017. *Transformative Transitional Justice and the Malleability of Post-Conflict States*. Cheltenham and Northampton: Edward Elgar.

McEvoy, Kieran. 2007. "Beyond Legalism: Towards a Thicker Understanding of Transitional Justice." *Journal of Law and Society* 34(4): 411–441.

McKnight, Janet. 2015. "The Fourth Act in Socio-Legal Scholarship: Playing with Law on the Sociological Stage." *Qualitative Sociological Review* 11(1): 108–124.

Millar, Gearoid. 2011. "Local Evaluations of Justice through Truth Telling in Sierra Leone: Postwar Needs and Transitional Justice." *Human Rights Review* 12(4): 515–535.

Miller, Zinaida. 2008. "Effects of Invisibility: In Search of the 'Economic' in Transitional Justice." *The International Journal of Transitional Justice* 2: 266–291.

Misztal, Barbara A. 2003. *Theories of Social Remembering*. Maidenhead and Philadelphia: Open University Press.

Nouwen, Sarah M.H. 2014. "As You Set Out for Ithaka: Practical, Epistemological, Ethical and Existential Questions about Socio-Legal Empirical Research in Conflict." *Leiden Journal of International Law* 27(1): 227–260.

Palmer, Nicola; Jones, Briony and Julia Viebach. 2015. "Introduction: Ways of Knowing Atrocity: A Methodological Enquiry into the Formulation, Implementation, and Assessment of Transitional Justice." *Canadian Journal of Law and Society* 30(2): 173–182.

Payne, Leigh; Olsen, Tricia. and Andrew, G. Reiter. 2010. "The Justice Balance: When Transitional Justice Improves Human Rights and Democracy." *Human Rights Quarterly* 32(4): 980–1005.

Pham, Phuong and Patrick Vinck. 2007. "Empirical Research and the Development and Assessment of Transitional Justice Mechanisms." *The International Journal of Transitional Justice* 1: 231–248.

Rauschenbach, Mina; Staerklé, Christian and Damien Scalia. 2015. "Accused for Involvement in Collective Violence: The Discursive Reconstruction of Agency and Identity by Perpetrators of International Crime." *Political Psychology* 37(2): 219–235.

Robins, Simon and Eric Wilson. 2015. "Participatory Methodologies with Victims: An Emancipatory Approach to Transitional Justice Research." *Canadian Journal of Law and Society* 30(2): 219–236.

Roht-Arriaza, Naomi. 2009. "Foreword." In *Assessing the Impact of Transitional Justice: Challenges for Empirical Research*, edited by van der Merwe, Hugo; Baxter, Victoria and Audrey R. Chapman, vii–xi. Washington, D.C.: United States Institute of Peace Press.

Schmidt, Evelyne. 2011. "Book Review: Methods of Human Rights Research." *The International Journal of Transitional Justice* 5(1): 159–165.

Simić, Oliveira. 2016. "Feminist Research in Transitional Justice Studies: Navigating Silences and Disruptions in the Field." *Human Rights Review* 17(1): 95–113.

Somers, Margaret R. 1994. "The Narrative Constitution of Identity: A Relational and Network Approach." *Theory and Society* 23: 605–649.

Srivastava, Prachi. 2006. "Reconciling Multiple Researcher Positionalities and Languages in International Research." *Research in Comparative and International Education* 1(3): 210–222.

Temple, Bogusia. 1997. "Watch your Tongue: Issues in Translation and Cross-Cultural Research." *Sociology* 31 (3): 607–618.

Temple, Bogusia. 2008. "Narrative Analysis of Written Texts: Reflexivity in Cross-Language Research." *Qualitative Research* 8 (3): 355–365.

17

READING LAW SPATIALLY

Antonia Layard

Legal geography

Legal geography investigates the co-production of space, law and society. It focuses on "the where of law", the social spaces, lived places and landscapes that are inscribed with legal significance, that "are not simply the inert sites of law but are inextricably implicated in how law happens" (Braverman et al., 2014, 1). Reflexivity between spatial and legal processes is key, so that, "by reading the legal in terms of the spatial and the spatial in terms of the legal, our understanding of both 'space' and 'law' may be changed" (Blomley et al., 2001, xvii).

As a relatively new cross-discipline, legal geography lets us investigate legal practices, provisions and phenomena from a different angle. Research brings in landscapes, places, non-human beings, objects, practices and concepts, rather than only seeing law as relationships between people. The approach holds particular promise for environmental, urban, constitutional, property and land-use scholars interested in the legal rules and practices that, for example, co-produce wildlife reserves and police protests or help us plan for sustainable cities. In these projects, lawyers, regulators and administrators are not engaging with static forms of nature, history or sustainability; there is an interaction between the world and the rules. Looking at law from the ground up, or from within a network of interacting people, places and things, brings a new perspective to legal work. A shift in focus from "law first", starting with the legal rules, to a grounded perspective beginning in the site or event helps us better understand how spatial and legal practices co-produce (for example) wildlife reserves, protests or homelessness.

Of course, legal geography is not the first interdisciplinary project to shift the scholarly gaze. Legal anthropology, feminist legal studies, critical race studies, indigenous law and science and technology studies have all long introduced more material approaches to investigate both law's place in the world as well as the world within law. Legal geography is distinctive in bringing a specific attention to space and spatiality, to the interrelationships between people and environments, analysing how these operate across and between humans, places and non-humans, as well as core geographical concepts of place, networks, mobility, scale, relationality, distance and temporality.

The central legal geographic concept is "space", the "fundamental stuff of geography" in the words of Nigel Thrift (2003). Notoriously difficult to define, space is what we move in, that through which we connect, argue, live and work. Spatiality is space's effects indicating how location, context and relationships, for example, impact on environments, people and activities. For many years, Euclidean understandings provided workable definitions for space as three-dimensional: "with meters or miles as its units is the geometric system that adequately describes the structure of the space of the physical world" (Sack, 1973, 16). And yet, such "deterministic, and one-dimensional treatments inherited from the 'scientific' approaches of the 1960s and early 1970s" were problematic for geographic practitioners, including planners who rejected understandings of cities as "laid out within a bounded, Euclidean, gridded plain" (Graham and Healey, 1999, 626).

An absolute conception of space has legal consequences, including when understandings of space as empty and inert are applied in colonial contexts – for instance, enrolled into legal assumptions of *terra nullius*, justifying the grant of land to some people and the exclusion of others (Kedar et al., 2018). The effects of absolute conceptions of space continue generations later, telling, as Irene Watson writes, "The tale of terra nullius, its capacity to bury us and its own capacity to survive and go on burying us" (2002, 253). Even municipal governance practices draw on absolute spatial conceptions of borders and territories, implemented to govern people and places, as Marie-Eve Sylvestre et al. (2015) illustrate in their study of the use of "red zones" or "no go areas" attached to bail conditions in Vancouver.

Western and Northern human geographers have, for some decades now, moved away from such absolutist conceptions of space, suggesting that, instead, space should be understood as relationally as possible, as a product of relationships rather than as a container within which the world proceeds. In Doreen Massey's phrase that has so captured scholars' imagination, space can be understood as "the simultaneities of stories so far" (and places as "collections of those stories, articulations within the wider power-geometries of space"; 2005, 130). Relational understandings of space "assume that space can be acted upon, that its properties and descriptions are dependent on the distribution of mass and energy and that, by itself, space therefore would not exert physical effects" (Sack, 1980, 55). Absolute and relational understandings of space are not, however, a binary. Rather, they are identifiable and overlapping, often distinct, sometimes in tension. To borrow from actor network theory, this enables us to think of space as the *explandum* rather than the *explanans* (the thing to be explained, not the explanation). Understanding how the geographical concept under investigation – be it space, territory, place, networks or mobility – is being conceptualised by legal actors can explain decisions in a more rounded way than focusing on highly abstracted legal doctrine alone, prioritising as it does "legally relevant" rules and facts.

None of this is to assume that space or spatiality can be universally defined, as a concept neatly bound and packaged up to travel. Spatiality is not like political modernity, which, as Dipesh Chakrabarty explains, "is impossible to *think* of anywhere in the world without invoking certain categories and concepts, the genealogies of which go deep into the intellectual and even theological traditions of Europe" (2009, 4). Spatiality – the attributes of space – travels. Spatiality will depend upon how "space" is understood, and not all jurisdictions or legal practices use space as an object on to which law is projected. Indigenous understandings of space often focus on space and time concurrently. Maori language, for example, makes no distinction between time and space, and locations are both temporal and spatial (Smith, 2012, 52). Legal geography cannot assume a certain form of spatiality or automatic aspatiality. John Borrows' work on Anishinaabe law reveals with extraordinary clarity the spatial and temporal specificity embodied in these representations of indigenous legal knowledge. As he reminds us, our legal systems are dominated by linguistic and conceptual practices: "Some traditions, like those of the Algonkian speaking nations with which we work, are linguistically verb-based languages. Nouns or words that categorise the world into persons, places, or things are not a dominant way of organizing life" (Borrows, 2016a, 808).

For all of these reasons, there is a growing commitment to provincialism underpinning the shared threads of legal geography. Scholars acknowledge the totalising effects of concepts and neologisms, accepting the critique that Western and European thought and thinkers can push for an apparent unilateral analytical framework rather than inviting a plurality of approaches. Legal geographic scholars are wary of universalism given legal geography's conceptual and methodological grounding, with practitioners cautious to acknowledge "the Imperial legacy of Western knowledge", in Linda Tuhiwai Smith's words (2012, xii). Although much legal geography has so far been both North/Western and critical, the shared aim is to address the gap between legal representation and spatial experiences wherever and however they are observed. The commitment to better spatial understanding binds legal geographers together, rather than any commitment to a single way of achieving this. Scholars take provincialism seriously, disavowing any unitary taxonomy, a scholarly canon or a single set of methodological tools.

Methodology within legal geography

So far, most legal geographic research has used empirical and phenomenological methodologies undertaken in the shared space of social science. Ethnographic methods, for instance, are highlighted as particularly effective as legal geographers are "insiders of the legal world" (Braverman et al., 2014, 121), enabling scholars to make observations or ask questions in the field to explore administrative and structural intricacies. Alternatively, ethnographic methods can also be kept separate within a legal geographic project. Michele Statz and Lisa Pruitt, for example, allocated the interviewing part of their research project to Michele Statz, on the basis that she had "training and experience as a qualitative researcher" and, without formal legal training, could offer a "forthright admission of *not* having a Juris Doctorate" to her lawyer interviewees (2017, 3).

Many legal geographers use mixed methods, including, incorporating legal analysis with interviews, site visits and visual records. Nicholas Blomley (2005) used all three methods in his study of urban gardening, seeking to explore how residents of Strathcona, a suburb in Vancouver, practise and understand urban gardening, as well as how people think about and act in relation to property. Scholars have also used visual approaches to interrogate the ocular, observational emphasis in legal geography. Frode Flemsæter, for instance, has used photographs in his research on Norwegian smallholdings "to put the property in the centre of attention rather than the informant, and to help informants recall memories and histories related to the properties" (2009, 412). Theoretical research methods, probing and expanding our understandings of law and spatiality, have also made productive and important contributions to the cross-discipline, particularly in critiquing spatial backdrops as "an adjectival context, a background against which considerations of the surrounding space are thrown into relief" (Philippopoulos-Mihalopoulos, 2010, 204; see also Butler and Mussawir, 2017).

The shared thread in all of these methods is a commitment to using geographic concepts in conjunction with these empirical or phenomenological methods, critically analysing the roles of both law and space in societies (Freeman, 2017). This includes established geographical concepts – space, scale, territory, place, networks, mobility – as well as legal geographic neologisms – "splices", "nomospheres", "lawscapes", chronotopes – to represent a shared understanding of the interactions between legal and geographical thinking (Blomley, 1994;

Delaney, 2010; Graham, 2010; Philippopoulos-Mihalopoulos, 2014; Valverde, 2015). These shared concepts underpin the methodology (the why) chosen to investigate both law and geography, justifying the selection of individual methods (the how). One reason for scholarly diversity has undoubtedly been the collegial resistance of legal geographic pioneers requiring that either a legal or geographical qualification should be a price of admission to debates. Legal geography is open to scholars in many disciplines: being a qualified lawyer or geographer is not a prerequisite; the shared focus is the interaction (Blomley, 1994).

Diversity of method is also inevitable. For, as geographers and legal geographers know well, the academy in which we produce our research inevitably affects the production of research. Achile Mbembe (2015, 10) points out that universities are "large systems of authoritative control, standardization, gradation, accountancy, classification, credits and penalties". This has both practical and intellectual implications, as Mbembe explains:

> This hegemonic notion of knowledge production has generated discursive scientific practices and has set up interpretive frames that make it difficult to think outside of these frames. But this is not all. This hegemonic tradition has not only become hegemonic. It also actively represses anything that actually is articulated, thought and envisioned from outside of these frames.
>
> *(2015, 10)*

Legal geography can push towards interdisciplinarity, but it is still usually produced within universities where knowledge production processes are embedded within different political economies, jurisdictions and systems. Methodology and research ethics processes can become sticks with which we can beat each other, particularly if they are emphasised as signifiers of intellectual sophistication. What we really need here is methodological reflexivity – some contemplation of the "how" of our research – rather than an apparent, universally testable, methodological rigour. There is no single or right way to *do* legal geography.

This preference for contemplation and inclusivity rather than strict schema is increasingly widespread, both for scholars and for institutions pursuing interdisciplinary research goals. Within social science, John Law has argued persuasively for a "broader or more generous sense of method", adapting standard methods to study "the ephemeral, the indefinite and the irregular" (2004, 4). If something is an "awful mess" he asks, "then would something less messy make a mess of describing it?" (2004, 3). And even here, he suggests, with Wen-yuan Lin, we must be careful not to universalise a provincial insight. Calling for empirical versatility across scholarly settings, they recall how uncomfortable John Law felt when speaking about STS, ANT and mess in Taiwan, suddenly realising that "the need for messy method was [itself] a decontextualized truth" (2017, 215). There are simply no universal rules.

Reading law spatially

All this is to say that there is no single way to read law spatially: much will depend on jurisdiction and cultural legal practices. Investigating both spatial and legal practices requires work on the interactions between both law and geography and their disciplinary ways of understanding the world. Academic research and scholarship consist of knowledge practices with claims to legitimacy, validated in different ways. Doctrinal legal scholarship, the bulwark of legal analysis, has long occupied a disputed place in the academy, with particular criticism of exposition, setting out what the law "is" in the form of treatises or textbooks as a "black letter" analysis (Chynoweth, 2008; Cownie, 2004). Of course, legal scholarship is far broader than this, particularly when used to understand society, as the Canadian Law and

Society Association puts it, to understand "the place of law in social, political, economic and cultural life" (CLSA, 2018; and, conversely, social, political, economic and cultural life in law). When legal geography scholars engage in reading, analysing and interpreting law, they do so to understand how geographic concepts appear (or not) in legal decision-making, their effects on dispute settlement and the creation of both legal and spatial precedents.

To use critical legal scholarship in legal geography, it is still useful to draw on Harry Arthurs's report on Canadian legal scholarship, where he distinguished between four types of legal research: law reform, expository, fundamental research and legal theory (Consultative Group on Research and Education in Law, 1983). Although the report caused some professional fireworks (Backhouse, 2003), Arthurs's taxonomy emphasises the difference between stating what the law "is", as a lawyer might do in advising a client by producing expository legal writing, and asking how law constructs and is constructed by cultural, economic, political and social processes. This interrogative form of legal research falls into Arthurs's category of "fundamental research" (where he put critical legal studies and law and economics). This questioning approach emphasises that, to use Austin Sarat and Thomas Kearns' phrase, "Law shapes society from the inside out by providing the principal categories that make social life seem natural, normal, cohesive and coherent" (2009, 22). Interrogating legal categories for their spatial effects on the world, be they contracts, crimes, property or human rights, as well as identifying the spatial assumptions these categories contain, perpetuate or undermine, is fundamental legal (geographic) scholarship.

Reading law spatially is, then, a growing strand of legal geography, turning, in Rebecca French's words, our "lens on basic 'black-letter law' as a fieldsite" (2009, 127). David Delaney notes that "spatial metaphors ... are ubiquitous in social thought – and particularly in legal thought" (2010). He identifies lawyers and judges as "nomospheric technicians", illustrating how actors create particular world-models through legal moves and spatial imaginaries while also foreclosing alternative worlds. Melinda Harm Benson also explores "the idea that litigation is *itself* a space creating process" in her work on the spatiality of (American) rules on judicial review (2014, 215). Spatial readings of cases and legislation enable us to use geographical concepts and techniques within legal analysis to understand better how legal decisions and practices produce and are produced by the world. Disciplinary expertise matters, whether in empirical, analytical or conceptual work for, as Laura Nader has warned: "We have much to learn from each other, but if we try to do each other's work, the work suffers from our naiveté and inexperience" (Nader, 2002, 73). By acknowledging disciplinary strengths, including in reading law, we can expand legal geography's scholarly and policy reach.

Realist, feminist and critical race legal scholars have long demonstrated that legal practice is replete with choices, enrolling assumptions about people or places into governance. The vividly spatial metaphor of the doctrine of *stare decisis* ("to stand by things decided") is not a fixed and static edifice building *ratio* by *ratio* but involves judgement and discretion. This scope for indeterminacy is not always acknowledged in doctrinal legal analysis. Law students still learn to read for rules apparently stripped of their worldly context, the *ratio* of the decision, even if, as feminist and critical race scholars have repeatedly shown, this means incorporating biases and prejudice. Such a focus on the "legally relevant" details relies, as Oliver Wendell Holmes explained in his 1897 lecture to new law students, on processes of abstraction. Cases, Holmes told the new students, eliminate "all the dramatic elements with which [a] client's story has clothed it, and retaining only the facts of legal import, up to the final analyses and abstract universals of theoretic jurisprudence" (Holmes, 1897, 847). Students today are still routinely taught how to perform these reductions. Reading law spatially lets us read for presence and absence, for spatial assumptions, metaphors, absences and biases, putting a geographic spin on Holmes's "facts of legal import" and "abstract universals of theoretic jurisprudence" to see "facts of spatial import" and "situated applications of theoretic jurisprudence".

Reading cases and legislation spatially, looking for spatial assumptions and biases or evidence of abstraction, lets us draw on the orthodox legal technique of asking questions but ask different ones instead. The formal legal *ratio* will still matter, but for legal geographers the questions will also reveal how this *ratio* was reached: are geographical details or concepts assumed or ignored? Are spatial imaginaries present (whether explicitly or implicitly)? Is the site presented as a regulatory "fact", or is there any evidence of spatial particularism that the legal category of place *should* be that way? How are understandings of space and place reconciled with established legal categories of rights, property or judicial review? Are time or temporalities used as discursive or judicial devices? How (if at all) is the history of the site explained? Is there mention of spatial specificity, fauna or flora, noise or smells? Are spatial metaphors used? Is there mention of a site plan or visit? Taking a routine legal technique (asking questions to interrogate judgment) to understand the decision's spatial effects, assumptions and absences sheds light on how law engages with the world beyond doctrine.

There are many lessons for reading law spatially to be drawn from other forms of results-orientated jurisprudence, including critical, Marxist and critical race legal studies. The book cover of the Australian *Feminist Judgments Project* depicts one woman standing on another woman's shoulders, reaching for a volume of Law Reports. Legal geographers also have significant intellectual debts. Observing feminist scholars "ask the woman question" (Bartlett, 2012, 405; Baer, 2009), or critical race scholars asking how "[u]nacknowledged White privilege helps maintain racism's stories" (Solórzano and Yosso, 2002, 27), empowers legal geographers to ask spatial questions, questioning whether law *is* anti-geography, and, if so, why or how and what consequences this brings. Feminist legal scholars challenge gender bias in legal doctrine and judicial reasoning, explicitly seeking to remedy injustices and to improve the conditions of women's lives, particularly by focusing on particularity and context, giving voice to women who have been silenced or side-lined (Conaghan, 2013). Legal geographers can challenge law's biases, particularly in property, administrative or international law, excavating assumptions about place, networks, boundaries, spatialities and practices, which are doing legal work.

This raises the question: are all legal decisions, practices and legalities spatial? For legal geographers, the answer is, yes. Scholars can read any decision or legal provision spatially, so that, even when spatial characteristics are not immediately obvious, legal geographers can find them. The foundational 1932 Scottish case of *Donoghue v Stevenson*, for instance, concerns the finding of a snail in a bottle of ginger beer, a cloudy drink with natural sedimentation poured into bottles that were "washed and allowed to stand in places to which it was obvious that snails had freedom of access from outside the defender's premises, and in which, indeed, snails and slimy trails of snails were frequently found" (1932 HL 31, 32). The problem – the snail in the bottle – can be understood as one of movement and the creation of a manufacturing network that was open and permeable, consisting of spatial relationships between animals and glass, manufacturers and bottle caps. It was the movement of the snails, the lack of physical boundaries (bottle caps were not put on the bottles until after they were filled) and the network of manufacture (including the label with the manufacturer's name and address, enabling the pursuer to identify the respondent and bring her claim) that came together to produce the dispute. This is, no doubt, a minor example, but legal geographers embrace the chance of being "spatial detectives" (Bennett and Layard, 2015) investigating the absence or presence of spatiality as well as its legal and social effects.

And so, one reason to read cases spatially is to read for assumptions and biases, perhaps understood in geography but not interrogated in law. In Michele Statz and Lisa Pruitt's analysis of the use of the word "distance" in American abortion law, for example, they found that, although the judges might find quantitative assessments relatively easy to relate to (driving for 550 miles to the nearest Texan clinic, for instance), this "doesn't require too much of a mental leap to realize how difficult that is". And yet, if immigration, childcare or work commitments are factored in, "it only tells a small piece of the story, that's for sure ... You know, it could still be difficult if it's 30 miles" (2017, 13). Distance, Statz and Pruitt conclude, becomes only partially "legally cognizable". As feminist scholars have long explained, this partial or embodied knowledge is inevitable. Given the power dynamics and legal tactics involved in putting together litigation in an apparently (spatially) objective legal system, litigators assume that quantitative versions of distance are more persuasive in court than subjective, embedded understandings of the concept. This matters enormously to women on the ground, dependent on activist lawyers to protect abortion rights, knowing which spatial tactic to pick.

A second reason to read law spatially is to identify any spatial imaginaries invoked or implied. Decisions with effects for types of place are often built on distinctive spatial visions that may sometimes be quite explicitly articulated. Nicholas Blomley, for instance, has noted how a prevailing legal and liberal imaginary of bounded selves underpins a critique of begging for crossing prevailing cultural and normative boundaries between people. This imaginary of self underpins an understanding of spaces for encounters with difference (including pavements or sidewalks) as threats to autonomy and liberty rather than as spaces of interaction. If the social imaginary of self can be changed, then the spatial imaginary of a "safe" street, public space and pan-handling can also change (Blomley, 2010). Similarly, fearful spatial imaginaries can also do governance work, as Mariana Valverde explains in her book *Everyday Law on the Street*. Writing about the campaign to put "diversity on the menu" for street traders in Toronto, she notes that regulation to control vendors "may well be due to an unconscious fear of a descent into 'Third World' urban chaos ... the 'Third World city' specter ... looms large in the 'regulatory imagination' as a possibility to be avoided in Toronto" (Valverde, 2012, 144). This particular imaginary was to be avoided.

A third advantage of reading law spatially is that cases can illustrate the difficulties of fitting in. This is a well-established concern in critical race studies. Patricia Hill Collins has highlighted how "Oppressed groups are frequently placed in the situation of being listened to only if we frame our ideas in the language that is familiar to and comfortable for a dominant group" (Collins, 2008, vii). We are in the earliest days of academic understanding how race and legal geography explicitly interact, but it is evident that, particularly in Northern and Western jurisdictions, spatial concepts may not necessarily "fit in" to existing legal discourse and practice producing systematic repression and discrimination. In *Subversive Property*, Sarah Keenan (2014) has explained how Australian property practices imposed leasehold arrangements on to aboriginal ways of living and cultural practices, requiring communities to fit in with the leases' conceptual grids rather than the other way around. Sherene Razack, meanwhile, has demonstrated how the litigation following the rape and killing of Pamela George in 1995 attached a space of violence to her wherever she went: "While Pamela George remained stuck in the racial space of prostitution where violence is innate, the men were considered to be far removed from the spaces of violence". For Pamela

George, wherever she went, the "implicit spatial underpinning" went with her: "She was of the space where murders happen; [her attackers] were not" (Razack, 2000, 126). Pamela George had to fit into her allocated space, the men into theirs. And, if spatial ontologies do not fit, results can be violently or legally imposed, with an end result that produces victory for one worldview over another (Watson, 2014). Reading cases for spatial fit can identify when such spatial mismatches occur and the work they are doing in legal decision-making.

A fourth reason for reading law spatially is profoundly practical. Reading cases to glean geographic details about the setting or event provides a basis from which to ask future questions (both conceptual or practical). Indigenous legal scholar Val Napoleon (Napoleon, 2016) reminds us that, "Law is an intellectual process, not a thing, and it is something that people actually do". This is a particularly important lesson within legal geography, with its commitment to the world, particularly if we take on board Aja Y. Martinez's (2014) caution that academia prefers "the strength of logos" to pathos in academic exchanges. Reading from the perspective of the place, the network or the type of event rather than the *ratio* provides a far clearer guide to how other places, networks or events might be regulated in the future.

Applying the method

By way of illustration, let us read the decision by the House of Lords, *DPP v Jones* ([1999] 2 AC 240), spatially. *DPP v Jones* is hugely significant for English highways law, a category of place where it is still possible (largely thanks to this judgment) to act in public regardless of whether the land itself is publicly or privately owned. The facts were that, on 1 June 1995, at about 6.40 p.m., 21 protestors held banners saying: "Never Again", "Stonehenge Campaign 10 years of Criminal Injustice", and "Free Stonehenge". The police asked the protestors to move off the verge, and, although many did, the litigants, Mr. Lloyd and Dr. Jones, did not. Arrested and convicted for taking part in a "trespassory assembly", they eventually appeared before the House of Lords, then the highest court in the UK. The court held, by majority, that an assembly of this type would not be an unreasonable use of the highway (Lords Irvine, Hutton and Clyde), rejecting the minority view that only activities incidental to passing and repassing would be acceptable (Lords Slynn and Hope). In English and Welsh law, a highway includes the road as well as pavements and verges (where these protestors stood), and so the finding creates an important legal and spatial precedent for people wanting to be on pavements and verges – rather than in the middle of the road – for quite everyday activities.

In his leading decision in favour of the protestors, Lord Irvine performed the remarkable feat of making the dispute fit in with his view of the law rather than applying the law to the site. Rather than beginning with questions of highway obstruction, Lord Irvine, then Lord Chancellor, began with a bold legal, and spatial, move, challenging spatial fit. His opening paragraph began: "My Lords, this appeal raises an issue of fundamental constitutional importance: what are the limits of the public's rights of access to the public highway?" ([1999] 2 AC 240, 251). He held that understandings of highways had to mesh with constitutional law, particularly given the incoming Human Rights Act 1998 and its direct implementation of the European Convention on Human Rights. This technique of making the site fit the law rather than applying the law to the site is all too common, as Sandy Kedar et al.'s book *Empty Lands* illustrates, analysing the litigation brought by Bedouin people displaced from parts of the Negev Desert. Here, as Kedar et al. show, a particular – limited, contemporary and rather absolute – specification of how to define a village or settlement produces assessments about land ownership claims that are apparently legally quite straightforward. Adopting a modern "law first" approach and assessing historical use patterns against current legal and geographic definitions misses the detail and specificity of how Bedouin people in the nineteenth century moved *and* farmed, a way of life that was (and still can be) dynamic and relational, not easily fixed by coordinates or conceptual boundaries. The test for ownership, however, had to fit more bounded spatial and legal norms.

Spatial assumptions are clearly evident in *DPP v* Jones. As Nicholas Blomley (2010) demonstrated in his book on sidewalks, *Rights of Passage*, mobility is the leitmotif for pavements and highways. Lord Irvine confirmed this point, saying that protest could only be permitted if people and things did not cause an obstruction and were neither a nuisance nor unreasonable. The spatial assumption of the primacy of mobility did not go away, although it was only Lord Hope, dissenting, who was concerned with the rights of landowners in this context, seeing the highway in terms of property, involving access by the public "to their land". The spatial assumption that highways are property belonging to an owner was otherwise noticeable by its absence, as the remaining judges preferred to see highways as a spatial category largely unaffected by ownership. This work done by spatial categories and assumptions here echoes the analysis by Sarah Keenan in her 2014 study of migrant workers, where an absolute conception of space with hard borders creates a binary between citizens and non-citizens, underplaying the plural and dynamic relationships migrant workers create between global communities and networks. Legal geography surfaces these assumptions, identifying biases even if they are remarkably mundane (highways are for mobility; they are not envisaged as property), illustrating the work these spatial moves are doing in apparently abstract legal reasoning (see also Delaney, 2010).

DPP v Jones is unusual in that the judges were unusually explicit about their spatial imaginaries of the highway. Lord Irvine, held that,

> the public highway is a public place which the public may enjoy for any reasonable purpose, provided the activity in question does not amount to a public or private nuisance and does not obstruct the highway by unreasonably impeding the primary right of the public to pass and repass: within these qualifications there is a public right of peaceful assembly on the highway.
>
> *([1999] 2 AC 240, 257)*

This framed the highway as a public place, where being in public entailed a wide array of activities, in which:

> ordinary and usual activities as making a sketch, taking a photograph, handing out leaflets, collecting money for charity, singing carols, playing in a Salvation Army band, children playing a game on the pavement, having a picnic, or reading a book, would qualify.
>
> *([1999] 2 AC 240, 255)*

This framing underpinned his rejection of a view of the highway as solely for activities incidental to passing and repassing. In contrast, Lord Clyde, dissenting, presented a much narrower spatial (and explicitly Christian) imaginary, allowing for the singing of hymns or Christmas carols, looking in shop windows, queuing to enter the shop or using the highway for a moving procession. These imaginaries underpin both spatial and legal precedents, which, thanks to Lord Irvine's judgment, frame highways as a "public place", albeit one that prioritises flow and movement, restricting obstructions (whether by people, animals or things), nuisance or, that great legal weasel word, "unreasonable" use. As Luke Bennett (2016) has illustrated in his analysis of Arkwright's "place-models" at his Cromford mills in eighteenth-century England, "place-forms" such as factories or highways can be replicated, both locally and globally, once the key material, economic, cultural and legal assumptions are worked out.

Lastly, reading the case spatially provides the spatial and temporal insights that emerged in subsequent protest litigation, giving profoundly practical advice. The site of the dispute in *DPP v Jones* was a "roadside verge of the A344, next to the perimeter fence of Stonehenge". Their Lordships distinguished other spatial contexts, including, "a narrow road" (Lord Irvine) or "a small, quiet country road" (Lord Hutton). In narrow or smaller locations, the exercise of these public activities in a public place might not be possible as – though this point is implicit rather than expressly made – obstruction would be more likely to occur. Similarly, Lord Irvine's judgment, for example, permits only temporary activities ("a picnic" but not "a protest") and no camping, a temporal limitation that proved decisive in the 2012 Occupy litigation (Layard, 2016).

Conclusion: imaginative leaps

Reading cases spatially requires a leap of imagination analogous to that in the *Feminist Judgment Projects*, where "the imaginative gap between the legal establishment and feminist legal theory is at last being reduced" (Davies, 2012, 167). Imaginative leaps are often central in reform, where believing that things might be different requires visualisation and faith. It also requires hope, as Kristie Dotson has written of Patricia Hill Collins's book *Black Feminist Thought*: "Collins's book became one of my epistemological cornerstones. It made all the difference in the world to me and once that difference was made, it could not be unmade" (2015, 2322). Extending our vision and lifting our eyes, as legal geography exhorts us to do, enable us to draw on imaginations whether sociological (Mills, 2000; Taylor, 2004) or geographical (Gregory, 1994; Harvey, 1990) to look up from the familiar routines of daily life, including the familiar routines of reading law.

Once imaginations are invoked, we can explore alternative spatial imaginaries, borrowing insights from critical race studies that rhetoric, composition and narrative are all productive "tools by which to interrogate the effects of racial bias" to develop "counterstories" (Martinez, 2014, 36). Alternative tellings or representations enable marginalised people (or perspectives) to challenge "master narratives" (Yosso, 2006, 10). Shifting perspective – using composition or narrative – enables "voices from the margins to become the voices of authority" in researching experiences (Solorzano and Bernal, 2001, 314). Similarly, the intellectual threads shared with wild law scholars centring the Earth in scholarship teach how – practically – to change perspective (Maloney and Rogers, 2017). Once we understand and expose the spatial assumptions, imaginaries and presumed "fit" that are being presented as ostensibly neutral, abstract *ratios*, we can demonstrate how alternative imaginaries might lead us to different legal results that acknowledge spatiality, producing more geographically sensitive and representative legal rules and practices. Most of all, perhaps, legal geographers can learn progressive lessons of imagination from indigenous jurisprudence, where place, sovereignty and authority have for centuries been interwoven in spatially sensitive ways, where "laws are lived as a way of life", as Irene Watson explains (2014, 255) or, in John Borrows' words, understand that, "A well-functioning legal system is built through good living" (Borrows, 2016b, 3).

References

Backhouse, C., 2003. Revisiting the Arthurs report twenty years later. *Canadian Journal of Law & Society/La Revue Canadienne Droit et Société*, *18*(1), pp. 33–44.

Baer, J.A., 2009. Feminist theory and the law. In Goodin, R.E. ed, *The Oxford Handbook of Political Science* (pp. 305–318). Oxford: Oxford University Press.

Barnett, H., 2012. Feminist legal methods. In *Sourcebook on Feminist Jurisprudence* (pp. 111–138). Abingdon: Routledge-Cavendish.

Bartlett, K.T., 2012. Feminist legal scholarship: A history through the lens of the *California Law Review*. *California Law Review*, 1, pp. 381–429.

Bennett, L., 2016. How does law make place? Localisation, translocalisation and thing-law at the world's first factory. *Geoforum*, 74, pp. 182–191.

Bennett, L. and Layard, A., 2015. Legal geography: Becoming spatial detectives. *Geography Compass*, 9 (7), pp. 406–422.

Benson, M., 2014. Rules of engagement: The spatiality of judicial review. In Braverman, I., Blomley, N., Delaney, D. and Kedar, A. eds., *The Expanding Spaces of Law: A Timely Legal Geography*. Stanford, CA: Stanford University Press.

Blomley, N., 1994. *Law, Space and the Geographies of Power*. New York: Guilford.

Blomley, N., 2005. The borrowed view: Privacy, propriety, and the entanglements of property. *Law & Social Inquiry*, 30(4), pp. 617–661.

Blomley, N., 2010. *Rights of Passage: Sidewalks and the Regulation of Public Flow*. Abingdon: Routledge.

Blomley, N. and Delaney, D., eds., 2001. *Legal Geographies Reader* (p. 118). Oxford: Blackwell.

Blomley, N.K. and Blomley, N.K., 1994. *Law, Space, and the Geographies of Power* (pp. 112–113). New York: Guilford Press.

Borrows, J., 2016a. Heroes, tricksters, monsters, and caretakers: Indigenous law and legal education. *McGill Law Journal/Revue de droit de McGill*, 61(4), pp. 795–846.

Borrows, J., 2016b. Seven gifts: Revitalizing living laws through indigenous legal practice. *Lakehead Law Journal*, 2(1), pp. 2–14.

Braverman, I., Blomley, N., Delaney, D. and Kedar, A., eds., 2014. *The Expanding Spaces of Law: A Timely Legal Geography*. Stanford, CA: Stanford University Press.

Butler, C. and Mussawir, E., 2017. *Spaces of Justice: Peripheries, Passages, Appropriations*. Abingdon: Routledge.

Canadian Law and Society Association, 2018. Available at www.acds-clsa.org/

Chakrabarty, D., 2009. *Provincializing Europe: Postcolonial Thought and Historical Difference – New Edition*. Princeton, NJ: Princeton University Press.

Chynoweth, P., 2008. Legal research. In Knight, A. and Ruddock, L. eds., *Advanced Research Methods in the Built Environment* (pp. 28–38). Oxford: Blackwell.

Collins, P.H., 2008. *Black Feminist Thought: Knowledge, Consciousness, and the Politics of Empowerment*. New York, London: Routledge.

Conaghan, J., 2013. *Law and Gender*. Oxford: Oxford University Press.

Consultative Group on Research and Education in Law, Law and Learning. 1983. *Report to the Social Sciences and Humanities Research Council of Canada*. Ottawa: Minister of Supply & Services.

Cownie, F., 2004. *Legal Academics: Cultures and Identities*. Oxford: Hart.

Davies, M., 2012. The law becomes us: Rediscovering judgment [book review]. *Feminist Legal Studies*, 20(2), pp. 167–181.

Delaney, D., 2010. *The Spatial, the Legal and the Pragmatics of World-Making: Nomospheric Investigations*. Abingdon, New York: Routledge-Cavendish.

Dotson, K., 2015. Inheriting Patricia Hill Collins's black feminist epistemology. *Ethnic and Racial Studies*, 38(13), pp. 2322–2328.

Flemsæter, F., 2009. From "home" to "second home": Emotional dilemmas on Norwegian smallholdings. *Scandinavian Journal of Hospitality and Tourism*, 9(4), pp. 406–423.

Freeman, L., 2017. Governed through ghost jurisdictions: Municipal law, inner suburbs and rooming houses. *International Journal of Urban and Regional Research*, 41(2), pp. 298–317.

French, R., 2009. Ethnography in ordinary caselaw. In Freeman, M. and Napier, D. eds., *Law and Anthropology: Current Legal Issues* (Vol. 12; pp. 126–143). Oxford: Oxford University Press.

Graham, N., 2010. *Lawscape: Property, Environment, Law*. Abingdon, New York: Routledge-Cavendish.

Graham, S. and Healey, P., 1999. Relational concepts of space and place: Issues for planning theory and practice. *European Planning Studies*, 7(5), pp. 623–646.

Gregory, D., 1994. *Geographical Imaginations*. Oxford: Blackwell.

Harvey, D., 1990. Between space and time: Reflections on the geographical imagination. *Annals of the Association of American Geographers*, 80(3), pp. 418–434.

Holmes, O.W. Jr., 1897. The path of the law. *Harvard Law Review*, 10, p. 457.

Kedar, A., Amara, A. and Yiftachel, O., 2018. *Emptied Lands: A Legal Geography of Bedouin Rights in the Negev*. Stanford, CA: Stanford University Press.

Keenan, S., 2014. *Subversive Property: Law and the Production of Spaces of Belonging*. Abingdon, New York: Routledge.

Law, J., 2004. *After Method: Mess in Social Science Research*. London, New York: Routledge.

Law, J. and Lin, W.Y., 2017. Provincializing STS: Postcoloniality, symmetry, and method. *East Asian Science, Technology and Society: An International Journal*, *11*(2), pp. 211–227.

Layard, A., 2016. Public space: Property, lines, interruptions. *Journal of Law, Property, and Society*, *2*(1) pp. 1–47.

Maloney, M. and Rogers, N., 2017. The wild law judgment project. In *Law as if Earth Really Mattered* (pp. 21–36). Abingdon, New York: Routledge.

Martinez, A.Y., 2014. A plea for critical race theory counterstory: Stock story versus counterstory dialogues concerning Alejandra's "fit" in the academy. *Composition Studies*, *42*, p. 2.

Massey, D., 2005. *For Space*. Thousand Oaks, CA: Sage.

Mbembe, A., 2015. Decolonizing knowledge and the question of the archive. *Aula magistral proferida*. Available at https://wiser.wits.ac.za/system/files/Achille%20Mbembe%20-%20Decolonizing% 20Knowledge%20and%20the%20Question%20of%20the%20Archive.pdf

Mills, C.W., 2000. *The Sociological Imagination*. Oxford: Oxford University Press.

Nader, L., 2002. *The Life of the Law: Anthropological Projects*. Oakland: University of California Press.

Napoleon, V., 2016. What is indigenous law? A small discussion. Available at www.uvic.ca/law/assets/ docs/ilru/What%20is%20Indigenous%20Law%20Oct%2028%202016.pdf

Philippopoulos-Mihalopoulos, A., 2010. Spatial justice: Law and the geography of withdrawal. *International Journal of Law in Context*, *6*(3), pp. 201–216.

Philippopoulos-Mihalopoulos, A., 2014. *Spatial Justice: Body, Lawscape, Atmosphere*. Abingdon, New York: Routledge.

Razack, S.H., 2000. Gendered racial violence and spatialized justice: The murder of Pamela George. *Canadian Journal of Law & Society/La Revue Canadienne Droit et Société*, *15*(2), pp. 91–130.

Sack, R., 1980. *Conceptions of Space in Social Thought: A Geographic Perspective*. London, Basingstoke: Macmillan.

Sack, R.D., 1973. A concept of physical space in geography. *Geographical Analysis*, *5*(1), pp. 16–34.

Sarat, A. and Kearns, T.R. eds., 2009. *Law in Everyday Life*. Ann Arbor: University of Michigan Press.

Smith, L.T., 2012. *Decolonizing Methodologies*. Dunedin: University of Otago Press.

Solorzano, D.G. and Bernal, D.D., 2001. Examining transformational resistance through a critical race and LatCrit theory framework: Chicana and Chicano students in an urban context. *Urban Education*, *36*(3), pp. 308–342.

Solórzano, D.G. and Yosso, T.J., 2002. Critical race methodology: Counter-storytelling as an analytical framework for education research. *Qualitative Inquiry*, *8*(1), pp. 23–44.

Statz, M. and Pruitt, L.R., 2017. To recognize the tyranny of distance: A spatial reading of *Whole Woman's Health v. Hellerstedt*. In *Environment and Planning A: Economy and Space* (pp. 1–22). https://doi.org/10.1177 %2F0308518X18757508

Sylvestre, M.E., Damon, W., Blomley, N. and Bellot, C., 2015. Spatial tactics in criminal courts and the politics of legal technicalities. *Antipode*, *47*(5), pp. 1346–1366.

Taylor, C., 2004. *Modern Social Imaginaries*. Durham, NC, London: Duke University Press.

Thrift, N., 2003. Space: The fundamental stuff of geography. *Key Concepts in Geography*, *2*, pp. 85–96.

Valverde, M., 2012. *Everyday Law on the Street: City Governance in an Age of Diversity*. Chicago: University of Chicago Press.

Valverde, M., 2015. *Chronotopes of Law: Jurisdiction, Scale and Governance*. Abingdon: Routledge.

Watson, I., 2002. Buried alive. *Law and Critique*, *13*(3), pp. 253–269.

Watson, I., 2014. *Aboriginal Peoples, Colonialism and International Law: Raw Law*. Abingdon, New York: Routledge.

Yosso, T.J., 2006. *Critical Race Counterstories along the Chicana/Chicano Educational Pipeline*. New York: Routledge.

18

LEGAL CONCEPTS IN FLUX

The social construction of legal meaning

Maayan Ravid and Alice Schneider

Introduction: socio-legal approaches to the study of legal change

That law changes is an empirically observable phenomenon in all existing and historical legal systems. Legal professionals and academics, as well as socio-legal (Dror 1970; Friedman 1986; Moore 1973) and legal theorists (Hart 2012; Unger 1983), acknowledge the occurrence of legal change. In modern legal systems, the paradigmatic ways in which the content of legally valid rules is changed are legislative reforms and judicial precedent. Such institutionalised changes of law typically depend on, or entail, amendments of legal text: for example, reformulations of statute and terminological amendments of legal concepts in court judgments. Such textual changes are usually promulgated publicly and documented in official records. They are correspondingly easy to spot and provide the subject matter for much doctrinal legal scholarship.

But this institutional, officially mandated change of the content of law is just one type of legal change. In addition, there exist more covert forms of legal change. Though more subtle, they are nevertheless socially significant. Most obviously, even when the 'black-letter law' or 'law in the books' remains constant, a shift in enforcement and application practices affects the significance of law in society. For example, changes in criminal prosecution practices – such as the police practice of not prosecuting the possession of small amounts of controlled substances – are immensely consequential for the social effects of black-letter laws. Thus, changes in executive practices count as another kind of legal change that is of interest to socio-legal scholars.

Furthermore, we can identify a third, intermediate way in which law changes. What we have in mind here is a kind of change that concerns the ways in which concepts in black-letter law acquire new meaning. Arguably, such changes in meaning of legal concepts can have immense social significance. For example, subtle changes in what judges consider to count as 'negligent' may be decisive in whether a given behaviour counts as criminally offensive or not. Such changes in legal meaning can occur in incremental ways that fall short of explicit legislative or judicial amendments. In such cases, the meaning of a legal concept – that which it signifies – shifts, even though the signifiers used – the terms and formulations in legal text – remain constant.

It should be noted that, in distinguishing, first, official legislative change, second, change in legal enforcement practices, and, third, change in legal meaning, we are not implying that these different types of legal change can always be demarcated clearly. They are not mutually exclusive; changes in the meanings attributed to legal concepts will often manifest in tweaks of judicial and administrative decision-making and may even prompt proposals for legislative change. Here, we propose to focus research investigations on the subtle and therefore oft-overlooked ways in which the meaning of legal terms fluctuates, alongside formal legislative change, or when no official change takes place at all.

In this chapter, we are concerned with the effects of society on legal norms, rather than with the arguably more typical socio-legal concern of how law and legal institutions affect social processes. The first subsection considers why changes in legal meaning may be significant and how they can be explored empirically. Given that the social practices that determine legal meaning will be affected by the power relations between social actors, as well as by culturally dominant norms and values, we recommend qualitative discourse analysis as a research method. The second subsection reflects in more detail on the peculiarities of the legal field, specifically its professionalised autonomy. It explains that, in exploring change in legal meaning, socio-legal scholars may be justified in focusing primarily on professional legal discourse. The third section contains an exemplary case study that explores change and variability in legal meaning through discourse analysis. It offers some insights into the method by sharing the process of analysing legal discourse on asylum seekers in Israel as an example.

Exploring changes in legal meaning: using discourse analysis

Meanings in language depend on socio-linguistic practices. A 'change in meaning' can encompass a change to various dimensions of practice and signification. It could be the case that the set of things a concept refers to broadens, or that it becomes narrower, its associative framework might change (Hall 1978), or its normative valence – the value judgements we tend to make in relation to said concept – may shift (Foucault 2006). This is not a comprehensive taxonomy, but simply flags up types of change in legal meaning that researchers may want to explore.

Even though changes in the meaning of words are usually such broad socio-cultural phenomena that they are beyond the control of individuals, critical scholarship has stressed that semantic changes are nonetheless often tied up with social power. Analyses have demonstrated that power in shaping language is related to social capital and political influence. In particular, the tradition of critical discourse analysis that follows the works of Michel Foucault has focused on how discursive practices reproduce and solidify inequality and domination (Fairclough 2003; Foucault 1982). At the same time, linguistic practices equally play a role in subversive and subcultural efforts. Particularly, sociolinguistic scholarship that focuses on the ways in which language is used in youth and minority groups reveals that semantic changes are often a key trope in subversion and identity formation. So, a change in the meaning of concepts depends on social processes that are often far from neutral and, thus, may allow insight into social realities of power and conflict that shape meaning in language.

Empirical explorations of legal meaning are bound to focus on these linguistic practices and may include various social-scientific research methods, such as different forms of semantic analysis or case studies. To be sure, the aptness of any given research method or research strategy will depend on the nature and pertinence of the research question. We recommend discourse analysis as a particularly applicable method for rigorous exploration of questions concerned with socio-legal interactions in discursive practices. In our assessment, the kinds of question that may guide socio-legal researchers towards an understanding of the role of social power in legal change include:

- Do terms and trends travel between social, political and legal discursive fields?
- Which social actors or groups exert power in determining and amending legal meaning? And
- Which values or norms accompany changes in meanings attributed to a given legal concept?

These questions resonate with queries pursued by anthropologists of law (Goodale 2017; Mundy 2002; Pirie 2013). However, in discourse analysis, we focus on things said or written as the chosen site for empirical examination. Discourse theories have in common the understanding that discourse is indicative, if not constitutive, of social dynamics and power interplays that yield change in social life. The practicalities of discourse analysis entail the systematic study of discourse: the way people talk, write or conduct themselves around generally agreed upon social structures. It involves 'analysis of collections of texts, the ways they are made meaningful through their links to other texts, the ways in which they draw on different discourses, how and to whom they are disseminated' (Phillips et al. 2004: 636). By surveying empirical material this way (including interviews, meeting transcripts, judicial texts, and decisions), discursive themes, trends, and interactions over time can be identified, and implications can be explored. Such analysis is concerned with the way knowledge is produced through the use of distinctive language and terms (Ritchie and Lewis 2013: 200).

Beyond the appropriateness of discourse analysis as a method of analysing change in legal meaning, the following sections focus on some difficulties that may arise in relation to this method, and how socio-legal researchers might approach them. The next section addresses the question of how researchers may define and demarcate the respective 'discourse' they seek to analyse. The fourth section contains a case study that sheds light on some analytical strategies involved in discourse analysis. The study explores the use of the term 'infiltrator' as it is applied to Sudanese and Eritrean migrants under the Israeli Prevention of Infiltration Law. Our findings illustrate that the absence of discussion on the use of the term 'infiltrator' contributes to its solidification and to the institutionalisation of securitisation themes in reference to Sudanese and Eritrean migrant populations. We argue that the persistent use of the term 'infiltrator', with its security connotations, by legal actors in legal settings, contributes to its institutionalisation for an asylum-seeking population.

Demarcating law-changing 'discourse': the autonomy of legal meaning

In adopting the method of discourse analysis, the first task that socio-legal scholars will find themselves confronted with is to identify and demarcate the relevant discourse they seek to analyse. This involves making boundary decisions on the kinds of speech act that will be taken to be part of the relevant discourse. In this section, we explain why it may be justifiable for socio-legal researchers to focus on legal doctrine and institutional debates. In particular, as the 'legal autonomy thesis' asserts, legal professionals such as judges, legislators, and other officials have a more immediate influence on the content of law than other social groups. We simultaneously emphasise that researchers need to maintain an awareness of how these narrower legal discourses may be influenced by their social environments.

Legal concepts are part of the technical-professional language of a specific subgroup in society. The members of this group have typically received legal education or have otherwise acquired knowledge of legal terminology. This means that legal terms are properly viewed as 'terms of art': they have a particular significance in the specific context of the legal system in which they are operative (Schauer 2015). Importantly, this means that legal terms such as 'intention', 'causality', and even 'weapon' have specific meanings that differ from the ways in which these terms feature in ordinary language use. For example, an alarm pistol arguably does not count as a 'weapon' in ordinary language, but it falls within the specialised legal definition of 'weapon' in German criminal law (Wessels and Hillenkamp 2015: 119). The fact that legal language is professionalised in this way has a variety of implications for those who seek to research changes in legal meaning. Most importantly, it means that legal meaning is somewhat autonomous from more general social meaning. For example, even when the ordinary language usage of the term 'injury' changes over time to encompass non-physical harm within its signification, it is not automatically the case that the specialised legal meaning of 'injury' in tort law shifts accordingly.

That legal meaning is somewhat insulated from broader social changes is a salient observation in socio-legal theory and scholarship. The 'legal autonomy thesis' describes the detached relationship between modern legal systems and the broader sociopolitical fabric in which they are embedded. Niklas Luhmann articulates this insight in employing the terms 'normative and operational closure', viewing law as a self-reproducing 'autopoietic' communicative system that only takes note of its social environment insofar it translates social facts into its specific legal rationality (Luhmann 2002). Similarly, thinkers such as Jürgen Habermas describe law as a communicative system with its own discourse-specific rationality, and the social theorist Pierre Bourdieu views actors in the 'legal field' as operating according to a field-specific logic that differs from that of the political and economic fields. Just as social practices are not always amenable to legal intervention, the content of law responds selectively to certain kinds of social influence, meaning that many social norms and movements are never reflected in legal meaning and content. In this way, the 'autonomy thesis' echoes the so-called 'gap problem' in socio-legal studies: the widely observed discrepancy between the official purpose of legal regulations and their de facto social effects (Banakar 2015: 12).

Applied to the social construction of legal meaning, the 'autonomy thesis' implies that, when we seek to determine which speech acts are constitutive to changing the meaning of a legal concept, we ought to focus on professional legal discourse. This entails defining 'discourse' in such a way that it privileges the interpretative contributions of lawyers, judges, legal academics, administrators, and other officials. That way, studying changes in legal meaning becomes primarily about the social and linguistic practices of legal professionals. Within this approach, researchers might expect that legal concepts are deliberated more explicitly within the discourses of the legal profession than concepts in ordinary language typically are. Legal professionals tend to be acutely aware of the fact that much hinges on terminological details. This means that researchers may expect professional legal discourse to display comparatively high degrees of reflexivity in relation to the concepts it employs, albeit within a technical, professional frame of reference.

At the same time, legal meaning – despite its autonomous nature – is not entirely disconnected from broader socio-linguistic productions of meaning. When we consider that legal professionals simultaneously operate in a multiplicity of social roles, it seems safe to presume that there is a certain amount of overspill in terms of how meaning is socially constructed. For example, scholarship has demonstrated well that extra-legal considerations routinely enter judicial decision-making through biases and ideology (Klein and Mitchell 2010), but also as a routine part of discretion (Galligan 1990). This is one way in which more general social norms – what we consider as proper, good, or bad – influence how professionals make sense of specifically legal concepts.

Additionally, the development of legal terms of art draws heavily from general parlance. For this reason, it seems safe to presume that legal and ordinary language terms are not usually homonymous (i.e. the term 'intention' in law and ordinary language does not refer to entirely different things as does the term 'bank', which denotes both financial institutions and land alongside a river). Instead, legal systems are often explicitly committed to develop concepts in close analogy to the way these concepts are employed in everyday life. In some legal systems, it is even an established rule of legal interpretation that, when faced with ambiguities, one ought to first consider the ordinary language use in deciding what a legal concept refers to and what it does not (MacCormick and Summers 2016). Particularly regarding the matter of normative evaluations, legal scholars have long emphasised that law bears an arguably irreducible commitment to popular morality (Dworkin 1995; F.G.L. 1979; Fuller 1978). Additionally, insofar as legal regulation seeks to be efficacious, it is essential that legal norms be communicated in ways that are accessible to legal laypeople. All this indicates links between the general meanings of a concept and its technical legal significance.

To be sure, the 'legal autonomy' thesis does not deny that there are some channels through which law is influenced by what happens in its social vicinity. Habermas describes the way professionalised legal speak borrows from broader communicative practices as 'parasitic' and 'colonizing' (Habermas 2001). But there are various ways in which we can make sense of the relation between the meanings of legal concepts and more general social productions of meaning. Oftentimes, the meaning of concepts in social life is itself unsettled, and law may act as a mediator in this regard. For example, in the 1983 case of *Nix v Hedden*, the US Supreme Court held that, under customs regulations, tomatoes should be classified as a vegetable, even though tomatoes are technically fruits (*Nix v Hedden*, 1893). In deciding on the specific meaning of 'vegetable' in trade law, the Court explicitly opted in favour of the ordinary language usage and popular perception, rather than the conflicting botanical categorisation. Oftentimes, the complexity of social life provides for a range of ways in which concepts can be read. That legal discourse navigates this semantic plurality, favouring some understandings over others, allows insight into the importance that non-professional meaning production – like political discourse – may have in shaping legal concepts.

So, even though legal professionals have a privileged role in determining legal content, they might not be the only participants in the discourses that shape legal meaning. Although legal professionals do (authoritatively) decide on legal meaning, they are themselves susceptible to more general linguistic norms and discursive practices. Thus, the links between the somewhat autonomous professional legal discourses and other social communicative arenas are of particular interest to those exploring socio-legal change. This is where socio-legal researchers can take on a novel role – in understanding the way law operates autonomously and examining critically the ways it is influenced by its social environment.

It is advisable that researchers approach the (semi-) autonomy of legal meaning thesis as a matter of degree. Alongside focusing explorations on the professional legal discourse, we can trace the ways in which other actors and discursive spheres exert influence on legal terms. The following section contains an exemplary methodological approach that illustrates how the legal meaning of a specific category is actively changing in a sociopolitical setting. The case study utilises discourse analysis to trace changing meanings denoted by the legal category 'infiltrator' over the course of 10 years.

How to approach case studies for discourse analysis – tracing change in legal meaning through the case of the 'infiltrator' in Israel

In the final section of this chapter, we provide findings from an illustrative case study of changing legal meaning through discourse analysis. In this section, we describe the process of setting up for a discourse analysis approach. In the example provided we examine discursive themes and interactions in the amendment process of the Prevention of Infiltration Law between 2010 and 2015. This is the law used to regulate persons from Sudan and Eritrea who entered Israel through unauthorised border points. The law's origin in early security legislation attaches security connotations to the term 'infiltrator' and seems distant from the more commonly used category of 'refugee' or 'asylum seeker'. Furthermore, amendments to the law facilitated the construction of a detention facility solely for these populations, a controversial and extreme way to physically exclude specific migrant populations. This prompted our enquiry into the way this term's meaning has shifted. We sought to ascertain whether legal debates regarding this group featured increased security concerns, as had been previously identified in sociopolitical discourse. Using discourse analysis, we follow discussions on the law, tracing the constitutive power of discourse in the changing meaning of the term 'infiltrator'.

Identifying and demarcating the discourse

Locating the empirical site – the discursive field – for examination will depend on the objectives that drive any particular research project. The core motivation behind our case study was to gain a better understanding of the role of legal discourse in immigrant categorisation and its relation to sociopolitical discourse and actors. Analysing the legal category assigned to Sudanese and Eritrean immigrants ('infiltrators'), and the meanings attributed to it, has the potential to shed light on law's role in discourse and understandings regarding this group.

In demarcating the discourses that determine legal meaning, we focus on two communicative sites: Supreme Court decisions on amendments to the Prevention of Infiltration Law and legislative committee debates on the law between 2010 and 2015. This choice is motivated by the insight that judicial and legislative speech acts have a pre-eminent status in determining legal concepts (and the ensuing social impact of their implementation) and are also sites of deliberation and contestation of legal meaning. Although legal language is viewed as semi-autonomous (see the discussion in the third section), analysing debates along a legislative process provides insights into how law is negotiated within broader social and political environments.

All previous works analysing discourse about Sudanese and Eritrean migrants in Israel focused largely on political and public discourse (Kalir 2015; Paz 2011; Yacobi 2011). A few works included some Israeli legal texts in juxtaposition with international law (Kritzman-Amir and Berman 2009) or governmental and media discourse (Ziegler 2015). We therefore knew that there was room for an analysis focused on legal debates.

Additionally, identification of relevant discourse can be informed by a researcher's observation that the existing literature is homogeneous on a particular issue. In such cases, the research motivation may be to affirm or challenge the consensus. For example, academic literature on Sudanese and Eritrean asylum seekers in Israel (cited above) commonly stipulates that protection of migrants' rights may be upheld through the litigation efforts of civil society organisations and through the discretion of courts as guardians of minority rights.

The presumption that legal institutions such as courts would be entirely insulated by the above-identified discursive tropes seemed suspicious. Therefore, the current study was particularly attentive to whether and how themes present in broader political discourse were received in legal discourse.

In practical terms, official legal texts can be accessed on most governmental or court websites. Such texts include official legislation, records of governmental meetings and debates, court decisions, legislative amendments, or intermediary communications in official institutions. One must identify which documents are most important to the phenomena at hand. Methodical collection and organisation of materials must follow to ensure that the examination is sound and impartial and could be reproduced by others in the field. Texts analysed in this case study were collected from official Israeli government websites.

Analysing discourse: what to look out for

The analysis of discourse involves reading through chosen constitutive texts and locating dominant themes that emerge, repeat, and interact. Analysis of the data in the present study began with a brisk reading of empirical data (e.g. court decision or meeting transcription) to intuitively pick up on repeating concepts and themes in use.

We were specifically concerned with the formal categorisation of a particular migrant group as 'infiltrators'. We were therefore particularly attentive to the synonyms that were employed in relation to the group, to metaphors and comparisons used to describe it, to other terms or associations commonly raised in the concept's vicinity, and to the kind or group of social actor(s) that raises them. This list is certainly not exhaustive, and researchers are encouraged to draw on literary and semantic analysis more generally.

Another important consideration for coding themes is existing literature on the topic. Developing an informed expectation of what a given discourse analysis is likely to draw out is particularly crucial for noting meaningful absences of themes. Five prominent themes were acknowledged from existing literature cited above: securitisation, negative social influence, economic influence, state identity, and Holocaust memory. These themes presented across different studies as dominating debates on Sudanese and Eritrean migrants across various discursive sites.

It seemed pertinent to examine whether dominant themes similarly emerge in legal discourse, and how they may affect legal meaning if they do. Relying on past literature, we sought out known themes from other discursive sites. These were utilised as 'preset' or a priori themes, sought out in the data, in contrast to 'emergent themes' that arise upon researcher engagement with the text. The point was to explore whether thematic categories elucidated in earlier research on political and public discursive arenas would also dominate in the legal one. It was done by methodically reviewing legal discourse to decipher whether the same themes appear, theme frequency, and if patterns, trends, or interactions could be identified. Below is an example of a single examination around the theme of securitisation.

Case study findings

This final part of the chapter includes a small portion of the findings from our sample case study. It begins with a brief descriptive introduction to the case study, followed by a sample of discourse analysis focused on the theme of securitisation in legal discourse. Existing literature on the topic had stipulated that security debates regarding Eritrean and Sudanese migrants in sociopolitical discourse increased over time and criminalizes them (Kalir 2015; Yaron et al. 2013; Ziegler 2015). We set out to explore if the same applied for legal discourse.

Brief case study introduction: how migrants became 'infiltrators'

Starting in 2005, growing numbers of persons from Sudan, and later Eritrea, entered Israel through its southern border via non-authorised border points. Such persons were held in jails for extended periods of time and were only released upon the understanding that they did not pose a security threat. Initially, they were afforded identification documents by the United Nation's High Commissioner for Refugees (UNHCR), stating they were recognised as persons of concern in process and were not to be detained or deported.

Up until 2006, Sudanese who entered Israel's border unlawfully were regulated under the 1952 Entry to Israel Law, the legislation used to manage all other non-Jewish migrants entering the state. From January 2006 onwards, they were given visas under the 1954 Prevention of Infiltration Law, an administrative law allowing for extensive state power to detain with few procedural protections. This law originated from early state security legislation, endowing vast administrative detention powers to circumvent perceived terrorist threats.

Between 2006 and 2010, deliberations continued regarding the impact of the Prevention of Infiltration framework on access to asylum and the gap it introduced between the potential refugee population and its status in practice. In 2010, the gap was made more distinct with new regulations on the treatment of asylum seekers and the beginning of an amendment process of the 1954 law (Prevention of Infiltration Law (Amendment No. 3), 2011).

From 2010 to 2015, Israeli legislators sought to amend and ratify a new version of the Prevention of Infiltration Law, equipped to deal with the 21st century reality of irregular migration and to detain people en masse and for long periods of time. The 1954 law was amended multiple times (Law for the Prevention of Infiltration and Securing the Departure of Infiltrators from Israel, 2014; Prevention of Infiltration Law (Amendment No. 4 and Temporary Order), 2013). It was challenged in the Supreme Court three times, owing to its infringements upon Basic Law Human Dignity and Liberty (*HCJ 7146/12 Adam v The Knesset*, 2013; *HCJ 8425/13 Gebrselassie, HCJ 7385/13 Eitan et al. v The Government of Israel et al.*, 2014; *HCJ 8665/14 Desete et al v The Knesset et al.*, 2015). On August 11, 2015, a nine Justice panel of the Supreme Court ruled the 5th Amendment to the law constitutional, and a detention facility was permitted to operate solely for Sudanese and Eritrean migrants (Ziegler 2015).

Thus, in 2018, the largest group seeking asylum (MPI 2017; UNHCR 2016) in Israel remains officially titled 'infiltrators'. More than 10,000 of them were held in immigration detention in Holot Facility in Israel's Negev Desert, during its 5 years of operation. Over half submitted asylum requests in Israel (Lior 2016), and, in 2016, 90% of Eritreans and 57.4% of Sudanese were recognised as refugees in applications submitted worldwide (UNHCR 2016). Nonetheless, Israel terms this group 'infiltrators' and regulates them under the Prevention of Infiltration Law.

Example from empirical data

Every research case will have its own context-specific terminologies that are embedded in national discourse and through historical events. Every researcher must become well versed in the researched societies' history, codes, and narratives, to recognise subtext, signalling, and framing. In Israel, security-related discursive strategies, connecting to national narratives of existential threat and struggle, were conjured in describing African migrants as a security threat to the state from the early days of their arrival.

In the present case study, the securitisation theme encompasses references to national security, connections to the Israeli–Arab conflict and Palestinian refugee issue, and metaphoric use of threatening water imagery (flood, wave, tsunami) to insinuate existential menace. Examples of these are provided below. Existing research on Israel's migration practices has revealed that this theme was strongly present in early political and media discourse on Eritrean and Sudanese migrants and remained dominant over time (Paz 2011; Stevens 2013). Scholars furthermore argue that heightened securitisation debates about these particular migrant groups facilitate their increased criminalisation, but all scholars maintained that legal debates are removed from such discursive influences as sites of professional legal deliberation rather than political speech acts (Kritzman-Amir and Berman 2009: 648; Stevens 2013: 154; Ziegler 2015: 190–191).

Relying on the theme of 'securitisation' as a preset category, we approached legal discourse on the topic, coding all references to security or subcategories related to the term (coalescing eventually into an overarching theme). Findings indeed revealed a gradual decrease in security theme prominence over time. This was consistent with the observation, established in existing literature, that legal discourse is typically somewhat autonomous from sociopolitical influence. In the first verdict on the amendment of the law, the word 'security' was mentioned 24 times and, in the second verdict, it appeared 10 times; the word 'terror' appeared 3 times in the first verdict and once in the second; the word 'hostile' appeared 3 times in the first verdict, twice in the second, and once in the third; the word 'threat' appeared 3 times in the first verdict and 3 times in the second; and the word 'wave' appeared twice in the second verdict. In the final verdict, the word security appeared twice, and none of the other words appeared at all.

This preliminary analysis enables us to answer the questions about *terms and trends travelling between social, political, and legal discursive fields*. But it does not shed light on *which actors are employing which terms*, or *how they are employing* them and *what power they exert*. In this case, for example, it did not account for the absence of securitisation discourse in the continuing security legal framework of the Prevention of Infiltration Law.

Methodical coding of security speech acts enabled a return to the data, to contextualise terms in use and provide a deeper understanding through further analysis. It emerged that highest levels of security discourse were employed in early legal debate around contestation of the term 'infiltrator'. Additional usage appeared in state arguments for continued use of this legal category. All mentions gradually disappeared in later debates and legal decisions. However, use of the term 'infiltrator' and the 'Prevention of Infiltration' framework continued. The infiltrator category persists and denotes the regulatory framework to date. Below are several examples from the data analysis:

In legislative committee debates

The security theme had a strong presence from the start of legislative debates regarding Amendment No. 3. On February 3, 2010, the 18th Knesset (Israel's parliament) Committee on Internal and Environmental Affairs first discussed a suggested amendment to the Prevention of Infiltration Law. The deputy attorney general for legislation explained the amendment's purpose:

This is meant to establish the relations between Prevention of Infiltration Law and Entry to Israel Law. This law is meant to address, eventually, anyone who enters the state borders unlawfully, and following early screening is found to have a security background to his infiltration … For those who do not have a security background, another mechanism exists for handling them … the Entry to Israel Law.

(Balas 2008: 2–3)

By the second debate on the amendment, mentions were made of the incorrectness of security language, the contested choice of a security-related legislative framework, and its inappropriateness for an asylum-seeking population, by committee members, legal professionals, and external experts. By the third meeting on the topic, the committee's legislative advisors recommended changing the legal framework from the Prevention of Infiltration to the Entry to Israel Law, tailoring new sections for those entering unlawfully. However, the representative of the Ministry of Justice's Counselling and Legislation Department responded on behalf of the government:

The government chose the Prevention of Infiltration Law, in order to send a strict message to those who are not refugees. This law falls under the Defence Minister's responsibility … we insist that the amendment be implemented specifically within the Prevention of Infiltration Law.

(Sternberg 2008)

In the fourth debate, she referred to the security threat – 'Sudan is an enemy state, how can I know about every single Sudanese national?'

Michael Ben Ari, an MK representing the right-wing National Union party also expressed such a position in several committee debates, mentioning Al Qaeda activity in Sudan and the threat they pose to the state:

This is an imminent threat. The state of Israel will be flooded by 200 of these coming in every night … I want to protect the state of Israel because it too is under threat. The major threat now is for the state of Israel and its weak neighbourhoods. It continues to spread.

(Ben Ari 2011: 20–30)

Following the quashing of the 3rd Amendment by the Supreme Court, the 4th Amendment was proposed. It contained special clauses that entailed monetary sanctions and finance and asset limitations on 'infiltrators' or those who assist them in transferring money out of the country. Israel's Money Laundering and Terror Financing Prohibition Authority was invited to take an active role in these debates. Representatives from the authority spoke about money transfers and possible connections to terrorism. Rotem Yadlin, assistant to the government secretary in the PM's office explained:

'One guy collects funds from 30 or 50 people … he sends that through a trafficker who gets it out of the country, sometimes in ways connected to funding terrorism … funds are collected in South Tel Aviv by a trafficker who is also an infiltrator … funds are taken into the occupied territories, and from there they are transferred to Gaza.

(Yadlin 2012: 69)

Another legal advisor dealing with terrorism funding continued in this vein:

We have not yet gauged the extent of this phenomenon, the research and intelligence information don't really deal with it … even if a small proportion of these funds end up in the West Bank or Gaza, they may create tremendous damage … The involvement of these two countries, Eritrea and Sudan, is very natural in terms of terror organisation.

(Yadlin 2012)

The 4th Amendment was also ruled unconstitutional by the Court. Committee discussions were held again regarding a fifth amendment of the Prevention of Infiltration Law. In these debates, the theme of securitisation using terminology of national threat was barely in use. State actors no longer argued group hostility or threat in legislative committees, and the 'infiltrator' category was no longer contested. The Prevention of Infiltration Law was maintained as the appropriate framework owing to the technical legal act of crossing the border at an unauthorised border point.

In judicial decisions

The use of the term 'infiltrator', with its security connotations, was discussed by Justice Vogelman extensively in the first verdict *Adam v Knesset*. Vogelman cites the state's choice of the Prevention of Infiltration law as problematic:

The term infiltrator is loaded with the historical baggage that rests on its shoulders … a person who has crossed the border of the state, alone or with a gang of others, for the purpose of carrying out hostile activity such as theft, robbery, murder, damages, or even spying.

(Vogelman 2013: 10)

Given the limited ability of the Court to scrutinise the rhetorical choices of the legislator, Vogelman uses the term 'infiltrators' in his decision while stating: 'We must remember throughout the debate the complex make-up of the new "infiltrators" and that a substantial number of them define themselves as asylum seekers' (Vogelman 2013).

Little focus is given to the securitisation theme in justice opinions. Minor references are made to it, such as Justice Amit stating in the second verdict:

Some of the infiltrators do arrive from hostile states such as North Sudan … we should mention Israel's unique geopolitical situation as a crowded state, with a small territory and population, surrounded by a ring of hostility.

(Amit 2014: 15)

In the last verdict, Chief Justice Naor discusses preceding legislation and decisions, reviewing the process and motivations for the law. She considers Israel's challenge in dealing with increased, irregular migration, as in many other states, and the difficulties of balancing state sovereignty with the rights of those seeking refuge. She recalls the original legal framework:

Another policy Israel applied was detention of infiltrators under the 1952 Entry to Israel Law. Alas, infiltrators were released from detention following a relatively brief period, as the Entry to Israel Law does not allow for detention periods over 60 days … as the infiltration phenomena grew state authorities employed additional means, including erecting a physical barrier at the border with Egypt and legislation meant to facilitate unique legal arrangements for infiltrators. Such arrangements are stricter than those applied to others unlawfully residing under Entry to Israel Law.

(Naor 2015: 7–8)

As Justice Naor reflects, developments in the law stemmed from state efforts to provide exceptional and stringent legal arrangements.

Whereas, in the first verdict, much debate was devoted to the term 'infiltrator' and the securitising baggage it carries, in the second and third verdicts, there is no debate. All judges employ the legal term 'infiltrator' in their opinions, though security concerns had faded. The prevention of infiltration legal framework had been 'transplanted' from early state security legislation to 21st-century migration and asylum control sought for a specific population. The persistent use of the term 'infiltrator', with its security connotations, had become not only accepted, but institutionalised by the Court.

Discourse analysis example conclusion

By using the method of discourse analysis to examine legal debate about Israel's largest group of potential refugees, one can trace and classify change over time. Whereas Sudanese and Eritreans were first handled as were all other migrants, under the Entry to Israel Law, and their treatment was monitored by UNHCR, over time their legal treatment was passed to the Israeli state. State actors amended the Prevention of Infiltration Law in order to apply it for this group. Whereas early debates on the law considered the 'infiltrator' category's security implications for asylum seekers' rights, deliberations decreased, resistance dwindled, and the legal framework was accepted over time. Though the frequency of security language decreased along the process, the use of prevention of infiltration framework and language remained.

The word 'infiltrator', evoking associations of threat and enmity, became official. The semantic distinction between the 'infiltrator' category and labels such as 'asylum seeker' or 'refugee' became increasingly blurred and ultimately futile, as the legal terminological choice of 'infiltrator' prevailed as the dominant referent to Sudanese and Eritrean migrants. What follows is that the persons seeking asylum or 'refugee' status become increasingly associated (if not synonymously linked) with concepts of 'risk', 'threat', 'damage', the invocation of considerations concerning security, and the Israeli–Palestinian conflict. This can be read as evidence of a change in legal meaning, as the 'infiltrator' legal category and legal engagements with this migrant group become permanently fused.

In this process, legal language maintains its semi-autonomous nature as claims of a technical neutrality accompanied legislative debates – that the 'infiltrator' category relates to the act of border entry, with no additional connotations. We argue that, in the treatment of asylum seekers, the title 'infiltrator' might have a technical legal meaning, but its sociopolitical connotations almost inevitably bring in security considerations that are not appropriate for this group, illustrated by reduced security discourse in the legal deliberation process. The term's regularised deployment by the Court, government workers, and legal professionals enhances its acceptance as an authoritative, technical term, and disregards the potentially harmful sociopolitical meaning officially associated with the groups it denotes.

Conclusion

This chapter maps out the study of change in legal meaning from a socio-legal perspective through discourse analysis. Understanding that (a) the attribution of meaning to concepts is a process of social construction bound with unequally distributed knowledge and power, and (b) that legal language operates with a professionalised sense of autonomy and authority, we employ this method to critically engage with changes in legal meaning over time, even when black-letter law remains the same.

In the first section, we reflected on the linguistic peculiarities of the legal field, specifically its professionalised autonomy. We then pointed out what socio-legal scholars might want to take into consideration when they study legal meaning. Finally, we provided an illustrative study of change in legal meaning, through discourse analysis in a specific case study.

In the case study, the terms and formulations in legal text ('infiltrators') remained constant, even though the group that it signified (asylum seekers) became far removed from the term's original legal meaning (individuals who entered the border unlawfully to do harm to the state). It ended up being applied to a very different group (i.e. those who seek refuge). Reduced appearances of a securitisation theme in discourse about the law signalled reduced resistance to the term 'infiltrator', reduced evidence and justification of the threat, and the eventual acceptance of the formal legal category.

The Israeli case explored in this chapter is only one example we drew from our research experience. In it, we show where a change in legal meaning has taken place, as the legal category 'infiltrator', introduced by lawmakers, became the uncontested and legally accepted signifier of the country's largest asylum-seeking population. Past research indicated that increased securitisation in media and political discourse has been instrumental in criminalising asylum seekers. So far, however, scholars have taken legal actors to inhabit a more neutral and less ideological discursive context. In contrast to this conception of the legal field, we show that reduced contestation of the 'infiltrator' category in legal discourse over time in fact signals tacit acceptance of the legal category of 'infiltrator' and complacency about its harmful connotations.

This case study illustrates the importance of empirical study of change in legal meaning and suggests discourse analysis as a useful method to elucidate subtle ways that change creeps in, and the power of law in the process. Understanding law as a social construction, as well as a constitutive force in shaping social life, it is clear that socio-legal scholars must critically engage with the law, rather than accept the authoritativeness with which law asserts itself.

Further reading

A very helpful reading on the process of law's institutionalisation can be found in Brian Tamanaha's *General Jurisprudence of Law and Society* (Tamanaha 2001).

Additional reading on qualitative methods can be found in the book *Qualitative Research Practice: A Guide for Social Science Students and Researchers* (Ritchie and Lewis 2013), particularly Chapter 9, which focuses on analysis applications.

Similarly, Gläser and Laudel's 'Life With and Without Coding' (Gläser and Laudel 2013) provides insights on the practicalities of coding in discourse analysis, and other methods.

For enhancing theoretical foundations on legal change, see:

Watson, Alan. (1983) Legal Change: Sources of Law and Legal Culture. *University of Pennsylvania Law Review*, 131(5), pp. 1121–1157. *JSTOR*, JSTOR, www.jstor.org/stable/3311936.

Halperin, Jean-Louis. (2011) Law in the Books and Law in Action: The Problem of Legal Change. *Maine Law Review*, 64(1).

Krieken, Robert van. (2004) 'Legal Reasoning as a Field of Knowledge Production: Lhumann, Bourdieu and Law's Autonomy', *in Law, Power & Injustice: Confronting the Legacies of Sociolegal Research, Law & Society Association Conference*, Chicago May 27–29.

Ohana, Natalie. (2016) 'Portraying the Legal in Socio-Legal Studies through Legal-Naming Events' in David Cowan and Daniel Wincott (eds), *Exploring the 'Legal' in Socio-Legal Studies*. London: Palgrave Macmillan.

References

Banakar R (2015) *Normativity in Legal Sociology: Methodological Reflections on Law and Regulation in Late Modernity*. Cham: Springer.

Dror Y (1970) Law as a Tool of Directed Social Change: A Framework for Policy-Making. *American Behavioral Scientist* 13 (4): 553–559. https://doi.org/10.1177/000276427001300406

Klein DE and Mitchell G (eds) (2010) *The Psychology of Judicial Decision Making*. American Psychology-Law Society Series. Oxford, New York: OUP.

Galligan DJ (1990) *Discretionary Powers: A Legal Study of Official Discretion*. Oxford: OUP.

Dworkin R (1995) *Law's Empire*. 9. print. Cambridge, MA: Belknap Press of Harvard University Press.

F.G.L. (1979) The Distinction between the Normative and Formal Functions of Law in H. L. A. Hart's The Concept of Law. *Virginia Law Review* 65(7): 1359–1381. DOI: 10.2307/1072670

Fairclough N (2003) *Analysing Discourse: Textual Analysis for Social Research*. London, New York: Routledge.

Foucault M (1982) *The Archaeology of Knowledge*. New York: Pantheon Books.

Foucault M (2006) *Madness and Civilization*. New York: Vintage Books.

Friedman LM (1986) The Law and Society Movement. *Stanford Law Review* 38 (3): 763. https://doi.org/10.2307/1228563

Gläser J and Laudel G (2013) Life With and Without Coding: Two Methods for Early-Stage Data Analysis in Qualitative Research Aiming at Causal Explanations. *Forum Qualitative Sozialforschung/Forum: Qualitative Social Research* 14(2). DOI: 10.17169/fqs-14.2.1886

Goodale M (2017) *Anthropology and Law: A Critical Introduction*. New York: New York University Press.

Habermas J (2001) *Between Facts and Norms: Contributions to a Discourse Theory of Law and Democracy*. 4th ed. Cambridge, MA: MIT Press.

Hall S (1978) *Policing the Crisis: Mugging, the State, and Law and Order*. 1978 ed. London: Macmillan

Hart HLA (2012) *The Concept of Law*. 3rd ed., Clarendon Law Series. Oxford: OUP.

Kalir B (2015) The Jewish State of Anxiety: Between Moral Obligation and Fearism in the Treatment of African Asylum Seekers in Israel. *Journal of Ethnic and Migration Studies* 41(4): 580–598. DOI: 10.1080/1369183X.2014.960819

Kritzman-Amir T and Berman Y (2009) Responsibility Sharing and the Rights of Refugees: The Case of Israel. *Geo. Wash. Int'l L. Rev* 41: 619.

Lior I (2016) 15,000 Asylum Requests Pending – The State Has not Approved a Single Request since the Start of the Year. *Haaretz*, 20 July. Available at: www.haaretz.co.il/news/education/.premium-1.3012510 (accessed September 15, 2018).

Fuller LL (1978) *The Morality of Law*. Rev. ed., 15. New Haven, CT: Yale University Press.

Luhmann N (2002) *Die Politik der Gesellschaft*. Kieserling A (ed.) Frankfurt am Main: Suhrkamp.

MacCormick N and Summers RS (2016) *Interpreting Statutes: A Comparative Study*. London; New York: Routledge.

Moore SF (1973) Law and Social Change: The Semi-Autonomous Social Field as an Appropriate Subject of Study. *Law & Society Review* 7 (4): 719. https://doi.org/10.2307

MPI (2017) Asylum Recognition Rates in the EU/EFTA by Country, 2008-2017. Available at: www.migrationpolicy.org/programs/data-hub/charts/asylum-recognition-rates-euefta-country-2008-2017 (accessed September 15, 2018).

Mundy M (2002) *Law and Anthropology*. Aldershot: Ashgate Press.

Ohana N (2016) Portraying the Legal in Socio-Legal Studies through Legal-Naming Events, in Cowan D and Wincott D (eds), *Exploring the 'Legal' in Socio-Legal Studies*. London: Palgrave Macmillan. 80–96.

Paz Y (2011) *Ordered Disorder: African Asylum Seekers in Israel and Discursive Challenges to an Emerging Refugee Regime*. UNHCR, Policy Development and Evaluation Service. Available at: www.refworld.org/pdfid/4d7e19ab2.pdf (accessed February 15, 2017).

Phillips N, Lawrence TB and Hardy C (2004) Discourse and Institutions. *The Academy of Management Review* 29(4): 635–652. DOI: 10.2307/20159075

Pirie F (2013) *The Anthropology of Law*. Oxford: OUP.

Ritchie J and Lewis J (2013) *Qualitative Research Practice: A Guide for Social Science Students and Researchers*. 2nd ed. London: Sage.

Schauer F (2015) Is Law a Technical Language? *San Diego Law Review*. Available at: https://papers.ssrn.com/abstract=2689788 (accessed October 19, 2018).

Stevens D (2013) Between East and West: The Case of Israel. In Lambert H, McAdam J, and Fullerton M (eds) *The Global Reach of European Refugee Law*. Cambridge: CUP. 132–155.

Tamanaha BZ (2001) *A General Jurisprudence of Law and Society*. Oxford Socio-Legal Studies. Oxford: OUP.

Unger RM (1983) The Critical Legal Studies Movement. *Harvard Law Review* 96(3): 561. DOI: 10.2307/1341032

UNHCR (2016) UNHCR Statistical Yearbook 2016, 16th edition. Available at: www.unhcr.org/statistics/country/5a8ee0387/unhcr-statistical-yearbook-2016-16th-edition.html (accessed September 25, 2018).

Wessels J and Hillenkamp T (eds) (2015) *Strafrecht Besonderer Teil 2: Straftaten gegen Vermögenswerte*. 38., neu bearb. Aufl. Lehrbuch, Entscheidungen, Gesetzestexte. Heidelberg: C. F. Müller.

Yacobi H (2011) 'Let Me Go to the City': African Asylum Seekers, Racialization and the Politics of Space in Israel. *Journal of Refugee Studies* 24(1): 47–68. DOI: 10.1093/jrs/feq051

Yaron H, Hashimshony-Yaffe N and Campbell J (2013) 'Infiltrators' or Refugees? An Analysis of Israel's Policy towards African Asylum-Seekers. *International Migration* 51(4): 144–157. DOI: 10.1111/imig.12070

Ziegler RR (2015) No Asylum for 'Infiltrators': The Legal Predicament of Eritrean and Sudanese Nationals in Israel. Available at: https://papers.ssrn.com/sol3/papers.cfm?abstract_id=2632503 (accessed February 15, 2017).

Laws

Entry to Israel Law 5712-1952 (1952).

Prevention of Infiltration Law (Crimes and Jurisdiction) 5714 (1954).

Prevention of Infiltration Law (Crimes and Jurisdictions) (Amendment No. 3) 5772-2012 (2011).

Prevention of Infiltration Law (Crimes and Jurisdiction) (Amendment No. 4 and Temporary Order) 5774-2013 (2013).

Law for the Prevention of Infiltration and Securing the Departure of Infiltrators from Israel (Legislative Amendments and Temporary Orders) 5775 (2014).

Cases

HCJ 7146/12 *Adam v The Knesset*. (2013).

HCJ 8425/13 Gebrselassie, HCJ 7385/13 *Eitan* et al. *v The Government of Israel* et al. (2014).

HCJ 8665/14 *Desete* et al *v The Knesset* et al. (2015).

Justice Amit (2014) HCJ 8425/13 Gebrselassie, HCJ 7385/13 *Eitan et al v The Government of Israel et al.* Israel High Court of Justice (IsrSC).

Justice Naor (2015) HCJ 8665/14 *Desete et al v The Knesset et al.* Israel High Court of Justice (IsrSC).

Justice Vogelman (2013) HCJ 7146/12 *Adam v The Knesset.* Israel High Court of Justice (IsrSC).

Nix v Hedden (1893).

Legislative Committee Meetings

Balas M (2008) Proposal to Prevention of Infiltration Law (Offences and Jurisdictions) (Amendment No. 3 and Temporary Order). Committee on Internal and Environmental Protection. Jerusalem: Knesset of Israel.

Ben Ari M (2011) Proposal to Prevention of Infiltration Law (Offences and Jurisdictions) (Amendment No. 3 and Temporary Order). Committee on Internal and Environmental Protection. Jerusalem: Knesset of Israel.

Proposal to Prevention of Infiltration Law (Offences and Jurisdictions) (Amendment No. 3 and Temporary Order) 2008. 151. Jerusalem: Knesset of Israel. 09:30, February 3, 2010.

Proposal to Prevention of Infiltration Law (Offences and Jurisdictions) (Amendment No. 3 and Temporary Order) 2011. 436. Jerusalem: Knesset of Israel. 11:30, August 10, 2011.

Proposal to Prevention of Infiltration Law (Offences and Jurisdictions) (Amendment No. 3 and Temporary Order) 2011. Preparation for second and third readings. 467. Jerusalem: Knesset of Israel. 09:30, December 19, 2011.

Proposal on Prevention of Infiltration Law (Offences and Jurisdictions) (Prohibition of Extracting Infiltrator Funds from Israel – Temporary Order) 2012 Proposal on Money Laundering Prohibition Law (Extracting Funds from Israel on behalf of an Infiltrator-Original Offence). 605. Jerusalem: Knesset of Israel. 09:30, September 10, 2012.

Sternberg A (2008) Proposal to Prevention of Infiltration Law (Offences and Jurisdictions) (Amendment No. 3 and Temporary Order). Committee on Internal and Environmental Protection. Jerusalem: Knesset of Israel.

Yadlin R (2012) Proposal on Prevention of Infiltration Law (Offences and Jurisdictions) (Prohibition of Extracting Infiltrator Funds from Israel – Temporary Order) 2012 Proposal on Money Laundering Prohibition Law (Extracting Funds from Israel on behalf of an Infiltrator- Original Offence). Committee on Internal and Environmental Protection. Jerusalem: Knesset of Israel.

19

FEMINIST APPROACHES TO SOCIO-LEGAL STUDIES

Rosemary Hunter

Introduction

Feminist approaches to socio-legal studies involve the combination of feminist theory with socio-legal methods and preoccupations. There is a strong affinity between feminist scholarship and socio-legal scholarship to the extent that both are concerned with the social experience and effects of law, and both reject the 'separation thesis' – that is, the notion that law operates according to its own internal logic, autonomously from society. Hence, much (though by no means all) feminist scholarship in law has taken a socio-legal approach. The scope of feminist socio-legal scholarship has been very broad, ranging from critiques of law's failure to reflect or respond to the reality of women's lives (see, for example, Graycar and Morgan 2002) to critiques of law's role in constructing and reinforcing gendered subjectivities (see, for example, Enright, McCandless and O'Donoghue 2017; Smart 1989) and analyses of gendered processes of exclusion in the legal profession (see, for example, Sommerlad and Sanderson 1998; Thornton 1996).

Feminist socio-legal scholarship has also reflected trends and developments in both feminist theory and socio-legal studies over the past 30-odd years. Feminist socio-legal scholars have embraced a range of feminist theoretical positions; worked within positivist and interpretivist paradigms; utilised qualitative, quantitative and mixed methods; and drawn upon a variety of interdisciplinary perspectives. Feminists have employed and explored classic socio-legal frameworks such as law in the books versus law in action, studies of legal institutions and decision-making by legal actors, legal mobilisation and legal consciousness, along with newer concerns with visual culture, spatiality and temporality (see, for example, Valverde 2015). Each of the separate topics covered in this collection has (or could have) a feminist strand. The common thread running through feminist approaches to socio-legal studies is a concern to highlight and consider the implications of gendered power relations in law and society (see, for example, Hunter 2007, 2013a). Beyond this, however, they are plural and non-prescriptive. Given the impossibility of representing the full range of feminist socio-legal work in the space available, this chapter will focus on one particular example of an emerging feminist socio-legal approach, the practice of rewriting judgments from a feminist perspective.

Since the mid-2000s, feminist judgment projects (FJPs) have been conducted in a number of common law jurisdictions, including Canada (Women's Court of Canada 2006), England and Wales (Hunter, McGlynn and Rackley 2010a), Australia (Douglas, Bartlett, Luker and Hunter 2014a), the USA (Stanchi, Berger and Crawford 2016), the Republic of Ireland and Northern Ireland (Enright, McCandless and O'Donoghue 2017) and New Zealand (McDonald, Powell, Stephens and Hunter 2017). Further projects are under way in international law (Hodson and Lavers 2019) and in Scotland (Cowan, Kennedy and Munro 2019), India and Africa, and are being planned or proposed in Mexico and Germany. These projects have inaugurated a new form of socio-legal scholarship that seeks to demonstrate in a sustained and disciplined way how judgments could have been written and cases could have been decided differently. As such, they use an innovative methodology to interrogate and contest the practice of judicial decision-making and show how knowledge of gendered social experience can inform the process of judging. The following sections explain the origins, premises, processes, outcomes and ongoing development of the FJPs and consider what they add to socio-legal studies more broadly.

Writing feminist judgments

The origins, objectives and methods of FJPs

One of the long-standing tensions within feminist legal scholarship is between feminist critiques and reconstructions of law. Although academic research and teaching readily lend themselves to critique, reconstruction is harder to achieve. Theoretically, there are debates as to whether law is impervious to feminist revision, and, practically, attempts at reconstruction require the cooperation of those who make and implement law, who tend not to be feminists and may, at best, be indifferent or, at worst, actively hostile to feminist goals. This difficulty was faced by members of the Canadian Women's Legal Education and Action Fund (LEAF), an organisation established in 1985 to educate and litigate about equality rights under section 15 of the Canadian Charter of Rights and Freedoms. Through a series of interventions in section 15 cases, LEAF advanced a substantive interpretation of equality that had initially been received favourably by the Canadian Supreme Court. By the mid-2000s, however, LEAF felt that the Court had stopped listening – it was now prioritising other issues, and its equality jurisprudence was going backwards. In considering how they could recapture the Court's attention, LEAF activists came up with the idea of showing the Court how it should be done. Rather than simply putting arguments to the Court, they would write the judgments they would like the Court to have written (see Majury 2006). The first group of six rewritten judgments of the Canadian Supreme Court emerged four years later (Women's Court of Canada 2006).

Although the FJPs had activist roots, they quickly became established as a new form of scholarship engaged in mainly by academics. The model for most of the subsequent projects was established by the FJP run in England and Wales in 2008–2010. Whereas the Canadian project focused on a specific line of jurisprudence – Canadian Supreme Court decisions under section 15 of the Charter of Rights and Freedoms – the England and Wales FJP and those following it have ranged more widely across the entire body of law within a particular jurisdiction or dealt with by a particular court (such as the US Supreme Court). Further, whereas the Canadian project invented a new court, the Women's Court of Canada, whose role was to 'review' the decisions of the Canadian Supreme Court, the England and Wales FJP and its successors have generally been premised on imagined feminist judges sitting on the bench alongside or in place of the original decision-makers. As such, the feminist judges must decide as if at the same time and subject to the same constraints (with regard to the law, known facts, known context, judicial norms) as the original judges in the case. If, within these constraints, it is possible to reach a different decision, or to reach the same decision by means of reasoning that incorporates rather than ignores feminist concerns, then that is a powerful argument that the original decision was not inevitable. It both exposes the contingency of judicial decision-making and demonstrates the real possibility for the introduction of a feminist approach within the bounds of judging-as-usual.

Subsequent FJPs have introduced further variations to the model, extending beyond appellate decision-making to first instance decisions, sentencing judgments and tribunals of inquiry. The Feminist International Judgments Project has involved rewriting decisions from a number of different international and regional courts and tribunals, often emulating the decision-making process of those bodies by producing a single judgment emanating from a 'chamber' of judges, rather than judgments representing the opinions of individual judges. The Australian FJP introduced imaginative variations to acknowledge indigenous sovereignty, and the FJP of Aotearoa New Zealand incorporated a separate strand of *mana wahine* judgments alongside the feminist judgments, embodying a specifically bicultural and intersectional Maori women's jurisprudence. In all of the FJPs, the feminist judges have drawn upon a diversity of feminist theories and approaches within and between the judgments, illustrating that feminism is far from monolithic and does not produce either singular or predictable results. This is especially the case when the reasoning in the judgments is considered, rather than the ultimate decision. None of the FJPs so far has included two or more differently rewritten feminist judgments within the same case, although this would clearly be a possibility for future projects.[1]

Anatomy of a feminist judgment

In order to provide a practical illustration of the construction of a feminist judgment, I describe here one feminist judgment chosen almost at random from the body of published work. The judgment selected for analysis is the first judgment in the English book, the case of *Evans v Amicus Healthcare Ltd* (Harris-Short 2010). The case concerned one of the classic gender issues, including reproduction, marriage, motherhood, domestic violence, rape and sexual violence, equal pay, discrimination and social welfare, which many – although by no means all – of the feminist judgments have dealt with. In this case, a woman, Natallie Evans, suffered from ovarian cancer. Before her ovaries were removed, a number of eggs were harvested from them and fertilised with the sperm of her partner, Howard Johnston, so that they would be able to have children following her cancer treatment. The embryos created were frozen, but the pair subsequently separated, and Mr Johnston withdrew his consent to their continued storage. Under the terms of the Human Fertilisation and Embryology Act 1990 (HFEA), this meant that the embryos would be destroyed. As they represented Ms Evans's only opportunity to have her own biological child, she argued (among other things) that destruction of the embryos would infringe her right to respect for her private life under Article 8 of the European Convention on Human Rights and,

---

1 Cf Appleby and Dixon (2016); Balkin (2001, 2007) and Hutchinson and Morgan (1984), all of which involved rewritten judgments in the same case adopting different theoretical perspectives.

consequently, she should be allowed to use the embryos without requiring the consent of her ex-partner.

The first question for the feminist judge was what feminist position to take on these facts. On the one hand, feminists have long fought for women's right to reproductive autonomy, to be able to make their own decisions about having children, rather than those decisions being constrained or dictated by priests, doctors or fathers. But, on the other hand, feminists have also contested the valorisation of motherhood and resisted the notion that having (biological) children should be women's ultimate aspiration in life. Although an equally plausible feminist judgment could have been written the other way, Sonia Harris-Short was sympathetic to Ms Evans's desire for a child in her particular situation and was also concerned to locate the case in the context of 'the gendered reality of daily life' (Sheldon 2010: 61). Like it or not, we live in a society in which reproduction and parenting continue to have different meanings for women and men. As Harris-Short notes in the judgment, 'The mother–child relationship is still widely perceived as being of unique significance. ... The majority of women still take the primary role in providing day-to-day care for a child' and 'For many women motherhood lies at the heart of who they are or what they hope to become. It sits at the core of their identity.' Further, she cites feminist research that establishes that, despite social changes, 'fatherhood still does not have the same core meaning for men' (Harris-Short 2010: 74).

The second question for the feminist judge was how she could legally decide in Ms Evans's favour. In the Court of Appeal (and subsequently in the European Court of Human Rights), although Ms Evans's right to private life was found to be engaged, so too was Mr Johnston's right to private life, and these rights cancelled each other out. As equal gamete donors, both had the right to grant or withhold consent to the creation and storage of the embryos. In this situation, the infringement of Ms Evans's rights under Article 8(1) was justified by the need to protect Mr Johnston's rights under Article 8(2). Harris-Short draws on feminist theory to reject the assumption of formal equality between Ms Evans and Mr Johnston, instead (like the Women's Court of Canada) adopting a substantive equality approach that takes into account relevant differences. Here, Ms Evans and Mr Johnston were clearly not similarly situated – although they had both donated the gametes to create the embryos, it was Ms Evans who would bear the child through pregnancy and give birth to it, it was Ms Evans who faced the social expectations of motherhood noted above, and, in particular, it was Ms Evans who was no longer able to conceive biological children in any other way. In these circumstances, treating the two in the same way was unfair and unjustified. There was greater justification for the relatively minor infringement of Mr Johnston's rights than the major infringement of Ms Evans's rights, and thus the consent regime under the HFEA should be modified in this particular case. This analysis is also consistent with the feminist critique of rights, which questions taken-for-granted hierarchies of rights and assumptions about 'balancing' rights in favour of a careful examination of the rights involved and the weight to be given to them in the particular circumstances of the case (see also Cheer and McLean 2017; McGlynn 2010).

The third question for the feminist judge concerned the rhetorical strategies to be used in the judgment to support the substantive legal argument. The judgment opens: 'My Lords, it is difficult to imagine the extreme distress experienced by a woman who is called into her doctor's consulting room' to be told she has ovarian cancer, which requires almost immediate removal of both ovaries. 'Those who have suffered the pain of infertility may have some understanding of the sense of devastation and despair that Natallie Evans must have felt' (Harris-Short 2010: 64). The invocation in a judgment of the subjectivity and experience of an infertile woman is entirely novel. And, throughout the judgment, Harris-Short fore-grounds Evans's story – her shock, vulnerability and powerlessness – as a means of building empathy and making the point that at issue in the case is not an abstract legal principle but a human being seeking justice, whose life is deeply affected by law. These three elements – feminist analysis of the facts, legal reasoning and purposive story-telling – are present in one way or another in most feminist judgments – the former generally implicitly, the latter two evident on the face of judgment.

Feminist judgment projects as socio-legal methodology

Realism about judging

The socio-legal nature of the FJPs can be seen in a multiplicity of ways. First, the FJPs approach judging as a socially engaged practice. Rather than judges being understood as standing outside society and answerable only to the law, the FJPs position judges as firmly embedded in society, conscious of the social and political contexts and power structures in which they operate and ethically responsible in their decision-making to litigants and the wider public. In this respect, the FJPs follow in the footsteps of legal realism, which insisted that law is a human creation and understood judges as makers and implementers of policy, with legal reasoning serving more as a post hoc justification (and often mystification) of policy choices than as the sole operative factor in producing judicial decisions (Llewellyn 1931, 1960).

The FJPs also highlight the fact that writing as a judge involves a particular form of authoritative performance, which is invested with juridical power and which historically has been associated with masculinity. Finding ways of performing convincingly as a judge while investing the performance with a feminist inflection is something that many participants have found challenging and, sometimes, uncomfortable (see, for example, Douglas et al. 2014b: 19–23; Fitz-Gibbon and Maher 2015). At the same time, feminist appropriation of the judicial role produces several effects that go beyond the usual bounds of academic schol-arship. Naming power structures, biases, inequalities and injustices and making violence vis-ible *in a judgment* invest feminist knowledge with the authority of law and make it available for future authoritative citation (Fitz-Gibbon and Maher 2015: 267). Moreover, academic and feminist performances of judging decentre the traditional figure of the judge (Hunter 2012: 144) and subvert judicial norms, demonstrating that those norms are not inevitable, and that judging could be done differently (Davies 2012: 173; Hunter, McGlynn and Rack-ley 2010b: 8). More generally, the FJPs remind us that law is a living system performed by a multitude of actors, and the choices they exercise about how they perform those roles matter (Davies 2012: 174).

Connecting with the social

In addition to 'rule scepticism', FJPs have rediscovered legal realism's fact scepticism (Frank 1930, 1949). As described by Hugh Collins:

> According to the Realists, the facts are not 'out there' but are selected and described with a view both to a rhetorical justification of the judge's decision, and to a construction of events so that a relevant legal rule or principle apparently determines the result.
>
> *(Collins 2005: 282)*

Thus, '[w]hen describing the events, a judge is likely to present the facts in a way that suggests the merits of the outcome that the judge proposes to reach' (ibid.; see also Rackley 2010). The way in which judges construct facts becomes evident when one compares different accounts of the facts of a case given by the trial court and different levels of appellate courts, and sometimes even when one compares different accounts of the facts given in the different opinions of judges on the same court. In many instances in the FJPs, part or all of a feminist judge's contribution (as seen in the *Evans* case above) has been to tell the story differently (Hunter 2010: 36–37), to acknowledge the realities of women's lives, to highlight previously excluded social experience and to include that experience in the text of the law. This might involve emphasising particular facts that were downplayed in the original judgment/s, interpreting those facts through a feminist lens, or reframing the analysis of the case to focus on the people concerned rather than the abstract legal issues. As Margaret Davies has written of the English project, 'The objective of seeing, comprehending, and foregrounding the interests of those marginalised or even erased by abstract individualism is a common theme in these judgments' (2012: 177), and she gives a particular illustration of a case involving 'sexually transmitted debt' – the situation where a husband's business borrowing is secured by the bank against the family home, and where his wife's consent to this arrangement may be obtained without proper information or disclosure and/or by means of undue influence:

> In [the feminist] judgment, the broader cultural situation of married women is an integral element of understanding the facts fully as is the absolute imperative to ensure that the women are treated with equal respect by legal professionals, banks, and ultimately the judges who decided the case.
>
> *(Davies 2012: 177)*

Often, too, as the realists observed and the *Evans* case demonstrates, a different telling of the story of the case lays the groundwork for the feminist judge to reach a different result.

Another characteristic feature of the feminist judgments (also seen in *Evans*) is the introduction of contextual or 'social framework' material in order to gain a full understanding of both the facts and the law (Hunter 2010: 37–40). This might include research evidence, demographic information, international and comparative legal materials, policy documents, reports of committees and law reform bodies, parliamentary debates and so forth. As a consequence, rather than dealing in abstractions, feminist judges engage in feminist practical reasoning (Bartlett 1990), reasoning that is rooted in social realities and understands both the causes of problems and the consequences of decisions. For example, in interpreting new sexual offences or anti-discrimination or environmental legislation, feminist judges have been concerned to understand the impetus for the enactment of the legislation and to implement fully its progressive purposes. As a result, rather than trying to assimilate the new law as far as possible with existing precedent (an inherently conservative process that can undermine the statutory objectives), they have construed it in such a way as to give effect to the remedies it was designed to provide (see, for example, McGlynn 2010; Stumcke 2014; Van Wagner 2017).

[handwritten margin note: feminist practical reasoning]

Further, the FJPs are conscious of the material effects of judicial discourse. Judicial constructions and reiterations of gendered norms contribute to their normalisation – to their acceptance and sedimentation in the social world. By contrast, when a judge instead contests established gender norms and asserts an alternative view, she disrupts this process (Fitz-Gibbon and Maher 2015: 261) and may even provide the foundation for the development of new, more open and less constraining norms. The FJPs are replete with instances in which feminist judges have refused to collaborate in the ongoing citation of legal stereotypes of women as mothers, wives, victims and perpetrators of crime, workers, carers, welfare recipients and citizens, and have sought to deconstruct these categories in favour of more nuanced, complex and inclusive possibilities. Although the feminist judgment in *Evans* does not take such a disruptive approach, it is careful to ensure that its account of social conventions regarding motherhood and fatherhood is descriptive rather than normative.

Institutional practices

As well as considering the social role and effects of judging as explained above, the FJPs have taken up the idea of judging as a social practice in a further sense, in terms of the way in which judges – and particularly appellate judges – make decisions not in isolation, but in dialogue with both the lawyers putting arguments to the court and other judges (see, for example, Paterson 2013). In order to emulate this aspect of judicial decision-making, most of the FJPs have established collaborative working methods, particularly involving workshops in which draft judgments are discussed and debated and judgment-writers receive feedback from other participants as well as invited lawyers and judges. These workshops have provided opportunities for judgment-writers to consider and respond to alternative approaches to their chosen case, as well as to receive input in relation to the law, facts and context and technical aspects of their judgment. The workshops held as part of the Northern/Irish FJP were consciously multidisciplinary, with invited speakers addressing themes raised in the judgments – such as issues of reproduction, attitudes towards unmarried mothers, dominant discourses around women's bodies – from (among others) historical, medical and nursing, literary, sociological, activist and artistic perspectives. Working collaboratively in this way is also a feminist process in the sense that participants provide mutual support and encouragement, and it emphasises the figure of the scholar (and the judge) not as an atomistic thinker and creator, but as a relational subject always engaged in conversations with others and in a shared enterprise of production.

What the FJPs do not challenge, however, is the institution of judgment-writing per se. If the strategic objective is to demonstrate that a different but equally plausible judgment can be written from a feminist perspective, then the outcome has to be a plausible judgment deploying conventional legal reasoning, including the citation of relevant legal precedents and authorities, the introduction of extrinsic materials in ways that are institutionally acceptable, the application of standard canons of statutory interpretation, the adoption of an appropriately authoritative voice, and so forth. This approach has been the subject of some complaint within the FJPs, as judgment-writers have chafed against the perceived constraints imposed by norms of judgment-writing (see, for example, Fitz-Gibbon and Maher 2015: 262). It has also been the subject of more sustained critique of the FJPs. In the Australian FJP, for example, Irene Watson explains in an essay why it is impossible for her as an indigenous woman to write the kind of judgment she wants to write within the confines of an Australian judicial institution, the very existence of which is premised on the denial of indigenous sovereignty (Watson 2014a; cf. 2014b). Stewart Motha has also argued that the FJPs, in trying to make a social impact, have taken too narrow and instrumental an approach and have sacrificed the possibility of an incalculable justice (Motha 2016).

Nevertheless, the FJPs do demonstrate a further important legal realist point about styles of judgment-writing. That is, just as legal doctrine gives judges more room to manoeuvre than formalists might represent, so too is there room to manoeuvre within the practice of writing judgments. Llewellyn (1960) identified two dominant judgment styles in US courts – formal style and grand style. Judges adopting formal style write judgments as if their decision followed logically by deduction from precedent, and they present policy issues as matters for the legislature rather than the courts. Judges adopting grand style, by contrast, treat precedents as persuasive, but are prepared to test them against principle and policy and to allow for ongoing renovation and reworking of legal doctrine in line with social developments and needs. In Llewellyn's account, these are 'period styles', that is, dominant approaches adopted generally by judges at different time periods. But individual judges might also adopt one or other style strategically in particular cases. And minority styles must also be possible. Whether or not we can or might wish to identify feminist style, it is certainly the case that feminist judges within the FJPs have drawn on a range of judgment-writing techniques that have lent themselves to feminist purposes.

Further developments

As indicated above, each new FJP has introduced new elements to the FJP methodology, whether that be extension to new locations and levels of decision-making, the addition of new theoretical perspectives or engagement with different judicial traditions. Whereas many of the FJPs to date have focused on domestic law in common law countries, the Feminist International Judgments Project will reimagine judgments in several regional and international fora with their own (often hybrid) judicial norms. The proposed German FJP will tackle squarely the as yet largely unexplored issue of how the feminist judgments methodology might apply in a civil law system, in which the role of the judge and of judgments is conceived of differently from the individual opinions offered by common law judges.

In addition to the collective FJPs, individual scholars are beginning to publish articles that consist of or include stand-alone feminist judgments. This might be done in order to consider how a particular legal issue would be dealt with by a feminist judge (for example, Barker 2016), to demonstrate that existing law can be interpreted in accordance rather than in conflict with women's rights (for example, Sauls Avolio 2017), or to show how the law would look if women were treated as legal persons (for example, Mukherjee 2011). In the latter two cases, the articles were developed from student work – a chapter of a PhD thesis (Mukherjee 2011) and an undergraduate student dissertation (Sauls Avolio 2017). In each case, the rewritten judgment enables the author both to illustrate her general argument in concrete terms and to demonstrate that an alternative judgment would have been not only desirable, but practically possible.

The wider socio-legal significance of feminist judgments

The most immediate wider influence of the FJPs is that they have inspired similar judgment rewriting projects by socio-legal scholars concerned with the achievement of justice for others traditionally excluded from legal subjectivity. The Wild Law Judgments Project, for example, produced a series of rewritten judgments putting earth jurisprudence into practice (Rogers and Maloney 2017). The Children's Rights Judgments Project rewrote judgments from a variety of jurisdictions illustrating how children's rights could be given greater effect in judicial decision-making (Stalford, Hollingsworth and Gilmore 2017). In a chapter in an edited collection, Tamara Hervey

> imagines what EU law could be like if, in its reasoning and its presuppositions, it
> took social rights seriously, by rethinking and rewriting, in an exercise of 're-

imagined jurisprudence' a central internal market judgement [sic] on health care. In doing so, by foregrounding the collective dimensions of health care, and their allocation on the basis of democratic national or sub-national processes, she makes explicit both the non-inevitability of the Court's current jurisprudence and the opportunity to re-orient it towards greater constitutional symmetry between the supranational and the national, and between market liberalisation and other values worthy of protection.

(De Búrca, Kilpatrick and Scott 2014: xi–xii; and see Hervey 2014)

In a slightly different vein, the Ethical Judgments Project took a series of medical law cases and rewrote them from two different perspectives – one legal and one ethical – in order both to illustrate how judges might draw upon ethical principles and insights and to highlight the differences between legal and ethical approaches (Smith et al. 2017).

Second, the FJPs have made a substantive contribution to socio-legal debates relating to judging and the judiciary. One of these debates concerns judicial diversity. The unrepresentative nature of the judiciary in most English-speaking common law countries has been the subject of extensive policy discussion and academic analysis. Although much of the debate has focused on the symbolic effects of a judiciary that reflects only a small and elite minority of the population it serves, scholars and policymakers have also addressed the question of whether judges from non-traditional backgrounds do or would make different decisions. However, theoretical arguments and empirical studies as to whether women judges make a difference have tended to remain at a fairly unsophisticated level, focusing on the existence or otherwise of essentialised gender differences (see, for example, Schultz and Shaw 2013). The FJPs add a different dimension to this debate, providing evidence that a differently constituted judiciary might indeed judge differently, while shifting attention from *women* judges as an undifferentiated whole to *feminist* judges – a category that neither includes all women nor is necessarily confined to women. The experience of the FJPs has also prompted reflection not just on the identity of the judge, but also on the institutional conditions that are likely either to permit or promote – or, conversely, to inhibit – a different judicial approach (Hunter 2015; see also Douglas and Bartlett 2016). A second debate concerns judicial reference to social science evidence. As noted above, this has been a characteristic feature of feminist judgments. But, in some jurisdictions, this is a controversial practice, both in terms of *whether* judges should introduce such material on their own initiative and *how* they do so (see, for example, Burns 2012; Rathus 2014, 2016). The FJPs have provided a new angle on these debates and provoked further comment and reflection on the uses of social science evidence in judicial decision-making.

Third, the FJPs have contributed to interdisciplinary theoretical developments. In political science, for example, much of the work on judges as political and institutional actors and on the impact of judicial diversity has taken a quantitative approach based on measuring associations between judicial identity factors and the outcomes of cases – for example, whether judges voted for plaintiffs or defendants in sexual harassment cases, for husbands or wives in spousal maintenance cases, or for the government or the individual in judicial review cases. The FJPs, on the other hand, show that focusing only on the outcomes of cases is at best limited and at worst misleading. In some of the cases rewritten as part of FJPs, the feminist judge found she could not achieve the result she wanted, as the law at the time would not allow her to get there. In other cases, the feminist judge reached the same result as the original court, but for different reasons. The experience of the FJPs is that the reasoning is at least as, if not more, important than the result, and it is in the reasoning rather than the result that the specifically feminist contribution is most likely to be found (see, for example, Hunter, McGlynn and Rackley 2010b). This, in turn, suggests that qualitative or mixed methods may be more useful for discerning the impact of judicial difference, or at least quantitative methods applied to judicial discourse rather than only to the outcomes of cases. A further contribution has been to the theorisation of prefigurative practices – that is, enactments of an imagined future in the present (Davies 2017: 16–17). To the extent that the FJPs are a form of prefigurative practice, they have provided a new source of material on which theories of prefiguration can draw (see, for example, Cooper 2017).

Finally, the FJPs have inspired further socio-legal research on feminist judging in the 'real world'. Although there are well-known examples of feminist judges on top courts – such as Justices Bertha Wilson and Claire L'Heureux-Dubé on the Canadian Supreme Court, Justice Ruth Bader Ginsburg on the US Supreme Court, Lady Hale on the UK Supreme Court, and Justice Mary Gaudron on the Australian High Court, it has tended to be assumed that these prominent feminist judges, and a handful of other judges who have publicly identified as feminists, are relatively unusual. But is that actually the case? One of the research questions of the Australian FJP was the extent to which feminist jurisprudence has had an influence on Australian law, and, in answering that question, the project organisers conducted a series of interviews with more than 40 Australian judges in federal and state courts and tribunals at all levels of the judicial hierarchy below the High Court. These interviews revealed accounts of feminist judging taking place unobtrusively but on a day-to-day basis throughout the Australian legal system (see Douglas 2016; Hunter 2018). In addition, my own research following the English FJP has included several studies of individual feminist judges (see Hunter 2013b; Hunter and Tyson 2017), as well as more sustained investigation and theorisation of the nature of feminist judging in lower courts (see Hunter et al. 2016).

Conclusion and further references

The FJPs have opened up a rich new seam in socio-legal scholarship, one that looks set to develop further in the coming years. The interaction of feminist theories and socio-legal studies in the FJPs has been multidimensional and has resulted in the enrichment of both elements. Rewriting judgments is clearly a socio-legal methodology that can be adopted by scholars with other kinds of theoretical and political interest, and the FJPs have also made a significant contribution to socio-legal studies of courts and judging. To return to this chapter's focus on feminist approaches to socio-legal studies, the FJPs follow on from an established line of feminist socio-legal work motivated by feminism's concern to understand the operations of gendered power relations and the role of law in perpetuating, reinforcing or ameliorating those power relations. The FJPs bring together feminist interests in women's social position, women's legal subjectivity and the position of women in the legal profession while, as indicated above, encompassing the ways in which gender and other power structures such as race, class, age, colonialism and religion intersect. Furthermore, they bring together feminist legal theory, feminist research methods and feminist activism, combining socio-legal studies' urge to understand the social operation of law with feminism's urge to change it.

The substantive feminist theoretical and sociological understandings deployed by the participants in FJPs are, of course, drawn from the much wider body of feminist (legal) theory and feminist socio-legal research. Having been invited by the editors to conclude the chapter with a list of up to five further references, I would like to give a flavour of the excellent feminist socio–legal work available, while once again being faced with the impossibility of representing adequately the substantial body of work being produced. To reduce the potential arbitrariness of imposing my own preferences, the following is a list of feminist socio-legal books that have been awarded book prizes by the Socio-Legal Studies Association in recent years.

Further reading

Barker, N (2012) *Not the Marrying Kind: A Feminist Critique of Same-Sex Marriage*. Basingstoke: Palgrave Macmillan.

Barlow, A, Hunter, R, Smithson, J and Ewing, J (2017) *Mapping Paths to Family Justice: Resolving Family Disputes in Neoliberal Times*. Basingstoke: Palgrave Macmillan.

Hayes, L (2016) *Stories of Care: A Labour of Law*. Basingstoke: Palgrave Macmillan.

Kotiswaran, P (2011) *Dangerous Sex, Invisible Labour: Sex Work and the Law in India*. Princeton, NJ: Princeton University Press.

Westwood, S (2016) *Aging, Gender and Sexuality: Equality in Later Life*. Abingdon: Routledge.

References

Appleby, G and Dixon, R (eds) (2016) *The Critical Judgments Project: Re-reading Monis v The Queen*. Sydney: Federation Press.

Balkin, J (ed) (2001) *What Brown v. Board of Education Should Have Said: The Nation's Top Legal Experts Rewrite America's Landmark Civil Rights Decision*. New York: NYU Press.

Balkin, J (ed) (2007) *What Roe v. Wade Should Have Said: The Nation's Top Legal Experts Rewrite America's Most Controversial Decision*. New York: NYU Press.

Barker, NJ (2016) Rethinking Conjugality as the Basis for Family Recognition: A Feminist Rewriting of the Judgment in *Burden v United Kingdom*. *Onati Socio-Legal Series* 6(6): 1249–1275.

Bartlett, KT (1990) Feminist Legal Methods. *Harvard Law Review* 103: 829–888.

Burns, K (2012) The Australian High Court and Social Facts: A Content Analysis Study. *Federal Law Review* 40: 317–348.

Cheer, U and McLean, J (2017) *Brooker v Police* [2007] NZSC 307. In: E McDonald, R Powell, M Stephens and R Hunter (eds), *Feminist Judgments of Aotearoa New Zealand – Te Rino: A Two-Stranded Rope*: 73–84. Oxford: Hart.

Collins, H (2005) Law as Politics: Progressive American Perspectives. In: J Penner, D Schiff and R Nobles (eds), *Jurisprudence and Legal Theory: Commentary and Materials*: 279–333. Oxford: OUP.

Cooper, D (2017) Transforming Markets and States Through Everyday Utopias of Play. *Politica & Società* 2/2017: 187–214.

Cowan, S, Kennedy, C and Munro, V (eds) (2019) *Scottish Feminist Judgments: (Re)Creating Law from the Outside In*. Oxford: Hart.

Davies, M (2012) The Law Becomes Us: Rediscovering Judgment. *Feminist Legal Studies* 20: 167–181.

Davies, M (2017) *Law Unlimited: Materialism, Pluralism and Legal Theory*. Abingdon: Routledge.

De Búrca, G, Kilpatrick, C and Scott, J (2014) Editors' Preface. In: G De Búrca, C Kilpatrick and J Scott (eds), *Critical Legal Perspectives on Global Governance: Liber Amicorum David M Trubek*: v–xiii. Oxford: Hart.

Douglas, H (2016) Sexual Violence, Domestic Abuse and the Feminist Judge. *Journal of International and Comparative Law* 3: 317–343.

Douglas, H and Bartlett, F (2016) Practice and Persuasion: Women, Feminism and Judicial Diversity. In: R Ananian-Welsh and J Crowe (eds), *Judicial Independence in Australia: Contemporary Challenges, Future Directions*: 76–88. Sydney: Federation Press.

Douglas, H, Bartlett, F, Luker T and Hunter, R (eds) (2014a) *Australian Feminist Judgments: Righting and Rewriting Law*. Oxford: Hart.

Douglas, H, Bartlett, F, Luker, T and Hunter, R (2014b) Reflections on Rewriting the Law. In: H Douglas, F Bartlett, T Luker and R Hunter (eds), *Australian Feminist Judgments: Righting and Rewriting Law*: 19–36. Oxford: Hart.

Enright, M, McCandless, J and O'Donoghue, A (eds) (2017) *Northern/Irish Feminist Judgments: Judges' Troubles and the Gendered Politics of Identity.* Oxford: Hart.

Fitz-Gibbon, K and Maher, JM (2015) Feminist Challenges to the Constraints of Law: Donning Uncomfortable Robes? *Feminist Legal Studies* 23: 253–271.

Frank, J (1930) *Law and the Modern Mind.* New York: Brentano's.

Frank, J (1949) *Courts on Trial: Myth and Reality in American Justice.* Princeton, NJ: Princeton University Press.

Graycar, R and Morgan, J (2002) *The Hidden Gender of Law*, 2nd edn. Sydney: Federation Press.

Harris-Short, S (2010) *Evans v Amicus Healthcare Ltd* – Judgment. In: R Hunter, C McGlynn and E Rackley (eds), *Feminist Judgments: From Theory to Practice*: 64–82. Oxford: Hart.

Hervey, TK (2014) Re-judging Social Rights in the European Union. In: G de Burca, C Kilpatrick and J Scott (eds), *Critical Legal Perspectives on Global Governance: Liber Amicorum David M Trubek*: 345–368. Oxford: Hart.

Hodson, L and Lavers, T (eds) (2019) *Feminist Judgments in International Law.* Oxford: Hart.

Hunter, R (2007) Would You Like Theory with That? Bridging the Divide Between Policy-Oriented Empirical Legal Research, Critical Theory and Politics. *Studies in Law, Politics and Society* 41: 121–148.

Hunter, R (2010) An Account of Feminist Judging. In: R Hunter, C McGlynn and E Rackley (eds), *Feminist Judgments: From Theory to Practice*: 30–43. Oxford: Hart.

Hunter, R (2012) The Power of Feminist Judgments? *Feminist Legal Studies* 20: 135–148.

Hunter, R (2013a) The Gendered 'Socio' of Socio-Legal Studies. In: D Feenan (ed), *Exploring the 'Socio' of Socio-Legal Studies*: 205–227. Basingstoke: Palgrave Macmillan.

Hunter, R (2013b) Justice Marcia Neave: Case Study of a Feminist Judge. In: U Schultz and G Shaw (eds), *Gender and Judging*: 399–418. Oxford: Hart.

Hunter, R (2015) More than Just a Different Face? Judicial Diversity and Decision-making. *Current Legal Problems* 68: 119–141.

Hunter, R (2018) Feminist Judging in the 'Real World'. *Onati Socio-Legal Series* 8(9): 1275–1306.

Hunter, R, McGlynn, C and Rackley, E (eds) (2010a) *Feminist Judgments: From Theory to Practice.* Oxford: Hart.

Hunter, R, McGlynn, C and Rackley, E (2010b) Feminist Judgments: An Introduction. In: R Hunter, C McGlynn and E Rackley (eds), *Feminist Judgments: From Theory to Practice*: 3–29. Oxford: Hart.

Hunter, R, Roach Anleu, S, and Mack, K (2016) Judging in Lower Courts: Conventional, Procedural, Therapeutic and Feminist Approaches. *International Journal of Law in Context* 12: 337–360.

Hunter, R and Tyson, D (2017) Justice Betty King: A Study of Feminist Judging in Action. *UNSW Law Journal* 40: 778–805.

Hutchinson, A and Morgan, D (1984) The Canengusian Connection: The Kaleidoscope of Tort Theory. *Osgoode Hall Law Journal* 22: 69–113.

Llewellyn, K (1931) Some Realism about Realism – Responding to Dean Pound. *Harvard Law Review* 44: 1222–1256.

Llewellyn, K (1960) *The Common Law Tradition: Deciding Appeals.* Boston, MA: Little Brown.

Majury, D (2006) Introducing the Women's Court of Canada. *Canadian Journal of Women and the Law* 18: 1–12.

McDonald, E, Powell, R, Stephens, M and Hunter, R (eds) (2017) *Feminist Judgments of Aotearoa New Zealand – Te Rino: A Two-Stranded Rope.* Oxford: Hart.

McGlynn, C (2010) *R v A (No 2)* – Judgment. In: R Hunter, C McGlynn and E Rackley (eds), *Feminist Judgments: From Theory to Practice*: 211–227. Oxford: Hart.

Motha, S (2016) Mistaken Judgments. In: A Sarat, L Douglas and M Umphrey (eds), *Law's Mistakes*: 18–43. Amherst: University of Massachusetts Press.

Mukherjee, M (2011) Judging in the Presence of Women as Legal Persons: Feminist Alternative to the Indian Supreme Court Judgment in. *Sakshi v Union of India. feminists@law* 1(2).

Paterson, A (2013) *Final Judgment: The Last Law Lords and the Supreme Court.* Oxford: Hart.

Rackley, E (2010) The Art and Craft of Writing Judgments: Notes on the Feminist Judgments Project. In: R Hunter, C McGlynn and E Rackley (eds), *Feminist Judgments: From Theory to Practice*: 44–56. Oxford: Hart.

Rathus, Z (2014) The Role of Social Science in Australian Family Law: Collaborator, Usurper or Infiltrator. *Family Court Review* 52: 69–89.

Rathus, Z (2016) Mapping the Use of Social Science in Australian Courts: The Example of Family Law Children's Cases. *Griffith Law Review* 25: 352–382.

Rogers, N and Maloney, M (eds) (2017) *Law as if Earth Really Mattered: The Wild Law Judgment Project.* Abingdon: Routledge.

Sauls Avolio, V (2017) Rewriting Reproductive Rights: Applying Feminist Methodology to the European Court of Human Rights' Abortion Jurisprudence. *feminists@law* 6(2).

Schultz, U and Shaw, G (eds) (2013) *Gender and Judging.* Oxford: Hart.

Sheldon, S (2010) *Evans v Amicus Healthcare Ltd* – Commentary. In: R Hunter, C McGlynn and E Rackley (eds), *Feminist Judgments: From Theory to Practice*: 59–63. Oxford: Hart.

Smart, C (1989) *Feminism and the Power of Law.* London: Routledge.

Smith, SW, Coggon, J, Hobson, C, Huxtable, R, McGuinness, S, Miola, J and Neal, M (eds) (2017) *Ethical Judgments: Rewriting Medical Law.* Oxford: Hart.

Sommerlad, H and Sanderson, H (1998) *Gender, Choice and Commitment: Women Solicitors in England and Wales and the Struggle for Equal Status.* Dartmouth: Ashgate.

Stalford, H, Hollingsworth, K and Gilmore, S (eds) (2017) *Rewriting Children's Rights Judgments: From Academic Vision to New Practice.* Oxford: Hart.

Stanchi, K, Berger, L and Crawford, B (eds) (2016) *Feminist Judgments: Rewritten Opinions of the United States Supreme Court.* New York: CUP.

Stumcke, A (2014) *JM v QFG and GK* – Judgment. In: H Douglas, F Bartlett, T Luker and R Hunter (eds), *Australian Feminist Judgments: Righting and Rewriting Law*: 397–404. Oxford: Hart.

Thornton, M (1996) *Dissonance and Distrust: Women in the Legal Profession.* Melbourne: OUP.

Valverde, M (2015) *Chronotopes of Law: Jurisdiction, Scale and Governance.* Abingdon: Routledge.

Van Wagner, E (2017) *West Coast ENT Inc v Buller Coal Ltd* – Judgment. In: E McDonald, R Powell, M Stephens and R Hunter (eds), *Feminist Judgments of Aotearoa New Zealand – Te Rino: A Two-Stranded Rope*: 398–419. Oxford: Hart.

Watson, I (2014a) First Nations Stories, Grandmother's Law: Too Many Stories to Tell. In: H Douglas, F Bartlett, T Luker and R Hunter (eds), *Australian Feminist Judgments: Righting and Rewriting Law*: 46–53. Oxford: Hart.

Watson, N (2014b) *In the matter of Djappari (Re Tuckiar)* – Judgment. In: H Douglas, F Bartlett, T Luker and R Hunter (eds), *Australian Feminist Judgments: Righting and Rewriting Law*: 442–451. Oxford: Hart.

Women's Court of Canada (2006) Rewriting Equality. *Canadian Journal of Women and the Law* 18(1): 1–371.

20

INTERSECTIONALITY AS THEORY AND METHOD

Human rights adjudication by the European Court of Human Rights

Charlotte Helen Skeet

Introduction

Kathy Davis, writing in 2008, described 'intersectionality' as a 'buzz word' viewed as 'essential for any feminist theory' (Davis, 2008, 67). Despite this and despite the early development of the theory and its application to legal analysis (Crenshaw, 1989), outside the USA it is less often used in legal research than in sociological or political projects. Lutz notes the absence of a 'dialogue between jurisprudence and other social sciences on intersectionality' (Lutz et al., 2011, 7). Its relative absence is still particularly noticeable in my area, gender and human rights, more than ten years on from Joanna Bond's exhortation for greater recognition of intersectionality in human rights law at both the international and domestic level (Bond, 2003, 2004).

I hope that this chapter will encourage more people to think about employing an intersectional approach in their socio-legal research. So much has now been written about intersectionality, but the first part of this chapter gives a brief introduction to the theory and methodology and some examples of its use and development. It also charts the development of intersectionality theory in its application to the field of human rights and explains the value of an intersectional approach. The third section uses an example from my own work to show how an intersectionality framework can be used to interrogate human rights adjudication on claims by visibly Muslim women. My method involved looking at the claims from an intersectional perspective. Using textual analysis of the cases to locate the presence of Orientalist tropes identified by Edward Said (2003) in *Orientalism* and I noted how the construction of the claimants as rights holders and the construction of the respondent state impacted on their claims. Finally, the chapter offers suggestions for further reading to assist the translation of theoretical discussions in intersectionality into a practical method that can be used to design socio-legal research projects.

Intersectionality, methodology and method: an overview

Intersectionality is a feminist methodology that counters the tendency to treat different categories of experience and analysis, such as race and gender, as mutually exclusive (Crenshaw, 1989, 139). Intersectionality analysis as applied to law examines the continuance of historical discrimination and the social construction of marginalisation in differential treatment and discrimination within current law and legal adjudication. It also examines representations in law and popular culture and the relationship between marginalized groups and the political priorities of equality-seeking groups that might represent marginalised people.

Collins and Bilge note the varied responses to the question: 'What is intersectionality?' They argue that, as a general description, the following fits core understandings:

> Intersectionality is a way of understanding and analysing the complexity in the world, in people and human experiences … when it comes to social inequality, people's lives and the organization of power in a given society are better understood by not being shaped by a single axis of social division, be it race or gender or class, but by many axes that work together and influence each other.
>
> *(Collins and Bilge, 2016, 2)*

Intersectionality cannot be dismissed, as either merely an 'exhortation to take complexity into account' (Conaghan, 2009, 29) or a call to reject categories completely; it is rather a call to reconsider the fundamental understandings of groups and categories and how those constructions relate and contribute to oppression. As McCall notes, '[t]he point is not to deny the importance – both material and discursive – of categories, but to focus on the process by which they are produced, experienced, reproduced, and resisted in everyday life' (McCall, 2009, 58). Sometimes criticised as too focussed on identity and not enough on context (Conaghan, 2009, 29), intersectionality should address and understand the consequences of categorical perception or imperception, as well as 'structural and cultural context' (Collins and Bilge, 2016, 124) for peoples' lived experiences (May, 2015, 116).

The literature on intersectionality theory is vast, and there have been considerable critique and discussion of its 'uncertainties' or heteronormativity. In response to this and to what has been described as an academic 'whitening' or 'decontextualization' of the origins of intersectionality, there have been three recent monographs that address the intellectual history, origins and development of intersectionality and assert its potential as an analytic method against critiques. Patricia Hill Collins and Sirma Bilge (2016), Ange-Marie Hancock (2016) and Vivien M. May (2015) approach the development and intellectual history of intersectionality from different perspectives but are clear in viewing intersectionality as a theory and methodology that has a number of diverse origins but is ultimately rooted in praxis. All locate its recent history in the social activism against oppression in the 1970s and 1980s across a range of locations, including the US and Latin America. It is argued that the element of praxis when 'doing' intersectionality is crucial. For example, Vivien May suggests that merely recognising that people are differently situated, without going on to use that analysis to address the social construction of discrimination, is not intersectionality (May, 2015, 15).

History and origins can also be traced further back to the 19th century and the struggle against slavery and colonialization. Sojourner Truth, an abolitionist activist and former slave, highlighted the differences in the construction of white and black women in the USA in her 1851 speech 'Aren't I a woman?' She pointed out that the reasons given for not allowing women to vote presented as universal a specific social construction of 'woman' that was only ever applied to white women of a certain class. She had never been described or treated as 'delicate' and in need of protection, nor had any other black women in her position (May, 2015, 69–70). Other histories note the differential construction of men and women under colonialism and the use of female norms against women who did not conform and the use of particular notions of 'women's rights' as a justification for intervention.

Intersectionality is sometimes wrongly described as limited by its connection to the historical context of slavery and its link to Afro-American black oppression in the USA. In fact, its focus on specific histories in the construction of oppression means that it can be applied to other historical contexts. In particular, indigenous groups have both developed and utilised intersectionality as an analytical framework (Collins and Bilge, 2016, 71–77). Similarly, although its application to sexuality is argued to be a recent development, sexuality as an axis of oppression was present in the analysis by the Combahee River Collective in the 1970s: intersectionality does not preclude combination with other theoretical discussions on the construction of sexuality and gender.

The application of intersectionality to law developed in the USA alongside critical race theory, LatCrit and postcolonial feminist legal theory. Intersectionality recognises and analyses why those whose experience of discrimination is at the intersections of different recognised groups may be overlooked or less able to bring successful legal claims against discrimination. Kimberlé Crenshaw (1989) developed a concept of legal intersectionality by analysing a number of US discrimination claims to reveal how discrimination categories were centred around a dominant norm of who represents the category. Crenshaw underpinned this case-law analysis by reference to the wider historical construction of and discrimination against black women in the US. In 'Demarginalizing the Intersection of Race and Sex: A Black Feminist Critique of Antidiscrimination Doctrine, Feminist Theory and Antiracist Politics', Crenshaw argues that the unstated norm in claims for gender discrimination envisages the claimant as a white heterosexual woman, and yet claimants in race discrimination claims are typified as male and heterosexual. These hidden norms operate in such a way that those who either do not experience discrimination in the same way as the 'elite' or 'privileged' group within a classification or who are perceived to be 'different' within the category may be unable to claim at all or may only able to make a partial claim. In 'Demarginalizing', Crenshaw provides the example of *DeGraffenreid v General Motors* (Crenshaw, 1989, 141–142). Historical discrimination meant that no black women at all had been employed by General Motors in the USA before the Civil Rights Act was introduced in 1964. In the 1970s, a 'last in first out policy' on redundancy hit black women particularly hard, and all the black women hired after 1970 were made redundant. This did not show up as having a differential impact on either black people as a group or women as group, as black men and white women had been employed before 1964. The women's claim for discrimination failed because the court did not see that it was based on either 'sex' or 'race'. The court did not recognise black women as a 'special class' to be protected. Contrast this with *Moore v Hughes Helicopter*, where the US court found that the black complainant was unable to bring a class claim on behalf of white women as well as black women, although there was a large sex disparity in pay at the plant she worked at. This was because the court determined that Moore was claiming discrimination as a 'black woman' not as a 'woman', and they refused to let her rely on the sex-disparity data (Crenshaw, 1989, 144). Crenshaw also uses *Payne v Travenol* to illustrate how black women were disqualified from bringing a race-discrimination claim for back pay for the whole of the black workforce (Crenshaw, 1989, 146). They were told they could only represent black women, not black men as well. Once again the court denied them the right to use the whole of the data set on pay disparity. In each case, because the claimants were denied use of the full statistics, which showed discrimination, their claims were unable to succeed. Crenshaw found that sometimes courts will recognise a claimant's difference in relation to the unstated norm that typifies the classification in order to distinguish and set aside that claim. In other cases, the court may overlook a claimant's experience of discrimination because it is experienced differently to other members of the category as a whole.

Methods

Method and methodology are sometimes used interchangeably but can be distinguished if we view methodology as the overarching theoretical approach for analysis of collection data and method as what is chosen for analysis and how the data are collected.

Structural, political and representational intersectionality

In Crenshaw's second seminal article, 'Mapping the Margins', which applied intersectionality to law, she further explored this methodology by distinguishing different methods for focussing intersectional analysis: structural, political and representational. The socio-legal field may engage all three. Research might look at all these aspects or only focus on one. Structural intersectionality helps to identify and map the way that a person's positionality affects their everyday lived experience. This may be because of their economic circumstances, which contribute to oppression, or because of institutional and societal discrimination due to race, gender or some other axis of oppression (Crenshaw, 1990/91, 1245). Structural intersectionality explains the ways in which lived experience is conditioned and mediated by the application of the law or the impact of its absence, including an inability to obtain remedies. Enquiry asks how a group experiences oppression, what factors are material to the experience and whether there is a history of oppression. Political intersectionality (Crenshaw, 1990/91, 1252) focusses on the failure to recognise or prioritise oppression or aspects of the oppression of a subject by one or more equality-seeking groups. For example, rights activists may unwittingly undermine some claims by favouring strategies that reflect or emphasise the experience of the dominant members of their group. They may themselves even show prejudice in relation to non-dominant group members. We can see an example of political intersectionality in the failure of women's rights groups to oppose the policy of mass sterilisations (350,000) of indigenous women in Peru between 1996 and 2000 because speaking out did not accord with their overall aims (Skeet, 2019a). Fujimori had spoken of the importance of contraceptive choice for women at the Beijing conference for Women's Rights in 1995 and rolled out a programme of family planning in Peru (Ewig 2006, 640). International rights NGOs were concerned that, if they highlighted the abuses of the programme, contraceptive choice for middle-class Peruvian women would be compromised. Local NGOs led by non-indigenous elites had a vested interest in the programme continuing as they were receiving money and support from international population agencies (Ewig, 2006, 648). In relation to representational intersectionality, Crenshaw, 1990/91, 1263) discusses the representation of members of marginalised groups in cultural and legal imagery. She argues that we need to both examine how these are produced through the confluence 'of prevalent narratives … as well as [give] a recognition of how contemporary critiques of racist and sexist representation marginalise' a group (Crenshaw, 1990/91 1283). One current example of this in the UK that instrumentalises a women's rights rhetoric is the presentation and representation of 'Asian grooming gangs' by some tabloid papers and far-right groups as the biggest threat to young white women and girls. This utilisation of race erases the threat of sexual abuse from white men and those in the establishment and hides abuse of Asian and black young women and girls, as well as abuse of young men and boys. The role of state agencies in failing to listen to vulnerable young people is also masked.

Forms of categorical analysis

Other methods specific to intersectionality are suggested by McCall, who suggests that we can distinguish three types of enquiry: anti-categorical, intra-categorical and inter-categorical. Anti-categorical might investigate the false premise on which categories are based and might deconstruct categories (McCall, 2009, 50) Inter-categorical study uses existing categories strategically to look at unequal relationships between categories (McCall, 2009, 50) Intra-categorical takes a critical stance towards categories by utilising them to focus on the intersections between them (McCall, 2009, 51). These are not necessarily mutually exclusive approaches. McCall's own project looked at differences both between categories and within them to refute the contention that women as a group had benefitted from new economic models in the 1970s because gender equality as measure was the only inequality not to have risen (McCall, 2009, 64). Crenshaw and McCall's divisions look at what might be analysed through an intersectional lens, but what other methods might be used to collect data? The section below illustrates a use of close textual analysis of case law. Other studies have employed both quantitative and qualitative methods, using interviews and ethnographies, among other methods. There are no specific methods that are excluded. Intersectionality methodology will determine how you frame your research questions and how you design your research. For example, if using a quantitative method, you will have to ensure that your method of collection allows you to disaggregate data so that you can examine the interconnectedness between different axes or categories, McCall's work provides a useful example of this type of research. McCalll's project required careful data collection and disaggregation. The need for this poses a problem for researchers wanting to apply an intersectional approach but having to rely on existing data sets. The data may not have been collected in a way that allows for disaggregation. At my own university, we found that data collected on equal pay had been collected in such a way that it was not possible for us to carry out any cross-categorical or intersectional investigation of the findings. Most importantly, whichever method you use to enable an examination through this methodology, your research must seek to address social justice.

Intersectionality and international human rights

Adopting an intersectional approach to human rights addresses some of the longstanding critiques of rights by feminists, particularly the tendency to individualise breaches caused by structural inequalities and their presumption of an 'abstract' rights holder. Eighteenth-century declarations of human rights were described as universal but were explicitly exclusive: the subject was transparently a male, white, free citizen who could 'afford' private property. In 20th-century international declarations of human rights, no one was explicitly excluded, but the 'abstract human' who was not to be discriminated against in relation to sex, race, ethnicity or nationality in fact masked an accepted norm of a rights holder as a white, male, heterosexual subject. The Convention on the Elimination of all Forms of Discrimination against Women and the International Convention on Racial Discrimination were introduced to give greater specificity for the application of human rights to the experience of women and people discriminated against on grounds of race or ethnicity. It is argued that, even within these more directed conventions – designed to address discrimination in human rights formulations – the understandings of, respectively, women's rights and race discrimination are too narrowly understood and exclusionary. Most rights conventions also contain non-discrimination provisions that either 'stand alone' or act in relation to the

CEDAW

ICRD

other rights under the convention. There is a tendency, as with discrimination provisions in civil rights law, to view a classic recipient in the terms of the most privileged members of these groups and to see them as operating separately rather than being viewed as intertwined or complementary protections. A failure to adopt an intersectional approach to human rights may lead to only a partial finding of a rights breach, or it may fail to recognise the context or cause of the breach and therefore fail to award a remedy that goes beyond individual recompense; it may even lead to no finding of a breach at all.

A classic example in relation to the partial finding and the problems it can cause is famously illustrated by *Abdulaziz, Cabales and Balkandali v The United Kingdom* ([1985] 7 EHRR 471). In this case, women who had immigrated to the UK from a number of different countries and had permanent residence in the UK were not allowed to bring husbands into the UK, even though men who had come from the same named countries were able to bring wives. The applicants argued that the UK government breached both their Article 8 right to private and family life and their Article 14 right not to be discriminated against on grounds of sex and of race or birth. They advanced evidence that the development in UK immigration policy that excluded their rights to reunification were based on racist ideology. The European Commission of Human Rights (now defunct) accepted the claim that this was both sex and race discrimination, but the European Court of Human Rights (ECHR) found for the women only as victims of sex discrimination and not on race grounds. This left the UK free to accept the court's decision yet remove the sex discrimination by 'levelling' down so that men in that situation could no longer bring in wives either. This meant no substantive victory for the women. In relation to the second issue, the failure to address context, *AS v Hungary* ([2006] CEDAW/C/36/D/4/2004) provides a good illustration. AS was a woman of Roma heritage who had been sterilised in a hospital in Hungary without her consent. The CEDAW Committee found this to be a 'woman's right' breach and that her rights under the convention had been breached, but they addressed this as an individual rights breach rather than contextualising it as part systematic structural oppression of Roma in Hungary. Therefore, its recommendations did not hold Hungary to account for this. In the section below, I discuss how I analysed the third example, where the failure to adopt an intersectional approach led to no finding of breach at all. Collins and Bilge refer to Crenshaw as the 'bridge' between the discussion of intersectionality in the context of the domestic civil rights movement in the US and its application to international human rights issues (2016, 97). In 2000, in the run up to the UN World Conference Against Racism, the UN appointed Crenshaw as a Special Rapporteur on the Gender Dimensions of Race Discrimination. Her work on this led to the adoption of a Recommendation by the Committee on the Elimination of Racial Discrimination (ICERD/C/56/Misc.21/Rev.3) and to the production of a paper on the Gender Dimensions of Racial Discrimination from the Office of the High Commissioner for Human Rights United Nations (OHCHR UN; UN, 2001) and to a UN Expert Group Meeting over several days that issued a report providing clear examples of intersectional rights breaches (DAW et al., 2000). The OHCHR paper and later Bond (2003, 2004) argue for greater cooperation between rights institutions so that all the dimensions of rights breaches are recognised. A set of initiatives from 2012 brought together several UN agencies, including CEDAW, with the Inter-America Commission of Human Rights and the African Commission of Human Rights. A further tripartite initiative started in 2016. So far, the ECHR has not been involved. Despite these positive initiatives, there has still not been the integration recommended in 2000, and, for example, CEDAW reporting guidelines still only require the data it receives from countries to be disaggregated by sex.

The European Court of Human Rights reinforcing intersectional discrimination against visibly Muslim women

This section discusses how I used an intersectional approach to my textual analysis of Orientalist discourses in the case law in the ECHR. The focus here is on *Sahin v Turkey* (2005). Vakulenko argued the Court was moving towards an intersectional analysis in this case (Vakulenko, 2007), but that Sahin's gender was invisible to it. The research presented here sees Sahin's gender as key in the Court's construction of her as different to an unstated norm of a rights holder. Use of an intersectional methodology to analyse this case asserts the importance of race as a category in Europe against claims that it is a less relevant category in the European context. Bilge provides a clear counter to these positions (Bilge, 2013). Although the analysis below focusses on religion and gender as axes of discrimination, race is a clear factor. For example, Sherene Razack argues that the religious and secular divide has operated as a 'colour line, marking the difference between the white, modern, enlightened West, and people of colour, and in particular, Muslims' (Razack, 2007, 6). Darien-Smith also argues that discourses on race have been shaped by the historical religious context that formed initial Western ideas about minorities (Darien-Smith, 2010).

Background to the case

The ECHR has not been noted for a strong analysis of gender equality (O'Connell, 2009) or religious freedom (Dembour, 2000). A line of cases involving women who had been dismissed from work or ejected from school and university for wearing the headscarf were rejected by the Court, which cited equality principles and women's rights themselves as a justification for rejecting claims. Earlier claims were found to be inadmissible; *Sahin v Turkey* was the first case to be found admissible by the ECHR and heard on its merits. Sahin's claims were rejected by the Chamber at a first hearing and then heard again by the Grand Chamber. The analysis below contextualises the Court's findings in *Sahin* with the earlier cases.

Sahin was ejected from the University of Bursa several years into her medical degree when an ordinance banning the headscarf was reinstated in Turkish universities and she refused to stop wearing it to classes and exams. Her claim to the Court was that her ejection for refusing to comply breached her right to privacy under Article 8, her right to religion under Article 9, also her right to freedom of expression under Article 10 and her right to education under Article 2 of the first protocol. She also claimed that she was discriminated against on religious grounds, Article 14, in trying to claim the rights. The Court declined to look separately at Articles 8, 10 and 14. It found no interference with her right to education and, although it found an interference with freedom of religion, it considered this justified in the interests of protecting the rights and freedoms of others.

The construction of visibly Islamic women in Sahin

An intersectional analysis helps to uncover the ways that the Court was constructing the claimants in order to deny the claims and justify these distinctions. I looked at this from the perspective of structural, political and representational intersectionality. In relation to the structural positioning of visibly Muslim women, at the time the case was heard there was a clear context of discrimination against Muslim people, and particularly Muslim women, in relation to access to services and employment and as illustrated through reports of hate crimes in Council of Europe countries where Islam was not the majority religion. It was in these countries that many of the previous unsuccessful cases that generated stereotypical discourses about visibly Muslim women had originated. In 2000, the Council of Europe Commission against Racism and Intolerance (ECRI) issued a recommendation highlighting the discrimination faced by Muslim women as both Muslims and as women, and ECRI specifically asked member states to remove discrimination in access to education (Skeet, 2009, 55). There was also clear underrepresentation and discrimination against women in the education system in Turkey. This was recorded by the Committee on the Elimination of All Forms of Discrimination against Women and by Human Rights Watch; both reports particularly focussed on the problems for women accessing education and the impact of the headscarf ban in worsening access to education (Skeet, 2009, 56). The case was heard in a context of widespread recognition by NGOs and rights bodies that Muslim women, and particularly visibly Muslim women, were experiencing discrimination because of both their gender and religion, and that this was racist. In these circumstances, the expectation might be that the ECHR would have no difficulty in supporting Leyla Sahin's case against the discrimination she claimed. Applying a political intersectional analysis, as discussed above, it can be seen that Leyla Sahin's position as an autonomous rights holder was undermined, and she herself was presented as someone seeking to undermine women's rights by some of the groups who might have represented her. This allowed the Court to use women's rights and equality principles against her claim. The Court may not have been able to do this if there had been strong third-party interventions or amicus curiae in Leyla Sahin's support – for example, interventions that drew attention to the wider context of gender discrimination against Muslim women or drew attention to the harmful stereotyping that previous courts had used. The later case of *SAS v France* (2014) was also unsuccessful, but the strong third-party interventions on behalf of SAS prevented the ECHR from using women's rights to dismiss the claim. There were no third-party interventions on Leyla Sahin's behalf. Françoise Tulkens, a judge in the case, recalls how women campaigners were camped out on the grass outside the Court the night before the Grand Chamber hearing (Skeet, 2009). They were not there to support Sahin but to ask the court not to uphold her claim. Women Living Under Muslim Laws, a group that campaigns against both the coercion of women into wearing religious clothing and the prevention of women from wearing religious clothing, noted the polarisation in the wider women's movement on this issue, with some feminist groups believing that women who wore the headscarf were 'traitors' to the feminist cause (WLUML, 2009).

An analysis of the stereotypical media representations of visibly Muslim women, which were both reflected in and supported by the constructions of visibly Muslim claimants in the case law from the ECHR, shows them to be intersectional. Visibly Muslim women are differentiated from other women and from Muslim men to their disadvantage. These representations seemed redolent of the colonial discourses that Said (2003) termed Orientalism and that constructed Orientalised women differently to 'Western' women and to Orientalised men. My method was to examine how the core tropes identified in Said's work and in feminist critiques of Orientalism had been used to carry Orientalist representations of women in the ECHR cases. I used a close textual analysis of the case decisions to trace these tropes and representations in the determinations on claims by Muslim women and particularly in the *Sahin* case, which was heard in full. I found all three tropes present in those claims and in other claims that referenced women's position.

Orientalism

In the colonial period, constructions of Islam and particularly constructions of Muslim women were used to assert the superiority of European culture and to justify colonialism itself. Edward Said's work recorded this systematic production of knowledge through art, literature, histories and records of current affairs, and he refers to these productions of knowledge as 'Orientalism', a term he defines in his work as a

> 'corporate institution for dealing with the Orient' a 'Western style for dominating, restructuring, and having authority over the orient' through 'making statements about it, authorizing views of it, describing it, by teaching it, settling it and ruling over it'.

> *(Said, 2003, 8)*

We can identify three tropes that serve to produce these representations as knowledge (Skeet, 2019b, 38–40). First, discourses essentialise and homogenise Islam. Second, these essentialising presentations are incorporated into a binary model that always presents Europe or the West in a superior position. Third, Orientalism operates through a 'cumulative and accumulative' (Said, 2003, 122–123) methodology that repeats observations about the 'Orient' and presents them as knowledge. So, self-referentialism becomes a way of presenting as impartial truths observations that were initially unsubstantiated.

Said recognised as inherent in this production of knowledge a binary notion of gender and acceptable masculinism. Women subject to Orientalist discourses are always presented in contrast to 'Western' women, and, in contrast to the agency of 'Western women', Orientalised women are presented as both lacking in agency and as temptresses carrying an alien culture and posing a threat to 'Western men' and 'Western culture' (Said, 2003, 16–188). Feminist writers – for example, Meyda Yeğenoğlu (1998) and Rana Kabbani – focussed on Orientalist constructs as specifically applied to women. Kabbani notes the ambivalence in writings, finding fluctuation between 'desire, pity contempt and outrage' and casting Orientalised women as both 'erotic victims and scheming witches' (Kabbani, 1986, 53). Yeğenoğlu, among others, identifies the 'veil' or headscarf as viewed as synonymous with the Orient, and therefore its control as synonymous with control of the Orient and therefore a lynchpin of imperial policy (Yeğenoğlu, 1998).

In reading *Sahin* and the earlier cases, I was looking for statements that matched discourses identified as Orientalism by feminist writers and for evidence of the tropes used to carry these discourses in the cases. My close references to the case texts alongside the theoretical discussions on Orientalism provided my data. An essentialist approach to Islam was very clearly evidenced in all the cases. In the earliest cases of *Karaduman v Turkey* ([1993] 16278/90) and *Dalab v Switzerland* ([2001] 42393/98), the Commission characterised the 'headscarf' as associated with fundamentalism and characterised Islam itself as incompatible with women's equality, tolerance and respect. These findings were repeated in both later cases concerning the headscarf and other cases that discussed or defined Islam. Positional superiority, the second trope, was also present. The references in *Dahlab* to the headscarf as a 'powerful external symbol' posits an internal or European culture that holds opposite values. This was made even more manifestly clear in a later case of *Lautsi v Italy* (2009), where a Christian cross and Islamic symbols were directly compared: the former was deemed a passive and unthreatening symbol compatible with democracy, and the latter was deemed a threat to the beliefs of children and parents and incompatible with equality and democracy. The third trope of self-referentialism and a cumulative and accumulative method of construction was also present. This 'referentialism' differs from the referentialism in a system of precedent, where the reference back is to legal analysis or interpretation. Here, the re-presentation refers to statements about Islam and the headscarf. Opinions of the Court are presented as facts. These 'facts' about Islam that are presented in later cases are then supported by reference to the 'facts' found in earlier cases. I found that all references that the Court uses on the nature of the headscarf, through a series of cases over many years, go back to just one source: a reference to a single academic source cited in a Swiss court and picked up by the Commission in *Dahlab*.

In *Sahin*, we can see how these three tropes are used, on the one hand, to construct Sahin as lacking in sufficient agency. The quote from *Dahlab* is repeated, referring to the headscarf as 'imposed on women by a religious precept that was hard to reconcile with the principle of gender equality' (para 111) and suggesting that wearing a headscarf was not truly Leyla Sahin's choice. On the other hand, Leyla Sahin is characterised as a threat to others, as presented in this extract:

> In such a context, where the values of pluralism, respect for the rights of others and, in particular, equality before the law of men and women are being taught and applied in practice, it is understandable that the relevant authorities … consider it contrary to such values to allow religious attire, including, as in the present case, the Islamic headscarf, to be worn.
>
> *(para 116)*

Gender in construction of the claims

Some claims for a breach of 'religious freedom' brought by men were also dismissed; other claims were successful and were not met with the same 'margin of appreciation' – or deference to the state's position. Françoise Tulkens noted this anomaly in her dissenting opinion in *Sahin v Turkey*, when she asked why Leyla Sahin wearing her personal headscarf to university was accepted as a 'threat' to the rights of others, when a male preacher on television preaching intolerance (*Gundez v Tukey*, 2005) was not (*Gundez v Turkey*, 2005, Dissenting Opinion, 3). Decisions in later cases seem to create a stark contrast: for example, *Arslan v Turkey* (2010) in relation to prohibited religious dress in Turkey for men. Orientalist discourses are also found in the claims brought by men. Although the same homogenisation and essentialism of Islam is present, the same binary presentation and referentialism, male claimants are not presented as lacking in autonomy. The construction of Orientalist discourses differs in relation to men and women. In the cases against Turkey, there is a further difference in the way the Turkish state itself is constructed: in the claims brought by men, the Turkish state is also presented as Orientalised and 'backward', in contrast to the presentation of the Turkish state in *Sahin*, where it is viewed as 'modern' and equality seeking (Skeet, 2019b, 54–58). The Court in *Sahin* refers to Attaturk's 1922 constitution, placing an emphasis on the protection of the rights of women (para 27–28); criticisms of the Turkish state and women's rights made by human rights NGOS and the UN are not referred to. We can compare and contrast this with *Gundez*, where the Court discusses the need for individual freedom in order for a society 'to progress' (para 37). Similarly, in *Arslan*, the Court refers to the law as a disproportionate response that is outmoded and pre-modern (paras 20, 21, 34, 41, 52). A very opposite view of the Turkish state as 'equality seeking' is also presented in women's claims where religious freedom is not an issue. In *Opuz v Turkey* (2010), Turkish law is again characterised as pre-modern and to be brought into line with 'international standards in respect of the status of women in a democratic and pluralistic society' (para 192). Using these comparisons, we can see how the Court not only Orientalises the claimant but also constructs the Turkish state differently when it deals with claims for rights to religion from visibly Muslim women. The constructions are used to justify a differential treatment or intersectional discrimination in relation to the claimant (Skeet, 2019b, 53). This construction of the state as 'modern' when it seeks to ban the headscarf accords with the broader historical literature and analysis of Orientalism and gender (Yeğen-oğlu, 1998, 134–135).

The representations of visibly Muslim women used by the Court in these cases match the stereotypical representations in popular media and those used by right-wing groups to justify attacks on Muslim women. Using intersectional analysis shows how the Court not only failed to address those harmful stereotypes, but has perpetuated them. It traces the current oppression and discrimination of visibly Muslim women back to colonial discourses.

It is not suggested that this is a deliberate policy by the Court. Said argues that Orientalist discourses are precisely so compelling because they are so ingrained in Western thought and language (Said, 2003, 2), and Crenshaw notes that it is often the case that courts' 'privileging of maleness or whiteness' is so 'implicit it is not perceived at all' (Crenshaw, 1989, 151). Any lack of intention by the Court does not make the need to address this approach any less urgent. Discrimination against visibly Muslim women is increasing, and the Court is not using human rights to address this.

Conclusion

This chapter has looked at intersectionality as a methodology. It discussed the use of identified tropes that create Orientalist discourses and how these could be traced to the decisions of the ECHR and used against claims by visibly Muslim women. This illustrates the difference in approach towards rights of men and women in relation to religious freedom and a difference in approach to the role of the state in relation to women's rights when religious freedom is not being claimed. Bringing together specific postcolonial analysis of Orientalism and intersectionality, I used textual and contextual analysis to show how the broader context and structural positioning of the claimants within discourses about women's rights were ignored, and instead Orientalist discourses were used by the ECHR to represent visibly Muslim women both as lacking in autonomy, and therefore not valid holders of women's rights, and as posing a threat to democracy and women's rights.

What methods might you employ? This will depend on what your research question is, as discussed above Intersectionality lends itself to a variety of different methods.

As noted earlier, there is a vast literature in this area. It is worth reading in full the first two articles that Crenshaw wrote on this subject: the first deconstructs the actions of courts in determining discrimination claims (Crenshaw, 1989), and the second discusses the application of intersectionality to study structural positioning, politics and representations (Crenshaw, 1990/91). The three recent histories I referred to in the text above also provide engaging reading. The collection edited by Grabham et al. (2009) is focussed on law and contains the piece by Leslie McCall and other chapters that provide both useful examples of the application of intersectionality to diverse legal topics and illustrations of very different methods including quantitative data collection, interviews, textual analysis and organisational ethnography.

Be wary of literatures that suggest that, if you want to examine intersections other than race and gender, you need to look for an alternative methodology. The emergence of 'multidimensionality' as more relevant or flexible fails to consider the breadth of writing in intersectionality and its existing use in masculinity and sexualities studies (Hancock, 2016, 138). These are not developments of a theoretical approach and it is argued they cannot be considered truly separate theories since they cannot describe their position without referring to intersectionality theory itself. Davis argues the criticism of intersectionality and debate around its use are not a sign of its weakness, but rather an indication that it has all the elements of a 'good' feminist theory (Davis, 2008, 79). Similarly, Collins and Bilge believe that intersectionality's 'heterogeneity' is a source not of weakness, but of its 'tremendous potential' (Collins and Bilge, 2016, 204).

Finally, you may decide not to employ intersectionality as a methodology, but, whatever the scope of your enquiry, be aware of the possibility of intersectionality as a factor. Feminist legal historian Constance Backhouse, writing about the first ever prosecution of a lesbian women for indecent assault in Canada in 1955, puzzled over why this prosecution for an 'attempted kiss' had ever gone forward. The nature of the allegation did not fit the usual standards for prosecution of sexual assault, and Yellowknife in the 1950s was a place that had a society beyond the usual narrow social mores of the time. The transcripts of the trial did not hold a key. Then, Backhouse found the reflections of the defence lawyer years after the case: he 'offered the startling *coup de grace*. She probably would never have been prosecuted, he mused "if she hadn't been Black"' (Backhouse, 2008, 226).

Further reading

Collins P. H., and S. Bilge (2016) *Intersectionality*, Cambridge, Polity Press.

Crenshaw, K. (1989) 'Demarginalizing the Intersection of Race and Sex: A Black Feminist Critique of Anti-Discrimination Doctrine, Feminist Theory and Antiracist Politics', *Univeristy of Chicago Legal Forum* 140, pp. 139–167. article 8.

Crenshaw, K. (1990/91) 'Mapping the Margins: Intersectionality, Identity Politics, and Violence against Women of Colour', *Stanford Law Review* 43:6 p. 124.

Grabham, E., D. Cooper, J. Krishnadas, and D. Herman (2009) *Intersectionality and Beyond: Law, Power and the Politics of Location*, Abingdon, Routledge Glasshouse.

May, V. M. (2015) *Pursuing Intersectionality, Unsettling Dominant Imaginaries*, New York, Routledge.

References

Gundez v Turkey (2005) [2005] 41 EHRR 59

Lautsi v Italy (2011) 54 EHRR 60

Opuz v Turkey (2010) 50 EHRR 28

Sahin v Turkey (2005) 44 EHRR 4.

Arslan v Turkey (2010) ECHR 41135/98

Backhouse, C. (2008) *Carnal Crimes: Sexual Assault in Canada, 1900–1975*, Toronto, Irwin Law.

Bilge, S. (2013) 'Intersectionality Undone: Saving Intersectionality from Feminist Intersectionality Studies', *Du Bois Review: Social Science Research on Race* 10:2, pp. 405–424.

Bond, J. (2003) 'International Intersectionality: A Theoretical and Pragmatic Exploration of Women's International Human Rights Violations', *Emory Law Journal* 52, pp. 71–186.

Bond, J. (2004) 'Intersecting Identities and Human Rights: The Example of Romani Women's Reproductive Rights', *Georgetown Journal of Gender & the Law* 5, pp. 897, 916.

Collins P. H., and S. Bilge (2016) *Intersectionality*, Cambridge, Polity Press.

Conaghan, J. (2009) 'Intersectionality and the Feminist Project in Law', in Grabham, E., D. Cooper, J. Krishnadas and D. Herman, *Intersectionality and Beyond: Law, Power and the Politics of Location*, Abingdon, Routledge Glasshouse.

Crenshaw, K. (1989) 'Demarginalizing the ntersection of Race and Sex: A Black Feminist Critique of Anti-Discrimination Doctrine, Feminist Theory and Antiracist Politics', *University of Chicago Legal Forum*, 140, pp. 139–167.

Crenshaw, K. (1990/91) 'Mapping the Margins: Intersectionality, Identity Politics, and Violence against Women of Colour', *Stanford Law Review* 43:6, p. 124.

Darien-Smith, E. (2010) *Religion, Race and Rights: Landmarks in the History of Modern Anglo-American Law*, Oxford, Hart.

Davis, K. (2008) 'Intersectionality as Buzzword: A Sociology of Science Perspective on What Makes a Feminist Theory Successful', *Feminist Theory* 9:1, pp. 67–85.

Dembour, M. B. (2000) 'The Cases that Were Not to Be: Religious Freedom and the European Court of Human Rights', in I. Pardo (ed.), *Morals of Legitimacy: Between Agency and System*, pp. 205–228. New York, Berghahan Books.

Ewig, C. (2006) 'Hijacking Global Feminism: Feminists, the Catholic Church, and the Family Planning Debacle in Peru', *Feminist Studies* 32:3, pp. 632–659.

Grabham, E., D. Cooper, J. Krishnadas, and D. Herman (2009) *Intersectionality and Beyond: Law, Power and the Politics of Location*, Abingdon, Glass House.

Hancock, A. M. (2016) *Intersectionality: An Intellectual History*, Oxford, Oxford University Press.

Kabbani, R. (1986) *Europe's Myths of the Orient: Devise and Rule*, Basingstoke, Macmillan.

Lutz, H., M. T. Herrera, and L. Supik (2011) *Framing Intersectionality: Debates on a Multi-Faceted Concept in Gender Studies*, Surrey, Ashgate.

May, V. M. (2015) *Pursuing Intersectionality, Unsettling Dominant Imaginaries*, New York, Routledge.

McCall, L. (2009) 'The Complexity of Intersectionality', in Grabham, E, D. Cooper, J. Krishnadas and D. Herman, *Intersectionality and Beyond: Law, Power and the Politics of Location*, Abingdon, Routledge Glasshouse, pp. 49–76.

O'Connell, R. (2009) 'Cinderella Comes to the Ball: Art 14 and the Right to Non-discrimination in the ECHR', *Legal Studies* 29:2, pp. 211–229.

Razack, S. (2007) 'The Sharia Law Debate in Ontario: The Modernity/Premodernity Distinction in Legal Efforts to Protect Women from Culture', *Feminist Legal Studies* 15:1, pp. 3–32.

Said, E. (2003) *Orientalism*, London, Penguin.

Skeet, C. (2009) 'Globalisation of Women's Rights Norms: The Right to Manifest Religion, and "Orientalism" in the Council of Europe', *Public Space: The Journal of Law and Social Justice* 4:3, p. 3473.

Skeet, C. (2019a) 'Forced and Coerced Sterilizations – The Need for an Intersectional Approach in International Rights Adjudication', in I. Iyioha (ed.) *Women's Health and the Limits of Law Domestic and International Perspectives*, Abingdon, Routledge.

Skeet, C. (2019b) 'Orientalism in the European Court of Human Rights', *Human Rights and Religion* 14:1, pp. 31–63.

United Nations Division for the Advancement of Women (DAW), Office High Commissioner for Human Rights (OHCHR), United Nations Fund for Women (UNIFEM). (2000) *Women and Racial Discrimination: Report of the Expert Group Meeting*, 21st–24th November, Zagreb, Croatia, www.un.org /womenwatch/daw/csw/genrac/report.htm

UN. (2001) *Gender Dimensions of Racial Discrimination*, Geneva, Office of the High Commissioner for Human Rights.

Vakulenko, A. (2007) 'Islamic Headscarves and the European Convention On Human Rights: An Intersectional Perspective', *Social & Legal Studies* 16:2, pp. 183–199.

Women Living Under Muslim Laws (WLUML). (2009) Interview with Four Francophone Feminists on the Headscarf Ban, www.wluml.org/english/newsfulltxt.shtml?cmd[157]=x-157-44910 (accessed May 2009).

Yeğenoğlu, M. (1998) *Colonial Fantasies: Towards a Feminist Reading of Orientalism*, Cambridge, CUP.

PART III

Methodological choices

21

ENCOUNTERING THE ARCHIVE

Researching race, racialisation and the death penalty in England and Wales, 1900–65

Lizzie Seal and Alexa Neale

Introduction

This chapter explores issues related to studying documents in historical socio-legal research. We discuss this in relation to a project entitled 'Race, Racialisation and the Death Penalty in England and Wales, 1900–65', which employs archival methods. This interdisciplinary project was funded by the Leverhulme Trust (RPG-2016-352) and draws on concepts, methodologies and modes of analysis from both history and criminology to explore the over-representation of black and other minority ethnic (BME) people among those hanged in the twentieth century (roughly 5% of civilian executions were of BME people, despite their constituting only 0.3% of the British population in 1950). The research includes all 56 cases of men of colour sentenced to death in twentieth-century England and Wales; there were no cases of BME women sentenced to death in the period.

By examining these cases, the project explores issues of racial discrimination in relation to capital punishment, including the ways in which prosecutions for murder were in practice made racist. In addition to identifying how racialised discourses and stereotypes played out in capital cases, we analyse how these were shaped by shifting constructions of racial meaning over time. We employ critical reading of archival material and newspaper reporting of individual cases to identify narratives and stereotypes of racial difference and racialised interpretations of defendants' behaviour. We situate case studies within their wider social, cultural and political contexts, including colonialism and postcolonialism, shedding new light on the penal culture of England and Wales in the past, which has implications for the present in terms of understanding the deep roots of racialised assumptions in the criminal justice system.

In this chapter, we explain how we have gone about researching capital cases from archival case files and also reflect on the methodological issues associated with archival research. We illustrate this through examination of one of the cases from our project, that of Lee Kun, who was executed at Pentonville Prison in 1916. Before turning our attention more fully to our project and the Kun case, we discuss 'the Archive' as a contested site of research about the past and related methodological issues. These are examined in relation to researching crime and criminal justice, and we highlight some pertinent examples from the existing literature.

Encountering the archive

Discussions of the archive entail 'debates about the production and institutionalization of knowledge' (Arondekar, 2005: 10), meaning that research conducted in official archives is intertwined with the 'legitimation of state power' (King, 2012: 15). The case files that contain the main sources for researching our project are held in the National Archives in Kew, which constitute the state's official record and, as such, are the home of institutional memory. The founding of national archives in the nineteenth century was part of the development of nation states, and the political history that they enabled was part of nation building (King, 2012: 15–16). Archives therefore played a practical role in 'making and sustaining' European empires and in the governance of colonised populations (Steedman, 2011: 332).

Understanding this role of the archive is crucial in relation to a project such as ours, which seeks to examine processes of racialisation, and the role of racism and racist discourses in capital cases. Archives are not simply repositories of neutral sources. They contain documents that were an active part of bureaucratic practices that had real effects on people's lives, as well as being sources of representations of people and events. Arondekar has described these elements as 'truth effects' and 'fiction effects', respectively (2005: 12). Both need to be analysed by the researcher. For our project, we need to understand how the different documents held in case files related to one another and were *part* of the case, not simply a record of it. We also need to interrogate the constructions of defendants' racial identities.

Archives help to maintain power by controlling what can be known about the past and what will be known about it. Policies and practices of retention and destruction shape memories and histories of people and institutions, including in relation to criminal justice in England and Wales (Rock, 2016: 60–62). Decisions about what to preserve are not only choices about what becomes the archive, but also choices that shape social memory and 'shared cultural understanding' as archives exteriorize collective memory (Schwartz and Cook, 2002: 3–6). What has been preserved may have been chosen to reflect well on the government of the day, with what has been destroyed being part of the erasure of the misuse of power. Though murder case files from the twentieth century were all retained and remain available for our project, entire subfolders of papers, for example, were destroyed by government departments before they reached the National Archives.[1] The archive acts as the 'originary site of "real" history' and subordinates the histories of the non-powerful (Burton, 2003: 38). The stories of women, working-class, colonised and queer people are harder to find in official archives, underlining Arondekar's argument that there is always a politics of the archive, and 'rarely is it a simple matter of revealing secrets that are waiting to be found' (2005: 27).

Our project is critical of the workings of state power, making analysis of the records of that power a vital source. We acknowledge the politics of the archive and bring techniques of reading drawn from discourse analysis, as well as concepts from critical scholarship, to deconstruct dominant portrayals. Stoler (2009) highlights how colonial archives enable researchers to map the 'colonial common sense' that formed colonial mindsets. One of our other research objectives relates to understanding the lived experiences of BME people sentenced to death. This is harder to reach through an analysis of official records, which primarily represent the perspective of the officials who created the documents, rather than the individuals that the documents are about.

---

1 Marginalia records that subfolders .6, .11, .14, .15 and .18 of Kun case file HO 144/1443/303,791 were destroyed.

Practices of 'reading against the grain' – that is, reading documents for other than their officially intended purpose and with an awareness of the social hierarchies that produced them – can challenge the interpretations of the powerful and recover subaltern perspectives (Guha, 1983).

There are significant challenges to reconstructing individuals' consciousness from records that they did not author and that were only intended to serve narrow, bureaucratic purposes. However, murder case files are rich sources for researching everyday lives (Neale, 2017). The police took witness statements from a wide range of individuals living lives similar to the defendant and their victim. The purpose of these was to provide the basis for the prosecution's case, and they were not verbatim records (Jackson, 2000). Nevertheless, even if they do not reveal people's thoughts, they provide access to real experiences (Watson, 2018). Sources such as witness statements and depositions reveal much about relationships, household composition, the jobs people held and the ways in which they gave support to one another. They are an example of how some documents in the National Archives are a valuable source for the lives of 'ordinary' working- and middle-class people. In combination with other records, such as newspaper reports, the census and birth, marriage and death certificates, official crime records can be used to construct narratives of the lives of those who passed through the criminal justice system (see Johnston, 2015).

National and other official archives are conventionally viewed as containing sources that are more reliable than, for example, personal memory, underscoring their status as providing the stuff of 'real' history. The official archive has a seductive allure as the place where knowledge is contained and that will satisfy the historian's search for meaning – what Derrida (1996) famously described as 'archive fever'. It seems to offer 'panoptical possibilities' of knowing everything about the past if one looks hard enough (Burton, 2003). This is, however, not the case, whether the researcher hopes to write an official history or a revisionist one. The National Archives have only retained 2% of government documents since the mid twentieth century. Burton argues that all archives are liminal, porous and permeable. Far from being panopticons, they actually represent 'fragmentation and ghostliness' (2003: 144). None are fully reliable, and this is the starting point from which historians must engage in their craft. The archive does not contain historical knowledge; it contains the materials that historians work with in order to create this. Steedman cautions that, '[t]he past is gone, and it was never there in the first place' (2011: 333), meaning what 'really' happened is irretrievable. Historians must instead practise a kind of magical realism in which they make the dead come to life.

Sources of crime history

Historical researchers must bring this awareness of the possibilities and limitations of the archive to their research as part of bringing the dead to life. In this section, we discuss the kinds of document that are the basis for researching crime history and highlight select illustrative examples from the existing crime history literature. The National Archives hold court records, the records of the Metropolitan Police, files from the Prison Commission and Home Office Prison Department, records from the Department of Public Prosecutions, Home Office criminal case files, and records related to criminal appeals. Within these files are documents such as witness statements, depositions, case summaries, trial transcripts, police reports, prison medical officer and psychiatrists' observations, applications for leave to appeal, reports on whether to exercise the royal prerogative of mercy or not, and official notices of execution. Files also contain newspaper clippings about the different stages of the trial process and occasionally have sources such as letters from and to the defendant, or diaries kept by the defendant and/or victim, if these were collected as evidence. They also contain telling visual sources such as crime scene photographs, floorplans and maps (Neale, 2017).

Crime historians have used such sources to highlight the shifting regulation of sexual behaviour over time. Jackson (2000) employs court records in her history of child sexual abuse in England 1830–1914, identifying narratives in depositions from doctors, victims and defendants. Bates (2016) uses similar cases to highlight the significance of perceptions of victim identities in such narratives, arguing that values of sexuality and gender were more influential in court than the testimony of medical 'experts'. The regulation and control of commercial sex has been researched via analysis of Metropolitan Police, Home Office and court files to examine its meanings as they related to gender, class, race and nationality and the social and cultural anxieties that these produced (Laite, 2011). Police and court files have been invaluable sources in mapping the history of queer urban culture – in London particularly – but also of how queer sexualities were regulated and criminalised through prosecution of individuals for offences such as importuning and keeping a disorderly house (Houlbrook, 2005).

Historical analysis of cases of murder and other types of homicide have been a fruitful means of researching prevalent social and cultural expectations in the context of their breach (Nash and Kilday, 2017). In particular, there is a thriving literature on homicides by women and the ways in which their portrayal reveals norms and ideologies of femininity, which more widely underpin women's formal and informal social control. Grey (2010: 446), for example, explores how 'cultural ideas of gender' played out in relation to an infanticide case from 1921, which, alongside the greater participation of women in the administration of justice as jurors and magistrates, helped lead to the Infanticide Act 1922. This made infanticide a legally distinct (and female-specific) crime, which was less serious than murder and not subject to the death sentence.

Capital punishment, as a matter of life and death and the most severe penalty that the state can enact, is both symbolically rich and an extreme indication of how different social groups are valued and treated. Ballinger's (2000) deconstruction of court and Home Office documents in relation to women executed in twentieth-century England and Wales highlights the role of judicial misogyny in the minority of women's capital cases that resulted in hanging (most women sentenced to death were reprieved), and how women's voices and experiences were subjugated in the criminal justice system. Black (2018) discusses rationales and reasons for mercy as they were applied to condemned women in post-independence Ireland through analysis of documents and case files held in the National Archives of Ireland.

As discussed, case files can contain personal as well as bureaucratic documents, such as letters and diaries if they were collected and retained as evidence. Houlbrook (2010) reads the letters that Edith Thompson, hanged for the murder of her husband in 1923, sent to her paramour and co-accused, Freddie Bywaters, as a form of 'self-fashioning'. These letters were a key part of the prosecution's case against Edith, but Houlbrook analyses them instead for their use of language and the ways in which this was influenced by the fiction Edith read, and as a performance of emotional intimacy. Home Office files relating to capital cases contain letters sent by relations of the condemned and members of the public as they related to the case. Seal (2014b) examines these as sources of the construction of imagined local and national communities, and as revealing the interrelationship between perceptions of justice and meanings of Britishness.

We read our sources for the Race, Racialisation and the Death Penalty project both along the grain to identify colonially inflected discourses of race, and against the grain to uncover everyday lives and historical agency. Next, we outline one of the cases from our project, that of Lee Kun, before explaining which documents are available about it in the National Archives and illustrating how we analysed them. We have selected a case about which there are law reports to demonstrate the much larger scope for understanding provided by historical documents.

The case of Lee Kun

On the evening of 16 October 1915, Lee Kun, a 27-year-old Chinese sailor resident in Limehouse, London, stormed into the house of Harriet Wheaton. He was looking for Elsie Goddard, with whom he had previously lived. Finding her in the house, he took her by the arm, saying, 'I want to speak to you, Elsie'. They went into the backyard. Harriet heard Elsie scream 'Oh mother' and rushed out to find Lee stabbing her. Harriet hit him with a broom and called for help, but Elsie, who had wounds on her head, face and neck, died in the yard. A deep cut to her jugular caused her death. Lee was detained by Harriet and some neighbours, arrested when police arrived and taken to Limehouse Police Station. There he gave a brief statement through an interpreter, allegedly stating 'she was robbing money; I asked her to pay it back, but she would not' (Trial transcript, p. 20: examination of Tsoi Chung Kingston by Mr. Bodkin for the prosecution).

A few days before Elsie's murder, a Chinese man who may have been Lee had walked up and down the street in which she lived, rushing in one night and hitting Elsie in front of her landlord, William Fossey. Police Constable Walter Fagg arrived and removed the man but did not arrest him, as he 'looked on it then as an ordinary squabble and I made no note. It is an ordinary thing' (Transcript, p. 6: examination of PC Fagg by Bodkin). William Fossey turned Elsie out, and she was homeless for a few days. She went to Harriet Wheaton's house on 15 October, wearing a petticoat and skirt but no blouse. Harriet offered to give her place to stay in exchange for help with the cleaning.

Lee Kun was found guilty of murder at the Central Criminal Court, Old Bailey on 17 November. He made an appeal against his conviction on the grounds that not all of the evidence given at his trial was interpreted into Cantonese. There were also concerns about the interpreter's lack of proficiency in English. The appeal was dismissed, the reason cited being that a defendant was, at the time, only entitled to have evidence translated if they were undefended, and Lee was defended. The prosecution also stated that the evidence had already been translated in the police court and did not differ at the trial. The Appeal Court found that, 'no substantial miscarriage of justice has actually occurred', and that translation where the accused was defended 'is not a matter of law, but of practice in our Courts'. However, the judgment also stated that it should be the court's responsibility to make sure the defendant understands the evidence against them. Lee Kun was hanged at Pentonville Prison on 1 January 1916.

Reconstructing the Lee Kun case from the archives

There are two files available for Lee Kun's case: the Central Criminal Court file and the Home Office file. These are the documents from which the case must be reconstructed. In order to do so, it is necessary to explain which documents are in the files and to contextualise them in relation to the various stages of the prosecution process. The Central Criminal

Court file (TNA/CRIM1/159/2) contains depositions (statements of witnesses) taken at the Thames Police court in front of the magistrate. This was the hearing at which the indictment would be read and the charge – in this case for murder – would formally be made. The magistrate would decide if the charge required a jury trial (inevitably so for a murder charge) and whether there was enough evidence for the case to proceed. A process of filtering would also take place, where the magistrate would review the evidence and ensure that it met the rules and standards of the higher court (Central Criminal Court, Old Bailey) before it went there. This file, therefore, represents a highly filtered version of exhibits of evidence and depositions. Each deposition made before the magistrate would be a further filtered version of the statement taken by police, in itself merely a response to closed questions put to the witness. The answers to the questions would be written into prose by clerks or note-takers in the courtroom, constructing 'enforced narratives' – that is, 'written accounts produced by questioning, but from which, in transcription, the interlocutor has been removed' (Steedman, 2001: 47).

Depositions were therefore shaped by the questioning prosecution counsel, representing the Director of Public Prosecutions and furthering the interests of the police in the sense that they were pursuing a successful conviction rate. The depositions in the Kun file, CRIM1/159/2, were recorded by a court official in handwritten cursive longhand. These can be difficult to read, although the file also contains typed versions. Questioning by the prosecution was followed by a short cross-examination by the defence. From reading the depositions, it is not always obvious why certain issues were raised and what their relevance was. It is difficult, for example, to understand the significance of the description given by one witness of the facial hair of the man with whom the victim had recently been living (Depositions p. 9: cross-examination of Hannah Sharp). The evidence presented at the police court was the basis for the legal arguments made during the trial and meant that the defendant and their counsel knew the case against them and could plan their defence strategy (though they did not have to reveal the grounds for the defence until the trial at the higher court). Copies of the depositions were also sent to the Home Office and were scrutinised as part of the decision-making about whether to commute a death sentence or not.

In the early part of the twentieth century, coroners would also question witnesses at inquests conducted to determine how a non-natural death had occurred. Inquests created similar depositions to those emerging from the police court, which, in the Kun case, were printed in the form of a booklet (*No. 151: Inquest on the Body of Clara Thomas, otherwise Elsie Goddard ...*). The Kun files also include copies of a brief report by the Senior Prison Medical Officer at HMP Brixton that commented on the accused's behaviour while awaiting trial, whether there any signs of insanity and whether they were fit to plead to the indictment. The report on Kun noted he was 'quiet, well behaved and rational, and [has] shown no signs of insanity' (Sidney R. Dyer, M.D., Senior Medical Officer, H.M. Prison Brixton, to the Director of Public Prosecutions).

The second file, HO144/1443/303791, compiled by the Home Office, contains documents that were needed in order for the Assistant Permanent Under-Secretary, Ernley Blackwell, to write a report summarising the case for the Permanent Under Secretary of State to the Home Office, Edward Troup, and the Home Secretary, John Simon, making a recommendation about whether the prisoner should be reprieved from the death penalty or executed. This is longer than the court file and contains the record of the bureaucratic process of prosecution for murder, such as short official letters and receipts for copies of depositions sent from the courts. Handwritten minutes on the front of the folders contained in the file provide insight into the impressions that civil servants at the Home Office gained from the documents. Underlining and marginalia, for example on copies of depositions, indicate which parts were significant or pertinent in terms of decision-making; Elsie Goddard's life-style and relationship history seem to have been perceived as important. These bureaucratic details are significant because they record, as no other documents do, the perceptions and impressions of the evidence by those who had the ultimate power over whether a person accused of murder lived or died.

In cases where there was an appeal, the Home Office file contains copies of sections of the trial transcript (or the full transcript of the entire trial). As death was the mandatory sentence for murder until 1957, cases were usually appealed in an attempt to avert execution. If available, the transcript is invaluable, as it is the only document that makes clear how the evidence was framed into a legal argument by the prosecution and what the defence to this was. This cannot be gleaned from the depositions by themselves. The transcript also reveals further information not found in the depositions, such as that Lee was already fairly well known to the local police (Transcript, p. 7: cross-examination of PC Walter Fagg by Mr. Beresford for the defence). Issues related to language and interpretation emerged at the beginning of the trial. Lee's barrister, Mr Beresford, requested a new interpreter as Lee could not understand the one provided, but this was refused by Justice Darling (Transcript, pp. 2–5). Under examination from prosecution counsel Mr Bodkin about whether Lee could speak English, PC Walter Fagg replied 'Broken English; I could manage to understand what he meant' (Transcript, p. 7). The issue of the level of Lee Kun's English proficiency therefore appears nuanced. He could communicate conversationally, but most likely could not understand the technical, legal language of the court.

The Home Office file contains documents related to making an appeal, such as the notification of appeal, application for leave to appeal and appeal court transcript. The Court of Criminal Appeal was established in 1907, so had only existed for a few years prior to Lee Kun's case. Although the appeal court judgment agreed that the evidence should have been properly translated during the trial, it did not find that a miscarriage of justice had occurred and dismissed the appeal. The reason given was that, had the defendant received the benefit of full translation, the verdict of the jury would still have been the same. However, the case did set a precedent making it the court's responsibility to ensure that the accused can understand the evidence presented, and that the defendant cannot waive this right. It was the precedent rather than the outcome of the trial (Lee Kun's death by hanging) that was remembered in law reports, with *R v Lee Kun* cited in legal practice as recently as 1993 (*Kunnath v The State* [1993] 4 All ER 30). This highlights the ways that archive documents can offer uniquely rich detail about the social, historical and legal contexts of a case.

Transcripts also offer greater detail and nuance than can be achieved by reading contemporary newspaper reports alone. As Wood (2016) has highlighted, newspapers have long prioritised the least common types of crime, including capital cases and particularly where the accused is BME, creating skewed popular perceptions of criminality. The police, courts and Home Office had significant interest in what was being reported about cases, as shown by the fact that many of their files collected and annotated copies of relevant newspaper clippings. Home Office minutes, for example, commented on press inaccuracies and negative publicity regarding judicial processes, issuing letters as correctives that were also recorded in the files. In Lee Kun's case, the Home Office was eager to see that *The Times* published a reference to their circular correcting 'the impression which might have been given … to the effect that the sentence would be carried out on the day following the dismissal of an appeal' (HO minutes: *The Times*, 18 December 1915). Other references in the case suggest that maintaining the public image of justice and capital punishment was prioritised over concerns specific to individual cases. Lord Chief Justice Rufus Isaacs, Lord Reading, dismissed Lee's appeal but commented,

> The prosecution of criminals and the administration of the criminal law are matters which concern the State. Every citizen has an interest in seeing that persons are not convicted of crimes and do not forfeit life or liberty except when tried under safeguards so carefully provided by the law.

(Appeal transcript, Judgment p. 6)

Analyses of sources of public opinion on the death penalty in the twentieth century by Seal (2014a) and Langhamer (2012) support the idea that maintaining the status quo was of paramount interest. However, the extent to which concern for public opinion may have impacted decisions in individual cases is an area for further research.

The Home Office file also contains petitions on Lee's behalf signed by local people. These did not carry any legal weight and also did not appear to sway the decision about whether to commute the sentence. However, petitions are valuable sources in terms of understanding which elements of a case or a condemned person's identity and/or circumstances were mobilised in pleas to show them mercy. Petitioning for mercy was a well-established tradition and was part of the public negotiation of justice (Seal, 2014a). In the next section, we demonstrate our analysis of these documents, derived from reading them both along and against the grain.

Reading race in the Lee Kun case

The main evidence for racialisation in Lee Kun's case is his continual identification as a 'Chinaman'. For example, in Justice Darling's summing-up, he described a possible interpretation of the case according to the defence: 'There was a Chinaman following her [Elsie Goddard] about and she desired to protect herself against the Chinaman; that she feared a Chinaman wanted to do her some injury and thereupon she bought a knife' (Transcript, pp. 29–30). Auerbach (2009) highlights that portrayals of Chinese men in popular fiction and theatre as violent and murderous were very well established by the time of the Kun case, and it was notable for being the first conviction in England of a Chinese man murdering a white British woman. The judge's repetition of 'Chinaman' does appear to evoke stereotypes of foreign threat, compounded by repeated evidence that Lee or another 'Chinaman' sent by him was following Elsie, evoking contemporary tropes of Chinese people as devious, cunning and sneaky (Auerbach, 2009).

News reporting of the case also highlighted Lee's race, carrying headlines such as 'Chinaman Charged with Murder' (*Derby Daily Telegraph*, 17 November 1915, p. 3) and 'Chinese Murderer's Appeal Dismissed' (HO minutes: *The Times*, 7 December 1915). The convention in *The Times* was to report murders in London according to the area in which they took place, but identification of Lee by race took precedence (Auerbach, 2009). This is typical in press reporting of the cases included in our project across the time period: the accused's race is nearly always identified.

The evidence given by PC Walter Fagg under cross-examination indicates how he perceived Limehouse and Poplar and the people who lived there. In relation to the incident that happened at Elsie's lodgings a week before the murder, he stated, 'I just treated it as a common street quarrel which so often happens in that quarter between these women and men, it is nearly a nightly occurrence' (Trial transcript, p. 7, cross-examination of PC Fagg by Beresford for the defence). A community of Chinese sailors, shopkeepers and lodging house landlords had existed in Limehouse since the mid nineteenth century. This grew in size just before the First World War (Forman, 2013). The Chinese people living in the East End were nearly all men; the majority of women in the area would have been white. Limehouse was perceived in racialised terms as a site of danger, crime and opium taking, and as a slum. Early twentieth-century popular fiction that featured Limehouse evinced 'stereotypical middle class views of the equivalence between Britain's urban poor and the teeming poor of the nation's overseas colonies' (Forman, 2013: 204). PC Fagg's reference to 'in that quarter between these women and men', meaning working-class white women and working-class Chinese men, evokes these views of Limehouse. It also shows how intimately class and race were imbricated in colonial understandings of multicultural urban areas.

Although criminal justice personnel and civil servants may well have held stereotypes about Chinese men as murderous and calculating, Lee Kun does not seem to have been perceived as negatively as Elsie Goddard. The Home Office report on the case describes her as 'a sailor's prostitute in Poplar and Limehouse'. In relation to a Chinese man, possibly Lee Kun, having called at her lodgings the day after Lee assaulted her and accused her of stealing money from him, the report states this 'shows the sort of life the deceased was leading'. Noting that, 'The suggestion that the deceased had robbed or cheated the prisoner out of his money may be true enough', the report concluded she had 'broken off relations with him' too far before the murder for this to amount to provocation (Home Office Report, p. 3). In his summing up, Justice Darling emphasised to the jury that Elsie had not gone to Harriet Wheaton's house for the purposes of prostitution, stating, 'There was no immorality about this. Whatever the woman was, in Mrs Wheaton's house there is no suggestion of any impropriety' (Transcript, p. 30). This indicates he believed that the jury might have assumed otherwise.

Negative assessments of Elsie as a disreputable working-class woman who worked as a prostitute illustrate further the interrelationships between gender, class and race. For Elsie, being white did not accrue any advantages in terms of how she was perceived, and this can be explained with reference to Victorian constructions of whiteness as a bourgeois identity, which would not have been available to Elsie (Bonnett, 1998). Lee's murder of Elsie was not figured in the criminal justice system or by the Home Office as especially shocking, even though it was the first murder of a white woman by a Chinese man, and that is because she was seen as belonging to the same urban social milieu as he did.

Reading case file material such as depositions against the grain, it is possible to glimpse through this case the everyday lives and survival strategies of poor working-class women in early twentieth-century London. The deposition of Hannah Sharp, Elsie's aunt, states that Elsie was married but her husband had left eleven years previously, and she had not seen him since. She had lived with Lee Kun in the past, but shortly before the murder lived with a Russian man known as Swanney, who had sailed on a ship on 6 October. This is likely to have made Elsie more vulnerable to the attack prior to the murder. Once she had lost her room in William Fossey's house, Elsie was clearly destitute. Whether he 'turned her out' for moral reasons or, perhaps more likely, because he did not want more trouble or attention from the police cannot be determined from the documents. What is clear, however, is that Harriet Wheaton provided a brief period of salvation for Elsie after several days of homelessness by offering her shelter and a bed for the night (shared with Harriet) in exchange for helping to clean the house. Elsie's lack of a full set of clothing, being without a blouse, further underlines her extreme need (Transcript, p. 30).

Finally, the petitions sent on Lee Kun's behalf demonstrate that racialised stereotypes were not the only available way to portray him, and that Chinese people living in Britain could oppose perceived injustices and contribute to their community's portrayal. The petition was initiated by Lee's solicitors and distributed in his local area, a common practice in terms of attempting to get the death sentence commuted via a non-legal route. This was signed by Chinese people from Poplar and Limehouse and stated that Lee had 'only resided in this country on and off over a space of 18 months and does not understand the English language'. Further to this legally based argument, it also asserted this injustice would 'cause considerable uneasiness in the minds of large numbers of Your Majesty's subjects and subjects of other countries', including China (Petition, p. 1). An accompanying letter from Ballantyne, Clifford and Hett solicitors argued for a reprieve 'in view of the strong feeling which exists amongst the Chinese community in London' and the 'feeling of great uneasiness with regard to the present case amongst the Chinese community in England' (Ballantyne, Clifford and Hett to the Under Secretary of State, Home Office, 31 December 1915). The petition invoked Britain's imperial role and the need to appear just and fair to maintain legitimacy, to subjects within and beyond the metropole. It strategically aligned with an imperial viewpoint in order to ask for mercy.

Conclusion

A close reading of the case file documents in relation to Lee Kun's murder of Elsie Goddard is necessary in order both to understand the assumptions about race, class and gender that emerged in the criminal justice system and Home Office, and to glean the lived experience of Lee and Elsie. Sources such as news stories and petitions can reveal the wider cultural perception of murder trials, and petitions are good sources of counter-narratives to the dominant narratives constructed in legal and press portrayals. These findings can only emerge from archival research and from employing the kind of approach that we have outlined in this chapter. There are law reports of the Kun case as it set a precedent in relation to the translation of evidence in court for defendants who did not speak English or did not speak it sufficiently well to follow their trial proceedings. These and the accompanying judgment of the Court of Criminal Appeal make clear the case's legal significance. Analysis of the case file documents reveals the process of prosecuting a murder and the involvement of other criminal justice actors, such as police officers and prison medical officers. The documents written by these actors had 'truth effects' (Arondekar, 2005) – they provided the basis for the prosecution and defence cases and for the decision not to grant a reprieve.

The archival documents must be consulted in order to understand the social, cultural and historical importance of a case. The Kun case demonstrates how they are invaluable as a window onto the everyday lives of working-class people, and that such stories can be reconstructed from official archives by reading against the grain. 'Mixed' relationships between men of colour and white women in the early twentieth century were not unusual in multicultural areas such as Limehouse and Poplar, although they are perhaps more readily associated with later migrations. The details of the murder illuminate particularly clearly Elsie's marginalisation as a poor working-class woman whose daily life involved precariousness of accommodation and little protection from violence – but Hannah Sharp's willingness to offer shelter also demonstrates how working-class women could help one another and is an example of their historical agency.

Close reading of case file documents enables analysis of contemporary attitudes towards race, and its interconnection with class and gender. These are what Arondekar (2005) describes as the documents' 'fiction effects' – the representations they portray of people and events. Reading along the grain to identify dominant portrayals reveals the significance of bourgeois colonial understandings of similarities between the urban poor in Britain and in overseas colonies to processes of racialisation. It indicates the role of 'colonial common sense' in early twentieth-century penal culture in the metropole (Stoler, 2009). By combining these methods of 'along-' and 'against-the-grain' in cases of BME men sentenced to death, something of the long history of racialised justice, the legacy of which is still felt today, can begin to be understood.

Further reading

Ballinger, A (2000) *Dead Woman Walking*, Dartmouth: Ashgate.

Nash, D and Kilday, A, eds. (2017) *Law Crime and Deviance since 1700: Microstudies in the History of Crime*, London: Bloomsbury.

Seal, L (2014a) *Capital Punishment in Twentieth-Century Britain: Audience, Justice, Memory*, Abingdon: Routledge.

Steedman, C (2011) After the Archive, *Comparative Critical Studies*, 8(2/3); 321–340.

Stoler, A L (2009) *Along the Archival Grain: Epistemic Anxieties and Colonial Common Sense*, Princeton, NJ: Princeton University Press.

References

Contemporary sources

R v Lee Kun, [1914-15] All ER Rep 603.

The National Archives: CRIM 1/159/2: Central Criminal Court Depositions, 'Defendant: KUN, Lee. Charge: Murder. Session: November 1915.'

The National Archives: HO 144/1443/303791: Home Office, Registered Papers, 'CRIMINAL: Kun, Lee; Court: C.C.C.; Offence: Murder; Sentence: Death.'

Secondary literature

Arondekar, A (2005) Without a Trace: Sexuality and the Colonial Archive, *Journal of the History of Sexuality*, 14(1/2): 10–27.

Auerbach, S (2009) *Race, Law, and the 'Chinese Puzzle' in Imperial Britain*, Basingstoke: Palgrave.

Ballinger, A (2000) *Dead Woman Walking*, Dartmouth: Ashgate.

Bates, V (2016) *Sexual Forensics in Victorian and Edwardian England*, Basingstoke: Palgrave.

Black, L (2018) 'On the Other Hand the Accused is a Woman': Women and the Death Penalty in Post-Independence Ireland, *Law and History Review*, 36(1): 139–172.

Bonnett, A (1998) How the British Working Class Became White: The Symbolic (Re)formation of Racialized Capitalism, *Journal of Historical Sociology*, 11(3): 316–340.

Burton, A (2003) *Dwelling in the Archive: Women Writing House, Home, and History in Late Colonial India*, Oxford: Oxford University Press.

Derrida, J (1996) *Archive Fever: A Freudian Impression*, Chicago: University of Chicago Press.

Forman, R G (2013) *China and the Victorian Imagination: Empires Entwined*, Cambridge: Cambridge University Press.

Grey, D J R (2010) Women's Policy Networks and the Infanticide Act 1922, *Twentieth Century British History*, 21(4): 441–463.

Guha, R (1983) *Elementary Aspects of Peasant Insurgency in Colonial India*, Oxford: Oxford University Press.

Houlbrook, M (2005) *Queer London: Perils and Pleasures in the Sexual Metropolis, 1918–1957*, Chicago: Chicago University Press.

Houlbrook, M (2010) 'A Pin to See the Peepshow': Culture, Fiction and Selfhood in Edith Thompson's Letters, 1921–1922, *Past and Present*, 207(1): 215–249.

Jackson, L A (2000) *Child Sexual Abuse in Victorian England*, London: Routledge.

Johnston, H (2015) *Crime in England 1815–1880: Experiencing the Criminal Justice System*, London: Routledge.

King, M T (2012) Working with/in the Archives, in *Research Methods for History*, S Gunn and L Faire (eds.), Edinburgh: Edinburgh University Press, 13–29.

Laite, J (2011) *Common Prostitutes and Ordinary Citizens: Commercial Sex in London 1885–1960*, Basingstoke: Palgrave.

Langhamer, C (2012) 'The Live Dynamic Whole of Feeling and Behavior': Capital Punishment and the Politics of Emotion, 1945–1957, *Journal of British Studies*, 51(2): 416–441.

Nash, D and Kilday, A (2017) Introduction, in *Law Crime and Deviance since 1700: Microstudies in the History of Crime*, D Nash and A Kilday (eds.), London: Bloomsbury, 1–16.

Neale, A (2017) Murder at the 'Love Hut': At Home with Elvira Barney, in *Beyond the Boundaries of Home: Interdisciplinary Approaches*, M Barrios Aquino et al. (eds.), Brighton: University of Sussex Library, 10–23.

Rock, P (2016) A Brief History of Record Management at The National Archives, *Legal Information Management*, 16: 60–64.

Schwartz, J M and Cook, T (2002) Archives, Records, and Power: The Making of Modern Memory, *Archival Science*, 2(1/2): 1–19.

Seal, L (2014a) *Capital Punishment in Twentieth-Century Britain: Audience, Justice, Memory*, Abingdon: Routledge.

Seal, L (2014b) Imagined Communities and the Death Penalty in Britain, 1930–65, *British Journal of Criminology*, 54(5): 908–927.

Steedman, C (2001) *Dust*, Manchester: Manchester University Press.

Steedman, C (2011) After the Archive, *Comparative Critical Studies*, 8(2/3): 321–340.

Stoler, A L (2009) *Along the Archival Grain: Epistemic Anxieties and Colonial Common Sense*, Princeton, NJ: Princeton University Press.

Watson, K (2018) In Their Own Words? Criminal Depositions and the Voices of the Past, Legal History Miscellany, 17 March: https://legalhistorymiscellany.com/2018/03/17/in-their-own-words-criminal-depositions-and-the-voices-of-the-past/ (accessed 15 April 2018).

Wood, J C (2016) Crime News and the Press, in *The Oxford Handbook of the History of Crime and Criminal Justice*, P Knepper and A Johansen (eds.), Oxford: Oxford University Press, 301–319.

22

LAW, THE ENVIRONMENT AND NARRATIVE STORYTELLING

Angus Nurse

Introduction

This chapter examines the extent to which critical understanding of environmental protection and the development of environmental enforcement policy is enhanced by socio-legal method, particularly narrative storytelling as a case analysis tool. Despite growing environmental awareness and the efforts of a variety of non-governmental organisations (NGOs) to enhance environmental protection policy, environmental enforcement remains outside mainstream criminal justice (Nurse 2011; Lynch and Stretesky 2014). Understanding environmental enforcement involves constructing narratives around this fringe area of 'policing', the public policy and enforcement response of which significantly rely on NGOs (Nurse, 2012, 2013a). White's (2012) regulation theory analysis identifies that third parties (e.g. NGOs) often play significant roles in investigating and exposing environmental harm and offending and are a necessity for effective environmental law enforcement. But, within such environmental enforcement discourse, a range of narratives are often at play that, when examined via narrative storytelling, allow for a deeper understanding of the roles and perspectives of different actors within a legal dispute. As Tait and Norris explain, 'narrative enables us to make sense of time, and to locate ourselves in it. Narratives do this by demarcating beginnings, middles and endings' (2011: 21).

Using narrative storytelling as its core method(s), this chapter explores how mainstream justice failures and the construction of environmental harm as being other than 'crime' result in flawed or at least difficult to enforce environmental laws that arguably fail to provide effective redress for much environmental harm. This chapter's narrative case study explores environmental harm via a green criminological lens, one that considers green crimes (e.g. pollution) and harms to the environment and non-human nature (Lynch and Stretesky 2014; Nurse 2016). In this context, ecological justice perspectives are at play. Such concerns contend that our justice systems need to do more than just consider human victims of crime and must also consider non-human victims and harm to the environment itself (Benton 1998; Beirne 2007; Nurse 2013b). The narrative method used within this chapter's case study analysis examines the application of EU law within the UK, illustrating how environmental protection is socially constructed such that the enforcement and policy approach differ between jurisdictions, and even within the UK there are contrasting perspectives on what is necessary to achieve effective environmental protection. Environmental enforcement is rarely a core policing priority and remains NGO-dependent (White 2012; Nurse 2013a). Narratives reveal how environmental offending (including pollution and waste offences) is often regulatory or administrative in nature, rather than being covered by the criminal law and mainstream criminal justice responses (Situ and Emmons 2000; Nurse 2016). This chapter employs regulation theory, arguing that an understanding of contemporary environmental protection and its enforcement requires drawing on mechanisms for examining not only the legal framework within which environmental protection takes place, but also the involvement of civil society as enforcers and policymakers. It explores the tension between protection of the environment and the drive for sustainable exploitation of natural resources within neoliberal markets. This results in law that simultaneously seeks to protect the environment while allowing its continued exploitation (Stallworthy 2008). The purpose of this chapter is to show how narrative method can be employed as a socio-legal analytical tool, particularly in respect of exploring conflicting narratives within complex legal issues and examining how the overarching narrative revealed through analysis relates to a wider social problem.

Narrative storytelling and environmental harm

This chapter's case study examines a five-year legal battle by campaigning NGO ClientEarth against the UK government over illegal levels of air pollution. The narrative method employed analyses different perspectives employed throughout a lengthy legal battle during which the UK Supreme Court ordered the UK government to act to address high air pollution. The case came out of admitted and continuing failure by the UK since 2010 to secure compliance in certain zones with the limits for nitrogen dioxide levels set by European law, under Directive 2008/50/EC. Yet analysis of the relevant narratives constructed during the legal dispute illustrates contrasting understanding of the legal requirements, as well as illuminating differing motivations and perspectives of the various actors involved. The narrative method employed in case analysis examines the narratives overtly told by the two parties and explicit in the source documents examined. This chapter's deployment of narrative method thus reveals that multiple and conflicting narratives were at play within the case under examination, and it explores narrative method as an analytical tool. The chapter also constructs a narrative of environmental activism in this case that contrasts with alleged government complacency and inaction. It highlights the role of NGOs as monitors of environmental and human rights compliance (Marcinkutė 2011; Nurse 2016) and demonstrates how NGO action, particularly via environmental litigation, can serve to highlight and remedy government failures in environmental protection that might otherwise go unnoticed.

Within ecological justice discourse (Benton 1998), debates continue over whether green crimes are best addressed through criminal justice systems or via civil or administrative mechanisms. Indeed, a central discussion within green criminology is that of whether environmental *harm* rather than environmental *crime* is important, with the environmental harm perspective currently dominating green criminological discourse (Hall 2013). Green criminology's ongoing debate concerns whether green crimes should be the focus of mainstream criminal justice and dealt with by core criminal justice agencies (e.g. the police) or whether they should be considered as being beyond the mainstream.

The argument for the harm perspective is dominated by the transnational nature of environmental 'crimes', their location within government environmental policy departments rather than criminal justice ones, and the reality of environmental harms primarily being dealt with by specialist environmental agencies (in)appropriately constituted (and resourced) to deal with the specifics of green offending (Nurse 2013a, 2016). Arguably, much environmental harm is regulatory in nature rather than being categorized as crimes within the focus of criminal law on individualized victims and property. Thus, strictly speaking, much green or environmental harm is not in fact defined as crime and is dealt with other than by criminal justice agencies. Environmental regulators and local authority enforcers often have a significant role to play (Situ and Emmons 2000; Nurse 2016).

The environmental justice and ecological justice conceptions of green criminology include theoretical and ideological considerations arguing for protection of nature because of its intrinsic value. This includes the right of non-human species and nature to be protected from human interference and/or to be given rights that are upheld by justice systems and environmental laws. Ecological justice acknowledges that human beings are only one part of the planet, and thus justice systems need to consider the wider biosphere and species that depend on nature (Benton 1998; Beirne 2007). Within an ecological justice perspective, there is scope to incorporate what is referred to as a consequentialist ethic: a theoretical conception concerned with goodness or badness as being more important than 'rightness' or 'wrongness' (Brennan and Lo 2008). Philosophers Jeremy Bentham (1748–1832) and John Stuart Mill (1806–1873) illustrated this conception within their writings on utilitarianism, which argues that consequences are the measure of whether an action is right or wrong, and that the 'value' of consequences can be measured by how much happiness or well-being is caused by an action (Bentham, 1962; Mill, 1993). But utilitarianism also incorporates the idea that doing the right thing means that everybody has an equal share in happiness, and no individual's happiness has greater value than another's. In this respect, ecological justice draws on notions of the public good in order to address environmental harm concerns. Thus, environmental litigation can incorporate a narrative concerning the intrinsic value of nature and the need to consider the public good.

For this chapter's discussion of narratology and deployment of narrative method, this raises some challenges. First, this chapter's discussion raises issues around the nature of environmental activism and litigation against the state, including how NGOs construct narratives of government failings in order to justify and sustain legal action. Second, the analysis explores how environmental compliance at state level is monitored. The surface narrative is that mechanisms exist in EU enforcement processes for scrutinising government failures. But more detailed examination and analysis of the conflicting narratives identify not only that this mechanism may not be truly effective, but also that the role of NGOs as monitors is integral to identifying where problems of non-compliance and policy failure may exist. Consistent with White's (2012) discussion of regulation theory, without NGOs playing a role in enforcement and monitoring activity, problems in policy and persistent failures in government action relating to the environment might well go undiscovered. Thus, the wider narrative of environmental problems and the implementation of environmental protection policy are of interest.

Law and narrative storytelling

Wolff (2014: 4) argues directly that, 'law is narration: it is narrative, narrator and the narrated'. At its most basic level, legal cases are constructed from a variety of texts that can be read as a series of intertwining stories. Establishing what happened, when and to whom, and determining liability arguably requires constructing, understanding and assessing a clear narrative to reach a judgment on the facts. In this regard, narrative storytelling can be distinguished from standard content analysis approaches as its function is both to identify the key narratives being developed and explicitly advanced by each side in a case and, through critical analysis, to construct appropriate alternative and wider narratives. As Wolff (2014:4) puts it, 'cases are narrative contests of facts and rights; statutes are recitations of the substantive and procedural bases for social, economic and political interactions; and private agreements are plots for future relationships whether personal or professional'. Narrative method can, thus, be applied to a wide range of legal disputes as a tool to both identify key (and often contrasting) narratives running throughout a dispute and to construct a fresh narrative that makes sense of a dispute (as the case study of UK environmental litigation in this chapter illustrates).

Wolff (2014: 20) identifies that, 'narratives are everywhere in law: stories of disputes source the common law; chronicles of efficiency, injustice or unaccountability inspire legislative reform; and debates about the findings, explanations, meanings, scope, influences and impacts of the law inform legal scholarship'. Arguably law is a narrative medium, particularly within the confines of adversarial trial systems where both prosecution and defence seek to convince jurists of the factual accuracy and adequacy of their 'story'. Thus, the competing narratives of criminal trials lend themselves to analysis understanding and adjudication, whereas environmental disputes can incorporate broader narratives about societal harm, often encompassing wider consideration of varied stakeholders including NGOs, enforcers and the environment itself (Lynch and Stretesky 2014).

Love (1998: 92) explains that one of the most valued benefits of 'storytelling' is that the listener can empathize with the narrator. Thus, one challenge for jurists in criminal trials is potentially that of distinguishing between an accomplished storyteller – for example, the seasoned advocate – and a compelling narrative based on legal coherence (and, more generally, distinguishing between truth, lies and misunderstandings). The risk exists that a good storyteller articulating a compelling narrative is both better understood and more readily believed by a jury than a complex challenging narrative woven by a less accomplished advocate. Yet, the basic principle of law as a collection of stories generally aids in its understanding; as Brooks states, 'law needs a narratology' (2008: 425), and critical analysis of narratives can provide a means through which underlying legal (and social) discourse can be explored and understood. Thus, this chapter contends that narratology (the theory of narrative structures) arguably provides a strong framework for better understanding of complex legal issues and their wider social significance. Johnston and Breit (2010: 6) proposed a three-stage structure for their narrative analysis of court reporting. This consisted of: Stage 1 – story level: the superficial level on which stories are told; Stage 2 – discourse level: analysis of the type of language used in telling stories and the professional knowledge deployed in construction of those stories; and Stage 3 – interpretative context: understanding of the audience and the environment in which a narrative is interpreted. Thus, narrative analysis arguably goes beyond simple content analysis and assessment of the surface 'story' and can engage with more complex aspects of legal and policy disputes that end up in litigation.

The analysis conducted later within this chapter's discussion of environmental harm, via the chapter's case study, applies Johnston and Breit's (2010) approach. The case study indicates how employing narrative method in complex problems (e.g. this chapter's environmental case study) requires narrative interrogation beyond Stage 1, the superficial story of a case. Instead, it requires analysis of language and interpretative context. This illustrates the reality that narrative analysis that goes beyond studying the basic plot lines of a case can uncover and examine multiple contested narratives and contested stories of a case that generate a deeper understanding of legal disputes.

At its most basic level, narrative method as applied to legal cases and disputes consists primarily of an investigation into a contest of narratives by extracting the visible narratives from available sources (e.g. court documents). In this respect, narrative method provides for *construction* of legal narratives within a case, potentially within a binary structure of prosecution versus defence or claimant versus respondent. But this focus on contesting narratives and on the issues raised once a case has made it to court risks being too narrow and fails to explore wider issues arising in legal discourse. Although courtroom storytelling and the construction of narratives around the contrasting versions of events presented at trial might influence the 'master' narrative of a judge (Grunewald 2013: 382), this does little to examine wider issues impacting on courtroom events, except where these are explicitly referred to in courtroom discourse. Environmental protection issues can touch on wider issues, noting that environmental law engages with a range of issues (Stallworthy 2008). As Lynch and Stretesky (2014: 9) put it, 'it has become increasingly clear in recent years that the environment around us is under expanded assault, that it is routinely harmed and damaged by humans'. Thus, there is a need to examine the law alongside relevant policy imperatives and arguably to also consider the social context in which alleged environmental harm takes place. This chapter uses narrative method by constructing and analysing the different narratives of harm, interpretations of law, and policy requirements at play within a contemporary environmental issue the resolution of which required litigation.

Narrative method can also be employed by examining the operation of law in narrative literature or that of law as rhetoric. The law and literature movement studies law and legal meaning through analysis of literary texts (see, for example, Posner 2009). Law *as literature* discourse, however, examines law as rhetoric. Sarat and Kerns (1996), for example, not only identify law as a profession of language, but contend that this language can be examined and understood from a range of perspectives, including feminism and interpretive social science. Arguably, the rhetoric inherent in legal discourse conveys authority, but also meaning. Rhetoric's purpose is primarily to convince, influence or please an audience, whether that be the large audience of a jury (and any attendant media reporting on a case), or the single judge as sole audience. Rhetorical narratology offers an opportunity to study the deployment of language and meaning in the construction of legal meaning, as well as the use of rhetoric to convey and enhance understanding. This may, for example, be useful in respect of examining the personal accounts and experiences of marginalized individuals within dominant legal narratives. Rhetoric can also be employed to evoke sympathy for victims who cannot speak for themselves. In respect of the environment, for example, the understanding that jurists may have of environmental harm and environmental law issues is potentially problematic (Woolf 1992). Thus, rhetorical devices might be employed to advocate for the rights of the environment or to critique hegemonic legal practices that are based on anthropocentric notions of justice (Stone 2010). The rhetoric deployed in legal discourse around the environment as victim, as in this chapter's case study, can provide for wider understanding of ecocentric perspectives centred around the intrinsic value of nature, contrasting with the human-centred (anthropocentric) approach dominating policy that allows environmental harm (Attfield 2014).

Although a full analysis of narratology as a discipline is beyond the scope of this chapter, this brief discussion of its benefits illustrates how narrative method can be employed in the study of law and legal meaning. Arguably, narrative storytelling risks being confined to discourse around courtroom narratives and the behaviour of actors within adversarial criminal trials. But the method can be employed to examine wider issues and to analyse the narrational qualities of a wide range of legal discourse. This approach is at the heart of this chapter's discussion.

The case study at the heart of this chapter involves an examination of NGO environmental activism and the use of environmental litigation to address perceived failures in state environmental protection policy. It also explores the use of socio-legal action (White 2008) by way of using existing laws and legal methods to achieve effective environmental protection. The case study also explores persistent government failures that arguably raise concerns about 'state crime', albeit criminal law was *not* in play within this case study. Thus, the intent of this chapter's case study is to examine, through application of narrative method, how environmental protection is socially constructed. Through the construction of varied narratives, the underlying attitudes of enforcers, policymakers and other actors can be revealed.

Narrative method, environmental harm and NGOs

Statutory enforcement failures and the perceived inadequacy of policy leave a vacuum that has increasingly been filled by NGOs adopting policy development and practical enforcement roles in addition to sometimes taking direct action to prevent a green crime or to take enforcement action when the statutory regulator has failed to achieve this (Nurse 2013a). NGOs in both the UK and US already act as policy advisors, researchers, field investigators, expert witnesses at court, scientific advisors, casework managers and, in the case of a small number of organisations, independent investigators and prosecutors. Acting together, NGOs also contribute greatly to public debates on environmental crime, generating considerable publicity for the issue and co-ordinating (and undertaking or funding) much of the research. Some NGOs take a hands-on approach to prosecution and challenging government enforcement inadequacies, whereas others view themselves as primarily having an advisory or scientific role (Nurse 2013a).

The role of environmental NGOs is linked to notions of environmental citizenship and Beck's (1992) risk society theory. Beck argues that events such as the Chernobyl nuclear meltdown require us to reconsider our conceptual framework, the role of scientific knowledge and our policy responses. Thus, our social and political institutions and mechanisms need to transform, particularly as regards how they deal with contemporary environmental risks. In this respect, there is a need for a new form of environmental citizenship that does not just focus on developing environmental policy to deal with obvious risks. In contemporary society, there is a need for ecological citizenship that looks at the potential unity between legal, political and moral systems, and it is here that a range of NGOs operate, from the small community grass-roots group to the major 'conservation corporation' that combines professional activism and policy development with local action.

Contemporary NGOs sometimes combine policy development and advocacy with practical enforcement roles in addition to occasionally taking direct action to prevent a green crime or to address regulatory shortfalls. Previous research and analysis (Nurse 2013a) identified socio-economic (Parkin 1968) and ideological (Jasper 1997; Lowe and Ginsberg 2002) factors that create a typology of three different types of environmental NGO: campaigning NGOS, law enforcement NGOs and political lobbying NGOS. Although, in principle, NGOs can operate in more than one of these areas, they generally adopt one of these functions as a primary role (e.g. direct law enforcement), which dictates how their environmental protection goals are pursued, even though a secondary objective (e.g. political lobbying to improve environmental or wildlife protection legislation) may be pursued alongside this.

On a broader level, environmental justice NGOs represent a varied set of interests that include radical environmentalists (i.e. those with a 'pure' view of environmental protection) and middle-class movements that have a general environmental concern and the resources to 'indulge' those interests. Analysis of the available literature on NGO policies and their ideological perspectives reveals that environmental NGOs broadly develop their policies from the primary ideological positions of:

1. Moral culpability – censuring activities that they believe are morally wrong;
2. Political priorities – censuring activities that they consider should be given a higher profile in public policy (which may include issues that they consider are worthy of a higher law enforcement priority or those that should be the subject of law enforcement activity and/or legislative change); and
3. Environmentalism/animal rights – a belief in ensuring and protecting environmental rights or rights for animals that includes policies that demonstrate either the case for animal/environmental rights or that demonstrate breaches of these existing rights.

(Nurse 2013a)

Uncovering the extent to which different perspectives are at play within a case requires consideration of a range of contested aims and objectives such that dedicated narrative analysis may be required. The following case study illustrates the application of Johnston and Breit's (2010: 6) three-stage process as narrative case study analysis.

Case study: ClientEarth versus the UK government

The case study at the heart of this chapter highlights environmental litigation as an environmental activism tool. White (2012) applies contemporary regulation theory to environmental crime (and harm), recognising the poor level of resources, meagre budgets and low staffing levels that exist in environmental law enforcement given the size and scale of environmental problems. Accordingly, a number of NGOs actively investigate and prosecute environmental and wildlife crimes and adopt policy enforcement roles to address perceived failures by state agencies (White 2012; Nurse 2013a). The case study illustrates one issue around the right of NGOs to take action in environmental harm cases. This is linked to the notion of 'standing' in judicial review (JR) cases, which relates to having 'sufficient interest' in a case.

Although it is not within this chapter's scope to examine JR law in detail, it is perhaps useful to identify that, broadly, two different perspectives exist. The *US perspective* rests on causation and the redress of injury arising from the decision – that is, you must have been directly affected, suffering an injury in fact – in other words, a concrete and particularized, actual or imminent invasion of a legally protected interest (*Lujan v. Defenders of Wildlife* 504 U.S. 555 [1992]). The *UK perspective*, by contrast, allows NGOs broader standing to pursue judicial review of government decisions affecting wildlife and the environment, particularly where a 'recognised' NGO is taking a case on behalf of its members. Arguably, UK NGOs have greater power to challenge government decisions, whereas US NGOs are better placed to bring court actions for damages and compensation. The environmental activism discussed in this chapter's case study illustrates where the public environmental interest is often not served by statutory authorities or the state, thus requiring

Table 22.1 Possible narratives within ClientEarth v the UK Government

Narrative	Analytical approach/method
Narrative on NGO action	Analysis of NGO policy documents and press releases
Narrative on the purpose of the law	Analysis of legal texts and policy documents
Narrative on government policy	Analysis of policy documents clarifying government intention and belief
Narrative on positional differences	Analysis of court documents to clarify different narratives and positions between the parties
Narratives on interpretation of the law	Analysis of court documents identifying what has happened and to identify the 'master' narrative from source documents
Narratives on required action	Analysis of court documents and subsequent press releases that tell their own 'stories'

NGO action. The greater the amount of public importance that is involved in an environmental issue before a court, in the UK at least, the more likely the courts will allow NGOs to have standing to bring a case. The absence of another responsible challenger (e.g. a regulator) is frequently a significant factor, so that a matter of public interest or concern is not left unexamined if only an NGO is willing to bring a case or pursue an issue. In *R v Secretary of State for Foreign Affairs ex p. The World Development Movement Ltd* [1994] EWHC Admin, the judge commented that, had the respected pressure group not mounted its challenge, it was unclear whether anybody else would or could question the decision. In addition, courts have considered cases brought by Greenpeace, Friends of the Earth, the Child Poverty Action Group and the Joint Council for the Welfare of Immigrants (among others).

Johnston and Breit's (2010: 6) three-stage structure was deployed as part of the analysis of this case, and the remainder of this chapter explores the case in detail by applying the three-stage narrative method. The approach taken is broadly one of tracing the narrative within the sources examined. Table 22.1 illustrates the possible narratives to be explored.

Whereas Table 22.1 lists the possible narratives, subsequent analysis via Johnston and Breit's (2010: 6) three-stage structure identifies that, within different aspects of the case documents, a specific narrative is being advanced. To illustrate this, the following discussion examines each analytical stage to identify how a case might be explored to critically analyse the conflicting narratives.

Narrative analysis Stage 1: basic case story

Stage 1 of narrative analysis examines the 'superficial' level of the case story through analysis of relevant legal documents. This identifies a straightforward story of EU law requirements as follows:

The 2008 Ambient Air Quality Directive (2008/50/EC) contains the following overall objective:

In order to protect human health and the environment as a whole, it is particularly important to combat emissions of pollutants at source and to identify and implement the most effective emission reduction measures at local, national and [European] level. Therefore emissions of harmful pollutants should be avoided, prevented or reduced and appropriate objectives set for ambient air quality taking into account relevant World Health Organisation standards, guidelines and programmes.

(Para 2)

Accordingly, the Directive sets legally binding limits for concentrations in outdoor air of major air pollutants that impact public health (e.g. nitrogen dioxide [NO_2]). By virtue of its (current) membership of the EU, the UK government is required to comply with the law and thus is required to meet 'limit values' that specify the legal limitations that can be placed on pollutants. The UK government is also required to produce a national air quality strategy setting out how it will comply with EU air quality requirements. However, the arguments of NGOs and the scientific and monitoring evidence suggest that the UK has consistently failed to meet its targets, and NGOs and the media have constructed a narrative of UK air quality being problematic and harmful to citizens' health (Carrington 2016; Ares and Smith 2017), as the harm caused was integral to discussing alleged government failings. In principle, a legal mechanism exists that would result in action being taken against the UK government for the failures in air quality by reference to the European Commission's monitoring process. However, in the absence of effective enforcement action being taken, and given the lack of improvements in air quality over a period of time, NGOs have become involved in pursuing a resolution through the courts. Article 23 of Directive 2008/50/EC specifies that, where levels of pollutants in ambient air exceed the set limits, a member state must adopt an air quality plan. In 2010, 40 out of 43 UK 'zones' were in breach of one or more of the nitrogen dioxide limit values. The UK government had adopted a plan in accordance with Article 23, but did not notify the European Commission with a plan for achieving the limits by 2015 as required by Article 22 of the Directive. NGO ClientEarth requested the UK government to confirm how it would comply with limits in 16 'zones' by 2015. Government failure resulted in litigation. The UK Supreme Court judgment (May 2013) included a declaration that the UK was in breach of its obligations under Article 13 of Directive 2008/50/EC.

Thus, at Stage 1, a surface-level narrative emerges. In its simplest form, the narrative is one of the UK government failing in its obligations to take the requisite action over air quality plans, and of court action taking place to determine that it is required to do so. However, narrative method, as applied to this case study, provides for a more detailed analysis of events, including exploration of deeper understanding, which the following Stage 2 analysis identifies.

Narrative analysis Stage 2: discourse level

Integral to narrative construction and application of narrative method to this case is understanding of the actors involved and the language employed to achieve their objectives. Analysis of the language used by the courts in reaching case judgment is also necessary.

In analysing the NGO legal action, construction of the NGO narrative considered not just the legal arguments themselves, but also press releases issued by NGO ClientEarth at each stage of proceedings and following proceedings. This analysis shows the combative nature of the action by use of language such as 'fight' and 'dirty air'. Press releases issued in April 2018 summarising the case quote ClientEarth CEO James Thornton as stating, 'it's incredible that the UK government has used public money to try to avoid tackling a public health crisis. Air pollution in this country is not only illegal, it's harming people's health and cutting lives short' (ClientEarth 2018). The matter was then referred to the Court of Justice of the European Union (CJEU) for ruling on a technical point regarding forcing the UK government to comply with EU law. The CJEU instructed the UK Court to adopt 'any necessary measure' on the UK government to establish plans for air quality.

The CJEU also clarified that 'natural or legal persons' *directly concerned* by limit values must be able to *require* the authorities to establish an air quality plan that *demonstrates* how limits will be achieved. In addition, the CJEU concluded that national courts should interpret their national laws in ways that are compatible with EU environmental directives and, when such interpretation is not possible, they must disregard national rules incompatible with the directives. Finally, the CJEU ruling confirmed that the supremacy of EU law means that individuals should be able to take legal action in national courts where a failure to comply with EU law was at issue in respect of government policy.

As a result of the litigation, the UK government's Draft Air Quality Plan was ordered to be produced by 24 April 2017. The government attempted to delay until after the General Election,[1] but ClientEarth successfully obtained a High Court order to require the plans to be produced. ClientEarth's contention is that the published plan fails to come up with specific measures for devolved nations, including Wales and Northern Ireland, and so is unlawful. Both parties were back in court on the 5 July 2017. Unfortunately, the UK's High Court ruled that there was 'nothing unlawful' in the government's draft air quality plan, but Mr Justice Garnham suggested that final plans could well be open to legal challenge if they did not deal with some of the concerns laid out by ClientEarth.

Subsequently, the parties were back in court in February 2018. In *R (on the application of ClientEarth) No 3* [2018] EWHC315, the Court concluded that the Department for Environment, Food and Rural Affairs's 2017 air quality plan was unlawful in that, in its application to 45 local authority areas, it did not contain measures sufficient to ensure substantive compliance with Directive (EC) 2008/50 and the Air Quality Standards Regulations 2010, SI 2010/1001. The Administrative Court further held that the plan did not include the information required by Annex XV to the Directive and Schedule 8 to the Regulations in respect of those same areas. However, to fully assess the case issues, interpretative narrative analysis was also required, as illustrated by the following Stage 3 discussion.

Stage 3: interpretative context

Integral to understanding of the audience and the environment in which the narrative(s) of the case is interpreted is examination of two perspectives on narratives:

First, this case illustrates how NGOs construct narratives about environmental harm to facilitate action through the courts. ClientEarth, claimant in these proceedings, is

---

1 The UK Prime Minister Theresa May called a General Election to take place on 8 June 2017. The Prime Minister's stated intention was to increase her parliamentary majority which would arguably aid efforts to challenge the supremacy of the EU and EU law and provide an enhanced mandate for a 'hard Brexit'; facilitating a clear break from the EU. However, the gambit failed and the Government majority was actually decreased as the opposition parties made gains.

a registered charity whose objectives include promoting and encouraging the enhancement, restoration, conservation and protection of the environment, including the protection of human health, for the public benefit. Thus, ClientEarth, as an environmental NGO, is concerned with constructing a narrative concerning government failure and the associated environmental harm. ClientEarth's narrative is not just an anthropocentric one concerned with human health (although human harm and pollution-related deaths are integral to its narrative); it also portrays the environment as a victim, developing a secondary narrative in which government failure goes unpunished but for the actions of NGOs like itself. The UK government sought to employ a technical argument that it had arguably complied with the letter of the law. However, the narrative employed by the NGO illustrated that, even if that were the case (a point strongly contested during litigation), an environmental harm problem persisted in respect of the failure to improve air quality. Accordingly, the NGO narrative contended that both the spirit and the letter of the law could not have been complied with; thus, there was a need for further action to be taken to meet EU law's stated objective of improving air quality.

Seen through the analysis of narrative method, this chapter identifies and constructs a narrative of environmental activism as a tool to resolve environmental problems in the face of government complacency and inaction. Although, in principle, a mechanism existed to address the government's failure to resolve air quality problems, in practice this was not working. Instead, the role of NGOs as monitors of environmental compliance and NGOs' willingness to use environmental litigation became the tool through which government failure in environmental protection was exposed and ultimately resolved. Within the court discourse, it became clear that the courts were willing to uphold the NGOs' ability to take action, as well as to reinforce their role as monitors of compliance, taking into account the importance of environmental protection. Indeed, in the Court's February 2018 judgment, Mr Justice Garnham stated:

> Proper and timely compliance with the law in this field matters. It matters, first, because the Government is as much subject of the law as any citizen or any other body in the UK. Accordingly, it is obliged to comply with the Directive and the Regulations and with the orders of the court. Second, it matters because, as is common ground between the parties to this litigation, a failure to comply with these legal requirements exposes the citizens of the UK to a real and persistent risk of significant harm. The 2017 Plan says that 'poor air quality is the largest environmental risk to public health in the UK. It is known to have more severe effects on vulnerable groups, for example the elderly, children and people already suffering from pre-existing health conditions such as respiratory and cardiovascular conditions'. As I pointed out in the November 2016 judgment, DEFRA's own analysis has suggested that exposure to nitrogen dioxide (NO_2) has an effect on mortality 'equivalent to 23,500 deaths' every year.
>
> *(Para 5)*

Thus, the Court: enforced the rule of law in such environmental cases; identified and raised concern about the wider harm caused to society and citizens by the government's failure; and reiterated the need for effective action to improve air quality. Although the last point was arguably the core objective of the case at the Stage 1 surface level (discussed earlier), it is inextricably linked to the wider narrative issues identified through in-depth analysis of the case and its surrounding discourse.

Conclusion: narrative method, environmental harm and beyond

This chapter's analysis identifies the importance of narrative method as a tool that can be applied in ways beyond the traditional, standard approach of narrative method examining contested stories that exist within adversarial trials. Fludernick (2014: 101) identifies that narration plays an integral part in legal discourse by facilitating the communication of law and allowing its principles to be explained. In Fludernick's examples, the 'plot lines' of cases combine such that 'the law code and judgments concern what one can clearly conceive of as stories' (2014: 108), albeit Fludernick acknowledges that legal discourse often downplays the inherent narrativity of criminal cases, based as they are in cause-and-effect logic.

The case discussed in this chapter's analysis has multiple narratives at play. First, the government's 'story' was that it was complying with the *technical* requirements of the law by producing air quality plans. However, the NGO's competing narrative was that the government was not complying with the *spirit* of the law. Although air quality plans had been produced, ClientEarth was effectively questioning the use and effectiveness of the plans if they did not, in fact, result in any tangible improvement in air quality, and did not apply to all affected parts of the UK. A secondary government narrative identified that its approach was arguably *minimal* compliance, albeit this approach may well have been unintentional. But, in respect of government failings, a secondary *NGO* narrative related to monitoring the actions of government and confirming the role of NGOs as ad hoc regulators. The Court narrative was one that identified government failings dating back to 2010, and, thus, a final 'hidden' narrative identified failings in the regulatory system such that the EU monitoring mechanism failed to address the issues identified by ClientEarth in its litigation.

Having identified these differing narratives through the use of the three-stage method, this chapter's contention is that narrative method can be employed to uncover deeper understanding of legal disputes and issues surrounding the analysis of particular legal discourse. Arguably, the nature of environmental disputes, such as the case discussed within this chapter, falls outside the norm of mainstream crime and justice narratives. In part, this is because the 'offender' at the heart of this case study was the state itself, such that the 'offender' narrative under discussion is not just one of the individualized offender breaking the law. Instead, the offending under discussion links to non-compliance with an aspect of EU law and is inextricably tied up with government policy approaches.

Further reading

Brooks, P. (2006) Narrative Transactions – Does the Law Need a Narratology? *Yale Journal of Law & the Humanities*, 18(1), 1–28.

Fludernick, M. (2014) A Narratology of the Law? Narratives in Legal Discourse, *Critical Analysis of Law*, 1(1), 87–109.

Johnston, J. and Breit, R. (2010) Towards a Narratology of Court Reporting, *Media International Australia*, 137, 47–57.

Lejano, R., Ingram, M. and Ingram, H. (2013) *The Power of Narrative in Environmental Networks*, Cambridge, MA: MIT Press.

Meretoja, H. (2017) *The Ethics of Storytelling: Narrative Hermeneutics, History, and the Possible*, Oxford: Oxford University Press.

References

Ares, E. and Smith, L. (2017) *Air Pollution: Meeting Nitrogen Dioxide Targets* (Parliamentary Briefing Paper, No. 8179), London: House of Commons.

Attfield, R. (2014) *Environmental Ethics*, Cambridge: Polity Press.

Beck, U. (1992) *Risk Society: Towards a New Modernity*, London: Sage.

Beirne, P. (2007) 'Animal rights, animal abuse and green criminology' in Beirne, P. and South, N. (eds.), *Issues in Green Criminology: Confronting Harms against Environments, Humanity and Other Animals*. Cullompton: Willan, pp. 55–83.

Bentham, J. (1962) 'Principles of Penal Law', in J. Bowring (ed.), *The Works of Jeremy Bentham*. New York, NY: Russell & Russell, p. 660.

Benton, T. (1998) Rights and Justice on a Shared Planet: More Rights or New Relations? *Theoretical Criminology*, 2(2), 149–175.

Brennan, A. and Lo, Y. (2008) Environmental Ethics. *Stanford Encyclopedia of Philosophy*. Available at: https://plato.stanford.edu/archives/fall2011/entries/ethics-environmental/ (accessed 28 April 2018).

Brooks, P. (2008) 'Narrative in and of the Law', in Phelan, J. and Rabinowitz, P.J. (eds.), *A Companion to Narrative Theory*. London: Blackwell, pp. 415–426.

Carrington, D. (2016) MPs: UK Air Pollution Is a 'Public Health Emergency'. *The Guardian* (Online). Available at: www.theguardian.com/environment/2016/apr/27/uk-air-pollution-public-health-emergency-crisis-diesel-cars (Accessed 20 April 2018).

ClientEarth (2018) UK Government Spends £500,000 Defending Long-Standing Inaction on Air Quality. Online at: www.clientearth.org/uk-government-spends-500000-defending-longstanding-inaction-on-air-quality/ (accessed 20 April 2018).

Fludernick, M. (2014) A Narratology of the Law? Narratives in Legal Discourse. *Critical Analysis of Law*, 1(1), 87–109.

Grunewald, R. (2013) The Narrative of Innocence, or Lost Stories. *Law and Literature*, 25, 366–389.

Hall, M. (2013) 'Victims of Environmental Harm', in Walters, R., Westerhuis, D. and Wyatt, T. (eds.), *Emerging Issues in Green Criminology: Exploring Power, Justice and Harm*, Basingstoke: Palgrave Macmillan, pp. 218–241.

Jasper, J M. (1997) *The Art of Moral Protest: Culture, Biography, and Creativity in Social Movements*, Chicago, IL: The University of Chicago Press.

Johnston, J. and Breit, R. (2010) Towards a Narratology of Court Reporting. *Media International Australia*, 137, 47–57.

Love, C. (1998) The Value of Narrative in Legal Scholarship and Teaching. *Journal of Gender, Race and Justice*, 2(1), 87.

Lowe, B.M. and Ginsberg, C.F. (2002) Animal Rights as a Post-Citizenship Movement. *Society & Animals*, 10(2), 203–215.

Lynch, M. and Stretesky, P. (2014) *Exploring Green Criminology: Toward a Green Criminological Revolution*, Farnham: Ashgate.

Marcinkutė, L. (2011) The Role of Human Rights NGO's: Human Rights Defenders or State Sovereignty Destroyers? *Baltic Journal of Law & Politics*, 4(2), 52–57.

Mill, J.S. (1993) *On Liberty*, New York, NY: Bantam.

Nurse, A. (2011) Policing Wildlife: Perspectives on Criminality in Wildlife Crime. *Papers from the British Criminology Conference*, 11, 38–53.

Nurse, A. (2012) Repainting the Thin Green Line: The Enforcement of Wildlife Legislation. *Internet Journal of Criminology*, October 2012, 1–20.

Nurse, A. (2013a) Privatising the Green Police: The role of NGOs in Wildlife Law Enforcement. *Crime Law and Social Change*, 59(3), 305–318.

Nurse, A. (2013b) *Animal Harm: Perspectives on Why People Harm and Kill Animals*, Farnham: Ashgate.

Nurse, A. (2016) *An Introduction to Green Criminology and Environmental Justice*, London: Sage.

Parkin, F. (1968) *Middle Class Radicalism: The Social Bases of the British Campaign for Nuclear Disarmament*, Manchester: Manchester University Press.

Posner, R. (2009) *Law and Literature*, Cambridge, MA: Harvard University Press.

Sarat, A. and Kerns, K. (eds.) (1996) *The Rhetoric of Law*, Ann Arbor, MI: University of MichiganPress.

Situ, Y. and Emmons, D. (2000) *Environmental Crime: The Criminal Justice System's Role in Protecting the Environment*, Thousand Oaks, CA: Sage.

Stallworthy, M. (2008) *Understanding Environmental Law*, London: Sweet & Maxwell.

Stone, C. (2010) *Should Trees Have Standing? Law, Morality and the Environment*, Oxford: Oxford University Press.

Tait, A. and Norris, L. (2011) Narrative and the Origins of Law. *Law & the Humanities*, 5(1), 11–22.

White, R. (2008) *Crimes against Nature: Environmental Criminology and Ecological Justice*, Cullompton: Willan.

White, R. (2012) NGO Engagement in Environmental Law Enforcement: Critical Reflections. *Australasian Policing*, 4(2), 7–12.

Wolff, L. (2014) Let's Talk About Lex: Narrative Analysis as Both Research Method and Teaching Technique in Law. *Adelaide Law Review*, 35(1), 3–21.

Woolf, H. (1992) Are the Judiciary Environmentally Myopic? *Journal of Environmental Law*, 4(1), 1–14.

23

LEGAL AESTHETICS AS VISUAL METHOD

Thomas Giddens

> Without an appreciation of its visual and aesthetic forms ... it is impossible to comprehend either the method of Law – its hermeneutic – or the procedures by which Law as judgment and measure ... inscribes itself upon everyday life.
>
> *(Goodrich 1991, p. 235)*

Introduction

This chapter seeks to introduce the reader to a method that is hard to schematise. It is a method that is fluid and open, and grounded in processes of interpretation and thus arguably the idiosyncrasies of academic judgement. It is a method that seeks to go beyond the boundaries of orthodox law and rational schematics. It aims to query not just the impact and effects of doctrine and policy in social situations, or even the identification and understanding of representations of traditional legal phenomena (courts, lawyers, judgment, moral dilemma) in ostensibly non-legal materials. It aims, instead, to reflect upon and thus transcend the limited way law is often encountered in mainstream texts and analysis. The method in question is legal aesthetics, but with a specific focus upon the use of legal aesthetics within a visual context of analysis (this is what I mean by 'legal aesthetics as visual method'). It is not about reading images through traditional visual methods such as semiotics or quantitative content analysis, but instead it is about heightening one's critical sensitivities in the visual encounter as part of the wider plethora of sensory experience.

As any meaningful reflection on methodology will appreciate, every method inevitably results in a fundamental limitation and shape to the knowledge and understanding – and thus the particular imagination of law – that can be produced, enabled, or given rise to. Formulated with respect to law, it is our methods that in a very real sense enable and delimit legal knowledge. The way we think about and approach law and the legal institution fundamentally – and I mean that quite technically – gives rise to the law we know. Method grounds what we are capable of knowing, which is true not just in legal studies, but also in academic study and experience more generally. To reflect upon images, and to do so aesthetically rather than, for example, as a content analysis, opens up to questions over this epistemic production, this unavoidable methodological limitation. As indicated, any discussion of method raises the same questions – but, in turning to images, as this chapter will indicate, these questions are made more overt for lawyers, because images are arguably farther removed from the familiar territory of most (socio-)legal study. Approaching aesthetically, the awareness and questioning of epistemic form becomes deeper, because the common scholarly paradigm of reading and writing textual documents in the development and communication of law and legal knowledge is overtly challenged by visuality.

As a method, doing this kind of visual analysis requires understanding not only of the images being encountered, but also of the legal context within which that reading is being done, and the effects this has on legal knowledge. It is also a key assumption of this kind of method that law appears visually: in the layout and formatting of statutes, the gowns and costumes of judges and police officers, the architecture of courtrooms, the theatricality of the trial, the embodied presence of the lawyer, the cultural symbolism of law. As Peter Goodrich describes it:

> The legal art … stands against an imagistic background of architecture, statuary, dress, heraldry, painting and insignia – gold rings, rods, coifs, seals, rolls, banquets and dramatics – which provide popular consciousness with a Justice which can be seen and so remembered.
>
> *(Goodrich 1991, pp. 234–235)*

Interrogating this visual dimension through legal aesthetics seeks something different from an attempt to make sense of or interpret the substantive content of the law, its practical adjudication, or its social contexts of effect and influence. It seeks, instead, to understand the way images – as part of the sensory array of legal encounter – are related to such legal substance, operation, and effect. That is, legal aesthetics as a visual method engages the relations between the form and content of law. Aesthetics in general can be understood as focusing on questions of sensory encounter; it is about the embodied encounter with form. Legal aesthetics accordingly asks about the sensory encounter with law: what form law takes, what forms it used to take or could come to take, and how this changes or contributes to our understanding of what the law is, how it operates, and how it might be changed for the better. In being a form that challenges textual dimensions of legal knowledge and practice, the specific sensory aspect of visuality engages similar questions.

My focus in this brief chapter is on the visual dimensions of law, which – as part of the sensory realm – an aesthetic approach can help us encounter and reduce to understanding. Indeed, thinking about aesthetics – about the appearance of things, about their sensory quality – quickly takes us to important questions about what form law *should* take, querying the common reliance upon textual articulation, or indeed a material connection with traditional state legal institutions. Indeed, to think about appearances ultimately leads us to question what legal knowledge itself looks like – as, for instance, text, reason, logic, performance, managed relation, ritual, or the rhetoric of argument – and to ponder alternative forms and thus alternative sources. This in turn opens up legal analysis to emanations of visual culture more broadly – to film, painting, television, comics, sculpture, architecture – through analysis of which we can step outside existing or hegemonic forms of legality and knowing, and continue to reflect upon the value, history, and possibilities of law and its institution.[1] A key thing to note is that this method in no way necessitates any representative elements

---

1 By institution, I simply mean the encoding or establishing of certain elements into (typically state-sponsored) bureaucratic or administrative form.

of traditional forms of legality such as lawyers, courts, judges, and so on. This is not a method that seeks only to read *representations* of law in the artefacts of visual culture; it is rather a method that reads such artefacts not only as law themselves, but as discourses upon legal form. Accordingly, one does not ask, 'where is the law in this?', but instead one asks, 'what does this emanation of legality – this expression of culture, of value and meaning, of theoretical stance – tell us about other emanations of legality or the form that legality can take?'

This chapter will proceed in three parts. The first will give a short overview of the ways in which law has been read as a visual phenomenon in recent scholarship. The following section will then provide a case study from my own work, examining in more detail a particular visual reading of the legal institution, as encountered in the context of visual culture, in order to demonstrate more fully some of the potential insights that attending to the visual dimensions of legality can afford. The chapter will finally close with a short reflection on the wider relevance of this method for socio legal studies, and for law more generally, particularly in relation to the production of legal knowledge.

Overview: law as a visual phenomenon

To elaborate the aesthetic approach to legal study with which this chapter is concerned, it is suitable for us to begin with what is arguably the most foundational practical aspect of a legal system or tradition, as well as an institutional and epistemic threshold of entry: jurisdiction. Jurisdiction can be conceived of as 'the material legal forms of sovereign, state and territory' (Dorsett & McVeigh 2012, p. 5). As a practical legal concept, the question of jurisdiction arguably has to come before any attempt at enunciating substantive law: we must know if we are in the realm of law before we are able to discuss its substance or content (see Dorsett & McVeigh 2012, p. 6). Jurisdiction engages concerns of when, where, and over whom law is able to speak and produce legitimate effects. As Goodrich inscribes:

> In that jurisdiction precedes law, in that it marks the point of entry into the juridical sphere and speech, it has to be visible in advance of utterance and hence must be a property of communal space, of the architecture of the institution, of context and vestment that can be apprehended prior to any discursive intervention in the name of legality.
>
> *(Goodrich 2008, p. 214)*

Because it is the first or primordial encounter with law – inchoate and thus lacking the full opportunity to convince the subject of its legitimacy or existence – jurisdiction must display itself, it must be, in Goodrich's terms, a visive power (see, generally, Goodrich 2008). Jurisdiction itself 'signals nothing, it has no content, but [is] rather only an enigmatic signification of something else' – of the space of legal authority (Goodrich 2008, p. 216), within which is subsequently enabled the articulation and application of substantive legal rules. And in this we can see an overarching point that trickles down through all the frames and structures of law and its institution: law appears. It has a visual form, it involves an aesthetic encounter – with its material structures (buildings, documents) as well as its inhabitants (agents, subjects). Indeed, Goodrich goes further and describes law's normative universe as a 'theatre of emblems', a visual order within which the person or legal subject is *seen* or enabled to appear (see Goodrich 2012). And this visual appearance is effusive throughout law's institution in its wholehearted embrace of images and theatrics in the demonstration of its social and communal presence. Obvious examples of this can be observed in the multiple elements of judgment, which is a key if not central practical activity of any common law system. The concrete adjudication, interpretation, and application of legal rules – judgment – involves a whole host of aesthetic and visual dimensions, and we will now very briefly consider the way many of these have been encountered in legal studies in order to set out the potential for such visual attention to elaborate meaningful and important aspects of law as a social and cultural phenomenon.

As one of the visual signals of entry into law's jurisdiction noted above, we shall begin with the architecture of justice, understood here as the physical context or place of judgment. The grandiose and often intimidating edifices of a 19th-century courthouse (think, for example, of the Royal Courts of Justice) are perhaps a leading image of what a court looks like – at least in the popular imagination. Yet such a courthouse is neither a necessary nor a neutral backdrop for the administration of justice – imagine, for example, the informal set-up of an employment tribunal, or the accessible and level arrangement of the UK Supreme Court. Linda Mulcahy's historical examination of the architectural practices in the development of courtrooms (Mulcahy 2011) highlights the shift from provincial, privileged, and a largely discretionary justice to a grand centralised system of adjudication – a shift that was celebrated and memorialised in the lavish expenditure and increasing architectural sophistication of courthouses across the 19th century (see Mulcahy 2011, pp. 112–138). The development of this particular kind of courthouse can be seen to some degree as a reflection of wider trends in architectural fashion in the 1800s (Mulcahy 2011, pp. 124–126), but the legal dimensions of court buildings within the emerging industrial society at the time meant their urban presence 'conferred a status which went beyond recognition of a new city as a seat of culture; it conferred symbolic status as an instrument of state-sanctioned and centralised power' (Mulcahy 2011, p. 127). Although many contemporary courts do not share these extravagant trappings, architects borrowed ecclesiastical styles and designs in an effort to legitimate the emerging centralised legal system amid the flow of industrialisation against which many reacted negatively, with the visual appearance and the material structures of the law seeking to display and present the institution as being not only powerful and legitimate – but divine (see Mulcahy 2011, pp. 130–131).

And this 'divinity' of the institution can be seen not just in such practices of court building: the judges who sit in these courtly constructions have a similarly 'divine' aspect that can be detected through engagement with their visual appearance. Leslie J Moran's work on judicial portraiture, for example, encounters both the visual dimensions of the institution of justice as well as the presentation of legal phenomena in wider visual culture. In judicial portraits, the 'voluminous robes and other paraphernalia of judicial dress dominate the painted surface ... [involving] an aesthetics that negates individuality' (Moran 2008, p. 96).[2] And in this negation, the famous split within the sovereign body identified by Kantorowicz – between mortal flesh and immortal office – is encountered (see Moran 2009, p. 300):

> Likeness and individuality in the judicial portrait are produced according to a rigorous aesthetic language associated with the values and virtues of the judicial institution. ... Flaws, blemishes, imperfections and idiosyncrasies are of little relevance. The subject is made in the image of an exemplar: the embodiment of the

---

2 On dress and law more widely, see Watt (2013). In a more recent engagement with dress and authority in the context of Japanese manga, see Taylor-Harding (2018).

ideal. … In this pictorial tradition, the differentiation of one sitter from another is not an aesthetic preoccupation. The opposite is the case; visual continuity is used to shape each judicial subject by way of the virtues of sameness, repetition, endurance and consistency.

(Moran 2009, p. 300)

Similar observations can be made in the emergence of standardised documentary forms in the history of bureaucratic systems, whereby official documents' 'unchanging parts are endowed with authenticating force' (Vismann 2008, p. 73). In the context of dress, even the non-grandiose attire of the business suit that might be found in less extravagant courts can be seen on one level to enable access to a realm that suppresses one's physical embodiment in favour of rational discourse.[3] But the appearance of the judge in portraits can also inform us not just about practices of portraiture, but about the appearance of the institution of the judiciary itself. As Moran's work with the German TV judge Ruth Herz indicates, 'producing, evaluating, and managing voice and gestures are [not just part of TV production, but are] also a routine part of the image work of the judge' (Moran et al. 2010, p. 205). Moreover, the features and characteristics of a created judicial image can be seen to reflect and augment key features and characteristics of the judicial institution, such as majesty, independence, and impartiality, and thus engaging meaningfully with the wide array of judicial images that can be identified across visual culture encounters important questions and insights in relation to the function, operation, and presence of law as part of the complex social world (see, for instance, Moran 2015).

Images also abound within the intricacies of judicial process. Richard Sherwin's seminal study of the encroaching presence of visual artefacts within legal processes – from jury presentations and video evidence to the circulation of procedural images in popular culture – warns of the potential erosion of legal authority as popular imagery takes over (see Sherwin 2000). But the use of visual evidence is a common occurrence and often taken as simply a practical window to the truth of an event. These images, however, bring with them the unavoidable baggage of the aesthetic, of sensory encounter, that feeds and shapes their meaning (Stoehrel 2013). In recognition of the broad scope of the aesthetic, the visual artefacts that are employed as plain or neutral evidence of fact are never so innocent: 'we seek knowledge with our whole being and it is the representation as a whole that affects the perception of reality', even if this fullness is not consciously acknowledged (Stoehrel 2013, p. 558). As Desmond Manderson puts it, 'the aesthetic realm suffuses our engagement with everything about us … It is part of what it means to be a human being, part of our relationship with the world … Nothing remains untouched by the aesthetic temperament' – not even law (Manderson 2000, pp. 23–24). And, if we place visual evidence within this wider context of aesthetic or sensory encounter, it becomes apparent that it has dimensions beyond those attributed to it by traditional institutional law. As Katherine Biber's work evocatively demonstrates, the evidentiary archive of law has a 'cultural afterlife' in its circulation within the visual arts long after the bureaucratic procedures of justice have ceased their administrative machinations (see Biber 2018). The images of evidence are not just transparent windows to the past that can enable and legitimate a judicial ruling, but are

---

3 See Collier (1998, pp. 45–46), who also notes that the supposed neutrality of the business suit, when compared with the historical lack of an equivalent in female attire, plays into women's exclusion from public life under patriarchy.

aesthetic productions with particular associations and cultural resonances, with significant aspects of meaning beyond those demarcated as 'fact' in legal processes.

The above is but a brief indication of the kinds of analysis and insight that engagement with visuality has brought to law in recent years. It is hoped that this has shown that taking seriously the visual aspects of law opens analysis up to questions of broader scope and relevance than a close reading of doctrine, of substantive content without reference to its form, or of distinctly sociological context(s), might produce. To think about the appearance of the institution, about the visual aspects of justice as well as the cultural presentation or querying of legal and judicial forms, is to reflect on the nature of law itself, but without falling down the well-mapped rabbit hole of natural versus positive law – we are not tracing the relationships between law and morality, nor examining whether law is just or how we might conceive of a just system. Here, the 'nature of law' becomes a question about form and appearance, about methodological progenesis and epistemic shape – about the sensory encounter with visuality. As we will see from the sections below, employing legal aesthetics as visual method means encountering the form – and the formation – of legal knowledge in a vast and open array of contexts, and, in doing so, in engaging meaningfully in methodologically reflexive legal study, it raises wide-ranging questions about the practices of both the legal profession and the legal academy.

Case study: Tom Kaczynski's 'White Noise'

In my own work, I have expressed a visual approach to legality in terms of reading law within the multimodal – textual and visual, inter alia – form of comics. If law is profoundly visual in its social, cultural, and political appearance, then encountering it through an engagement with visual media has a number of benefits and logical foundations. On the one hand, it permits the elaboration and development of critical resources for reading visual (or multimodal) phenomena through an immersion in, and interdisciplinary engagement with, well-founded and on-going attempts to theorise the visual articulation and decoding of meaning. On the other hand, once it is accepted that law is a multimodal, predominantly visual, and certainly sociocultural phenomenon, reading it within multimodal, predominantly visual culture becomes an eminently suitable and appropriate thing to do. It might be possible to map these on to two aspects of legal aesthetics as a method for approaching law as a visual phenomenon, with one aspect examining the traditionally delineated realm of law and its institution as a visual or aesthetic phenomenon, and the other visual and aesthetic culture as legal discourse to be examined and interrogated. This is a somewhat artificial distinction, however, because the two practices are ultimately identical: in examining law as an artefact of visual culture, one is encountering just one of many examples of legally significant visual culture, and looking for law 'in' non-traditional sources such as comics, film, and so on, has the effect of maintaining this artificial segregation of certain traditional forms of law (as courts, texts, and so on) from the wider ranges of cultural discourse. The more profound question thus becomes why it is that a certain form of law has become authoritative, binding, and pre-eminent not just in the management of human relations and conduct, but also in the scholarly and pedagogic imagination of what law 'looks like'.

As I say, it is to comics that my attention has been drawn, with the medium's multimodality raising significant questions in relation to the primacy of text and its relations with other – notably visual – forms of knowledge (note, in particular, Giddens 2012, 2018, and, in comics form, Giddens 2015). Within this broader project, and as a way to demonstrate how law might be approached visually in the context of legal aesthetics, I want here to focus on one particular aspect that continues some of the themes set out above, in particular in relation to the epistemic form of law and the question of an expanding interdisciplinary context of legal understanding. If we think about the development of interdisciplinary legal scholarship, notably the protracted debates in relation to law and literature and the wider suitability of using humanities methods and cultural artefacts in the theorisation and evaluation of law (see, for example, Weisberg 1984; White 1985; Ward 1995; Williams 2002; Dolin 2007), one can identify a resistance on the part of the mainstream or orthodox regions of the legal academy and profession. Richard Posner's infamous treatise on law and literature is undoubtedly a case in point (Posner 1988). But the current state of the discipline demonstrates that attention to context and alternative forms of disciplinary knowledge beyond the close reading of doctrine is de facto what most legal study is about (see, for example, Goodrich 2009; Williams 2009). In many ways, socio-legal studies has become the new 'mainstream' of the legal academy in relation to which critical and humanities scholars often (but not always consciously) position themselves antagonistically, or the 'centre ground' they seek to occupy or speak to, or a space where the legal humanities can be meaningfully elaborated – depending upon one's intellectual positioning, as it can be said that, 'academic lawyers hold sharply opposed views as to what "counts" as relevant legal research, positioning differing scholarship on, or outside, a perceived periphery' (Williams 2009, p. 247). But, despite this disciplinary disputation, it is clearly now the case that the sociological context of law – its contexts of practice, of social and policy impact, of empirical encounter – is a large part of what not just socio-legal studies, but law in general is about (see, for instance, Feenan 2013); even if the place of the humanities in relation to sociological method might remain somewhat ambiguous, an exclusive reliance on traditional doctrinal methods is now far from central within academic law's self-identity.

But how far can we extend this context, or is the 'socio' the only or 'best' context within which to study law, and can we readily separate 'law' from its 'context(s)' in any case? And is it really now the case that such an opening up no longer brings trepidation in certain avenues of the (socio-)legal conurbation? I do not think such broad questions can be answered in a short tract such as this, so instead we shall consider the more substantive implications of visually opening up the context of law, to a point where we can reflect upon the very formation of legal knowledge and institution, of its appearance out of the primal abyss of the universe. Such a context goes beyond that of sociological and empirical method to the broader or more precedent dimensions of aesthetics – of sensory engagement and the phenomenal or epistemic emergence of knowledge more generally. In doing this, we shall also necessarily reflect upon the methodological implications of aesthetically engaging law's visuality.

To encounter law's abyssal context, it is to the achingly concise and deeply evocative work of Tom Kaczynski that I turn for this case study, and more specifically to his one-page work 'White Noise' (Kaczynski 2012b), reproduced in Figure 23.1. As set out in the introduction, what the method I am elaborating here seeks is not any representation of traditional law or its institution, but rather the capacity to read visual form as discourse upon law, its institution, its forms, or its knowledge-making. Accordingly, at first glance there might appear to be no law in Figure 23.1 – but the exact point of the legal aesthetic method as I am expressing it is that through it one cannot fail to see law here. The precision, order, and efficiency of Kaczynski's work doubtless, on one level, indicates why a lawyer or legal academic might be attracted to it – especially, in a psychoanalytic context, when Kaczynski uses such structural integrity to encounter radical otherness and the chaos of infinity, of that without structure, and thus excavates the legal unconscious on a grand

Figure 23.1 'White Noise' (Kaczynski 2012b, p. 45). Copyright 2012 Tom Kaczynski

scale. In this sense, it is a rendering of the melancholia of the lawyer (see Goodrich 1995) in a speculative context, for those living in times of globalisation, ecological catastrophe, and digital revolution. In this sense, 'White Noise' is profoundly a work of law, of legal discourse, of seeking to come to terms with the limitations of structural legal forms and methods within an expanded context or recognition of wide-ranging alternatives.

To make this more explicit, in 'White Noise', a basic trajectory of increasing context can be read. The single page narrative begins with a man waking in the dead of night, and thereafter being unable to sleep. The narrative text links this depicted man's experience to a more general encounter in late modern attempts to sleep at night; in insomnia, Kaczynski figures, one gradually becomes aware of the background of existence. The everyday distractions melt away, and we are left to encounter the planet without civilisation. The integrated systemic context of one's life is the first awareness that comes into focus, with the possible 'fluctuation of the power grid'. This expands to a more 'natural' context of insects and creepy-crawlies, living beyond the human. The biological aspects of one's own body then appear, along with the forgotten evolutionary history of the corporeal self that links us to the complex life of the Earth's biosphere. The planet itself then emerges more fully, as geological time crystallises, and the 'uneasy' movements of the planet's surface are perceived. From here, the context explodes into the abyss of space and the infinite expanse within which the planet spins, surrounded by the 'countless solar holocausts' of exploding stars across the universe – a context without end. An abyss that is opened up methodically, efficiently, inexorably, across half a dozen small comics panels. But the point here is not so much Kaczynski's particular genius, but the significance of this single page as a work of law.

The central theme of 'White Noise' for my current purpose is that of the anxiety of context; of the potential threat to meaning and certainty that a recognition of genealogy and repressed or background dimensions can bring. Indeed, as much of the debate around the legitimacy of law and humanities indicates – especially in the American legal academy – concerns with the objectivity of meaning are of high significance. 'White Noise' opens up to a context so vast that it threatens meaninglessness – if we are fleas on the back of existence, specks of dust in the infinite archive of the cosmos, to what purpose or end, what meaning or significance, are the categorisations, descriptions, moral reflections, and judgments of law? A fear or anxiety in relation to this loss of meaning is clearly a part of the resistant reactions against so-called 'postmodern' critical legal theory that sought to question the unitary, primary, and authoritative nature of law's texts and institution. This is not necessarily a reaction unique to the postmodern moment, but can be traced as a generally repressed or forgotten dimension of the legal academy since its inception (Goodrich 1992). Indeed, in large part what 'White Noise' excavates is precisely the unconscious of law, which is a significant dimension also of what legal aesthetics encounters and where the visuality of law is typically located. Thus, in this examination of legal aesthetics as visual method, we shall now turn in more detail to the key contextual movements of 'White Noise' in relation to interdisciplinary legal study in order to show what is at stake in encountering the visual in this way.

The first panel in many ways prefigures the whole movement of expansion, in that it presents its character without any boundary, in a panel without edge. The first specific context to think about here is thus figured in the second panel: that of the power grid, of the socio-economic embeddedness of human life. Here, our conduct and experience are recognised as existing within not a vacuum or as the abstractions of rational choice, but in relation to a variety of social institutions and wider systems and structures of socially organised life. The power company provides electricity to power one's home, in turn regulated (directly and indirectly) by institutional law and state mechanisms, as well as being influenced by economic forces and private interests, by social and cultural developments, and scientific and technological change. In many respects, this is the context most familiarly associated with the 'socio-legal'. Here, we are engaged not just with doctrine, not with the bartering of purposive or mischievous interpretation, but with the wider sociological context of law's function. A mild anxiety is present here, in that reliance on these somewhat intangibly large structures puts the subject in quite a vulnerable position. What if the power were to fail? What if institutional adjudication no longer took place? And the more familiar jurisprudential or legal question: how can we ensure that it does not fail, and that it operates correctly, towards justice? Images can be encountered here – there are a variety of empirical and semiotic methods for reading the visual on this level of the 'socio' (see, for an introductory range of examples, Margolis & Pauwels 2011) – but thinking images in terms of aesthetics can go much further.

The third panel evokes nature, and the boundary between the human – the social, the cultural – and the natural. It presents nature as something distinct from the human, and something bigger than the human. Nature exists without us, before and after us. It is an intricate and troubling context, filled with bugs and microbes and interconnected ecosystems. Socio-legal studies ventures here, too, in its engagement, for example, with questions of ecology and environmental law (see, for example, Philippopoulos-Mihalopoulos 2011). But the line between human and nature is not so easily maintained, as the fourth panel indicates in its bringing forth of an awareness of the biological, the animal nature of the human body. Here, the recognisable human face is replaced with a muddle of veins and arteries, suggesting that the person – the subject, the mask of persona – does not have a 'human' face, but a biological or animal one. In biopolitical work, the human–nature divide is argued to be a human construct that always delineates the boundaries, ultimately, of political life, of membership of the sovereign order – and thence of law (see, for example, Agamben 2004; Parsley 2010, 2013). Here, the persona is indicated as biology and evolution, thus opening the doctrinal and social orders of law up to a vast history and genealogy far beyond that of the institution of the state, of jurisdiction and judicial adjudication. Panel six shifts a little further, indicating not just the evolutionary history of *homo sapiens* and its problematic relationship or integration with what is often thought as 'natural' and thus separate, but instead the geological planet spinning and undulating in deep time. Law's context starts to become too big, and the anxiety increases accordingly as indicated in the figure's alarm as his bed – that symbol of safety, comfort, and recuperation – is tipped around at the whims of geological becoming.

Finally, the planet itself is placed into its cosmic context, and the petty concerns of law seem to fade into insignificance. If 'White Noise' is not concise enough in its movement to this context, Figure 23.2, an excerpt of three panels from another of Kaczynski's works, provides a more

Figure 23.2 Excerpt from '10,000 Years' (Kaczynski 2012a, p. 28). Copyright 2012 Tom Kaczynski

efficient movement from a closed to an infinite context – and the anxiety or disquiet this can bring about. Perhaps we can cite Nietzsche here to summarise something of what is at stake in this interdisciplinary and aesthetic expansion in Kaczynski's legal discourse:

> Once upon a time, in some out of the way corner of that universe which is dispersed into numberless twinkling solar systems, there was a star upon which clever beasts invented knowing.
>
> *(Nietzsche 1990, p. 888)*

And, in this endless context, as Nietzsche himself argued, it becomes apparent that general systems of thought, understanding, and – for our purposes – categorisation and regulation, can never capture or represent the infinite variety of the embodied surface of life and existence (see, generally, Nietzsche 1990, and, for more on this point, reading the rupture by difference as a 'Nietzschean sublime', see Battersby 2007). Recognising the abyss outside law, its context within the boundless universe, on one level shows up the relatively artificial and potentially pointless quality of, not only law, but any physical or epistemic structure we could build. Such is the horror that keeps us awake at night, in Kaczynski's ironically introspective vision. And, as a work of introspection, an introspection that moves outwards from the subject by delving into the awareness gleaned in insomnia, this rendering of law's outside becomes a recalling of the repressed within, of the unconscious. This is reinforced – psychologically, culturally, epistemically – in the final two panels where Kaczynski's character blanks out this terrifying abyssal context with the gentle, reassuring hum of an electric fan. In this movement of covering up, of blanking out, is a repression of the awareness of context. In the silence of the night, the boundlessness of our location is gradually recalled until it becomes too troubling, too disruptive – 'Vertigo. Nausea.' – and it is repressed again outside or beneath conscious thought. And such repression enables the peace of sleep, the stasis of rest, and the stability of epistemic form.

To interpret or read this legally, to engage in an aesthetic rendering of this item of visual culture as legal discourse, says something about law, the legal discipline, the nature and limits of legal study, and, in particular, about the implications and effects of visual engagement and aesthetics. On its most profound level, this reading says that law is the hum of a fan – it is part of the reassuring or soothing background noise of social and cultural life that blanks out or protects us from the abyss of the universe (see Legendre 1998). Which is to say only that law is an epistemic form, a rendering or reduction of the ultimately unknowable complexity of a reality that in its fullness exceeds all conscious structure: the hum of discourse against the abyss without structure. What it says, also, is that this is a visual phenomenon as much as a conceptual one, as is most clearly demonstrated in the final panel. Here, the blank page is masked with the visual representation of text – of the hum of discourse and knowing just outlined. This is a visual depiction of text over a blank background, of the limited symbolic forms of written language over the infinite potential for figuration that a blank space represents (see Goodrich 1999; Pont 2012), as well as over the actual material of the page itself as part of the phenomenal, pre-structural lifeworld (see also, for example, Giddens 2018, pp. 172–173). The printed word masks the potential infinity of the unmarked page; discourse masks the infinity of the unstructured universe. In law, legal texts, and those of the legal academy, become a mask over the infinite context that threatens to disrupt or challenge the legitimacy or authority of law and its academic study, as well as over the expanse of alternative forms and sources that can be read within legal studies.

Wider relevance: towards a reflexive legality

The method I have demonstrated above is reflexive; it seeks not only to read alternative forms of law, but also, in doing so, remains aware of the epistemic or methodological shift that is entailed in such a reading. It is this reflexivity in terms of epistemology that makes this approach part of legal aesthetics, rather than other ways of approaching images (e.g. through semiotics or other qualitative methods). As an aesthetics, we are asking how sensory encounter becomes epistemic form – how knowledge and law appear. In the above example, visual form was read and analysed in a way that opened up to alternative forms of law and enabled reflection on the appearance of law more generally. Although my example worked expressly in the context of self-reflection in terms of method, other studies could remain true to this ethos while taking different tacks. For example, in adverting to the visual appearance of courtrooms in cinema, one can become aware of sociocultural encodings of legal authority, opening up to spheres and forms of legal knowledge beyond the texts of doctrine or of sociological study. One might even study something as ostensibly mundane as roads, reading them as law, as material expressions of sovereignty and as technologies of jurisdiction in the colonial expansions of empire (see Barr 2015).

Such an approach to law is an exercise, ultimately, in interpretation: it requires academic judgement and intellectual insight, under a radical openness and generosity in terms of what 'counts' as law or legal knowledge, and an ability to see law without its traditional institutional or scholarly trappings. Indeed, a core premise of this approach is that law does not have any boundaries, and thus that any object or artefact or cultural product can be read or unpacked legally or with some legal relevance, and thus as law. The methodological rigours of such an exercise are not strict or able to be delineated into a step-by-step guide in a handbook, but rather involve an attitude or stance, a feeling for legality and its expression all around, and a persistent questioning that leads an analyst to profoundly legal questions (interpretation, administration, authority, choice, morality, hierarchy, identity, structure, justice, politics, institution, and so on) in relation to their chosen object. In many ways, the same questions are asked that we would ask of any other legal source: How do I interpret this? What is its authority? How does it relate to other sources?

With its wider impact and significance, this method of approaching legal study, of engaging in the visuality of law, legal knowledge, and the institution of justice, thus operates on something of a disciplinary level. In one respect, it is a method that simply engages legal questions in a particular and significant context – that of visual appearance. But the significance goes deeper than just another context or another 'law and'. The aesthetics of legal visuality is a method that queries the very form of legal knowledge, questioning well-rooted and heavily sedimented practices within the legal academy. It is a method that can be added to any study, as a meta-reflection on the particular form of one's own work, and the justifications and effects of those choices.

But, taken further, done fully and seriously, it questions academic and institutional practice and the production of legal knowledge across the discipline and beyond. Is law only to be found in texts, in journal articles and empirical engagement, in theory texts and monographs and handbooks, in judgments and policy documents? What is the relation between all these texts and the clearly more expanded presence of law? Such questioning opens up to a fuller range of legal materials for study, but also to reflective questions on one's own practice: How does my practice shape my knowledge? How does my method shape the law I imagine? Why am I writing this down?

Further reading

Gearey, A. 2001. *Law and Aesthetics*. Hart.

Goodrich, P. 2016. *Legal Emblems and the Art of Law: Obiter Depicta as the Vision of Governance*. Cambridge University Press.

Manderson, D. (ed.). 2018. *Law and the Visual: Representations, Technologies, Critique*. Toronto University Press.

Sousanis, N. 2015. *Unflattening*. Harvard University Press.

Wagner, A. & Sherwin, R. (eds.). 2013. *Law, Culture and Visual Studies*. Springer.

References

Agamben, G. 2004. *The Open: Man and Animal*, Stanford, Stanford University Press.

Barr, O. 2015. A Jurisprudential Tale of a Road, an Office, and a Triangle. *Law and Literature*, 27, 199–216.

Battersby, C. 2007. *The Sublime, Terror, and Human Difference*, Abingdon, Routledge.

Biber, K. 2018. *In Crime's Archive: The Cultural Afterlife of Evidence*, Abingdon, Routledge.

Collier, R. 1998. *Masculinities, Crime, and Criminology*, London, Sage.

Dolin, K. 2007. *A Critical Introduction to Law and Literature*, Cambridge, Cambridge University Press.

Dorsett, S. & McVeigh, S. 2012. *Jurisdiction*, Abingdon, Routledge.

Feenan, D. (ed.). 2013. *Exploring the 'Socio' of Socio-Legal Studies*, London, Palgrave.

Giddens, T. 2012. Comics, Law, and Aesthetics: Towards the Use of Graphic Fiction in Legal Studies. *Law and Humanities*, 6, 85.

Giddens, T. 2015. Lex Comica: On Comics and Legal Theory. In Giddens, T. (ed.) *Graphic Justice: Intersections of Comics and Law*, pp. 8–15, Abingdon, Routledge.

Giddens, T. 2018. *On Comics and Legal Aesthetics: Multimodality and the Haunted Mask of Knowing*, Abingdon, Routledge.

Goodrich, P. 1991. Specula Laws: Image, Aesthetic and Common Law. *Law and Critique*, 2, 233.

Goodrich, P. 1992. Critical Legal Studies in England: Prospective Histories. *Oxford Journal of Legal Studies*, 12, 195.

Goodrich, P. 1995. *Oedipus Lex: Psychoanalysis, History, Law*, London, University of California Press.

Goodrich, P. 1999. The Iconography of Nothing: Blank Spaces and the Representation of Law in *Edward VI and the Pope*. In Douzinas, C. & Nead, L. (eds.) *Law and the Image: The Authority of Art and the Aesthetics of Law*, pp. 89–114, London, University of Chicago Press.

Goodrich, P. 2008. Visive Powers: Colours, Trees and Genres of Jurisdiction. *Law and Humanities*, 2, 213–231.

Goodrich, P. 2009. Intellection and Indiscipline. *Journal of Law and Society*, 36, 460.

Goodrich, P. 2012. The Theatre of Emblems: On the Optical Apparatus and the Investiture of Persons. *Law, Culture and the Humanities*, 8, 47–67.

Kaczynski, T. 2012a. 10,000 Years. In *Beta Testing the Apocalypse*, pp. 18–29, Seattle, Fantagraphics.

Kaczynski, T. 2012b. White Noise. In *Beta Testing the Apocalypse*, p. 45, Seattle, Fantagraphics.

Legendre, P. 1998. The Other Dimension of Law. In Goodrich, P. & Carlson, D. G. (eds.) *Law and the Postmodern Mind*, pp. 175–192, Ann Arbor, University of Michigan Press.

Manderson, D. 2000. *Songs without Music: Aesthetic Dimensions of Law and Justice*, London, University of California Press.

Margolis, E. M. & Pauwels, L. (eds.). 2011. *The Sage Handbook of Visual Research Methods*, London, Sage.

Moran, L. J. 2008. Judicial Bodies as Sexual Bodies: A Tale of Two Portraits. *The Australian Feminist Law Journal*, 29, 91–108.

Moran, L. J. 2009. Judging Pictures: A Case Study of Portraits of the Chief Justices, Supreme Court of New South Wales. *International Journal of Law in Context*, 5, 295–314.

Moran, L. J. 2015. Judicial Pictures as Legal Life-Writing Data and a Research Method. *Journal of Law and Society*, 42, 74–101.

Moran, L. J., Skeggs, B. & Herz, R. 2010. Ruth Herz Judge Playing Judge Ruth Herz: Reflections on the Performance of Judicial Authority. *Law Text Culture*, 14, 198–219.

Mulcahy, L. 2011. *Legal Architecture: Justice, Due Process and the Place of Law*, London, Routledge.

Nietzsche, F. 1990. On Truth and Lies in a Nonmoral Sense. In Bizzell, P. & Herzberg, B. (eds.) *The Rhetorical Tradition: Readings from Classical Times to the Present*, pp. 1171–1179, Boston, MA, Bedford Books.

Parsley, C. 2010. The Mask and Agamben: The Transitional Juridical Technics of Legal Relation. *Law Text Culture*, 14, 12–39.

Parsley, C. 2013. The Animal Protagonist: Representing 'the Animal' in Law and Cinema. In Otomo, Y. & Mussawir, E. (eds.) *Law and the Question of the Animal: A Critical Jurisprudence*, pp. 10–34, Abingdon, Routledge.

Philippopoulos-Mihalopoulos, A. (ed.) 2011. *Law and Ecology: New Environmental Foundations*, Abingdon, Routledge.

Pont, X. M. D. 2012. Confronting the Whiteness: Blankness, Loss and Visual Disintegration in Graphic Narratives. *Studies in Comics*, 3, 253–274.

Posner, R. 1988. *Law and Literature: A Misunderstood Relation*, Harvard, Harvard University Press.

Sherwin, R. K. 2000. *When Law Goes Pop: The Vanishing Line Between Law and Popular Culture*, London, University of Chicago Press.

Stoehrel, R. F. 2013. The Legal Image's Forgotten Aesthetics. *International Journal for the Semiotics of Law*, 26, 555–577.

Taylor-Harding, R. 2018. Caught in Couture: Regulating Clothing and the Body in *Kill la Kill*. In Pearson, A., Giddens, T. & Tranter, K. (eds.) *Law and Justice in Japanese Popular Culture: From Crime Fighting Robots to Duelling Pocket Monsters*, pp. 112–125, Abingdon, Routledge.

Vismann, C. 2008. *Files: Law and Media Technology*, Stanford, CA, Stanford University Press.

Ward, I. 1995. *Law and Literature: Possibilities and Perspectives*, Cambridge, Cambridge University Press.

Watt, G. 2013. *Dress, Law and Naked Truth: A Cultural Study of Fashion and Form*, London, Bloomsbury.

Weisberg, R. H. 1984. *The Failure of the Word: The Protagonist as Lawyer in Modern Fiction*, London, Yale University Press.

White, J. B. 1985. *The Legal Imagination: Abridged Edition*, London, University of Chicago Press.

Williams, M. 2002. *Empty Justice: One Hundred Years of Law, Literature, and Philosophy*, Abingdon, Routledge-Cavendish.

Williams, M. 2009. Socio-Legal Studies and the Humanities – Law, Interdisciplinarity and Integrity. *International Journal of Law in Context*, 5, 243.

24

A CONTENT ANALYSIS OF JUDICIAL DECISION-MAKING

Richard Kirkham and Elizabeth A. O'Loughlin

Introduction

Legal academia is littered with discussion about the techniques of judicial argumentation. It is surprising, then, that there is comparatively little research systematically studying how judges make decisions, upon what grounds, and using what strategies. This chapter makes the claim that empirical studies recording what doctrinal strategies judges employ in their decision-making are a valuable tool for enriching legal debate. Such research offers a fuller picture of the application of the law by the courts and is capable of informing existing rich doctrinal debate that is traditionally based on isolated pockets of lead cases from the highest courts.

The chapter explores the technique of content analysis, which is one important methodological strategy for evidencing how judges use legal doctrine. Content analysis applies a form of discourse analysis in order to capture more comprehensively specific features of judicial decisions. The first section outlines how content analysis studies have been used to date, noting in particular that, whereas the method has been used more readily in the US, its potential has yet to be fully realised elsewhere, particularly in the UK.

The second section sketches our recent experience in engaging with this methodological approach. The study in question related to a discrete area of judicial practice: judicial review of ombudsman decisions in UK public law.[1] We elucidate how we designed a content analysis study to interrogate how judges make decisions, upon what grounds, and using what interpretive strategies in judicially reviewing the decisions of ombudschemes. We designed a coding method that, in particular, sought to test empirically the claim that the courts are commonly deferential to the work of ombudschemes. This section concludes by reflecting upon some of the challenges we faced in the design and implementation of the method and highlighting pitfalls that we would avoid in the future.

The third section reflects upon the wider relevance of this method. The excavation of our methodology in the second section provides helpful introductory guidance of a number of ways to record empirically, for example, judicial approaches to statutory interpretation, or

---

1 Our study included case law on ombudschemes in the legal systems of England and Wales, Northern Ireland, and Scotland.

a bench's approach to judicial review or appeal grounds. Such methods are broadly relevant to any socio-legal scholar seeking to capture a rigorous record of judicial practice and are a mechanism to test doctrinal claims in the field. The chapter concludes by reflecting briefly upon the hitherto unrealised potential and function of content analysis methodologies for the study of law in the UK academy.

An introduction to content analysis

In the study of judicial decision-making, bold claims are often made about the meaning and practice of law based upon the selective interrogation of appropriately sourced examples. The focus in such study is on establishing the legal reasoning that underpins case law. When it comes to the study of legal doctrine as developed in the courts, this method is almost certainly the most common form of legal scholarship and establishes a powerful foundation upon which to understand not just the meaning of the law, but how it develops and is best applied. However, other questions are less well answered through this approach to legal study. For instance, patterns of judicial decision-making, or anomalies, are harder to pick up if the form of study is too selective. Such trends and other analytical questions can only be sensibly addressed if multiple cases are considered alongside each other through a structured approach that treats like cases equally.

To establish a deeper understanding of the practice of the judiciary, various forms of empirical legal research are available. A common quantitative approach towards analysing judicial decision-making is to establish, across a large body of cases, a statistical correlation between judicial attitudes towards policy or doctrine and decisions made (Hanretty, 2012). However, although attitudinal studies might assist in indicating a propensity among the judiciary to behave in a certain way, by themselves they do not fully evidence 'the values, ideas and interests underlying legal arguments' (Kalimo et al., 2018, 287) or how the language of law is used 'to construct problems and frame solutions' (288). To arrive at finer-tuned analysis of judicial decision-making, therefore, discourse analysis offers an alternative technique through which to interrogate the text of judgments according to preselected criteria connected to the research question being asked.

Discourse analysis is a broad field and comprises 'a cluster of methodologies' rather than one uniform technique (Kalimo et al., 2018, 286), with one variant being the content analysis method explored in this chapter. Content analysis is a form of discourse analysis that comprehensively and systematically analyses the content of a sample of documents, in our case judicial decisions, and records consistent or inconsistent features (Murchison and Jochelson, 2015). Content analysis studies are used to bring a degree of scientific rigour to legal scholarship, creating what has been termed 'a distinctively legal form of empiricism' (Hall and Wright, 2008, 64). Given their familiarity with legal tools of argumentation, legal and socio-legal scholars are well equipped to employ this social science technique.

In North American legal scholarship in particular, the diversity of studies using the method demonstrates its utility. For example, systematic methods have been deployed to capture whether the tools of judicial argumentation indicate activism or restraint on the part of the bench (Canon, 1982, Cohn and Kremnitzer, 2005, Jochelson et al., 2012, Riddell, 2016). Content analysis has also been used to record empirically the prevalence of particular canons of statutory interpretation (Krishnakumar, 2017) and the prevalence of originalist interpretative methods in the US Supreme Court (Rosenthal, 2019). Additionally, there exist a number of studies that use content analysis to shed light on strategies employed in, and the influences upon, judicial decision-making more generally (Muttart, 2007). These assess judicial argumentation in relation to a variety of subject-specific areas, such as the use of the death penalty, negligence, labour law, administrative law, antitrust law, and promissory estoppel (Hall and Wright, 2008). The method's use has 'accelerated' since the 1990s, and such studies are now 'widespread' in the US legal academy (Hall and Wright, 2008, 70).

In the UK, socio-legal empirical methods are also commonly adopted. For example, in response to increasing government rhetoric that the courts were flooded with judicial review claims, Bondy et al. (2002) responded with a comprehensive empirical account of the nature of judicial review claims, their outcomes, and the consequences of such findings. Similarly, in a number of specialisms within legal academia, there have been empirical studies assessing the impact of systemic changes to the judicial system across various sectors (Arrowsmith and Craven, 2016, Burton, 2018).[2] More generally, there is now a steady use of empirical legal research across UK legal academia (Mitchell and MacKay, 2011, Opeskin, 2015, Lewis, 2017).[3] The turn to empiricism provides all-important overarching context to the debates to be had about both doctrine and the legal system generally. Content analysis is, however, a subtly different subset within such empirical legal scholarship. Although some basic or general empirical data may well be recorded as part of this method, within it there is a greater focus on finely reading an entire set of documents, usually judgments, in order to draw conclusions about patterns in legal reasoning. Case coding in content analyses goes further than recording basic facts, as it requires an appraisal of the 'substance of judicial reasoning as expressed through the legal and factual content of written opinions' (Hall and Wright, 2008, 72–73). So far, in the UK there have been surprisingly few studies engaging in this kind of systematic documentary analysis (Favale et al., 2016, Goudkamp and Katsampouka, 2018, Kalimo et al., 2018).[4]

Lessons from our experience

Our project

The content analysis study looked at in this chapter was one part of a larger project funded by the Nuffield Foundation that explored various mechanisms for monitoring decision-making quality in the ombudsector.[5] Ongoing restructuring in the civil justice system has led to ever more reliance being placed on ombudschemes to resolve disputes. In turn, these developments have increased the potential for critical scrutiny and the need for processes that provide reassurance. The research project was aimed at interrogating those processes

---

2 Arrowsmith and Craven used questionnaires and interviews to isolate factors influencing low levels of supplier-complaint litigation in respect of EU public procurement law in the UK. Burton conducted interviews and observations to reveal the impact on legal advice of the shift to telephone-services–only social welfare legal aid.

3 By way of example, Mitchell and MacKay recorded basic features concerning convictions for involuntary manslaughter; Opeskin pursued an international comparative empirical assessment of tenure practices of three different 'top-level' courts; and Lewis outlined tactics in personal injury litigation drawn from structured interviews with practitioners.

4 Favale, Kretschmer, and Torremans trace patterns of legal reasoning in the CJEU towards copyright and database right cases. Goudkamp and Katsampouka conducted a systematic study of 146 claims for punitive damages, including classifying claims according to the *Rookes* set of categories of punitive claims. Kalimo, Meyer, and Mylly's discourse analysis studies copyright cases in the CJEU.

5 For more details, see www.sheffield.ac.uk/law/research/directory/ombudsman-1.765390

designed to deliver that reassurance, such as internal review, transparency initiatives, and, most relevant to this chapter, judicial oversight.

The ombudsman design and role make its relationship with the court an interesting prism through which to view the nature of judicial decision-making, and explore the strategies that judges deploy in resolving cases about them. Adjudicating over administrative discretion as defined through ambiguously worded powers is a generic challenge for the judge in administrative law, which is managed through the adoption of various flexible interpretation techniques and legal doctrine. The ombudsector illustrates this challenge well, as the office is commonly a statutory one deliberately provided with significant autonomous and wide-ranging discretionary powers to deliver a particular form of justice. In ombudsman litigation, as in other areas of administrative law, this dynamic creates a sizeable scope for the judiciary to wield its decision-making in either a 'thick', controlling manner or 'thinly' and with considerable constraint and deference towards the administrative body under review.

The role and importance of judicial review in providing control over administrative bodies is a matter of significant debate, but there have been very few systematic studies of how the judiciary performs its functions in this area of law. In tackling this deficit, this study used a content analysis methodology to interrogate how judges make decisions, upon what grounds, and using which strategies. We were particularly interested in the role judicial review plays in maintaining or distilling service standards into ombudschemes. The technique was applied to a complete cache of case law relating to the ombudsman in the UK, thus providing a full, rather than selective, picture of targeted aspects of judicial decision-making.

This ambition to analyse more comprehensively the content of judicial decisions is the primary rationale for the content analysis method (Murchison and Jochelson, 2015). Through content analysis, 'a scholar collects a set of documents, such as judicial opinions on a particular subject, and systematically reads them, recording consistent features of each and drawing inferences about their use and meaning' (Hall and Wright, 2008, 64). In other words, a fine-grained reading of judgments is attempted to establish the underlying factors used to justify a decision.

In our study, this approach entailed reading cases and recording and coding targeted aspects of the decisions made. The most thorough and recent doctrinal research shows that judicial oversight of the ombudsector exhibits high degrees of deference to the authority of the original decision-maker, a few outliers notwithstanding (Kirkham and Allt, 2016). This study sought to test this claim through a more robust empirical approach, by capturing the approach of courts at all stages of the judicial hierarchy in judicial review. If we take judicial restraint at the basic level to mean that, empirically, there are very few instances where the courts intervene with a decision conducted by an ombudsman, what does this mean for the function of judicial review? What role does judicial review have in respect of the ombudsector? By employing a content analysis methodology, we were able to analyse outcomes, types of grounds used, and judicial statements on the legal framework of operation for ombudschemes. Asking such questions in a systematic manner shed light on the role that judicial review plays vis-à-vis the ombudsector.

In order to frame our approach to coding design, we drew upon previous research aimed at isolating factors that indicate judicial activism or restraint. This approach went some way to answering our first research question (whether the bench adopts a policy of deference towards the ombudsector), but also acted as a useful framework to design a coding system that would comprehensively capture the modes of judicial reasoning employed. We hypothesised that judicial activism may be indicated by a judgment that:

- *Readily circumvents 'threshold' hurdles*: where the court is willing to wield its discretion to get around barriers to hearing the case, such as out-of-time applications;
- *Quashes or supersedes the decision of a public authority, or majoritarianism*: where policies or, for our purposes, the decisions of schemes adopted through the democratic process are rendered invalid;
- *Employs non-traditional approaches to legislative interpretation, or interpretive fidelity*: the degree to which legislation is interpreted beyond its 'ordinary meaning';
- *Departs from precedent, also known as interpretive stability*: the degree to which earlier court decisions or interpretations have been departed from;
- *Reliance on substantive, rather than procedural, judicial reasoning*: greater readiness to rely upon substantive grounds, such as irrationality, over procedural grounds;
- *Develops the common law*: the tendency to flesh out, or even create, an area of law, particularly in relation to the restrictions and obligations upon a public authority (Cohn and Kremnitzer, 2005, Dickson, 2015, Canon, 1983, Kmiec, 2004).[6]

The general tenor of these indicators formed the basis for our approach to designing coding to capture the decision-making style of the bench in navigating oversight of ombudschemes. In terms of case selection, a number of challenges and choices were taken away from us by virtue of our selection of the discrete area of ombudsman case law. As well as raising a number of bespoke points of analysis connecting to the ombudsman institution, this choice of research focus offered the advantage of avoiding the need for sampling, which is required where the field of study deployed is too wide. Thus, as there were only 107 cases, the full data set was manageable, given that the case range needed to study comprehensively one well-defined subset of cases is relatively limited.

The purpose of the content analysis method is to provide a systematic way in which empirically to record or test the questions that the study is designed to answer, or the position of 'conventional' scholarship that the researcher wishes either to prove or refute. The code system focuses the attention of the researcher while they read the cases (Hall and Wright, 2008). In order to address our research questions, our coding was required to record:

- the core outcomes of ombudsman judicial reviews, appeals, and permission hearings;
- the grounds of review used by the judiciary to resolve cases;
- the judicial strategies deployed in decision-making.

Core outcomes

These coding questions involved recording basic facts about the cases in the data set and required little by way of interpretation. Non-coded fields entailed recording: the case name, the date of the case, and the interested party. Coded fields involved recording the type of

---

6 This list was adapted from, and influenced by, these previous studies, taking into account relevance for the purpose of our research question. Some of these studies used additional categories to ours, but we either considered that they were not appropriate for a study of the courts in the UK, or that different aspects could be captured under the broader headings we provided, or through our mixed methods approach of combining content analysis with doctrinal analysis.

claimant; the court; whether the parties had representation; whether the decision was judicial review, appeal, or permission; what stage of the ombudsman process was being challenged; whether permission to apply was granted; why permission was not granted; the outcome of judicial review; and the remedy.

Grounds of review

The exercise of coding the basis upon which judges quash ombudsman decisions required some consideration of methods for choosing a taxonomy of administrative law. As a starting point, we relied upon Nason's (2016) study of 482 cases heard in the Administrative Court during two periods, from 1 January 2013 to 31 July 2013, and from 1 January 2015 to 31 July 2015. Instead of applying a prescribed taxonomy, Nason applied a method of constructive interpretation to 'look from the bottom up and peel off a taxonomy of grounds by considering the legal arguments advanced and reasons for deciding in a sample of cases' (2016, 246). In other words, she interrogated the grounds that the Administrative Court actually used in deciding cases, and from that derived a workable taxonomy. As Nason's method most approximated our own, we used her taxonomy as a starting template for our study. Mirroring the best-practice guidance on designing coding, as outlined above, we refined and added to Nason's categories by subjecting them to a pilot test, which led to an adaptation of the coding scheme in order to make it more appropriate for the research questions being asked and more closely aligned to the detail of case law on the ombudsman. We further mirrored Nason's approach by tweaking categories based upon the actual reasons and language advanced by the court. Table 24.1 summarises the coding scheme developed. A full defence and description of the coding scheme can be found on the web page of the research project.[7]

Modes of judicial reasoning

Overlaying the doctrinal grounds deployed in administrative law cases, our study sought to examine the modes of judicial reasoning adopted within judgments. The most relevant prior content analysis study for this purpose is that conducted into the decision-making of the Court of Justice of the EU (CJEU) on copyright law by Favale et al. (2016). Through coding, Favale et al. capture two sources of information: the extent to which the CJEU used precedent in its decision-making and the interpretive techniques it used to apply legislation within its decisions. Both questions we explored in this study through the coding scheme outlined in Table 24.2.

Overall, the categories of coding that we deployed strived to record interim conclusions on the way judicial reasoning, and decision-making strategy, has been exercised in the case law, and whether it displays any obvious indicators of activism.

The value of recording the types of case law relied upon allowed a picture to be painted about the approach of the bench towards jurisprudence relating to the ombudsman sector. Is it treated rather simply as a public authority capable of judicial review, with reliance on general administrative law? Is jurisprudence relating only to the ombudsector developing? Does this jurisprudence capture the entire sector, or are different approaches advocated for each specific scheme? Kirkham and Allt have found, through traditional doctrinal analysis, that

---

7 www.sheffield.ac.uk/polopoly_fs/1.792260!/file/researchstudy2018.pdf

Table 24.1 Coding scheme for the grounds used in ombudsman case law

1. Ordinary common law statutory interpretation	2. Mistake	3. Discretionary impropriety	4. Quality of decision
1.1 Did the ombudsman act within their statutorily delegated power/juris-diction (including abuse of discretion) 1.2 Did the ombudsman misinterpret statute/law	2.1 Error of fact 2.2 Mistaken	3.1 Relevant/irrelevant considerations 3.2 Failure to exercise discretion 3.3 Fettering discretion	4.1 No reasons given 4.2 Inadequate reasons given 4.3 Incorrect remedy 4.4 Irrational 4.5 Incorrect application of fair and reasonable test

5. Procedural impropriety		6. Significant claims based on common law constitutional values, rights, or allocation of powers	7. Breach of ECHR
5.1 Unfair hearing 5.2 Lack of hearing 5.3 Bias 5.4 Independence 5.5 Undue delay	5.6 Inadequate notice 5.7 Refusal to review decision 5.8 Right to reply 5.9 Bad service 5.10 Legitimate expectation 5.11 Duty to disclose	6.1 Breach of fundamental constitutional values (e.g. democracy, dignity, access to justice, judicial independence, rule of law) 6.2 Turns upon allocation of powers between particular institutions of the state (abuse of power)	

there is a 'unified interpretation of the powers of ombudsman schemes across the sector' (2016, 211). This coding empirically tested that conclusion.

In relation to statutory interpretation, generally, instances of the last category, *contextual*, would indicate a greater degree of 'activism' on the part of the court, for it gives the bench considerable space in their interpretations and leaves the court open to criticism over the wielding of this interpretive power. Such decision-making strategy may be applied by fleshing out the contours of the obligations upon the ombudsman to conform to a particular standard on judicial review grounds, or it may involve taking a contextual or purposive approach to the statutory parameters of the ombudsman's powers and obliga-tions. Where such initial findings were made, we then fact-checked them through a more doctrinal reading of the judgment. The coding also records instances where the court has given authoritative statements on the law, and on good practice, relating to the ombudsec-tor. Statements on the law may take the form of conclusive interpretations of the ombuds-man's power, as outlined by its constitutive legislation. It can also be witnessed through common law development of the ombudsman's obligations on various review grounds, for example by fleshing out to what extent the ombudsman is required to comply with the duty to give reasons. Statements on good practice, or *obiter dicta*, may not carry the same authoritative weight, but take a more speculative tone about the standards that the ombudsman may be expected to reach. Such coding gave an indication of the role or function of judicial review in respect of ombudschemes. If there was evidence of statements of law or practice, the coding acted as a flag in order for us to return to the case to give it a more doctrinal reading.

Overall, our findings were that, in ombudsman case law, the general picture is one of deference. In most instances, ombudsman case law is best characterised as providing a 'safety valve' for managing dissatisfied users of ombudsman services and applying thin interpretations to the rule of law. However, our study also demonstrates that there is a significant strand of ombudsman case law in which thicker interpretations of the rule of law are developed. We found, however, that this limited tendency towards what some might describe as 'activist' decision-making is generally concentrated around probing the quality of reasoning in ombudsman decision-making and encouraging higher standards in operational practice, areas that match traditional judicially claimed expertise. Further, judicial messages are more likely to be delivered through subtle dicta and in cases upholding ombudsman decisions, than in those quashing ombudsman decisions.

Lessons learned

We encountered a series of challenges and learned a number of lessons in the practical application of our coding scheme. In designing the methodology, we spent many hours carefully delineating judicial review grounds for coding. It is inevitable that some measure of ambiguity will remain in how coding categories should apply to particular cases. Often, there is no obvious right way to resolve these judgement calls, but such ambiguity is not disabling as long as coders are reasonably consistent in how they apply coding categories across a range of cases (Hall and Wright, 2008). In our study, to establish 'reasonable consistency' in application, a few ground rules were applied. First, in the event of ambiguity, either because of the nature of the facts or because of an apparent vagueness in the judge's application of the law to the facts, to decide in which category to code a judgment we followed Nason's constructivist example. In other words, we chose to be true to the wording of the judgment, rather than favouring our own intuition about the dividing line between the two grounds (which is inherently more subjective). Second, we captured all the arguments that were considered in depth within the judgment, noting those that were successful and those that were not. This allowed us to avoid reliance upon multiple and potentially repetitive grounds that may have been put forward by the claimant, and to focus only on the way in which they were demarcated by the court. Where the wording of the judge was directly synonymous with one of the above grounds, it would be recorded expressly. For example, the right to make representations obviously correlates to the right of reply. Third, where there were two separate submissions, both of which relied upon the same ground, these were recorded as two separate grounds. Where a case concerned multiple respondents, including an ombudsman, the only grounds recorded would be those that relate to the ombudsman. Finally, to add confidence to the results, we both coded a pilot set of cases separately. On comparison, the differences in the coding of the grounds deployed by the judiciary were extremely small and were resolvable by way of subsequent discussion. In practice, many other cases were also double-read at the subsequent analysis stage.

Table 24.2 Coding scheme for recording modes of judicial reasoning deployed in ombudsman case law

Cases cited	Case law interpretation	Statutory interpretation
1. General legal principle case law (non–ombudsman) only	1. Confirm case law	1. Literal
2. Ombudscheme-specific case law only	2. Distinguish	2. Textual
3. Other ombudsman case law only	3. Reject/reverse	3. Contextual
4. 1 + 2		
5. 1 + 2 + 3		
6. 1 + 3		
7. 2 + 3		

Judicial strategy	Any authoritative judicial statements	
1. Judicial guidance with finding against ombudsman	1. Law	
2. Judicial guidance without finding against ombudsman	2. Good practice	

Painstaking care was therefore taken to ensure that exact judicial review grounds were recorded in a manner as consistent and as independently reproducible as possible. When we came to analysing the data, however, it became apparent that the level of detail that we had entered into in our coding exercise was unnecessary. What was most interesting about the grounds being recorded was their nature rather than the detail – that is, whether the matter turned on a matter of statutory interpretation, or on the substance of the decision that was being reviewed, or on a flaw in the process by which the decision was made. The analysis therefore did not necessarily require such specific demarcations of, for instance, the form of procedural fairness being considered, such as between 'lack of hearing' or 'fair hearing'. Although this latter realisation does not undermine the set of rules we established to ensure that the findings could broadly be reproduced by another coder, it nonetheless would have sped up the data gathering process had we adopted a simpler coding scheme.

The above example relates to a situation whereby we realised we had coded in too much detail. Upon reaching the point where we analysed our findings, we faced a different problem. Here, we realised that, in relation to coding on the type of statutory interpretation, we had provided too little detail. It was only upon reaching the data analysis stage of the study that we realised that, between us, we had inconsistently recorded the types of statutory interpretation. Whereas Elizabeth left out instances where it appeared that there had been no real attempt at an interpretive exercise, Richard recorded such instances as 'literal'. This difference in approach required us to return to all the data, inputting an extra code, that of 'no interpretation approach applied'. This discrepancy highlights the importance of ensuring that coding methods and operational definitions are tightly defined, with clear coder training prior to commencement of the study. It also sheds light on the need to test intercoder reliability, particularly in larger content analysis studies (Johnson, 1987).

The above hiccups hint at the presence of an internal researcher bias in our approach to designing the coding. Given that we are both administrative lawyers, it follows that we naturally gravitated towards focusing more heavily upon the role of 'grounds' in judicial decision-making. This highlights the importance of revisiting the coding exercise and, in particular, cross-checking a portion of each researcher's findings, in order to identify and iron out deviation in the application of the codes.

More generally, the identification of these issues demonstrates that content analysis studies do raise significant 'methodological concerns' (Jochelson et al., 2012, 191). Indeed, Muttart, in his SSRN published paper, reveals that his article 'was rejected for such reasons' (2011, 29). A key challenge with some of the more ambitious models is the method's manageability (Canon, 1983, Muttart, 2011). On a practical level, the complexity of the method can risk over-burdening the researcher, and large-scale studies require considerable background support and funding. More fundamentally, if the method is overloaded with research questions, it comes to rely upon multiple points of input judgements being applied to the analysed text and requires a process of relative weighting of the different parameters being tested (Cohn and Kremnitzer, 2005). Some of those judgement calls may be relatively straightforward (e.g. what the result of the case was). Others, though, will require technical resolution (e.g. what weight to give dissenting judgments). Such resolution may be rationally explainable, but the more criteria deployed, the more the numbers of judgement calls being made will increase, creating entry points for subjectivity within the research. This is by no means a fatal problem – empirical research in the social sciences often has to face such dilemmas – but, where the variables are numerous, then the ability of the researcher to be clear about the choices being made is reduced. In turn, the sceptic's ability to offer differing interpretations of the final results will also increase. Riddell's response to Murchison and Jochelson's research demonstrates this (Riddell, 2016).

Given these methodological challenges, we posit that the argument for systematic empirical scholarship is primarily a supportive one, as the method has weaknesses that render it incomplete as a tool to explain in full the nature of judicial reasoning. Any endeavour to reduce the meaning of a large body of cases to a uniform system of coding will always risk losing the full subtleties and nuances upon which a judicial decision is balanced. However, the method is of value in order to offset the various shortcomings of conventional legal scholarship. For example, in relation to the research questions in our study, it must be noted from the outset that judicial activism 'cannot be synonymous with merely exercising judicial review' (Kmiec, 2004, 1464). By this, we mean that it cannot be taken that any instance of a finding against a decision-making authority, in this case an ombudsman, is evidence of judicial activism. There is, then, a need to blend the coding approach with a more doctrinal reading of the cases, which inevitably entails an exercise of judgement on the part of the analyser. The coding we used, therefore, registers the grounds and the judicial tools of argumentation pursued in judicial review, which in turn will reveal more context to the question of how interventionist the courts are in relation to the ombudsector.

The value of the method

Content analysis studies have rich potential in offering a complementary role to broader doctrinal studies aimed at making sense of judicial practice. In particular, systematic studies can provide an objective means by which to critique conventional and alternative positions and identify 'anomalies which may escape the naked eye' (Tyree, 1981, 23). In this regard empirical research has a powerful role in forcing us to consider revising our theories in the face of evidence that contradicts pre-held positions or isolating incorrectly decided cases.

There is no question that doctrinal legal scholarship is highly adept at interrogating judicial reasoning and the legal grounds employed in leading cases; there exists a substantial literature on the topic. There is also a very active theoretical debate on the legitimate approaches that the judiciary should employ. In public law, for example, there are significant differences of viewpoint, based upon underlying principle, as to the extent to and manner in which the judiciary should exercise restraint when deciding legal disputes (King, 2008). Within this debate, forceful claims about the practice of the judiciary are sometimes made. For instance, it has been suggested that there is an increasing tendency for the judiciary to rule upon matters that would be better left to the political branches of the state, implying that the judiciary is prone to overreach (Ekins and Forsyth, 2015).

The difficulty is that, in understanding the import of these debates, empirical conclusions are often drawn from a narrow methodological approach based upon selected high-profile cases, rather than a more widespread systematic empirical analysis of how the judiciary rationalises its decision-making function. The absence of an offsetting field of systematic empirical analysis exposes the legal discipline to several risks. First, it is possible that a wider understanding of judicial decision-making is warped by the selective focus of legal commentators. Some cases, particularly strong precedent-setting cases, might deserve enhanced attention, but individual cases may be explainable as one-off instances of a certain judicial strategy being employed and do not by themselves demonstrate the existence of a systematic practice. A linked concern is the potential for abstract arguments about the law to become informed and driven more by conscious or unconscious biases than by the real practice of the law. In studies that do not offer a systematic or holistic overview of court practice, it is also plausible that cases that do not fit the argued-for pattern are deliberately excluded (Chilton and Posner, 2015). A further problem in not analysing legal decision-making systematically is that, without the full evidence being tested, it is difficult to ascertain whether or not accounts of the law represent an accurate portrayal of practice, or whether they are being shaped by selective, and skilfully argued, references to case law. Even with extensive supporting citation, the claims made in doctrinal scholarship are supported by variable theoretical preferences, and the extent of the supporting evidence is 'unclear or difficult for others to probe or falsify' (Baude et al., 2017, 37). Without an agreed method to distinguish between rival interpretations of case law, readers might be tempted to rely in part on the author's reputation as a proxy for accuracy (Baude et al., 2017).

The value of the content analysis method, then, is its capability to test more comprehensively assumptions that exist in doctrinal legal scholarship about the practical application of the law. Although such assumptions can often be confirmed or disputed through other kinds of empirical research, content analysis provides a method that interweaves doctrinal tools of legal scholarship into the exercise, thereby ensuring that the study captures nuances that purely numerical appraisals may overlook. It therefore better fits the 'toolkit' that legal scholars have acquired through years of doctrinal legal study by importing legal methods into an empirical exercise, rather than drawing on methods and approaches that have been developed in other fields.

Content analysis is also a valuable mechanism for addressing the aforementioned risks that may come with doctrinal study. Indeed, it is a common claim, one not just confined to socio-legal circles (Besbris and Khan, 2017), that academic commentary on the law would benefit from a more rigorous approach towards evidencing doctrinal claims (Baude et al., 2017). Rather than seeking meaning of the law through a focus on a few isolated lead cases, the approach advocated through content analysis is to study the application of the law by the courts through a study of an entire body of decided cases. The benefit of doing so is demonstrated by a number of key examples in existing content analyses. For example, one recent study claims to have debunked several prevalent assumptions about the manner in which the judiciary deploy substantive canons, including the assumption that the canons were used to displace legislative preferences with those of the judiciary (Krishnakumar, 2017). Another study of the controversial private law remedy of punitive damages found that their use in practice was 'contrary to textbook gospel' (Goudkamp and Katsampouka, 2018, 92). More studies of this kind would therefore make an important contribution to the field. Such studies allow doctrinal claims about the status and practice of the law, many implications of which are discussed, to be tested. The sheer variety of the method's use in North American legal scholarship demonstrates just how far-reaching its potential utility is. This approach – under-used in the UK – has a function in any corner of the legal academy.

Recommended reading

Baude, W., Chilton, A. and Malani, A. 2017. Making Doctrinal Work More Rigorous: Lessons from Systematic Reviews. *University of Chicago Law Review*, 84(1), pp. 37–58.

Cohn, M. and Kremnitzer, M. 2005. Judicial Activism: A Multi-Dimensional Model. *Canadian Journal of Law and Jurisprudence*, 18(2), pp. 333–356.

Favale, M., Kretschmer, M. and Torremans, P. 2016. Is There an EU Copyright Jurisprudence? An Empirical Analysis of the Workings of the European Court of Justice. *Modern Law Review*, 79(1), pp. 31–75.

Hall, M. and Wright, R. 2008. Systematic Content Analysis of Judicial Decisions. *California Law Review*, 96(1), pp. 63–122.

Rosenthal, L. (2019). An Empirical Inquiry into the Use of Originalism: Fourth Amendment Jurisprudence During the Career of Justice Scalia. *Hastings Law Journal*, 70(1), pp. 79–169.

References

Arrowsmith, S. and Craven, R. 2016. Public Procurement and Access to Justice: A Legal and Empirical Study of the UK System. *Public Procurement Law Review*, 6, pp. 227–252.

Baude, W., Chilton, A. and Malani, A. 2017. Making Doctrinal Work More Rigorous: Lessons from Systematic Reviews. *University of Chicago Law Review*, 84(1), pp. 37–58.

Besbris, M. and Khan, S. 2017. Less Theory. More Description. *Sociological Theory*, 35(2), pp. 147–153.

Bondy, V., Platt, L. and Sunkin, M. 2002. *The Value and Effects of Judicial Review: The Nature of Claims, their Outcomes and Consequences*. Public Law Project, available from: http://publiclawproject.org.uk/wp-content/uploads/data/resources/210/Value-and-Effects-of-Judicial-Review.pdf (accessed 16 July 2018).

Burton, M. 2018. Justice on the Line? A Comparison of Telephone and Face-to-Face Advice in Social Welfare Legal Aid. *Journal of Social Welfare and Family Law*, 40(2), pp. 195–215.

Canon, B.C. 1982. A Framework for the Analysis of Judicial Activism. In: Halpern, S.C. and Lamb, C. M. eds., *Supreme Court Activism and Restraint*. Lanham, MD: Lexington Books, pp. 385–419.

Canon, B.C. 1983. Defining the Dimensions of Judicial Activism. *Judicature*, 66(6), pp. 236–247.

Chilton, A.S. and Posner, E.A. 2015. An Empirical Study of Political Bias in Legal Scholarship. *Journal of Legal Studies*, 44(2), pp. 277–314.

Cohn, M. and Kremnitzer, M. 2005. Judicial Activism: A Multi-Dimensional Model. *Canadian Journal of Law and Jurisprudence*, 18(2), pp. 333–356.

Dickson, B. 2015. Activism and Restraint within the UK Supreme Court. *European Journal of Current Legal Issues*, 2(1), available from: http://webjcli.org/article/view/399/515

Ekins, R. and Forsyth, C. 2015. *Judging the Public Interest: The Rule of Law vs the Rule of Courts*. Policy Exchange, available from: https://policyexchange.org.uk/wp-content/uploads/2016/09/judging-the-public-interest.pdf (accessed 16 July 2018).

Favale, M., Kretschmer, M. and Torremans, P. 2016. Is There an EU Copyright Jurisprudence? An Empirical Analysis of the Workings of the European Court of Justice. *Modern Law Review*, 79(1), pp. 31–75.

Goudkamp, J. and Katsampouka, E. 2018. An Empirical Study of Punitive Damages. *Oxford Journal of Legal Studies*, 38(1), pp. 90–122.

Hall, M. and Wright, R. 2008. Systematic Content Analysis of Judicial Decisions. *California Law Review*, 96(1), pp. 63–122.

Hanretty, C. 2012. The Decisions and Ideal Points of British Law Lords. *British Journal of Political Science*, 43(3), pp. 703–716.

Jochelson, R., Weinrath, M. and Murchison, M. 2012. Searching and Seizing after 9/11: Developing and Applying Empirical Methodology to Measure Judicial Output in the Supreme Court's Section 8 Jurisprudence. *Dalhousie Law Review*, 35(1), pp. 179–213.

Johnson, C.A. 1987. Content-Analytic Techniques and Judicial Research. *American Politics Quarterly*, 15(1), pp. 169–197.

Kallimo, H., Moyer, T. and Mylly, T. 2018. Of Values and Legitimacy – Discourse Analytical Insights on the Copyright Case Law of the Court of Justice of the European Union. *Modern Law Review*, 81(2), pp. 282–307.

King, J. 2008. Institutional Approaches to Judicial Restraint. *Oxford Journal of Legal Studies*, 28(3), pp. 409–441.

Kirkham, R. and Allt, A. 2016. Making sense of the case law on Ombudsman Schemes. *Journal of Social Welfare and Family Law*, 38(2), pp. 211–227.

Kmiec, K. 2004. The Origin and Current Meanings of Judicial Activism. *California Law Review*, 92(5), pp. 1441–1478.

Krishnakumar, A.S. 2017. Reconsidering Substantive Canons. *University of Chicago Law Review*, 84(2), pp. 825–908.

Lewis, R. 2017. Tort Tactics: An Empirical Study of Personal Injury Strategies. *Legal Studies*, 37(1), pp. 162–185.

Mitchell, B. and MacKay, R. 2011. Investigating Involuntary Manslaughter: An Empirical Study of 127 Cases. *Oxford Journal of Legal Studies*, 31(1), pp. 165–192.

Murchison, M. and Jochelson, R. 2015. Canadian Exclusion of Evidence Under Section 24(2) of the Charter: An Empirical Model of Judicial Discourse. *Canadian Journal of Criminology and Criminal Justice*, 57(1), pp. 115–154.

Muttart, D. 2007. *The Empirical Gap in Jurisprudence: A Comprehensive Study of the Supreme Court of Canada*. Toronto: University of Toronto Press.

Muttart, D. 2011. One Step Forward, One Step Back: Measuring Activism in the Supreme Court of Canada. Available from: http://dx.doi.org/10.2139/ssrn.1470709 (accessed 16 July 2018).

Nason, S. 2016. *Reconstructing Judicial Review*. Oxford: Hart.

Opeskin, B. 2015. Models of Judicial Tenure: Reconsidering Life Limits, Age Limits and Term Limits for Judges. *Oxford Journal of Legal Studies*, 3(4), pp. 627–663.

Riddell, T. 2016. Measuring Activism and Restraint: An Alternative Perspective on the Supreme Court of Canada's Exclusion of Evidence Decisions under Section 24(2) of the Charter. *Canadian Journal of Criminology and Criminal Justice*, 5(1), pp. 87–111.

Rosenthal, L. 2019. An Empirical Inquiry into the Use of Originalism: Fourth Amendment Jurisprudence During the Career of Justice Scalia. *Hastings Law Journal*, 70(1), pp. 75–169.

Tyree, A. 1981. Fact Content Analysis of Case Law: Methods and Limitations. *Jurimetrics*, 22(1), pp. 1–33.

25

INTELLECTUAL PROPERTY, BIOTECHNOLOGY AND PROCESS TRACING

Applying political research methods to legal study

Benjamin Farrand

Introduction: studying the politics of law-making

The study of biotechnology in the social sciences often falls into discrete disciplinary categories, whether it is in the form of doctrinal legal study of biotechnological inventions in patent law (Bonadio 2012), the consideration of social implications of these inventions in bioethics (Savulescu 2009), or the analysis of interest group interventions in areas of controversy such as genetically modified organisms and agriculture in politics and public policy (Skogstad 2003). In my research, I attempt to bring these various fields together in interdisciplinary analysis of what could broadly be called biotechnology regulation. Whereas doctrinal study of biotechnology patenting tends to focus on questions of what 'is' or 'ought' to be patented, or compares approaches under different regimes, it does so in a way that focuses very much on textual analysis of legislation and legal decisions. Similarly, bioethics is more akin to a philosophical perspective on the 'ought' of biotechnology patenting (where it considers patents at all, as opposed to macro-level discussions of the morality or ethics of biotechnology research or application), comprising a more normative approach to the study of emerging technologies. Finally, public policy approaches have tended towards the study of the role of different stakeholders in making their voices heard on controversial biotechnological subject matter. My research is centred at a nexus between these approaches, seeking to better understand how different ideas, norms or beliefs (relating to the 'bioethics' dimension of this field of study) can influence legislative bodies or courts by focusing on how actors are able to change the approaches or perspectives of these bodies in areas considered controversial (the public policy dimension), resulting in specific legal outcomes (the legal dimension). A different way of putting this is that my research in the field of biotechnology seeks to better understand or explain legal change in areas of controversy, exploring the ways in which a multitude of different law and policy actors are able to take their vision of what law 'ought' to be and effectively make it what law 'is'. In order to do this, however, it is necessary to answer these questions in a coherent way, using an appropriate theoretical and methodological approach tailored to explaining change.

Process tracing: explaining legal change

This chapter considers the application of a change-explaining methodology, process tracing, to a project that explored the history of the patentabilty of inventions derived from human embryonic stem cell (hESC) research in the systems of the EU and China (Farrand 2016). Process tracing 'attempts to identify the intervening causal process [...] between an independent variable and the outcome of the dependent variable' (George & Bennett 2005: 6) by providing an analysis of evidence of 'processes, sequences and conjunctures of events within a case for the purpose of either developing or testing hypotheses about causal mechanisms that might causally explain the case' (Bennett & Checkel 2014: 7). To put it another way, process tracing is a method used to analyse the intermediate steps between an action and an outcome that may help us to explain or understand how a particular outcome was reached. In the context of legal study, process tracing as used in this project makes its most valuable contribution in providing a rigorous methodology for uncovering the processes by which particular norms, beliefs, ideas or ideological positions produce concrete legal results. Socio-legal scholars can apply this approach to a range of different issues or questions, going beyond purely biotechnological research. Hypothetical examples of how this could be used include: a family lawyer seeking to explore how a change in government may result in a shift in discourses concerning how a family is constituted, and how this may impact upon legislative initiatives in fields such as equal marriage or gender recognition; a contract lawyer who wants to understand how hegemonic ideas concerning market freedoms represented in contemporary capitalism shape understandings of bargaining power and privity of contract represented in legislation; or an EU lawyer working to identify how Euroscepticism as a phenomenon works to facilitate opt-outs from particular fields of EU activity such as justice and home affairs. Process tracing can of course go beyond the ideational – socio-legal scholars of a more positivist bent could instead be interested in, for example, how decision-making in House of Commons committees may influence the content or wording of Acts of Parliament, or how the wording used by a judge in a decision is used to distinguish a new set of circumstances from an existing precedent in an interesting or controversial case, so as to achieve (and, indeed, justify) a preferred outcome. In this way, process tracing can be applied to a wealth of different issues in socio-legal analysis; it is not tied to any particular subject matter of disciplinary perspective, but can be used to interrogate change in a range of different areas of law, focusing on very different institutions in very different contexts, as explored further in the section of this chapter on my research on biotechnology patenting.

These causal mechanisms can be unobservable physical, social or psychological processes through which actors are able to effect change in other entities, such as individuals or organisations, whether in terms of attitudes, behaviours or actions, until another intervening causal mechanism acts upon them (George & Bennett 2005: 37). This means that it goes beyond discourse analysis as a methodological tool, or indeed doctrinal legal analysis, insofar as it seeks to provide not a descriptive account of 'A happened, then B', but rather 'A led to change/result B, because of X'. Process tracing seeks to explore the role of X in more detail, identifying the relationships between it and A and B, as well as considering why X is a more convincing explanation than Y. It is at its most useful when seeking to explain or understand a particularly interesting, unusual or puzzling outcome, or one that appears, on the surface at least, to be counter-intuitive. In terms of theoretical approach, according to Beach and Pedersen, the ontology of process tracing is *deterministic*, insofar as it relates to the identification of necessary and sufficient causes in individual cases, and *mechanistic*, in that the focus of analysis is upon causal mechanisms that explain outcomes (2012: 27–28). Bennett and Checkel recommend a three-part best practice standard, based in meta-theory, context and method (2014: 21). Meta-theoretically, the theories used to explain the function of these mechanisms must be ontologically consistent with a mechanism-based understanding of social reality, requiring researchers to consider carefully the hypothesised causal mechanism and underlying theoretical framework (2014: 23). Contextually, researchers should place the phenomenon in its wider context with a clearly stated hypothetical causal process (2014: 21), indicating the importance of conceptual clarity. Methodologically, the work should take into account the issue of 'equifinality' – the possibility that multiple paths may result in the same outcome, and that these alternative explanations should also be considered in order to determine whether they or the hypothesised mechanism are more likely to have resulted in the observed effect (George & Bennett 2005: 153–160; Bennett & Checkel 2014: 20).

Brady, Collier and Seawright state that an essential characteristic of process tracing is making causal process observations, defined as 'observations on context, process, or mechanism [… which] provide depth of insight [… and] are routinely used in qualitative research based on within-case analysis' (2010: 12). Through the observation of these processes, process tracing allows for qualitative researchers to more effectively explain or understand particular outcomes. For example, in 'International Actors on the Domestic Scene: Membership Conditionality and Socialization by International Institutions', Kelley (2004) sought to identify the causal mechanisms that resulted in Eastern European states passing ethnic minority protection legislation in the 1990s. In this work, Kelley stated that 'socialization-based methods […] were not very effective when used alone, and I show […] that more rational choice-based efforts such as membership conditionality were crucial in changing policy' (2004: 426). In this explanation, Kelley identifies both the theoretical framework in which the mechanism is to be assessed, namely rational choice, and the mechanism by which this effect was achieved, that of membership conditionality, in which the desire to become part of international organisations such as the EU influenced domestic actors to pursue policy changes (2004: 431–433). Furthermore, Kelley provides clear consideration of alternative explanations, including the threat of sanctions from Russia if minorities of Russian origin were mistreated or domestic application of principles of democracy, determining them to be insufficient in explaining the outcomes observed (2004: 433–434).

Process tracing as a method of understanding the ways in which certain legal outcomes are reached is something of a novelty in legal research; indeed, its use thus far has predominantly been by political scientists and international relations scholars seeking to place legal change in a broader context of existing theoretical models or explanations for the actions of policymakers or judicial bodies. Examples come from different disciplinary fields: Obermaier's (2009) work on European Court of Justice (ECJ) jurisprudence, analysing the applicability of several different explanations for the Europeanisation of controversial legal decisions is firmly grounded in political science. Mantilla's (2017) study of the reasons why the US and UK joined the 1949 Geneva Conventions is a key example of the application of international relations theories to why political actors make legal commitments. Yildirim's (2018) consideration of the causes of significant differences in the time it takes different WTO members to facilitate compliance with an adverse WTO panel ruling is based in political economy. This, admittedly non-exhaustive, body of work nevertheless indicates that, historically, the application of process tracing to law is done from an external disciplinary perspective, in which law or legal change constitutes an interesting case study or puzzle, rather than it being used as an internal means of critiquing or analysing socio-legal issues. The project I will expand on in the next section of this chapter was an attempt to bridge these disciplinary boundaries. By taking an interdisciplinary approach to legal study, using process tracing to explore an interesting question about similar legislative outcomes in very different legal regimes, new insights into legislative development could be made possible.

Process tracing in socio-legal research: theoretical and methodological synthesis

The project I applied this approach to originally began as a relatively 'simple' comparative analysis of the patentabilty of inventions derived from hESC research in the systems of the EU and China. The initial research had been conducted as part of a workshop in 2014 exploring synergies between EU and Chinese law, bringing together scholars from the EU and China working on issues such as financial regulation, environmental protection and intellectual property law. At this time, debates over the extent to which hESCs constituted a form of 'life' and the extent to which the granting of a patent over inventions derived from them would be contrary to *ordre public* or morality under the EU's Biotechnology Directive Article 6 (98/44/EC) appeared to have been settled after the *Brüstle* case. In *Brüstle*, the Court of Justice concluded that, as hESCs could only be derived from the destruction of the embryo, which it considered to constitute life as it has the potential to develop into a human being, a patent could not be granted over the invention derived from this destruction of life (Farrand 2016: 270–271). In the event of hESCs being derived from artificial electrical stimulation of an oocyte, which could not develop into a human being, then no destruction of life occurs (Farrand 2016: 271).

In the context of the workshop I was involved in, I became curious about the restrictions on patentability in the field of biotechnology that may arise in the Chinese legal system, and how these may differ from those of the EU, in order to assess a potential area of legal divergence between the two regimes. On this basis, I decided to consult the official translation of the Chinese Patent Act held by the World Intellectual Property Organisation, where I made an interesting finding. Although the specific language used in the Chinese Patent Act was not identical to that of the Biotechnology Directive, it was remarkably similar. Where Article 6 of the Biotechnology Directive states that, 'inventions shall be considered unpatentable where their commercial exploitation would be contrary to *ordre public* or morality', Article 5 of the Chinese Patent Act states that, 'patent rights shall not be granted for invention-creations that violate the law or social ethics, or harm public interests'. Interestingly, the 2010 Guidance accompanying the Chinese Patent Act on how this should be interpreted indicates that, 'the use of human embryos for industrial or commercial purposes is considered contrary to public morality and derived inventions not granted patent rights' (p. 131). In fact, there is compelling evidence to suggest a chain of legislative development beginning with the Biotechnology Directive and ending with the Chinese Patent Act and its Guidelines – the European Patent Convention (EPC) and the guidelines established by the European Patent Office (EPO) were directly based on the Biotechnology Directive as it relates to biotechnology-related patents, and the EPO guidelines were highly influential on the Chinese Guidelines. But why was this the case? Why did the Chinese law mirror the EU and EPO standards?

In order to better understand this puzzle, I used process tracing as a method to determine what causal mechanisms may help us to understand the means by which two very different legal systems nevertheless implemented very similar restrictive approaches to patenting hESC-derived inventions. Referring back to Bennett and Checkel's best practice standards, I needed to ensure that consideration was paid to the theoretical, contextual and methodological dimensions of the research. In terms of theory, epistemologically my work is of a social constructivist nature; this epistemological position holds that, 'people do one thing and not another due to the presence of certain "social constructs": ideas, beliefs, norms, identities or some other interpretive filter through which people perceive the world' (Parsons 2010: 80). In particular, my research is governed by the belief that, in order to understand the decisions made by policymakers, it is important to consider the introduction of new ideas (see, generally, Beland & Cox 2010), starting from 'the recognition that we cannot hope to understand political behaviour without understanding the ideas that actors hold about the environment in which they find themselves' (Hay 2002: 208). But is process tracing compatible theoretically with a social constructivist perspective? Beach and Pedersen perceive process tracing as being firmly within positivist epistemology, in which the emphasis is on making observations regarding 'facts' in the real world and providing clear causal *explanations* in the form of independent variable A impacting upon dependent variable B. Goertz and Mahoney take a similar position, holding that positivist qualitative analysis is concerned with 'explaining outcomes' (Mahoney & Goertz 2006: 230–231), with Hall arguing that, ultimately, process tracing is positivist in nature and therefore incompatible with a strongly interpretivist epistemology (2013). However, Hall does acknowledge that there could be benefit in considering more fully the meaning actors ascribe to their actions (that may constitute the causal mechanism itself; 2013: 24), with Vennesson maintaining that process tracing can be used in both positivist and interpretivist research designs, and that the combination of the two may indeed be useful (2008: 224). Constructivist approaches to causal mechanisms allow for the consideration of the reasons that actors give for their chosen actions, and investigate relations between belief and behaviour (Vennesson 2008: 233). In this respect, Wendt argues that there is a difference between 'traditional' considerations of causation and constructivist considerations of 'constitutive' relations (1998) that help us to better understand how certain changes occur, or '[how] we construct certain meanings and so "constitute" certain political arenas and actions' (Parsons 2010: 87). However, as Parsons makes clear, this is not to say that constructivism does not allow for causal inference (Parsons 2010: 88), only that it does so by considering how meaning is constructed by actors, which may help us to better understand why and how they take the actions that they do.

Theoretically, then, my approach was consistent – my intention was to consider the role of ideas in institutional settings, seeking to better understand how ideas serve to constrain or facilitate legislative approaches to controversial issues by focusing on the processes by which that legislation is created. In this instance, I wanted to understand how very different systems of legislative development in different contexts resulted in very similar outcomes, focusing on the role of ideas, beliefs and norms. Institutions, and those operating within them, work to a 'logic of appropriateness' – in essence, rules of the game that determine what is acceptable or unacceptable within a particular context, or, in the case of policy and legislative development, what solutions are deemed to be appropriate and facilitated, and what are inappropriate, and therefore hindered or discounted. In this respect, institutional path-dependence means that the governing contexts, rules and history of decision-making bind the decision-making of the future, absent a significant rupture or external shock that results in a change in decision-making (see, for example, Lewis & Steinmo 2012). Therefore, in this project, I wanted to apply this theoretical approach to institutional approaches to hESC-related patents, in order to assess the role of this path-dependence on the decision-making processes resulting in similar policies.

The next consideration was context. In this project on hESC patentability, context was twofold: I needed to place the analysis in the context of intellectual property (IP) law generally, including the position of both the EU and China as WTO members and, subsequently, party to the Trade-Related Aspects of Intellectual Property Rights (TRIPS) Agreement, and the context of the law-making systems of the EU and China specifically. Beginning with the issue of IP law, TRIPS requires compliance with a set of minimum standards that form the basis of the international framework for IP protection. This prevents considerable divergences between states in what may be patented, with Article 27 outlining what constitutes patentable subject matter. The exceptions to patentability are listed under Article 27(2), which states that:

> Members may exclude from patentability inventions, the prevention within their territory of the commercial exploitation of which is necessary to protect *ordre public* or morality, including to protect human, animal or plant life or health or to avoid serious prejudice to the environment.

The emphasis here, however, is on the 'may', meaning that, although states are required to conform to the patentability criteria set out in Article 27(1), the exceptions carved out in 27(2) are optional, meaning that states are not obliged to incorporate these exceptions into their national laws (see Henckels 2006). Furthermore, other states party to TRIPS, such as the US and Israel, do not impose restrictions to the patentability of hESC-derived inventions on this basis. Therefore (as will be discussed in more detail below), the existence of this permissible exception in the TRIPS Agreement is not sufficient to explain the similarities between the EU and Chinese regimes, despite their institutional differences. This also means that a legal doctrinal approach would be insufficient in explaining the similarities, given this legal flexibility, requiring the use of a different approach and necessitating the use of interdisciplinary methodology.

In terms of institutional design, the EU and China have very different processes for legislative development. Without covering all the complexities of EU law-making (and at the risk of simplification), the Commission has the right of legislative initiative, with the Council of the European Union and the European Parliament having the ability to approve, modify or reject legislation. Stakeholders can become involved in the legislative process at the stage of agenda-setting in the Commission through participation as experts (Farrand 2015), or later through the lobbying of the European Parliament (and, to a lesser extent, the Council of the European Union) in a form of participative deliberation over the content of legislation (Farrand 2015, 2016; see also Coen & Richardson 2009). In China, however, the legislative process is more closed and opaque. It instead gains its legitimacy not through general participation, but instead through the formalisation of processes and institutions. However, experts are still involved in law-making processes, both in formulating policy as well as legitimating the decisions made, in a form of authoritarian deliberation (He & Warren 2011; Farrand 2016). Here, then, was a divergence in institutional design, but with one commonality, namely the involvement of expert groups. However, from a social constructivist perspective, the notion of expertise is in itself a constructed one – *who* is considered an expert, and *how* is expertise used? Therefore, focusing solely on the commonality of expertise and ignoring the other divergences as a means of understanding the similarities in law would also be insufficient. A deeper understanding of the processes at work in the formulation of the EU Biotechnology Directive and the Chinese Patent Act was therefore required in order to identify potential causal mechanisms for these similarities.

Methodologically, process tracing is something of a laborious undertaking, requiring review of large volumes of information in the form of speeches, preparatory works, Commission working papers, resolutions of the European Parliament and other sources that may be of relevance when following the course of legislation from initial idea to final adopted text. By analysing these documents – and, in particular, how and when these documents are modified – it is possible to gain a better understanding of the ideas or beliefs that had an impact on the finalised text of the legislation, or, in other words, to identify potential causal mechanisms for legislative outcomes. Tracing the development of the Biotechnology Directive, it was possible to determine that the Directive was significantly modified during its passage from Commission proposal to finalised legislation. In particular, the first version of the Directive made no specific references to morality, and exclusions concerning the patenting of living matter were not present – in other words, the current Articles 5 and 6 of the Directive did not exist in the original proposal. This was the cause of some concern in the European Parliament, which was being heavily lobbied by interest groups representing secular and religious concerns concerning biotechnology-related inventions and patenting. Consideration of European Parliament resolutions, as well as the use of Eur-Lex as a means of reviewing each document published during the passage of the Directive, including the ultimate rejection of the first draft and the passing of a subsequent draft that included the provisions on morality and life matter, was useful in determining the role of interest groups and participative processes in the European Parliament in facilitating a significant change in the content and wording of legislation (for a more comprehensive analysis, see Farrand 2016: 273–275).

In comparison, the process for the passage of the legislation and guidelines in China was a more closed process, with a notable absence of interest group representation. Instead, based on the interviews conducted by Sleeboom-Faulkner (2014), the process in China was instead expert- and elite-driven, with legislation and guidelines being drafted on the basis of coordination with medical scientists working in the field, who were themselves sceptical of public involvement in the legislative process. Furthermore, the authoritarian deliberation of the Chinese system was undertaken in a context in which China was investing significant resources in developing its national biotechnology and IP-intensive industries. Why then did it decide to pursue a more restrictive and limited regime for hESC-derived patents? The explanation provided in my project was the role of learned practice and internalisation. Many of the Chinese biotechnology researchers who returned to China as a result of the government's policies and were involved in the drafting of the legislation and guidelines were partly educated (either as postgraduate or doctoral researchers) in European nations, subsequently becoming involved in post-doctoral projects in research institutions. These research institutions were required to comply with the standards of best practice, ethical compliance and adherence to the rules of the Biotechnology Directive when it came to the publication of results. Through this process of institutional learning, in which legislation dictated that inventions involving the destruction of embryos could not be patented, researchers came to internalise the appropriateness of these rules. When they returned to China, these internalised rules and understandings then guided their responses to government requests for information regarding the drafting of its own biotechnology-patenting regulations. In addition, by complying with these stricter standards, cross-state collaboration with European partners in existing research relationships could be more easily facilitated, as standards of institutional research practice would be seen as compatible (Farrand 2016: 275–277). Therefore, despite significantly different institutional designs, with different means of legislating and with different logics of appropriateness, the EU and China nevertheless drafted similarly restrictive legislation and guidelines on patenting hESC-derived inventions.

Yet could there be other, more convincing explanations? With process tracing, it is important to consider the issue of equifinality – the possibility that multiple paths may result in the same outcome, and that these alternative explanations should also be considered in order to determine whether they or the hypothesised mechanism are more likely to have resulted in the observed effect (George & Bennett 2005: 153–160). As discussed above, the requirements of the TRIPS Agreement for the EU and China were not sufficient – it was ultimately left up to states to determine the appropriateness of morality or *ordre public* excep tions to patenting, resulting in different approaches in different states, with the US taking a much more liberal approach than that taken by the EU and China. Another consideration was different moral statuses of the embryo in the different cultures. Could it be that a strong conviction that an embryo reflected the starting point of life would be sufficient for both regimes to exclude from patentability inventions that resulted in their destruction? Based on the process tracing research, the answer was 'no'. Not only were moral statuses significantly different *within* European states, with regard to differing levels of religious objection between Catholic and non-Catholic countries, but secular objections based in historical atrocities also led to divergences between various EU states on the level of protection that should be afforded to an embryo. In China, where Christianity arguably holds less influence than Confucian thought, the embryo has lesser moral status than in Europe, and life is predicated on the development of social relationships, with embryonic research actively encouraged and the regime for regulating the research undertaken being much more liberal than that permit ted in EU states (for a more comprehensive comparison of the different approaches, see Farrand 2016: 269–272). This leads, as Jiang has stated, to the 'paradoxical' situation in China where human embryos have low moral status in practical scientific application, but high moral status in patent law (2015: 81–82). For this reason, this other competing explanation is also less convincing than the one of institutional learning and divergences in logics of appropriateness, helping to support the main argument made.

Improving the analysis: lessons learned and refining the approach

Perhaps the most interesting finding of this research project was the discovery that divergent institutional decision-making structures, with very different approaches to moral claims in the field of biotechnology research, could nevertheless design very similar regulatory solutions to perceived problems. By using process tracing to better understand the origins and development of the EU and Chinese approaches to hESC-derived invention patentability, the importance of institutional learning and the transfer of ideas as a source of regulatory best practice could be uncovered. If this analysis had been performed using a more standard comparative doctrinal legal approach, this interesting insight may have been lost. Although a perfectly serviceable comparison of the two regimes *may* have been possible, an understanding of the underlying factors resulting in such a level of regulatory similarity would not have been.

This is not to suggest that the approach used here was perfect, or that it could not be improved upon. Although the application of the method was rigorous, and adherence to the theoretical and contextual dimensions was maintained, I could have been more explicit in the discussion of the use of process tracing and clearer on the issue of equifinality. On the first issue, as noted above, the use of process tracing was informed by a social constructivist perspective in which the key independent variable was that of institutional design, with the casual mechanism linking the independent variable to the dependent variable of legislative outcome being ideational path-dependence. As Dür and De Bièvre state, it is important in process tracing work to be explicit about methodological choices, by necessity 'spelling out the causal mechanism' (2007: 8). In my article, although I do use process tracing to demonstrate this mechanism, conceptualising and defining terms such as path-dependence and constructivism, I do not explicitly refer to the use of process tracing as the method for conducting the research, nor do I discuss these concepts in terms of variables and causal mechanisms, leaving this implicit in the analysis. An improvement would have been to make this explicit.

As with the use of process tracing as a method, the use of equifinality as a way of demonstrating the convincingness of the identified causal mechanism was implicit rather than explicit. Although independent variables such as membership of the WTO (and therefore being states party to the TRIPS Agreement) and the moral status of the embryo in the comparator regimes were demonstrated as being insufficient to explain the similarity of legislative outcomes, the analysis was not conducted using these specific terms. This is in part owing to the narrative style of the work, written for a legal audience rather than a political science or international relations one. An example of a work that is more explicit in its discussion of process tracing methodology and clear use of equifinality as a means of considering and discounting competing explanations is that undertaken by Deters, which was written with the intention of demonstrating the utility of process tracing in qualitative research (2013: 75, 79). Deters states that the form of process tracing used in his work combines theory generating with theory testing, seeking to explain why environmental policies in the EU are subject to a wide level of variance, with different causal mechanisms explaining the different outcomes, or complex combinations of mechanisms achieving the result (2013: 79–80). There is also consideration of equifinality in the discussion of counterfactual examples that may have changed outcomes or alternative mechanisms that may explain the same result. The explicit identification and explanation of the methodology of process tracing in order to explain policy decisions in a contentious area are particular strengths of this work and can improve research using process tracing as a means of identifying causal mechanisms.

It may have been interesting to consider a counterfactual in order to demonstrate the importance of ideas concerning legislative process and institutional design as an explanation for the similar regimes for the patentability of hESC-derived inventions in the EU and China. A counterfactual can be used to dispel an alternative hypothesis (Haas 2015: 123), where the presence or absence of a particular causal mechanism can help to reinforce or weaken an argument regarding the importance of the identified causal mechanism to the outcome observed. For example, what might have happened in the EU regarding the passage of the Biotechnology Directive, had the participative element of citizen and interest group engagement with the European Parliament been absent? As stated above, in the Commission's proposal for a Directive, there was no specific exclusion as currently contained in Article 6, and it was the involvement of interest groups appealing to the European Parliament to reject the initial proposal that resulted in the redrafting of the Directive with a specific morality exclusion to patentability. Had the role of the European Parliament been purely consultative, and had interest groups not protested the content of the Directive, then the original draft may have entered into law, with the result that inventions derived from hESCs could be patented. In the event of a case such as *Brüstle* being heard on the basis of an objection to the destruction of an embryo in order to obtain stem cells, the absence of Article 6 could have led to a different decision by the CJEU regarding patentability, if indeed the case would have been referred there to begin with. Similarly, what if the academics involved in the legislative process in China had not been educated and involved in research projects in European countries? In the absence of the institutional learning and internalisation of ideas regarding best practice and the conduct of research within the context of the Biotechnology Directive and EPC, would the recommendations of the Chinese researchers have been the same? This cannot be definitively proven, but, in the event of dispelling alternative explanations such as the moral status of the embryo, cannot be easily dismissed either. Would an externalised international (and potentially abstract) concept of best practice have been as influential in the event that it had not been experienced by the Chinese researchers involved in informing the legislative process of the Chinese Patent Act? From a social constructivist perspective, this would appear somewhat unlikely. Nevertheless, these are interesting questions, and ones in which the introduction of a hypothetical counterfactual could provide additional avenues for analysis.

Process tracing and socio-legal research: the broader implications

Having considered how process tracing was used in the context of my biotechnology-related research, I must now turn to considering how this approach can be used by other socio-legal researchers. Process tracing provides both a method and a methodology for approaching these example objects of study, allowing for scholars to conduct a robust analysis by ensuring a theoretical, contextual and methodological synthesis in the consideration of these phenomena. For it to be used in this form of socio-legal study, the researcher must consider the theoretical approach to be taken – is their causal mechanism compatible with their underlying epistemology? They must also take into account the broader context in which that decision to distinguish the case was made, and to consider alternative explanations. Applying this in the hypothetical example, let us assume the researcher considers that social pressures upon the judiciary to change their attitude to a particular issue are the causal mechanism linking the independent variable (the particular case in question) to the dependent variable (namely, the change in the law as a result of judicial reasoning). Epistemologically, the researcher may hold that judges are ultimately rational actors acting in the interest of ensuring the legitimacy of decision-making, requiring adherence to social norms. Therefore, when social norms change, so too will the decisions of the judiciary. The researcher must then consider the context – are there indications that society's view of that issue *has* changed? This may require exhaustive documentary evidence, whether in the form of media reporting, opinion polling, interviews, statements by politicians or other sources that may help to identify that potentially changing social norm. Methodologically, does that indication of the awareness of social change appear in the decision, and does it appear influential in the justification of the overruling of existing precedent? To be effective process tracing, the researcher should also consider the issue of equifinality and the possibility of more convincing alternative explanations. Are the facts significantly different to demonstrate a reason to take a different position? Has the judge released a statement or been interviewed subsequent to the decision, where they make it clear that social pressures had no bearing on the decision? Although these alternative explanations may not necessarily be exhaustive, they should nevertheless be potential avenues for a socio-legal scholar to explore. This does, of course, require that evidence is obtainable – this may be more difficult in the case of judicial decision-making, particularly in legal systems in which this reasoning is not made public. For this reason, the use of process tracing is dependent upon the ability to gather the body of information required to consider various explanations for an observed outcome.

The relevance of process tracing to socio-legal studies is that it can assist in opening up the 'black box' of politics that is often considered outwith the domain of legal study or, alternatively, hinted at or discussed with little in the way of methodological consideration. As Unger once stated, an approach to law founded in doctrinal formalism and a dismissal (or, at the least, an absence of consideration) of the politics and contestation of law was a misguided enterprise, 'for how could law, produced through conflict among interests and ideologies, come to look, after the fact, in the hands of professional interpreters, as if a single mind and will had conceived it?' (Unger 2015: 11–12). If, as socio-legal scholars, we wish to place law in its greater social, cultural and historical contexts, then the black box of politics and policy must be opened, rather than the use of 'policy' being adhered to as a fashionable addition to the study of 'law and ...', with little in the way of conscious thought behind it. Process tracing is one of the methods that can be used to carefully open that box and examine its contents, helping to link origins, causes and effects in a way that withstands scrutiny and is cognisant of the counter-arguments and competing explanations. To put it another way, process tracing can go beyond telling us the 'what' of law, or even the 'why' of law, to understand the 'how' of law. It allows us to go beyond saying (as one example) 'this law is the result of lobbying', to better explore and understand *how* different types of lobbyist (or interest group) were able to effectively lobby, *how* they were able to influence the language or scope of legislation by consideration of their strategies, and *how* this explanation is more convincing than another based in the idea of an impartial and uninfluenced parliament. Being able to unpack these processes is highly beneficial to socio-legal studies at this time of political and legal uncertainty and contestation, whether or not we consider the role of 'populist' parties and communication (for more on this see Laclau 2007) in serving to influence both general understandings of law and specific approaches to legal issues. Process tracing could be useful in considering the regulation of the Eurozone and responses to the Stability and Growth Pact by new political parties, challenges to judicial reform in Poland and the use of 'rule of law' as a rhetorical device to both facilitate and hinder such reforms, or how the broader context of revelations regarding political manipulation and use of data such as in the case of Cambridge Analytica may serve to change approaches to both data protection law, as well as electoral laws concerning advertising and political communication. Process tracing could be used to explore how national developments and concerns regarding refugees and the knock-on effects on parliamentary politics then shape European responses to migration, such as current debates over the reform of the Dublin processes. It could also be used to search for alternative explanations that may be as, if not more, convincing than current understandings of anti-immigrant hostility, particularly in Southern Europe. But perhaps most importantly, process tracing methodologies allow for this analysis to be done with the application of rigorous appreciation of theory, context and application of method, as a means of ensuring that the socio-legal research performed in highly contentious or controversial areas can be done in a way that withstands scrutiny.

Conclusions and further reading

In conclusion, process tracing can be a highly useful method of analysis for socio-legal scholars. It assists the researcher in unpacking political and social contexts, linking actions to their outcomes through the identification of causal mechanisms or processes and helping them to better understand *how* changes in law may come about, particularly in areas of political or moral controversy. Process tracing also helps the socio-legal researcher to explore these processes in a methodological way, requiring the researcher to carefully consider the compatibility of their approach with their epistemological position, with awareness of the broader context in which their research and observed phenomena are placed, and with due consideration of equifinality and alternative explanations. Its flexibility, in terms of both perspective (whether positivist or interpretivist) and its potential for use in a wide range of different scenarios, makes it a valuable asset in critiquing legal developments in a way not often undertaken in contemporary legal scholarship.

Suggested further reading

Bennett, A. & Checkel, J.T., 2014. Process Tracing: From Philosophical Roots to Best Practices. In A. Bennett & J.T. Checkel, eds. *Process Tracing: From Metaphor to Analytic Tool*. Cambridge: Cambridge University Press, pp. 3–37.

Farrand, B., 2016. Human Embryonic Stem Cells and Patent Law in the EU and China: Convergence in Standards through Divergence in Institutions. *Intellectual Property Quarterly*, 3, pp. 260–277.

Haas, P.M., 2015. *Epistemic Communities, Constructivism, and International Environmental Politics*, 1st edn, London, New York: Routledge.

Lewis, O.A. & Steinmo, S., 2012. How Institutions Evolve: Evolutionary Theory and Institutional Change. *Polity*, 44(3), pp. 314–339.

Sleeboom-Faulkner, M., 2014. *Global Morality and Life Science Practices in Asia: Assemblages of Life*, New York: Palgrave Macmillan

References

Agreement on Trade-Related Aspects of Intellectual Property Rights, Apr. 15, 1994, Marrakesh Agreement Establishing the World Trade Organization, Annex 1C, 1869 U.N.T.S. 299, 33 I.L.M. 1197 (1994)

Beach, D. & Pedersen, R.B., 2012. *Process-Tracing Methods: Foundations and Guidelines*, Ann Arbor, MI: The University of Michigan Press.

Beland, D. & Cox, R.H., 2010. Introduction: Ideas and Politics. In D. Beland & R.H. Cox, eds. *Ideas and Politics in Social Science Research*, Oxford, New York: Oxford University Press, pp. 1–26.

Bennett, A. & Checkel, J.T., 2014. Process Tracing: From Philosophical Roots to Best Practices. In A. Bennett & J.T. Checkel, eds. *Process Tracing: From Metaphor to Analytic Tool*, Cambridge: Cambridge University Press, pp. 3–37.

Bonadio, E., 2012. Biotech Patents and Morality after *Brüstle*. *European Intellectual Property Review*, 34(7), pp. 433–443.

Brady, H.E., Collier, D. & Seawright, J., 2010. Refocusing the Discussion of Methodology. In H. E. Brady & D. Collier, eds. *Rethinking Social Inquiry: Diverse Tools, Shared Standards*, 2nd edn, Lanham, MD: Rowman & Littlefield, pp. 3–20.

Coen, D. & Richardson, J., eds., 2009. *Lobbying the European Union Institutions, Actors, and Issues*, Oxford, New York: Oxford University Press.

Deters, H., 2013. Process Tracing in the Development and Validation of Theoretical Explanations: The Example of Environmental Policy-Making in the EU. *European Political Science*, 12(1), pp. 75–85.

Dür, A. & Bièvre, D.D., 2007. The Question of Interest Group Influence. *Journal of Public Policy*, 27(1), pp. 1–12.

Farrand, B., 2015. Lobbying and Lawmaking in the European Union: The Development of Copyright Law and the Rejection of the Anti-Counterfeiting Trade Agreement. *Oxford Journal of Legal Studies*, 35 (3), pp. 487–514.

Farrand, B., 2016. Human Embryonic Stem Cells and Patent Law in the EU and China: Convergence in Standards through Divergence in Institutions. *Intellectual Property Quarterly*, 3, pp. 260–277.

George, A.L. & Bennett, A., 2005. *Case Studies and Theory Development in the Social Sciences*, Cambridge, MA: MIT Press.

Haas, P.M., 2015. *Epistemic Communities, Constructivism, and International Environmental Politics*, 1st edn, London, New York: Routledge.

Hall, P.A., 2013. Tracing the Progress of Process Tracing. *European Political Science*, 12(1), pp. 20–30.

Hay, C., 2002. *Political Analysis: A Critical Introduction*, Basingstoke, New York: Palgrave Macmillan.

He, B. & Warren, M.E., 2011. Authoritarian Deliberation: The Deliberative Turn in Chinese Political Development. *Perspectives on Politics*, 9(2), pp. 269–289.

Henckels, C., 2006. The Ostensible Flexibilities in TRIPS: Can Essential Pharmaceuticals be Excluded from Patentability in Public Health Crises? *Monash University Law Review*, 32, p. 335.

Jiang, L., 2015. Between Scylla and Charybdis: Patentability and Morality Related to Human Embryonic Stem Cells. *Intellectual Property Brief*, 6(1), pp. 53–97.

Kelley, J., 2004. International Actors on the Domestic Scene: Membership Conditionality and Socialization by International Institutions. *International Organization*, 58(03), pp. 425–457.

Laclau, E., 2007. *On Populist Reason*, reprint edn, London, New York: Verso.

Lewis, O.A. & Steinmo, S., 2012. How Institutions Evolve: Evolutionary Theory and Institutional Change. *Polity*, 44(3), pp. 314–339.

Mahoney, J. & Goertz, G., 2006. A Tale of Two Cultures: Contrasting Quantitative and Qualitative Research. *Political Analysis*, 14(3), pp. 227–249.

Mantilla, G., 2017. Conforming Instrumentalists: Why the USA and the United Kingdom Joined the 1949 Geneva Conventions. *European Journal of International Law*, 28(2), pp. 482–511.

Obermaier, A.J., 2009. *The End of Territoriality? The Impact of ECJ Rulings on British, German and French Social Policy*, Oxford: Oxford University Press.

Parsons, C., 2010. Constructivism and Interpretive Theory. In D. Marsh & G. Stoker, eds. *Theory and Methods in Political Science*, Houndmills, UK, New York: Palgrave Macmillan, pp. 80–98.

Patent Law of the People's Republic of China (2008).

Savulescu, J., 2009. Genetic Interventions and the Ethics of Enhancement of Human Beings. In D. M. Kaplan, ed. *Readings in the Philosophy of Technology*, Lanham, MD: Rowman & Littlefield, p. 417.

Skogstad, G., 2003. Legitimacy and/or Policy Effectiveness? Network Governance and GMO Regulation in the European Union. *Journal of European Public Policy*, 10(3), pp. 321–338.

Sleeboom-Faulkner, M., 2014. *Global Morality and Life Science Practices in Asia: Assemblages of Life*, New York: Palgrave Macmillan.

Unger, R.M., 2015. *The Critical Legal Studies Movement*, reissue edn, London, New York: Verso.

Vennesson, P., 2008. Case Studies and Process Tracing: Theories and Practice. In D.D. Porta & M. Keating, eds. *Approaches and Methodologies in the Social Sciences: A Pluralist Perspective*, Cambridge, New York: Cambridge University Press, pp. 223–239.

Wendt, A., 1998. On Constitution and Causation in International Relations. *Review of International Studies*, 24(5), pp. 101–118.

Yildirim, A., 2018. Firms' Integration into Value Chains and Compliance with Adverse WTO Panel Rulings. *World Trade Review*, 17(1), pp. 1–31.

26

EXPERIMENTS IN CRIMINAL JUSTICE CONTEXTS

Julia Yesberg and Ben Bradford

Introduction

In the summer of 1854, England was in the grip of its third cholera epidemic. Although the most popular theory for the cause of the epidemic was foul air or miasma, John Snow – a British physician – was convinced the disease was spread by contaminated drinking water. In what became known as the Grand Experiment, Snow set out to test his hypothesis. At the time, two water companies supplied the same South London neighbourhoods with water. One company took its water supplies untreated from the River Thames, near where the sewers were discharged, whereas the other had recently moved to a freshwater site upriver, away from the contamination. This set the scene for a natural experiment, where residents formed two groups: one exposed to the contaminated water, the other not – and Snow found that those who were exposed to contaminated water were eight to nine times more likely to die of cholera. Although there was no intentional manipulation of variables, Snow's Grand Experiment illustrates the primary use of the experimental method: to test a hypothesis and answer questions about cause and effect. Experiments are conducted to support, refute, or validate a hypothesis and provide insight into causation by measuring an outcome after a particular variable is manipulated – in Snow's case, the source of water.

Today, experimental methods are commonplace in the natural and social sciences. Experimental clinical trials are used in medicine to test whether a potential new treatment is safe and effective. Experiments are used frequently in psychology to test different theories about psychological phenomena. After what might be termed a delayed start, criminology, perhaps particularly in the field of policing studies, has recently taken a significant 'experimental turn'. Experiments – some of which will be described in this chapter – are increasingly common – for example, to test the effect of particular policing interventions on crime prevention. Criminal justice organisations in the UK and beyond are increasingly committed to experimental evaluations of new policies and existing practices. With a few exceptions, such as Harvard University's Access to Justice lab, socio-legal studies as a discipline seems to be (yet further) behind this curve, for reasons that may relate partly to the severe ethical challenges posed by attempts to manipulate court outcomes, sentencing decisions, and so on.

The aim of this chapter is to introduce the reader to different types of experimental method and to provide examples from our own work of how these methods have been applied in criminal justice contexts. First, we briefly describe the main types of experimental design that can be used to test hypotheses and discuss their relative strengths and weaknesses. Then, we present two detailed case studies of how we have applied these methods in two different criminal justice contexts: one to test procedural justice theory in Scotland; the other to measure the effect of a violent offender treatment programme in New Zealand. Lastly, we outline the different threats to validity in experiments and the importance of replication and discuss some of the limitations of experimental methods.

Experimental designs

Experiments are used when a researcher is interested in answering questions about causation. The key feature of experiments is the process of intentionally varying something to discover what happens to something else later, although, as the example of Snow's work on cholera shows, 'natural' variation can also be the basis of experimental studies. There are different types of experimental design, which vary in terms of the strength of the conclusions that can be drawn from the research. What design is best to use depends on the question being asked, the assumptions that can be reasonably made, and what is already known about the topic (Deaton and Cartwright 2018).

Randomised control trials

Randomised control trials (RCTs) provide the most powerful design for testing causal hypotheses. Three conditions must be met for a study to be considered an RCT: (1) there need to be at least two groups (one receiving the treatment or intervention and the other(s) receiving no treatment or a different intervention); (2) random assignment of the units of analysis (people, police units, courts, etc.) to the groups; and (3) an assessment of an outcome measure.

Treatment and control groups

RCTs must have at least one *treatment or experimental group* and at least one *control or comparison group*. The treatment group receives some form of intervention or experimental manipulation – for example, exposure to a particular policing tactic; we will use 'hotspots policing' as a running example. This is a policing strategy wherein areas with particularly high levels of crime and/or disorder are targeted for additional police patrols and other activity (Weisburd *et al.* 2012). The control group either receives a different intervention from the treatment group (e.g. exposure to a *different* policing tactic) or, more often, receives no intervention at all – 'business as usual' – which, in the case of hotspots policing, means that areas in the control group receive the same amount and type of policing they would have received should the experiment not have been taking place. The main purpose of the control group is to estimate the *counterfactual* – what would have happened to the treatment group had it not received the intervention (Shadish *et al.* 2002).

Random assignment

Randomisation is the key feature of RCTs that makes them the most powerful design (Bachman and Schutt 2007). *Random assignment* of the units of analysis – for example, individuals, groups of people, geographic areas, police units, or courts – to treatment and control groups provides assurance that the only difference between the two groups is whether or not they received the intervention. For example, random assignment to conditions in a hotspots experiment – wherein, most commonly, a number of high-crime locales in a particular city are identified, and then extra police resource is assigned to some but not others – means the only *systematic* difference between the two groups is that one receives the intervention and the other does not. Because it ensures that exogenous causal factors (i.e. the characteristics of local areas that cause crime and change in crime levels) are evenly distributed across control and experimental conditions, randomisation ensures the effect of the intervention can be isolated. However, because it relies on chance randomisation does not necessarily mean the two groups will be perfectly identical. This can be a particular challenge when only a few units are available for the experiment. Equality of theoretically relevant variables across experimental and control groups should be demonstrated wherever possible by the collection of data on the composition of the two.

Outcome measure

Along with random allocation to at least two groups, RCTs must have a measurement of the outcome of interest – the *dependent variable* – for both groups *after* the treatment group has received the intervention. For example, an experiment on hotspots policing may choose recorded crime rates as the outcome measure. The *effect* of the intervention is the difference between the crime rate in the treatment group and the crime rate in the control group. Some experiments may also include measurements of the dependent variable *prior* to the intervention. Including a pre-measure is useful for determining how much change has occurred over time in the treatment group relative to the control group, and allows the researcher to verify that the randomisation was successful (i.e. that there were no systematic differences in crime rates between the two groups prior to the treatment). Experiments with 'pre' and 'post' measures of outcomes are generally considered more robust than those with only 'post' measures. Box 26.1 provides an example of an RCT in policing studies.

Box 26.1 Randomised control trials: body-worn video

A prime example of an RCT in policing comes from a study of body-worn video in Rialto, California (Ariel *et al.* 2015). The researchers tested the effect of body-worn cameras on incidents of police use-of-force and public complaints. Over a one-year period, officers were randomly assigned to either 'experimental shifts' where they were equipped with body-worn cameras that recorded all contacts with the public, or 'control shifts' where the officers were told not to wear the cameras. In this study, the shifts, rather than the officers, were the units of experimental analysis (a total of 988 shifts were randomly allocated during the trial period). The integrity of assignment was verified by measuring the number of 'footage hours' in the experimental and control shifts, as well as dip-sampling dates of footage and checking the officers wore the cameras as assigned. The two outcome measures were incidents of police use-of-force and citizen complaints against the police. Findings of the trial showed a reduction in police use-of-force in experimental shifts relative to the control shifts. Officers were roughly twice as likely to use force in shifts without cameras than in shifts where body-worn cameras were used. The study also included a quasi-experimental aspect where citizen complaints were measured before and after the intervention, and change over time was examined (see next section).

Quasi-experimental studies

Although RCTs are often described as the 'gold standard' approach, sometimes it is not feasible or ethical to randomise to conditions. Other designs that still retain some components of RCTs – often called quasi-experimental designs (Campbell and Stanley 1963) – are an alternative that still allows for valid conclusions about causality. Quasi-experiments share the purpose of testing causal hypothesis as well as including many of the features of RCTs (e.g. control groups, 'pre' and 'post' measures), but they lack random allocation to conditions.

Non-equivalent control group designs

In non-equivalent control group designs, the experimental and comparison groups are assigned before the intervention occurs but are not randomly allocated to conditions. In the hotspots policing example, control areas may be selected that match experimental areas as closely as possible on crime rates, deprivation, and other relevant indices. That way, the researcher can be fairly certain that any effect of the intervention is not caused by any pre-existing observable differences. But there may still be unobservable differences (on variables that were not measured and were not criteria for matching) between the two groups, and it is unlikely the two groups would be as similar as they would be if assigned randomly. Matching the control group can be done on an individual basis (e.g. subjects who receive the intervention are matched to similar subjects who do not receive the intervention) or on an aggregate basis (e.g. a control group is selected that matches the experimental group in the aggregate rather than on an individual basis). See Box 26.2 for an example of a non-equivalent control group design.

Before and after designs

The key feature of a before and after design is the lack of a comparison group. In these designs, all subjects are exposed to the intervention and serve, at an earlier time, as their own controls. Pre-test measures are used to compare with measures following the intervention; the *effect* is the difference between these measures over time. For example, a researcher could measure the crime rate of an area prior to the introduction of hotspots policing; then, following the intervention, the crime rate could be measured again to observe what change has occurred. There could be just two measures (pre-test and post-test) or many observations over time; the latter is preferable because it enables the researcher to study the *process* by which an intervention has an effect (Bachman and Schutt 2007). Before and after designs are considered the weakest type of quasi-experimental design because there may be many variables other than the intervention that cause the 'effect' – the researcher cannot rule out the possibility that the same effect would have been observed in the absence of the intervention.

Box 26.2 **Quasi-experiments: mounted police and public opinion**

An example of a quasi-experimental design comes from a study that investigated the effect of horseback community patrols on public trust and confidence in police (Giacomantonio *et al.* 2015). The design of the study included six areas, in three matched pairs, none of which had recent experience of mounted community patrols. One area in each pair received a series of mounted patrols (allocation was not randomised), numbering seven or eight over a four-week

---

period. The control area operated business as usual. Pre and post surveys were conducted with local residents living in the six areas to measure the effect of mounted patrols on trust and confidence. The findings of the study showed that: (1) the introduction of mounted community patrols was noticed by residents, (2) having recently seen mounted patrols was associated with significantly higher levels of trust and confidence, and (3) public trust in police increased in the test areas relative to the control areas after the mounted patrols had taken place, suggesting that this form of visible policing may indeed have a positive effect on trust and confidence. The intervention appeared to have a buffering effect: in the control areas, trust declined, whereas, in the treatment areas, it remained constant. A qualitative aspect – systematic social observation – was also included in this study and showed that both visibility and the mode of deployment generated the effect on public trust.

Natural experiments

Unlike RCTs and quasi-experimental designs, natural experiments are made possible by events outside the control of the researchers. Variables are not intentionally manipulated, and the dependent variable is simply measured after exposure to the independent variable. John Snow, for example, took advantage of a company's decision to change the location of its water supply to test his theory about the cause of cholera. 'Naturally' occurring variation offers researchers the opportunity to analyse populations as if they had been part of an experiment, such as when there is divergence in policy or practice between countries or regions, between schools or classrooms, or between other geographical or social populations. The validity of these studies relies on the assumption that the assignment of units to 'treatment' or 'control' groups mirrors randomisation. However, the assignment to treatment and control groups is rarely truly random, and there may be many extraneous variables influencing assignment. Box 26.3 provides an example of a natural experiment.

Box 26.3 Natural experiments: residential change and recidivism

In a study made possible by the devastation caused by Hurricane Katrina in 2005, Kirk (2009) tested the effect of residential change on rates of recidivism. Previous research looking at the effect of residential relocation on the likelihood of recidivism has suffered the issue of selection bias (i.e. there may be unmeasurable characteristics about an individual that determine where they choose to reside after release). The residential destruction resulting from Hurricane Katrina created an exogenous source of variation in where parolees resided after release from prison. Some parolees were unable to return home and were forced to relocate to a new parish. Therefore, assignment to the 'treatment' group (parolees who relocated) and the 'control' group (parolees who returned home) was not determined by the researcher and was not subject to selection bias. Kirk found that around half of all prisoners released from Louisiana correctional facilities post-Katrina (who resided in affected areas prior to incarceration) relocated to a new parish, whereas half returned to their home parish. Parolees who moved to a different parish upon release from prison were significantly less likely to be re-incarcerated than those who returned to the parish where they were originally convicted. In other words, moving away from familiar territory seems to decrease offending rates among those released from prison.

Statistical analysis

All experiments involve quantification of some kind, and almost all therefore involve statistical analysis of data. Although this can be enough to deter some from engaging in experimental research, the analysis of data from a well-designed randomised experiment often needs little more than basic statistical tests of sample means or proportions – for example, the difference in mean levels of crime between the experimental and control sites in a hotspots experiment. A key strength of the method is that the research design can obviate the need for complex analysis. Analysis of data from less robust designs, however often needs to be substantially more sophisticated, precisely because the relative weakness of the design needs to be taken into account.

Case studies

In this section, we present two detailed case studies, taken from our own work, of experimental methods applied in two very different criminal justice contexts. The first example is an RCT that tested procedural justice theory using road police units in Scotland. The second example is a quasi-experimental study measuring the effect of an intensive psychological rehabilitation programme for high-risk violent offenders housed in New Zealand prisons. In both cases, we describe not only the experiments themselves, but also wider issues of implementation and context that affected the studies and interpretation of their results.

Scottish Community Engagement Trial

The Scottish Community Engagement Trial (ScotCET, MacQueen and Bradford 2015) was an RCT that tested the impact of a procedural justice intervention. This experiment was intended to be a replication of the Queensland Community Engagement Trial (QCET), the first large-scale randomised field trial of procedural justice policing (Mazerolle *et al.* 2012, 2013). Procedural justice theory posits that the experience of fair treatment during encounters with authority figures, such as police officers, generates trust and legitimacy, enhances decision acceptance and satisfaction with the decision-maker, and promotes subsequent cooperation and compliance (Tyler and Huo 2002). Results from QCET demonstrated that improving the quality of routine interactions between public and officers during random breath-testing operations had a direct positive effect on public satisfaction with the process and outcome of the encounter, perceptions of police procedural fairness, overall trust and confidence in the police, and police legitimacy. The QCET intervention comprised officers in the test condition delivering a scripted series of remarks, comments, and questions designed to communicate the core elements of procedural justice (such as dignity, respect, voice, neutrality, and trustworthy motives), and it was one of the first studies to demonstrate a causal link between implementation of procedurally just forms of policing and change in public opinion.

Although, in the event, ScotCET cannot be considered a replication of QCET, not least because of differences in the legal frameworks of Australia and Scotland (e.g. random police stops are not allowed under Scottish law), the two studies shared many characteristics in common. All 20 road police units in Scotland were involved in the Scottish experiment, which took place during the 4-week 2013–14 Festive Road Safety Campaign, wherein police focus on road safety, drunk-driving, and poor driving behaviour. Units were randomly assigned to experimental or control conditions via a matched-pair design: units were first paired on geographical (Edinburgh was paired with Glasgow) or functional (the two motorcycle units were paired with each other) bases; then, on a coin toss, one unit in each pair was assigned to the experimental group. During the first week of the campaign, all units conducted 'business as usual', merely distributing a questionnaire to drivers once encounters (i.e. interactions triggered by police pulling them over for some reason) had finished. The questionnaire asked drivers to rate their experience, indicate their level of trust in police, and so on. A week-long hiatus followed while materials were distributed to units in the experimental condition and officers were briefed on the intervention. They were asked to verbally deliver a set of key messages during encounters, and to distribute a leaflet designed to enhance perceptions of procedural justice. The aim was to introduce a level of consistency into encounters such that each encounter included *all* of the core elements of the procedural justice model, while allowing officers to continue acting responsively and naturally. Units in the control condition continued to operate 'business as usual'. Analysis of the survey returns from across the period allowed a 'difference in differences' analysis, which compared change in opinions in the control group with change in the experimental group – with difference between the two groups being attributable to the experimental intervention.

The basic hypothesis of ScotCET was that the intervention would enhance perceptions of procedural justice and levels of satisfaction, trust, confidence, and legitimacy in the experimental units compared with those in the control condition. Pre-test and post-test measures were used to measure the key outcomes. Findings showed the opposite pattern to that expected: in the control areas, consistent improvements were observed on the key outcome measures over the course of the trial. In the experimental areas, assessments of procedural justice during encounters and driver satisfaction fell, relative to the control areas. ScotCET therefore produced a negative 'buffering' in the experimental group – the intervention *inhibited* an uplift in public perceptions that was observed in the control areas and would, therefore, have also been observed in the experimental areas had the intervention not been in place.

These results were unexpected, to say the least. Possible reasons for these apparently perverse results are discussed in MacQueen and Bradford (2017), a follow up study that involved group interviews with the officers who had delivered the intervention. It seems that communication breakdowns during the implementation phase led to misunderstandings about the aims and objectives of the experiment and about the requirements it placed on those delivering it, leading to implementation failure – a failure to properly carry through the requirements of the experimental manipulation. Within a context of reform and perceived organizational 'injustice' current in Police Scotland at the time of ScotCET – largely a result of its recent formation from eight regionally based 'legacy forces' in summer 2013 – officer non-compliance with the requirements of the intervention was moreover enabled and exacerbated by recourse to some well-known aspects of 'police culture' (Reiner 2010). Among the officers tasked with delivering the experiment, there was scepticism and cynicism about the motivation of senior officers, the knowledge and ability of external 'experts', and indeed the possibility of generating more positive relations with the public. The nature of the experimental intervention – which aimed at increasing levels of procedural justice – and the time and place in which it was delivered not only seem to have led to implementation failure, but also triggered a diffuse negative response in the experimental units that shifted attitudes and behaviours and resulted in the overall negative results outlined above. There was, in other words, a backfire effect.

ScotCET illustrates well some of the perils of RCTs in policing and many other criminological and socio-legal contexts. Researchers often require the assistance of a group of professionals to deliver the intervention, and, should this cooperation be patchy or indeed not forthcoming, the experiment will likely fail. Equally important, though, is the danger of backfire effects. In the case of ScotCET, this was mild: driver assessments of the stops were generally high, on average, and the effects noted above reflected blocked improvement in the experimental group. In other contexts, however, backfire could be ethically challenging and even disastrous – consider, for example, interventions aiming to reduce crime or reoffending, or to improve the experience and/or outcomes of victims.

Quasi-experimental study of violent offender treatment

Our second case study is a quasi-experimental evaluation of a prison-based psychological treatment programme for violent offenders carried out in New Zealand (Polaschek *et al.* 2016). Meta-analytic research shows that most offender treatment outcome studies are methodologically poor in quality (Koehler *et al.* 2013). RCTs can rarely be fulfilled in correctional settings, most notably because of ethical issues, high attrition rates, and concerns about the generalisability of findings to real-world therapeutic settings (Lipsey and Cullen 2007). Quasi-experimental approaches are more common in this field and most often involve taking a group of offenders who received an intervention and retrospectively matching them to a group of offenders who did not receive the intervention, with matching based on risk of reoffending and other relevant variables (e.g. age; Lipsey and Cullen 2007; Polaschek and Collie 2004).

Our study took this approach. It examined whether New Zealand's High-Risk Special Treatment Units (HRSTUs) reduced subsequent recidivism rates for the men who completed them. The HRSTUs are purpose-built units housed in New Zealand's prison system and target high-risk, mostly violent, male offenders. The programme is a hybrid, combining a closed-group cognitive-behavioural intervention with a hierarchical democratic therapeutic community approach. Prisoners attend group sessions – on a variety of areas such as offence-supportive thinking, mood management, problem solving, and relapse prevention planning – for approximately 250 hours over 25 weeks, and remain in the treatment unit for 10–12 months (Kilgour and Polaschek 2012). A sample of 121 men was selected from among those who completed one of the HRSTU programmes and were subsequently paroled between 2010 and 2013. The comparison sample of 154 men was recruited from men who were eligible to attend a HRSTU but had not done so. Both groups were recruited as part of a larger longitudinal study called the 'Parole Project', which prospectively followed a cohort of high-risk offenders for 1 year following their release from prison.

Because allocation to groups was not randomised, analysis was undertaken to ensure there were no pre-existing differences between the two groups on variables that may be related to recidivism (e.g. age, risk of reoffending, sentence length, number of previous convictions). The two samples were well matched in most respects on available data; however, treated men were older at release, had been given longer sentences, and had served more time in prison. We planned to control for any such differences, but none of the variables predicted recidivism on their own, and, combined, the variables were not able to significantly predict whether men were members of the treatment or comparison group. Therefore, the two groups were considered statistically equivalent on relevant risk-related variables.

Findings showed consistently positive results in favour of the treatment group. Men in the treatment sample were significantly less likely to breach parole, to be reconvicted for any type of offence, to be reconvicted for violence, or to be re-incarcerated for a new offence in the first 12 months after release from prison. One of the challenges of treatment outcome studies is that most provide no information about the underlying mechanisms that may be involved (i.e. what it is about the treatment that has brought about the reductions in recidivism). Our study explored two potential pre-release mechanisms: dynamic risk for violence and readiness for release. Findings showed that dynamic risk for violence fully accounted for differences between the treatment and comparison groups in reconvictions for violence; however, in all other cases, the proposed mechanisms did not explain treatment-related differences in recidivism.

In a context where randomisation is rarely possible, quasi-experimental approaches such as this offer a robust approach to measuring the effect of correctional treatment, provided there are no systematic differences between the treatment and control groups. Yet, even if the two groups are equivalent on the variables measured, as was the case here, we cannot rule out the possibility that other systematic differences between the two groups (on variables that were not measured) are causing the effect. Furthermore, because the groups were not matched prospectively, there was no pre-test available for the control group on the proposed mechanisms (dynamic risk for violence and readiness for release). Including a pre-test would have allowed us to examine change over time, for both the treatment and control group, which would provide more compelling evidence of a treatment effect.

Validity in experiments

The ability for experiments to yield valid conclusions is of central concern when weighing up which research design to employ. There are different sources of validity in experimental methods that relate both to the effects of the study and the generalisability of findings.

Internal validity

Internal validity refers to determining whether a causal relationship actually exists: can we be sure the effect of the experiment was caused by the treatment or intervention? We have already talked about *selection bias* in one of our examples, which occurs when there are unmeasured pre-existing differences between the treatment and comparison groups (i.e. differences in the types of people who choose to return home or move to a new location after prison; Kirk 2009). Randomisation deals with this bias by equalising the characteristics of the two groups. Quasi-experiments can reduce the likelihood of selection bias by including a pre-test measure and collecting equivalent data about the composition of both groups. Another challenge to internal validity is *endogenous change* – that is, natural developments among the subjects that occur independent of the treatment, which can include testing effects, maturation, and 'regression to the mean'. Before and after designs that do not include a control group are most at risk of these threats to validity.

Other threats to internal validity include *external events* that can alter the outcome under consideration (e.g. a newsworthy event that relates to the focus of the experiment, such as a high-profile case of police corruption in an experiment designed to increase trust in the police). This threat to validity is not an issue if both treatment and control groups are exposed to the same event, but it can cause serious problems if only one group is exposed. *Contamination* occurs when the control group is in some way aware of the experiment and/or receives certain features of the intervention. For example, if police units that operate out of the same headquarters are assigned to different conditions in a hotspots experiment, there is the possibility that elements of the intervention – that is, particular practices not currently standard – will filter into the control group. This often leads researchers to randomise or allocate to conditions at particular levels that minimise the risk of contamination. Lastly, *treatment misidentification* occurs when something other than the intervention is responsible for the apparent effect of treatment (e.g. expectancies of the experimenter, placebo effect).

External validity

External validity refers to the generalisability of findings of an experimental study. In other words, to what degree would the findings hold for other people in other places at other times? Paradoxically, the design components essential to minimise threats to internal validity may make it more difficult for an experiment to achieve external validity. Being able to apply the findings from the specific sample that was studied to a larger population is referred to as *population validity*. The extent to which the findings can be generalised from the set of specific experimental or environmental conditions is referred to as *ecological validity*. The external validity of an experiment will be stronger, the more the study is replicated (see below).

Replication and meta-analysis

Replication is considered to be the 'cornerstone of science' because only replication can determine whether an effect demonstrated by a single study is a true finding. As an original finding may be subject to bias or error, multiple replications are needed to confirm or discount particular findings. Psychology and other disciplines have recently been going through a 'replication crisis' after efforts to replicate past study findings have frequently proven unsuccessful, leading to concern about whether the original study results were false positives. *Meta-analysis* is a statistical procedure for synthesising data from replication (or near-replication) studies, thus capitalising on the existence of multiple versions of the same experiment. It is used to find a common effect across studies that may report differing treatment effects. Meta-analysis is a powerful tool to improve the precision and accuracy of estimates and to increase statistical power.

Limitations of experimental methods

Despite a proliferation of experimental studies in the field of criminology, there has been a long history of scepticism about experimental methods within the discipline, most especially in relation to RCTs. This has stemmed from diverse sources, and some of it, if correct, would have serious implications for the experimental paradigm in criminology and, indeed, more widely. In this section, we outline some of this criticism.

Perhaps most obviously, experiments, particularly those with random assignment of the treatment, pose significant ethical concerns in criminal justice contexts. Some interventions and practices, such as police, jury, or sentencer decision-making, are extremely difficult if not impossible to randomise. It seems prima facie unlikely, for example, that many ethics committees would allow an experiment that proposed to randomly assign a group of convicted offenders to shorter or longer prison sentences. The potential for backfire effects, as occurred in ScotCET, is also troubling when research involves life-changing experiences and outcomes for victims as well as offenders, and indeed for wider communities who might, for example, be over- or under-exposed to a particular police intervention (Kochel 2011). It is worth noting that some such concerns can be overcome by the argument that units in the control group receive the 'same' intervention they received previously, whereas those in the experimental group receive an intervention that is in some sense 'better' (e.g. diversion from prosecution into what is believed to be a more effective programme for reducing recidivism; Neyroud 2017). This would imply that no unit is worse off for being included in the experiment than would otherwise have been the case, and the potential benefits of the intervention are decided by what amounts to a lottery.

Epistemological concerns about the ability of experiments to generate truly 'accurate' or even 'useful' knowledge in criminological contexts have also been raised (see Hope 2009). Perhaps the most serious challenge here is that the overall selection of units to be assigned to the experimental and control groups is itself rarely random, and this selection is often based on highly imperfect criteria such as administrative data, such that it is unsure whether the patterns upon which the selection is made reflect the 'real' distribution of the phenomenon of interest (ibid.). For example, the areas included in hotspots experiments are usually all, by definition, 'high-crime' locations. Yet this categorisation is based on police-recorded data that both under-represent many forms of crime, such as domestic violence and white-collar crime, and can constitute something of a self-fulfilling prophecy, wherein police are 'attracted' to areas of high crime and, once there, identify more crime, thus generating more reasons to go there, and so on. The outcome of the intervention (crime) may therefore be co-produced by the intervention itself (greater police presence) – although hotspot experiments regularly find that hotspots interventions reduce recorded crime, of course (Braga et al. 2014). Hope (2009) argues that a counterfactual geographical or temporal *distribution* of hotspots is needed to compare against the actual observed distribution from which units are selected for the intervention: without this, it is uncertain whether the observed distribution is meaningful in terms of the 'real' distribution of crime over place and time; even with it, it is not clear a *particular* hotspot at the time of selection would, absent the experiment, still be a hotspot in a week's, month's, or year's time. Pertinent here is the point that randomisation is an imperfect tool. It cannot simply be assumed that hotspots where crime would have fallen anyway are evenly distributed across experimental and control groups. All this generates uncertainty that poses fundamental questions about selection bias in the inclusion of units into the experiment, about the certainty of conclusions drawn about the effect of the intervention, and, therefore, about the validity of many RCTs and other experiments. Another way to state this argument is to note that, although hotspots policing does seem to reduce recorded crime in high-crime locations, it is far from certain whether this has any impact on the underlying spatial or temporal distribution of offending.

A second and related question concerns the extent of the 'control' needed to select appropriate units for inclusion in an experiment. As noted, units are rarely randomly selected from some larger population but are usually pre-determined (e.g. all roads traffic units in Scotland) or selected on the basis of administrative or other data. In the latter case, exclusion criteria are often applied to determine which can be assigned to treatment or control groups. Experiments involving those charged or convicted of an offence, for example, often exclude serious crimes, or particularly sensitive or troubling offences such as domestic abuse or hate crime (e.g. Neyroud 2017). Such decisions are often highly context-dependent – because, for example, what constitutes sensitive varies from jurisdiction to jurisdiction – and are subject to the preferences and prejudices of the practitioners and others making decisions on implementation. Essentially, the argument moves from 'this intervention produces this outcome' to 'this intervention, fielded in relation to the particular set of units included in this particular study, produces this outcome'. If different exclusion criteria had been applied, then different outcomes would have been possible, even likely. This poses significant challenges for the realism of experiments – how closely they map to the underlying 'real-world' phenomenon they are trying to assess (Pawson and Tilley 1997; c.f. Cartwright 2007). It also poses significant challenges when studies are replicated in other locations, times, or circumstances. If the type and nature of units included differ systematically from study to study, it can be difficult, if not impossible, to compare them.

The final concern with experiments in criminal justice contexts we address here relates to the ways knowledge is produced within academic disciplines. There is widespread concern within the discipline of criminology that an over-emphasis on the 'gold standard' of experiments undermines the legacy of much seminal research within the field – including many of its 'classics', which were rarely based on experimental methods – and ongoing attempts to use more diverse research methods (Lumsden and Goode 2018). A particular issue is the 'technocratic' application of results from experimental studies that provide what appear to be concrete, demonstrably 'true' and 'correct' recommendations for policy, but that miss or even deliberately obscure both their inherent uncertainty and the importance of wider social and political factors in determining 'what works' and where (Hough 2010). Moreover, the idea of the gold standard, as well as use of tools such as the Maryland Scale of Scientific Methods to determine the validity of knowledge (Farrington *et al.* 2002), risks discounting knowledge produced in other ways. There is no a priori reason why experimental methods produce 'better' evidence and knowledge, which is always a context-dependent question: experimental methods do not provide the 'final word' on an issue that trumps all that came before, and researchers should not be compelled to use experimental methods where these are inappropriate, and/or better methods are available to address the question at hand.

Deaton and Cartwright (2018) recount a cautionary tale that summarises some of the points above and is worth repeating here in a little detail. They note that, because it ignores prior information about the topic of study, whether this is derived from theory, existing research, or analysis of the current case, randomisation can be 'wasteful' in discarding useful knowledge and also, in the process, expose people to potential harm from experiments that did not need to take place. They describe what they accept is the extreme case of extracorporeal membrane oxygenation (ECMO):

> a new treatment for new-borns with persistent pulmonary hypertension that was developed in the 1970s by intelligent and directed trial and error within a well-understood theory of the disease and a good understanding of how the oxygenator should work. In early experimentation … mortality was reduced from 80 to 20 percent. The investigators felt compelled to conduct an RCT, albeit with an adaptive 'play-the-winner' design in which each success in an arm increased the probability of the next baby being assigned to that arm. One baby received conventional therapy and died, 11 received ECMO and lived. Even so, a standard randomized controlled trial was thought necessary. With a stopping rule of four deaths, four more babies (out of ten) died in the control group and none of the nine who received ECMO.
>
> *(Deaton and Cartwright 2018: 6)*

In others words, the researchers felt compelled to conduct RCTs owing to existing disciplinary norms that required 'gold standard' evidence of treatment effectiveness, leading to the deaths of five infants. Obvious tragedy aside, the key point here is that the RCTs were unnecessary, as non-randomised experiments and other observations had already amply demonstrated that ECMO worked.

A final word

Although we opened this chapter with clear statements about the strength, even necessity, of experimental methods, it should by now be clear that, along with others, we have significant reservations about the use of experiments in criminal justice contexts. To be sure, experimental methods provide a very powerful research tool for some questions, and, in some circumstances, experiments are clearly the best way to proceed. But in others they are not, and decisions about how to proceed need to be taken on a case-by-case basis. Nor should researchers necessarily shy away from causal claims if they are unable or unwilling to conduct experiments. As the example of ECMO demonstrates, non-experimental methods can isolate causal effects of treatments that are sufficiently convincing to support wider policy implementation. More widely, a 'mosaic' or plurality of methods can be used to explore, and support, causal claims in the absence of experimental evidence (Johnson *et al.* 2019).

Conversely, researchers should not shy away from experiments when and where they seem appropriate. There is little doubt that the policy relevance and impact of criminology has in the past been inhibited by the reluctance or inability of researchers working in the field to conduct experiments. When done properly, and in the correct context, experiments produce clear, actionable policy recommendations. They can also provide for the specific ways to implement those recommendations, as they must, by definition, consider what the intervention is and how it should be delivered, although it should be noted that many experimental interventions do not necessarily live up to this promise. An issue with many hotspots experiments, for example, has been a lack of clarity in relation to which specific elements of the policing intervention produced observed reductions in crime, making wider implementation more difficult. Such concerns notwithstanding, calls for increasing the methodological diversity of many academic disciplines are commonplace, and, within the field of criminology and related subject areas, experiments can and should constitute a vital part of this diversity.

Recommended reading list

Deaton, A. and Cartwright, N. (2018). Understanding and misunderstanding randomized controlled trials. *Social Science & Medicine*, 210: 2–21.

Johnson, R.B., Russo, F. and Schoonenboom, J. (2019) Causation in mixed methods research: The meeting of philosophy, science and practice. *Journal of Mixed Methods Research*, 13 (2): 143–162.

MacQueen, S. and Bradford, B. (2015). Enhancing public trust and police legitimacy during road traffic encounters: Results from a randomised controlled trial in Scotland. *Journal of Experimental Criminology* 11 (3): 419–443.

Polaschek, D.L.L., Yesberg, J.A., Bell, R.K., Casey, A.R. and Dickson, S.R. (2016). Intensive psychological treatment of high-risk violent offenders: Outcomes and pre-release mechanisms. *Psychology, Crime & Law* 22 (4): 344–365.

References

Ariel, B., Farrar, W.A. and Sutherland, A. (2015). The effect of police body-worn cameras on use of force and citizens' complaints against the police: A randomized controlled trial. *Journal of Quantitative Criminology* 31 (3): 509–535.

Bachman, R. and Schutt, R.K. (2007). *The Practice of Research in Criminology and Criminology Research*. Thousand Oaks, CA: Sage.

Braga, A.A., Papachristos, A.V. and Hureau, D.M. (2014). The effects of hot spots policing on crime: An updated systematic review and meta-analysis. *Justice Quarterly* 31 (4): 633–663.

Campbell, D.T. and Stanley, J.C. (1963). *Experimental and Quasi-Experimental Designs for Research. Handbook of Research on Teaching*. Chicago: Rand McNally.

Cartwright, N. (2007). Are RCTs the gold standard? *Biosocieties* 2 (1): 11–20.

Deaton, A. and Cartwright, N. (2018). Understanding and misunderstanding randomized controlled trials. *Social Science & Medicine*, 210: 2–21.

Farrington, D.P., Gottfredson, D.C., Sherman, L.W. and Welsh, B.C. (2002). The Maryland scientific methods scale. In L.W. Sherman, D.P. Farrington, B.C. Welsh and D.L. MacKenzie (eds.) *Evidence-Based Crime Prevention*, 13–21. London: Routledge.

Giacomantonio, C., Bradford, B., Davies, M. and Martin, R. (2015). *Making and Breaking Barriers: Assessing the Value of Mounted Police Units in the UK. Full Report*. Santa Monica, CA: RAND.

Hope, T. (2009). The illusion of control: A response to Professor Sherman. *Criminology and Criminal Justice* 9 (2): 125–134.

Hough, M. (2010). Gold standard or fool's gold? The pursuit of certainty in experimental criminology. *Criminology and Criminal Justice* 10 (1): 11–22.

Johnson, R.B., Russo, F. and Schoonenboom, J. (2019). Causation in mixed methods research: The meeting of philosophy, science and practice. *Journal of Mixed Methods Research*, 13 (2): 143–162.

Kilgour, T.G. and Polaschek, D.L.L. (2012). *Breaking the Cycle of Crime: Special Treatment Unit Evaluation Report*. Wellington: Department of Corrections Psychological Services.

Kirk, D.S. (2009). A natural experiment on residential change and recidivism: Lessons from Hurricane Katrina. *American Sociological Review* 74 (3): 484–505.

Kochel, T.R. (2011). Constructing hot spots policing: Unexamined consequences for disadvantaged populations and for police legitimacy. *Criminal Justice Policy Review* 22 (3): 350–374.

Koehler, J.A., Lösel, F., Akoensi, T.D. and Humphreys, D.K. (2013). A systematic review and meta-analysis on the effects of young offender treatment programs in Europe. *Journal of Experimental Criminology* 9: 19–43.

Lipsey, M.W. and Cullen, F.T. (2007). The effectiveness of correctional rehabilitation: A review of systematic reviews. *Annual Review of Law and Social Sciences* 3: 297–320.

Lumsden, K. and Goode, J. (2018). Policing research and the rise of the 'evidence-base': Police office and staff understandings of research, its implantation and 'what works'. *Sociology*, 52 (4): 813–829.

MacQueen, S. and Bradford, B. (2015). Enhancing public trust and police legitimacy during road traffic encounters: Results from a randomised controlled trial in Scotland. *Journal of Experimental Criminology* 11 (3): 419–443.

MacQueen, S. and Bradford, B. (2017). Where did it all go wrong? Implementation failure – and more – in a field experiment of procedural justice policing. *Journal of Experimental Criminology* 13 (3): 321–345.

Mazerolle, L., Antrobus, E., Bennett, S. and Tyler, T. (2013). Shaping citizen perceptions of police legitimacy: A randomized field trial of procedural justice. *Criminology* 51 (1): 33–64.

Mazerolle, L., Bennett, S., Antrobus, E. and Eggins, E. (2012). Procedural justice, routine encounters and citizen perceptions of police: Main findings from the Queensland Community Engagement Trial (QCET). *Journal of Experimental Criminology* 8 (4): 343–367.

Neyroud, P. (2017). *Learning to Field Test in Policing: Using an Analysis of Completed Randomised Controlled Trials Involving the Police to Develop a Grounded Theory on the Factors Contributing to High Levels of Treatment Integrity in Police Field Experiments*. PhD thesis, University of Cambridge. Available at: www.repository.cam.ac.uk/bitstream/handle/1810/268177/Neyroud-2017-PhD.pdf

Pawson, R. and Tilley, N. (1997). *Realistic Evaluation*. Thousand Oaks: Sage.

Polaschek, D.L.L. and Collie, R.M. (2004). Rehabilitating serious violent adult offenders: An empirical and theoretical stocktake. *Psychology, Crime and Law* 10: 321–334.

Polaschek, D.L.L., Yesberg, J.A., Bell, R.K., Casey, A.R. and Dickson, S.R. (2016). Intensive psychological treatment of high-risk violent offenders: Outcomes and pre-release mechanisms. *Psychology, Crime & Law* 22 (4): 344–365.

Reiner, R. (2010). *The Politics of the Police*. Oxford: Oxford University Press.

Shadish, W.R., Cook, T.D. and Campbell, D.T. (2002). *Experimental and Quasi-Experimental Designs for Generalized Causal Inference*. Boston, MA: Houghton Mifflin.

Tyler, T.R. and Huo, Y. (2002). *Trust in the Law: Encouraging Public Cooperation with the Police and Courts Through*. New York: Russell Sage Foundation.

Weisburd, D., Groff, E.R. and Yang, S.-M. (2012). *The Criminology of Place*. Oxford: OUP.

27

LEGAL EPIDEMIOLOGY, EVIDENCE-INFORMED LAW AND ADMINISTRATIVE DATA

New frontiers in the study of family justice

Matthew A. Jay[*]

Introduction

It is well recognised that law, compared with other sectors of human endeavour, is deficient in its scientific evidence base. My first contention is that there is no 'evidence-informed law'. In medicine, we expect interventions and decisions to be informed by sound research evidence. Getting a drug to market requires extensive testing on animals and humans to establish safety and efficacy. When it is on the market, continual surveillance is required to monitor the incidence of adverse events. Practitioners can then consult the published literature when deciding what treatments to offer.[1] This approach to healthcare—that interventions are underpinned by the best available evidence—is commonly referred to as evidence-informed (or evidence-based) medicine, a process that incorporates research, clinical judgement and patient preferences and values (Sackett *et al.*, 1996). Although they have obvious outward differences, decision-making in medical and legal settings, particularly regarding decisions that have future consequences, share significant commonalities: they are both complex and concerned with balancing the benefits and risks associated with an intervention and making decisions that could result in a range of different outcomes, never knowing in advance what those outcomes will be for any given individual. A lack of research generation and use has, however, been highlighted as a particular problem within the context of the family justice system (FJS) and means that we lack answers to even basic questions about how the system operates, and that life-altering decisions are made without a real appreciation of how individuals will likely be

* I am grateful to Dr Ania Zylbersztejn for her comments on an early draft of this chapter.

1 Guidelines from the National Institute for Health and Care Excellence, based on the best available evidence, are also available.

affected (Rodgers, Trinder and Williams, 2015; Broadhurst et al., 2017; Jay et al., 2017). Clearly, if we do not know how well the system is doing, we cannot hope to improve it.

My second contention is that research evidence therefore has a role to play in law. Epidemiology and administrative data are both well suited to this enterprise, especially when approached from a social, life course perspective. This chapter is therefore about the use of epidemiology to study law and its outcomes (legal epidemiology) and the implementation of research evidence in practice (evidence-informed law). There are some caveats: First, I focus on the English FJS, particularly as it relates to the upbringing of children.[2] This has the advantage of focusing on using epidemiology on particular problems: a good research question, after all, must be precisely specified, albeit with the inevitable drawback that we do not see how epidemiology is applied in other contexts. Second, my focus on epidemiology is not intended to be hegemonic. I have argued before that research teams should have appropriate expertise, including those with quantitative and qualitative research skills, as well as local and national policymakers, social care practitioners, lay people and black-letter lawyers (Jay et al., 2017).

The next section gives a brief introduction to epidemiology and administrative data. This is followed by discussion of three themes arising from the data scoping exercise for the Family Justice Observatory (FJO) that I carried out with colleagues from University College London and Lancaster University and that was funded by the Nuffield Foundation (Jay et al., 2017): individual case prediction versus research, a conceptual framework, and evidence-informed law. I round off with a brief discussion of barriers to moving legal epidemiology and evidence-informed law forward.

Epidemiology

Branches

Epidemiology is the branch of science that investigates the distribution and determinants of health outcomes in populations (Hennekens and Buring, 1987). To describe a pattern of disease, a traditional study involves estimating its prevalence (the proportion of the population that have the disease at a given point) or its incidence (the rate at which people in the population develop the disease during a given period). As such, epidemiology is essentially quantitative. It is not, however, limited to morbidity and mortality: epidemiologists study a range of outcomes such as cognitive function; general health, well-being and quality of life; healthcare delivery; and other outcomes, including social problems. To identify determinants of outcomes, epidemiologists define not just their outcomes, but also their *exposures*: factors thought to be influential in causing the outcome, such as health behaviours (e.g. smoking and exercise), socioeconomic factors, work-place structure, or the built environment. Nor is the field limited to studies *describing* the health and well-being of a population. *Analytical* studies quantify associations between different variables to identify determinants of outcomes. Such studies give clues as to causation between exposure and outcome and potential interventions.

Social epidemiology is a subspeciality that investigates structural factors that determine well-being (Kaufman, 2008), taking a step back to look upstream to the 'causes of the causes' of outcomes.

---

2 I use the term 'family justice system' in a broad sense to mean not only the family courts, but also children's social care services in the discharge of their duties under the Children Act 1989 and other legislation. This is because one cannot be fully understood in isolation from the other. For the same reason, I am concerned both with public family law, such as applications for care orders, and private family law, such as disputes about with whom a child should live following parental separation (Jay et al., 2017).

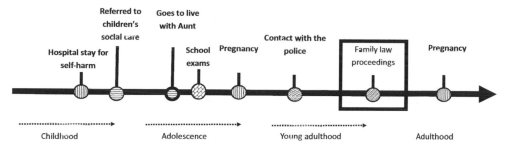

Figure 27.1 A diagram depicting a hypothetical life course and examples of the multiple, intertwined events that can determine outcomes across life

Source: Adapted from Jay *et al.* (2017).

Countless studies have been conducted showing that poorer or more disadvantaged groups, on average, have worse health and social outcomes. This applies more or less consistently to a remarkably wide range of outcomes measured against a wide range of socioeconomic position indicators (Marmot, 2015). Epidemiologists might also adopt a *life course* perspective by studying exposures and outcomes at different stages of life, acknowledging (a) that what happens in early life has far-reaching consequences for health in later life; (b) that many exposures are time-varying (e.g. one may not be consistently poor across life, and changes in exposure status or the cumulative impact of exposures may be important); and (c) that the same exposure may operate differently at different times (Kuh *et al.*, 2003).[3] A hypothetical example of the intertwined nature of different life events at different times is depicted in Figure 27.1.

Within the context of the FJS, the need for a social, life course perspective is clear when one considers the notion of 'welfare', which is the court's paramount consideration in decisions concerning the upbringing of the child.[4] This concept 'extends to and embraces everything that relates to the child's development ... and to the child's present and future life as a human being'.[5] Taking a social and longitudinal perspective across life (and across generations) encourages us to examine individuals and families holistically in research by considering factors that predict entry into the FJS in the first place, the operation of the FJS itself and longer-term outcomes for the individuals whose lives it affects.

Methods

The epidemiologist's toolbox is varied and constantly developing and is the subject of an extensive literature (Hennekens and Buring, 1987; Rothman, Greenland and Lash, 2008). An alternative to the descriptive/analytic dichotomy noted above is to consider observational

---

3 Thalidomide is a clear medical example. This drug, when the foetus is exposed *in utero*, has severe impacts on the developing foetus. However, it was used, before this was known, to treat morning sickness in pregnant women. This is a 'critical period' model: most examples, especially in social epidemiology, are less clear-cut and are usually 'sensitive period' models, in that the exposure can have an effect outside the sensitive window, albeit with less force.

4 Children Act 1989, s 1(1).

5 *Re G (Education: Religious Upbringing)* [2012] EWCA Civ 1233, [26].

and interventional designs, an overview of which is given in Table 27.1; each has its own strengths and weaknesses.

A distinction is also often drawn between retrospective and prospective designs with, it is claimed, prospective studies being superior to retrospective ones. This is partly because data collected after the fact might be less reliable if, for example, participants are required to recall past events. However, determining whether any particular study is 'superior' to another requires a careful assessment of whether the chosen design is appropriate to the research question, whether the data are of high quality, and whether the study accounts for chance, bias and confounding as potential alternative explanations for the findings (Table 27.2), not simply whether the study was designed after or before the fact.

Legal epidemiology

Legal epidemiology, which brings together the above methods with the study of law, is a nascent field. The necessity of integrating epidemiology and law was highlighted by Burris, Kawachi and Sarat (2002), who also noted a limited availability of empirical evidence in support for their hypothesised links between law and health. Addressing this challenge requires interdisciplinary expertise and a well-defined subject matter. I propose a definition for this subspecialty as the branch of epidemiology that seeks to bridge the gap between the field of legal research and that of health and well-being in order to provide answers to policy- and practice-relevant questions. It seeks to understand how law and legal processes operate on a population level, as well as the short- and long-term outcomes for the individuals whom they affect, in all domains of law's activity and of health and well-being. Promoting the use of empirical methods to understand law and effectively disseminating research findings to improve the quality of policy and individual-level decision-making should both be central to the discipline. Legal epidemiology therefore draws together the expertise of epidemiologists with that of lawyers, with the ultimate goal of improving the law and its operation in line with the best available evidence. Legal epidemiology understands law to take place not only on the statute books and law reports, but also in everyday life (Burris, Kawachi and Sarat, 2002). As such, it has particular relevance for socio-legal scholars in that it provides a direct conduit between the law, wider society and health and well-being outcomes.

Data sources

All research needs data, and these could be collected from a variety of sources. Here, I discuss fresh data collection, existing research resources and administrative data. Fresh data collection includes postal or telephone surveys, face-to-face interviews and clinical assessments undertaken to answer some specific research question. The advantage is that the researcher has total control over what questions to ask, and how and when to ask them, but she also has total responsibility. The researcher must identify the target population and a sampling frame, design the questionnaire/interview schedule, assess its reliability and validity, invite and consent participants, conduct the research and everything else besides. This is costly. If done badly, serious biases can be introduced. To take one example, it is well known that people of lower socioeconomic position are less likely to take part in research in the first place and are more likely to drop out if they do, and this can skew results (Howe *et al.*, 2013). Similarly, if the sample is recruited in a non-random fashion, results

Table 27.1 Common epidemiological study designs

Study type	Description	Main advantages	Main disadvantages
Ecological	Assesses correlations between several variables, often over time or regions. Analysis is only at the group level	Comparatively quick and inexpensive as data are readily available. Useful for hypothesis generation, describing trends and international comparisons	Subject to the ecological fallacy: correlations at the group level may not hold at the individual level
Case reports and series	Detailed report of a case or series of cases	Useful for describing novel observations and hypothesis generation	No control group and highly susceptible to selection bias. Sample sizes are small or n = 1. 'Results' may not therefore be generalisable
Cross-sectional	Surveys exposures and outcomes contemporaneously	Often used for hypothesis generation and describing a population	Difficult to discern temporality of associations. May be unsuitable for rare outcomes
Case-control	A sample with the outcome and a control group without are recruited. The groups are then compared on exposures	Can test hypotheses relating to rare outcomes	May be difficult to recruit a suitable control group, leading to biases
Cohort	A sample is followed up from some common inception point (e.g., birth), and data are collected on at least one subsequent occasion	Useful for testing hypotheses as well as population description and hypothesis generation. Temporality of exposure–outcome is usually clear	Can be much costlier and logistically difficult. May be unsuitable for rare outcomes
Interventional	Investigators implement some intervention and measure outcomes before and after. The archetype is the randomised-controlled trial (RCT) whereby participants are randomised to receive the intervention or not	RCTs are generally considered the highest forms of evidence as the act of randomisation addresses confounding, including of unmeasured variables	Costly and logistically difficult. May not be suitable for rare outcomes. Subject to recruitment biases. May be practically or ethically impossible (e.g. a child cannot be randomised to being abused to test the effect of abuse on outcomes)

Table 27.2 Alternative explanations for findings

Possible alternative explanation	Description	Possible solutions
Poor data quality or variation in quality	If data are poorly recorded, inaccuracy and bias may ensue, especially if quality of coding varies. Missing data can also reduce a study's ability to detect differences and/or lead to biased estimates	Researchers collecting data must implement quality assurance such as double data entry. Those using existing resources should carefully investigate data collection and processing and changes over time
Random chance	Estimates of quantities of interest (e.g. averages, proportions or differences) are subject to sampling variability. The smaller the sample, the more volatile the estimate. There is therefore a degree of random chance	Larger sample sizes provide more stable and precise estimates. Statistics can be employed to determine the degree of an estimate's precision and calculate the probability of observing the data, assuming no real difference (frequentist probability values) or the probability of the observed difference given the data and prior knowledge (Bayesian probability). Formulae exist to determine a priori how many participants are required to achieve a level of precision (sample size calculations)
Bias	Biased (systematically incorrect) results arise from a number of sources. Examples: selection bias (certain groups more likely to take part than others); attrition bias (more likely to drop out); recall bias (more or less likely to accurately recall past events); or misclassification bias (more or less likely to be correctly classified as having the outcome)	Best addressed in study design. Researchers can, e.g., oversample from groups known to be less likely to take part and offer incentives such as small cash payments. Carefully defining and measuring exposure and outcome status are also crucial. Blinding researchers and participants to exposure/outcome/treatment status also assists where feasible
Confounding	Occurs where a spurious association between two variables is induced by their relationship with a third. Alternatively, a negative confounder might mask an association. A confounder is considered a 'nuisance', the effect of which we wish to control	Confounding can be addressed by study design (e.g. by restricting analyses or matching participants on confounders) or statistical adjustment. Multivariable models such as multiple regression can be employed to control for confounders, and these have become the mainstay in the epidemiologist's armamentarium

may not be generalisable to the target population. Finally, fresh data collection may be unsuitable for certain outcomes, particularly rare ones as the number of participants required would be prohibitively large.

Epidemiologists might therefore consider existing research resources. Britain has a number of established birth cohorts: studies of individuals recruited at birth[6] and followed up regularly throughout their lives. Investigators can request access to the data to investigate their own hypotheses. The earliest cohort was established in 1946, and there have been several since: 1958, 1970 and the millennium (Institute of Education, no date). A number of regional studies also exist such as the Avon Longitudinal Study of Parents and Children, established in 1991 (Boyd *et al.*, 2013), and many surveys, often commissioned by government, that recruit different samples at each data collection wave (Office for National Statistics, no date). These resources contain rich data on a variety of life aspects, including socioeconomic conditions, family circumstances, personal development and health and social outcomes, all of which may be relevant to socio-legal scholars.

The research resources, however, are also subject to selection and attrition biases. They may also not contain the necessary information on exposures or outcomes and may be too small, even though they recruit thousands of individuals, to study certain topics. A third resource to consider is therefore administrative data. Administrative data refers to:

> [i]nformation about people, business and other organisations that is collected by any government department or agency, for delivering their day-to-day services. It can include information such as tax records, school records, health information, etc.

> *(Administrative Data Research Network, 2017)*

For example, the Children Looked After (CLA) data set, held by the Department for Education (DfE), contains information on all children who become looked after[7] in England (Mc Grath-Lone *et al.*, 2016; Jay *et al.*, 2017). Data are held on, among other things, demographics (age, gender and ethnicity), date of each episode and period of care per child, local authority, legal status (e.g. whether the child became looked after through a care order or some other route), placement type (e.g. foster carers or care home) and reason for exit from care. Researchers working on these data will be working with files that contain hundreds of thousands of rows, one for each time a child enters care, and therefore the data are said to be at the individual or episode level.[8]

Data sets from the FJS have to date been under-utilised. Nevertheless, where they have been used, results have been eye-opening. The CLA data set has been exploited to show that 3.3% of all children born in 1992–4 entered out-of-home care before their 18th birthday, that this rate is rising with more recent birth cohorts and that rates of entry varied by ethnicity (Mc Grath-Lone *et al.*, 2015). Linked to data from all schools in England, Sebba *et al.* (2015) demonstrated the ways in which educational outcomes differ among CLA, children in need[9] and the general population. Researchers using administrative data from the Children and Family Courts Advisory and Support Service

---

6 Or, rather, mothers recruited during pregnancy. The children recruited can, of course, opt out of future participation if they wish.

7 That is, who are 'in care': these are children whom a local authority considers it necessary to look after, usually because they have experienced, or are at risk of, neglect or abuse.

8 In contrast to data at the aggregate level. Individual-level data are always presented in the aggregate in publication in order to make sense of them and to preserve data subjects' anonymity.

9 Per the Children Act 1989, s 17, a child in need is a child who is unlikely to achieve or maintain a reasonable standard of health or development without local authority services, or whose health or development is likely to be impaired without such services or who is disabled.

(CAFCASS)[10] were able to demonstrate that 24% of mothers subject to public family law proceedings experienced at least one further set of proceedings within seven years (Broadhurst *et al.*, 2015), and work is underway to examine the role of fathers in these cases—a difficult group to study in social work settings (Nuffield Foundation, 2017).

It would likely be impossible to carry out these studies without administrative data. Because data are collected on every service contact with the whole population, it is possible to overcome sampling-related problems (such as selection biases and loss to follow-up) and small sample sizes. The use of such data also means there is no burden on study participants; data are collected contemporaneously, meaning that there is limited or no risk of recall bias or recall-related inaccuracies; and, because the data already exist as part of the service's normal operations, research costs are reduced. Different data sets can also be linked together to provide further depth of analysis (Harron *et al.*, 2017). It is therefore possible to overcome many of the limitations of the study designs in Table 27.1.

It is worth mentioning at this stage the (dis)connections between administrative data and big data, especially given the intense interest that has arisen around the opportunities and challenges of such data sets. There is no universally agreed definition of 'big data', though such data sets are typically extremely large to the extent that they provide computational challenges not present in more traditional forms of data (Connelly *et al.*, 2016). Connelly *et al.* (2016), despite considering administrative data sources to be a form of big data, nonetheless draw several distinctions between them and other types. These include the fact that administrative data tend to be more structured, with a known target population, whereas other big data sources are not (Connelly *et al.*, 2016). For example, although Twitter holds data on all Twitter posts, it is not known necessarily who the population is that tweets. The CLA data set, by contrast, contains all data on looked after children, which is a clearly defined population of children drawn from another clearly defined population (i.e. all other children). The size of administrative data sets might also distinguish them from other sources. The CLA data set held data for 99,230 children in 2014–15 (Mc Grath-Lone *et al.*, 2016). This is extremely large compared with many studies of children in care, but is small compared with the billions of data points generated by Twitter.

It will be noted that I have specifically referred to big data as a data source. A sound methodological framework—whether epidemiological or otherwise—is still required to analyse them. They cannot stand on their own if we are to draw meaningful conclusions from them. The possible alternative explanations mentioned in Table 27.2 apply equally to big data as to any other source. Big data, as with administrative data, may provide more precise answers, but they will not necessarily provide more reliable, valid or reproducible answers. The conversation around big data is often centred on the use of algorithms for predictive purposes. This is distinct from their use in an epidemiological framework and discussed further in the next section.

Legal epidemiology and evidence-informed law

I discuss in this section certain aspects of the data scoping exercise I carried out with colleagues at University College London and Lancaster University for the FJO (Jay *et al.*, 2017). This was one exercise in a broader study that aimed to inform the structure and

---

10 A body that represents all children who go through care proceedings. CAFCASS also has some involvement where children are involved with private cases that reach the courts such as disputes about where a child should live following relationship breakdown.

functions of a new organisational structure (the FJO), whose purpose will be to improve the generation and use of research evidence within the FJS (Rodgers, Trinder and Williams, 2015). The review is an example of the kind of work that researchers must do when using administrative data to better understand the resources being used. For the purposes of the present chapter, its value lies in the methodological and conceptual developments that the review necessitated. I do not intend to précis the report (it is freely available online and contains a concise executive summary and table of key points), but instead to draw out three issues that are particularly important for legal epidemiology with administrative data: (1) a distinction between data for individual case level prediction and research-based inference; (2) the development of an epidemiological conceptual framework; and (3) evidence-informed law.

Individual case predictive analytics vs research inference

It is essential to delineate a distinction between the use of data for prediction and the use of data for research. Failure to distinguish between these two could undermine public trust in the use of administrative data (in the legal sector and elsewhere), and this would have knock-on effects for service operation and research. The use of data for prediction refers to bodies using data on identified individuals or groups in order to target services at them. This could be, for example, exploiting big data with machine learning algorithms or implementing screening tests to predict who may require services and thereby put in place an early intervention in order to secure better outcomes sooner and at lower cost. There are two broad considerations pertinent to the use of administrative data about people in such a way: (1) evidence as to efficacy and (2) infringements of privacy.

As to the first, such methods should only be used if underpinned by strong research evidence that they are effective. A review of screening protocols used in emergency departments to detect child abuse, for example, found no evidence that any test was highly predictive of abuse, and that the addition of screening protocols to clinical screening assessment increased false positives far in excess of the additional abused children detected (Woodman *et al.*, 2008). A DfE systematic review concluded that, of tools available to analyse data to identify whether a child is suffering, or likely to suffer, significant harm, there was significant variability in their validity, with many tools performing poorly in many domains of validity and reliability (Barlow, Fisher and Jones, 2012). If tools are inaccurate or prone to false positives and false negatives, they might in fact result in more harm than good. If a false positive occurs, stigma and antagonization might ensue, and resources will be wasted; if a false negative occurs, an opportunity to intervene is missed.

The second issue—privacy—can essentially be rephrased as: even if we can predict outcomes reliably and validly using administrative data, should we? Administrative data are usually, by necessity, collected and used by a public body without the data subject's express consent, and as such the subject's right to privacy is engaged. Given that groups under consideration are generally of poorer socioeconomic circumstances, any such infringement may be discriminatory. The DfE systematic review also identified concerns among practitioners that such tools may be too simplistic and represent a threat to their professional judgement and decision-making (Barlow, Fisher and Jones, 2012). Indeed, automated decision-making is a concern legally, particularly under the General Data

Protection Regulation,[11] which contains specific provisions that determine under what circumstances wholly automated decision-making and profiling are lawful.[12] There are therefore both ethical and legal obstacles to the use of predictive algorithms in this field that must be studied, and that must have public support, if such tools are to be made part of day-to-day practice.

By contrast, the use of administrative data for research purposes involves approved and trained researchers accessing de-identified data and, after a process of careful scrutiny and analysis, drawing conclusions about defined populations. Rather than predicting a result for a given individual, epidemiological research is concerned with eliciting the causal mechanisms between exposure and outcome at a group level and thereby predicting what happens, on average, at a group level. Data access and linkage are done in a secure manner and in a way that limits the risk of re-identification (Harron *et al.*, 2017). This enables researchers to analyse the data without needing the original identifiers, thus ensuring anonymity of data subjects is maintained. Published data are in anonymised, aggregate form only, using appropriate summary statistics. It is the published data from such a process of turning data into research evidence with which I have been concerned in this chapter.

An epidemiological conceptual framework

In epidemiology, it is often useful to develop a conceptual framework in diagrammatic form for a given problem. Such frameworks aid in explaining complex relationships among different variables operating at different levels (individual, family, local, national) and can be useful for hypothesising, directing interventions and informing analytical approaches (Paradies and Stevens, 2005). It was therefore useful to develop such a framework for legal epidemiological investigations into phenomena that are, as noted in the introduction, inherently complex and multifaceted.

The framework developed for the FJO review is depicted in Figure 27.2. This should be considered preliminary in that it is necessarily a simplified representation, and work will be required to test specific hypotheses at various points of the system and, if necessary, modify the framework. It should also be noted that this model is broadly consistent with other epidemiological models such as the World Health Organization's social determinants of health framework (Commission on the Social Determinants of Health, 2008) and not intended to challenge them. A high-level framework linking law to health more generally is given in Burris, Kawachi and Sarat (2002). What our framework adds is a focus on child maltreatment and welfare need and the interventions intended to deal with them. Here I detail the most important aspects of the framework and provide illustrative examples from research that underpin it.

Central to the framework is the operationalisation of child maltreatment and high welfare need (the entity that the FJS exists to remedy) and the population of children at risk. More than 3% of children enter out-of-home care at least once before their 18th birthday (Mc Grath-Lone *et al.*, 2015), and an estimated one in five is referred to social services before

---

11 Regulation 2016/679 of the European Parliament and of the Council of 27 April 2016 on the protection of natural persons with regard to the processing of personal data and on the free movement of such data, and repealing Directive 95/46/EC (General Data Protection Regulation) OJ L 119/1.

12 In particular, art 22(1) states that, '[t]he data subject shall have the right not to be subject to a decision based solely on automated processing, including profiling, which produces legal effects concerning him or her or similarly significantly affects him or her'. An exception to this is where the decision is authorised by Union or member state law that also contains 'suitable measures to safeguard the data subjects' rights and freedoms and legitimate interests': art 22(2).

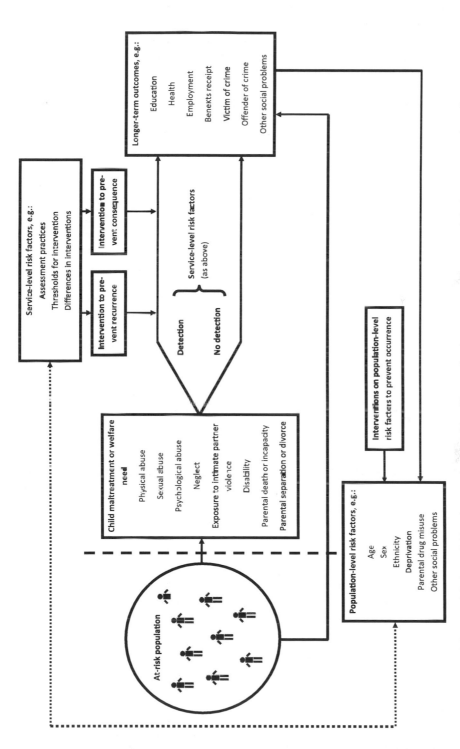

Figure 27.2 A conceptual framework linking child maltreatment and child welfare need to longer-term outcomes and the interventions along the way

Source: Adapted from Jay *et al.* (2017).

the age of 5 (Bilson and Martin, 2016). A set of risk factors determine who is more likely to be affected: this is depicted by the thick dashed line. It is known that rates of children entering out-of-home care vary by ethnic status: for children born in 2001–03, 4.2% of mixed-ethnicity children and 4.5% of black children entered care by age 9, compared with 1.6% of white children, 0.8% of Asian children and 2.7% of children with other ethnicities (Mc Grath-Lone *et al.*, 2015). Deprivation is also a major predictor, with children living in more deprived areas being significantly more likely to enter care than those in less deprived ones (Bywaters *et al.*, 2017). Younger maternal age is associated with an increased likelihood of having recurrent care proceedings (Broadhurst *et al.*, 2015). Understanding risk factors such as these is important not only for planning purposes, but also for identifying interventions to reduce the occurrence of need in the first place.

The second elements of the framework worth emphasising are the interventions. Where need exists, it will not always be detected, and, where it is detected, there will not always be an intervention, or the intervention may change over time and space. Examples include the Family Drug and Alcohol Court (FDAC, 2017), provision of services under section 17 of the Children Act 1989 or care and adoption orders. Whether an intervention is offered will depend on a set of service-level risk factors such as local authority assessment practices and the thresholds at which various state actors will intervene. Crucially, these risk factors may interact with the characteristics of the populations served, in that different services might deal with different groups in different ways (represented by the dotted double arrows). Thus, a child living in a deprived neighbourhood is less likely to enter care if they live in a deprived local authority compared with a less-deprived one (Bywaters *et al.*, 2017), indicating that 'richer' authorities might be dealing with 'poorer' families in different ways to 'poorer' authorities.[13]

Finally, all children will experience longer-term outcomes, the precise extent, nature and mechanisms of which may be elucidated through research. It is well known that CLA and children in need have worse educational attainment than the general population (Sebba *et al.*, 2015). Much remains to be understood, however, such as the role that special educational needs and disabilities have to play and, given that being 'in care' or 'in need' are statuses that vary over time (Mc Grath-Lone, 2017), how complex care trajectories affect educational outcomes. In the realm of mental health, 55% of looked after children aged 5–10 years and 49% of those aged 11–15 years were identified by Meltzer *et al.* as having a mental disorder, proportions 6.8 and 4.5 times higher than the general population, respectively (Meltzer *et al.*, 2000, 2002). Interventions to improve long-term outcomes (and the research that must underpin these interventions) will improve the lives not only of these vulnerable children, but also of their families and future generations, as these longer-term consequences will inexorably determine the conditions of future generations.

I do not propose that this framework is immutable. It is a general theory linking social conditions, admission to the FJS and long-term outcomes. As such it is, in essence, a scientific theory to be fleshed out, tested, refined, disproved and improved by continual research initiatives. In the process, novel interventions can be formulated, piloted and, if successful, rolled out for the benefit of all.

---

13 I use inverted commas because the measure of deprivation used in that study was the Index of Multiple Deprivation, which is an area-based measure of deprivation, not affluence, and not all people living in deprived areas are individually deprived.

Evidence-informed law

I now return to the theme with which I opened this chapter—the use of research evidence in legal decision-making—and I stress the similarities that I drew between legal and medical decisions. Both are complex and probabilistic. In both, someone will be offered some intervention that will have some intended outcome at some point in the future.[14] In medicine, it might be a surgeon deciding whether to operate to remove a brain tumour; in law, it might be a judge deciding whether a child should be adopted against the wishes of his or her parents. In both, nobody knows beforehand what will happen to the affected individual. But, in healthcare, we often have a good idea of what is *likely* to happen because of decades of population-level research and evidence-informed medicine. In the FJS, the lack of these is conspicuous (Rodgers, Trinder and Williams, 2015). We expect that the use of even common, everyday drugs is based on sound research evidence. We owe to our children at least the same level of scrutiny of the interventions offered by local authorities and courts, the very nature of which can only have life-long consequences.

It is worth emphasising that basing decisions on research evidence does not mean allowing that evidence to dictate those decisions, undermining judicial and administrative discretion and independence. Research evidence can be used to *inform* the likely possible outcomes, but can never say whether any particular individual will actually experience them. Under a model of evidence-informed law, the discretion of the judge is maintained, and the decision must still be made with reference to the black-letter law, the circumstances of the individual and her family and other relevant factors. What differs to the present situation is that decision-makers would use research evidence in their day-to-day work to make decisions that are more conducive to the welfare of the child and result in better long-term outcomes.

Unto the breach

I have aimed to make a case that legal epidemiology and administrative data have a role to play both in the legal academy and on the front line. Epidemiological methods coupled in particular with administrative data can provide unique insights into the operations of the system as well as predictors for entry and long-term consequences. The latter are particularly important for decisions made within the FJS that have profound effects upon the lives of children and families. In this section, I discuss some difficulties and opportunities with moving the field forward and getting research evidence into day-to-day practice.

Perhaps the most fundamental challenge is the well-known lack of empirical training on undergraduate and postgraduate law curricula (Genn, Partington and Wheeler, 2006). This is true of both qualitative and quantitative disciplines, but is perhaps most acute with the latter, evidenced by the fact that the present volume contains few chapters dedicated to quantitative methodology. It is not difficult to see how a lack of even a basic understanding of research methodology could lead to misunderstandings and misconceptions among practitioners and a failure to generate a critical mass of researchers to take the discipline forward, especially where this is technical and highly complex, as in the case of legal epidemiology and administrative data. The epidemiological analysis of large data sets requires skills in: data storage and

---

14 The same is not true for all legal decisions. Deciding whether A assaulted B, or whether C breached her contract with D, are essentially retrospective fact-finding missions that, when established, have logical legal consequences. Whether a given decision is in a child's best interests, however, requires a probabilistic prediction of the future.

management, data cleaning, coding programming skills, general research methods and critical appraisal, and advanced quantitative statistical methods. Such skills require specialist training, yet even basic quantitative methods are conspicuously absent from legal curricula.

A second problem lies in the practical difficulties of working with administrative data and the technical infrastructure required (Jay *et al.*, 2017). Applications to data providers for access to administrative data can be complex and time-consuming, and researchers will be required to demonstrate that they are qualified to handle the data appropriately. Data are generally used without the express consent of the data subject. A legal basis for sharing data is therefore required,[15] and the processing, sharing and storage of data must be conducted ethically and in accordance with stringent information governance requirements. Precedents for such sharing exist (e.g., the 'Safe Havens' of the Secure Anonymised Information Linkage Databank; SAIL Databank, 2018), but researchers will have to ensure that they are in a position to process data safely if they are to work with administrative data.

These challenges are not insurmountable, and research progress could be made immediately without radical changes to the academy or the court. All science is done in teams, and there is no reason why those with the necessary skills in epidemiology and administrative data could not enter into collaborations with lawyers, socio-legal scholars and others. Such collaborations would enable lawyers to access methodological expertise as well as the data, and they would give scientists access to legal expertise necessary for the interpretation of findings. Legal epidemiology has enormous promise for the field but is at present a nascent discipline. The establishment of a community of family justice researchers was one of the key recommendations arising from the FJO data scoping review, and it will be through such a community that the greatest gains will be made in terms of research endeavours.

Conclusion

Legal epidemiology has a necessary role to play in socio-legal scholarship. Legal epidemiological research evidence can also be used to inform legal decisions, with the ultimate goal of making better decisions. Both legal epidemiology and evidence-informed law, as I have outlined them on these pages, are perhaps relatively novel developments, but I hope I have begun to convince the reader that they are important. They sit alongside other approaches and can be used to draw out the causative mechanisms between exposures and outcomes of interest at a population level, in a manner that is robust, transparent and generalisable and that has direct implications for policy and practice. All researchers should seek to improve the law and how it operates: legal epidemiology can be a crucial part of ensuring that we know whether what we are doing is working or not.

Further reading

Berkman, L. F., Kawachi, I. and Glymour, M. (eds) (2014) *Social Epidemiology*. 2nd edn. Oxford: Oxford University Press.

Burris, S., Kawachi, I. and Sarat, A. (2002) 'Integrating Law and Social Epidemiology', *Journal of Law, Medicine & Ethics*, 30, pp. 510–21.

Jay, M. A. *et al.* (2018) 'Harnessing Administrative Data for Family Justice Research and Practice' *Family Law*, Mar., pp. 315-19.

15 E.g., data in respect of family proceedings held by CAFCASS can be shared for research purposes by virtue of the Criminal Justice and Court Services Act 2000, s 13(5).

Marmot, M. (2015) *The Health Gap: The Challenge of an Unequal World*. London: Bloomsbury.

Rothman, K., Greenland, S. and Lash, T. (eds) (2008) *Modern Epidemiology*. 3rd edn. Philadelphia, PA: Lippincott Williams & Wilkins.

References

Administrative Data Research Network. (2017) *Glossary*. Available at: www.adrn.ac.uk/public-engagement/glossary/ (accessed: 11 December 2017).

Barlow, J., Fisher, J. D., and Jones, D. (2012) *Systematic Review of Models of Analysing Significant Harm: Research Report DFE-RR199*. Available at: https://assets.publishing.service.gov.uk/government/uploads/system/uploads/attachment_data/file/183949/DFE-RR199.pdf (accessed: 6 August 2018).

Bilson, A. and Martin, K. E. C. (2016) 'Referrals and Child Protection in England: One in Five Children Referred to Children's Services and One in Nineteen Investigated before the Age of Five', *British Journal of Social Work*, 47(3), pp. 793–811. doi: 10.1093/bjsw/bcw054

Boyd, A. *et al.* (2013) 'Cohort Profile: The "children of the 90s"—The Index Offspring of the Avon Longitudinal Study of Parents and Children', *International Journal of Epidemiology*, 42(1), pp. 111–27.

Broadhurst, K. *et al.* (2015) 'Connecting Events in Time to Identify a Hidden Population: Birth Mothers and Their Children in Recurrent Care Proceedings in England', *British Journal of Social Work*, 45(8), pp. 2241–60. doi: 10.1093/bjsw/bcv130

Broadhurst, K. *et al.* (2017) *Towards a Family Justice Observatory—A Scoping Study: Main Findings Report of the National Stakeholder Consultation*. Available at: http://wp.lancs.ac.uk/observatory-scoping-study/ (accessed: 12 December 2017).

Burris, S., Kawachi, I. and Sarat, A. (2002) 'Integrating Law and Social Epidemiology', *Journal of Law, Medicine & Ethics*, 30, pp. 510–21.

Bywaters, P. *et al.* (2017) *Identifying and Understanding Inequalities in Child Welfare Intervention Rates: Comparative Studies in Four UK Countries*. Available at: www.nuffieldfoundation.org/inequalities-child-welfare-intervention-rates (accessed: 12 March 2018).

Commission on the Social Determinants of Health. (2008) *Closing the Gap in a Generation: Health Equity through Action on the Social Determinants of Health*. Available at: http://apps.who.int/iris/bitstream/10665/43943/1/9789241563703_eng.pdf (accessed: 15 December 2017).

Connelly, R. *et al.* (2016) 'The Role of Administrative Data in the Big Data Revolution in Social Science Research', *Social Science Research*, 59, pp. 1–12. doi: 10.1016/j.ssresearch.2016.04.015

SAIL Databank. (2018) *SAIL Databank - The Secure Anonymised Information Linkage Databank*. Available at: https://saildatabank.com/ (accessed: 1 February 2018).

FDAC. (2017) *FDAC National Unit*. Available at: http://fdac.org.uk/ (accessed: 15 December 2017).

Genn, H., Partington, M. and Wheeler, S. (2006) *Law in the Real World. Improving Our Understanding of How Law Works. Final Report and Recommendations*. Available at: www.nuffieldfoundation.org/nuffield-inquiry-empirical-legal-research-law-real-world

Harron, K. *et al.* (2017) 'Challenges in Administrative Data Linkage for Research', *Big Data & Society*, 4(2), doi: 10.1177/2053951717745678

Hennekens, C. H. and Buring, J. E. (1987) *Epidemiology in Medicine*. Philadelphia, PA: Lippincott, Williams & Wilkins.

Howe, L., *et al.* (2013) 'Loss to Follow-up in Cohort Studies: Bias in Estimates of Socioeconomic Inequalities', *Epidemiology*, 24(1), pp. 1–9.

Institute of Education. (no date) *Birth Cohort Studies*. Available at: https://cls.ucl.ac.uk/ (accessed: 23 May 2019).

Jay, M. A. *et al.* (2017) *Who Cares for Children? Population Data for Family Justice Research*. Available at: http://wp.lancs.ac.uk/observatory-scoping-study/

Kaufman, J. (2008) 'Social Epidemiology,' in Rothman, K., Greenland, S. and Lash, T. (eds) *Modern Epidemiology*, pp 532–548. 3rd edn. Philadelphia, PA: Lippincott Williams & Wilkins.

Kuh, D. *et al.* (2003) 'Life Course Epidemiology,' *Journal of Epidemiology and Community Health*, 57(10), pp. 778–83. doi: 10.1136/jech.57.10.778

Marmot, M. (2015) *The Health Gap: The Challenge of an Unequal World*. London: Bloomsbury.

Mc Grath-Lone, L. *et al.* (2015) 'Changes in First Entry to Out-Of-Home Care From 1992 to 2012 Among Children in England', *Child Abuse & Neglect*, 51, pp. 163–71. doi: 10.1016/j.chiabu.2015.10.020

Mc Grath-Lone, L. *et al.* (2016) 'Data Resource Profile: Children Looked After Return (CLA)', *International Journal of Epidemiology*, 45(3), pp. 716–17f. doi: 10.1093/ije/dyw117

Mc Grath-Lone, L. (2017) *Using Longitudinal Administrative Data to Characterise the Use of Out-of-Home Care Among Looked After Children in England*. Thesis (PhD). University College London.

Meltzer, H. *et al.* (2000) *The Mental Health of Children and Adolescents in Great Britain*. London: The Stationery Office.

Meltzer, H. *et al.* (2002) *The Mental Health of Young People Looked After by Local Authorities in England*. London: The Stationery Office.

Nuffield Foundation. (2017) *Understanding the Scale, Pattern and Dynamics of Birth Fathers' Recurrent Appearance in Care Proceedings*. Available at: www.nuffieldfoundation.org/birth-fathers-recurrent-appearance-care-proceedings (accessed: 23 May 2019).

Office for National Statistics. (no date) *Household and Individual Surveys*. Available at: www.ons.gov.uk/surveys/informationforhouseholdsandindividuals/householdandindividualsurveys (accessed: 12 March 2018).

Paradies, Y. and Stevens, M. (2005) 'Conceptual Diagrams in Public Health Research', *Journal of Epidemiology and Community Health*, 59(12), pp. 1012–13. doi: 10.1136/jech.2005.036913

Rodgers, B., Trinder, L. and Williams, T. (2015) *Towards A Family Justice Observatory to Improve the Generation and Application of Research*. Available at: www.nuffieldfoundation.org/towards-family-justice-observatory

Rothman, K., Greenland, S. and Lash, T. (eds) (2008) *Modern Epidemiology*. 3rd edn. Philadelphia, PA: Lippincott Williams & Wilkins.

Sackett, D. L. *et al.* (1996) 'Evidence Based Medicine: What It Is and What It Isn't', *BMJ*, 312, pp. 71–2. doi: 10.1136/BMJ.312.7023.71

Sebba, J. *et al.* (2015) *The Educational Progress of Looked After Children in England: Linking Care and Educational Data*. Available at: http://reescentre.education.ox.ac.uk/research/educational-progress-of-looked-after-children/ (accessed: 12 March 2018).

Woodman, J. *et al.* (2008) 'Performance of Screening Tests for Child Physical Abuse in Accident and Emergency Departments', *Health Technology Assessment*, 12(33), pp. iii, xi–xiii, 1–95.

28

SOCIO-LEGAL APPROACHES TO ONLINE HATE SPEECH[*]

Nicole Stremlau and Iginio Gagliardone

As part of his tradition to set an annual personal challenge at the start of the year, Mark Zuckerberg pledged to "fix Facebook" in 2018. Efforts following his statement, and significant setbacks, have demonstrated just how challenging this commitment could be (Bever 2018). From growing evidence of Russian interference in the 2016 US elections, to widespread breaches of privacy in the Cambridge Analytica scandal, to rising concerns about the spread and prevalence of hate speech online, questions of whether and how Facebook can be "fixed" are growing (Battelle 2018; Osnos 2018). The company has increasingly been investing in research – once regarded as a tangential part of its business. Facebook has long argued it is a "platform" rather than a "publisher" and therefore not liable for the content found on its site. But, over the past year, as criticism has mounted and the scale of the problems became increasingly clear to the company's leadership, thousands more content monitors have been hired to identify and flag hate speech online, and there has been an increase in investment in research around areas such as how the platform is used for misinformation, particularly around elections, and new ways of identifying hate speech online through artificial intelligence.

This chapter explores what methods a socio-legal approach offers to address some of these challenges, particularly around online hate speech. Although there is no unified "socio-legal" perspective, adopting some of the tools and theoretical frameworks socio-legal scholars use enables us to ask questions that have been overlooked, particularly in the traditional legal approaches that have dominated much of the contemporary scholarship on hate speech and its regulation. These approaches have largely revolved around doctrinal disputes about the limits of free speech and have mostly involved European and American scholars.

Three areas related to socio-legal perspectives on hate speech online are explored in the following sections: first, the challenges of defining "hate speech", especially when it is on a global, borderless platform; second, the difficulties of actually identifying hate speech online in particular contexts when language may be coded, or there may be different social

[*] This project has received support from the European Research Council under the European Union's Horizon 2020 research and innovation programme (agreement no. 716686, ConflictNET).

mores; and, third, a concrete project analysing the nature and proliferation of hate speech online is illustrated, highlighting the challenges of both definition and research in practice.

Hate speech: a definitional challenge

Over the last decade, there has been a proliferation of different types of authority seeking to define what is and is not allowed to be said or written in the public domain. Multi-stakeholder processes have been initiated to bring greater clarity and suggest mechanisms to identify hateful messages. The United Nations Office of the High Commissioner for Human Rights has been leading the effort and initiated a process of global consultations under the name of the Rabat Plan of Action to clarify the scope of obligations under Article 20 of the International Covenant on Civil and Political Rights that prohibits incitement of hatred. Despite harmonization efforts at a global level, national governments have taken radically different positions, seeking to enforce conceptions of civility that lead to a stricter application of hate speech regulations or, on the contrary, failing to recognize the role of their own political discourse in fuelling a language of hate.

Social networking platforms, as expanding private spaces for public expression, have created unprecedented conditions for the regulation of speech and, in their quest to create global standards or rules, have somewhat unexpectedly become involved in new forms of law-making, creating the boundaries of what can be defined acceptable speech and setting trends for national policymakers. These companies have advanced their own definitions of hate speech, binding users to a set of rules and becoming arbiters of what constitutes an infringement of those rules. They often rely on their users as "flaggers" to identify content that violates their community standards and bring it to the attention of these companies, which then decide how to act on the content. Social media companies have also been active in influencing policy and government approaches to determining what might constitute hate speech. In the US, this has been done with expensive and extensive lobbying efforts in Washington. In 2017, Alphabet, Google's parent company, spent the most of all social media companies (US$18.2 million) on lobbying with 102 registered lobbyists (Lanard 2018). And social media companies are increasingly investing in attempts to shape policy and regulations abroad through funding civil society groups, working closely with the US State Department on shared "freedom of expression" or "Internet freedom" agendas (the comparatively lax US approach to information regulation more closely matches the interests of social media companies than that of the governments in many markets they are seeking to grow their business in), and through providing technical or media policy assistance to governments, particularly in developing countries (Hanson 2012).

In this complex and diverse scenario, socio-legal studies' rich engagement with legal pluralism can offer an important complement to current debates, analysing in practice how different sources of authority coexist and compete, and with what consequences. There are tensions between a desire to develop global definitions of what constitutes "hate speech" and, at the same time, a desire to localize them and have culturally interpretive approaches to making decisive judgements about what exactly hate speech might be, at a particular moment and in a particular space. But there are also increasing calls for narrower definitions of hate speech, so that it can be better identified and targeted and not misused by actors (often more powerful ones) justifying speech as hateful as a means of taking down or restricting speech that might be unappealing to them personally or challenge their authority.

"Hate speech" is a broad and emotive concept. It lies in a complex nexus with freedom of expression, individual, group and minority rights, as well as concepts of dignity, liberty and equality. As a phenomenon, it calls into question some of the most fundamental principles on which societies are built (Gagliardone et al. 2015). The answers each society has developed to balance freedom of expression with respect for equality and dignity have created unique rifts and alliances.

Despite multiple efforts to define the contours of hate speech, in everyday discourse the term has tended to be used well beyond the boundaries set by international and national bodies and Internet companies. Incidents (e.g. hate crimes against immigrants or members of a minority group) and critical events (e.g. elections) have played an important role in raising awareness around the power of speech to lead to violence but have also promoted debates that largely ignore long-term definitional efforts and have been open to manipulation by political entrepreneurs. Empirical studies that have explored popular perceptions of hate speech and compared them with those used among scholars and in policy circles (iHub Research 2013) have highlighted how personal insults, propaganda and negative commentary about politicians also tend to be referred to as hate speech.

Building on these expansive definitions, accusations of "hate speech" have also been employed by governments and those in positions of power to shut down legitimate debates on matters of public interest. This has extended to judgments that assume speakers intentionally advocated harm when their intent may have been more frivolous – an ill-judged or flippant comment on social media – or nuanced – to satirize, or provoke a debate on a challenging issue, including through art (Rowbottom 2012). In instances where the speech is offensive or provocative, the labelling of the expression as hate speech could overstate the connection between the speech and the alleged harm – either by misjudging the influence of a speaker or the likelihood of harm occurring and/or overlooking the propensity of individuals to engage in counter speech that has a strong and positive impact. This is especially the case in deeply divided societies that are transitioning to democracy, and where the government is often in a hegemonic position with limited accountability, and where there is censorship or control of media outlets. Such practices have led to the implication that all hate speech is unlawful, with calls for criminal or other sanctions that might be inappropriate or ineffective and might indeed hinder democratic outcomes. For instance, it could lead to increased policing and state or private surveillance of discourse, including online, and encourage over-reliance on censorship instead of systemic discrimination being addressed.

In cases where there are open hostilities between groups, the use of the term hate speech could have the opposite consequence than intended. Indeed, defining an expression as a hate speech act and attempts to counter it could actually increase the audience of its speaker, especially if they are able to position themselves as "martyrs" of censorship or frame unsuccessful attempts at censorship as a vindication of their views. Arguably, this could have more severe consequences than a lack of response (Mouffe 2018).

For these reasons, alternative, more narrowly defined concepts, such as "dangerous speech" or "fear speech", have been proposed, focusing more on the propensity of expression to cause widespread violence. In some contexts, such as in resolutions of the UN Human Rights Council, the term "hate speech" is avoided in favour of more elaborate formulations such as "intolerance, negative stereotyping and stigmatization of, and discrimination, incitement to violence, and violence against persons based on religion or belief", or "the spread of discrimination and prejudice", or "incitement of hatred". This perhaps demonstrates reluctance to normalize, or give legitimacy, to the use of the expression "hate speech", given its status as a heavily contested term.

Dangerous speech, as a term, has been used in the context of inciting mass violence or, as advocated by Benesch, expressions that have a significant probability of "catalyzing or amplifying violence by one group against another, given the circumstances in which [they were] made or disseminated" (Benesch 2012, p. 2). More specifically, dangerous speech is considered to be speech that increases the risk of mass violence targeting certain people because of their membership of a group, on an ethnic, religious or racial basis. It intends to be broad enough to capture any form of expression that constitutes incitement to violence or conditions its audience to accept, condone and commit violent acts against people who belong to a targeted group. For example, Hutu extremists were able to incite genocide in Rwanda in part because years of propaganda had influenced Hutus to view Tutsis as less than human and so dangerous that they must be eliminated from the country. The propagandists' goal may not have been genocide, but their work prepared Hutus to understand and answer the call to act when extremist leaders launched the genocide.

In this context, the definition of dangerous speech attempts to include a wide range of expressions, such as verbal or written speech, traditional print and broadcast media pieces or blogs and social media posts, or even images or symbols, or music and poetry. Its message may be interpreted as a call to violence against a specific group or may portray this group in a way that legitimizes or justifies violence against it. To this end, such speech often uses dehumanizing imagery or symbols when referring to that group (e.g. by analogizing its members to vermin that must be exterminated), accuses the group of planning to harm the audience and generally presents the group's existence as a threat to the audience. Determining the context is critical, as speech could be dangerous even if its intention is not to cause violence – for example, a false rumour that a rival group is planning attack could provoke violence against that group in what is considered to be justified self-defence (Marcus 2012).

"Cyberhate" is another broad term, closely tied to hate speech, that is also increasingly used to refer to online speech with the potential of inciting violence. It has been referred to as the "globalization of hate" or having the ability to use the virtual environment to stretch across borders and encourage transnational groups and communities that are able and willing to incite violence (Bakalis 2018; Burnap and Williams 2015; Glassman 2000; Perry and Olsson 2009). The Anti-Defamation League (ADL) defines cyberhate as any use of electronic communications technology to spread anti-Semitic, racist, bigoted, extremist or terrorist messages or information. These electronic communications technologies include the Internet (i.e., websites, social networking sites, "Web 2.0" user-generated content, dating sites, blogs, online games, instant messages and email) as well as other computer- and mobile phone-based information technologies (Anti-Defamation League 2016).

Similarly, in recent years, the term "microaggression" has gained increasing salience and has been applied, particularly in university and college environments, to identify behaviour and unconscious biases that threaten a particular group. It is often used in reference to racial groups. The term microaggression was advanced by Derald Wing Sue as "the brief and commonplace daily verbal, behavioural and environmental indignities, whether intentional, that communicate hostile, derogatory or negative racial, gender, and sexual orientation, and religious slights and insults to the target person or group" (Sue et al. 2007). However – and crucially – these indignities do not necessarily have to be the outcome of intentional behaviour. Instead, he argues that, "perpetrators of microaggressions are often unaware" of the indignities that they inflict on others.

This focus on the unconscious or unwitting dimension of microaggression is important – and in part distinguishes microaggression from more intentional forms of hate speech or dangerous speech. According to Sue, "microaggressions are often unconsciously delivered in the form of subtle snubs or dismissive looks, gestures, and tones." Rather than a framework of analysis to assess whether a speech act conforms to an act of microaggression, encounters are underpinned by a pervasive unconscious bias against those of different ethnicities and racial groups, women, LGBT individuals and disability groups. Indeed, the increasing use of the term in college campuses has led UCLA to formulate a tool to categorize and monitor the use of microaggressions, with the caveat that the context and relationship are critical to this. Categories of statements that could be conceived of as microaggressions are those that refer to an individual as an alien in their own land; the ascription of intelligence; criminality/assumption of criminal status; pathologizing cultural values/communication styles; ascription as a second-class citizen; use of sexist/heterosexist language; as well as the use of traditional gender role prejudicing and stereotyping. In this context, microaggressions can be seen as an important component of laying the groundwork for mass violence; the term reflects an ongoing process of subtle "othering".

Microaggressions can be humiliating, especially if people are exposed to a lot of them, and, in their most pernicious forms, can compromise a person's dignity and give them a sense that important people think they do not really belong; they can impose real psychological damage (Sunstein 1995). However, he notes that microaggressions can also have detrimental effects on the groups that produce them – typically white, male, heterosexual and middle-class – contributing to a sense of prejudice and superiority, potentially even hatred. Although the issue of microaggression has risen in the popular consciousness, and associated policies have been adopted to counter it, it is important to recognize that, if charges of microaggression are taken too far, they can impose a stifling orthodoxy, undermining freedom of thought and expression. In other words, as speech acts have the ability to inflict verbal violence and trauma, this can lead to excessive scrutiny of dialogue and conversation.

As this section has suggested, from "hate speech" to "microaggressions", there is a wide variety of terminology that is particularly used in North America and Europe as part of an attempt to capture the kind of harmful and hurtful speech that is increasingly being used on social media. How speech is categorized and defined, and for what purpose, has a major impact on what types of research methods are available. Terminology differs in other regions of the world, although "hate speech" (translated) can be the most common term and is often associated with the capacity to catalyse violence. How one defines such speech is important because it sets the scope of how it is identified and addressed.

Methodological approaches to researching hate speech online

The definitional problem affecting hate speech has clear implications for how such forms of expression can be identified and studied. Both scholarly and policy work around hate speech may have recognized the importance of a better understanding of the phenomenon, but have tended to prioritize the need to recognize, isolate and combat expressions considered potentially harmful. Although the emphasis in the literature – and, more dramatically, in campaigns driven by public authorities and political entrepreneurs – has tended to be on cataloguing and combating expression of hatred, calls have been growing that stress the need to better understand an increasingly defining trait of contemporary communication. As Robert Post has observed:

> hate speech regulation imagines itself as simply enforcing the given and natural norms of a decent society [...] but from a sociological or anthropological point of

view we know that law is always actually enforcing the mores of the dominant group that controls the content of law.

(Post 2009, p. 130)

The increasing availability of tools able to collect and analyse large quantities of text has led researchers to embark on ambitious programmes of research to chart the emergence of hate speech in different national contexts or targeting specific groups (Faris et al. 2016; Fortuna and Nunes 2018; Olteanu et al. 2018). Correlations between online hate speech and offline cases of violence have started to be more systematically mapped (Müller and Schwarz 2017). Many of these efforts, however, have been informed by a need to identify and catalogue speech in ways that can be algorithmically processed and automated, erasing some of the complexities of how hate speech often functions in subtle and coded forms and beyond the most widely spoken languages. Facebook itself, despite its ability to deploy incredible processing power and ambition to ultimately recur to artificial intelligence to map online speech, has reacted to criticism about being a vehicle for the propagation of hateful messages by hiring an increasing number of human coders, rather than uniquely reverting to automatized techniques (Solon 2017; Tangermann 2018).

The dangerous speech framework mentioned above suggests moving beyond text and developing a greater sensitivity to the climate in which a dangerous speech act takes place. It invites practitioners, researchers and policymakers to consider factors such as: the speakers' influence (speakers with a high degree of influence over the audience – for example, a political, cultural or religious leader or media personality – will likely have influence over a crowd); audience receptiveness (the audience may have grievances and fear that the speaker can cultivate); speech content (content that may be taken as inflammatory by the audience and understood as a call to violence; coded language can be used to do this); medium of dissemination (this includes language used and the medium for dissemination, which may be the sole or primary source of news for the relevant audience, replacing the "marketplace of ideas"); and the social/historical speech context (long-standing competition between groups for resources, lack of efforts to solve grievances or previous episodes of violence may provide a climate propitious for violence; Benesch 2012, 3–5). In this way, dangerous speech is seen as a potential early warning signal for violence, as it is often a precursor – if not also a prerequisite – of mass violence. It may therefore also be possible to limit such speech or its dangerousness. Dangerous speech also attempts to provide a framework through which speakers could be held accountable for speech that constitutes crime. Nevertheless, it is extremely difficult to accurately and systematically predict the likely effect of speech on an audience, and applying the framework in different contexts is challenging (as we found in the case of our research in Ethiopia, discussed below). A small change in the political climate, or indeed the audience's responsiveness to a particular speaker, can significantly alter the propensity of a violent corollary of a speech act.

Approaches that have attempted to combine content and context and add rigour to the process of identifying specific forms of speech have contributed little to explaining *why* hate speech emerges and proliferates. The hideousness of this type of speech has often prevented in-depth, ethnographic analyses to be widely employed, as research aimed at combating hate speech has been prioritized. The few cases available where researchers have sought to reach out to individuals and communities engaging in forms of speech considered derogatory and potentially dangerous, however, have produced powerful findings. Erjavec and Kovačič (2012), for example, have analysed hateful messages in the comments on Slovenia's most popular news websites and have been able to interview some of their authors. Their research strategy has led to the identification of different categories of speaker, each motivated by unique factors: from the "soldiers" who belong to political parties and non-governmental organizations and use online means systematically to disseminate stereotypes and damage the reputation of their opponents to the "watchdogs" who use hate speech to draw attention to social problems. This type of research offers important insights into what motivates certain users to resort to extreme language. As the authors explain, referring to how "soldiers" justify hate speech: They claim that online hate speech cannot be compared to hate speech in the traditional media, as this is the only possible means of communication in online comments: "'This is the only way of communication; otherwise your voice is simply not heard.'" Thus, they justify the use of hate speech in comments as "'sharp,'" "'military,'" "'the only convincing,'" and "'the only possible'" way of communication, which the "'enemies'" understand (Erjavec and Kovačič 2012, p. 910). Findings such as these resonate with research on "Internet trolling" (Buckels, Trapnell and Paulhus 2014; Herring et al. 2002; Shin 2008), which is the practice of deliberately provoking users through inflammatory language and upsetting content, and they offer some indications of how the medium can influence the message. More generally, such research seeks a more grounded understanding of the unique characteristics and of some of the causes of a fast-evolving phenomenon, rather than simply seeking "solutions" to it. Socio-legal studies' emphasis on empirical investigations of the practice and perception of law connects it with efforts of this kind, made by anthropologists and media scholars, to develop a finer-grained understanding of hate speech and its regulation.

A practical example: studying hate speech around elections

In this chapter, we have sought to address some of the complexities of defining and identifying hate speech. We now turn to some of the challenges of implementing socio-legal research projects attempting to identify hate speech online in the very politically charged environment around Ethiopia's elections. The project, called *Mechachal* ("tolerance" in Amharic), sought to pay attention to the historical, political and socio-economic context in which online communications take place, but also to address another key challenge highlighted above: the fact that an excessive focus on the dangerous sides of digital communication can be exploited by political entrepreneurs to persecute dissenting voices.

Mechachal developed around the 2015 Ethiopian elections and, as with similar projects examining hate speech and disinformation around elections, it attracted interest – and funding – because of concerns about the possible consequences of the "darker" side of the Internet. The international community was concerned about the possible rise of violence, especially after having witnessed riots, killings and displacements in the aftermath of the Kenyan elections of 2007, where the media played a significant role in inciting animosity and suspicion between different ethnic groups (Dercon and Gutiérrez-Romero 2012; Somerville 2011).[1] The Ethiopian government, as it had done on the occasion of previous elections (Gagliardone 2016; Stremlau 2018), had an interest in stressing the destabilizing aspects of hate speech, also as a way to justify the need for increasing control and surveillance, including the shutting down of the Internet.

---

1 The project was funded by the UK Foreign and Commonwealth Office with the support of the UK High Commission in Ethiopia. It involved a large number of researchers including more than 10 Ethiopian coders who regularly monitored social media.

In the very initial stages of the project, we were faced with the dilemma of possibly developing a research project that might allow, for the first time, a systematic analysis of the nature and quality of hate speech online in Ethiopia (Gagliardone, Patel and Pohjonen 2014) and the risk that the results of our work could further exacerbate the perception of hate speech as a destabilizing force, possibly leading to even more repressive measures in a country already characterized by tight control of the media.

The nature of digital communication in Ethiopia also offered a rare opportunity. The uniqueness of the languages spoken in Ethiopia, and by the Ethiopian diaspora, and the relatively limited Internet penetration in the country made it possible to elaborate a sampling strategy that would essentially map almost all Facebook spaces of public interest targeting Ethiopian audiences and, furthermore, to locate possible instances of hate speech in the broader context of the overall set of communications occurring on the social networking platform (for more details on the sampling strategy, see Gagliardone et al. 2016). This allowed identification of how, contrary to expectations, hate speech constituted only 0.7 per cent of the overall set of conversations occurring on Facebook ahead of the 2015 elections (Gagliardone et al. 2016). This strategy allowed Mechachal to develop a fine-grained understanding of how hate speech emerges and proliferates online – working with statements included in that 0.7 per cent as further illustrated below – but also to systematically remind public authorities of the marginality of those forms of speech.

Mechachal's conceptual framework was tailored towards examining how online communication occurs in highly polarized political environments. It was not obsessed with finding hate speech, but was rather interested in locating it in the long-term trajectory of historical grievances in the country. Hate speech was considered a subset of what the project termed "statements going against", messages displaying conflict-producing or conflict-maintaining behaviours (the "name-calling" that has characterized the debates in Ethiopia's traditional and new media, using terms such as "anti-peace" and "chauvinist" as ways to dismiss adversaries, fell into this category as they remove possibilities of engaging with an issue a priori). These were confronted with "statements going towards", statements that help initiate, maintain and/or build a communicative relationship – for example, acknowledging another person's or group's position, offering additional information about the topic being discussed, joking (in a non-hostile way) and facilitating engagement and conversation with the other members in the discussion. Such statements may also contain strong criticism but, in the context of a polarized debate, they offer a premise for recognizing adversaries as legitimate, rather than simply dismissing them. Again, contrary to expectations, statements "going towards" were found to be the vast majority – 59 per cent – compared with just 16 per cent of statements categorized as "going against" (25 per cent of statements could not be categorized as either against or towards).

The concepts of going against and going towards are aimed at dividing the continuum of statements uttered in online debates into two broad categories and represent the beginning of more in-depth analysis. In the case of statements going against, four subcategories were created in such a way that statements could be categorized as: offensive speech; hate speech; dangerous speech with limited possibility for the speakers (or the groups they appeal to) to carry out violence; and dangerous speech with high risk that the speakers (or the groups they appeal to) could carry out violence. The identification of these typologies was based on an equation that factored in different parameters within which each selected statement could be categorized.

A first layer considered the grounds on which an individual or group is being targeted. Although statements that go against in general can be antagonistic on any grounds, including politics, in the case of these subcategories, we only considered statements that targeted people based on their ethnicity, religion, gender or sexual affiliation. This is to comply with international, regional and national legal frameworks defining hate speech, which exclude purely political statements from their definitions. In the case of Ethiopia, where the constitution recognizes ethnic federalism as a building block of the Ethiopian nation–state, the distinction between politics and ethnicity proved particularly complex (Stremlau 2011, 2014), and its operationalization emerged as the result of numerous discussions within the research team and during the stakeholders' meetings in Addis Ababa. Many political parties in Ethiopia are historically ethnically based, such as the Tigrayan People Liberation Front or the Oromo Peoples' Democratic Organization (OPDO). The team agreed that, if a statement targeted a party or one of its members directly, it had to be considered under the label of "politics". However, if in the same statement the speaker attacked, for example, both the OPDO and Oromos in general, the statements had to be flagged under both labels of "politics" and "ethnicity", and this would be computed in the equation.

The second layer focused on the content of the statement. The analysis at this level is the one that builds most significantly on research on "dangerous speech" and "fear speech". We thus investigated whether or not, for example, a statement uses derogatory terms; contains a rumour based on a particular group's ethnicity, religion or gender that cannot be easily or factually verified; or suggests that the audience faces a serious threat of violence from another group.

The third layer of analysis asked whether or not a statement encourages the audience to do something specific against an individual or group identified on the basis of ethnicity, religion or gender. The call to action can refer to psychological forms of violence (e.g. the speaker suggests that immigrants deserve to be treated differently from citizens) or to physical violence (e.g. there is a call to beat, or kill, a specific person or group). The analysis at this level takes into account the arguments put forward by many legal scholars that the content of a speech act alone is not sufficient for it to be considered to be hate speech. An exhortation should be present instead towards performing an action that can cause harm to a specific subject.

Finally, a fourth layer of analysis poses questions related to the imbalance of power between the speakers and the target. This layer is important in providing context, as there is significant difference between a statement by a prominent government official or religious leader targeting a group that is already persecuted in their country, and one posted by a loner who uses the Internet as a means of venting his anger against a public figure. This type of analysis, however, poses some particular challenges, as it requires the person coding the statement to make judgements about the world that exists beyond the statements itself. What is being examined in particular is: whether the speakers and/or those who are likely to support their statements may be able to carry out the actions suggested against the target individual or group; and whether the targeted individual or group is able to call on officially recognized institutions to defend itself against the threat of violence. Given the complexities of making these types of judgement, after having tested different approaches, we settled for a 'conservative' interpretation of this question. This means that, if the coder could not clearly assess whether the speaker or the group he appealed to was able to carry out violence, the statement had still to be identified as "dangerous speech, but with limited risk of violence". Similarly, if the coder could assess that the speaker or the group he appealed to was able to carry out violence, but could not clearly assess whether or not the target group could call on officially recognized institutions to defend itself, the statement had to be categorized as "dangerous speech, with high risk of violence".

The combined answers to the questions posed for each of these layers led to classifying statements in one of the four subcategories. For example, if a statement contained only derogatory terms against followers of a particular religion, it was categorized as offensive; if, in addition to this, it also contained an incitement for other people to discriminate against members of that religious group, it was categorized as hate speech. Following a different path, if a statement contained a rumour that members of ethnic group A were going to attack or reclaim land from members of ethnic group B, and called for people of ethnic group B to arm themselves and be ready to act (i.e. what is called accusation in a mirror), it was categorized as dangerous speech.

Despite the discussion among scholars about whether or not dangerous speech has to be considered a subset of hate speech – for example, statements that do not explicitly call for attacking a specific group can still be instrumental in creating a sense of resentment and suspicion that can later lead to violent actions – we considered the four subcategories as part of the same continuum, with an increasing risk of violent outcomes going from the left to the right end of the spectrum.

Our framework is the result of multiple rounds of testing and refinement, but it is not infallible. The connections between speech and violence are complex, and, despite regular conversations within our group to analyse how each coder coded specific statements and improvements in our intercoder reliability tests, some messages still posed significant challenges to attempts to clearly categorize them using one of the available options. Our goal is to contribute to the growing debate on the likelihood of certain types of speech leading to violence, using tools that are able to take this complexity into consideration, and offer rigorously sourced and analysed empirical evidence, rather than being alarmist.

The full methodology adopted for Mechachal is outlined in the series of publications cited above, but, to prevent the risk of being misinterpreted as presenting speech on Facebook as less threatening than some expected, we ensured that the evidence collected in different phases of the project could be shared with and challenged by a broad variety of stakeholders, representing different components of Ethiopian society. Before the publication of each report, we presented and debated preliminary results in Addis Ababa with a group that included leading figures from the government of Ethiopia, the major opposition parties (Semayawi, Medrek, EDP), the new and traditional media scene (from *The Reporter* and *Addis Standard* to *Horn Affairs* and Zone 9), academics, representatives of regional and international organizations (African Union, UNESCO) and members of the national and international civil society (PEN Ethiopia). This process offered a unique opportunity to test the convening power of evidence of a kind that is usually scarcely available, but that allows academic insights on hotly debated topics. Individuals sitting at opposite ends of the political spectrum found common ground and agreed on the ability of academically informed research to create a space for individuals and groups holding competing views to engage with one another using evidence as their starting point, rather than personal grievances.

Conclusion

Hate speech – in its contemporary form – is strictly interconnected to what Chantal Mouffe has referred to as the moralization of politics (Mouffe 2005). The distinction between right and left has become less relevant, replaced instead by a distinction between right and wrong, good and evil. As she pointed out, politics has not disappeared; it is increasingly played on the moral register. The communities adopting the various terms of "hate speech", and the answers or findings they have sought to produce, have been caught in this dilemma.

Different communities, at different points in their histories, have coined terms that serve to affirm this distinction, disconnecting a group from another, severing the need to know more about a specific issue because the source from which it is being discussed has been judged a priori as one from which nothing worth listening to can be coming. In Silvio Berlusconi's Italy, this disconnecting, antagonizing word was "communist". In Trump's America, "liberal" has increasingly served this function. In contemporary Ethiopia, the term "Woyane" has been used to target the ruling class, "chauvinist", "anti-peace" or "anti-constitution" to target the opposition. This disconnection clearly does not amount to hate speech. It is instead the beginning of the relationship of antagonism, the creation of an enemy, the start of a process that can lead to more or less aggressive forms of expression. Much depends on what the group being targeted is, what power it holds in relation to other groups in a given society, and how much its presence threatens existing balances.

This paradox also depends on the fact that a lot of hate speech – as observed, as read, as witnessed – is hideous, and that the response that it is likely to trigger in the researcher and in the outsider peeking in (rather than the intended audience that may be sympathetic or welcome the type of speech) is one of judgement and disconnect. This reaction also plays on the moral register.

As Stanley Fish (1997) noted, this moral response often amounts to a kind of "Oh dearism": it express discomfort, disdain, and it is likely to emerge from a supposedly higher moral ground from which the observer claims to be speaking. It ties with what Fish has defined as "boutique multiculturalism", flagging liberal responses to hate speech as hypocritical and self-righteous, something that can read more or less as, "you hater are not allowed to sit at our dinner table of rational thinkers". This liberal, moral gaze is what – as described in research by Polletta and Callahan (2017), for example – is likely to infuriate extremists even more.

A change of perspective is needed. Carol McGranahan's anthropology of lying (2017), for example, has stressed the need not to ask how to correct lies, but how to understand lies and liars in their cultural, historical and political context. Francesca Polletta's take on fake news has similarly stressed the importance of not interrogating why people believe such stories, but rather examining the pleasure that comes from reading surprising news (Polletta and Callahan 2017).

Recognizing some forms of expression as a type of hate speech means suppressing the urge to catalogue and judge and accepting, with Chantal Mouffe, conflict as the natural site of democracy. Hate speech, against this background, should thus not be considered the exception, but the extreme form of a relation of contestation.

This recognition does not come without risks. Researchers may be accused of condoning practices considered abhorrent, and potentially dangerous. This potential criticism cannot be solved a priori. Only the rigour and sensitivity of researchers accepting the challenge of engaging in these types of enquiry and the balance achieved in each individual case can offer an answer and practically illustrate the value of this approach. It also opens the possibility of investigating processes and relationships that are often ignored, overwhelmed by the need to classify, contain and combat. What is, for example, the relationship between hate speech and inequality? In research conducted in Ethiopia, it was found that the majority of antagonistic speech, as well as the most virulent forms of hate speech, came from individuals with little or no influence, not from ringleaders or political entrepreneurs. Vitriolic comments appeared as a bitter response to power and to those who represent it. In Trump's America, emerging research has begun to pinpoint links between hate crimes and rising inequalities (Majumder 2017).

These findings must be substantiated by additional research but suggest that the links between power inequalities and the more aggressive tones used by individuals with little influence should be further examined before certain types of speech are dismissed as inappropriate. Especially in contexts where individuals enjoy few opportunities to effect change in a concrete way or have limited access to outlets in which they can voice discontent or criticism, social media offer an opportunity to voice frustration, not just towards the speakers, but at the processes through which power is exercised more broadly.

Socio-legal approaches to hate speech are not framed here as a way to surpass other efforts to map online vitriol, but to unlock paths that have been so far been rarely pursued, and to contribute to developing a fuller understanding of the reasons why certain behaviours are on the rise, rather than simply flagging them as unacceptable at the table of rational thinkers.

Further reading

Gagliardone, I., Gal, D., Alves, T., and Martinez, G. (2015). *Countering Online Hate Speech*. UNESCO Series on Internet Freedom. Paris: United Nations Educational, Scientific and Cultural Organisation.

Hare, I., and Weinstein, J. (2010). *Extreme Speech and Democracy*. Oxford University Press.

Pohjonen, M., and Udupa, S. (2017). "Extreme Speech Online: An Anthropological Critique of Hate Speech Debates." *International Journal of Communication* 11: 19.

Rowbottom, J. (2012). "To Rant, Vent and Converse: Protecting Low Level Digital Speech." *The Cambridge Law Journal* 71 (02): 355–383.

Waldron, J. (2012). *The Harm in Hate Speech*. Cambridge, MA: Harvard University Press.

References

Anti-Defamation League. 2016. "Responding to Cyberhate. Progress and Trends." www.adl.org/sites/default/files/documents/assets/pdf/combating-hate/2016-ADL-Responding-to-Cyberhate-Progress-and-Trends-Report.pdf

Bakalis, Chara. 2018. "Rethinking Cyberhate Laws." *Information & Communications Technology Law* 27 (1): 86–110.

Battelle, John. 2018. "Facebook Can't Be Fixed." Quartz. 2018. https://qz.com/1178636/mark-zuckerberg-facebook-fb-news-feed-cant-be-fixed-without-gutting-its-advertising-driven-business-model/.

Benesch, Susan. 2012. "Dangerous Speech: A Proposal to Prevent Group Violence." World Policy Institute, New York. www.worldpolicy.org/sites/default/files/Dangerous%20Speech%20Guidelines%20Benesch%20January%202012.pdf

Bever, Lindsay. 2018. "Mark Zuckerberg Pledges 'to Do the Job He Already Has,' Basically." *Washington Post*. www.washingtonpost.com/news/the-switch/wp/2018/01/04/mark-zuckerberg-pledges-to-do-the-job-he-already-has-basically/

Buckels, Erin E., Paul D. Trapnell, and Delroy L. Paulhus 2014. "Trolls Just Want to Have Fun." *Personality and Individual Differences* 67: 97–102.

Burnap, Pete, and Matthew L. Williams 2015. "Cyber Hate Speech on Twitter: An Application of Machine Classification and Statistical Modeling for Policy and Decision Making." *Policy & Internet* 7 (2): 223–242.

Dercon, Stefan, and Roxana Gutiérrez-Romero. 2012. "Triggers and Characteristics of the 2007 Kenyan Electoral Violence." *World Development* 40 (4): 731–744.

Erjavec, Karmen, and Melita Poler Kovačič. 2012. "'You Don't Understand, This Is a New War!' Analysis of Hate Speech in News Web Sites' Comments." *Mass Communication and Society* 15 (6): 899–920.

Faris, Robert, Amar Ashar, Urs Gasser, and Daisy Joo. 2016. *Understanding Harmful Speech Online*. Cambridge, MA: Berkman Klein Center for Internet & Society Research.

Fish, Stanley. 1997. "Boutique Multiculturalism, or Why Liberals Are Incapable of Thinking about Hate Speech." *Critical Inquiry* 23 (2): 378–395.

Fortuna, Paula, and Sérgio Nunes 2018. "A Survey on Automatic Detection of Hate Speech in Text." *ACM Computing Surveys (CSUR)* 51 (4): 85.

Gagliardone, Iginio. 2016. *The Politics of Technology in Africa.* Cambridge: Cambridge University Press.

Gagliardone, Iginio, Danit Gal, Thiago Alves, and Gabriela Martinez. 2015. *Countering Online Hate Speech.* UNESCO. https://books.google.co.uk/books?hl=en&id=WAVgCgAAQBAJ&oi=fnd&pg=PA3&dq= countering+online+hate+speech&ots=Tabj3oLSWx&sig=P1rADlv5Fa4toM5qfsEIrBJUWxA

Gagliardone, Iginio, Alisha Patel, and Matti Pohjonen. 2014. "Mapping and Analysing Hate Speech Online: Opportunities and Challenges for Ethiopia." University of Oxford and Addis Ababa University. http://Pcmlp.Socleg.Ox.Ac.Uk/Sites/Pcmlp.Socleg.Ox.Ac.Uk/Files/Ethiopia%20hate% 20speech.Pdf

Gagliardone, Iginio, Matti Pohjonen, Zenebe Beyene, Abdissa Zerai, Gerawork Aynekulu, Mesfin Bekalu, Jonathan Bright, et al. 2016. "Mechachal: Online Debates and Elections in Ethiopia-From Hate Speech to Engagement in Social Media." https://papers.ssrn.com/sol3/papers.cfm? abstract_id=2831369

Glassman, Elliot. 2000. "Cyber Hate: The Discourse of Intolerance in the New Europe." In Lengel, Laura (ed.), *Culture and Technology in the New Europe: Civic Discourse in Transformation in Post-Communist Nations,* 145–164. Stamford: Ablex.

Hanson, Fergus. 2012. "Internet Freedom. The Role of the U.S. State Department." *Brookings* (blog). www.brookings.edu/research/internet-freedom-the-role-of-the-u-s-state-department/

Herring, Susan, Kirk Job-Sluder, Rebecca Scheckler, and Sasha Barab 2002. "Searching for Safety Online: Managing 'Trolling' in a Feminist Forum." *The Information Society* 18 (5): 371–384.

iHub Research. 2013. "Umati Final Report." Nairobi, Kenya. www.research.ihub.co.ke/uploads/2013/ june/1372415606__936.pdf

Lanard, Noah. 2018. "Google, Amazon, and Facebook Go Big on DC Lobbying. How Do Their Efforts Stack Up?" *Washingtonian* (blog). June 5, 2018. www.washingtonian.com/2018/06/05/google-amazon-and-facebook-go-big-on-dc-lobbying-how-do-their-efforts-stack-up/

Majumder, Maimuna. 2017. "Higher Rates of Hate Crimes Are Tied to Income Inequality." *FiveThirtyEight* (blog). January 23. https://fivethirtyeight.com/features/higher-rates-of-hate-crimes-are-tied-to-income-inequality/

Marcus, Kenneth. 2012. "Accusation in a Mirror." https://papers.ssrn.com/sol3/papers.cfm? abstract_id=2020327

McGranahan, Carole. 2017. "An Anthropology of Lying: Trump and the Political Sociality of Moral Outrage." *American Ethnologist* 44 (2): 243–248.

Mouffe, Chantal. 2005. *On the Political.* London: Routledge.

———. 2018. "Populists Are on the Rise but This Can Be a Moment for Progressives Too." *The Guardian,* September 10. www.theguardian.com/commentisfree/2018/sep/10/populists-rise-progressives-radical-right

Müller, Karsten, and Carlo Schwarz. 2017. "Fanning the Flames of Hate: Social Media and Hate Crime." https://warwick.ac.uk/fac/soc/economics/staff/crschwarz/fanning-flames-hate.pdf

Olteanu, Alexandra, Carlos Castillo, Jeremy Boy, and Kush R. Varshney. 2018. "The Effect of Extremist Violence on Hateful Speech Online." ArXiv Preprint ArXiv:1804.05704.

Osnos, Evan. 2018. "Can Mark Zuckerberg Fix Facebook before It Breaks Democracy?" September 10. www.newyorker.com/magazine/2018/09/17/can-mark-zuckerberg-fix-facebook-before-it-breaks-democracy

Perry, Barbara, and Patrik Olsson 2009. "Cyberhate: The Globalization of Hate." *Information & Communications Technology Law* 18 (2): 185–199.

Polletta, Francesca, and Jessica Callahan 2017. "Deep Stories, Nostalgia Narratives, and Fake News: Storytelling in the Trump Era." *American Journal of Cultural Sociology* 5 (3): 392–408.

Post, Robert 2009. "Hate Speech." In Hare, Ivan and Weinstein, James (eds), *Extreme Speech and Democracy,* 123–138. Oxford: Oxford University Press.

Rowbottom, Jacob. 2012. "To Rant, Vent and Converse: Protecting Low Level Digital Speech." *The Cambridge Law Journal* 71 (02): 355–383.

Shin, Jiwon. 2008. "Morality and Internet Behavior: A Study of the Internet Troll and Its Relation with Morality on the Internet." In *Society for Information Technology & Teacher Education International*

Conference, 2834–2840. www.editlib.org/index.cfm?fuseaction=Reader.ViewPresentation &paper_id=27652&paperfile_id=46654

Solon, Olivia. 2017. "Facebook Is Hiring Moderators. but Is the Job too Gruesome to Handle?" *The Guardian*, May 4. www.theguardian.com/technology/2017/may/04/facebook-content-moderators-ptsd-psychological-dangers

Somerville, Keith. 2011. "Violence, Hate Speech and Inflammatory Broadcasting in Kenya: The Problems of Definition and Identification." *Ecquid Novi: African Journalism Studies* 32 (1): 82–101.

Stremlau, Nicole. 2011. "The Press and the Political Restructuring of Ethiopia." *Journal of Eastern African Studies* 5 (4): 716–732.

Stremlau, Nicole. 2014. "Media, Participation and Constitution-making in Ethiopia." *Journal of African Law* 58 (2): 231–249.

Stremlau, Nicole. 2018. *Media, Conflict, and the State in Africa*. New York: Cambridge University Press.

Sue, Derald Wing, Christina M. Capodilupo, Gina C. Torino, Jennifer M. Bucceri, Aisha Holder, Kevin L. Nadal, and Marta Esquilin 2007. "Racial Microaggressions in Everyday Life: Implications for Clinical Practice." *American Psychologist* 62 (4): 271.

Sunstein, Cass. 1995. "Democracy and the Problem of Free Speech." *Publishing Research Quarterly* 11 (4): 58–72.

Tangermann, Victor. 2018. "Facebook Needs Humans ★and★ Algorithms to Filter Hate Speech." Futurism. https://futurism.com/facebook-human-algorithm-hate-speech

INDEX

Page numbers in *italics* indicate figures or tables.

399

Printed in Great Britain
by Amazon